ADVANCING YOUR CAREER:
Concepts of Professional Nursing

ADVANCING YOUR CAREER:
Concepts of Professional Nursing

Rose Kearney Nunnery, RN, PhD
Director
Technical College of the Lowcountry
Beaufort, South Carolina

Formerly,
Associate Professor and Director
Department of Nursing
State University of New York College
   at New Paltz
New Paltz, New York

 F. A. DAVIS COMPANY • Philadelphia

F. A. Davis Company
1915 Arch Street
Philadelphia, PA 19103

Copyright © 1997 by F. A. Davis Company

Printed in the United States of America

Last digit indicates print number: 10 9 8 7 6 5 4 3 2

Managing Publisher: Lisa A. Biello
Acquisitions Editor: Joanne P. DaCunha, RN, MSN
Cover Designer: Louis Forgione

As new scientific information becomes available through basic and clinical research, recommended treatments and drug therapies undergo changes. The author and publisher have done everything possible to make this book accurate, up to date, and in accord with accepted standards at the time of publication. The author, editors, and publisher are not responsible for errors or omissions or for consequences from application of the book, and make no warranty, expressed or implied, in regard to the contents of the book. Any practice described in this book should be applied by the reader in accordance with professional standards of care used in regard to the unique circumstances that may apply in each situation. The reader is advised always to check product information (package inserts) for changes and new information regarding dose and contraindications before administering any drug. Caution is especially urged when using new or infrequently ordered drugs.

Library of Congress Cataloging-in-Publication Data

Kearney Nunnery, Rose.
    Advancing your career : concepts of professional nursing / Rose
Kearney Nunnery.
       p.   cm.
    Includes bibliographical references and index.
    ISBN 0-8036-0235-9
    1. Nursing—Vocational guidance.   2. Career development.
3. Nursing—Vocational guidance—United States.   4. Nursing—
Philosophy.   I. Title.
    [DNLM: 1. Nursing. 2. Career Mobility. WY 16 N972a 1997]
RT82.N85   1997
610.73′06′9—dc21
DNLM/DLC
for Library of Congress
                                   96-29493
                                      CIP

PREFACE

The nursing profession has undergone major changes in the past two decades, and the pace of change seems to accelerate daily. We have grown from defending nursing as a profession to our present pivotal role in health care. Focusing on people in their respective environments with their unique health-care needs that are addressed through nursing care is increasingly important with our rapidly expanding knowledge base and the dynamic changes occurring in the health-care system. In essence, our quest in our respective nursing roles is to expand knowledge, become involved, and broaden the vision of professional practice.

This book is directed to the RN student returning to school. The intent is to provide you, the practicing RN, with professional concepts to advance your practice. These concepts build on your prior nursing education, and their application will greatly enhance your professional practice and growth. The aim is to intellectually engage you in an ongoing professional dialog with your peers, colleagues, and instructors, broaden your professional development, and build on your preexisting knowledge and experiences. You, the RN student, are challenged to delve further into professional education and conceptual practice. This book is written for the adult learner with the characteristics of self-direction, prior experiences, applicability to practice, and motivation to meet the challenge to increase her or his knowledge base.

This book is divided into six sections. Each chapter includes chapter objectives, key terms, and key points, along with exercises to assist the reader in meeting each of the chapter objectives, references, and a bibliography. Section I introduces the concepts of professional nursing practice. Chapter 1 focuses on the characteristics of professional nursing, as a profession and as a unique professional discipline. Readers are challenged to develop personal perspectives of professional nursing as a philosophy statement. Coping with returning to school is the theme of Chapter 2. Dr. Bernadette

Dersch Curry's presentation of study tips and strategies for success are highlighted for the arduous process of returning to the student role.

Section II addresses the theoretical bases of nursing. First, Chapter 3 presents the Evolution and Use of Formal Nursing Knowledge, by Dr. Jacqueline Fawcett and Barbara Swoyer. In addition to a discussion of the evolution, vocabulary, and advantages of these nursing models, the chapter presents applications for selecting and using the models as a guide for practice. Chapter 4 presents theory development, description, and use. Terminology is applied to theories borrowed from other disciplines but successfully applied in professional nursing, including Maslow's hierarchy of basic needs, developmental theories, and systems theory. Section II concludes with a discussion of health and illness models that have been successfully used to guide nursing practice (Chapter 5). The theories of health and illness presented include Dunn's high-level wellness, the health belief model, a health promotion model, and a chronic illness model. Focusing on health, the section includes levels of prevention and cultural influences.

Section III features the critical components of professional nursing practice. Eight critical components of professional nursing are reviewed: communication, critical thinking, leadership, management, organizations, change, teaching and learning, and group theory. The first of these critical components is presented by Dr. Nancy Courts in Chapter 6, with a discussion of communication models, essential ingredients of effective communication, nonverbal communication forms, and specific communication techniques. Critical thinking is essential to professional nursing practice. In Chapter 7, Dr. Rebecca Parrish and Dr. Genevieve M. Bartol trace the historical aspects of critical thinking in nursing, along with the characteristics, measurement, and further development of critical thinking skills. Drs. Theresa M. Valiga and Sheila Grossman addresses leadership as a critical component of professional nursing practice in Chapter 8. Included along with definitions, theories, and styles of leadership is a description of the components of effective leadership.

Management is an essential part of professional practice. Dr. Maureen Murphy-Ruocco provides a discussion of management theories, types of power, negotiation arts, delegation principles, and strategies for difficult management situations in Chapter 9. Application of leadership and management are influenced by the practice environment. Chapters 10 and 11 present organizational and change theories. Organizations have redefined themselves radically during the past decade. Organizational theory focusing on systems theory, structure and function, culture, communication, and negotiation for power are applied to a variety of organizational designs. Dealing with organizational change is an involved process. Chapter 11 presents theories of change, the characteristics of change agents, and change in individuals, families, groups, and organizations. Chapter 12 focuses on the teaching and learning process, learning styles, adult learning theory, and learning readiness. Included in this chapter is a discussion on writing behavioral objectives, developing lesson plans, teaching skills and methods, and outcome evaluations. Section III concludes with a chapter on group theory. Dr. Joanne Lavin assists with a presentation of information on group process, including characteristics and roles of groups and group leaders and skills needed for collaboration and coordination within the organization and among organizations.

Section IV delves into the concepts needed for providing care as a major activity in professional nursing practice. In Chapter 14, Phyllis B. Heffron assists the reader in a review of the nursing process, with a presentation of the historical aspects along with the components of assessment, diagnosis, planning, implementation, and evaluation. In Chapter 15, Vicki L. Buchda continues to address managing and providing professional nursing care with a review of methods for organizing care activities, models of care delivery, use of clinical pathways, and documentation systems. Research as a basis for practice is discussed in Chapter 16. Legal and ethical considerations, the research process, and utilization and critique of research are highlighted. This section on providing care concludes with Dr. Kathleen Winter's discussion of the politically active nurse in Chapter 17.

Section V confronts the reality of moving health care into the twenty-first century. In Chapter 18, Sister Rosemary Donley addresses the health-care agenda and health-care reform issues debated in both legislative and professional areas that have major implications for our imminent move into the next century. Chapter 19 addresses our changing demographics, with a growing aging population. To assist in dealing with these changing demographics, theories of aging, demographics, and major health problems of older adults, family, societal, and care issues are described. In Chapter 20, Kathy Malloch addresses one of the major issues driving today's health-care system: economics. Issues related to types of payers, location of care provisions, and marketplace considerations are discussed. The issue of quality care is discussed in Chapter 21 by Francoise Dunefsky. The issues of quality assurance, quality improvement, continuous quality improvement, and total quality management are differentiated. Our ongoing move into the community is examined by Troy W. Bradshaw in Chapter 22. Community roles, priorities, and intervention strategies are presented, along with a view of the differentiation between public health and community health nursing, applicable theoretical models, and future predictions. Section V concludes with a presentation of nursing informatics by Dr. Cassy D. Pollack. Chapter 23 illustrates nursing informatics roles along with ongoing development in the area.

The final section of this book concludes with challenges for the future. Topics include professional ethics and future visions. In Chapter 24, Dr. Joseph T. Catalano discusses professional ethics, focusing on basic human rights, the right to privacy and dignity, access to care, informed consent, advance directives, organ procurement, client endangerment, and workplace hazards. This section concludes with an expanded vision for the profession, including the Pew Commission challenges for the health professions.

This book is intended to enhance your professional practice and continued professional development through further education. Your personal characteristics of self-motivation, a thirst for information, and commitment to your clients and the profession will be enhanced as you develop a more conceptual approach to professional nursing practice. Advance your practice through ongoing education and the basic concepts of professional nursing practice.

Rose Kearney Nunnery

ACKNOWLEDGMENTS

Numerous people have been a large part of this process. Family members, friends, and colleagues have more than tolerated my preoccupation with the nursing profession for the past two years. My particular thanks are extended to all the contributors who have shared their expertise and insights in these pages. Joanne DaCunha merits particular credit for the completion of this project for her endless encouragement, enthusiasm, and belief in the potential for our profession. And a special note of thanks to Helen Kearney who served as an informal editor, supportive mother, and a true friend. I have experienced endless encouragement from my professional colleagues, friends, parents, and students, all who added to this kaleidoscope into the future. And to my husband, Jimmie, for his innumerable golf games that lowered his handicap and provided me the time to fill these pages.

Rose Kearney Nunnery

CONTRIBUTORS

Genevieve M. Bartol, RN, EdD
Professor and Chair, Psychosocial/Community/Gerontology Division
The University of North Carolina at Greensboro
School of Nursing
Greensboro, North Carolina

Troy W. Bradshaw, RN, C, MS
Assistant Professor
Angelo State University
San Angelo, Texas

Vicki L. Buchda, RN, MS
Director, Patient Care Resources
Mayo Arizona
Scottsdale, Arizona

Joseph T. Catalano, RN, PhD
Professor
East Central University
Ada, Oklahoma

Nancy Courts, RN, PhD
Assistant Professor/Chair of Adult Health Division
The University of North Carolina at Greensboro
Greensboro, North Carolina

Bernadette Dersch Curry, RN, PhD
Associate Professor and Department Chair
Niagara University College of Nursing
Niagara, New York

Sister Rosemary Donley, PhD, RN
Executive Vice President
The Catholic University of America
Washington, DC

Francoise Dunefsky, RN, MS
Vice President for Patient Care Services
The Kingston Hospital
Kingston, New York

Jacqueline Fawcett, PhD, FAAN
Professor
University of Pennsylvania
School of Nursing
Philadelphia, Pennsylvania

Sheila Grossman, PhD, RN
Associate Professor
School of Nursing
Fairfield University
Fairfield, Connecticut

Phyllis B. Heffron, RN, MSN
Former Faculty Facilitation-RN/BSN Program
University of Iowa
Iowa City, Iowa

Joanne Lavin, RN, CS, EdD
Associate Professor
Kingsborough Community College
Brooklyn, New York

Kathy Malloch, RN, MBA, PhD(c)
Former Vice President, Patient Care Services
Del E. Webb Memorial Hospital
Sun City West, Arizona

Maureen Murphy-Ruocco, RN, EdD, CNP
Chairperson and Associate Professor, Department of Professional Nursing
Felician College
Lodi, New Jersey

Rebecca Parrish, RN, PhD
Assistant Professor
The University of North Carolina at Greensboro
Greensboro, North Carolina

Cassy D. Pollack, RN, MSN, MPPM
Assistant Professor/Associate Dean Masters Studies
Yale University School of Nursing
New Haven, Connecticut

Barbara Swoyer, BSN, RN
Graduate Student
University of Pennsylvania School of Nursing
Philadelphia, Pennsylvania

Theresa M. Valiga, RN, EdD
Dean and Professor
Fairfield University School of Nursing
Fairfield, Connecticut

Kathleen Winter, RN, PhD
Associate Professor
Duquesne University
Pittsburgh, Pennsylvania

CONSULTANTS AND REVIEWERS

Barbara J. Banik, RN, PhD
Former Assistant Professor
University of Massachusetts at Amherst
Amherst, Massachusetts

Mary Ann Camann, RN, MN, PhD(c)
Assistant Professor Baccalaureate Degree Nursing
Kennesaw State University
Marietta, Georgia

Jan B. Corder, RN, DSN
Associate Director
Northeast Louisiana University School of Nursing
Monroe, Louisiana

A. Barbara Coyne, RN, PhD
Professor of Nursing
LaRoche College
Pittsburgh, Pennsylvania

Patricia A. Cullen, RN, EdD
Associate Professor of Nursing
Gwynedd Mercy College
Gwynedd Valley, Pennsylvania

Anne D'Antuono, RN, PhD
Faculty, Coordinator Psychiatric-Mental Health Nursing
Catholic Medical Center School of Nursing
Woodhaven, New York

Mary B. Dressler, RN, EdD
Associate Professor of Nursing
Gwynedd Mercy College
Gwynedd Valley, Pennsylvania

Mary Letitia "Tish" B. Gallaher, RN, CS, MS
Assistant Professor
Wilmington College
New Castle, Delaware

Pamela E. Hosang, RN, EdD
Associate Professor
Medgar Evers College, City University of New York
New York, New York

Mary Ann Lavin, ScD, RN, CS, FAAN
Assistant Professor
Saint Louis University School of Nursing
St. Louis, Missouri

Mary Lou McHugh, RN, EdD
Associate Dean of Academic Affairs
Allegheny University of the Allied Health Sciences
School of Nursing
Philadelphia, Pennsylvania

Barbara K. Scheffer, RN, MS
Assistant Professor
Eastern Michigan University
Department of Nursing Education
Ypsilanti, Michigan

Susanne M. Tracey, RN, MN, MA
Associate Professor of Nursing
Rivier-St. Joseph School of Nursing and Health Sciences
Nashua, New Hampshire

Charlotte Torres, RN, CS, EdD
Associate Professor
Grand Valley State University
Allendale, Michigan

Mary Jane M. Williams, RN, PhD
Associate Professor
Central Connecticut State University
New Britain, Connecticut

Katherine E. Yutzy, RN, MSc
Associate Professor
Goshen College
Goshen, Indiana

CONTENTS

Section II

THEORETICAL BASIS OF NURSING PRACTICE, 39

Chapter 3
EVOLUTION AND USE OF FORMAL NURSING KNOWLEDGE, 41

Jacqueline Fawcett, PhD, FAAN
Barbara Swoyer, BSN, RN

Chapter 4

WHAT IS THEORY, 64

Rose Kearney Nunnery, RN, PhD

Section IV

PROVIDING CARE, 227

Chapter 22
NURSING IN THE COMMUNITY, 348

Troy W. Bradshaw, RN,C, MS

Chapter 23
NURSING INFORMATICS AND HEALTH MANAGEMENT INFORMATION SYSTEMS, 360

Cassy D. Pollack, RN, MSN, MPPM

Section VI

NURSES WITH VISION, 369

Chapter 24
PROFESSIONAL ETHICS, 371

Joseph T. Catalano, RN, PhD

Chapter 25
EXPANDING THE VISION, 389

Rose Kearney Nunnery, RN, PhD

Section I

INTRODUCTION

Chapter 1

PROFESSIONAL NURSING PRACTICE

Rose Kearney Nunnery

CHAPTER OBJECTIVES

On completion of this chapter, the reader will be able to:

1. Relate the attributes of a profession to professional nursing practice.
2. Describe the clients of professional nursing practice.
3. Discuss responsibility and accountability in professional nursing practice.
4. Describe ethical responsibilities in professional nursing practice.
5. Discuss the formal and informal educational expectations for professional nursing practice.
6. Develop a personal philosophy of professional nursing.

KEY TERMS

Theory
Paradigm
Metaparadigm
Person
Environment
Health
Nursing
Authority
Community Sanction
Standards
Code of Ethics

Professional Culture
Professional
    Development
Professional
    Organizations
Educational Background
Continuing Education
    and Competency
Communication and
    Publication

Autonomy and
    Self-Regulation
Responsibility and
    Accountability
Community Service
Theory Use, Develop-
    ment, and Evaluation
Research Involvement
Philosophy

I n pursuing a baccalaureate in nursing, the registered nurse student must reevaluate personal and collegial perspectives on what truly constitutes professional nursing practice. You are at a gateway for advancing your nursing practice. To advance in one's professional career one must broaden and build on the knowledge base. This involves Mezirow's (1991) theory of adult development and adult education as transformative learning. This theory proposes that the adult moves from technical and practical learning modes into the reflective learning necessary to understand perceptions of oneself and the world. Callin (1996) describes this "perspective transformation" in nursing as requiring the opportunity for reflection, review, and critical thinking. This concept of perspective transformation provides an ongoing process in both personal and professional development. From the professional, armed with technical skills and expertise in the practice setting, we charter a course into the conceptual components that embody and expand professional nursing practice. These conceptual tools allow for creativity and refinement within the paradigm of professional nursing practice. As a start, consider the concepts that characterize both a profession in general and professional nursing practice in specific.

CHARACTERISTICS OF A PROFESSION

A classic work was done on the characteristics of the profession of social work as that discipline struggled with the issue of its professional status. Greenwood (1957) proposed five characteristics of a profession: (1) systematic theory, (2) authority, (3) community sanction, (4) ethical codes, and (5) professional culture. These were then applied to social work to defend its professional status, but they are applicable to any profession, including professional nursing practice.

Systematic Theory and Knowledge Base

All professions are guided by systematic theory, on which their knowledge base is built. As Greenwood (1957) noted, "the skills that characterize a profession flow from and are supported by a fund of knowledge that has been organized into an internally consistent system called a body of theory" (p. 46). This system includes theoretical foundations unique to the profession as well as those borrowed from or adapted from other scientific disciplines.

Kerlinger (1986) defines a **theory** as "a set of interrelated constructs (concepts), definitions, and propositions that present a systematic view of phenomena by specifying relations among variables, with the purpose of explaining and predicting the phenomena" (p. 9).

This theory base is also referred to as the **paradigm** used by professionals or the practitioners in a particular scientific community. Kuhn (1970) has provided us with the well-established definition of a paradigm as "universally recognized scientific achievements that, for a time, provide model problems and solutions to a community of practitioners" (p. vii). The paradigm consists of the beliefs and the belief system shared by members of a particular scientific community. When the paradigm is no longer useful in explaining, practicing, and conducting research in that community, the paradigm shifts and a new belief structure is promoted, adopted, and used by its members.

The paradigm is merely the phenomenon of concern that guides nursing practice. In Chapter 3, we see that Fawcett proposes that a conceptual model and a paradigm are interchangeable terms relative to the phenomena of nursing. Various nursing paradigms or conceptual models are currently used in practice. The selection is based on the belief structure of the particular nursing community, for example, care of people who are chronically ill and need major assistance with health needs versus wellness initiatives in occupational settings. The paradigm is the type of nursing that meets some health needs of a particular client group, in a certain environment or setting. This brings us to the metaparadigm of nursing.

The **metaparadigm** is the overall concern of nursing common to each nursing model, whether a conceptual model/paradigm or formal theory. Fawcett (1995) has described the following four requirements for a discipline's metaparadigm: identity, inclusiveness, neutrality, and internationality. First, the metaparadigm must provide an identity for the profession that is distinctly different from others. Second, the metaparadigm must address all phenomena of interest to the profession in a manageable and understandable manner. Third, the metaparadigm must be neutral, that is, all smaller practice paradigms must be appropriate under the umbrella metaparadigm. And finally, the metaparadigm must be "international in scope and substance" (p. 6) to represent the profession across national, social, cultural, and ethnic boundaries. The metaparadigm of professional nursing incorporates four concepts: person, environment, health, and nursing.

The **person** represents the individual, family, group, or community receiving care, each with unique characteristics.

The **environment** includes the physical, social, cultural, spiritual, and emotional climate or setting(s) in which the person(s) lives, works, plays, and interacts.

Health is the focus for the particular type of nursing and specific care provisions needed.

Nursing is defined by its activities, goals, and services.

In any area of professional nursing practice, we can evaluate *who* is the person, that is, the client or recipient of nursing care, *where* the person and the caregiver are seen and are influenced by others, *why* the person needs professional nursing care, and *how* the professional nurse functions as a provider of care. These concepts are present whether the client is the frail elder in an acute care setting, the expanding family in a birthing center, or an employee group in an occupational setting. Investigate these concepts specific to your own practice setting for an initial view of the systematic theory and knowledge base of your disciplinary paradigm.

Authority

The next characteristic of a professional is authority, as viewed by the client. This **authority** occurs through education and experience, which provide the professional with the knowledge and skills to make professional judgments. The client perceives the professional as having the knowledge and expertise to assist in meeting some need. The professional is therefore viewed as an authority in the area, and his or her judgments are trusted. Authority is the basis for the competence the client perceives and the client-professional relationship.

In the client-nurse relationship, the nurse is perceived as the authority figure whether providing a selected care technique or filling an informational need. The competence and skill demonstrated justify the client's trust in the professional nurse. Benner (1984) has described five levels of competency in clinical nursing practice: novice, advanced beginner, competent, proficient, and expert (p. xvii). The higher the levels of competence or expertise clients perceive in any profession, the greater trust or authority they place in the practitioners of that profession. Clients who see nurses as experts in providing needed health care view the profession as having more authority in health-care judgments. Based on this perception of authority, society grants the pro-

fession and its practitioners certain rights, privileges, and responsibilities.

Community Sanction

Society grants the profession certain powers and obligations to practice the specific profession. *Nursing's Social Policy Statement* (ANA, 1995c) states that "the authority for the practice of nursing is based on a social contract that acknowledges professional rights and responsibilities as well as mechanisms for public accountability" (p. 3). The professional community is responsible for ensuring safe and effective practice within the discipline. Professional and legal regulation of nursing practice as a **community sanction** occurs through statutes, definition of practice, and expectations for practitioners. Powers for entry and continuity in the profession are granted through licensure and professional practice parameters dictated in the state practice acts. These laws define a specific practice and provide regulatory powers at the state level for the board, licensing of professionals and protection of title (e.g., RN), general practice standards, approvals for educational programs, and disciplinary procedures.

Definition of practice and specific practice standards are further specified within the professional community through major nursing associations. The American Nurses Association (ANA) has specified a variety of practice standards for the profession, both general and specific to certain practice areas. The ANA has prepared several specialty standards documents jointly with the particular specialty organization to reflect the expectations for specialized professional practice. These **standards,** which illustrate the sanction by the community of the nursing profession, are described as "authoritative statements by which the nursing profession describes the responsibilities for which its practitioners are accountable. . . . Standards also define the nursing profession's accountability to the public and the client outcomes for which nurses are responsible" (ANA, 1991, p. 1). *The Standards of Clinical Nursing Practice,* (ANA, 1991), for example, prescribes general standards of care and standards of professional performance. Standards of care address safe practice and use of the nursing process with the actions of assessment, diagnosis, outcome identification, planning, implementation, and evaluation (ANA, 1991). Standards of professional performance are expected professional roles and behaviors, including quality of care, performance appraisal, education, collegiality, ethics, collaboration, research, and resource utilization (p. 2). Further standards of specialty practice are provided through the certification process with specialized education, testing, and ongoing learning requirements.

Another area in which the community grants a profession certain privileges based on professional knowledge and expertise is the education process. Educational programs are both approved at the individual state level, as with the Board of Nursing, and accredited at the national level by the National League for Nursing. Development, implementation, and evaluation of the organization, curriculum, faculty, students, graduates, facilities, and program resources are important considerations granted to professional groups. Here again, the profession is granted the power and has the responsibility to provide the community with practitioners who are appropriately educated for safe and effective practice.

Greenwood (1957) identified one of the most important professional privileges as confidentiality. Professional nursing enjoys this privilege and conscientiously guards the confidentiality of client information. As discussed in relation to ethical codes, confidentiality is a major consideration in professional nursing practice.

Code of Ethics

A professional abides by a certain **code of ethics** applicable to the practice area. Developed within the profession, these codes address general ethical practice issues. As Greenwood (1957) illustrates, although ethical codes vary among professions, they are uniform in describing client-professional and colleague-colleague relationships (p. 50). The *American Nurses Association Code for Nurses* is the major code for professional nursing practice (Table 1–1). In its preamble, the metaparadigm concepts of the profession are related as the purpose of the code: "To provide guidance for conduct and relationships in carrying out nursing responsibilities consistent with the ethical obligations of the profession and with high quality nursing care" (ANA, 1985, p. 1). The interpretative statements provided by the ANA promote understanding for appropriate application of the code in professional practice. The ANA Code embodies both the formal and informal ethical codes referred to by Greenwood. Unlike the Hippocratic Oath in medicine, neither the Nightingale Pledge nor the Professional Nursing Pledge is consistently used on entry into the nursing profession. Achieving professional status, however, requires ethical standards for our expected behaviors with clients, colleagues, and other professionals.

Professional Culture

The fifth characteristic of a profession is a **professional culture.** Greenwood (1957) described this as the formal and informal groups represented in the profession. *Formal groups* refer to the organizational systems in which the professionals practice, the educational institutions that provide for basic and continued learning, and the professional associations. *Informal groups* are the collegial settings that provide for collaboration, stimulation, and sharing of mutual values. These informal groups exist within each formal group, providing further professional, collegial inclusiveness.

Organizational systems in which professional nursing is practiced are diverse and multidimensional. As you will see in later chapters, hospital and home health agency settings are complex parts of a larger system. Professional nursing practice provides a unique culture with the values and norms expected of its practitioners. Organizational philosophies and mission statements provide information on the expressed culture of these settings. Further expression of the professional culture is apparent in the behaviors of professional nurses who practice in these settings.

Formal educational settings for professional nursing practice occur in institutions of higher learning with liberal and specialized learning requirements. In addition, values and norms for professional practice are transmitted as expectations for professional practice. Beyond basic educational practice, professional development is provided for with continuing education and specialty preparation. Cherry (1990) defines **professional development** as any organized program that facilitates maintenance and enhancement of competence, including the cognitive, affective, and psychomotor abilities to provide quality patient care, whether through direct patient care, management, or collaboration with other disciplines (p. 385). As with formal basic education, values and norms for professional practice are communicated as expectations for professional practice.

Professional organizations or associations are a major component of the culture of professional nursing practice, but they vary in purpose or mission and membership. The purpose of some **professional organizations,** such as the ANA, is to globally represent the profession. Specialty groups, with a more specific focus, promote education, skills, standards, and perhaps certification opportunities for a particular segment of the profession, for example, the American Association of Critical Care Nurses (AACN). Each organization has a unique philosophy or mission directed at professional nursing practice.

TABLE 1 – 1. American Nurses Association Code for Nurses

Ethical Standard	Subtopics of Interpretative Statement
1. The nurse provides services with respect for human dignity and the uniqueness of the client, unrestricted by considerations of social or economic status, personal attributes, or the nature of health problems.	1.1. Respect for human dignity 1.2. Status and attributes of clients 1.3. Nature of health problems
2. The nurse safeguards the client's right to privacy by judiciously protecting information of a confidential nature.	2.1. Client's right to privacy 2.2. Protection of information 2.3. Access to records
3. The nurse acts to safeguard the client and the public when health care and safety are affected by incompetent, unethical, or illegal practice by any person.	3.1. Safeguarding the health and safety of the client 3.2. Acting on questionable practice 3.3. Review mechanisms
4. The nurse assumes accountability and responsibility for individual nursing judgments and actions	4.1. Acceptance of responsibility and accountability 4.2. Responsibility for nursing judgment and action 4.3. Accountability for nursing judgment and action
5. The nurse maintains competence in nursing.	5.1. Personal responsibility for competence 5.2. Measurement of competence in nursing practice 5.3. Intraprofessional responsibility for competence in nursing practice
6. The nurse exercises informed judgment and uses individual competency and qualifications as criteria in seeking consultation, accepting responsibilities, and delegating nursing activities.	6.1. Changing functions 6.2. Accepting responsibilities 6.3. Consultation and collaboration 6.4. Delegation of nursing activities
7. The nurse participates in activities that contribute to the ongoing development of the profession's body of knowledge.	7.1. Nurse and development of knowledge 7.2. Protection of rights of human participants in research 7.3. General guidelines for participating in research
8. The nurse participates in the profession's efforts to implement and improve standards of nursing.	8.1. Responsibility to the public for standards 8.2. Responsibility to the profession for standards
9. The nurse participates in the profession's efforts to establish and maintain conditions of employment conducive to high-quality nursing care.	9.1. Responsibility for conditions of employment 9.2. Maintaining conditions for high-quality nursing care
10. The nurse participates in the profession's efforts to protect the public from misinformation and misrepresentation and to maintain the integrity of nursing.	10.1. Protection from misinformation and misrepresentation 10.2. Maintaining the integrity of nursing
11. The nurse collaborates with members of the health care professions and other citizens in promoting community and national efforts to meet the health needs of the public.	11.1. Collaboration with others to meet health needs 11.2. Responsibility to the public 11.3. Relationships with other disciplines

Source: Courtesy of American Nurses Foundation.

Values and norms for professionals are communicated in official publications, position statements, and specified standards. These organizations promote professional practice parameters for clinical practice, education, administration, and research. They provide educational opportunities and foster expansion of the knowledge base of individual professionals and the profession in general. Some organizations focus specifically on the science of the profession. Their purpose is to promote the scholarly aspects of the profession through education, publications, and conferences along with the refinement and building of skills through these media.

Consider the organizations that represent professional nursing practice and education illustrated in Table 1–2. ANA and its 53 state and territorial associations focus mainly on the professional as an entity, with concern for the health of society as well as the welfare of professional nurses through standards, official position statements, political action initiatives, and certification options for specialty practice. Specific to an area of specialty practice, the AACN, with more than 76,000 members worldwide, is the largest specialty organization. The National League for Nursing (NLN) has two types of membership, individual and agency, with initiatives related to accreditation of nursing education programs and community health agencies. The American Associa-

TABLE 1 – 2. Characteristics of Selected Professional Organizations

Organization	Mission	Membership	National Headquarters and Major Journal
American Nurses Association (ANA) and associated state and district associations Founded 1897	**Focus:** Professional nursing **Mission:** The purposes of ANA are to work for the improvement of health standards and health services for all people, foster high standards of nursing, and promote the professional development of nurses including their economic and general welfare. (ANA, 1995a)	Professional nurses at the state level obtain national and district membership.	American Nurses Association 600 Maryland Ave., SW Washington, DC 20024-2571 (800) 637-0323 http://www.nursingworld.org **Journal:** *The American Nurse*
American Association of Colleges of Nursing (AACN) Founded 1969	**Focus:** Nursing education **Mission:** The mission of AACN is to advance the quality of baccalaureate and graduate nursing education, promote research, and provide for the development of academic leaders. (AACN, 1994)	Member schools with baccalaureate and higher degree nursing programs	American Association of Colleges of Nursing 1 Dupont Circle, NW Suite 530 Washington, DC 20036 (202) 463-6930 http://www.aacn.nche.edu **Journal:** *Journal of Professional Nursing*
American Association of Critical-Care Nurses (AACN) Founded 1969	**Focus:** Specialty care **Mission:** The vision of AACN (1995) is the health care system, driven by the needs of patients, and where critical care nurses make their greatest contribution.	Individual membership	American Association of Critical-Care Nurses 101 Columbia Aliso Viejo, CA 92656-1491 (714) 362-2000 http://www.aacn.org **Journals:** *American Journal of Critical-Care, Critical-Care Nurse*
National League for Nursing (NLN) and associated constituent leagues Founded 1952	**Focus:** Nursing education and community health **Mission:** "The mission of the NLN is to improve education and health outcomes by linking communities and information. It achieves its mission through collaborating, connecting, serving, [and] learning." (NLN, 1995)	Individual members at the national level also obtain membership in a council of interest and a local constituent league. Agency membership for nursing education as: ▪ diploma programs ▪ associate degree programs ▪ baccalaureate and higher degree programs	National League for Nursing 350 Hudson Street New York, NY 10014 (800) 669-9656 http://www.nln.org **Journal:** *N & HC: Perspectives on Community*
Sigma Theta Tau International and member chapters (Honor Society of Nursing) Founded 1922	**Focus:** Nursing scholarship **Mission:** The mission of this international honor society is to improve global health through the development, dissemination, and use of nursing knowledge. (Dickenson-Hazard, 1996)	Individuals are invited to membership in chartered chapters with selection criteria as baccalaureate or higher degree students, faculty members, or community leaders	Sigma Theta Tau International Center for Nursing Scholarship 550 West North Street Indianapolis, IN 46202-3191 (317) 634-8171 http://stti-bl.iupui.edu **Journals:** *Image: Journal of Nursing Scholarship Online Journal of Knowledge Synthesis for Nursing*

tion of Colleges of Nursing focuses on collegiate education, serving member schools with baccalaureate and higher degree programs through educational standards, programs, policies, and legislative initiatives directed at high-quality professional education. Sigma Theta Tau International, as the honor society for nursing, has a distinctly scientific focus. This organization promotes knowledge development through research, dissemination of scientific information, technology, education, interdisciplinary collaboration, and adaptability. Appendix A provides a comprehensive listing of professional organizations.

PROFESSIONALISM IN NURSING

The nursing profession is characterized by Greenwood's attributes of a profession. But what of its uniqueness? Miller, Adams, and Beck (1993) have proposed that "nurses must disclaim the traditional analysis of professional and professionalism by other disciplines as the only method to determine definitions and characteristics of professionalism in nursing" (p. 290). They propose the use of a behavioral inventory to assist nurses in attaining higher degrees of professionalism (p. 294). This behavioral inventory consists of nine categories of professional nursing characteristics: educational background; adherence to the code of ethics; participation in the professional organization; continuing education and competency; communication and publication; autonomy and self-regulation; community service; use, development, and evaluation of theory; and research involvement (p. 291). Consider each of these criteria for professionalism in nursing.

The **educational background** required for professional practice is specified to ensure safe and effective practice. In nursing, the basic education required for entry into the profession varies with differences among baccalaureate, associate degree, diploma education, and even some entry-level graduate programs. But within each type of educational program, curricula and requirements are guided by general standards that must be met.

Although a school's curriculum is developed by its faculty members, certain standards are required for an educational program. Despite some variability in requirements and content, nursing curricula must contain essential content and hours as required by state boards of nursing, professional associations, and national accrediting bodies. Consumers of nursing care can be confused by the different educational routes leading to the title of registered nurse. As we will see in the final chapter, the Pew Health Professions Commission (1995) has recommended the following relative to basic nursing education:

Recognize value of multiple entry points to professional practice.

Consolidate professional nomenclature, e.g., a single title for each level of nursing preparation/service.

Differentiate practice responsibilities among levels and strengthen existing career ladder programs

A.D.N.: entry hospital and nursing home

B.S.N.: hospital care management and community practice

M.S.N.: specialty practice in hospital and independent practice. (p. 34)

Working to clarify these areas among professionals and consumers of nursing will have a beneficial impact on the view of nursing as a profession and **individual** nurses as true professionals.

Adherence to a **code of ethics** is expected in any profession. As illustrated previously, the *ANA Code for Nurses with Interpretative Statements* (1985) provides the broad guidelines. It is the responsibility of the practicing professional to know these guidelines and practice in accordance with the Code. As Miller, Beck and Adams (1993) reported, most professional nurse respondents did not have a copy of the ethical code, and many were unfamiliar with the document (p. 293). To meet this criterion of professionalism, nursing professionals need to demonstrate greater knowledge and understanding of the official ethical code. Periodic review of the 11 standards is an important responsibility for all professional nurses. This is especially true when the roles of nurses or clientele change, but it is also important to fully appreciate one's professional responsibilities, challenges, and talents when roles are stable.

Participation in the **professional organization** is an important criterion for a profession. Unfortunately, in nursing, this is quite a broad area, as is evident from the listing of professional organizations in Appendix A. Approximately 10 percent of the more than two million nurses in the United States belong to the major professional group, ANA. Many nurses prefer to associate with specialty groups that they believe better meet their educational and practice needs. This brings us to two critical considerations: multiple memberships and activity. Professionals are not limited to membership in one professional association. If all nurses belonged to one official organization representing professional nurses, that organization would have an enormous influence on health care by virtue of these numbers. But, because of different disciplinary paradigms, discussed at the start of this chapter, this is not the case. Professionals associate with organizations they view as most appropriate to their belief system views and practice, rather than with those not perceived to match their professional practice needs. Yet, ANA does represent the 2.2 million nurses in the United States and its territories. In the ANA (1995a) certificate of incorporation, the purpose of the association is stated as follows:

to promote the professional and educational advancement of nurses in every proper way; to elevate the standard of nursing education; to establish and maintain a code of ethics among nurses; to distribute relief among such nurses as may become ill, disabled, or destitute; to disseminate information on the subject of nursing by publications in official periodicals or otherwise; to bring into communication with each other various nurses and associations and federations of nurses throughout the United States of America; and to succeed to all rights and property held by the American Nurses Association as a corporation duly incorporated. (p. iii)

We are beginning to see more collaboration among organizations on key issues. This will further strengthen the profession and create a sense of professional community among nurses. Membership and participation in a major nursing organization are the important traits of professionalism in a professional nurse. Active involvement means more than paying dues; it is active support of and involvement in the issues addressed by the organization and the profession to promote high-quality health care for the consumer.

The fourth characteristic of professionalism in nursing identified by Miller, Adams, and Beck (1993) is **continuing education and competency.** These are crucial to safe, effective, and ethical professional practice. Ongoing improvement and knowledge are the goals of continuing education, which is required for relicensure in some states and recertification in specialty areas. To demonstrate nurses' involvement in formal continuing education, a 1992 study indicated that 21 percent of the RNs had completed additional formal education beyond their basic nursing education (ANA, 1995b, p. 2). But continuing education is more than obtaining required credits, in services, or formal degrees. Remaining current with ideas presented in the nursing and scientific literature is an important component of professional competency. Identifying learning and developmental needs is an expectation for competent professional practice. In essence, continuing education *for competency* involves self-assessment, ongoing learning, and self-evaluation. Self-assessment of individual learning needs is a continuous process for the professional. The focus is on discovery, as in baccalaureate and graduate education. Ongoing learning means that the mind is challenged every day with new ideas, building of a professional knowledge base and skills. Self-evaluation provides the satisfaction in one's progress and pursuit of further avenues of professional development.

Communication and publication were identified as the fifth characteristic of professional nursing. Although Miller, Adams, and Beck (1993) reported limited involvement in this area from the subjects in their research study, they did stress that "scholarly writing for publication and communica-

tion to others must become a requisite for the professional nurse to maintain and promote professionalism in nursing" (p. 294). This does not necessarily mean that every nurse needs to publish a scholarly article each year. Innovative ideas are communicated in a variety of ways, both within the practice setting and worldwide through publications or on the Internet. Communication among professionals through well-developed and presented memoranda, proposed institutional policies and practices, and reports at the agency level is important and shows professionalism. Sharing with colleagues through specialty, district, or state nurses' association newsletters or publications further promotes professionalism. Ideas can also be extended to professional education and development through professional journals, other publications, and telecommunication. It is the responsibility of the professional to share innovative ideas that can benefit other professionals.

This responsibility relates to the sixth characteristic of professionalism in nursing, **autonomy and self-regulation.** These attributes are involved in decision making for the nurse who is "willing to extend the time and talent to ensure quality patient care" (Miller, Adams, and Beck, 1993, p. 293). Autonomy involves independent judgment and self-governing within the scope of one's practice, which has changed in response to people's health care needs. As key professionals in organizational settings, nurses make the time and commitment to ensure that high-quality care and standards are present and upheld. This involves critical thinking, communication, collaboration, and leadership. Important concepts in this area are professional responsibility and accountability. The ANA Code for Nurses (1985) defines **responsibility** as carrying out the duties associated with the professional role and **accountability** as being answerable for one's judgments and actions in performing professional responsibilities (pp. 8–9). Professional responsibility and accountability involve upholding quality standards as well as developing and critically analyzing those standards and the outcomes. Professionals are responsible and answerable to clients for nursing care outcomes. Nurses are actively involved in supervising, delegating, and evaluating others. But their professional status can take the expectations of critical thinking, clinical judgment, expertise, and advocacy beyond a narrowly defined job description.

Community service was proposed as the seventh characteristic of professionalism in nursing. Nurses are well-equipped and talented in this area with their orientation of service to clients and society at large. Nurses frequently lead health-promoting activities in their employment role, their professional community, and among their families and acquaintances. Consider how residents in a defined community always seem to know who the nurses in the area are and how frequently those nurses are approached with questions or requests to get involved in projects or committees. Also consider how nurses reach out to others with information on health or means to foster wellness in their community. All of these activities are community services. Leadership skills of professional nurses promote the involvement in community service, in their practice, professionally, and in personal communities.

Although all professions have systematic theory and knowledge on which to base their practice, the eighth characteristic of professionalism in nursing involves greater activity in this process: **theory use, development, and evaluation.** Theory is essential for a profession to guide its practice and research. Nursing, as a developing and dynamic profession, demands that its professionals develop, refine, and evaluate theory. We not only use theory, but are constantly involved in critical analysis as clients, health care, and environments change. We are constantly expanding and refining our knowledge base. The challenge is to collect, analyze, and report data on efficacy related to trends in clients' outcomes. These trends, rather than individual cases, provide information that expands and refines the profession's knowledge base. This need for data collection and analysis leads to research, the final characteristic of professional nursing proposed by Miller, Adams, and Beck (1993).

In Chapter 16, research involvement is discussed as an expectation for professional nurses. **Research involvement** refers to much more than leading or participating in a research study. As stated in the interpretative statements of ANA Code for Nurses (1985), "each nurse has a role in this area of professional activity, whether as an investigator in furthering knowledge, as a participant in research, or as a user of theoretical and empirical knowledge" (p. 12). Ensuring ethical standards and protection of clients involved in research is critical for every professional nurse. Equally essential is the responsibility for incorporating current knowledge into professional practice and supporting the development of further knowledge. It is important to appreciate the process and rigor needed for research. In 1981, the ANA Commission on Nursing Research identified specific research activities for nurses according to their level of nursing education. These guidelines provide certain expectations for involvement in re-

search for all nurses, whether they are prepared at the associate degree, baccalaureate, master's, or doctoral level. Research involvement, whether by using findings, getting involved in an investigation, or protecting subjects, is a characteristic of professionalism in nursing. It adds to our knowledge base, enhances our practice, and promotes improved outcomes for our clients.

Fulfilling these characteristics well is the challenge to professionalism in nursing. The degree to which professionals demonstrate professionalism in nursing is apparent in their professional practice and how they define nursing. One's personal definition of nursing is one's philosophy of nursing, belief system, and guide for professional practice.

YOUR PHILOSOPHY OF NURSING

Virginia Henderson (1897–1996) was an outstanding leader in nursing. Her classic definition of nursing embodied her view of the unique role of the professional nurse as

> assisting the individual, sick or well, in the performance of those activities contributing to health or its recovery (or to a peaceful death) that he would perform unaided if he had the necessary strength, will, or knowledge. And to do this in such a way as to help him gain independence as rapidly as possible. (Henderson, 1966, p. 15)

This concrete definition was expanded and applied to nursing practice, education, and research. Her philosophy of nursing was one of caring, assisting, and supporting the person. In her writings, Henderson (1966) encouraged every nurse to develop a personal concept of nursing.

A **philosophy** of nursing presents a particular professional nurse's belief system or worldview of nursing—the nurse's personal definition of nursing. Bevis (1989) defines philosophy as providing a point of view of nature, relationships, and the value of things (p. 34). One common thread through any personal philosophy is the way the individual professional defines the concepts common to nursing: the metaparadigm concepts of person, environment, health, and nursing.

As discussed previously, the metaparadigm concept of the person relates to nursing clients. Nurses in different practices define the person uniquely within the practice, for example, as individuals versus families. This also influences the environment, for example, an intensive care unit in an acute care setting or a rural health care unit located in a community school or modular building. The concept of health also varies, from the professional who provides care for trauma victims to the nurse involved with health initiatives in an employee group. Specific nursing roles and the services provided influence the concept of nursing. In addition to the metaparadigm concepts in a personal philosophy of nursing, certain other commonalities are generally apparent. Bevis (1989) has identified the following philosophical propositions generally accepted despite divergent implications and implementation:

1. The individual has intrinsic value and there is worth inherent in human life.
2. Nursing is a rational activity.
3. Nursing's uniqueness is in the way the basic social and biological sciences are synthesized in functions that promote health.
4. The individual nurse-citizen has some control over and responsibility for the political and social milieu in which she lives.
5. Nursing is a process with a central subjective purpose, an inherent organization or system, and dynamic creativity. (pp. 43–45)

In addition, consider the four essential features of contemporary nursing practice identified in *Nursing's Social Policy Statement* (ANA, 1995):

1. Attention to the full range of human experiences and responses to health and illness without restriction to a problem-focused orientation
2. Integration of objective data with knowledge gained from an understanding of the client's or group's subjective experience
3. Application of scientific knowledge to the processes of diagnosis and treatment

4. Provision of a caring relationship that facilitates health and healing (p. 6)

At this point you must critically analyze your belief system and express your views of nursing. We all have prior experiences that influence our thinking and actions. Try to place those aside and begin to craft your philosophy of nursing. Consider the following questions:

- State your personal definitions of the concepts of person, environment, health, and nursing.
  Who is the recipient of nursing care?
  Where is the environment in which these persons are located?
  What are the influences (or the effects) of this environment on the person?
  What does this person perceive health to be?
  What does health mean to you, personally and as a nurse?
  Why does that person need the nursing care that you provide?
  What does the term "nursing" signify to you personally?
- List the assumptions (or statements you consider proven facts) about nursing and the characteristics of professional nurses.
  What does the concept of people, in general, signify to nurses?
  What characteristics do nurses demonstrate?
  What are the roles of nurses in the current health care delivery system?
  What is unique about nurses and the nursing profession?

Using these definitions and assumptions, develop your views into a one- or two-page personal philosophy of nursing. Evaluate this periodically to analyze how your professional practice is enhanced in your ongoing quest for knowledge and expertise in your profession.

KEY POINTS

- The following are characteristics of a profession: (1) systematic theory and knowledge base, (2) authority, (3) community sanction, (4) an ethical code, and (5) a professional culture.
- Kerlinger (1986) defines a **theory** as "a set of interrelated constructs (concepts), definitions, and propositions that present a systematic view of phenomena by specifying relations among variables, with the purpose of explaining and predicting the phenomena" (p. 9).
- A **paradigm** used by professionals in a scientific community includes the beliefs and the belief system shared by members of that particular community to explain phenomena, practice the profession, and conduct research.

- The **metaparadigm** of nursing is the overall concern of nursing common to each nursing model, whether a conceptual model/paradigm or formal theory, and it includes the concepts of person, environment, health, and nursing.
- The American Nurses Association Code for Nurses is the major code for professional nursing practice. It identifies expected professional practice behaviors with clients, colleagues, and other professionals in the ethical standards.
- Autonomy involves judgment and self-governing within one's scope of practice. This self-governing requires ongoing evaluation of both responsibility and accountability in professional practice. In the ANA Code for Nurses (1985), **responsibility** is defined as carrying out the duties associated with the professional role, and **accountability** is being answerable for one's judgments and actions while performing professional responsibilities (pp. 8–9).
- Miller, Adams, and Bell (1993) have proposed the use of a behavioral inventory to assist nurses in attaining higher levels of professionalism. The following characteristics of professionalism are included in this inventory: educational background, adherence to the code of ethics, participation in the professional organization, continuing education and competency, communication and publication, autonomy and self-regulation, community service, theory use, development and evaluation, and involvement in research.
- A personal **philosophy of nursing** presents the belief system or worldview of nursing for a particular professional nurse. Incorporated in a philosophy are definitions, values, and assumptions concerning the metaparadigm concepts of person, environment, health, and nursing.

CHAPTER EXERCISES

1. Relate each of the four metaparadigm concepts of nursing to your specific practice area and setting. Describe the paradigm under which you practice.

2. Locate another definition of professionalism or a profession in the literature. Apply this definition to the nursing profession.

3. Analyze your state nursing practice act for the powers, privileges, and responsibilities vested in the profession. Discuss how this act directs responsibility and accountability in professional nursing practice.

4. Select a professional organization listed in Appendix A. Investigate the mission, purposes, major initiatives, membership, and benefits of membership. Discuss the professional culture of the organization and the values related to nursing and health care.

5. Review one of the standards of practice listed in the bibliography. Identify the legal and ethical responsibilities of practice in this area. Discuss the formal and informal educational responsibilities for professional practice.

6. For each of the 11 ethical standards of the ANA Code for Nurses (1985), describe how these are applicable to each of the following environments for nursing practice:
a. Acute care in a hospital setting
b. Home care
c. Clinic or occupational health setting

7. Describe your present involvement in each of the following nine areas of professionalism in the behavioral inventory suggested by Miller, Adams, and Bell (1993):
- Educational background
- Adherence to the code of ethics
- Participation in the professional organization
- Continuing education and competency
- Communication and publication
- Autonomy and self-regulation
- Community service
- Theory use, development, and evaluation
- Research involvement. (p. 291)

8. Share your personal philosophy of professional nursing with a colleague. Explain and support your views. Identify commonalities between you and your colleague.

REFERENCES

American Association of Colleges of Nursing. (1994). *Member services*. Washington, DC: Author.

American Association of Critical Care Nurses (AACN). (1995). What is the American Association of critical-care nurses? *AACN Critical Care, http://www.aacn.org/aacn.html.*

American Nurses Association. (1995a). *Bylaws, as amended July 2, 1995* (Publication No. A01 10M 9/95). Washington, DC: American Nurses Publishing.

American Nurses Association. (1995b). *Nursing facts. Today's registered nurse — numbers and demographics* (Publication No. PR-17). Washington, DC: Author.

American Nurses Association. (1995c). *Nursing's social policy statement* (Publication No. NP-107 5M 9/95). Washington, DC: American Nurses Publishing.

American Nurses Association. (1991). *Standards of clinical nursing practice* (Publication No. NP-79 20M 12/91). Kansas City, MO: Author.

American Nurses Association. (1987). *The scope of nursing practice* (Publication No. NP-72 15M 6/87). Kansas City, MO: Author.

American Nurses Association. (1985). *Code for nurses with interpretative statements* (Publication No. G-56). Kansas City, MO: Author.

American Nurses Association, Commission on Nursing Research. (1981). *Guidelines for the investigative function of nurses*. Kansas City, MO: Author.

Benner, P. (1984). *From novice to expert: Excellence and power in clinical nursing practice*. Menlo Park, CA: Addison-Wesley.

Bevis, E. O. (1989). *Curriculum building in nursing: A process* (3rd ed.) (Publication No. 15-2277). New York: National League for Nursing.

Callin, M. (1996). From RN to B.S.N.: Seeing familiar situations in different ways. *Journal of Continuing Education in Nursing, 27,* 28–33.

Cherry, B. S. (1990). Professional development. In J. A. Dienemann (Ed.), *Nursing administration: Strategic perspectives and application* (pp. 385–402). Norwalk, CT: Appleton & Lange.

Dickenson-Hazard, N. (1996). Message from the executive officer. *Sigma Theta Tau International, http://stti-bu.iupui.edu/stti/nancy.html.*

Fawcett, J. (1995). *Analysis and evaluation of conceptual models of nursing* (3rd ed.). Philadelphia: F. A. Davis.

Greenwood, E. (1957). Attributes of a profession. *Social Work, 2*(3), 45–55.

Henderson, V. (1966). *The nature of nursing: A definition and its implications for practice, education, and research*. New York: Macmillan.

Kerlinger, F. N. (1986). *Foundations of behavioral research* (3rd ed.). New York: Holt, Rinehart and Winston.

Kuhn, T. S. (1970). *The structure of scientific revolutions* (2nd ed.). Chicago: University of Chicago Press.

Mezirow, J. (1991). *Transformative dimensions of adult learning*. San Francisco: Jossey-Bass.

Miller, B. K., Adams, D., Beck, L. (1993). A behavioral inventory for professionalism in nursing. *Journal of Professional Nursing, 9,* 290–295.

National League for Nursing. (1995). *National League for Nursing 1995–1997*. New York: Author.

Pew Health Professions Commission. (1995). *Critical challenges: Revitalizing the health professions for the twenty-first century*. San Francisco: USCF Center for the Health Professions.

BIBLIOGRAPHY

Allen, D. G. (1994). The social policy statement: A reappraisal. In P. L. Chinn (Ed.), *Advances in nursing science series. Exemplars in criticism: Challenge and controversy* (pp. 69–79). Gaithersburg, MD: Aspen.

American Nurses Association. (1995a). *Scope and standards of gerontological nursing practice* (Publication No. GE-14 7.5M 6/95). Washington, DC: American Nurse Publishing.

American Nurses Association. (1995b). *Scope and standards of nursing practice in correctional facilities* (Publication No. NP-104). Washington, DC: American Nurses Publishing.

American Nurses Association. (1995c). *Standards of clinical practice and scope of practice for the acute care nurse practitioner* (Publication No. MS-22). Washington, DC: American Nurses Publishing.

American Nurses Association. (1995d). *Standards of nursing informatics* (Publication No. NP-100). Washington, DC: American Nurses Publishing.

American Nurses Association. (1994a). *Scope of practice for nursing informatics* (Publication No. NP-90). Washington, DC: American Nurses Publishing.

American Nurses Association. (1994b). *Standards for nursing professional development: Continuing education and staff development* (Publication No. COE-17). Washington, DC: American Nurses Publishing.

American Nurses Association. (1994c). *Statement on psychiatric–mental health clinical nursing practice and standards of psychiatric–mental health nursing practice* (Publication No. PMH-12). Washington, DC: American Nurses Publishing.

American Nurses Association. (1994d). *Statement on the scope and standards of otorhinolaryngology nursing practice* (Publication No. NP-95). Washington, DC: American Nurses Publishing.

American Nurses Association. (1994e). *Statement on the scope and standards of respiratory nursing practice* (Publication No. NP-96). Washington, DC: American Nurses Publishing.

American Nurses Association. (1993a). *Nursing facts. Registered nurses: A distinctive health care profession* (Publication No. PR-12). Washington, DC: Author.

American Nurses Association. (1993b). *The scope of cardiac rehabilitation nursing practice* (Publication No. NP-86). Washington, DC: Author.

American Nurses Association. (1990). *A statement on the scope of college health nursing practice* (Publication No. CH-19). Washington, DC: Author.

American Nurses Association. (1988). *Standards for organized nursing services and responsibilities of nurse administrators across all settings* (Publication No. NS-31). Washington, DC: Author.

American Nurses Association. (1987a). *Standards of addictions nursing practice with selected diagnoses and criteria* (Publication No. PMH-10). Washington, DC: Author.

American Nurses Association. (1987b). *Standards of oncology nursing practice* (Publication No. MS-16). Washington, DC: Author.

American Nurses Association. (1987c). *Standards of practice for the primary health care nurse practitioner* (Publication No. NP-71). Washington, DC: Author.

American Nurses Association. (1986a). *Standards of community health nursing practice* (Publication No. CH-2). Washington, DC: Author.

American Nurses Association. (1986b). *Standards of home health nursing practice* (Publication No. CH-14). Washington, DC: Author.

American Nurses Association. (1985a). *Human rights guidelines for nurses in clinical and other research* (Publication No. D-46 5M 2/85). Kansas City, MO: Author.

American Nurses Association. (1985b). *Neuroscience nursing practice: process and outcome criteria for selected diagnoses* (Publication No. MS-13). Washington, DC: Author.

American Nurses Association. (1985c). *The scope of practice for the primary health care nurse practitioner* (Publication No. NP-61). Washington, DC: Author.

American Nurses Association. (1984). *Standards of practice for the perinatal nurse specialist* (Publication No. MCH-15). Washington, DC: Author.

American Nurses Association. (1983). Outcome standards for rheumatology nursing practice (Publication No. MS-12). Washington, DC: Author.

American Nurses Association. (1981a). *Standards of cardiovascular nursing practice* (Publication No. MS-4). Washington, DC: Author.

American Nurses Association. (1981b). *Standards of perioperative nursing practice* (Publication No. MS-2). Washington, DC: Author.

Taylor, J. W. (1994). *Implementation of nursing practice standards and guidelines* (Publication No. NP-98). Washington, DC: American Nurses Association.

Chapter 2

COPING WITH RETURNING TO SCHOOL

Bernadette Dersch Curry

CHAPTER OBJECTIVES

On completion of
this chapter, the reader
will be able to:

1. Evaluate personal and professional goals.
2. Identify personal and professional role conflicts and stressors.
3. Develop time management strategies for family, work, and educational demands.
4. Assemble resources to assist with family, work, and educational demands.
5. Develop a personalized study environment and study strategies.

KEY TERMS

Goals

Role Transition

Resources

Streamline

Returning to school for an advanced degree in nursing may begin as an academic and professional goal. But as the fullness of the college experience unfolds, you will come to realize that education is more than academic exercises and credits. It is an intellectual pursuit that leads to multifaceted personal growth. You have chosen the challenge and made the personal and professional commitment to goals, and with a positive attitude and a variety of resources you can experience the exhilaration of success and the satisfaction of accomplishment.

WHAT TO EXPECT

Using experiences with RN students in a baccalaureate nursing program, Donea Shane (1980) described observations and set forth what is known as The Returning to School Syndrome. She characterized emotional responses and captured the essence of the process. In addition to identifying and documenting the behaviors, she wanted to alert RN students to prepare for the challenges.

The syndrome has three phases. In the first phase, called the *honeymoon,* fascination with the new and different activities associated with academe casts a positive glow on the experience. The student can derive a strong sense of satisfaction and an optimistic outlook from making the decision and embarking on the journey. A heightened sense of purpose can provide confidence and motivation. Shane notes that the length of the honeymoon phase varies from hours to semesters. The phase most commonly ends when the student encounters the first course that addresses "substantial nursing theory or clinical practice" (Shane, 1980, p. 86). The RN student may have had minimal or no experience with nursing theory (Fawcett, 1995). The abstract nature of theory may elicit anxiety in students who previously learned in concrete and structured educational modes and functioned professionally with technical expertise.

In phase two, called *conflict,* new and different perspectives of nursing are presented, and students experience a growing discomfort with previous knowledge and familiar concepts, often accompanied by waning confidence. Insecurity and self-doubt can chip away at professional image and cause students to question their capabilities. Inability to accept the reality of a less than perfect grade can pose an emotional impasse. This assault on the once self-assured ego takes a serious toll. The barrage of emotions can be physically and emotionally draining. At this point fatigue, anger, and withdrawal are common, complicating already negative feelings, interfering with educational activities, and causing hostility toward the institution. The student may blame the institution, faculty, or just about anyone or anything else for his or her perceived unsatisfactory achievement in the program.

Biculturalism, the third phase, is described as the "ability to be as comfortable and effective in one culture (school) as in another (work)" and is considered the "most positive solution to The Returning to School Syndrome" (Shane, 1980, p. 86). By understanding their expectations of the academic experience and using coping skills, students can appreciate both their current and expanded nursing roles. Students learn that growth does not require destroying strong foundations but builds on them, and that all past education and professional experiences serve as a rich resource for professionals to measure growth.

SETTING PERSONAL GOALS

Deciding to return to school is a major lifetime decision and the beginning of a new phase of goal setting. **Goals** are powerful entities. They can provide a focus, sustain commitment, and reinforce priorities. Formulating goals provides a framework for current and future decisions. Goals help keep the decision maker focused by addressing both the time needed and the scope of the task. Their power can be overlooked if the goal is considered simply an endpoint of a process.

Remember these points when setting your goals:
- You alone are the goal maker and in command of your personal quest.
- You alone create the goal, establish the plan, and accomplish the task.
- You can expect to invest considerable time and attention in developing to your goals and their accompanying plans.
- Forethought, motivation, and creativity transform goals from ideas into reality.
- Personal goals are born of individual values, ambition, and abilities, and are the result of introspective and selective processes.
- Genuine personal goals are holistic and help you maintain perspective and respect priorities.

The planning associated with goals cannot be underestimated. Chenevert (1993) said that the "difference between a goal and a dream is a *workable* plan" (p. 135). Both long- and short-term goals, and the means to achieve them, must be realistic and acknowledge individual strengths and limitations, available resources, and personal flexibility. Capitalize on individual strengths, and use available resources to strengthen limitations.

Flexibility is particularly important. Things always change, and these changes may require adjustments to your original plans. Consider revising your goals or readjusting your plans as a positive response to the new developments. When establishing your goals and plans, be sure to develop a "plan B," to increase your ability to adapt quickly to the new situation.

Consider achieving an advanced degree as a long-term goal. It requires patience, time, and energy to succeed. Building in short-term goals helps to keep your achievements and remaining goals in perspective. Achieving these short-term goals provides a sense of satisfaction, which can energize and increase motivation. View each educational phase as a milestone and each course or semester completed as an accomplishment and progress toward the ultimate goal.

No matter how well you have set your goals, made realistic plans, or chosen appropriate actions, you will face occasional stress, frustration, discouragement, and low motivation. Achievement rarely occurs without challenge. During these times, it helps to recall the reasons for setting the goal and review the potential benefits. Achieving a goal is fulfilling a commitment to oneself. It is by working through challenges and succeeding that growth occurs. Being true to oneself when setting and living out goals, and heeding the words of Goethe that "things which matter most should never be at the mercy of things which matter least," are vitally important.

REFINING PROFESSIONAL IDENTITY

"Metamorphosis does not happen without our artful participation" (Moore, 1992, p. 76). Neither personal nor professional growth occurs without individual energy and creativity. The purposeful decision to return to school begins an ongoing series of transitions leading to the goal. Each of those transitions requires the thought, attention, and action of the individual and contributes to professional change and personal growth.

Change can be an uncomfortable and negative experience. However, it can also be invigorating, challenging, and have many positive results. Returning to the student role requires "self-redefinition," accompanied by motivation (Redman & Cassells,

1990). Factors that influence nurses to pursue further professional education have been studied and found to be both introspective and practical. Redman and Cassells (1990) found that the opportunity for career and educational mobility was the most influential factor for RNs' deciding to pursue the baccalaureate degree. Personal desire to have a bachelor's degree was the second. Interestingly, students in traditional baccalaureate nursing programs most often reported those same factors as being very influential in their decision to enroll (Curry, 1994). These motivators play an important part in the active roles expected of the student.

From the onset, you'll have the opportunity to chart your own course of action resulting in a change in professional identity. Planning is important because it allows time to seek assistance and develop mindset, time frame, and methods for the journey. Transition from RN to student can be gradual and meet your individual needs. Participating in educational decisions is a prime example of engaging in active change (Grant, 1994), and it sets the tone for establishing a new professional identity. In **role transition,** you not only assume but develop the new role (Strader & Decker, 1995); it is the opportunity for you to individualize educational and professional experiences and to use education as a vehicle for true change in the professional role.

Your professional experience and commitment can guide the transition and are integral to individual goals. The educational experience is an opportunity to develop abilities to expand a professional base, focus on an area of interest, or meet a specific health-care need in society. It enables you to formulate and work toward achieving your own expectations. Programs for advanced professional education in nursing build on prior learning and experiences. A paradigm shift in nursing focuses on the similarities rather than the differences in the profession and facilitates movement from one level to another (Grant, 1994). This shift can foster camaraderie, mentoring, and advancement. The presence of examples greatly assists role transition, and having a role model is extremely valuable in showing the importance of lifelong learning and in assisting with the process of refining professional identity (Strader & Decker, 1995).

Nursing education is designed to develop professionals who think critically and to provide the principles and guidelines for the myriad, diverse situations you encounter. The fullness of your nursing role is limited only by your own imagination, creativity, and ability. During this transitional period, remember that health care is also in transition. Claire Fagin (1994) notes that "nursing is a major player" in finding solutions for health-care reform. As a student, you can craft a professional identity in tune with contemporary nursing and your personal interests and professional talents. As you progress, the change and personal growth will gradually emerge in your professional persona, which will enrich your experience. Nor does this growth stop on graduation. This experience serves as an impetus for lifelong learning and the desire to maximize abilities and the professional role.

ROLE CONFLICTS AND STRESSORS

Returning to school creates a new and additional role for the nurse, and the time, attention, and energy it requires must be found from a finite supply. Rearranging an established lifestyle and pattern of daily activities to accommodate the additional workload is often necessary. The overall balance of life activities and parts of life roles can be affected.

Most nurses who return to school are employed, balancing concurrent roles of parent, nurse, student, and homemaker (Lengacher, 1993). Though they may be challenging, multiple roles can convey a number of rewards and pleasures, providing a positive synergy the individual might not experience from only one role. Functioning in multiple roles can be instrumental in redefining one's identity, goal setting, and personal achievement. Negative consequences, however, can also occur, particularly, role conflict in women (Lengacher, 1993).

What are the sources of role conflict, or stressors, a returning student might experience? Any facet of the student's life has the potential for conflict or stress, varying with the individual student. Adequate planning and flexibility can minimize difficulties.

Educational Conflicts and Stressors

FITTING INTO ACADEME

Being an adult learner may present your first challenge. For some, the label itself elicits a sense of not belonging, of not "fitting in," or of being behind the traditional education schedule. In most disciplines, however, adult learners currently constitute a significant percentage of college students. You will not be the lone adult in nursing courses or on campus.

Initial selection of courses presents a maze of choices and possibilities, which may seem overwhelming and strange. Keep in mind that the goal of the institution is to promote the success of each student. Faculty are available to help and advise you. Be prepared to seek out the faculty adviser and be an active participant in your education.

You have both a "right and responsibility to ask for guidance" (Bruner & Donahue, 1992, p. 143). Effective education includes two-way communication, and you will be both encouraged and expected to be an active student.

GRADES

Most educational endeavors involve criteria and some form of evaluation, and grades are the most common format. Although grades are usually important to all students, the mature student may place undue emphasis on them. Some students may assume that previous professional experience or age requires them to excel in their courses. This is both unrealistic and an unnecessary burden. Concern for grades can lead to a mental battle for self-esteem that focuses more on getting good grades than on assimilating information. A grade less than an "A" should not be perceived as a threat to one's identity. Grades do not automatically equal the time and money invested, despite the achievement. Contracting for a grade is an alternative that allows the student to select a grade and an accompanying level of performance criteria. Contracting permits the student to be independent and take ownership of planning and implementing objectives for the assignment (Knowles, 1988).

TEST ANXIETY

Test anxiety is common among all learners and can be a major problem. Remember that some degree of anxiety is expected. Excessive anxiety before and during exams can interfere with thinking, however. Adequate preparation and understanding of the material and a positive, self-confident attitude can control test anxiety. The following are some basic tips to reduce test anxiety:

- Plan and use adequate time for study.
- Don't cram.
- Study with others after you've studied alone.
- Take control.
- Think positively.
- Keep your normal reasonable routine.
- Use stress-reducing tapes.
- Pace your time to answer the questions.
- Don't be afraid to ask the professor for clarification.

WRITING PAPERS

Assembling the material and thoughts to write a paper may seem overwhelming at first. However, every college uses a format that can guide you through the process. Your course professor will give specific direction and be available to explain expectations. Ask the professor for feedback as you develop the topic, and use the library staff to help acquire the appropriate references. Make sure you have a copy of the writing format (APA, MLA, etc.) at home. Once you have the first draft written, put it aside and review it with an objective eye the next day. Pay attention to grammar and flow to convey thoughts accurately.

ACTIVE CLASSROOM—ACTIVE LEARNER

Today's classroom may vary significantly from your previous experiences. Note taking and passive learning have been replaced by group work, presentations, simulations, and many other creative educational strategies, producing a dynamic environment that addresses many learning styles and promotes critical thinking (Boyer, 1987).

COMPUTER ANXIETY

If you have little or no experience with computers, you may have doubts about doing computer-assisted exercises or submitting an assignment on disk. Developing keyboarding skills while taking courses can be time-consuming, and not necessarily a confidence booster at the start. However, computers can produce a high-quality, finished document and generate multiple copies. Assignments can be quickly edited and duplicated. Introductory courses to develop basic computer skills are usually available, and computer lab staff can assist you with problems.

> Tell me and I'll forget
>
> Show me and I may remember
>
> Involve me and I'll understand
>
> Chinese Proverb

ACADEMIC TRANSITION

As Shane (1980) noted, returning students may have difficulty accepting information from faculty they view as having less current clinical experience. Students may have limited exposure to nursing theory, because their experience is more technical. Advanced education focuses on incorporating theoretical concepts into the technical experience to allow for a new view of professional nursing.

Achieving maximum professional growth requires an understanding that college is more than attending classes and accumulating credits; it is about personal growth and expanding perspective. It is about the experience of blending into the college scene, making grades and deadlines while making dinner, and making it to work on time. The new and different demands may challenge one's time, intellectual reserves, and confidence. Simple tasks such as finding a parking space, a particular building or office on campus, or a specific book in the library can deplete resources needed for major tasks. The transition can be unnerving, and you may begin to question your own worth.

Work-Related Problems

Working while attending school presents a host of stressors. Though scheduling of classes around professional responsibilities may create some problems, it can also provide wonderful opportunities to implement new concepts learned in the classroom.

At times, academic responsibilities may be more time-consuming than anticipated, and the student may attempt to adjust work schedules as a solution. However, this may cause additional complications with finances, colleagues, or supervisors.

Family Complications

The biggest conflicts or stressors may arise from situations involving those people closest to the student, especially family. Reorganizing responsibilities during school sessions can help, but continuing an education should never require the student to choose sides against family. In fact, family support and understanding of the experience is essential from both practical and emotional standpoints (Campaniello, 1988).

A supportive partner can be the most important asset in the education experience. However, don't expect a partner to immediately understand the expectations and pressures of the process. You'll need to talk about the pressures of your new role, if you expect your partner to understand and support your endeavor. Accurate and adequate communication is essential to formulating new or different expectations within the family. When time with your family is curtailed to accommodate the demands of a course, you may experience considerable role strain and question the decisions and compromises made to pursue the degree.

The characteristically nurturant roles of wife and mother in American society have been compatible with the nursing profession for many decades. However, these roles can be significant stressors for nurses returning to school (Lengacher, 1993). Certainly, the parental role should not be taken lightly, and the addition of school-related activities to an already busy schedule can prompt feelings of guilt and anxiety. These feelings may be more intense for a single parent. In addition, the need for competent child care frequently extends beyond day care to evening care. Reliable supervision for school-age and teenage children is an equally important issue that may require much more coordination than the care of younger, less mobile children. It can be extremely difficult for a student to concentrate in class knowing that a teenage son with a new driver's license is driving home from school.

Students who are part of the "sandwich generation" may bear responsibility for parents and children. Even though the parents do not live in the students' home, they may require additional time, attention, and emotions.

Single students without children may have fewer family responsibilities but fewer resources and support to draw on while still being responsible for the multiple functions of a single-person household. Few people experience a totally uncomplicated return to school.

The number of men in nursing schools is growing. Besides the increasing percentage of young men who enter traditional baccalaureate nursing programs, there is a noticeable increase in the number of men choosing nursing as a second career (Curry, 1994). Men can be subjected to societal stressors and experience role conflict when they enter a primarily female profession. Returning to school may cause similar stressors when the male student is questioned about his continuing education or his career choice. The conventional roles of husband, father, and breadwinner are not often linked with nursing. Exposure to such narrow thinking can affect the many dedicated men striving to advance both themselves and the profession of nursing. The situation can be compounded when

male mentors, role models, and peer support are not readily accessible.

Multiple Roles

Multiple family roles added to the roles of nurse and student make a challenging combination. Yet multiple roles have positive aspects. Handling these roles can increase confidence, propel the student through activities, and provide a sense of satisfaction. The adage "if you want something done, ask a busy person to do it" has held true for decades. Adding or modifying roles does not necessarily have negative consequences. In fact, a study of RN students employed during their course work showed that they did not experience "burnout" more frequently than other nurses (Dick & Anderson, 1993). However, keep in mind that stress can result from almost any type of change, even positive change. Holmes and Rahe (1967) showed that both positive and negative life events can have a negative effect on health. It would be unrealistic to expect balance and harmony among all life roles during course work (Table 2–1).

Personal Stressors

The most intense stress or conflicts experienced by the student may be the pressures that come from within. Doubt, insecurity, and discouragement can become overwhelming enemies. Strive to be faithful to the commitment to yourself, and have trust in yourself, faith in your decisions, and courage to continue. It is vitally important to realize that the capital letter "I," when referring to oneself, does not stand for indispensable. To ensure success, embark on a plan of organization that will streamline activities, use resources, delegate tasks, maximize results of efforts, and not create unnecessary stress.

TIME MANAGEMENT

Time is a precious intangible commodity that cannot be stored, stopped, or renewed. It is invisible yet constantly makes its presence known, and it can hang heavily on the hands of some and quickly fly by for others. Contemporary society is fascinated with time and ways to save it. Time management is a popular but inappropriate phrase. People do not manage the clock but rather organize their activities within the framework of time. The returning student has considerable experience with time from both personal and professional perspectives, but the student

TABLE 2–1. Social Readjustment Rating Scale

Life Event	Mean Value
Death of spouse	100
Divorce	73
Marital separation	65
Jail term	63
Death of close family member	63
Personal illness or injury	53
Marriage	50
Fired from work	50
Marital reconciliation	47
Retirement	45
Change in family member's health	44
Pregnancy	40
Sex difficulties	39
Addition to family	39
Business readjustment	39
Change in financial status	38
Death of close friend	37
Change to different line of work	36
Change in number of marital arguments	35
Mortgage or loan more than $10,000	31
Foreclosure of mortgage or loan	30
Change in work responsibilities	29
Son or daughter leaving home	29
Trouble with in-laws	29
Outstanding personal achievement	28
Spouse begins or stops work	26
Starting or finishing school	26
Change in living conditions	25
Revision of personal habits	24
Trouble with boss	23
Change in work hours, conditions	20
Change in residence	20
Change in schools	20
Change in recreational habits	19
Change in church activities	19
Change in social activities	18
Mortgage or loan less than $10,000	17
Change in sleeping habits	16
Change in number of family gatherings	15
Change in eating habits	15
Vacation	13
Christmas season	12
Minor violation of the law	11

Source: Holmes, T., & Rahe, R. (1967). The social readjustment rating scale. *Journal of Psychosomatic Research 2*(4):213–218.

role can present new and different challenges. Time management can be effective for returning students, especially if approached with a positive attitude rather than a stopwatch mentality, and viewed as an opportunity to plan and use time to one's advantage.

Time is one of the most elusive entities an individual encounters. As one progresses through the decades of life, one can experience a true sense of the days, weeks, and months passing at an ever-increasing pace. The student's perception of time, the accuracy of that perception, and how the individual functions in relation to time are extremely important to the educational experience. Achievement of academic objectives requires time—time to read, write, review, and assimilate, among many other things.

The fleeting nature of time is very evident when you are sitting in front of a blank sheet of paper or computer screen. If concentration or creative thoughts don't come within a reasonable period of time, don't expect that more time will produce them. Taking a break is probably more beneficial. Forced thoughts are counterproductive because they may be quite tangential or unusable, and may be time-consuming and emotionally draining. Creativity doesn't necessarily flow on demand. If this happens when you are facing a deadline, don't panic. Seasoned adult learners usually know to expect academic tasks to take twice as long as the original time allotted. This allows opportunity to concentrate, develop and nurture thoughts, and provide for critical review. Allowing adequate time is especially crucial when other people are involved. Accurate timing is vital for "turnaround time" with a typist, availability of a book at the library, use of audiovisual equipment, or scheduling student study groups. Ironically, the word "holiday" may take on a totally new and different meaning to the student. Any opportunity for additional time may be viewed as a gift.

How to Organize

PRACTICAL PLANNING

A true gift is found when a student takes inventory of daily activities and develops a time plan that realistically addresses personal needs, family and professional responsibilities, and academic goals and expectations. The value of a schedule cannot be overrated. However, to be effective, it must be realistic and consider the time frame and importance of other people and things involved. When you develop and use your plan for time management, you should keep in mind some key elements:

- The plan is simply a blueprint and can be modified.
- Its purpose is to assist in, not hinder, the use of time.
- Periodic reassessment and necessary modification are wise.
- The semester system provides an automatic time frame for reassessment in educational matters.
- Feasibility of the plan is essential.

Neither the most worthy goal nor unbounded motivation can turn an unrealistic plan into reality. A poignant example of realistic timing given by Covey, Merrill, and Merrill (1994) is referred to as the "law of the farm." They state that to have a crop in the fall, seeds must be planted in the spring. You can't cram on the farm. They also note that shortcuts and cramming in education are not effective.

TIME PLANS

Realistic individualized time plans cannot be purchased at the campus bookstore. However, many time management methods and aids are available and can be used to meet individual student needs. Various forms of calendars and schedules can assist you in arranging activities into a reasonable time frame. Recording your schedule or list in writing is an important part of the time management process; it can serve as a point of direction, a reminder, and a visual commitment to the task. The written schedule tends to carry more importance and improve organization. It is important to organize from both short- and long-term perspectives. Within the framework of an academic year or semester, the student can plan according to monthly, weekly, and daily calendars. Meltzer and Palau (1993) state that these three time planning segments have slightly different functions: monthly calendars assist students in arranging activities for long-term projects, weekly calendars help with developing consistency, and daily calendars aid in prioritizing (p. 5).

To implement effective daily planning, you should set a few minutes aside the night before to determine and list things to do. Priorities can then be identified by ranking each item from 1 to 10, or assigning items a level of importance (A, B, or C). The list should be very specific regarding the activity and the time allotted (Table 2–2). Crossing off accomplished items can give the student satisfaction and motivation to continue. When items are still on the list at the end of the day, there are three choices. First, do the task then and be done with it. Second, plan it for the next day, and third, eliminate it because it was not important. Covey, Merrill, and Merrill (1994) suggest that organizing on a weekly rather than daily plan helps reduce the problem of operating on a crisis basis. It allows the individual more flexibility without the pressure of a fixed daily schedule.

It is advisable to "frontload" whenever possible, accomplishing partial or complete assignments at the earliest opportunity. This eliminates working

TABLE 2–2. Sample Daily Plan

Daily Plan			
Time	**Task**	**Priority***	**Done**
8:00–10:00 A.M.	Study for statistics exam	A	
10:00–10:20 A.M.	Get gas for car	A	
10:45–12:00 A.M.	Find article for history course in library	B	
	Buy birthday card for sister	C	
12:15–1:30 P.M.	Lunch with study group on campus	A	
7:00–8:00 P.M.	Revise floor manual on new admission procedure	B	
7:00–8:00 A.M.	Prepare dinner for family	A	
3:30–11:30 P.M.	Work	A	
6:00–6:30 P.M.	Dinner meeting with nurse manager	B	
	Pick up clothes at dry cleaners	C	
2:00–3:00 P.M.	Check the mail, change clothes for work	A	

*Key: A—must be done today; B—should be done today; C—not necessary today.

TABLE 2 – 3. Time Management Strategies

- Assess your energy and concentration
- Avoid marathon approach
- Allow for spillovers
- Plan travel time
- Use 5-minute fillers
- Prepare waiting-room portfolio
- Carry pocket calendar
- Do double work
- Use travel time
- Time your time
- Leave open time

under increasing pressure when unanticipated complications arise. All too often, students take time, health, and necessary people and things for granted. Assignments should always be planned to be completed before the due date. Though some claim to work better under pressure, working up to the last minute of a deadline regularly is physically and emotionally exhausting, and the possibility always exists that circumstances will arise to prevent you from completing the task. (See Table 2–3.)

Barriers to Time Management

PROCRASTINATION

Delaying the inevitable can geometrically increase the emotional pressure attached to accomplishing a task or meeting a deadline. Procrastination creates a domino effect, pushing the task into a time slotted for other activities. Guilt often accompanies the delays, adding even more pressure, which interferes with your concentration even when you finally address the task. Procrastinating in family responsibilities to meet academic requirements can elicit enormous self-imposed guilt when families are understanding and cooperative. If you find you are procrastinating, look for the core reason for the delaying tactic and act on it. If the task seems overwhelming, seek advice, break it down into smaller parts, and get started with a simple aspect. Simply thinking about a project does not accomplish the work, and perfection is not expected on the first attempt. Getting started can easily become the most energy- and time-consuming part of a project, especially when those involved allow themselves to be controlled by rather than to control the situation.

INTERRUPTIONS

Interruptions can easily derail the most well-planned schedule. The lost time can range from minutes to months, and the impact can be minuscule or monumental. Some interruptions are caused by other people or the environment, and others come from within. When you are attempting to meet responsibilities of multiple roles, the saying "timing can be everything in life" can be brutally true. One of the most common forms of interruption was invented by Alexander Graham Bell. The ring of the phone arrives without permission and often at inopportune times. A well-intentioned friend or relative who calls to say hello can not only take precious time but disrupt a line of thought that can never be retrieved again. At times you can feel victimized by the phone because it seems impolite to keep the call brief. Conversely, the phone may seem like a welcome distraction when you are involved in a difficult or unpleasant task. In either case, it takes time from the original plan. Arrange for other family members to answer the phone and field the questions or take messages or turn on the answering machine. The most endearing interruption can be from a child who wants to spend time with a parent. Those times are important and cannot be replaced.

Sometimes we interrupt ourselves and can be our own worst enemy. Human nature allows attention to wander even in the midst of complex tasks. Whether studying for an exam or paying household bills, staying focused will get the job done in time to take advantage of planned leisure time. Succumbing to daydreaming or distraction by any sights or sounds can lead to an afternoon of unproductive activity.

TIME SAVERS

There are many ways to successfully manage time and activities. As time is used more effectively, you may develop new and different strategies specific to your individual situations. Follow these time management methods to gain more productive and enjoyable days.

- Assess yourself. When are you best able to concentrate? When are you most energetic? Many people are most productive in the early morning, when the world is very quiet, the mind is clear, and the body refreshed.
- Avoid the marathon approach. Eight consecutive hours is a long time to focus on any one task, whether it is writing a paper or washing floors. The productivity level increases if activi-

ties are varied and performed in smaller blocks of time.

- Allow for time spillovers. Try to plan time with leeway between activities, to accommodate meetings that run late, unexpected appointments, or simply losing track of time.
- Plan adequate travel time. Not all trips from work to campus to home have to resemble the Indianapolis 500. Checking the most time-efficient routes, and having a backup plan for heavy traffic or inclement weather, can save valuable time and anxiety. Be familiar with school policy regarding communication of closings due to weather conditions. Allow sufficient time to find a parking space and walk to buildings.
- Use 5-minute fillers. While waiting for a meeting or class to start, use the 5- or 10-minute time slot to make a phone call, photocopy an article, or review a study question with another student.
- Make a "waiting room" portfolio. Keep a portfolio of portable tasks that can be accomplished in the 20 or 30 minutes spent in the dentist or doctor's waiting room, or in the car during practice before a youngster's soccer game, or when a class or meeting is canceled. Keep a supply of notepads and pencils to make "to do" lists, outline projects, or write overdue letters. Thirty minutes can make a visible difference on a piece of needlework planned as a gift.
- Keep a pocket calendar. Combine family, work, school, and social events to give an overview, and allow appointments or meetings to be made on the spot. Save time by writing the phone number with a name in the time slot in case of change. Keep a list of frequently used numbers on the calendar.
- Do double work activity. Always have some type of task ready to be done during telephone conversations. While conversing with a colleague about work or school you can do simple tasks, such as folding the laundry, washing dishes, polishing furniture, or sorting papers.
- Use travel time. Public transportation is a waiting room in motion and provides hands-free time for reading texts, reviewing policies for work, or keeping current with professional journals. Travel time by car can be valuable time with yourself. It can be used to mentally gear up for, or wind down from, a busy day. Newscasts and informational talk shows capsulize current issues. Listening to audiotapes for course review, relaxation, or motivation is an especially good way to pass this time.

- Consider a cellular connection. If a cellular phone is available, students can save time by calling ahead to confirm meetings or notify of delays. Telephone calls made in the car can open time slots in a busy schedule and accomplish personal business calls in privacy.
- Time your time. Keep track of time to stay on task without becoming obsessive. Be mindful of the positive or negative results in relation to the time being invested. If time escapes you easily, use a watch or pocket timer to time intervals. At home, the timer on the stove can alert you to keep on pace or move to the next task.
- Leave open time. Schedule times for nothing. An occasional blank space in a busy week can be a welcome event, to be used as you choose.

Time management involves developing a respect for the clock, because time continues even when your energy and ideas are diminishing or depleted. In addition, you cannot expect to successfully integrate the timing of academic responsibilities into an already busy schedule of personal, family, and professional activities overnight. It will take attention, effort, and time to be successful. However, as you work to create and stick to time lines, it is advisable to look at the word *time* and consciously plan not to habitually relegate the *me* part to the end.

SETTING LIMITS

Setting limits is not intended to cause a restrictive environment or mindset. In fact, it encourages you to be goal focused and proactive rather than reactive. Setting limits is about responsible assessment and knowing boundaries. It is being aware of capabilities and acknowledging limitations. Setting limits puts you in control. It allows you to be the decision maker and determine what is realistic and beneficial. The words "realistic" and "beneficial" are key elements in limits, and students can become painfully aware that things that could be helpful or desirable are not always possible.

Balance

Setting limits is not confined to time. Many aspects of daily life including energy, money, and activities of all types can be subject to limits. Effective limit setting involves balance among the various facets of life and within each facet (social, professional, intellectual, physical, etc.). Balance does not mean that each day will have a time slot for everything, but that a weekly or monthly calendar will show that needs and goals are being addressed appropriately regarding time and effort. Balance requires first-hand knowledge of priorities, and respect for individual needs, abilities, and interests. True balance includes both ends of the limit spectrum, both minimum and maximum boundaries. Meeting the minimum expectation is a vital beginning, and at times an appropriate end. Minimums cannot be ignored, but maximum limits are most often considered. Contemporary society often seems committed to the concept of maximum, sometimes to the point of excess. However, at times less is better, and keen judgment must be used to determine those circumstances. Work expands to fill the allotted time is a saying that may assist students in setting limits.

A prime principle of limit setting is learning to say "no." This two-letter, one-syllable word is often the most difficult word to articulate. The desire to participate, to please, and to be viewed as cooperative and competent is very human. The altruistic nature common among nurses adds to the difficulty in limiting time and efforts, resulting in time binds and exhaustion. Responsibility to oneself is an important part of setting limits. In addition, at times you may find it more difficult to say "no" to yourself than to others, especially if it involves curtailing something pleasurable. It takes considerable self-discipline to leave a social gathering early to study for an exam or write a paper. It takes even more self-control to say "no" and stay on task when no one else is present or will know of your efforts or infractions. In reality, you are responsible for determining the appropriate balance and limitations, regardless of the presence or pressure of others. You will be the prime beneficiary of thoughtfully constructed limitations. You can, however, become a victim if limits are ill conceived or not honored.

Pace

A positive attitude, motivation, and zeal for knowledge enhance learning; however, unbridled enthusiasm can also lead to pushing oneself beyond reasonable expectations. Overextending yourself at school can seriously limit the time and attention you have to devote to other responsibilities, and it can lead to academic burnout. Remember that achieving a degree is a growth process, not a race but a process of completion. Pace yourself so that adequate time is given to all your work activities.

Pace can result in frustration, diminished quality of effort and work, depletion of physical and mental resources, or abandonment of your goal. Set and abide by speed limits. Take advantage of opportunities, or address unanticipated events, but always keep your setpoint at a realistic level. Reasonable pacing allows you to comfortably complete academic assignments, courses, and curricula and to participate in other life activities. Setting limits is not meant to hinder but rather to help students achieve goals responsibly. Individual abilities are acknowledged, the need for realistic balance and pace to prevent a goal from becoming an obsession and to avoid overuse or depletion of resources are emphasized.

ASSEMBLING RESOURCES

Before embarking on a new venture, thoroughly assess the situation and take inventory of the available resources. Assess all aspects of life to develop a comprehensive picture and identify resources that are currently accessible. **Resources** can come in many forms, including human, inanimate, and intangible. They serve varied purposes and can provide information, support, motivation, and physical convenience among many other things. Take advantage of readily available assistance. Create a plan to determine how to use existing resources to meet your goal. Then be on the alert for new and additional sources for help. Just as new and different needs can emerge, so can resources. A proactive approach is necessary because resources do not necessarily come neatly packaged, labeled, and delivered. It is your responsibility to actively seek out and negotiate for resources and to know when and how to use them appropriately. Though it can be comforting to know that something is accessible, the true value of a resource lies in its use rather than its potential.

Resources fall into three basic categories—educational, professional, and family. Each category offers a variety of opportunities for assistance. Students are encouraged to take advantage of all types of resources (Table 2–4).

Educational Resources

The college campus, the very setting that facilitates achievement of the desired degree, is most likely the resource area about which the student is least informed. The first step is for you to make an all-out effort to become aware of all the services and opportunities connected with the institution. Some resources may be apparent or mentioned in the application and admission process. Once you are enrolled, however, become familiar with the aca-

TABLE 2 – 4. Examples of Where to Find Resources

Educational	Department chair
	Faculty
	Academic adviser
	Course professor
	Student orientation programs
	Adult and continuing education department
	Learning centers
	Library
	Financial aid office
	Bulletin boards
	Special-interest student groups
	Other students
Professional	Professional organizations
	Employer
Family/Friends	Available babysitters
	Family or friends with special talents, such as a computer whiz
	Neighbor willing to car pool
	Someone with library privileges at a nearby university
	Local groups that offer educational funding
	Access to computer or photocopying

demic expectations and the people, methods, and activities to help meet those expectations. College offers many forms of assistance, but you must spend time and energy to become knowledgeable.

CAMPUS COMMUNICATION

A number of resources are designed to distribute information. A brief review of your college's literature, such as the catalog, viewbook, and department brochures, can provide an overview of its program, policies, and services. A campus map is extremely helpful in orienting you to the physical layout and quickly identifying key locations and services. Semester schedules and an array of weekly announcements are posted to inform students of current curricular and extracurricular activities. Routine review of bulletin boards informs you of upcoming events that are beneficial to attend.

Student orientation programs, especially those designed for mature students, are extremely helpful. These sessions capsulize the information in the institution's literature and focus on the practical aspects of the college experience. Orientation usually provides answers to commonly asked questions and alleviates some anxiety. Besides information, the programs provide opportunity for interaction with the college people. Department chairs, faculty, and students are usually present and interested in talking with incoming students. An added benefit of attend-

ing orientation is meeting other incoming students—your academic peers.

ACADEMIC ADVISER

One key resource in the educational setting is the faculty member who serves as academic adviser. The importance of an adviser cannot be overestimated. Plan to meet with your adviser at the very beginning of the first semester, and regularly throughout the experience. The adviser will assist you in course selection and monitor academic progress, but the role entails much more. You can expect your adviser to help you assess strengths and weaknesses, maintain focus, and serve as a source of encouragement and information. By serving as a sounding board, the adviser can assist you in developing independence and critical thinking. An adviser guides each student through the education process in an individualized manner, to meet the specific learning needs and the criteria of the program. You must be a willing and active participant, however, and understand that the adviser's role is to guide and facilitate, not to handle the advisee's responsibilities or errands. The adviser can serve as a role model and an ongoing source of guidance and information for the process of socialization into academe. Developing knowledge and appreciation for the values, customs, and methods of academe takes time and effort and can be a difficult adaptation for the student whose previous education was different.

CAMPUS SERVICES AND PERSONNEL

An adviser may direct the student to a variety of resources on the campus. Many institutions have a specific department or office that works with adult learners. This unit may be known as Life Long Learning, Adult Education, or something else. It provides information on issues relevant to mature students, including transfer and life experience credit and financial opportunities for older students.

Every college also has a division that focuses on improving specific learning skills. Personnel with varied educational backgrounds work with students individually or in small groups to enhance abilities. Services can range from remediation in a specific learning area, such as mathematics, to supplemental instruction in sciences, to assistance in developing and writing papers. A variety of technological devices and methods may be available for educational goals such as increasing reading rate. These learning centers are designed for students who desire to improve their methods and abilities. Study groups in subject areas and tutors can be arranged through the center. Students can be referred by a professor or adviser, or they seek assistance on their own. International or culturally diverse students can expect to find an office on campus dedicated to bridging cultural variation in the educational setting. Courses such as English as a second language may come under the direction of this office.

One of the most traditional educational resources is the campus library. Students would benefit from a formal orientation to the facility or an individual appointment with a librarian to learn about the reference services available and the computerized catalog and information search operations. Libraries often have individual study carrels and typing and photocopy equipment for the convenience of students. Some college libraries provide free photocopying service. Copies of daily newspapers, weekly journals, and past issues bound in the stacks can help students develop current and historical perspectives for various courses. Also be aware of other libraries, public or university affiliated, that offer different or additional holdings. Some healthcare institutions have libraries and librarians at the worksite. Collections in these libraries often reflect the focus of the hospital or agency. The library can be a very convenient, quiet, and efficient place for a busy student to seek out and work on information away from home activities.

Financial aid is available for all students, not just those coming directly from high school. The nursing department and financial aid office can appraise students of their eligibility for public funding. Employee benefit programs are another possible source of funding. A variety of state and federal assistance programs exist in addition to Veterans Administration benefits for students associated with the military. RNs can also benefit from scholarships and stipends offered by professional and civic groups exclusively for adult students. Sometimes students have received funding from local organizations. Diligent monitoring of announcements can be financially advantageous.

An often overlooked resource is the course professor. The professor is the first point of communication and generally welcomes the opportunity to clarify or expand topics. The professor can provide the course perspective, develop criteria, and evaluate progress as well as refer students to other valuable resources, as needed. Faculty have office hours designated exclusively to interacting with students. Meetings with the course professor can correct assumptions, dispel rumors, and assist you in develop-

ing an understanding of the material. Students involved in work and family schedules that prevent them from being available to meet during office hours can arrange a telephone discussion.

STUDENT PEERS

One of the most valuable educational resources for the student is the student peer. Sharing the common educational experience can forge an intellectual and emotional bond. Student peers offer information, understanding, and unconditional support. Fellow students have similar goals and circumstances. They can comprehend the pressures of the return to school in a way that no family member does, and they can offer creative solutions that have worked for them. Study groups can be extremely helpful for reviewing course content, preparing for exams, or developing projects. Discussion and exchange of ideas in a group can energize individuals and the whole. Group interaction creates a network of additional eyes and ears to garner information for a course assignment. The interplay of common goals and varied experiences can expand perspectives, broaden understanding, and make the task more enjoyable.

The student peer group can provide immeasurable personal support. The camaraderie can help keep motivation at a productive level, or assist in overcoming disappointment. Some students act as role models and serve as sources of encouragement while others provide information or support. Each student brings unique characteristics, talents, and abilities that can be shared. Interaction may be as brief as a conversation during a class break but still be supportive. Instructors often promote support groups (Dick & Anderson, 1993). Students who choose not to belong to a student group should make a point of interacting with some students individually and become a more active participant. Exchanging telephone numbers helps, especially when students are on campus only 1 or 2 days a week. Occasional student social gatherings add pleasure and balance to a goal-oriented schedule.

ACADEMIC ITEMS AND TECHNOLOGY

Educational pursuits cannot take place in a vacuum, and certain items can be helpful in accomplishing academic tasks. Besides the required textbooks for each course, the student should have a current edition dictionary, a thesaurus, and a copy of the format for writing papers (APA, MLA, etc.) preferred by the college. A computer at home, or convenient access to one, provides an efficient tool for developing, storing, and retrieving of information. Depending on the capability of the computer and student, information can be accessed from libraries and many other sites. Students who do not have computers at home will find that most colleges have a computer facility for student use. When the campus location and times are not convenient, you can buy computer time and photocopy services at one of several franchise businesses located throughout the country. These businesses are usually open 24 hours a day, which is helpful to students with full schedules and erratic hours. Although it is not essential for success, owning a computer and acquiring computer skills can be an integral part of the college experience. A knowledgeable friend, computer lab personnel, and instruction books are valuable resources. Meanwhile, a competent typist to transfer your words to paper and disk is invaluable.

Professional Resources

The professional arena holds many resources. The cooperation of your immediate superior in the workplace is pivotal in facilitating meshing of professional responsibilities and educational goals. You should schedule a meeting to notify your superior of your decision to return to school. Be prepared to present a well-defined plan including how it will benefit the nurse, the unit, and the institution. It is important for the superior who is responsible for assignments, schedules, and evaluations to understand your circumstances and potential. This may be an appropriate time to ask about adjusting your workload and schedule in the future and to note any precedent. It is primarily your role to devise viable possibilities and options compatible with the function of the unit. Supervising personnel can provide additional input and insight into constraints for schemes presented. Enlist the cooperation of clinical colleagues to serve as interim backups or resources.

Many health-care agencies recognize the worth of continued education by subsidizing personnel for a portion of or the full cost of a course. Some institutions require that a specific grade be achieved for reimbursement. Such policies provide both financial and academic motivation for education.

Professional nursing organizations are resources in many ways. The continual dissemination of materials through associations provides students with a current supply of professional information and issues. Conferences and workshops sponsored by nursing organizations give students opportunity to listen to and possibly interact with leaders in the profession. Organization workshops or panels also offer opportunities to participate as a presenter. Local and state chapters of many groups may have funds available for student education. Sigma Theta Tau International, the International Nursing Honor Society, fosters student achievement and rewards it with induction into the membership. State nurse and student nurse associations provide a stream of information and an opportunity to speak on contemporary issues of the profession.

From within the professional milieu you may discover a person to serve as mentor. Developing a relationship with a mentor is especially beneficial. A mentor is more than a role model and can offer much more than intellectual substance. You can expect to receive support and guidance from a person attuned to the politics, power, and processes of career paths. Mentors characteristically assist in the development of personal and professional growth. Though adult learners are self-directed, seeking a mentor is tied to the desire to obtain the expertise and resources to actively meet practical needs (Knowles, 1988). Having a mentor is not essential, but it can be a positive experience and often increases your success potential, leading to your service as a mentor in the future. This chain of mentoring constitutes an ongoing form of repayment to the profession.

Participating in a professional position concurrently with your college studies places the student in regular touch with contemporary care. The clinical experiences put real faces on the pages of textbooks and make the lessons relevant. Involvement in the workplace maintains access to an interdisciplinary network, which is necessary with the changes of a health-care system in transition.

Family Resources

The most devoted family and friends can never have the identical perspective you have with returning to school. However, most families are eager to encourage and support you, despite a limited understanding of the total picture. The encouragement and admiration of your family can help sustain your motivation throughout the semesters. You can readily serve as a role model for both children and adults and can gain self-esteem and confidence from the experience. Additionally, the family can provide assistance in practical ways that save the student time and energy. Some family and household responsibilities can be adjusted to accommodate the student's schedule or workload, without overlooking the responsibilities and interests of other family members. The experience can benefit individual members in many practical ways, perhaps enhancing the sense of family for the group. Negotiate and delegate with partner, children or parents according to the needs of the family. Cultivate each individual's talents and abilities so everyone can successfully take on new responsibilities. Appreciate their help, no matter how small, and be sure to show it. Ease your standards. For instance, do not redo a task because the outcome does not meet your standards. It does not matter if the towels are not folded and stacked the way you would do it. Students who are parents should keep in mind that they can learn from how a child approaches a project. A child who is computer literate can help you learn to use the computer, and you can both benefit from the shared experience.

Do not eliminate the support you might get from a telephone conversation with a relative hundreds of miles away. Willing friends and neighbors can help by offering to assist with car pools, babysitting, or caring for an older parent.

Health: An Overlooked Resource

One very important resource that is frequently taken for granted is good health. Despite professional knowledge and experience, even nurses can undervalue personal wellness until they have a problem. To maintain the physical and mental stamina for a busy personal and professional schedule with additional educational responsibilities, students must attend to the basic premises of health promotion and wellness. Disregard for individual health can lead to illness and negatively influence academic schedules and goals. Regular exercise, good nutrition, and plenty of rest can help you approach responsibilities with a sense of vitality, and it helps you balance your activities and lifestyle. With a positive attitude toward personal health, you can achieve a higher level of wellness, feel better, enjoy the college experience, be more productive, and position yourself for academic success.

You will have many resources at your disposal. Initially, you may not recognize these resources and miss an opportunity for assistance. Give serious thought to the people and things in various aspects of your life, and to your contacts, both social and professional. Assembling resources consists of lining up assets and opportunities. It involves drawing on or using the knowledge, service, and access to resources available. Resources can be found as far as the Internet reaches or as near as your personal collection of nursing journals. Interaction and exchange

are important in identifying and developing resources. Talking about activities and projects to family, friends, coworkers, and fellow students can increase your "brain power" and extend your network of available assistance. Some resources are readily identified and available, and others may have to be created.

STREAMLINING WORK

Streamlined can be defined as "designed or organized to give maximum efficiency" (Flexner, 1993, p. 1881); it connotes concepts such as expertly assembled, minimal resistance, swiftness, smooth progress, and unencumbered. These are positive and desirable qualities for work. Try to streamline work in each of the various facets of life—family, social, professional, and educational. Streamlining work in one area of life can positively affect the other areas.

Streamlining involves carefully considering all your ideas and plans. It is the coordination of goals, limits, resources, and time management in an action-oriented process geared toward efficiency and energy saving. It requires more organization and fine tuning how things are usually done. Streamlining means eliminating the unnecessary and making work a pleasant and productive experience. Be careful not to eliminate everything because functioning with only the absolute essentials can turn work into "hard labor."

Educational Streamlining

The educational arena has many requirements and essential activities, yet you can simplify the process and still achieve your objectives. Life and your nursing career provide you with processes integral to streamlining educational activities. Educational streamlining does not focus on the study process per se, but rather helps create life circumstances that foster conditions conducive to study.

ACCRUING CREDIT

One aspect of streamlining is using resources effectively. This is particularly important in looking at the overall curriculum and various courses involved. The mass of information and number of academic courses necessary may seem overwhelming. However, you may already possess some of the required knowledge, and there is no reason to reinvent the wheel. Discuss your experience with an adviser and explore the variety of ways, besides taking courses, you can demonstrate knowledge and receive credits. This can be done during the application and admission process. However, once you have a better understanding of the requirements, you may want to analyze how your experience can earn you credits. You may qualify for transfer credits for courses taken at another institution that are comparable in content to those in the curriculum. You may also be eligible for credits by taking the Credit for Life Learning Experience exams or those designed by faculty. These tests are designed to demonstrate knowledge covered in the course. Be aware of fees associated with taking the challenge exam and receiving credit, and the university and department may stipulate a time for completion. In addition, some universities grant credit to adult learners toward elective courses for "life experience." This is usually granted through an adult learning office, and entails documenting achievement of specific objectives by the student in settings outside the classroom. The criteria are set by and vary according to the university; however, this type of credit is not usually awarded for work associated with your academic major.

COURSE TIMING

The time at which a course is offered, especially a required course, is crucial to busy adults with many roles. Always check course schedules carefully to note if it has multiple sections, and possibly one at a more convenient time or place. When you have a time conflict for an essential course, talk with your adviser about taking the class at a satellite location or another school. Explore the availability of telecourses. Distance education programs, which send live video broadcasts to one or more remote classroom locations, are also options. Whenever possible, it is helpful to chain courses together. This minimizes the number of trips to campus and saves transportation time and expense. When there are intervals between classes, it is wise to plan to use the time for a specific task, such as library research, review of notes, or study groups.

USING THE LIBRARY

Make trips to the campus library as productive as possible. If you did not receive a formal orientation to the library, ask a librarian to describe the policies and features. When using journal articles, it is best to photocopy the material for current and future use at home and highlight the important information. Students should make sure the photocopy shows the complete information for citation, including journal volume and edition. For books, note the ISBN number and citation information for quick retrieval in the future. It is helpful to keep a supply of index cards handy to write citations and any pertinent information. Honor due dates. Attach a note with the due date on the front of the book to remind yourself to return it on time. Review your books weekly the night before a campus day to avoid a needless return trip. When you go to the library for one course, check the availability of materials for other courses. Assist other students by being alert for materials relevant to their topics of interest. A class list with selected project or paper topics can guide you. Carefully monitor your time in the library. It is easy to spend inordinate amounts of time in the library because it is usually quiet and serene, with no signs of passing time.

PORTFOLIO SYSTEM

Organizing things is just as important as organizing your life. A portfolio system is extremely helpful for easy access to important materials. Devote one portfolio to academic progression, including such things as letters of acceptance, catalogs, course schedules, an advisement or curriculum plan, and any correspondence with the college. Transcripts, paid receipts, and other relevant materials can be added each semester. Keep a personal copy of any information requested by the college, such as an annual health history and physical forms, immunization records, or CPR documentation.

A second portfolio should pertain to course work, with pertinent materials for each course such as course outline, schedule, reading list, completed assignments, and papers for future reference. Copies of relevant journal articles can be included with the respective course or maintained in a separate portfolio for articles.

Another portfolio can contain printed copies of any computer materials. When using a computer, be sure to store information on a disk and the hard drive, appropriately catalogued. It is wise to have a "traveling disk" readily available in a briefcase or handbag, to access information when opportunities arise. Always check disks for viruses before using them in each machine, especially if you use a computer that has multiple users. A computer virus can easily destroy many hours of work.

A portfolio created for programs and brochures for conferences, workshops, and professional meetings is also useful. It can provide an overview of upcoming events for possible participation, and a record of events attended, along with names and information.

COMMUNICATION

Efficient communication is part of streamlining. Using fax machines can save considerable time in transmitting information. If you have no access to a fax at home, work, or school, many commercial locations can be used. Carrying a list of school-related places and people, with their phone and fax numbers and e-mail addresses, will also enhance communication. The names and number of other students, your adviser, the department secretary, and the library are a few frequently used items. Students who do not use business cards in their professional roles may consider cards with home address and appropriate numbers.

Forming a car pool with another student offers several advantages, including the opportunity to discuss class projects and review material. Students who audiotape courses can use travel time for review. As you progress in your educational program, your academic networks will expand, and more people and information will be available to use in the process of streamlining.

Professional Streamlining

Even those employed on a part-time basis usually have to assess and reorganize their situations to accommodate school. Adjustments range from exchanging a few hours to taking a leave of absence.

Negotiation with superiors, and sometimes peers, is often a successful approach to resolving the situation. Cost-conscious employers and supervisors can be extremely receptive to innovative plans that maintain quality performance and increase cooperation and morale. If timing of the work day is an issue, flex time may be the answer. Condensing work hours to fewer days may help. Sometimes arriving early or adding an hour on specified days is all that is necessary to allow a student to leave the workplace in time to attend a class. Trading holiday coverage for class time and job sharing are other options. If you are a manager or supervisor, delegate functions and authority as appropriate. A leave of absence is sometimes the most appropriate method. Most reasonable requests to realign work schedules to gain an education will be considered, and many are granted.

Streamlining Domestic Functions

One of the first tasks of streamlining is to get all involved to realize that you cannot continually relegate school work to the end of the night, after everything else is finished, or to an already crammed weekend. Most home tasks can be rearranged, reprioritized, or eliminated to improve your quality of life.

Have a family discussion and encourage new ideas for getting the work done, determining what can be eliminated or obtaining volunteers. Use incentives and rewards for a job well done. Do not expect to be relieved of all responsibilities or perfection from family members. Accept mistakes and jobs not done quite as well as you like. New interests and unrecognized talents may be developed in the streamlining process.

Hiring household help to clean periodically can provide significant assistance at moderate expense. Neighborhood teenagers or college students may be available. Grandparents or other relatives may be pleased to provide child care for a few hours a week. Arrange with neighbors to exchange childcare or carpooling responsibilities.

Thinking in quantities and doing two things at once can help. Buy and prepare food in quantity. One night a week, while you are cooking dinner, it is possible to prepare two dishes, with one to be served on another evening. Have a responsible child do the shopping. Schedule these activities early in the week, when ambition and energy are usually high. Plan to eat out once a week, for family enjoyment and less work.

Some basic practices to increase efficiency in domestic responsibilities are as follows:

- Select and lay out clothes the night before each working day.
- Do a morning check to make sure all necessary family items for the day are ready.
- Know the daily schedule and phone numbers for each family member.
- Plan a route for each day. Chain activities and errands together to avoid driving in circles.
- Handle mail only once—read and relegate.
- Post a list for needed household items, making an automatic grocery list.
- Make a monthly medicine cabinet check.
- Plan time for routine car maintenance so you can handle daily schedules without delay.

Reorganizing activities can result in better working conditions, greater productivity, more time for the important things and people, and an improved quality of life.

STUDY TIPS

You have already spent several years in a study mode and have an established learning style. However, a few years may have passed and you need to focus on recapturing successful study strategies and possibly developing new techniques.

By enrolling in college, you have voluntarily committed yourself to education. A positive attitude may be your most valuable tool, because it can facilitate the learning process and allow you to enjoy the experience.

Study Environment

Have a designated area at home that is conducive to studying and concentrating. The room should have functional furniture and be capable of holding educational equipment and materials. Furniture that is too comfortable may defeat the purpose. Adequate lighting is imperative, and the room temperature and noise level should be considered to prevent distractions. A quiet atmosphere is needed for activities involving concentration, yet some learners find background music or sounds are helpful and may even accelerate the pace of activity. Ellis (1985) uniquely expressed the traditional belief that "silence is the best form of music for study" (p. 49). Individual differences exist, however, and not everyone or all academic activities require total silence or isolation. Whatever your personal preferences, the environment should be designed to signal the brain that it is entering a work zone (Table 2–5).

TABLE 2–5. Study Tips at a Glance

- Designate a study area
- Provide adequate lighting
- Prevent distractions
- Get mind and body ready for business
- Have necessary materials on hand
- Develop concrete plan and sense of control
- Set routine time for study
- Use all parts of a textbook—key words, summaries, illustrations, etc.
- Preread material
- Create a mental picture
- Be an active listener
- Date and streamline all notes
- Request permission to tape lectures
- Reprocess information for use in other courses
- Bring questions to the professor

Preparation for Study

Just as you prepare the environment, you must prepare yourself for study. Your body and mindset have to be open to academic business. Hunger and fatigue are unwelcome distractions and should be addressed before work begins. Any necessary materials should be on hand and within reach, to allow an undisturbed flow of work. A positive attitude, a sense of control, and a concrete plan set the stage for a productive session. You will need to acknowledge the transition and allow time to enter into the task. To participate effectively, you must mentally shift gears and assume the appropriate level of concentration. When projects are ongoing, it can be difficult to immediately regain the mental perspective of the previous work session. A quick review of the last section completed helps focus your attention and reduces startup time. Ending each work session of a continuing project by attaching a note detailing specific directions and ideas for the start of the next session may be beneficial.

Be cautious about unnecessary delays. Activities may give the appearance of efficiency, organization, and productivity, and a sense of attending to the task at hand but, in fact, be time and energy demons. Spending excessive amounts of time on preparation or process does not produce substance or achieve goals. A neatly labeled, color-coded collection of folders is of little value if the time you took to acquire and assemble them came from the time you needed to create content. Procrastination in the disguise of preparation is not productive.

Study Process

Though individual study preferences exist and styles emerge, some practices have been successful and can benefit the returning student with a busy schedule. It is helpful to establish a routine time for study, if possible. A routine facilitates readiness for the work and helps the student stay on task during the allotted time. Short study sessions interspersed with breaks and alternated with some physical activity are usually more productive than one continuous day-long effort. A break to read the mail, have lunch, vacuum the carpet, or take a quick walk or run serves the student well.

Each textbook is a valuable resource, and you should know its layout to gain a comprehensive view of its content and features. Take advantage of all the information authors provide. Objectives, key words, headings, highlights, and summaries are not window dressing; they provide direction and facilitate understanding. Illustrations clarify concepts. Diagrams, pictures, graphs, listings, and tables expand and enhance the mental images constructed by the written words. A glossary defines terms from the perspective of the subject area. An index assists students in quickly locating relevant information. Marking frequently used pages with a labeled tab or note can be helpful.

Reading the introduction and summary and paying attention to key words and headings before you read the chapter may help you identify the main points and understand the total concept. Visualizing while reading can create a mental picture and may help increase your comprehension. When questions arise, or you do not understand the material, tab the page, write the question on an index card, and speak with the professor.

Though initial study must be done individually, you can benefit from a study group. To be effective, the group should have an agenda and a set time for each meeting. The gathering gives students an opportunity to compare notes from class, discuss content or questions from readings, and brainstorm about possible test questions. Group study works best when done on a regular, preferably weekly, basis.

Besides reading and discussion, a significant amount of information is gained through class notes. It is important to be an active listener and to record pertinent information. Note taking requires listening for and documenting key words and central thoughts and ideas. Verbatim notes are neither efficient nor realistic. Listen and understand first, and then summarize the information presented. Develop a consistent and efficient method of note taking to ease the process and improve the content. Always date your notes and indicate the topic. Use paragraphs and headings to group and identify information. Record any reference your professor makes to pages in the text or names of other works and authors, and be alert to the importance of listings and definitions. Streamline notes to those points that are necessary and meaningful without being too brief or cryptic. Use common abbreviations and symbols, or develop an individual form of shorthand. Drawings and diagrams offer additional perspective on the words.

The Cornell format for notes is a useful tool. The format uses a lengthwise border on the left side of the paper, with notes written on the right side, the left portion is used for questions, comments, and additional information. Most important, handwriting must be legible for your notes to be of value.

Taping lectures on an audiocassette reinforces the note-taking process. Tapes allow the student to add to notes already taken and clarify details. The portable nature of tapes permits convenient repetition of the material in private settings such as at home or in your car. Some international students may find tapes especially helpful in adapting to the English language and its nuances or to a professor who speaks rapidly. Any student who wishes to tape a lecture should have ample long-playing tapes available and request the permission of the presenter before taping. Some professors do not permit taping, and some students are reluctant to participate in discussion when being taped.

Cross-course activities help streamline and add depth to your education. The concept is to use information or processes from one course in another course or academic endeavor. It involves reprocessing information, reframing ideas, and implementing information or methods in new and creative ways. It does not mean submitting the same paper for two courses, but it can involve developing a new perspective on already researched material. For example, if appropriate to course objectives, a topic such as alcoholism could be used for papers in biology, sociology, psychology, and community nursing courses, among others. A different perspective directs the focus in each case. Students could merge aspects of work already produced to develop new perspectives and draw correlations. In the process, they increase their depth of knowledge, expand the scope of methods, and improve their critical thinking.

Bibliography cards are a simple, successful, and portable method of storing and transferring information. When researching any topic one should write the citation in the correct form on an index card, along with notation of any pertinent information, quotes or statistics. When the project or paper is completed, the bibliography will be complete, and merely rearranging the cards will produce the alphabetical order for typing. The cards can then be filed according to a variety of categories (topic, course, alphabetic, etc.) to be retrieved for use later. The information can be transferred to computer at home, or the entire process can be adapted to a laptop computer.

A future use file can contain any materials with potential for use. Contents can include articles, quotes, cartoons, and brochures among many other things. Categories for filing could be established according to academic courses or topics, with a miscellaneous category. This file gives students a place to put information received or discovered that is pertinent to a specific area, as well as a possible resource for any endeavor.

Advice on how to study could fill volumes, and many good publications on study strategies are available. Effective use of study methods can lead to cognitive energy and success. However, accept the responsibility for determining and implementing the sound study practices most appropriate and realistic for you.

If you honor the commitment to yourself, plan realistic strategies, use time and resources effectively, and maintain a balance in life activities, you can enjoy the challenge of the educational experience and achieve your goals.

KEY POINTS

- Knowledge of the experiences of returning RN students identified by Shane serve as a guideline for your educational journey.
- Personal goals involve commitment, require time and thought to formulate, and should be individualized and feasible. A series of short-term goals can help you accomplish long-term goals.
- Refining professional identity and role transition involve change that can be an uncomfortable but positive experience with personal and professional rewards.
- A mentor offers a role model, support, and assistance to avoid pitfalls.
- Responsibility to self can be both a key motivator and a monitor of actions.
- It is important to plan activities in realistic time frames to achieve goals and to focus on quality rather than be directed primarily by the cadence of the clock.
- Recognition of abilities, limitations, and resources is essential for realistic implementation and success.
- Work can be streamlined to direct time and attention to changing priority areas, maintain quality performance, and provide balance in a multiple-role lifestyle.
- Flexible thinking and change in perspective indicate growth related to the education experience.

CHAPTER EXERCISES

1. R&R

Recreation and relaxation are important aspects of life. List activities you enjoy that could serve as a break or a source of refueling or relaxation. Include and identify activities that can be considered a quick fix (Q), those of short duration, lasting a half hour or less, and extended enjoyables (E), those things that involve longer periods of time (e.g., hours, days, a weekend).

2. Support search

Write your name inside a small circle in the center of the page. Around this circle, place the names of each person who is a personal support inside another circle and the name of each professional support inside a square. The support each person provides can be indicated by the name's proximity to your name circle.

3. Time wasters

Take 5 minutes to list on paper all the ways you tend to waste time.

Review your list and identify items that waste large amounts and small amounts of time.

Picking one large time waster and one small time waster, make a plan for the next week to consciously work toward eliminating both of them.

At the end of the week, review your progress and mark a plus (+) or minus (−) next to the selected time wasters for each incident during the week.

Pick two additional time wasters to work on during the next week, following the same process until you have successfully eliminated the time wasters.

4. Time plan

This exercise is designed to help you assess the timing and balance of activities from a weekly perspective. At the beginning of the week, write all planned activities in the appropriate hour or half-hour intervals. Schedule all activities, major or minor, including time for meals, errands, travel, recreative, and so on. Be realistic in planning, and allow for flexibility.

As each day is completed, record the actual activity performed next to the planned activity in each time slot.

At the end of the week analyze the time frames.

- What activities took more time than planned? Why?
- What activities took less time than planned? Why?
- What patterns were noticeable during the week?
- Which activities were not planned in writing?
- What surprised you about your actual use of time?
- How will you change planned time for activities?

REFERENCES

Boyer, E. L. (1987). *College: The undergraduate experience in America*. New York: Harper & Row.

Bruner, B., & Donahue, A. (1992). Marketing for the returning adult population. *Symposium for the Marketing of Higher Education*. Chicago: American Marketing Association.

Campaniello, J. (1988). When professional nurses return to school: A study of role conflict and well being in multiple role women. *Journal of Professional Nursing, 4*(2), 136–140.

Chenevert, M. (1993). *Pro nurse handbook*. St. Louis: Mosby.

Covey, S. R., Merrill, A., & Merrill, R. (1994). *First things first* [audiocassette]. New York: Simon & Schuster, Audio Division.

Curry, B. D. (1994). Societal and marketing influences on enrollment into baccalaureate nursing programs. In *Symposium for the marketing of higher education* (pp. 211–216). Chicago: American Marketing Association.

Dick, M., & Anderson, S. E. (1993). Job burnout in RN to BSN students: Time commitments, and support for returning to school. *Journal of Continuing Education in Nursing, 24*(3), 105–109.

Ellis, D. B. (1985). *Becoming a master student*. Rapid City, SD: College Survival Inc.

Fagin, C. (1994). Women and nursing: Today and tomorrow. In E. Friedman (Ed.), *An unfinished revolution: Women and healthcare in America*. New York: United Hospital Fund.

Flexner, S. B. (Ed.). (1993). *Random House unabridged dictionary* (2nd ed.). New York: Random House.

Grant, A. B. (1994). *The professional nurse: Issues and actions*. Springhouse, PA: Springhouse Publishing.

Holmes, T. H., & Rahe, R. (1967). The social readjustment scale. *Journal of Psychosomatic Research, 2*(4), 213–218.

Knowles, M. (1988). *The adult learner: A neglected species*. Houston: Gulf Publishing.

Lengacher, C. (1993). Development of a predictive model for role strain in registered nurses returning to school. *Journal of Nursing Education, 32*(7), 301–308.

Meltzer, M., & Palau, S. M. (1993). *Reading and study strategies for nursing students*. Philadelphia: Saunders.

Moore, T. (1992). *Care of the soul*. New York: Harper Collins.

Redman, B. K., & Cassells, J. M. (Eds.). (1990). *Educating RN's for the baccalaureate*. New York: Springer.

Shane, D. (1980, June.). The returning to school syndrome. *Nursing 80*, 86–88.

Strader, M. K. & Decker, P. J. (1995). *Role transition to patient care management*. Norwalk, CT: Appleton & Lange.

BIBLIOGRAPHY

Aiken, L., & Fagin, C. (1992). *Charting nursing's future: Agenda for the 1990's.* Philadelphia: Lippincott.

Covey, S. R. (1990). *The 7 habits of highly effective people.* New York: Simon & Shuster.

Covey, S. R. (1995). *Living the 7 habits* [audiocassette]. New York: Simon & Shuster, Audio Division.

Ellis, J. R., & Hartley, C. L. (1995). *Nursing in today's world* (5th ed.). Philadelphia: Lippincott.

Fawcett, J. (1995). *Analysis and evaluation of conceptual models of nursing* (3rd ed.). Philadelphia: Davis.

Friedman, E. (Ed.). (1994). *An unfinished revolution: Women and health care in America.* New York: United Hospital Fund.

Hamilton, M. P. (1992). *Realities of contemporary nursing.* New York: Addison Wesley.

Hughes, E. C., Hughes, H., & Deutscher, I. (1958). *Twenty thousand nurses tell their story.* Philadelphia: Lippincott.

Kalisch, P., & Kalisch, B. (1986). *The advance of American nursing.* Boston: Little, Brown.

Khan, K., Schmidt, P. L., Schoville, R., & Williams, M. (1993, September). From expert to novice. *American Journal of Nursing,* September, 53–56.

Mirin, S. K. (Ed.). (1980). *Teaching tomorrow's nurse: A nurse educator reader.* Wakefield, MA: Nursing Resources.

Moloney, M. M. (1992). *Professionalization of nursing.* Philadelphia: Lippincott.

Yoder Wise, P. (1995). *Finding and managing in nursing.* St. Louis: Mosby.

Zerwekh, J., & Claborn, J. C. (1994). *Nursing today: Transitions and trends.* Philadelphia: Saunders.

Section II

THEORETICAL BASIS OF NURSING PRACTICE

Chapter 3

EVOLUTION AND USE OF FORMAL NURSING KNOWLEDGE

Jacqueline Fawcett
Barbara Swoyer

CHAPTER OBJECTIVES

On completion of
this chapter, the reader
will be able to:

1. Describe the progress and development of nursing knowledge as the basis for professional nursing practice.
2. Identify the different functions of conceptual models and theories.
3. Discuss the advantages and disadvantages of using selected conceptual models of nursing and nursing theories to guide professional nursing practice.
4. Apply a conceptual model of nursing or nursing theory to a particular clinical situation.

KEY TERMS

Formal Nursing
    Knowledge
Conceptual Models of
    Nursing

Grand Theories of
    Nursing
Middle-Range Nursing
    Theories

T his chapter describes the evolution of nursing knowledge, as it has been formalized in conceptual models of nursing and nursing theories, and identifies the impact of that knowledge on professional nursing practice.

FORMAL NURSING KNOWLEDGE

Conceptual models of nursing and nursing theories represent formal nursing knowledge. That knowledge has been obtained by several nurse scholars who have devoted a great deal of time to observing clinical situations, considering what is important to nursing in those situations, and then testing their thoughts by conducting nursing research (Fawcett & Downs, 1992). Nursing knowledge continues to evolve as nurse clinicians and researchers use conceptual models and theories to guide their clinical practice and research, and then report the results at conferences and in publications. Consequently, all nurses can contribute to the evolution of nursing knowledge.

Nightingale's (1859) book, *Notes on nursing: What it is, and what it is not,* contains the first ideas that can be considered formal nursing knowledge. More than 100 years later, Henderson (1966) published her definition of nursing, continuing the evolution of formal nursing knowledge. Although the intervening years were filled with many ideas about nursing, most of those ideas, unfortunately, were not presented as formal conceptual models and theories. The following summarizes the work of Nightingale and Henderson.

FLORENCE NIGHTINGALE'S NOTES ON NURSING

Nightingale's ideas about nursing, first published in 1859, represent the beginning of formal nursing knowledge. Nightingale maintained that *every* woman is a nurse because, at one time or another in her life, she has charge of the per-

sonal health of someone. Nightingale equated knowledge of nursing with knowledge of sanitation. The focus of nursing knowledge was on how to keep the body free from disease or in such a condition that it could recover from disease. According to Nightingale, nursing ought to signify the proper use of fresh air, light, warmth, cleanliness, quiet, and the proper selection and administration of diet—all at the least expense of vital power to the patient; that is, she maintained that the purpose of nursing was to put the patient in the best condition for nature to act on him.

Implications for Nursing Practice

Nursing practice encompasses care of both well and sick people. Nursing actions focus on both patients and their environments. Thirteen "hints" provided the boundaries of nursing practice:

1. *Ventilation and warming.* The nurse must be concerned first with keeping the air that patients breathe as pure as the external air, without chilling them.
2. *Health of houses.* Attention to pure air, pure water, efficient drainage, cleanliness, and light will secure the health of houses.
3. *Petty management.* All the results of good nursing may be negated by not knowing how to manage what you do when you are there and what should be done when you are not there.
4. *Noise.* Unnecessary noise, or noise that creates an expectation in the mind, hurts patients. Anything that wakes patients suddenly invariably puts them into a state of greater excitement and does them more serious and lasting mischief than any continuous noise, however loud.
5. *Variety.* Seeing the same walls, ceiling, and surroundings during a long confinement to one or two rooms affects the nerves of the sick. Most cheerful cases are found among those patients who are not confined to one room, whatever their suffering, and most depressed cases are seen among those subjected to a long monotony of objects about them.
6. *Taking food.* The nurse should be conscious of patients' diets and remember how much food each patient has had and ought to have each day.

Portions of this chapter are adapted from J. Fawcett (1995). *Analysis and evaluation of conceptual models of nursing* (3rd ed.). Philadelphia: F. A. Davis, with permission; and from J. Fawcett (1997). Conceptual models and theories of nursing. Appendix 20 in C. L. Thomas (Ed.), *Taber's cyclopedic medical dictionary* (18th ed.), pp. 2310–2326. Philadelphia: F. A. Davis, with permission.

7. *What food?* To watch for the "opinions" of the patient's stomach, rather than read "analyses of foods," is the business of all who have to decide what the patient should eat.

8. *Bed and bedding.* The patient should have a clean bed every 12 hours. The bed should be narrow, so that the patient does not feel "out of humanity's reach." It should not be so high that the patient cannot easily get in and out of it. The bed should be in the lightest spot in the room, preferably near a window. Pillows should be used to support the back below the breathing apparatus, to allow shoulders room to fall back, and to support the head without throwing it forward.

9. *Light.* Second only to their need of fresh air is the need of the sick for light. Light, especially direct sunlight, has a purifying effect on the air of a room.

10. *Cleanliness of rooms and walls.* The greater part of nursing consists of preserving cleanliness. The inside air can be kept clean only by excessive care to rid rooms and their furnishings of the organic matter and dust with which they become saturated. Without cleanliness, you cannot have all the effects of ventilation; without ventilation, you can have no thorough cleanliness.

11. *Personal cleanliness.* Nurses should always remember that if they allow patients to remain unwashed or in clothing saturated with perspiration or other excretion, they are interfering injuriously with the natural processes of health as much as if they were to give their patients a dose of slow poison.

12. *Chattering hopes and advices.* Invalids scarcely have a greater worry than the incurable hopes of their friends. All friends, visitors, and attendants of the sick should avoid the practice of attempting to cheer the sick by making light of their danger and exaggerating their probabilities of recovery.

13. *Observation of the sick.* The most important practical lesson nurses can learn is what to observe, how to observe, which symptoms indicate improvement, which indicate the reverse, which are important, which are not, and which are evidence of neglect and what kind of neglect.

VIRGINIA HENDERSON'S DEFINITION OF NURSING

Henderson contributed to the evolution of nursing knowledge by providing a definition that has been accepted around the world. According to Henderson, the unique function of the nurse is to help individuals, sick or well, perform those activities contributing to health or its recovery (or to peaceful death) that they would perform unaided if they had the necessary strength, will, or knowledge, and do this in such a way as to help them gain independence as soon as possible.

Implications for Nursing Practice

The practice of nursing requires nurses to know and understand patients by putting themselves in their place. Nurses should not take everything patients say at face value, but rather should interact with patients to ascertain their true feelings. *Basic nursing care* involves helping the patient perform the following activities unaided:

1. Breathe normally.
2. Eat and drink adequately.
3. Eliminate body wastes.
4. Move and maintain desirable postures.
5. Sleep and rest.
6. Select suitable clothes and dress and undress.
7. Maintain body temperature within normal range by adjusting clothing and modifying the environment.
8. Keep the body clean and well groomed and protect the integument.
9. Avoid dangers in the environment and avoid injuring others.
10. Communicate with others by expressing emotions, needs, fears, or opinions.
11. Worship according to one's faith.
12. Work in such a way that one has a sense of accomplishment.
13. Play or participate in various forms of recreation.
14. Learn, discover, or satisfy the curiosity that leads to normal development and health and use the available health facilities.

CONCEPTUAL MODELS OF NURSING

The terms "conceptual model," "conceptual framework," "conceptual system," "paradigm," and "disciplinary matrix," frequently used interchangeably, are defined in the same way: a set of abstract, general concepts and the statements that describe or link those concepts. Each conceptual model presents a particular perspective on the phenomena of interest to a particular discipline, such as nursing. Conceptual models of nursing present the diverse perspectives of the recipient of nursing, who can be an individual, a family, or a community; the environment of the recipient and the environment in which nursing occurs; the health state of the recipient; and the definition and goals of nursing, as well as the nursing process used to assess, label, plan, intervene, and evaluate.

Currently, the works of several nurse scholars are recognized as conceptual models. Among the best known are Johnson's Behavioral System Model, King's General Systems Framework, Levine's Conservation Model, Neuman's Systems Model, Orem's Self-Care Framework, Rogers' Science of Unitary Human Beings, and Roy's Adaptation Model (Johnson, 1990; King, 1990; Levine, 1991; Neuman, 1995; Orem, 1995; Rogers, 1990; Roy & Andrews, 1991). An overview of each of these nursing models, along with its implications for professional nursing practice, are presented in the following sections.

Functions of Conceptual Models of Nursing

One function of any conceptual model is to provide a distinctive frame of reference and "a coherent, internally unified way of thinking about . . . events and processes" (Frank, 1968, p. 45) that tells nurses what to observe and how to interpret what they observe in clinical practice. Each conceptual model, then, presents a unique focus that has a profound influence on nurses' ways of thinking about patients and their environments, as well as health-related events and situations.

Another function of conceptual models of nursing is to identify a particular "philosophical and pragmatic orientation to the service nurses provide patients—a service which only nurses can provide—a service which provides a dimension to total care different from that provided by any other health professional" (Johnson, 1987, p. 195). Conceptual models of nursing provide explicit orientations not only for nurses but also for the general public. The models identify the purpose and scope of nursing and provide frameworks for objective records of the effects of nursing assessments and interventions. Johnson (1987) explained, "Conceptual models specify for nurses and society the mission and boundaries of the profession. They clarify the realm of nursing

responsibility and accountability, and they allow the practitioner and/or the profession to document services and outcomes" (pp. 196–197).

A SUMMARY OF FORMAL KNOWLEDGE IN NURSING: CONCEPTUAL MODELS

Dorothy Johnson's Behavioral System Model

Johnson's conceptual model of nursing focuses on the person as a behavioral system, consisting of all the patterned, repetitive, and purposeful behaviors that characterize life. Seven *subsystems* carry out specialized tasks or functions needed to maintain the integrity of the whole behavioral system and manage its relationship to the environment:

1. *Attachment or affiliative.* Function is the security needed for survival as well as social inclusion, intimacy, and forming and maintaining social bonds.
2. *Dependency.* Function is the succoring behavior that calls for a response of nurturance as well as approval, attention or recognition, and physical assistance.
3. *Ingestive subsystem.* Function is appetite satisfaction in terms of when, how, what, how much, and under what conditions the individual eats, all of which is governed by social and psychological considerations as well as biologic requirements for food and fluids.
4. *Eliminative.* Function is determining when, how, and under what conditions the individual eliminates wastes.
5. *Sexual.* Functions are procreation and gratification, with regard to behaviors that depend on the individual's biologic sex and gender role identity, including, but not limited to, courting and mating.
6. *Aggressive.* Function is protection and preservation of self and society.
7. *Achievement.* Function is mastery or control of some aspect of self or environment, with regard to intellectual, physical, creative, mechanical, social, and care-taking (of children, partner, home) skills.

The *structure* of each subsystem includes four elements:

1. *Drive or goal.* The motivation for behavior.
2. *Set.* The individual's predisposition to act in

certain ways to fulfill the function of the subsystem.

3. *Choice.* The individual's total behavioral repertoire for fulfilling subsystem functions, which encompasses the scope of action alternatives from which the person can choose.

4. *Action.* The individual's actual behavior in a situation. Action is the only structural element that can be observed directly; all other elements must be inferred from the individual's actual behavior and the consequences of that behavior.

Each subsystem has three *functional requirements:*

1. *Protection* from noxious influences with which the system cannot cope.

2. *Nurturance* through the input of appropriate supplies from the environment.

3. *Stimulation* to enhance growth and prevent stagnation.

IMPLICATIONS FOR NURSING PRACTICE

Nursing practice is directed toward restoring, maintaining, or attaining behavioral system balance and dynamic stability at the highest possible level for the individual. The nursing diagnostic and treatment process has four steps:

1. *Determination of the existence of a problem* in behavioral subsystem functions or structural elements.

2. *Diagnostic classification of problems* as internal subsystem or intersystem problems.

3. *Management of nursing problems* through three types of treatments:

    Fulfill subsystem functional requirements by protecting the patient from overwhelming noxious influences, supplying adequate nurturance, and providing stimulation.

    Impose external regulatory or control mechanisms on behavior, such as setting limits for behavior, inhibiting ineffective behavioral responses, and assisting patients to acquire new behavioral responses.

    Change the structural elements of the subsystems by altering the set through instruction or counseling and adding choices by teaching new skills.

4. *Evaluating the efficacy of nursing treatments* by comparing the extent of behavior system

stability and balance before and after the treatments.

Imogene King's General Systems Framework

King's conceptual model of nursing focuses on the continuing ability of individuals to meet their basic needs to function in their socially defined roles and on individuals' interactions within three open, dynamic, interacting systems.

1. *Personal systems.* Individuals who are regarded as rational, sentient, social beings. The following concepts are related to the personal system:

    Perception. A process of organizing, interpreting, and transforming information from sense data and memory that gives meaning to one's experience, represents one's image of reality, and influences one's behavior.

    Self. A composite of thoughts and feelings that constitute a person's awareness of individual existence, of who and what one is.

    Growth and development. Cellular, molecular, and behavioral changes in individuals that are a function of genetic endowment, meaningful and satisfying experiences, and an environment conducive to helping individuals move toward maturity.

    Body image. A person's perceptions of his or her body.

    Time. The duration between the occurrence of one event and another.

    Space. The physical area, called territory, that exists in all directions.

    Learning. Gaining knowledge.

2. *Interpersonal systems.* Two or more individuals interacting in a given situation. The following concepts are associated with this system:

    Interactions. The actions between two or more persons; a sequence of verbal and nonverbal behaviors that are goal directed.

    Communication. The vehicle by which human relations are developed and maintained, encompassing intrapersonal, interpersonal, verbal, and nonverbal communication.

    Transaction. A process of interaction in

which human beings communicate with the environment to achieve valued goals; goal-directed human behaviors.

Role. A set of behaviors expected of one occupying a position in a social system.

Stress. A dynamic state in which an individual interacts with the environment to maintain balance for growth, development, and performance, involving an exchange of energy and information between the person and the environment to regulate and control stressors.

Coping. A way of dealing with stress.

3. *Social systems.* Organized boundary systems of social roles, behaviors, and practices developed to maintain values and the mechanisms to regulate the practices and rules. The following concepts are related to social systems:

Organization. Composed of human beings with prescribed roles and positions who use resources to accomplish personal and organizational goals.

Authority. A transactional process characterized by active, reciprocal relations in which members' values, backgrounds, and perceptions play a role in defining, validating, and accepting the authority of individuals within an organization.

Power. The process by which one or more persons influence other persons.

Status. The position of an individual in a group or a group in relation to other groups in an organization.

Decision making. A dynamic and systematic process by which goal-directed choices among perceived alternatives are made and acted on by individuals or groups to answer a question and attain a goal.

Control. Being in charge.

IMPLICATIONS FOR NURSING PRACTICE

Nursing practice is directed toward helping individuals maintain their health so they can function in their roles. The *Theory of Goal Attainment* describes an interaction-transaction nursing process depicting a sequence in which the nurse and the client meet in a situation.

1. *Assessment phase.* The nurse and client perceive each other, make mental judgments about the other, take some mental action,

react to each others' perceptions, communicate, and begin to interact.

2. *Planning phase.* Interactions between the nurse and client continue and can be observed directly. The specific data of interaction, which can be recorded, are the concerns, problems, or disturbances identified by client and nurse, their mutual goal setting, their exploration of means to achieve those goals, and their agreement on the means required to achieve them.

3. *Implementation phase.* Transactions are made and can be observed in the form of goal attainment measures.

4. *Evaluation phase.* A decision is made as to whether the goal was attained and, if necessary, why the goal was not attained is determined.

Myra Levine's Conservation Model

Levine's conceptual model of nursing focuses on conservation of the person's wholeness. Adaptation is the process by which people maintain their wholeness or integrity as they respond to environmental challenges and become congruent with the environment. The following are sources of challenges:

1. *Perceptual environment.* Encompasses that part of the environment to which individuals respond with their senses.

2. *Operational environment.* Includes those aspects of the environment that are not directly perceived, such as radiation, odorless and colorless pollutants, and microorganisms.

3. *Conceptual environment.* The environment of language, ideas, symbols, concepts, and invention.

Individuals respond to the environment by means of four integrated processes:

1. *Fight-or-flight mechanism*

2. *Inflammatory-immune* response

3. *Stress* response

4. *Perceptual awareness,* including the basic orienting, haptic, auditory, visual, and taste-smell systems

IMPLICATIONS FOR NURSING PRACTICE

Nursing practice is directed toward promoting wholeness for all people, well or sick. Patients are partners or participants in nursing care who are temporarily dependent on the nurse. The nurse's goal is to end the dependence as quickly as possible. The nursing process of this conceptual model is conservation, which is defined as "keeping together" and consists of three steps:

1. *Trophicognosis.* A nursing care judgment arrived at by the scientific method. Involves observation, awareness of provocative facts, and construction of a testable hypothesis, which is the trophicognosis.
2. *Intervention.* Two types of nursing interventions:

    Therapeutic, when nursing intervention influences adaptation favorably or toward renewed social well-being

    Supportive, when nursing intervention cannot alter the course of the adaptation but only maintain the status quo, or fails to halt a downward course

    Intervention is structured based on four conservation principles:

    Conservation of energy. Balancing the patient's energy output and input to avoid excessive fatigue.

    Conservation of structural integrity. Maintaining or restoring the structure of the body by preventing physical breakdown and promoting healing focuses attention on healing.

    Conservation of personal integrity. Maintaining or restoring the individual patient's sense of identity, self-worth, and uniqueness.

    Conservation of social integrity. Acknowledging patients as social beings and helping them preserve their place in a family, community, and society.
3. *Evaluation.* The trophicognosis is evaluated and revised in light of the results of the actions and necessity for change (Levine, 1966).

Betty Neuman's Systems Model

Neuman's conceptual model of nursing focuses on the wellness of the client system in relation to environmental stress and reactions to stress. The client system, which can be an individual, a family or other group, or a community, is a composite of five interrelated variables:

1. *Physiological variables.* Bodily structure and function.
2. *Psychological variables.* Mental processes and relationships.
3. *Sociocultural variables.* Social and cultural functions.
4. *Developmental variables.* Developmental processes of life.

5. *Spiritual variables.* Aspects of spirituality on a continuum from complete unawareness or denial to a consciously developed high level of spiritual understanding.

The client system is depicted as a central core, which is a basic structure of survival factors common to the species, surrounded by three types of concentric rings:

1. *Flexible line of defense.* The outermost ring; a protective buffer for the client's normal or stable state that prevents invasion of stressors and keeps the client system free from stressor reactions or symptomatology.
2. *Normal line of defense.* Lies between the flexible line of defense and the lines of resistance; represents the client system's normal or usual wellness state.
3. *Lines of resistance.* The innermost concentric rings; involuntarily activated when a stressor invades the normal line of defense. The system attempts to stabilize the client system and foster a return to the normal line of defense. If effective, it can reconstitute the client; if ineffective, death may ensue.

Environment comprises all internal and external factors or influences surrounding the client system:

1. *Internal environment.* All forces or interactive influences internal to or contained solely within the boundaries of the defined client system; the source of *intrapersonal stressors.*
2. *External environment.* All forces or interaction influences external to or existing outside the defined client system; the source of *interpersonal and extrapersonal stressors.*
3. *Created environment.* Subconsciously developed by the client as a symbolic expression of system wholeness, it supersedes and encompasses the internal and external environments; functions as a subjective safety mechanism blocking the true reality of the environment and the health experience.

IMPLICATIONS FOR NURSING PRACTICE

Nursing practice is directed toward facilitating optimal wellness by retaining, attaining, or maintaining client system stability. The nursing process includes three steps:

1. *Nursing diagnosis.* Based on assessment of variables and the lines of defense and resistance that make up the client system.

2. *Nursing goals.* Negotiated with the client for desired prescriptive changes to correct variances from wellness.
3. *Nursing outcomes.* Determined by evaluating the results of three types of prevention as intervention modalities:

   Primary prevention. Action required to *retain* client system stability; selected when the risk of or hazard from a stressor is known but no reaction has yet occurred. Interventions attempt to reduce the possibility of the client's encounter with the stressor or strengthen the flexible line of defense to decrease the possibility of a reaction when the stressor is encountered.

   Secondary prevention. Action required to *attain* system stability; selected when a reaction to a stressor has already occurred. Interventions deal with existing symptoms and attempt to strengthen the lines of resistance through the client's internal and external resources.

   Tertiary prevention. Action required to *maintain* system stability; selected when some degree of client system stability has occurred following secondary prevention interventions.

Dorothea Orem's Self-Care Framework

Orem's conceptual model of nursing focuses on the nurse's deliberate action related to systems of therapeutic self-care for individuals with limited abilities to provide continuing self-care or care of dependent others. The following are the six central concepts:

1. *Self-care.* Behavior directed by individuals toward themselves or their environments to regulate factors that affect their own development and functioning in the interests of life, health, or well-being.
2. *Self-care agency.* A complex capability of maturing and mature individuals to determine the presence and characteristics of specific requirements for regulating their own functioning and development, make judgments and decisions about what to do, and perform care measures to meet specific self-care requisites. The person's ability to perform self-care is influenced by 10 *power components:*
   - Ability to maintain attention and exercise requisite vigilance with respect to self as self-care agent and internal and external conditions and factors significant for self-care.
   - Controlled use of available physical energy sufficient to initiate and continue self-care operations.
   - Ability to control the position of the body and its parts in executing the movements required to initiate and complete self-care operations.
   - Ability to reason within a self-care frame of reference.
   - Motivation (i.e., goal orientations for self-care that are in accord with its characteristics and its meaning for life, health, and well-being).
   - Ability to make decisions about care of self and to put these decisions into operation.
   - Ability to acquire technical knowledge about self-care from authoritative sources, to retain it, and to put it into operation.
   - A repertoire of cognitive, perceptual, manipulative, communication, and interpersonal skills adapted to the performance of self-care operations.
   - Ability to order discrete self-care actions or action systems into relationships with prior and subsequent actions to achieve regulatory goals of self-care.
   - Ability to consistently perform self-care operations, integrating them with relevant aspects of personal, family, and community living.

The person's ability to perform self-care as well as the kind and amount of self-care required are influenced by ten internal and external factors, called *basic conditioning factors:*
   - Age
   - Gender
   - Developmental state
   - Health state
   - Sociocultural orientation
   - Health-care system factors; for example, medical diagnostic and treatment modalities
   - Family system factors
   - Patterns of living, including activities regularly engaged in
   - Environmental factors
   - Resource availability and adequacy

3. *Therapeutic self-care demand*. The action demand on individuals to meet three types of self-care requisites:

   Universal self-care requisites. Actions that need to be performed to maintain life processes, the integrity of human structure and function, and general well-being.

   Developmental self-care requisites. Actions that need to be performed in relation to human developmental processes, conditions, and events, and events that may adversely affect development.

   Health deviation self-care requisites. Actions that need to be performed in relation to genetic and constitutional defects, human structural and functional deviations and their effects, and medical diagnostic and treatment measures prescribed or performed by physicians.

4. *Self-care deficit*. The relationship of inadequacy between self-care agency and the therapeutic self-care demand.

5. *Nursing agency*. A complex property or attribute that enables nurses to know and help others know and meet their therapeutic self-care demands and regulate the exercise or development of their self-care agency.

6. *Nursing system*. A series of coordinated deliberate practical actions performed by nurses and patients toward meeting the patient's therapeutic self-care demand and protecting and regulating the exercise or development of the patient's self-care agency.

IMPLICATIONS FOR NURSING PRACTICE

Nursing practice is directed toward helping people meet their own and their dependent others' therapeutic self-care demands. The following six operations describe and give direction to nursing practice:

1. *Nursing diagnosis*. A professional operation focusing on determining why the person needs nursing care. This requires calculating the person's therapeutic self-care demand through assessment of the self-care requisites, assessment of self-care agency, including determination of the influence of the power components and basic conditioning factors, and identification of the self-care deficit.

2. *Nursing prescription*. A professional operation that specifies the means to be used to meet particular self-care requisites, all care measures needed to meet the entire therapeutic self-care demand, and the roles to be played by the nurse and the self-care agent in meeting the patient's therapeutic self-care demand and regulating the patient's exercise or development of self-care agency.

3. *Nursing system design*. A professional operation that involves selection of a nursing system and one or more methods of helping. Three types of regulatory nursing system designs exist:

   Wholly compensatory nursing system. Selected when the patient cannot or should not perform any self-care actions.

   Partly compensatory nursing system. Selected when the patient can perform some, but not all, self-care actions.

   Supportive-educative nursing system. Selected when the patient can and should perform all self-care actions.

   The five *methods of helping* are:

   □ Acting for or doing for another
   □ Guiding and directing
   □ Providing physical or psychological support
   □ Providing and maintaining an environment that supports personal development
   □ Teaching

4. *Planning*. A case management operation that requires specification of the time, place, environmental conditions, equipment and supplies, organization and timing of tasks to be performed, and the number and qualifications of nurses or others necessary to produce a designed nursing system, evaluate effects, and make needed adjustments.

5. *Regulatory care*. A professional operation that involves the actual production and management of the designated nursing system and methods of helping.

6. *Controlling*. A case management operation that encompasses observing and evaluating the efficacy of the nursing system.

Martha Rogers' Science of Unitary Human Beings

Rogers' conceptual model of nursing focuses on unitary, irreducible human beings and their environments. It includes four basic concepts:

1. *Energy fields.* Irreducible, indivisible, pandimensional unitary human beings and environments that are identified by pattern and manifesting characteristics specific to the whole that cannot be predicted from knowledge of the parts. Human and environmental energy fields are integral to each other.
2. *Openness.* A characteristic of human and environmental energy fields; energy fields are continuously and completely open.
3. *Pattern.* The distinguishing characteristic of an energy field. Pattern is perceived as a single wave that gives identity to the field. Each human field pattern is unique and integral to its own unique environmental field pattern. Pattern is an abstraction that cannot be seen; what is seen or experienced are manifestations of field pattern.
4. *Pandimensionality.* A nonlinear domain without spatial or temporal attributes.

Three principles of homeodynamics describe the nature of human and environmental energy fields:

1. *Resonancy.* Asserts that human and environmental fields are identified by wave patterns that manifest continuous change from lower to higher frequencies.
2. *Helicy.* Asserts that human and environmental field patterns are continuous, innovative, and unpredictable, and characterized by increasing diversity.
3. *Integrality.* Emphasizes the continuous mutual human field and environmental field process.

IMPLICATIONS FOR NURSING PRACTICE

Nursing practice is directed toward promoting the health and well-being of all persons, wherever they are. The Rogerian practice methodology encompasses two phases:

1. *Pattern manifestation appraisal.* The continuous process of identifying manifestations of the human and environmental fields that relate to current health events. Human field pattern is appraised by means of manifestations of the pattern in the form of experience, perception, and expressions. Experiences of pattern manifestation are accompanied by perception and expressed in such diverse forms as verbal responses, responses to questionnaires, and personal ways of living and relating. Relevant pattern information includes sensations, thoughts, feelings, awareness, imagination, memory, introspective insights, intuitive apprehensions, recurring themes and issues that pervade one's life, metaphors, visualizations, images, nutrition, work and play, exercise, substance use, sleep/wake cycles, safety, decelerated/accelerated field rhythms, space-time shifts, interpersonal networks, and access to and use of professional health care.
2. *Deliberative mutual patterning.* The continuous process by which the nurse, with the client, patterns the environmental field to promote harmony in relation to health events. The nurse helps create an environment in which healing conditions are optimal and invites clients to heal themselves as they participate in various modalities used in deliberative mutual patterning, including noninvasive modalities such as therapeutic touch, imagery, meditation, relaxation, unconditional love, attitudes of hope, humor, and upbeat moods, and the use of sound, color, and motion.

Callista Roy's Adaptation Model

Roy's conceptual model of nursing focuses on the responses of the human adaptive system to a constantly changing environment. Adaptation is the central feature of the model. Problems in adaptation arise when the adaptive system is unable to cope with or respond to constantly changing stimuli from the internal and external environments in a manner that maintains the system's integrity. Environmental stimuli are categorized as follows:

1. *Focal.* The stimuli most immediately confronting the person.
2. *Contextual.* The contributing factors in the situation.
3. *Residual.* Other unknown factors that may influence the situation. When these factors become known, they are considered focal or contextual stimuli.

Adaptation occurs through two types of innate or acquired coping mechanisms, used to respond to changing environmental stimuli:

1. *Regulator subsystem.* Receives input from the external environment and changes in the person's internal state, and processes these changes through neural-chemical-endocrine channels to produce responses.
2. *Cognator subsystem.* Also receives input

from external and internal stimuli involving psychological, social, physical, and physiologic factors, including regulator subsystem outputs. These stimuli are then processed through cognitive/emotive pathways, including perceptual/information processing, learning, judgment, and emotion.

Responses take place in four modes:

1. *Physiologic mode.* Concerned with basic needs requisite to maintaining the physical and physiologic integrity of the human system; encompasses oxygenation, nutrition, elimination, activity and rest, protection, the senses, fluids and electrolytes, neurological functions, and endocrine functions.
2. *Self-concept mode.* Deals with people's conceptions of the
      physical self—body sensation and body image, and
      personal self—self-consistency, self-ideal, and the moral–ethical–spiritual self.
3. *Role function mode.* Concerns people's performance of roles based on their positions within society.
4. *Interdependence mode.* Involves one's willingness and ability to love, respect, and value others and to accept and respond to love, respect, and value given by others; primarily concerns relationships with significant others and social support systems.

The four modes are interrelated. Responses in any one mode may have an effect on or act as a stimulus in one or all of the other modes.

Responses in each mode are judged to be one of the following:

1. *Adaptive.* Promoting the integrity of the person in terms of the goals of the human adaptive system, which include survival, growth, reproduction, and mastery.
2. *Ineffective.* Not contributing to the goals of the human adaptive system.

IMPLICATIONS FOR NURSING PRACTICE

Nursing practice is directed toward promoting adaptation in each of the four response modes, thereby contributing to the person's health, quality of life, and ability to die with dignity. The nursing process encompasses six steps:

1. *Assessment of behavior.* Collecting data regarding adaptive system behaviors; determining adaptive and ineffective responses; setting priorities for further assessment.
2. *Assessment of stimuli.* Identifying the focal and contextual stimuli that influence adaptive system behaviors.
3. *Nursing diagnosis.* Making judgments regarding adaptation status.
4. *Goal setting.* Stating behavioral outcomes of nursing intervention.
5. *Nursing intervention.* Managing environmental stimuli by increasing, decreasing, maintaining, removing, or otherwise altering relevant focal and contextual stimuli.
6. *Evaluation.* Making judgments regarding the effectiveness of the nursing intervention.

NURSING THEORIES

The terms "theory," "theoretical framework," "theoretical model," and "theoretical rationale" are frequently used interchangeably and defined in the same way: a set of relatively specific and concrete concepts and the statements that describe or link those concepts. Each theory presents a particular perspective about a particular phenomenon, such as the recipient of nursing, the environment, health, or a step in the nursing process.

Functions of Nursing Theories

The function of a nursing theory is to provide considerable specificity in describing, explaining, or predicting some phenomenon. Theories are more specific and concrete than conceptual models. A conceptual model is an abstract and general system of concepts and propositions, whereas a theory deals with one or more relatively specific, concrete concepts and propositions. In addition, conceptual models are general guides that must be further specified by relevant and logically congruent theories before action can be taken.

Grand Theories

Theories vary in scope; that is, they vary in their relative level of concreteness and the specificity of their concepts and propositions. Theories that are broadest in scope are called grand theories. These theories consist of rather abstract and general concepts and propositions that cannot be generated or tested empirically. Indeed, grand theories are developed through thoughtful and insightful appraisal of existing ideas or creative intellectual leaps beyond existing knowledge. Examples of grand theories in nursing include Leininger's (1991) Theory of Culture Care Diversity and Universality, Newman's (1994) Theory of Health as Expanding Consciousness, and Parse's (1992, 1995b) Theory of Human Becoming. An overview of each of these theories, along with implications for professional nursing practice, are presented in the following pages.

The less abstract nature of grand theories compared to conceptual models is illustrated by Parse's (1992) theory, which was derived in part from Rogers' (1970, 1990) conceptual model. Rogers' conceptual model is a frame of reference for all of nursing, whereas Parse's theory limits the domain of interest to the lived experience of health.

SUMMARY OF FORMAL KNOWLEDGE IN NURSING: GRAND THEORIES

Madeleine Leininger's Theory of Cultural Care Diversity and Universality

Leininger's grand nursing theory focuses on the discovery of human care diversities and universalities and ways to provide culturally congruent care. The concepts of the theory are as follows:

1. *Care.* Abstract and concrete phenomena related to assisting, supporting, or enabling experiences or behaviors toward or for others with evident or anticipated needs, to ameliorate or improve their human condition or lifeway.
2. *Caring.* The actions and activities directed toward assisting, supporting, or enabling another individual or group with evident or anticipated needs to ameliorate or improve their human condition or lifeway or face death.
3. *Culture.* The learned, shared, and transmitted values, beliefs, norms, and lifeways of a particular group that guides thinking, decisions, and actions in patterned ways; encompasses several cultural and social structure dimensions, including technological factors, religious and philosophical factors, kinship and social factors, political and legal factors, economic factors, educational and cultural values, and lifeways.
4. *Language.* Word usages, symbols, and meanings related to care.
5. *Ethnohistory.* Past facts, events, instances, experiences of individuals, groups, cultures, and institutions that are primarily people-centered (ethno) and describe, explain, or interpret human lifeways within particular cultural contexts and over short or long periods of time (history).
6. *Environmental context.* The totality of an event, situation, or particular experience that gives meaning to human expressions, interpretations, and social interactions in particular physical, ecological, sociopolitical, and cultural settings.
7. *Health.* A state of well-being that is culturally defined, valued, and practiced and that reflects the ability of individuals (or groups) to perform their daily role activities in culturally expressed, beneficial, and patterned lifeways.
8. *Worldview.* The way people tend to view the world or their universe to form a picture of, or a value stance about, their life or the world around them.
9. *Cultural care.* The subjectively and objectively transmitted values, beliefs, and patterned lifeways that assist, support, or enable another individual or group to maintain their well-being and health, to improve their human condition and lifeway, and to deal with illness, handicaps, or death. Two dimensions exist:
   Cultural care diversity. The variabilities and differences in meanings, patterns, values, lifeways, or symbols of care within or between collectivities that are related to assistive, supportive, or enabling human-care expressions.
   Cultural care universality. The common, similar, or dominant uniform care meanings, patterns, values, lifeways, or symbols that are manifest among many cultures and reflect assistive, supportive, facilitative, or enabling ways of helping people.
10. *Care systems.* The values, norms, and structural features of an organization designed to serve people's health needs, concerns, and conditions. Two types of care systems exist:
    Generic lay care system. Traditional or local indigenous health-care or cure practices that have special meanings and uses for healing or assisting people, which are generally offered in fa-

miliar home or community environmental contexts with their local practitioners.

Professional health-care system. Professional care or cure services offered by diverse health personnel, who have been prepared through formal professional programs of study in special educational institutions.

11. *Cultural-congruent nursing care.* Cognitively based assistive, supportive, facilitative, or enabling acts or decisions that are tailor-made to fit with individual, group, or institutional cultural values, beliefs, and lifeways to provide or support meaningful, beneficial, and satisfying health-care or well-being services. The following are three modes of cultural-congruent nursing care:

Cultural care preservation or maintenance. Assistive, supportive, facilitative, or enabling professional actions and decisions that help people of a particular culture to retain and preserve relevant care values so that they can maintain their well-being, recover from illness, or face handicaps and death.

Cultural care accommodation or negotiation. Assistive, supportive, facilitative, or enabling creative professional actions and decisions that help people of a designated culture adapt to, or negotiate with, others for a beneficial or satisfying health outcome with professional care providers.

Cultural care repatterning or restructuring. Assistive, supportive, facilitative, or enabling professional actions and decisions that help clients reorder, change, or greatly modify their lifeways for a new, different, and beneficial health-care pattern while respecting the clients' cultural values and beliefs.

IMPLICATIONS FOR NURSING PRACTICE

Nursing practice is directed toward improving and providing culturally congruent care to people. The three modes of cultural-congruent nursing care are used as the basis for nursing interventions.

Margaret Newman's Theory of Health as Expanding Consciousness

Newman's grand nursing theory focuses on health as the expansion of consciousness, emphasizing the idea that every person in every situation, no matter how disordered and hopeless, is part of the universal process of expanding consciousness. The theory includes the following concepts:

1. *Time.* The amount of time perceived to be passing (subjective time); clock time (objective time).
2. *Space.* Encompasses personal space, inner space, and life space as dimensions of space relevant to the individual and territoriality, shared space, and distancing as dimensions relevant to the family.
3. *Movement.* An essential property of matter; a means of communicating; the means by which one perceives reality and becomes aware of oneself; the natural condition of life.
4. *Consciousness.* The informational capacity of human beings, that is, their ability to interact with their environments. Consciousness encompasses interconnected cognitive and affective awareness; physiochemical maintenance, including the nervous and endocrine systems; growth processes; the immune system; and the genetic code. Consciousness can be seen in the quantity and quality of the interaction between human beings and their environments. The process of life is toward higher levels of consciousness; sometimes this process is smooth, pleasant, and harmonious; at other times it is difficult and disharmonious, as in disease.
5. *Pattern.* A fundamental attribute of all that provides unity in diversity; information that depicts the whole; relatedness. People are identified by their pattern. The evolution of expanding consciousness is seen in the pattern of movement-space-time.

IMPLICATIONS FOR NURSING PRACTICE

Nursing practice is directed toward facilitating pattern recognition by connecting with the client in an authentic way and assisting the client in discovering new rules for a higher level of organization or consciousness. The nurse-client relationship is a rhythmic coming together and moving apart that occurs in three ongoing steps:

1. *Meeting.* Occurs when a mutual attraction between nurse and client occurs via congruent patterns.
2. *Forming shared consciousness.* Sharing of the whole between the nurse and the client to form a connection; when the connection is formed, pattern recognition is facilitated by applying the four components of Newman's research methodology:

   Establishing the mutuality of the process of inquiry.

   Focusing on the most meaningful persons and events in the person's life.

   Organizing the data in narrative form and displaying it as sequential patterns over time.

   Sharing the person's perception of the pattern with him or her and seeking revision or confirmation.
3. *Moving apart.* Occurs when the client is able to center without being connected to the nurse.

Rosemarie Parse's Theory of Human Becoming

Parse's grand nursing theory focuses on human experiences of participation with the universe in the cocreation of health. The theory includes these concepts:

1. *Meaning.* Encompasses three subconcepts:

   Imaging. Symbolizing or picturing; making concrete the meaning of multidimensional experiences.

   Valuing. Choosing to confirm a cherished belief; the process of confirming cherished beliefs.

   Languaging. Expressing valued images; sharing valued images through symbols of words, gesture, gaze, touch, and posture.
2. *Rhythmicity.* Refers to cadent or ordered and encompasses several subconcepts:

   Revealing-concealing. The simultaneous disclosing of some aspects of self and hiding of others; a paradoxical rhythm in the pattern of relating with others.

   Enabling-limiting. A rhythmical pattern of relating; in choosing, there are an infinite number of opportunities and limitations; one is thus enabled-limited by all choices.

   Connecting-separating. A rhythmical process of moving together and moving apart.
3. *Cotranscendence.* Refers to going beyond the actual in interrelationships with others. The subconcepts include the following:

   Powering. Struggling with the tension of pushing-resisting.

   Originating. Springing from; emerging; creating anew, generating unique ways of living that surface through interconnections with people and projects.

   Transforming. The changing of change, co-constituting anew in a deliberate way; shifting views of the familiar as is shed on the known is seen in a different light.

The following are the three major principles of the theory of human becoming:

1. *Structuring meaning multidimensionally is cocreating reality through the languaging of valuing and imaging.* Humans construct what is real for them from choices made in many realms of the universe.
2. *Cocreating rhythmical patterns of relating is living the paradoxical unity of revealing-concealing and enabling-limiting while connecting-separating.* Humans live in rhythm with the universe, co-constituting patterns of relating.
3. *Cotranscending with the possibles is powering unique ways of originating in the process of transforming.* Humans forge unique paths with shifting perspectives as they cast a different light on the familiar.

IMPLICATIONS FOR NURSING PRACTICE

Nursing practice is directed toward respecting the quality of life as perceived by the person and the family. The practice methodology encompasses three dimensions and three processes:

1. The dimension *illuminating meaning* is shedding light by uncovering the what was, is, and will be, as it appears now. It happens in *explicating* what is. The process of explicating is making clear what is appearing now through languaging.
2. The dimension *synchronizing rhythms* happens in dwelling with the pitch, yaw, and

roll of the interhuman cadence. The process of *dwelling with* is giving self over to the flow of the struggle in connecting-separating.

3. The dimension *mobilizing transcendence* happens in moving beyond the meaning moment to what is not-yet. The process of *moving beyond* is propelling toward an imaged possible in transforming.

Middle-Range Theories

Middle-range theories are narrower in scope than grand theories, encompassing a limited number of concepts and a limited aspect of the real world. Middle-range theories therefore consist of concepts and propositions that are empirically measurable. Examples of middle-range theories in nursing include Orlando's (1961) theory of the deliberative nursing process, Peplau's (1952, 1992) theory of interpersonal relations, and Watson's (1985) theory of human caring. An overview of each of these theories, along with implications for professional nursing practice, are presented in this section.

The specificity of middle-range theory concepts and propositions is illustrated by Orlando's (1961) theory. This theory predicts that using a particular communication technique will be effective in identifying the client's immediate need for help. The technique requires the nurse, using a personal pronoun, to share with the client his or her perceptions, thoughts, and feelings about the client's behavior and to ask the client if those perceptions, thoughts, and feelings are correct. An example is: "I think you do not want morning care right now? Am I correct?"

SUMMARY OF FORMAL KNOWLEDGE IN NURSING: MIDDLE-RANGE THEORIES

Ida Jean Orlando's Theory of the Nursing Process Discipline

Orlando's middle-range predictive nursing theory focuses on an interpersonal process that is directed toward facilitating identification of the nature of the patient's distress and his or her immediate needs for help. The following are the concepts of the theory:

1. *Patient's behavior.* Behavior observed by the nurse in an immediate nurse-patient situation. It includes two dimensions:

Need for help. A requirement of the patient that, if supplied, relieves or diminishes immediate distress or improves the immediate sense of adequacy or well-being.

Improvement. An increase in the patient's mental and physical health, well-being, and sense of adequacy.

The need for help and improvement are expressed in both nonverbal and verbal forms. Visual manifestations of nonverbal behavior include such motor activities as eating, walking, twitching, and trembling, as well as such physiologic forms as urinating, defecating, temperature and blood pressure readings, respiratory rate, and skin color. Vocal forms of nonverbal behavior—nonverbal behavior that is heard—include crying, moaning, laughing, coughing, sneezing, sighing, yelling, screaming, groaning, and singing. Verbal behavior refers to what a patient says, including complaints, requests, questions, refusals, demands, and comments or statements.

2. *Nurse's reaction.* The nurse's nonobservable response to the patient's behavior has three dimensions:

Perception. Physical stimulation of any one of the five senses by the patient's behavior.

Thought. An idea that occurs in the nurse's mind.

Feeling. A state of mind inclining the nurse toward or against a perception, thought, or action; occurs in response to the nurse's perceptions and thoughts.

3. *Nurse's activity.* The observable actions taken by nurses in response to their reactions, including instructions, suggestions, directions, explanations, information, requests, and questions directed toward the patient; making decisions for the patient; handling the patient's body; administering medications or treatments; and changing the patient's immediate environment. The nurse's activity has two dimensions:

Automatic nursing process. Actions the nurse decides on for reasons other than the patient's immediate need.

Deliberative nursing process (process discipline). A specific set of nurse behaviors or actions directed toward the patient's behavior that ascertain or meet the patient's immediate needs for help.

IMPLICATIONS FOR NURSING PRACTICE

Nursing practice is directed toward identifying and meeting the patient's immediate needs for help through use of the deliberative nursing process, which occurs when three requirements are met:

1. What the nurse says to the patient must match the nurse's reaction, what the nurse does nonverbally must be verbally expressed, and the expression must match the nurse's reaction.
2. The nurse must clearly communicate to the patient that what is expressed belongs to himself or herself (*I* think that . . .).
3. The nurse must ask the patient about the item expressed to obtain correction or verification. (Is that so?)

Hildegard Peplau's Theory of Interpersonal Relations

Peplau's middle-range descriptive nursing theory focuses on the phases of the interpersonal process that occur when an ill person and a nurse come together to resolve a difficulty related to health. The one concept of the theory is the nurse-patient relationship, which has four discernible phases:

1. *Orientation.* Occurs as the patient has a felt need signifying a health problem and seeks assistance to clarify the problem. The patient participates by asking questions, trying to find out what needs to be known to feel secure, and observing ways in which professional people respond. The nurse participates by helping the patient recognize and understand the health problem and the extent of need for assistance, understand what professional services can offer, plan the use of professional services, and harness energy from tension and anxiety connected with felt needs.
2. *Identification.* Occurs as the patient learns how to make use of the nurse-patient relationship, as both come to know and respect one another as persons with likes and differ-

ences of opinions in ways of looking at a situation and in responding to events. The nurse makes use of professional education and skill to aid the patient in arriving at a point where full use can be made of the relationship to solve the health problem.
3. *Exploitation.* Occurs as the patient makes full use of available professional services.
4. *Resolution.* Occurs as the nurse helps the patient organize actions so that the patient will be free for more productive social activities and relationships.

IMPLICATIONS FOR NURSING PRACTICE

Nursing practice is directed toward promoting favorable changes in patients through the nurse-patient relationship. Within that relationship, the nurse's major function is to study the interpersonal relations between the client and others. The five characteristics of professional nursing practice are:

1. The focus of professional nursing is the patient.
2. The nurse uses participant observation rather than spectator observation.
3. The nurse is aware of the various roles she assumes in the nurse-patient relationship.
4. Professional nursing is primarily investigative, emphasizing observation and collecting data to make available to the patient rather than task-oriented.
5. Professional nursing is grounded in the use of theory.

Three interlocking performances in interpersonal relations make it possible for nurses to study what is happening in their contacts with patients:

1. Nurses *observe* the ways in which patients transform energy into patterns of action that bring satisfaction or security in the face of a recurring problem.
2. Nurses and patients *communicate* with each other in terms of their views of themselves and their expectations of others.
3. Nurses *record* the verbatim difficulties of patients and desymbolize the recordings to reveal hidden wishes and longings that may be the root of the problem.

Jean Watson's Theory of Human Caring

Watson's middle-range descriptive nursing theory focuses on the caring actions taken by nurses as they interact with others. The theory is based on the following concepts:

1. *Transpersonal caring.* Human-to-human connectedness in which each person is touched by the human center of the other; four components are included:

   Self. The organized, consistent conceptual gestalt, composed of perceptions of the characteristics of the "I" or "me" and perceptions of the relationships of the "I" or "me" to others and to various aspects of life, together with the values attached to those perceptions.

   Phenomenal field. The totality of human experience; the individual's frame of reference, which can be known only to the person; the person's subjective reality.

   Actual caring occasion of the person and the nurse. The event bringing the caregiver and the recipient of care together, which involves action and choice by both the nurse and the individual.

   Intersubjectivity. An intersubjective human-to-human relationship in which the person of the nurse affects and is affected by the person of the other. Both are fully present in the moment and feel a union with the other. They share a phenomenal field that becomes part of the life history of both and are coparticipants in becoming in the now and the future.

2. *Carative factors.* Ten nursing interventions or caring processes, as follows:

   □ Formation of a humanistic-altruistic system of values.
   □ Instillation of faith-hope.
   □ Cultivation of sensitivity to one's self and to others.
   □ Development of a helping-trusting, human care relationship.
   □ Promotion and acceptance of the expression of positive and negative feelings.
   □ Systematic use of a creative problem-solving caring process.
   □ Promotion of transpersonal teaching-learning.
   □ Provision for a supportive, protective, and corrective mental, physical, societal, and spiritual environment.
   □ Assistance with gratification of human needs.
   □ Allowance for existential-phenomenological-spiritual forces.

IMPLICATIONS FOR NURSING PRACTICE

Nursing practice is directed toward helping persons gain a higher degree of harmony within the mind, body, and soul that generates self-knowledge, self-reverence, self-healing, and self-care processes while increasing diversity, which is pursued through use of the 10 carative factors.

VOCABULARIES OF CONCEPTUAL MODELS AND THEORIES

The content of each conceptual model and nursing theory is stated in a distinctive vocabulary that should not be considered jargon. The terminology the author of each conceptual model or theory uses results from considerable thought about how to convey the meaning of that particular perspective to others (Biley, 1990). Furthermore, as Akinsanya (1989) points out, "Every science has its own peculiar terms, concepts and principles which are essential for the development of its knowledge base. In nursing, as in other sciences, an understanding of these is a prerequisite to a critical examination of their contribution to the development of knowledge and its application to practice" (p. ii). In fact, the differences in the vocabularies of the various conceptual models and theories are the same as those in the vocabularies of diverse medical specialties, such as obstetrics, gynecology, cardiology, neurology, psychiatry, and geriatrics.

ADVANTAGES AND DISADVANTAGES OF USING FORMAL NURSING KNOWLEDGE

Explicit use of formal nursing knowledge to guide nursing practice is the hallmark of a professional nurse. The use of formal nursing knowledge "distinguishes nursing as an autonomous health profession" and represents "nursing's unique contribution to the health care system" (Parse, 1995a, p. 128).

The most obvious practical advantage of using an explicit conceptual model of nursing is identifying the goals of nursing practice and of a nursing process format that encompasses particular parameters for assessment, labels for patient/client problems, a strategy for planning nursing care, a set of nursing interventions, and criteria for evaluating the outcomes of nursing practice. In other words, the conceptual model gives substance to the generic nursing process, which only tells the nurse to assess, diagnose, plan, implement, and evaluate. Each conceptual model tells the nurse *what* to assess, *what* diagnoses are possible, *how* to plan, *what* interventions are appropriate, and *what* outcomes to evaluate.

The major practical advantage a nursing theory provides is greater specificity in one or more phases of the nursing process. For example, Orlando's (1961) theory of the deliberative nursing process tells the nurse exactly how to identify the patient's immediate need for help. Orlando's theory can be used very effectively in combination with the Roy adaptation model (Roy & Andrews, 1991).

The number of nurses throughout the world who recognize the value of basing professional nursing practice on an explicit conceptual model of nursing or nursing theory is rapidly increasing. Indeed, Cash's (1990) claim that "there is no central core that can distinguish nursing theoretically from a number of other occupational activities" (p. 255) is offset by many claims to the contrary. Clearly, his claim fails to take into account the contributions made by explicit conceptual models of nursing and nursing theories to the development of practice that is unique to *nursing* (Parse, 1995a). As Chalmers (cited in Chalmers, Kershaw, Melia, & Kendrich, 1990) points out, "Nursing models [and theories] have provided what many would argue is a much needed alternative knowledge base from which nurses can practice in an informed way. An alternative, that is, to the medical model which for so many years has dominated many aspects of health care" (p. 34). Nursing models and theories also provide an alternative to the institutional model of practice, in which "the most salient values [are] efficiency, standardized care, rules, and regulations" (Rogers, 1989, p. 113). The institutional model, moreover, typically upholds, reinforces, and supports the medical model (Grossman & Hooton, 1993).

In fact, conceptual models of nursing and nursing theories provide explicit frames of reference for *professional nursing practice* by delineating the scope of nursing practice. They move the practice of nursing away from a medically or institutionally driven model, thereby fostering autonomy from medicine and a coherent purpose of practice (Bélanger, 1991; Bridges, 1991; Ingram, 1991). Furthermore, conceptual models and nursing theories specify innovative

goals for nursing practice and introduce ideas designed to improve practice (Lindsay, 1990) by facilitating the identification of relevant information, reducing the fragmentation of care and improving its coordination (Chalmers, cited in Chalmers, et al., 1990). In particular, conceptual models and theories provide a nursing knowledge base that has a positive effect on practice "by enabling well-coordinated care to take place, by providing a basis for the justification of care actions and by enabling nurses to *talk nursing*" (Chalmers, cited in Chalmers et al., 1990, p. 34) and to *think nursing* (Perry, 1985).

Hayne (1992) points out that, although some clinicians hold the "unfortunate view [that conceptual models and theories] are the inventions and predictions only of scholars and academics [that have] little significance for their own practice environments," many other clinicians recognize their beneficial effects on practice (p. 105). Indeed, conceptual model- or theory-based nursing practice "help[s] nurses better communicate what they do" (Neff, 1991, p. 534) and why they do it.

The importance of effectively communicating what nursing is and what nurses do is underscored by Feeg (1989), who identified the following three reasons for implementing conceptual model-based or theory-based nursing practice:

1. In this time of information saturation and rapid change, we know it is not valuable to focus on every detail and, therefore, we need [conceptual models and theories] to help guide our judgments in new situations.

2. In this time of technological overdrive, we need a holistic orientation to remind us of our caring perspective.

3. In this time of professional territoriality, it has become even more important to understand our identity in nursing and operationalize our practice from a . . . knowledge base. (p. 450)

Additionally, using conceptual model- or theory-based nursing practice highlights the need for nursing to be clear about its mission in today's climate of health-care reform. In this time of health-care reform, it is crucial that we explicate *what we know and why we do what we do*. It is crucial that we communicate out nursing knowledge and explain how that knowledge governs the actions we perform on behalf of or in conjunction with people who require health care. Thus, nursing practice based on an explicit conceptual model or nursing theory is "for our patients' sake" (Dabbs, 1994, p. 220).

Johnson (1990) noted that, although individual clinicians and nursing departments take risks when the decision is made to implement conceptual model- or theory-based nursing practice, the rewards far outweigh the risks. She states:

> To openly use a nursing model [or theory] is risk-taking behavior for the individual nurse. For a nursing department to adopt one of these models [or theories] for unit or institution use is risk-taking behavior of an even higher order. The reward for such risk-taking for the individual practitioner lies in the great satisfaction gained from being able to specify explicit concrete *nursing* goals in the care of patients and from documenting the actual achievement of the desired outcomes. The reward for the nursing department is having a rational, cohesive, and comprehensive basis for the development of standards of nursing practice, for the evaluation of practitioners, and for the documentation of the contribution of nursing to patient welfare. (p. 32).

Anecdotal and empirical evidence that the rewards of implementing conceptual model or theory to guide professional nursing practice include such benefits as reduced staff nurse turnover (Fernandez, Brennan, Alvarez, & Duffy, 1990; K. Frederickson, cited in Studio Three, 1992; Scherer, 1988), more rapid movement from novice to expert nurse (Field, 1989), and increased client satisfaction (Scherer, 1988).

Furthermore, as the use of conceptual models of nursing and nursing theories moves nursing practice from a base of implicit knowledge to explicit nursing knowledge, both nurses and the recipients of nursing care are empowered. Indeed, nursing "knowledge is power" (Orr, 1991, p. 218), which as Lister (1991) and Malin and Teasdale (1991) have pointed out, can be used to empower recipients of health care to participate fully in decisions about that care. The challenge, then, is to help each nurse select an explicit *nursing* model or theory to guide her or his nursing practice.

USING CONCEPTUAL MODELS TO GUIDE PROFESSIONAL NURSING PRACTICE

Use of an explicit conceptual model of nursing to guide professional nursing practice is exemplified by two case studies.

Case Study: Orem's Self-Care Framework

Thomas Johnson is a 39-year-old, moderately obese male with multiple sclerosis, diagnosed 1 year ago. He has experienced a steady decline in functioning since his diagnosis and became wheelchair-dependent 6 months ago. Mr. Johnson has pressure ulcers on his sacrum and both buttocks, and he is currently being hospitalized for management of these wounds. He requires sterile dressing changes twice daily. Mr. Johnson uses sliding board transfers with moderate assistance because of upper extremity weakness. He requires moderate assistance for dressing, toileting hygiene, bathing, meal setup, and transfers. Mr. Johnson has bowel control, but is currently experiencing urinary retention, which is managed by straight catheterization every 4 hours. He has been managing at home with the assistance of his live-in girlfriend of 15 years, Cheryl Wilson. She is very supportive and participates in all aspects of Mr. Johnson's care. Visiting nurses had been providing daily skin care treatments and were beginning to teach Mr. Johnson self-catheterization. He states that he copes by not dwelling on his disabilities, but he admits to feeling low at times and thinks about what life was like before his diagnosis of multiple sclerosis.

Initial Orem self-care framework–based nursing assessment indicates that Mr. Johnson is currently unable to meet what Orem call his therapeutic self-care demand. Therapeutic self-care demand is defined as "the known self-care requisites [that are] particularized for individuals in relation to their conditions and circumstances" (Orem, 1995, pp. 65, 123). Three types of self-care requisites make up the therapeutic self-care demand: universal self-care, developmental self-care, and health-deviation self-care requisites. Assessment of Mr. Johnson's self-care agency, that is, his ability to perform self-care, reveals that he is currently unable to meet his therapeutic self-care demand. Comparing the therapeutic self-care demand with Mr. Johnson's current self-care agency reveals several self-care deficits.

The nurse, Mr. Johnson, and Ms. Wilson agree that the goal is to enhance Mr. Johnson's self-care agency and Ms. Wilson's dependent care agency through the use of all three types of nursing systems. The wholly compensatory nursing system is needed to provide straight catheterization every 4 hours and sterile dressing changes twice a day. The partly compensatory nursing system is needed to assist Mr. Johnson with dressing, toileting hygiene, bathing, meal setup, and transfers. The supportive-educative nursing system is needed to teach Mr. Johnson and Ms. Wilson about his personal care and to provide psychological support to facilitate coping with a debilitating illness. Consequently, the nursing staff will initially provide wound care but also teach Ms. Wilson how to care for the open areas when Mr. Johnson goes home. Nurses will also continue to perform Mr. Johnson's straight catheterization every 4 hours, but he will be expected to participate in learning the self-catheterization procedure. In summary, the nursing staff will provide Mr. Johnson and Ms. Wilson with the necessary guidance and teaching to allow them to meet his therapeutic self-care demand once he is discharged.

Case Study: Roy's Adaptation Model

Brian Williams is a 29-year-old, thin, married male who was involved in a motor vehicle accident. Mr. Williams' blood alcohol level at the time of the accident was 0.29 mg/dL, and he has two previous arrests for driving under the influence. He suffered multiple injuries, including a severed spinal cord at T8-T9, left ear laceration, fractured left humerus, and three fractured ribs. Mr. Williams is experiencing paralysis below the waist and bowel and bladder dysfunction; his left arm is casted, and he requires dressing changes to his left ear twice daily. He is dependent for transfers, bowel and bladder management, dressing, bathing, and range of motion exercises. Mr. Williams appears withdrawn and depressed, repeatedly stating, "I should have known better." Lynn Williams, Mr. Williams' wife, is very supportive of him but admits that she feels some anger because of his drinking problems and his past refusal to get any kind of help. Mr. Williams' accident was 3 weeks ago, and he is about to be transferred to the rehabilitation unit at the hospital.

Initial Roy adaptation model–based nursing assessment indicates that Mr. Williams is exhibiting ineffective behaviors in all four response modes. More specifically, assessment of physiological mode responses reveals that Mr. Williams has a very poor appetite and is below average weight. Mr. Williams is also experiencing bowel and bladder incontinence, paralysis below his waist, and difficulty sleeping. Assessment of self-concept mode responses indicates that Mr. Williams

is struggling with guilt about causing his accident, the powerlessness he feels about his situation, and a negative body image. Assessment of role function mode responses reveals that Mr. Williams is beginning to feel like a failure. He is having difficulty accepting his dependence on others and expresses concern over "not being the head of my household anymore." Assessment of the interdependence mode responses indicates that Mr. and Mrs. Williams have had no time to spend alone together, and since Mrs. Williams has had to return to work, Mr. Williams is very lonely during the day. Mr. Williams has also indicated that he is concerned about the resumption of a sexual relationship with his wife.

On Mr. Williams' arrival at the rehabilitation unit, he and the rehabilitation nurse agree that their primary goal is to convert ineffective responses to adaptive ones, thereby contributing to his personal health and quality of life. Mr. Williams agrees that he needs to learn about his condition and how to manage his physical disabilities to become independent in his personal care. Mr. Williams also agrees with the nurse that rehabilitation is a full-time job, and he must fully participate in physical and occupational therapy. Together, the nurse and Mr. Williams begin to identify specific behaviors that need to be modified or developed. They also establish a "time table" of short- and long-term goals for behavioral changes. Nursing intervention for Mr. Williams focuses on increasing the focal stimulus of social support through individual counseling and teaching and participation in a support group for patients and their families and weekly Alcoholics Anonymous meetings.

SELECTING A CONCEPTUAL MODEL OR NURSING THEORY FOR PROFESSIONAL NURSING PRACTICE

The fact that formal nursing knowledge consists of many conceptual models and theories requires each nurse to select one as a guide for his or her own professional practice. The following six steps can help you select an appropriate conceptual model of nursing or nursing theory.

1. *Identify your own beliefs about and values related to the phenomena of interest to all nurses.* State your beliefs about the recipients of nursing, the relevant environment, health, and the goals of professional nursing practice. The following questions will help you identify your particular beliefs and values:

- □ Are all people, regardless of health state or diagnosis, potential recipients of professional nursing?
- □ Or are only people with documented illness legitimate recipients of professional nursing?
- □ Who are the significant people in the recipient's environment?
- □ What are the significant objects in the recipient's environment?
- □ In what settings can professional nursing practice take place?
- □ What is health?
- □ What are the appropriate goals of professional nursing practice?
- □ What part do recipients of professional nursing play in determining nursing goals and identifying interventions used to attain those goals?

2. *Identify the client population with which you would like to work.* The population may be based on a specific diagnosis, such as cancer or renal failure; an age group, such as children and adolescents or the elderly; a type of illness, such as an acute crisis or chronic illness; or a particular symptom, such as chest pain or an elevated temperature.

3. *Systematically analyze and evaluate the content of several conceptual models of nursing and nursing theories.* Review the summaries of Conceptual Models on theories presented earlier in the chapter as well as the primary source material for each conceptual model and theory. This will provide a firm foundation for selecting the conceptual model or theory.

4. *Compare the philosophic claims undergirding the conceptual model with your own beliefs and values.* Step 3 will help you identify the philosophic claims on which various conceptual models and nursing theories are based.

5. *Identify the conceptual models and nursing theories that are appropriate guides for nursing with the client population of interest.* Step 3 will also provide the needed information regarding how

well a particular nursing model and theory works in particular client populations.

6. *Choose the conceptual model or theory that most closely matches your beliefs and values and the client population with which you want to work.* Then use the model or theory to guide your practice with several clients so that you can determine its utility. If you find that the conceptual model you have chosen is not useful, select another model or theory and test its utility again.

Research findings indicate that nurses feel vulnerable and experience a great deal of stress as they attempt to achieve professional aspirations within a continuously and rapidly changing medically dominated, bureaucratic health-care delivery system (Graham, 1994). Conceptual models of nursing and nursing theories provide the intellectual focus and identify the practical skills that nurses need to survive and they enhance the well-being of individuals, families, and communities. As a novice user of a conceptual model of nursing or nursing theory, do not become discouraged if initial experiences with the model or theory seem forced or awkward. Adopting an explicit nursing model or theory does require using a new vocabulary and a new way of thinking about nursing situations. Repeatedly using the conceptual model or theory should, however, lead to more systematic and organized applications. Broncatello's (1980) words provide the encouragement needed to start using a conceptual model of nursing or nursing theory to guide professional nursing practice:

> The nurse's consistent use of any model [or theory] for the interpretation of observable [client] data is most definitely not an easy task. Much like the development of any habitual behavior, it initially requires thought, discipline and the gradual evolvement of a mind set of what is important to observe within the guidelines of the model [or theory]. As is true of most habits, however, it makes decision making less complicated. (p. 23)

KEY POINTS

 Conceptual models of nursing present diverse perspectives of the recipient of nursing, who can be an individual, a family, or a community; the environment of the recipient and the environment in which nursing occurs; the recipients health state; and the definition and nursing goals as well as nursing actions or interventions.

- The most practical function of a conceptual model is its delineation of goals for nursing practice and a nursing process format that encompasses parameters for assessment, labels for patient/client problems, a strategy for planning nursing care, a set of nursing interventions, and criteria for evaluating the outcomes of nursing care. A conceptual model of nursing provides a structure for documenting all aspects of the nursing process, from assessment to evaluation of outcomes. A conceptual model also helps identify standards of nursing practice and criteria for quality assurance reviews.
- The function of a nursing theory is to provide considerable specificity in describing, explaining, or predicting some phenomenon. Theories are more specific and concrete than conceptual models. A conceptual model is an abstract and general system of concepts and propositions, whereas a theory deals with one or more relatively specific and concrete concepts and propositions. In addition, conceptual models are general guides that must be specified further by relevant and logically congruent theories before action can occur.
- Conceptual models of nursing and nursing theories move the professional practice of nursing away from that driven by a medical or institutional model, and therefore foster autonomy from medicine and a coherent purpose for professional nursing practice.
- Six steps are used to select a conceptual model or nursing theory to guide professional nursing practice: (1) state your philosophy of nursing in the form of beliefs about and values related to the nursing recipient, the environment, health, and nursing goals; (2) identify the particular client population with which you wish to practice; (3) thoroughly analyze and evaluate several conceptual models of nursing and nursing theories; (4) compare your philosophy of nursing with the philosophical claims on which each conceptual model and nursing theory is based; (5) determine which conceptual models or nursing theories are appropriate for use with the client population of interest; and (6) select the conceptual model or nursing theory that most closely matches your philosophy of the nursing and the client population of interest.

CHAPTER EXERCISES

1. Select a conceptual model of nursing. Assess a client in your practice setting using an assessment format developed for that model.

2. Explain how the concepts of a selected conceptual model of nursing can be more fully specified by a selected middle-range nursing theory.

3. Review the nursing care plan for a client in your practice setting. Revise the nursing care plan to be consistent with a particular conceptual model of nursing or nursing theory. Explain how the revised nursing care plan reflects the unique contributions of nursing to health care.

REFERENCES

Akinsanya, J. A. (1989). Introduction. *Recent Advances in Nursing, 24,* i–ii.

Bélanger, P. (1991). Nursing models—a major step towards professional autonomy. *AARN Newsletter, 48*(8), 13.

Biley, F. (1990). Worldly wise. *Nursing (London), 4*(24), 37.

Bridges, J. (1991). Working with doctors: Distinct from medicine. *Nursing Times, 87*(27), 42–43.

Broncatello, K. F. (1980). Auger in action: Application of the model. *Advances in Nursing Science, 2*(2), 13–23.

Cash, K. (1990). Nursing models and the idea of nursing. *International Journal of Nursing Studies, 27,* 249–256.

Chalmers, H., Kershaw, B., Melia, K., & Kendrich, M. (1990). Nursing models: Enhancing or inhibiting practice? *Nursing Standard, 5*(11), 34–40.

Dabbs, A. D. V. (1994). Theory-based nursing practice: For our patients' sake. *Clinical Nurse Specialist, 8,* 214, 220.

Fawcett, J., & Downs, F. S. (1992). *The relationship of theory and research* (2nd ed.). Philadelphia: Davis.

Feeg, V. (1989). From the editor: Is theory application merely an intellectual exercise? *Pediatric Nursing, 15,* 450.

Fernandez, R., Brennan, M. L., Alvarez, A., & Duffy, M. R. (1990). Theory-based practice: a model for nurse retention. *Nursing Administration Quarterly, 12*(4), 47–53.

Field, P. A. (1989). Brenda, Beth, and Susan: Three approaches to health promotion. *The Canadian Nurse, 85*(5), 20–24.

Frank, L. K. (1968). Science as a communication process. *Main Currents in Modern Thought, 25,* 45–50.

Graham, I. (1994). How do registered nurses think and experience nursing: A phenomenological investigation. *Journal of Clinical Nursing, 3,* 235–242.

Grossman, M., & Hooton, M. (1993). The significance of the relationship between a discipline and its practice. *Journal of Advanced Nursing, 18,* 866–872.

Hayne, Y. (1992). The current status and future significance of nursing as a discipline. *Journal of Advanced Nursing, 17,* 104–107.

Henderson, V. (1966). *The nature of nursing. A definition and its implications for practice, research, and education.* New York: Macmillan.

Ingram, R. (1991). Why does nursing need theory? *Journal of Advanced Nursing, 16,* 350–353.

Johnson, D. E. (1987). Evaluating conceptual models for use in critical care nursing practice. [Guest editorial]. *Dimensions of Critical Care Nursing, 6,* 195–197.

Johnson, D. E. (1990). The behavioral system model for nursing. In M. E. Parker (Ed.). *Nursing theories in practice* (pp. 23–32). New York: National League for Nursing.

King, I. M. (1990). King's conceptual framework and theory of goal attainment. In M. E. Parker (Ed.). *Nursing theories in practice* (pp. 73–84). New York: National League for Nursing.

Leininger, M. M. (Ed.). (1991). *Culture care diversity and universality: A theory of nursing.* New York: National League for Nursing.

Levine, M. E. (1991). The conservation principles: A model for health. In K. M. Schaefer & J. B. Pond (Eds.). *Levine's conservation model: A framework for nursing practice* (pp. 1–11). Philadelphia: Davis.

Levine, M. E. (1966). Trophicognosis: An alternative to nursing diagnosis. In *American Nurses' Association Regional Clinical Conference* (Vol. 2, pp. 55–70). New York: American Nurses' Association.

Lindsay, B. (1990). The gap between theory and practice. *Nursing Standard, 5*(4), 34–35.

Lister, P. (1991). Approaching models of nursing from a postmodernist perspective. *Journal of Advanced Nursing, 16,* 206–212.

Malin, N., & Teasdale, K. (1991). Caring versus empowerment: Considerations for nursing practice. *Journal of Advanced Nursing, 16,* 657–662.

Neff, M. (1991). President's message: The future of our profession from the eyes of today. *American Nephrology Nurses Association Journal, 18,* 534.

Neuman, B. (1995). *The Neuman systems model* (3rd ed.). Norwalk, CT: Appleton & Lange.

Newman, M. A. (1994). *Health as expanding consciousness* (2nd ed.). New York: National League for Nursing Press.

Nightingale, F. (1859). *Notes on nursing: What it is, and what it is not.* London: Harrison and Sons. (Commemorative edition printed by J. B. Lippincott Company, Philadelphia, 1992.)

Orem, D. E. (1995). *Nursing: Concepts of practice* (5th ed.). St. Louis: Mosby.

Orlando, I. J. (1961). *The dynamic nurse-patient relationship: Function, process and principles.* New York: G. P. Putnam's Sons. (Reprinted 1990, New York: National League for Nursing.)

Orr, J. (1991). Knowledge is power. *Health Visitor, 64,* 218.

Parse, R. R. (1992). Human becoming: Parse's theory of nursing. *Nursing Science Quarterly, 5,* 35–42.

Parse, R. R. (1995a). Commentary: Parse's theory of human becoming: An alternative guide to nursing practice for pediatric oncology nurses. *Journal of Pediatric Oncology Nursing, 12,* 128.

Parse, R. R. (Ed.). (1995b). *Illuminations: The human becoming theory in practice and research.* New York: National League for Nursing Press.

Peplau, H. E. (1952). *Interpersonal relations in nursing.* New York: G. P. Putnam's Sons. (Reprinted 1991. New York: Springer.)

Peplau, H. E. (1992). Interpersonal relations: A theoretical framework for application in nursing practice. *Nursing Science Quarterly, 5,* 13–18.

Perry, J. (1985). Has the discipline of nursing developed to the stage where nurses do 'think nursing'? *Journal of Advanced Nursing, 10,* 31–37.

Rogers, M. E. (1970). *An introduction to the theoretical basis of nursing.* Philadelphia: Davis.

Rogers, M. E. (1989). Creating a climate for the implementation of a nursing conceptual framework. *Journal of Continuing Education in Nursing, 20,* 112–116.

Rogers, M. E. (1990). Nursing: Science of unitary, irreducible, human beings: Update 1990. In E. A. M. Barrett (Ed.). *Visions of Rogers' science-based nursing* (pp. 5–11). New York: National League for Nursing.

Roy, C., & Andrews, H. A. (1991). *The Roy adaptation model: The definitive statement.* Norwalk, CT: Appleton & Lange.

Scherer, P. (1988). Hospitals that attract (and keep) nurses. *American Journal of Nursing, 88,* 34–40.

Studio Three. (1992). *The Nurse Theorists: Excellence in Action— Callista Roy.* Athens, OH: Fuld Institute of Technology in Nursing Education.

Watson, J. (1985). *Nursing: Human science and human care. A theory of nursing.* Norwalk, CT: Appleton-Century-Crofts. (Reprinted 1988. New York: National League for Nursing.)

BIBLIOGRAPHY

Fawcett, J. (1993). *Analysis and evaluation of nursing theories.* Philadelphia: Davis.

Fawcett, J. (1995). *Analysis and evaluation of conceptual models of nursing* (3rd ed.). Philadelphia: Davis.

Parker, M. E. (1990). *Nursing theories in practice.* New York: National League for Nursing.

Parker, M. E. (1993). *Patterns of nursing theories in practice.* New York: National League for Nursing Press.

Chapter 4

WHAT IS THEORY

Rose Kearney Nunnery

CHAPTER OBJECTIVES

On completion of
this chapter, the reader
will be able to:

1. Define key terms in theory development.
2. Discuss Maslow's theory of motivation with the hierarchy of basic needs.
3. Describe the components of developmental theories and their application to individuals across the lifespan.
4. Describe the components and application of systems theory.
5. Discuss the impact of theory on practice.

KEY TERMS

Theory	Concepts	Internal Criticism
Model	Constructs	External Criticism
Framework	Variables	Hierarchy of Needs
Conceptual Model or Framework	Propositions	Developmental Theories
	Theory Description	General Systems Theory

A characteristic of a scientific discipline is that it is built on a theoretical base. This includes theoretical foundations unique to the discipline as well as those borrowed or adapted from other scientific disciplines. In Chapter 1, paradigms and the metaparadigm concepts of nursing were discussed. Kuhn (1970) described a paradigm as "universally recognized scientific achievements that for a time provide model problems and solutions to a community of practitioners" (p. vii). When the paradigm is no longer useful in explaining phenomena, practice, and conduct research in that particular scientific community, a paradigm shift occurs and a new structure evolves.

In 1957, Merton used a paradigm to analyze sociological theory. He viewed the paradigm as a "field glass" to illuminate and view concepts and interrelationships and make assumptions clear on the body of knowledge for analysis and testing. Merton (1957) identified the purposes of a paradigm as providing for the following:

1. Parsimonious arrangement of concepts and propositions showing interrelationships.
2. A logical guide showing derivations and avoiding hidden assumptions and concepts.
3. Culmination in theory development as a building process.
4. Systematic arrangement and cross-tabulation of concepts for analysis.
5. Codification of qualitative research methods (pp. 13–16).

From a cultural perspective, Leininger (1991) defined a worldview or paradigm as "the way people tend to look out on the world or their universe to form a picture or a value stance about their life or world around them" (p. 47). In the professional culture of nursing, these are the values, attitudes, beliefs, and practices unique to the discipline. Thus, a scientific community has the tools to create and test theory for knowledge development and use of this knowledge in practice. The paradigm or worldview furnishes the philosophical assumptions that are considered "givens" by the theorist or the scientific community. In nursing, this provides us with the process: the metaparadigm concepts to various paradigms, and the development of theory on which to base research, practice, administration, and education.

TERMINOLOGY IN THEORY DEVELOPMENT AND ANALYSIS

We believe professions such as nursing are based on unique theory. Kerlinger (1986) defined a **theory** as "a set of interrelated constructs (concepts),

definitions, and propositions that present a systematic view of phenomena by specifying relations among variables, with the purpose of explaining and predicting the phenomena" (p. 9). This definition provides us with the components and aims of a theory, which must initially be described and then evaluated for potential use in practice, education, and research in a discipline.

Before moving to the components of a theory, we need to address three similar terms frequently associated with theory: model, framework, and conceptual framework or model. A **model** is a graphic representation of some phenomena. It may be a mathematical model ($A + B = C$) or a diagrammatic model, linking words with symbols and lines. A theoretical model provides a visual description of the theory using limited narrative and displaying components and relationships symbolically. A **framework** is another means of providing a structural view of the concepts and relationships proposed in a theory. Again, use of words and narrative is limited, but the structure of the theory is presented and allows translation, interpretation, and illumination of the narrative or text.

A **conceptual model or framework** is similar to a theory in that it represents some phenomena of interest and contains concepts and propositions. However, with a conceptual model/framework, the concepts and especially the propositions are broader in scope, less defined, and less specific to the phenomena of concern. As Fawcett (1995) noted, in professional nursing practice, conceptual models provide explicit frames of reference by delineating the scope of practice, identifying the care recipient or client, relevant environment, aspects of health to be considered, and steps and substance of the nursing process.

A theory can evolve from a conceptual model/framework as concepts are further defined, specified, tested, and interrelated to represent some aspect of reality. Fawcett (1993) has described the structural hierarchy of contemporary nursing knowledge (Figure 4–1), with its components from the most abstract metaparadigm, influenced by different philosophies, to conceptual models that further evolve into theories and specific empirical indicators for testing. She applied this to nursing practice, describing the role of conceptual models as "guides for theory development, then, by focusing attention on certain concepts and their relationships, they place the concepts and their relationships in a distinct context. . . . Each theory is, therefore, more circumscribed than its parent conceptual model." (pp. 20–21).

As knowledge about some phenomena increases, a theory is proposed to address phenomena or real-

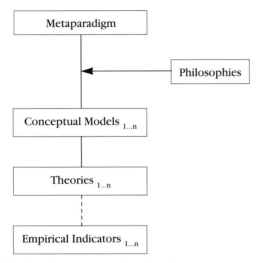

FIGURE 4-1. The structural hierarchy of contemporary nursing knowledge. (From Fawcett, J. [1995]. *Analysis and evaluation of conceptual models of nursing* [3rd ed.]. Philadelphia: F. A. Davis, with permission.)

ity within the discipline. The components of a theory are the constructs (concepts), with their specific definitions, and the propositions that link those constructs (concepts). At the simplest level, a **concept** is a view or idea that we hold about something. This can be something highly concrete, such as a pencil, or something highly abstract, such as quality. The more concrete the concept, the easier it is understood and consistently used. For instance, we are comfortable envisioning a pencil and can easily describe this to others. But the concept of quality is more abstract, and ensuring that all individual definitions are the same is difficult.

We strive to define a concept in operational terms, that is, how we view a specific entity and how it can be measured so that others know exactly what we mean. To meet the criteria of a theory, we need to define the concepts or constructs. Consider the concept of a pencil. We think of a pencil as a writing implement. This is the *theoretical or conceptual definition* of a pencil we read in a dictionary. But what do we truly mean by a pencil? It is a yellow-painted, wooden-covered graphite instrument that we use to make marks on a paper. Does it have an eraser? Does a mechanical pencil fit into this definition? An *operational definition* narrows the definition to precisely what we view and how it can be measured. In addition, concepts are broadened to constructs, such as with quality or identity, which can be multidimensional and difficult, if not impossible, to break down into component parts. A **con**struct is a more complex idea package of some phenomena that contains many factors but cannot be truly isolated or confined to a more concrete concept. The construct of identity contains many pieces, such as personal perception, role expectations, and status. However, we must still provide an operational definition of a construct by specifying certain elements it contains, such as self-image, ideal image, group image, role expectations, and status. The same multidimentionality occurs when we assess quality of health care.

In research, we often see the term "variables", referring to some concept in the theory under study. **Variables** are concepts that change and contain a set of values that can be measured in a practice or research situation. For example, a client's cholesterol reading is a variable. The concept of blood cholesterol has been operationally defined within certain parameters, and the level of the reading is the value for the variable.

Whether concepts, constructs, or a combination of both are included in a specific theory, these concepts/constructs are the building blocks of the theory. Definitions are provided to help us understand the nature and characteristics of each block in the construction. We then need to relate these building blocks to each other. Stating the relationships between or among the constructs (or concepts) provides the **propositions** of a theory. These are also called the relational statements, showing how the concepts are linked in the theory and relate to each other and to the total theoretical structure. They define how the structure is held together. In nursing theory, propositions refer to how the individual is characterized with specific abilities, knowledge, values, and traits and how these interrelate with the characteristics of health, the environment, and nursing.

As stated previously, Kerlinger defined the aims or purpose of theory as describing or explaining some phenomena of interest. In nursing, this is further differentiated into levels of theory that describe, explain, predict, and control. Dickoff and James (1968) developed a classic position paper proposing four levels of nursing theory:

1. Factor-isolating (naming) theories;
2. Factor-relating (situation depicting) theories;
3. Situation-relating (predictive or promoting/inhibiting theories); and
4. Situation-producing (prescriptive) theories.

Although the authors cited the need for significant theory at the highest level of theory, all levels may be present as a practice theory evolves (factor-isolating and then relating), is subjected to further research, and is refined, becoming predictive and prescriptive.

In application, testing, and refinement, theory is a continuum as long as the content meets the intent of the disciplinary paradigm and metaparadigm.

In addition, theories are classified according to their scope as grand, middle-range, and limited in scope or practice. This is the breadth of coverage of some phenomenon. General systems theory is an example of a grand theory, or one with a broad scope. This theory, discussed later in the Chapter, has been used in development, testing, and application in many scientific disciplines.

Merton (1957) was the first theorist to suggest "theories of the middle range: theories intermediate to the minor working hypotheses evolved in abundance during the day-by-day routines of research, and the all inclusive speculations comprising a master conceptual scheme from which it is hoped to derive a very large number of empirically observed uniformities of . . . behavior" (pp. 5–6). Many of our traditional nursing theories meet the characteristics of a middle range theory, including the models of King, Orem, Roy, and Watson, described in Chapter 3. Other middle-range theories include some of the developmental theories reviewed later in this chapter. Although these theories address psychosocial, cognitive, and moral development, they apply across disciplines as continual, incremental knowledge and skills developed by individuals. More limited nursing practice theories are evolving as hypotheses derived from middle-range theories are tested, clarified, and made specific to certain practice areas or types of health-care client. Chapter 5 shows examples of limited nursing practice models that are being tested and refined into theoretical frameworks, including Pender's health promotion model and the chronic illness trajectory framework.

THEORY DESCRIPTION AND EVALUATION

To understand theories for use and application in practice, we use certain criteria to describe and evaluate them. Theory development is an inductive process to generate concepts and make inferences by stating interrelationships (propositions) within a framework to view phenomena. From observations of phenomena, we can name concepts and enumerate proposed relationships. Once the theory is developed, it is applied, in whole or part, for testing. To evaluate nursing theory, we consider the following three sets of criteria.

Chinn and Kramer (1991) differentiate between *theory description* and *critical analysis of theory.*

The theory is described by answering questions in the following six areas: purpose, concepts, definitions, relationships, structure, and assumptions. This process provides an understanding of the components and aims of the theory. Once the theory has been described, five questions are addressed in critical analysis:

- Clarity and consistency in construction
- Simplicity and meaningfulness of relationships
- Generality or scope
- Accessibility, with potential for use and research
- Significance to the discipline

This differentiation allows us to discriminate between understanding the theoretical structure and evaluating the theory's soundness and usefulness in practice, education, or research.

Barbara Stevens Barnum (1994) proposes two categories of theory: *descriptive theory* and *explanatory theory.* Descriptive theory is factor-naming and factor-relating theory developed initially to characterize some phenomena. Explanatory theory addresses the next levels in theory development, looking at the "how" and the "why" for some phenomena of concern (Barnum, 1990). This brings us to the situating-relating and situation-producing levels of theory development. Theory description is delineated as theory interpretation, with questions addressing the following areas:

- Major elements of the theory and their definitions
- Relationships among the elements
- Differentiating between descriptive and explanatory theory
- How the theory addresses, defines, and differentiates nursing
- The focus on as client, nurse, action, or relationship
- Unique language used and defined by the theorist (pp. 17–18)

For critical analysis, internal and external criticism are differentiated. **Internal criticism** is used to evaluate how the theory components fit together in terms of clarity, consistency, adequacy, and logical development (Barnum, 1994). **External criticism** deals with real-world issues such as reality convergence, usefulness, significance, and discrimination from other health-care disciplines (Barnum, 1994). This process allows us to discriminate between understanding the theoretical structure and evaluating the soundness and usefulness of the theory for application in practice, education, or research.

Table 4–1 illustrates criteria for theory analysis and critique proposed by Fawcett (1993). Analysis

TABLE 4 – 1. Fawcett's Framework for Analysis and Evaluation of Nursing Theories

Questions for Analysis	*Questions for Evaluation*
1. What is the scope of theory?	1. Is the theory significant?
2. How is the theory related to nursing's metaparadigm?	■ Are the metaparadigm concepts and propositions addressed by the theory explicit?
■ Which metaparadigm concepts are addressed by the theory?	■ Are the philosophical claims on which the theory is based explicit?
Does the theory deal with the person?	■ Is the conceptual model from which the theory was derived explicit?
Does the theory deal with the environment?	■ Are the authors of knowledge from adjunctive disciplines acknowledged, and are bibliographical citations given?
Does the theory deal with health?	2. Is the theory internally consistent?
Does the theory deal with nursing processes or goals?	■ Are all the elements of the work (philosophical claims, conceptual model, theory) congruent?
■ Which metaparadigm propositions are addressed by the theory?	■ Do the concepts reflect semantic clarity and consistency?
Does the theory deal with life processes?	■ Are any concepts redundant?
Does the theory deal with patterns of human-environment interaction?	■ Do the propositions reflect structural consistency?
Does the theory deal with processes that affect health?	3. Is the theory parsimonious?
Does the theory deal with the health or wholeness of the human being in interaction with the environment?	■ Is the theory stated clearly and concisely?
3. What philosophical claims are reflected in the theory?	4. Is the theory testable?
■ On what values and beliefs about nursing is the theory based?	■ Can the concepts be observed empirically?
■ What worldview of the person-environment relationship is reflected in the theory?	■ Can the propositions be measured?
4. From what conceptual model was the theory derived?	5. Is the theory empirically adequate?
5. What knowledge from adjunctive disciplines was used in developing the theory?	■ Are theoretical assertions congruent with empirical evidence?
6. What are the concepts of the theory?	6. Is the theory pragmatically adequate?
7. What are the propositions of the theory?	■ Are education and special-skill training required before the theory is applied in clinical practice?
■ Which propositions are nonrelational?	■ For what clinical problems is the theory appropriate?
■ Which propositions are relational?	■ Is it feasible to implement clinical protocols derived from the theory?
	■ Are the nursing actions compatible with expectations for nursing practice?
	■ Does the clinician have the legal ability to implement the nursing actions?
	■ Do the nursing actions lead to favorable outcomes?

Source: Fawcett, J. (1993). Analysis and evaluation of nursing theories (p. 36) Philadelphia: F.A. Davis, with permission.

refers to the description of the theory. Fawcett (1993) describes this as "a nonjudgmental, detailed examination of the theory, including its scope, context, and content" (p. 37). Theory analysis is followed by theory evaluation, which requires thoughtful interpretation of the theory. Fawcett (1993) describes the process as requiring "judgments to be made about the theory's significance, internal consistency, parsimony, testability, empirical adequacy, and pragmatic adequacy" (p. 39). Application of this framework for theory analysis and evaluation was evident in Chapter 3, in Fawcett and Swoyer's presentation of information on specific nursing conceptual models and theories.

As we move to specific practice theories, we find that research is the means of supporting the concepts and relationships proposed. Research provides supportive evidence and suggests further study and possible gaps or revisions needed in the theoretical structure. We can see this in the next chapters covering refinement of nursing and other health models, such as the health belief model revision. Research can be qualitative and inductive for generating theory, or more quantitative, for deductively testing hypotheses as theoretical propositions.

BORROWED THEORIES

Nursing and other health-care disciplines have long used a variety of theories to guide practice. Some are discipline-specific, such as the nursing theories reviewed in Chapter 3. Other theoretical structures have been applied to or "borrowed from" other disciplines. As Barnum (1990) describes:

As an applied science, much of nursing's theory is "borrowed" from other disciplines. Every discipline has similar boundary ambiguities, where the inquiry and answers in one field overlap those in another. . . . Nursing's uniqueness in this respect does not lie in boundary overlap but in the number of boundary overlaps with which it must contend. A high number of overlaps occur in the discipline of nursing because it often attempts to deal holistically with a phenomenon (man) that has previously been dealt with in compartmentalized ways by other disciplines. (p. 218).

Chinn and Kramer (1991) agree on the usefulness of theories borrowed from other disciplines in some cases, but they recommend caution because some borrowed theories "do not take into consideration significant factors that influence a nursing situation" (p. 40).

Several classic theories have been borrowed and applied in nursing to view the person, family, community, and group. We use Maslow's hierarchy of needs to view the person and basic human needs. Developmental theories have been applied across the lifespan as we seek to understand the complexity of human behavior. In looking at the person or group, we have applied systems theory to understand the interaction of person and environment. The following section briefly describes selected theories applied to the nursing discipline and often used in the evolution of nursing models more specific to our metaparadigm concepts.

Maslow's Theory of Human Motivation and Hierarchy of Basic Needs

A theory widely used across disciplines is Maslow's theory of human motivation. In his original 1954 publication of *Motivation and Personality,* Maslow described how his work emerged and was published in segments in various journals and books. The book begins by presenting Maslow's philosophy as an approach to science. Human values are prevalent in the philosophy, and his worldview is described as holistic, functional, dynamic, and purposive. In his 1970 revised edition, Maslow reinforced his worldviews and described his theory as holistic-dynamic. He supported his original 16 propositions on motivation, on which his theory was based (see Chapter 12 on motivation in the teaching/learning process). This is a grand theory that views the complexity of human behavior, especially related to motivation of behavior. The theory of motivation was based on clinical and experimental data from psychology, psychiatry, education, and philosophy. It does not address specific nursing concerns except as they relate to human behavior with environmental influences.

Maslow's theory includes a hierarchical structure for human needs. Imagine a pyramid of human needs (Figure 4–2). At the base of the pyramid are the physiologic drives. Higher needs progress upward as safety, love and belonging, esteem, and

FIGURE 4-2. Maslow's hierarchy of human needs.

self-actualization needs. Maslow (1954, 1970) describes this as a "hierarchy of prepotency" to explain that the individual concentrates on the physiologic drives. The physiologic drives are considered the most powerful but, as these needs are satisfied, higher needs emerge on which the individual focuses. This is the general structure for the hierarchy.

Individual differences are provided for in this theory. Some individuals have altered placement of needs in the hierarchy. Maslow (1970) described differences among individuals in placement of some of the higher needs such as a reversal of esteem and love/belonging needs. In addition, individuals may have different levels of need satisfaction. For example, one person might meet the physiologic drives at a 75 percent level while another person's level for satisfaction is 85 percent. Individual differences also apply to the emergence of higher needs. Maslow (1970) described this as a gradual process; one person's safety needs may begin to emerge when his physiologic needs are being met at 25 percent while another person may not begin to satisfy her safety needs until 30 percent of her physiologic needs are met. Levels of satisfaction and emergence of higher needs therefore occur at different points in different people, as do pain thresholds in different people.

Looking again at the theoretical hierarchy, we see at the bottom level of the pyramid the physiologic drives, including the need to maintain homeostasis and the needs of hunger and thirst, sleep and rest, activity and exercise, sexual gratification and sensory pleasure, and maternal responses (Maslow, 1970). Meeting the physiologic hunger drive is very different from meeting one's nutritional requirements or treating anxiety or depression with a chocolate bar. When the individual is truly hungry or thirsty, not merely satisfying an appetite for food or drink, all energies and thoughts are directed to satisfying that drive for food or water. When the physiologic drives and needs are relatively satisfied, higher-level needs emerge.

Safety needs are the next level of the hierarchy. Safety, both physical and emotional, must be achieved. Threats to a person's safety can become all-consuming. Think of an isolated person in an inner-city apartment whose fear for his safety motivates him to place bars on the windows and multiple chains and dead bolt locks on the door. This person fears for his physical safety from a threat real or imagined of bodily harm. This is the main concern, not whether access is impeded in the case of a fire or accident. All focus is placed on the quest for freedom from perceived danger. Maslow (1954, 1970) also views safety needs more broadly in the

need for the familiar and spiritual, religious, or philosophical meaning in life. He described the use of rituals and ceremonial behaviors in children and individuals with psychological disorders as examples of focusing on safety needs.

Once the person satisfies these safety needs, the focus turns to the need for love and belonging. Inclusion and affection are important needs, not the isolated sex act, which is a physiologic drive. Maslow (1970) described a hunger and striving for affectionate relations and a place in a group, as opposed to the maladjusted person (pp. 43–44).

Satisfying the need for belongingness and love brings us to the next level of esteem needs. Esteem needs involve a sense of dignity, worth, and usefulness in life. Maslow (1970) described two sets of esteem needs: (1) the sense of self-worth, including perceptions of strength, achievement, competence, and confidence; and (2) the esteem of others, including perceptions of deserved respect, status, recognition, importance, and dignity (p. 45). Satisfying the sense of self-worth and respect allows the next, and highest, level of basic needs to emerge.

The need for self-actualization at the top of the pyramid is the desire for self-fulfillment. This is the sense of being able to do all that you can to answer the "why" of your existence. Maslow (1970) described self-actualization as "the full use and exploitation of talents, capacities, potentialities, ect., such [that] people seem to be fulfilling themselves and . . . developing to the full stature of which they are capable" (p. 150). Originally, Maslow (1954) proposed that self-actualized people included both older people and college students and children. But when Maslow (1970) further examined the concept of self-actualization, he separated psychological health from self-actualization, which he limited to older people whose human potentialities have been realized and actualized.

Maslow then developed support for his theory of basic needs and human actions using case studies and other research. Through observation of people he proposed specific phenomena that are determined by basic gratification of cognitive-affective, cognitive, character traits, interpersonal and miscellaneous needs. He cited characteristics of people in relation to the hierarchy. For example, the following characteristics of self-actualized people emerged from Maslow's (1970) research and analysis of historical figures, public people, selected college students, and children:

1. More efficient and comfortable perceptions of reality
2. Acceptance of self, others, and nature

3. Spontaneity, simplicity, and naturalness in thoughts and behaviors
4. Problem-centered rather than ego-centered
5. Desire for detachment, solitude, and privacy
6. Autonomy with independence of culture and environment
7. Continued freshness of appreciation
8. Mystic and oceanic feelings with limitless horizons
9. Genuine desire to help people
10. Deeper and more profound interpersonal relationships
11. Democratic character structure
12. Strong ethical sense that discriminates means/ends and good/evil
13. Philosophical and unhostile sense of humor
14. Creativeness
15. Resistance to enculturation with an inner detachment (pp. 203–228)

Maslow created further hypotheses for testing. He described cases that diverged from his theory, such as the martyr who ignores survival needs for a principle. He called for further research, hypothesizing that satisfying basic needs earlier in life allows the individual to weather deprivation easier in later life (Maslow, 1954, p. 99). Maslow's work continued until his death in 1970. His hierarchy has endured and applications have extended in health care, education, industry, and marketing to understand people and their motivators. Needs related to individual, environmental, and health concerns are applicable to the nursing discipline. However, this theory is still a grand theory and does not address the specific domain of nursing.

Developmental Theories

A group of theories widely used in health care and education are the developmental theories. These middle-range theories address personality (Erikson and Havighurst), cognitive (Piaget), and moral (Kohlberg) development using a lifespan perspective. This perspective is based on progression and complexity in motor, personal-social, cognitive, or moral behavior. A brief review of each of the theories demonstrates how the theorist moved from his philosophy or worldview to identify concepts, propositions, and a model or theory based on observations, existing research, or case study presentations. Common to the developmental theories are predictable steps or stages through which the individual progresses over the life cycle. This is a building process. These theories are based largely on research through observation or case studies. Subsequent applications and research have been guided by the use of these theories to explain more specific phenomena or test hypotheses.

Erikson's (1963) eight ages of man represents a theory of psychosocial personality development in which the individual proceeds through critical periods in a step-by-step or epigenetic process (Figure 4–3). This theory has been and continues to be used widely in health care and psychology. In the theory, Erikson presents his philosophy and case studies with Freudian and neo-Freudian applications. Each stage has positive and negative aspects that are defined and described. The basic goal is for the individual to develop a favorable ratio of the positive aspect for a healthy ego. Erikson (1963) further describes basic virtues and essential strengths for each of his "ages" or stages of development. These strengths and basic virtues define the positive aspects of ego development required in each stage. Propositions are developed for each of the stages. This theory is supported mainly by case study, with suggestions and encouragement of further hypotheses for research and testing. Erikson's theory has been used widely in nursing to foster positive ego development and empowerment in individuals. Al-

AGES	STRENGTHS & VIRTUES	DEVELOPMENTAL STAGE
8. Ego Integrity vs. Despair	Renunciation & Wisdom	Older Adulthood
7. Generativity vs. Stagnation	Production & Care	Middle Adulthood
6. Intimacy vs. Isolation	Affiliation & Love	Young Adulthood
5. Identity vs. Role Confusion	Devotion & Fidelity	Adolescence
4. Industry vs. Inferiority	Method & Competence	School Age
3. Initiative vs. Guilt	Direction & Purpose	Preschool
2. Autonomy vs. Shame & Doubt	Self-control & Will Power	Toddler
1. Trust vs. Mistrust	Drive & Hope	Infancy

FIGURE 4-3. Erikson's (1963) eight ages of man.

though this theory does not specifically address the domain of nursing, common concerns include the person, environment, and psychosocial health.

Havighurst's developmental tasks and education represents another theory of personality development that includes principles of cognitive and moral development as well. In this perspective the individual proceeds through six stages accomplishing critical tasks. Havighurst (1972) described his philosophy including the origins of the concept, and proposed a method for analyzing individual developmental tasks based on the following five criteria: (1) nature or definition, (2) biological basis, (3) psychological basis, (4) cultural basis, and (5) educa-

tional implications (pp. 17–18). Table 4–2 illustrates the tasks for each of the six age groups.

Although descriptions of the tasks represent some gender bias and cultural limitations, the concepts' biological and psychological bases are applicable to health care. The tasks represent major milestones in biological, psychological, emotional, and cognitive functioning or development that individuals must negotiate as they progress through the lifespan. Person, environmental, and health promotion concerns are apparent in the lifespan perspective. Age-specific tasks relate well to activities of daily living during specific life stages and can easily incorporated in care planning.

TABLE 4–2. Havighurst's Developmental Tasks

Stages	Tasks	Stages	Tasks
I. Infancy and early childhood	1. Learning to walk 2. Learning to take solid foods 3. Learning to talk 4. Learning to control the elimination of body wastes 5. Learning sex differences and sexual modesty 6. Forming concepts and learning language to describe social and physical reality 7. Getting ready to read 8. Learning to distinguish right and wrong and beginning to develop a conscience		6. Preparing for an economic career 7. Acquiring a set of values and an ethical system as a guide to behavior 8. Desiring and achieving socially responsible behavior
		IV. Early adulthood	1. Selecting a mate 2. Learning to live with a marriage partner 3. Starting a family 4. Rearing children 5. Managing a home 6. Getting started in an occupation 7. Taking on civic responsibility 8. Finding a congenial social group
II. Middle childhood	1. Learning physical skills necessary for ordinary games 2. Building wholesome attitudes toward oneself as a growing organism 3. Learning to get along with age-mates 4. Learning an appropriate masculine/feminine social role 5. Developing fundamental skills in reading, writing, and calculating 6. Developing concepts necessary for everyday living 7. Developing conscience, morality, and a scale of values 8. Achieving personal independence 9. Developing attitudes toward social groups and institutions	V. Middle age	1. Assisting teenage children to become responsible and happy adults 2. Achieving adult social and civic responsibility 3. Reaching and maintaining satisfactory performance in one's occupational career 4. Developing adult leisure-time activities 5. Relating oneself to one's spouse as a person 6. Adjusting and accepting the physiologic changes of middle age 7. Adjusting to aging parents
III. Adolescence	1. Achieving new and more mature relations with age-mates of both sexes 2. Achieving a masculine or feminine social role 3. Accepting one's physique and using the body effectively 4. Achieving emotional independence of parents and other adults 5. Preparing for marriage and family life	VI. Later maturity	1. Adjusting to decreasing physical strength and health 2. Adjusting to retirement and reduced income 3. Adjusting to death of a spouse 4. Establishing an explicit association with one's age group 5. Adopting and adapting social roles in a flexible way 6. Establishing satisfactory physical living arrangements

Source: Havighurst, R. J. (1972). *Developmental tasks and education* (3rd ed.). New York: David McKay.

Piaget's theory of cognitive development focuses on the development of the intellect. Piaget was an example of a self-actualized person. Moving from the publication of his first monograph on birds at age 10, he detailed the development of the intellect in children through observations. His techniques were sometimes criticized by the scientific community. But his theory has since been accepted and used in practice and research by many students and professionals. Piaget's theory looked at the innate and environmental influences on the development of the intellect. This theory has four major periods of cognitive development: sensorimotor, preoperational thought, concrete operations, and formal operations (Table 4–3).

Within his theory, Piaget provided us with the concepts of schema, object permanence, assimilation, and accommodation. *Schema* are patterns of thought or behavior that evolve into more complexity as more information is obtained through assimilation and accommodation. *Object permanence,* the knowledge that something still exists when it is out of sight, develops when the child is between 9 and 10 months of age. *Assimilation* is the acquisition and incorporation into the individual's existing cognitive and behavioral structures of new information. *Accommodation* is the change in the individual's cognitive and behavioral patterns based on the new information acquired. Piaget's theory has been translated and applied worldwide and across disciplines. His work continued until his death in 1980, and further research and theory is still evolving.

Piaget's work concentrated on cognitive development in children, including views on moral development. As such, it is more limited but has provided major insight into working with children. Applications are seen in health teaching, especially in chronic or terminal illness situations. But with these limitations on cognitive development for some environmental influences, it can address only a portion of the domain of concern to nursing.

Kohlberg's theory of moral development was developed as an outgrowth of Piaget's work on moral development in children. Kohlberg's (1984; Kohlberg et al., 1987) extensive work on moral development is based on research with children given scenarios to describe reactions and make judgments. His initial study was with only boys 10 to 16 years old from Chicago. Additional research with children of both genders and different backgrounds was added later. Kohlberg's theory includes six stages grouped into three major levels: preconventional, conventional, and postconventional (Kohlber, 1984), illustrated in Table 4–4.

Kohlberg' theory provides major insight into moral development. He provided the theoretical structure, the supportive research, and applications in educational practice. The individual progresses through the levels and stages, not as a natural process but through intellectual stimulation with a central focus on moral justice. As Crain (1985) observed, the stages emerge from thinking about moral problems and stimulation from social experi-

TABLE 4–3. Piaget's Theory of Cognitive Development

Period of Cognitive Development	Age	Stage Description
Sensorimotor stages		
Reflexive	Birth–1 month	Use of primitive reflexes, such as sucking and rooting
Primary circular reactions	1–4 months	Repeating an event for the result, such as thumb in mouth
Secondary circular reactions	4–10 months	Combining events for a result such as kicking a mobile over crib
Coordination of secondary schema	10–12 months	Creating a behavior for some result, such as standing in crib to reach mobile
Tertiary circular reactions	12–18 months	Looking for similar results from varying behaviors, such as shaking crib and jumping to observe movements of mobile
Representational thought begins	18–24 months	Symbolic representation in thought such as hanging objects to create mobile
Preoperational	2–7 years	Making overgeneralizations, such as all cats are named Tiger; egocentric
		Focuses only on one concrete attribute
		Magical thought and symbolic play present
Concrete operations	7–11 years	Logical and reversible thought appears; conservation of matter and numbers
Formal operations	After 11 years	Theoretical and hypothetical thinking now possible; higher-order math and reasoning

TABLE 4-4. Kohlberg's Theory of Moral Development

Level	Stage	Stage Description
Level I: Preconventional morality	1. Heteronomous morality	Egocentrically applies a fixed set of rules from authorities, e.g. parents, to avoid punishment.
	2. Individualism, purpose, and exchange	Sees that different individuals have different rules, e.g. parents and teachers, but selection bases on individual interests with some fair exchange.
Level II: Conventional morality	3. Interpersonal expectations, relationships, and conformity	Motives of other person now emerge when considering right and wrong; use of the Golden Rule in considerations.
	4. Social system and conscience	The good of society as a whole now emerges with the individual having certain roles and rules in the system.
Level III: Postconventional morality	5. Social contract and individual rights	Beliefs in upholding laws and legal contracts looking at the greatest good for greatest number; sees but cannot deal well with ethical-legal conflicts.
	6. Universal ethical principles	Principles of justice and human rights are followed and upheld as a personal and universal ethical system.

Source: Adapted from Kohlberg, L. (1984) *Essays in moral development: Volume II. The psychology of moral development* (pp. 174–176). San Francisco: Harper & Row.

ences rather than merely social development. Further research and practices have been based on this theory and are ongoing.

As with Piagetian theory, Kohlberg's theory is limited to a specific area of development. The focus is on the person, such as the child, with ramifications for adult life. Environmental (e.g., social and cultural) factors provide insight for social and psychological health. The limitation to moral development addresses only a portion of the domain of concern to nursing.

Many developmental models are used and applied in nursing. Examine the conceptual models and theories presented in Chapter 3 for their application of developmental concepts. Several nursing theories have a decidedly developmental focus, whether as a main component, as in Watson's theory, or with specific concepts included, defined, and built on, as in King's model. Riehl-Sisca (1989) has grouped the following nursing models and theories as types of developmental theories based on the theorists' views, the model's philosophy, and its primary focus or domain of nursing:

   Rogers' Nursing: A Science of Unitary Human Beings
   Watson's Theory of Human Caring in Nursing
   Parse's Theory: Man-Living-Health
   Chrisman and Riehl's Systems-Development-Stress Model

A lifespan, developmental, or life processes focus has major relevance for nursing as we view the person in the context of environment and effects on health status. The interrelationships with health and nursing are complex and must be specified for their applicability to the domain of nursing.

Systems Theory

Perhaps the most widely used theory in multiple disciplines is **systems theory**. Systems have been in existence for ages but, in the late 1930s, Bertalanffy introduced systems theory to represent an aspect of reality. Thus, general system theory was incorporated in the paradigms of many scientific communities. This is a grand theory, wide in scope, that has generated numerous theories in many disciplines. Bertalanffy (1968) explained the wide applicability in many scientific communities as the various disciplines became concerned with "wholeness," not just focusing on isolated parts, but the interrelationships among them and between the parts and the whole. A system generally contains the following basic components: input, output, boundary, environment, and feedback. Figure 4–4 illustrates a basic view of a simple system.

The initial step in understanding and applying systems theory is to view the grand theory. Bertalanffy (1968) defined a system as a complex of interacting elements and proposed that every living organism is essentially an open system. The general system theory applies the following principles to human and organizational systems:

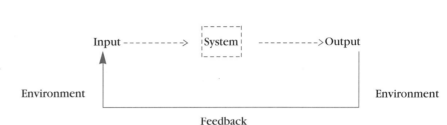

FIGURE 4-4. General systems model: A simple open system.

1. *Wholeness*. This indicates that the whole is more than merely the sum of the parts. To understand the whole, one must understand the components and their interactions with each other and the environment.

2. *Hierarchical order*. Some form of hierarchy exists in the system's components, structure, and functions.

3. *Exchange of information and matter (openness)*. In an open system there is an exchange and flow of information and matter with the environment through some boundary that surrounds the system. Inputs come through the boundary from the environment, are transformed through system processes (throughputs), and are sent as outputs through the boundary back into the environment. This exchange of information and matter is goal-oriented, whether to maintain the steady state or fulfill the functions of the system. An important component of this process is *feedback* from the environment.

4. *Progressive differentiation*. Differentiation within the system leads to self-organization. Applying the laws of thermodynamics, entropy is a measure of order or organization in the system in the process of seeking equilibrium or some final goal. In an open system, entropy is decreased or negative, allowing for differentiation and self-organization.

5. *Equifinality*. In open systems the final state can be reached from different initial conditions and in different ways. Initial conditions do not necessarily determine the final state or outcome of the system.

6. *Teleology*. Behavior in the system is directed toward some purpose or goal, as a human characteristic.

Environmental influences are a major consideration in health care. Systems theory provides a useful framework to visualize some phenomena (the system), focusing on the components, structure, and functions as the internal environment (throughputs), and influenced by (inputs and feedback) and influencing (outputs) the environment. It is important to carefully analyze the system for all component parts, structures, and functions. Recall that the basis for general systems theory is that "the whole is greater than the sum of the parts." This brings us to the need for a precise analysis of interrelationships among components and between the parts and the entire system. In addition, an open system has permeable boundaries receiving input and feedback from the environment. Problems occur when environmental factors are unknown, unclear, or ignored. Consider the broad health-service system in the United States. Duncan (1994) believes the health-care system does not take into account an extensive array of critical social factors, such as abuse, violence, illiteracy, and teenage pregnancy, that impinge on the health of individuals and affect their use of the health-care system (p. 84). If this is the case, environmental and societal influences are omitted or only partially visualized as crossing system boundaries.

In nursing, systems theory and various applications have been used to explain organizations, nursing and health-care delivery, and groups of people. Several nursing models are based in systems theory. Johnson's Behavioral Systems conceptual model views the person as a behavioral system and nursing as an external force. This exemplifies how a grand theory (General Systems Theory) from another scientific community provided a basis for developing the conceptual model of nursing (Johnson's Behavioral Systems). Specificity to the metaparadigm concepts and interrelationships unique to nursing have provided the basis for the nursing conceptual framework. Further delineation of concepts and propositions leads to more specific nursing theory. Certain middle-range nursing theories have been classified as systems models. Riehl-Sisca (1989) categorizes Neuman's Health-Care Model, Roy's Adaptation Model, and King's framework and theory as systems models. Other nursing models use various components of general systems theory. Further applications from systems theory are evident in subsequent sections on management, organizations, and change.

THE IMPACT OF THEORY ON PRACTICE

As Barnum (1990) states, "today the chief problem in theory application is not whether a theory is to be applied, but *how*" (p. 128). We use theory every day in our personal and professional lives, from the basic principles of asepsis in hygiene and Universal Precautions to understanding the complex communication channels of the organizational system in which we practice.

Theory, practice, and research are interrelated and interdependent. We need theory to guide practice predictably and effectively. We need research to support the significance and usefulness of the theory, since the dynamic nature of our metaparadigm concepts of person, evnironment, health, and nursing makes theories tentative and subject to refinement and revisions. Professional practice must provide the questions for study based on problems phenomena relevant to the discipline. As Chinn and Kramer (1991) have described, "deliberate application of theory places theory within the context of practice to ensure that it serves the goals of the profession" (p. 167).

Again, recall that nursing is a profession and a scientific community. We practice using principles provided by our paradigm and theoretical bases. This furnishes us with the tools for critical thinking, provision of care, education, administration, research, and interdisciplinary collaboration. As Kuhn (1970) has described, we have a paradigm that provides the models for problems and solutions in our knowledge base and practice community. Our paradigms and theories are designed to address problems and solutions in practice or we need to shift to a new structure with different theories and paradigms to explain our concerns for people, environments, health, and nursing.

The theory on which we base practice must be compatible and correspond to the phenomena of professional nursing practice. To ensure that the goals of theory and practice are consistent, Chinn and Kramer (1991) recommend considering the following questions:

1. Are the theory goals congruous with practice goals?
2. Is the intended context of the theory congruous with the situation in which the theory will be applied?
3. Is there, or might there be, similarity between theory variables and practice variables?
4. Are the explanations of the theory sufficient to be a basis for nursing action?
5. Does research evidence support the theory?
6. How will this new approach influence the practical function of the nursing unit? (pp. 168–171)

In the previous chapter, we reviewed conceptual models and theories unique to nursing. These models are the guides to practice in our highly complex disciplinary matrix. Implementing models for practice, whether unique to nursing or borrowed and adapted, is a necessary but arduous time-consuming task. The process is worth the effort to ensure quality care to recipients, but requires many of the skills addressed in subsequent chapters.

KEY POINTS

- Kerlinger (1986) defines a **theory** as "a set of interrelated constructs (concepts), definitions, and propositions that present a systematic view of phenomena by specifying relations among variables, with the purpose of explaining and predicting the phenomena" (p. 9).
- A **model** is a graphic representation of some phenomena. A theoretical model provides a visual description of the theory using limited narrative but displays components and relationships symbolically. A **framework** is another means of providing a structural view of the concepts and relationships proposed in a theory. A **conceptual model or framework** represents phenomena of interest and contains concepts and propositions that are broader in scope, less defined, and less specific to the phenomena of concern than those in a theory.

- A **concept** is a view or idea we hold about something, ranging from something highly concrete to something highly abstract. A **construct** is a more complex idea package of some phenomena containing many factors that cannot be isolated or confined into a more concrete concept. Definitions of concepts and constructs are theoretical or conceptual, such as those in dictionaries, or operational. An *operational definition* states precisely what we view as phenomena and how they can be measured. **Variables** are concepts that contain a set of values that can be measured in a practice or research situation.

- **Propositions** in a theory are the relationships among the constructs (or concepts) that propose how the concepts are linked and relate to each other and to the total theoretical structure.

- Dickoff and James (1968) developed a classic position paper proposing four levels of nursing theory: factor-isolating, factor-relating, situation-relating, and situation-producing theories.

- Theories are classified as grand, middle-range, or limited (practice) based on their scope or breadth of coverage of phenomena.

- Theory description is a careful, nonjudgmental analysis of the component parts of a theory, including assumptions, concepts, definitions, propositions, context, and scope.

- Theory evaluation requires thoughtful interpretation relative to the clarity, significance, consistency, empirical support, and usefulness in explaining a phenomenon of concern.

- *Maslow's theory of human motivation and hierarchy of basic needs* proposes a hierarchial structure for human needs, from physiologic drives and needs to safety needs, belongingness and love needs, esteem needs, and self-actualization needs at the top of the pyramid.

- Developmental theories are widely used in nursing and other health-care disciplines.
  - *Erikson's (1963) eight ages of man* represents a theory of psychosocial personality development in which the individual proceeds through critical periods in a step-by-step or epigenetic process.
  - *Havighurst's developmental tasks and education* represents another theory of personality development that includes principles of cognitive and moral development within six stages containing critical tasks for maturation.
  - *Piaget's theory of cognitive development* focuses on the development of the intellect within four major periods of cognitive development: sensorimotor, preoperational thought, concrete operations, and formal operations.
  - *Kohlberg's theory of moral development* was developed as an outgrowth of Piaget's six stages, grouped into three major levels: preconventional, conventional, and postconventional.

- A system generally contains the following basic component parts: input, output, boundary, environment, and feedback. **General systems theory** is a grand theory applied to many disciplines. Bertalanffy (1968) defined a system as a complex of interacting elements with the following principles: wholeness, hierarchial order, open exchange of information and matter, progressive differentiation, equifinality, and teleology.

- Theory, practice, and research are interrelated and interdependent. When selecting a theory on which to base practice, the theory must be compatible and correspond to the phenomena of professional nursing practice.

CHAPTER EXERCISES

1. Identify a theory used in your practice setting. Identify the concepts (constructs), how the component concepts are defined, the propositions that link the concepts, and the aims of this theory.

2. Using a theory evident in your practice setting, describe and evaluate the theory using Fawcett's (1993) criteria, listed as questions in Table 4–1.

3. Apply Maslow's theory of motivation, with its hierarchy of basic needs, to clients with the following nursing diagnoses:
   a. Caregiver role strain
   b. Decreased cardiac output
   c. Powerlessness
   d. Social isolation
   Contrast their placement on the hierarchy of needs.

4. Select three individuals of different age groups. Apply two developmental theories to behavior you have observed. Give examples of how they are progressing according to the selected theories.

5. Apply systems theory to a work group of which you are a member. Identify the components of input, output, boundary, environment, and feedback. Describe examples applicable to general systems theory principles of wholeness, hierarchial order, open exchange of information and matter, progressive differentiation, equifinality, and teleology.

6. Describe how theory is used in your practice setting, and propose how it could be used further.

REFERENCES

Barnum, B. J. S. (1990). *Nursing theory: Analysis, application, evaluation* (3rd ed.). Glenview, IL: Scott, Foresman/Little, Brown Higher Education.

Barnum, B. J. S. (1994). *Nursing theory: Analysis, application, evaluation* (3rd ed.). Philadelphia: Lippincott.

Bertalanffy, L. V. (1968). *General system theory: Foundations, development, applications.* New York: George Braziller.

Chinn, P. L., & Kramer, M. K. (1991). *Theory and nursing: A systematic approach* (3rd ed.). St. Louis: Mosby-Year Book.

Crain, W. C. (1985). *Theories of development: Concepts and applications* (2nd ed.). Englewood Cliffs, NJ: Prentice-Hall.

Dickoff, J., & James, P. (1968). A theory of theories: A position paper. *Nursing Research, 17,* 197–203.

Duncan, K. A. (1994). *Health information and health reform: Understanding the need for a national health information system.* San Francisco: Jossey-Bass.

Erikson, E. H. (1963). *Childhood and society* (2nd ed.). New York: W. W. Norton.

Fawcett, J. (1995). *Analysis and evaluation of conceptual models of nursing* (3rd ed.). Philadelphia: F. A. Davis.

Fawcett, J. (1993). *Analysis and evaluation of nursing theories.* Philadelphia: F. A. Davis.

Havighurst, R. J. (1972). *Developmental tasks and education* (3rd ed.). New York: David McKay.

Kerlinger, F. N. (1986). *Foundations of behavioral research* (3rd ed.). New York: Holt, Rinehart and Winston.

Kohlberg, L. (1984). *Essays in moral development: Volume II. The psychology of moral development.* San Francisco: Harper & Row.

Kohlberg, L., DeVries, R., Fein, G., Hart, D., Mayer, R., Noam, G., Snarey, J., & Wertsch, J. (1987). *Child psychology and childhood education: A cognitive-developmental view.* New York: Longman.

Kuhn, T. S. (1970). *The structure of scientific revolutions* (2nd ed.). Chicago: University of Chicago Press.

Leininger, M. M. (1991). The theory of culture care diversity and universality. In M. M. Leininger (Ed.), *Culture care diversity and universality: A theory of nursing* (Pub. No. 15-2402) (pp. 5–68). New York: National League for Nursing.

Maslow, A. H. (1954). *Motivation and personality.* New York: Harper & Brothers.

Maslow, A. H. (1970). *Motivation and personality* (2nd ed.). New York: Harper & Row.

Merton, R. K. (1957). *Social theory and social structure* (rev ed.). Glencoe, IL: Free Press.

Riehl-Sisca, J. P. (1989). *Conceptual models for nursing practice* (3rd ed.). Norwalk, CT: Appleton & Lange.

BIBLIOGRAPHY

Ault, R. L. (1977). *Children's cognitive development: Piaget's theory and the process approach*. New York: Oxford University.

Bevis, E. O. (1989). *Curriculum building in nursing: A process*. New York: National League for Nursing.

Erikson, E. H. (1980). *Identity and the life cycle*. New York: W. W. Norton.

Fawcett, J. (1984). The metaparadigm of nursing: Present status and future refinements. *Image: Journal of Nursing Scholarship, 16*(3), 84–87.

Fawcett, J., & Hayes, E. (1983). Using conceptual frameworks in nursing practice and research. In M. B. White (Ed.), *Curriculum development: The crisis theory framework* (Vol. 8) (pp. 195–212). New York: Springer.

Hardy, M. E. (1974). Theories: Components, development, evaluation. *Nursing Research, 23,* 100–107.

Lundh, U., Soder, M., & Waerness, K. (1988). Nursing Theories: A critical view. *Image: Journal of Nursing Scholarship, 20,* 36–40.

Power, F. C., Higgins, A., & Kohlberg, L. (1989). *Lawrence Kohlberg's approach to moral education*. New York: Columbia University.

Stein, K. F. (1995). Schema model of the self-concept. *Image: Journal of Nursing Scholarship, 27,* 187–193.

Chapter 5

HEALTH AND ILLNESS MODELS

Rose Kearney Nunnery

CHAPTER OBJECTIVES

On completion of this chapter, the reader will be able to:

1. Differentiate among the various health and illness models for applicability to professional nursing practice.
2. Discuss the advantages and disadvantages of the various models.
3. Apply a health belief or health promotion model to a given nursing care situation.
4. Analyze differences in health beliefs held by members of various cultural groups.

KEY TERMS

Health
Illness
High-Level Wellness
Health Belief Model
Modifying and Enabling
    Factors

Health Promotion Model
Chronic Illness Trajectory
    Framework
Health Promotion
Health Protection

Preventive Services
Primary Prevention
Secondary Prevention
Tertiary Prevention

Health is a condition we seek, promote, and hope to maintain. Health is more than a dichotomy. It is more than the absence of illness, disease, or infirmity. A multidimensional construct of health is determined by the individual's worldview and philosophical assumptions. If we subscribe to our four metaparadigm concepts of nursing, health is specified in the nursing theory that guides our practice. Health as a part of the metaparadigm is interrelated with concepts of person, environment, and nursing.

In Chapter 3, health was illustrated within individual theoretical structures. For example, consider the three definitions of health provided by King, Roy, and Leininger. King (1981) defines health as follows:

> dynamic life experiences of a human being, which implies continuous adjustment to stressors in the internal and external environment through optimum use of one's resources to achieve maximum potential for daily living. **Illness** is defined as a deviation from normal, that is, an imbalance in a person's biological structure or in his psychological make-up, or a conflict in a person's social relationships. (p. 5)

Roy defines health as "a state and a process of being and becoming an integrated and whole person. . . . Health as a state reflects the adaptation process and is demonstrated by adaptation in each of the four integrated adaptive modes. . . . Health is a process whereby individuals are striving to achieve their maximum potential" (Lutjens, 1991, pp. 9–10). And Leininger (1991a) defines health as "a state of well being that is culturally defined, valued, and practiced and which reflects the ability of individuals (or groups) to perform their daily role activities in culturally expressed, beneficial, and patterned lifeways" (p. 48).

In other nursing theories and models the concept of health may not be well defined but is interpreted, as in Rogers' theory, as a variable depending on cultural interpretation (Whall, 1987, p. 150). Still, health or well-being is represented in each framework on which practice is based.

THEORIES OF HEALTH AND ILLNESS

Aside from the nursing conceptual or theoretical frameworks, different models are available to guide assessment of health factors and promote and preserve health. Benner and Wrubel (1989) have described five theories of health as (1) an ideal, (2) the ability to fulfill social roles, (3) a commodity, (4) a human potential, and (5) a sense of coherence.

Health is more than an ideal. We strive for the person, family, community, or group to reach a positive state of well-being. Defining health as the ability to perform one's role is limiting and fails to meet our holistic concern for the person. As Benner and Wrubel (1989) state "this view focuses on doing rather than being and ignores the person's sense of fulfillment and well-being" (p. 151). Health as a commodity implies that it can be bought, sold, traded, and withheld. This fails to meet the intent of a caring professional practice discipline. As a commodity, health is described as a "medicalized view," promising instant cures without personal involvement (Benner & Wrubel, 1989, pp. 151–153).

Health defined as a human potential is consistent with the beliefs of many in nursing and other health care disciplines, and is the basis of the first three health models presented here. Health as a human potential includes physical, mental, and spiritual health. Benner and Wrubel (1989) based their model on the premise that all people have the potential for health, with the limitation that they are always pursuing but not attaining health. This definition depends on whether one views health as a defined goal or a dynamic state we continue to strive toward. Dunn's high-level wellness, the health belief model, and Pender's health promotion model are consistent with health viewed as human potential.

A fifth view of health takes a phenomenological approach. Phenomenology is the lived experience of the individual, from his or her unique perspective. As Munhall and Oiler (1986) define it, "Phenomenology is an approach that concentrates on the subject's experience rather than concentrating solely on subjects or objects" (p. 57). It focuses on one's lived experience rather than an opinion derived from another person's observations of the experience. Benner and Wrubel's (1989) approach to health as a mind-body-spirit integration in a state of becoming is an example of health as a sense of coherence. A focus on the person's belonging to a sociocultural group makes this integration unique. Benner and Wrubel define the term "well-being" as a better indication of health with challenges and involvement in the following definition: "Well-being is defined as congruence between one's possibilities and one's actual practices and lived meanings and is based on caring and feeling cared for" (Benner & Wrubel, 1989, p. 160). In this view, a model must be based on a qualitative approach to address individuals' well-being, since this depends on the lived experience of those persons in their context. As Benner and Wrubel (1989) state, "health as well-being comes when one engages in sound self-care, cares, and feels cared for—when one trusts the self, the body, and others. Breakdown occurs when that trust is broken. Well-being can be restored . . . " (p. 165). The chronic illness trajectory framework is consistent with the view of health as coherence.

Considering your particular view of the world and your concept of health, we can now approach ways of promoting health using a sample of different models. This selection is, again, determined by one's worldview and theoretical guide.

Dunn developed his model of **high-level wellness** starting with the 1947 definition of health from the World Health Organization emphasizing physical, mental, and social well-being. He stressed that well-being includes the positive, dynamic, and unique integration of mind, body, and spirit of the individual within his environment, including work, family, community, and society. Dunn (1973) defined high-level wellness for an individual as "an

integrated method of functioning which is oriented toward maximizing the potential of which the individual is capable. It requires that the individual maintain a continuum of balance and purposeful direction within the environment where he is functioning" (pp. 4–5).

High-level wellness was seen as an ongoing challenge to the highest level possible, the individual's maximum potential. Meeting basic needs and striving for higher needs were components of his view of individual health and well-being. Dunn (1973) views high-level wellness as "an open-ended and ever-expanding tomorrow with its challenge to live at full potential" (p. 223). He also considered high-level wellness, with similar components, for the family, community, environment, and society.

Dunn's beliefs about high-level wellness evolved into a health grid (Figure 5–1) that demonstrates a

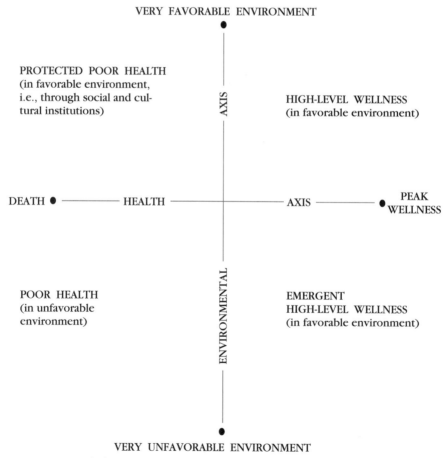

FIGURE 5-1. Dunn's high-level wellness. (From U.S. Department of Health, Education, and Welfare. Public Health Service, National Office of Vital Statistics.)

person or group at some point along a health continuum or horizontal axis, from death at the left side to peak wellness at the right. The person or group was further influenced by the environment (the vertical axis), from a very favorable environment at the top to a very unfavorable environment at the bottom. This illustrates the person or group in context, within one of the four quadrants ranging from poor health to protected poor health, high-level wellness, and emergent high-level wellness. This model provides an explanation of the person-environmental relationship in health, but it provides no direction as to movement among quadrants and compartmentalizes wellness.

The **health belief model** is a valuable tool for looking at both health promotion and actions directed at maintaining or restoring health. Originally, the model was based on the following hypothesis:

> Persons will not seek preventative care or health screening unless they possess minimal levels of relevant health motivation and knowledge, view themselves as potentially vulnerable and the condition as threatening, are convinced of the efficacy of intervention, and see few difficulties in undertaking the recommended action (Becker et al., 1977, p. 29).

The health belief model was designed as an organizing framework to advance health promotion activities by targeting interventions on certain individual variables. The three major concepts in the model were individual perceptions, modifying factors, and likelihood of action. *Individual perceptions* involve how the person considers the risk of susceptibility or the severity of the illness; in other words, how likely it is that the disease or condition could happen to that individual. *Modifying factors* are a set of demographic, sociopsychological cues to action from family, friends, professionals, or the media relative to the perceived threat of the disease. Sociopsychological variables include personality, interpersonal influences, and socioeconomic status. The modifying factors, along with individual perceptions, led to the likelihood of action in the direction of health. The concept of motivation was central to this model (Becker et al., 1977, p. 31).

An extensive review of research on variables in the health belief model led to a subsequent revision. The model was expanded from a diagram of health belief concepts and their relationships to explain and predict health-related behaviors (Figure 5–2). The three major concepts became (1) readiness to undertake recommended compliance behavior, (2)

modifying and enabling factors, and (3) compliant behaviors. Based on research, *readiness to undertake recommended compliance behavior* broadened individual perceptions from perception of susceptibility and severity to perceptions of motivations, values for threat reduction, and subjective risk/benefit considerations that the compliant behaviors would be safe and effective. Modifying factors were expanded to more inclusive **modifying and enabling factors** based on research findings. A reciprocal relationship between readiness and modifying/enabling factors also became more apparent in the revised model. The outcome in the revised model was the likelihood of *compliant behaviors* with preventive recommendations or prescribed regimens.

The original version of the health belief model focused on health promotion or preventive behaviors. Since its inception, the model has been widely used in research and practice. In addition to use in understanding utilization of health-care services and health promotion behaviors, the model has guided research in client compliance to health care. For example, in a study of chronically ill clients a considerable amount of adherence behaviors were explained by beliefs pertaining to benefits of and barriers to treatment in addition to client satisfaction with clinic services (Athey, 1988). An extensive body of research on patient compliance for the revised model demonstrated applicability in a wide range of health-care situations. Insights for use in practice and education were offered. Concerning education, Becker et al. (1977) recommended that health-care providers understand the following principles:

1. Behavior is motivated.
2. Certain beliefs seem central to a client's decision to act.
3. Not all persons possess these beliefs and motives to equal degrees.
4. Intellectual information, while necessary, is often not sufficient to stimulate needed beliefs.
5. Health providers need to view the importance of client education and accept substantial responsibility in this activity (p. 42).

These principles are consistent with the discipline of professional nursing practice and are routinely incorporated into care plans and health teaching. Consideration of the belief systems of the individual, family, or group is essential in assessing a client and choosing interventions. The extent of detail and inclusion of this information is the challenge to the nurse, whose health teaching role is an integral component of professional practice.

But the model has limitations. The language is di-

READINESS TO UNDERTAKE RECOMMENDED COMPLIANCE BEHAVIOR

MODIFYING AND ENABLING FACTORS

COMPLIANT BEHAVIORS

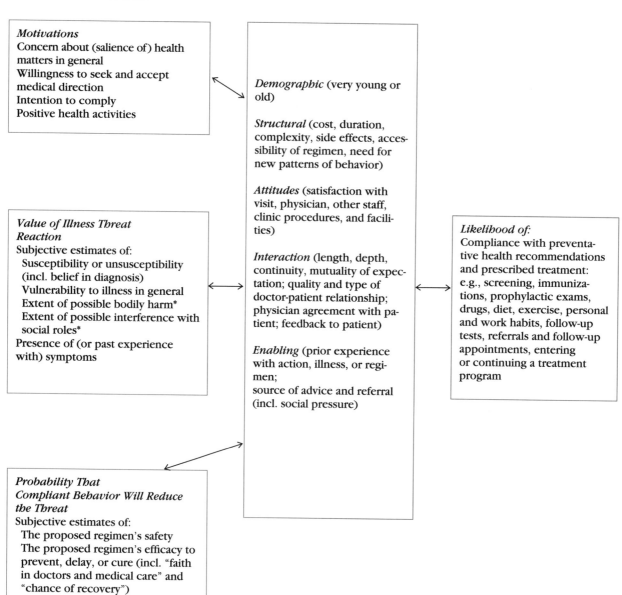

Motivations
Concern about (salience of) health matters in general
Willingness to seek and accept medical direction
Intention to comply
Positive health activities

Demographic (very young or old)

Structural (cost, duration, complexity, side effects, accessibility of regimen, need for new patterns of behavior)

Attitudes (satisfaction with visit, physician, other staff, clinic procedures, and facilities)

Value of Illness Threat Reaction
Subjective estimates of:
Susceptibility or unsusceptibility (incl. belief in diagnosis)
Vulnerability to illness in general
Extent of possible bodily harm*
Extent of possible interference with social roles*
Presence of (or past experience with) symptoms

Interaction (length, depth, continuity, mutuality of expectation; quality and type of doctor-patient relationship; physician agreement with patient; feedback to patient)

Enabling (prior experience with action, illness, or regimen;
source of advice and referral (incl. social pressure)

Likelihood of:
Compliance with preventative health recommendations and prescribed treatment:
e.g., screening, immunizations, prophylactic exams, drugs, diet, exercise, personal and work habits, follow-up tests, referrals and follow-up appointments, entering or continuing a treatment program

Probability That Compliant Behavior Will Reduce the Threat
Subjective estimates of:
The proposed regimen's safety
The proposed regimen's efficacy to prevent, delay, or cure (incl. "faith in doctors and medical care" and "chance of recovery")

* At motivating, not inhibiting, levels

FIGURE 5-2. Health belief model for explaining and predicting individual health-related behaviors. (From Becker, M. H., Haefner, D. P., Kasl, S. V., Kirscht, J. P., Maiman, L. A., & Rosenstock, I. M. [1977]. Selected psychosocial models and correlates of individual health-related behaviors. *Medical Care, 15* [5], 30. Reproduced with permission, Philadelphia: Lippincott-Raven Publishers.)

rected to physician-patient relationships, quite possibly a product of the roles and functions of other health-care providers in 1977. Expansion to other health professions is needed. As a part of the health history, readiness as motivations in health behaviors are easily included in the interview. Soliciting and understanding the client's "subjective estimates" of the threat, potential reduction, and care options are less frequently included in the assessment, depending on the professional's impressions of time restraints, knowledge of the client, and even cultural or interpersonal differences between professional and client. In a nursing health assessment, we frequently acquire demographic information and some structural information that provides insight into modifying and enabling factors. The challenge is to acquire the additional structural information, such as cost and accessibility, and confidently and voluntarily seek information from the client about quality, satisfaction, and social pressures for additional knowledge of attitudinal, interaction, and enabling factors. This information can increase compliant behaviors when this predictive health belief model is used.

As Pender (1987, 1996) indicates, however, the health belief model is directed at preventive services in the context of a provider-consumer relationship rather than individual health promotion behaviors. To be empowered consumers in today's health-care system, individuals must take personal responsibility for their own health long before they seek care from a health professional. This concept is not addressed in the health belief model.

Pender's health promotion model was an outgrowth of the health belief model, based on research and information on health and health-protecting behaviors. It is primarily a nursing model and has undergone two revisions with evolving knowledge. In the health promotion model, health promotion is motivated by the desire to increase the level of wellness and actualization of an individual or an aggregate group (Pender, 1996, p. 7). Pender (1996) states that the assumptions of the model "emphasize the active role of the client in shaping and maintaining health behaviors and in modifying the environmental context for health behaviors" (p. 55). Structurally, the model had been designed as a schematic representation similar to the original health belief model. Based on extensive research, the model was revised, and significant variables were reorganized (Figure 5–3). Three variables from the original versions were deleted after research studies demonstrated that they were poorly explained or insignificant as predictors. The knowledge obtained through this body of research also led to the addition of three new variables in the health promotion model: activity-related affect, commitment to a plan of action, and immediate competing demands and preferences.

The revised health promotion model contains two principal components that interact for participation in health-promoting behaviors: individual characteristics and experiences and behavior-specific cognitions and affect. *Individual characteristics and experiences* are similar to the individual perceptions in the health belief model, looking at health through past experiences (prior related behavior) and personal factors. Pender (1996) points out that "empirical studies indicate that often the best predictor of behavior is the frequency of the same or a similar behavior in the past" (pp. 66–67). Personal factors include biologic (age, gender, body mass, etc.), psychologic (such as self-esteem, motivation, perceived health status), and sociocultural (e.g., ethnicity, educational level, socioeconomic status) variables (Pender, 1996, p. 68). Based on research evidence, these biologic, psychologic, and sociocultural personal factors were included in the model as further predictors of individual health perceptions and behaviors. For example, consider the health-seeking behaviors demonstrated by clients of different socioeconomic groups, family backgrounds, and experiences in the health-care system. Later in this chapter, we address specific cultural differences in health beliefs that also influence health-seeking behaviors.

The *behavior-specific cognitions and affect* are similar to the health belief model's modifying or enabling factors but relate more to the nomenclature of nursing. As Pender (1996) has indicated, this category of variables is of "major motivational significance" and provides direction for nursing interventions (p. 68). These behavior-specific cognitions and affects include perceived benefits, perceived barriers, perceived self-efficacy, activity-related affect (subjective feelings), interpersonal influences, and situational influences. Pender (1996) explains that the variables of perceived benefits, barriers, and self-efficacy have been shown to be predictors of health promotion behaviors in most of the research studies completed. Activity-related affect, a new variable included in the health promotion model, addresses the individual's subjective feeling related to the health promotion behavior. Interpersonal and situational influences are identified as having both direct and indirect effects on health promotion behaviors. Consider the older adult walking through a shopping mall and noticing a free hypertension clinic. Indirect situational influences to action may

INDIVIDUAL
CHARACTERISTICS
AND EXPERIENCES

BEHAVIOR-SPECIFIC
COGNITIONS
AND AFFECT

BEHAVIORAL
OUTCOME

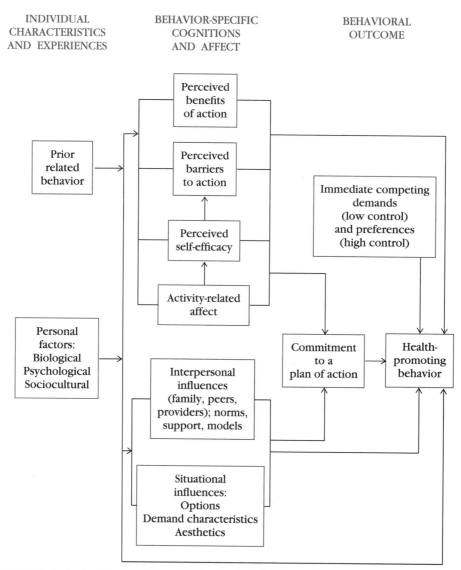

FIGURE 5-3. Pender's health belief model. (Pender, N. J. [1996]. *Health promotion in nursing practice* [3rd ed.]. Stamford, CT: Appleton & Lange. Reprinted with permission.)

include the perceived camaraderie of people in the clinic, compared with a tedious wait for an office appointment, leading to the action of confirming one's blood pressure is under control because of the dedication to a walking program. The direct influence is the availability of the screening during this older adults' routine exercise program at the mall.

Behavioral outcome, the third component of the model, includes actions toward the healthy behavior. These actions lead to the attainment of a positive health outcome. Variables that influence health-promoting behaviors are commitment to the plan of

action and competing demands and preferences. Pender (1996) describes the commitment to the plan of action with two distinct cognitive processes:

(1) commitment to carry out a specific action at a given time and place and with specified persons or alone, irrespective of competing preferences; and (2) identification of definitive strategies for eliciting, carrying out, and reinforcing the behavior (p. 72).

Commitment to the plan of action is affected by the immediate competing demands and preferences the individual perceives. This component is greatly influenced by nursing interventions related to values clarification, encouragement, and reinforcement of healthy behaviors.

In the earlier version of the health promotion model, Pender (1987) described the model as an organizing framework that is flexible and subject to revision after further testing. With the empirical support of variables, the revised model has increased potential to predict and intervene for health promotion activities. Health promotion settings are the social environment in which we live, work, and play such as family, school, workplace, health-care agencies, and the community at large. Ongoing research studies focused on a variety of client populations target theory testing for this model and further validating the utility of its theoretical structure in the discipline of nursing.

Table 5–1 compares the health belief model and the health promotion model. Both models propose that the health professional must understand how the person perceives the world and makes personal decisions through the identified readiness or individual characteristics and experiences. The modifying factors or behavior-specific cognitions and affect are the social, situational, and environmental influences related to the person's conception of healthy behavior. Both models include demographic variables, such as age, since research supports the importance of differences. For example, the choices between surgery and radiation is very different for

the person of 28 versus 82 years of age, in terms of not only physiologic differences but also past experiences. Attention to these differences turns the focus to health-care consumers, their specific outcomes, and success in the health-promotion activity.

CHRONIC ILLNESS MODEL

Although the health belief model has been used in research and practice settings with chronic illness clients, Corbin and Strauss' chronic illness model is specific to chronicity. Despite its focus on chronic illness, it is still a health promotion model. As Corbin and Strauss (1992a) state,

> the focus of care in chronicity is not on cure but first of all on the prevention of chronic conditions, then on finding ways to help the ill manage and live with their illness should these occur. Interventions are aimed at fostering the prevention of, living with, and shaping the course of chronic illnesses, especially those requiring technologically complex management, while promoting and maintaining quality of life. (p. 20)

The chronic illness trajectory framework (1992a) is a substantive theory, that applies to individuals with a broad range of chronic conditions. Benner and Wrubel's (1989) concept of health as coherence applies to this model. Corbin and Strauss (1992a)

TABLE 5–1. Comparing the Health Belief Model and the Health Promotion Model

Model	Individual Characteristics	Mediating Factors	Outcomes
Health Belief Model (Becker et al.,1977)	*Readiness for Recommended Behavior* Motivations including general health concerns, willingness and compliance behaviors, positive health attitudes Value of illness threat reduction including subjective estimates and past experiences Probability that compliant behavior will reduce threat (subjectively)	*Modifying/Enabling Factors:* Demographic Structural Attitudes Interaction Enabling	*Compliant Behaviors:* Likelihood of compliance with preventive health recommendations and prescribed regimens
Pender's Health Promotion Model (1996)	*Individual Characteristics and Experiences:* Prior related behavior Personal factors ■ biologic ■ psychological ■ sociocultural	*Behavior-specific Cognitions and Affect:* Perceived benefits Perceived barriers Perceived self-efficacy Activity-related affect Interpersonal influences Situational influences	*Behavioral Outcomes:* Commitment to a plan of action Immediate competing demands and preferences Health-promoting behaviors

describe the development of the framework as based on 30 years of qualitative, grounded theory research. The original framework was developed with the following concepts: key problems, basic strategies, organizational or family arrangements, and consequences (Strauss & Glaser, 1975: Strauss et al., 1984). It evolved into a nursing theory through its use and research base, but the developers maintain that potentially it applies to all health-care disciplines. The framework or model is based on the following assumptions:

1. The course of chronic conditions varies and changes over time.
2. The course of a chronic condition can be shaped and managed.
3. Technology involved is complex and can potentially create side effects.
4. The illness and technology pose potential consequences for the individual's physical well-being, biographical fulfillment (identify over time), and performance of daily activities.
5. Biographical needs and performance of daily activities can affect illness management choices and the course of the illness.
6. The course of illness is not inevitably downward.
7. Chronic illnesses do not necessarily end in death. (Corbin & Strauss, 1992a, p. 10; 1992b, p. 97).

Corbin and Strauss (1992a) describe the framework as a conceptual model organized under the central concept of "trajectory." This was proposed to indicate the management of the evolving course of the chronic condition, as "shaped" by the person, family members, and health-care providers. From this central organizing or umbrella concept flow the other major theoretical concepts:

Trajectory phasing	Eight phases: pretrajectory, trajectory onset, crisis, acute, stable, unstable, downward, dying; subphasing within each phase for fluctuations as improvements, plateauing, reversals, or deterioration occurs during course of illness
Trajectory projection	Vision of the illness course
Trajectory scheme	Shaping the course, controlling symptoms, and handling disability
Conditions influencing management	Technology used, resources, past experience, motivation, setting of care, lifestyle/beliefs, interactions/
	relationships, type of chronic condition and physiologic involvement, symptoms, political and economic climate affecting legislation
Trajectory management	Management of symptoms, side effects, crises, and complications through the trajectory scheme
Biographical and everyday living impact	Identity adjustments and management of limitations
Reciprocal impact	Consequences with management and problems related to illness, biography and everyday activities

These concepts are described as leading to the structure of the nursing process, with the following steps:

1. Locating the client and family and setting goals
2. Assessing conditions influencing management
3. Defining the intervention focus; the target of intervention
4. Intervention
5. Evaluating the effectiveness of intervention

This model focuses on the person to illustrate the management of an evolving course of a chronic condition the individual experiences that is influenced by that individual, the family, and health-care providers. This takes us a step further than the health belief model because this model is more grounded in the individual's unique, personal history, and patterns of life. The chronic illness experience is distinctively different for an elderly, frail Anglo-American woman living in an urban high-rise apartment than for the African-American elder with a physical disability living in a rural farm area. This involves more than the issue of compliance; it focuses on quality of life issues. As we see later with cultural diversity, the beliefs and values of individuals, families, communities, and groups, along with environmental factors, are major considerations in health care.

LEVELS OF PREVENTION

When considering health promotion activities, we frequently also refer to preventing illness and disability to achieve a healthier state. In 1990, national health promotion and disease prevention activities were developed under the auspices of the U.S. Department of Health and Human Services (USDHHS) and published as *Healthy People 2000*. Interestingly, the publication distinguished between health promotion and health protection strategies, with an individual versus a community focus, as follows:

> **Health promotion** strategies are those related to individual life-style—personal choices made in a social context—that can have a powerful influence over one's health prospects. These include physical activity and fitness, nutrition, tobacco, alcohol and other drugs, family planning, mental health and mental disorders and violent and abusive behavior. . . . **Health protection** strategies are those related to environmental or regulatory measures that confer protection on large population groups. These strategies address issues such as unintentional injuries, occupational safety and health, environmental health, food and drug safety, and oral health. **Preventive services** include counseling, screening, immunization, or chemoprophylactic interventions for individuals in clinical settings. (USDHHS, 1992, pp. 6–7)

These preventive activities and services address the three areas of prevention: primary, secondary, and tertiary. Health promotion activities are both protective and preventive, but they require consumers actively involved in all levels of prevention.

Primary prevention refers to healthy actions taken to avoid illness or disease. Examples include healthy nutrition, smoking cessation, exercise programs, parenting classes, community awareness programs, and mental health programs and activities. Primary prevention refers to the individual lifestyle health promotion strategies recommended in *Healthy People 2000*. These are becoming more popular and prevalent as people take responsibility for their health. Health columns have increased in daily newspapers as have health magazines, health food stores, televised health programs, and educational programs for the general public. But consumers can still have difficulty acquiring sufficient information on a selected topic before they become frustrated.

Secondary prevention involves screening for early detection and treatment of health problems. With secondary prevention, the individual is not seeking health care for a specific problem, but rather early detection of a potential problem, to mobilize resources and reduce its intensity or severity if the problem is identified. Secondary prevention usually involves use of some procedure or measurement tool in addition to the health history and physical assessment. Duncan (1994) proposed that the health-care system view prevention with this concept in mind in efforts to control costly care, such as

mammography, rather than actually trying to prevent illness or disease (p. 84).

Examples of secondary prevention include screening procedures used by health-care consumers or health-care professionals for physiologic, developmental, or environmental problems. Physiologic procedures include screening for hypertension or specific forms of cancer. Mental health screening procedures range from simple tests for orientation to more elaborate instruments such as mental status questionnaires for aging clients. In young children, examples of secondary prevention activities include use of growth charts to assess growth along established percentiles and the Denver II developmental screening test to detect problems in the areas of person-social skills, motor activities, and language. Note the difference between using parenting classes as primary prevention for developmental stimulation and screening for developmental problems with the Denver II, as secondary prevention. Environmental screening procedures include testing air and water quality and home safety assessments. If a problem is detected, a referral is made for a differential diagnosis and institution of early treatment.

Tertiary prevention occurs during the rehabilitative phase of an illness to prevent complications or further disability. The individual has already entered the health-care system and is recovering from or learning to cope with a health deficit. Tertiary prevention builds on this to prevent further deficits. Examples of tertiary prevention are counseling and teaching after recovery from a cardiovascular event, an accident or injury, an abusive situation, or any other physical, psychosocial, and mental or environmental disruption from usual health and functioning. Support from self-help groups is a large component in tertiary prevention. Continuing with the example of preventive activities for children with parenting classes and the Denver II, an example of tertiary prevention is family counseling following identification of a child in a physically abusive situation.

Professional nursing practice involves all three levels of preventive activities. Since the health of individuals, families, communities, and groups is a major concern in nursing, professional skill and expertise in the area of prevention activities is presumed in practice, education, research, and administrative functions.

CULTURAL INFLUENCE ON HEALTH PERCEPTIONS AND PROMOTION

Healthy People 2000 also targeted selected groups as at-risk populations requiring special health promotion strategies. The report illustrates significant health problems in some minority groups but, more important, it emphasizes individuals within subgroups. This report shows that individual differences, beyond racial group, socioeconomic status, and educational level, impact health status and access to health care.

> Rather than amalgamating into one single group, we have come to recognize and even celebrate our diversity as a basis for national strength. Nevertheless, our health care programs are characterized by unacceptable disparities linked to membership in certain racial and ethnic groups. (USDHHS, 1992, p. 31)

This points to the need for a concerted effort to understand and embrace diversity in our daily personal and professional lives. But much is implied within the construct of diversity. When people speak of ethnicity and race, they generally refer to a group, tribe, or nation of people united by some common characteristics, whether biological, environmental, or social. In the United States, we tend to classify people into five ethnic groups: African Americans, Asian and Pacific Islander Americans, Hispanic Americans, Native Americans, and white Americans. But this does little to help us understand the health beliefs, practices, needs, or diversity represented within each of these population classifications. It may, in fact, encourage us to impose stereotypical judgments on persons within these groups. This leads us to the concept of culture as a way of life.

One's cultural inheritance provides a powerful influence on health beliefs, both consciously and unconsciously. We bring into our personal and professional lives the influences from our ancestors, family, peers, and colleagues. We are affected by history, genetics, social customs, religion, language, politics, law, economics, education, and many other factors. We mutually influence and are influenced by others because of these endowments. When we talk about cultural diversity, we mean more than an inherited background. Culture implies social, familial, religious, national, and professional characteristics that affect the way we think and act. It is a combination of all of these things.

Research demonstrating individual differences and perceptions provides valuable data for the revision of the health belief model. Educational, ethnic, and social class differences were identified for careful assessment of client beliefs and perceptions (Becker et al., 1977). This is significant whether one is dealing with individual clients or families with a specific health-care deficit or a larger population group with informational needs for health promotion activities.

But it is important to consider the characteristics of both the client and the health professional. One of the functions of the American Nurses Association (ANA) Council on Cultural Diversity (1986) is "to promote an understanding of the health-related needs of individuals from diverse cultures, individuals with different life styles and values" (p. 1). This includes their proposed concept of cultural relativism: the culture of others should be approached with respect (ANA, 1986, p. 10). To this aim, it is important to understand individual, family, community, and group health beliefs.

Cox (1993) has identified the following six areas of cultural differences in behavior apparent in organizations: (1) time and space orientation, (2) leadership style orientations, (3) individualism versus collectivism, (4) competitive versus cooperative behavior, (5) locus of control, and (6) communication styles (p. 108). Although these are also relevant for health-care organizations, significant differences can exist in health beliefs and roles of the client with a health care need and the health-care provider, considered the "expert."

One's health beliefs are the result of cultural inheritance, educational information, reasoned opinions, and, often, unfounded impressions. The proportion of each of these factors is individually determined. Babcock and Miller (1994) describe three paradigms for cultural influence on health care: (1) magicoreligious, (2) scientific or biomedical, and (3) holistic (Table 5–2). The three different views show us how individuals differ in their beliefs in the supernatural, the scientific community, or the holistic mind-body-spirit interrelationship. It is worth noting that the American health-care system operates from the scientific worldview, which diverges from that of many cultures and their subgroups.

Lantz (1989) has defined a health culture as the traditional way that a group views health, illness, disease causation, the healer's role, the sick role, acceptable treatment modalities, and service systems (p. 51). In our health-care system, we have defined all these terms, and we usually present them through our words and behaviors as norms to which clients must adhere. Otherwise, they are termed "bad patients," "noncompliant," or even "problem cases." For example, the health-care community carefully conducts, evaluates, and uses research to identify biological, chemical, structural, or physical factors to treat, manage, or cure a disease. Faced with clients whose belief system includes the "hot/cold" theory of disease causation and treatment—that imbalance of the four body humors of yellow and black bile, phlegm, and blood resulting in "hot" infectious condition must be treated with appropriate foods or herbs—we may ignore or pa-

TABLE 5 – 2. Summary of Belief Systems about Health and Illness

	Magico-religious	Scientific/Biomedical	Holistic
Worldview	Fate of world is under control of supernatural forces. God(s) or other supernatural forces for good and evil are in control while humans are at the mercy of natural forces.	Life is controlled by physical and biochemical processes that can be studied and manipulated by humans.	Harmony, natural balance. Human life is only one aspect of nature and part of the general order of the cosmos. Everything in universe has a place and role according to laws that maintain order.
Illness/disease	Initiated by supernatural agent with or without justification, via sorcery. Cause of health or illness is not organic, but mystical. Causes: possession by evil spirits, breaching a taboo, supernatural forces (sorcery, witchcraft).	Wear and tear, accident, injury, pathogens, and fluid and chemical imbalance. Cause-effect relationship exists for natural events. Life related to structure and functions like machines. Life can be reduced or divided into smaller parts. Mind and body two distinct entities. Cause exists, if only it were known.	Disease, imbalance, and chaos result when these laws are disturbed.
Health	Gift or reward given as a sign of God's blessing and good will.	Illness prevention activities, restoration through exercise, medication, treatments, and other means.	Environment, behavior, and sociocultural factors are influential in maintaining health and prevention of disease. Maintaining and restoring balance are important to health.
Ethnic group	Hispanic Americans, African Americans: components found in other groups.	White Americans	Native Americans, Asian Americans: components found in other groups
Other concepts			Yin/yang Hot/cold Harmony/disharmony

Source: Babcock, D. E., & Miller, M. A. (1994). *Client education: Theory and practice*. St. Louis: Mosby. Modified from Albers, cited in Herberg, P. (1989). Theoretical foundations of transcultural nursing. In Boyle, J. S., & Andrews, M. M., *Transcultural Concepts in Nursing Care*. Boston: Scott, Foresman, with permission.

tronize them. Many scientific minds reject this theory, creating conflict and failure to provide health care. As Benner and Wrubel (1989) have stated, "changes in lifestyles and health habits work best when they are integrated into the person's own cultural patterns and traditions [for] it is hard to sustain new patterns if they go against the grain of one's normal social patterns" (p. 155).

Madeleine Leininger proposed a transcultural nursing theory entitled culture care diversity and universality. Leininger's (1970) early definition of culture referred to a way of "life belonging" to a designated group, through accumulated traditions, customs, and the ways the group solves problems that are learned and transmitted systematically, largely through socialization practices that are reinforced through social and cultural institutions (pp. 48–49). Within her culture care theory, Leininger (1991a) defined culture as "the learned, shared and transmitted values, beliefs, norms, and lifeways of a

particular group that guides their thinking, decisions, and actions in patterned ways" (p. 47). Taking this one step further as a health belief, Leininger (1991a) defined cultural care as "the subjectively and objectively learned and transmitted values, beliefs, and patterned lifeways that assist, support, facilitate, or enable another individual or group to maintain their well being, health, to improve their human condition and lifeway, or to deal with illness, handicaps, or death" (p. 47).

Based on in-depth qualitative research, Leininger has identified dominant cultural values and culture care meanings and action modes for 21 American subculture groups, showing differences with the Anglo-American health-care value structure. The Anglo-American cultural values include individualism, independence and freedom, competition and achievement, materialism, technology, instant time and actions, youth and beauty, equal rights (gender), leisure time, scientific facts and numbers, and a sense of generosity in time of crisis; action modes include stress alleviation, personalized acts, self-reliance, and health instruction (Leininger, 1991a, p. 355). These characteristics are consistent with the prevailing culture of the practitioners and organizations that make up the health-care system. Table 5–3 lists information on a sample of these American subgroups.

Difficulties arise when significant values are unknown, in conflict, or poorly understood. The client's cultural values can be quite different from those of the health-care provider. As we can see from the data in Table 5–3, of the 15 sample subgroups presented, 10 share none of the dominant characteristics of health-care systems and Anglo-American clients, and few characteristics are shared by the remaining subgroups. In addition, consider the importance of religious or dominant spiritual influence in all but three of the cultural subgroups presented. Knowledge of the dominant values can assist in providing health promotion or health maintenance activities and programs. An example of this was noted by Armmer and Humbles (1995), as the support from and linkages with church leaders was considered crucial to the success of a health promotion program for African Americans. Leininger (1994) stresses that nurses as primary, secondary, and tertiary care providers, through their close and continuous contact with culturally diverse clients, must move from unicultural personal and professional knowledge to provide meaningful culturally based nursing care (p. 255).

Other individual values may not be initially apparent or may grow more dominant. Alternative health-care practices, such as acupuncture and herbal medicines, are being tried as people become dissatisfied with the biomedical view and move to holistic care. These practices may differ from the inherited cultural background but be adopted or become more dominant. This points to the need for a comprehensive cultural assessment with the client and may require great openness, sensitivity, and time. As Bell (1994) points out, it took several months of living and working in the community for her to fully understand how closely the traditional Navajo value for a harmonious balance and relationship with all living things related to the health of land, family, and community (p. 237).

NURSING'S ROLE

Nurses have a primary responsibility in health promotion, health maintenance, and prevention activities, in fact, these are the essence of professional nursing practice. The focus of nursing is on the health of the individual, family, community, and societal group. Health promotion roles are guided within the theoretical framework on which nursing practice is based, including how you, as the professional, view the client, the concept of health, the environment, and the practice of nursing as well as your accord with a model's definitions and relationships. This is the point of the middle-range theory discussed in Chapters 3 and 4, from which you can move to a practice model that is applicable to your specific function or practice setting. Before you decide on the best framework to guide your own professional practice, consider the following two examples.

Example 1. Suppose your practice is guided by King's theory of goal attainment. In this theory, nursing is defined as "a process of human interactions between nurse and client whereby each perceives the other and the situation, and through communications, they set goals, explore the means to achieve them, agree to the means, their actions indicate movement toward goal achievement" (King, 1987, p. 113). Health promotion, health maintenance, and prevention activities are all implied in this definition of health as adjustment to stressors in the system environments and use of resources. Health is viewed as a potential and the goal of the process. Specific assessment and intervention activities must address the theory's theoretical concepts and propositions. Personal perceptions of the client are important components of the health beliefs model, Pender's health promotion model, and the chronic illness trajectory framework. If your practice setting is a clinic with a large population that needs health promotion strategies addressing individual lifestyles and the preventive services identified in *Healthy People 2000,* you may find the health beliefs model or Pender's model of health promotion quite useful with your clients. These same models can address health maintenance as secondary and tertiary prevention. On the other hand, if your practice setting is a hospice or you work primarily with cancer patients and their families, you may find the chronic illness trajectory framework more useful for guiding your practice and use of the nursing process.

Example 2. If your practice is guided by Leininger's (1991a) culture care diversity and universality model, three modes of cultural care guide your nursing judgment, decisions, and actions: preservation and maintenance, accommodation and negotia-

TABLE 5–3. Leininger's (1991b) Identification of Dominant
Culture Care Values and Actions for American Subgroups

American Subgroup	Extended Family	Religion—Spiritual	Home Remedies	Folk—Native Practices	Heritage—Traditions	Folk—Ethnic Foods	Hot-Cold Beliefs	Respect Authority	Respect Elders	Matriarchal	Patriarchal	Importance of Touch	Physical Presence	Individualism	Independence	Achievement	Materialism	Time Immediacy	Technology	Youth and Beauty	Leisure Time	Scientific Data	Work Ethic
Anglo-														X	X	X	X	X	X	X	X	X	
African-	X	X	X		X	X							X							X			
Mexican-	X	X	X	X	X	X	X	X	X	*	X		X										
Haitian-	X	X	X	X	X	X	X	X	X		†												
Native-	X	X		X	X			X	X		X												
Philippine-	X	X	X	X	X	X	X	X	X														
Japanese-	X			X	X			X	X		X						X			X		X	X
Vietnamese-	X	X		X		X	X	X	X			X											
Polish-	X	X	X	X	X	X												X	X				X
German-		X																X	X			X	X
Italian-	X	X			X	X						X	X	X		X							
Greek-	X	X	X	X	X																		X
Jewish-	X	X			X	X				*		X				X	X						
Arab/Muslim-	X	X		X	X	X		X	X		X												
Lithuanian-	X	X																					X
Finnish-		X	X	X	X																		X

*For care decisions.
†Decision maker.
Source: Adapted from Leininger, M. M. (1991b). Selected culture-care findings of diverse cultures using culture care theory and ethnomethods. In Leininger, M. M. (Ed.), *Culture care diversity and universality: A theory of nursing* (Pub. No. 15-2402) (pp. 355–368). New York: National League for Nursing.

tion, and repatterning or restructuring. In Leininger's concept of culturally congruent nursing care, these modes all focus on health promotion, health maintenance, and prevention activities within the context of the client's cultural belief system. Recall that culturally congruent nursing care was defined as "those cognitively based assistive, supportive, facilitative or enabling acts or decisions that are tailor-made to fit with individual, group, or institutional cultural values, beliefs, and lifeways in order to provide or support meaningful, beneficial, and satisfying health care, or well-being services" (Leininger, 1991a, p. 49). The practice models and assessment tools selected must be culturally sensitive and include individual focus on each of the assessment factors included in the sunrise model.

Selecting a health model involves a deliberate and reflective process that takes into account your worldview, the theory that guides your professional practice, and the unique characteristics of the people and environment in which you work. You may practice under several similar models, depending on a changeable environment or client group. In the next section of this book, we concentrate on several critical components of professional nursing practice, including communication, critical thinking, leadership, management, understanding organizations, effecting change, teaching and learning, and working with groups. The theoretical bases and the information we have about each of these components further influence professional nursing practice.

KEY POINTS

- **Health** is more than the absence of **illness**, disease, or infirmity. A concept of health is determined by one's worldview and philosophical assumptions.
- Benner and Wrubel (1989) have described five theories of health as (1) an ideal, (2) the ability to fulfill social roles, (3) a commodity, (4) a human potential, and (5) a sense of coherence.
- Dunn's **high-level wellness** stresses well-being, including the positive, dynamic, and unique integration of mind, body, and spirit of the individual functioning within his or her environment, and the individual's maximum potential.
- The **health belief model** was designed as an organizing framework to advance health promotion activities by targeting interventions to certain individual variables. Three major concepts explain and predict health-related behaviors: (1) readiness to undertake recommended compliance behavior, (2) modifying and enabling factors, and (3) compliant behaviors.
- **Pender's health promotion model** (1996) is a schematic representation with three components promoting health-promoting behaviors. *Individual characteristics and experiences* include prior related behavior and personal factors (biologic, psychologic, and sociocultural factors). *Behavior-specific cognitions and affect* include perceived benefits, perceived barriers, perceived self-efficacy, activity-related affect interpersonal influences, and situational influences. The *behavioral outcome* is attainment of a positive health outcome through commitment to the plan of action and competing demands and preferences.
- **Chronic illness trajectory framework** (Corbin and Strauss, 1992a) is a conceptual model organized under the main concept of "trajectory" for managing an evolving course of a chronic condition. Under the central concept are the major concepts of trajectory phasing, trajectory projection, trajectory scheme, conditions influencing management, trajectory management, biographical and everyday living impact, and reciprocal impact. These concepts lead to a five-step nursing process structure.

- **Health promotion** and **protection** strategies relate to individual lifestyle and environment influences on health status and health prospects. **Preventive** activities and **services** address three areas of prevention. **Primary prevention** refers to healthy actions taken to avoid illness or disease. **Secondary prevention** involves screening for early detection and treatment of health problems. **Tertiary prevention** during the rehabilitative phase of an illness prevents complications or further disability.
- Culture involves a combination of social, familial, religious, national, and professional characteristics that affect the way we think, act, and interact with others. Differences among groups and subgroups produce diversity that can lead from uniculturalism to appreciation of a multicultural environment and health-care behaviors.
- Leininger (1991a) defines cultural care as "subjectively and objectively learned and transmitted values, beliefs, and patterned lifeways that assist, support, facilitate, or enable another individual or group to maintain their well being, health, to improve their human condition and lifeway, or to deal with illness, handicaps, or death" (p. 47).
- Nursing focuses on the health of the individual, family, community, and societal group. Health promotion roles are guided by the theoretical framework on which practice is based.

CHAPTER EXERCISES

1. Select the definition provided for health from the nursing theories presented in Chapter 3. Discuss which of the five models of health they fit in, and suggest health promotion models for each.

2. Describe how the health beliefs model can be used with specific examples of primary, secondary, and tertiary prevention activities.

3. Use Pender's health promotion model to plan a health promotion campaign with one of the following groups:
   a. Immunization program in an urban apartment complex with a high density of families with young children.
   b. Home safety program at a senior citizens' center.
   c. Wellness program for employees in a manufacturing company.

4. Recall a client with a chronic illness for whom you provided nursing care in the past. Retrospectively apply the chronic illness trajectory framework to the client's experiences you were able to observe.

5. Select a cultural subgroup other than your own. Interview several representatives from that subgroup and representatives from your own extended family on the following topics:
   a. Personal, family, and group health beliefs, including how health and illness are viewed.
   b. Who makes most of health-care decisions in the family.
   c. How they seek care, and from whom.
   d. Home remedies used and the origins of these practices.
   e. Impressions of traditional American health care.
      Analyze the differences between the two groups, and compare them with your personal answers on the preceding topics.

6. Select a cultural subgroup other than your own. Identify differences between your beliefs and theirs. Choose an appropriate health promotion model for use with that group, and describe areas to which you will need to pay particular attention in assessment and intervention activities.

REFERENCES

American Nurses Association [ANA]. (1986). *Cultural diversity in the nursing curriculum: A guide for implementation (Publication No. G-171 2M 5/86)*. Kansas City, MO: Author.

Armmer, F. A., & Humbles, P. (1995). Parish nursing: Extending health care to urban African-Americans. *Nursing and Health Care: Perspectives on Community, 16,* 64–68.

Athey, J. L. (1988). The role of the health belief model and health locus of control construct as explanations of adherence to a chronic illness regimen. Unpublished doctoral dissertation, University of South Carolina, Columbia.

Babcock, D. E., & Miller, M. A. (1994). *Client education: Theory and practice.* St. Louis: Mosby.

Becker, M. H., Haefner, D. P., Kasl, S. V., Kirscht, J. P., Maiman, L. A., & Rosenstock, I. M. (1977). Selected psychosocial models and correlates of individual health-related behaviors. *Medical Care, 15*(5, Suppl), pp. 27–46.

Bell, R. (1994). Prominence of women in Navajo beliefs and values. *Nursing and Health Care, 15,* 232–240.

Benner, P. (1984). *From novice to expert: Excellence and power in clinical nursing practice.* Menlo Park, CA: Addison-Wesley.

Benner, P., & Wrubel, J. (1989). *The primacy of caring: Stress and coping in health and illness.* Menlo Park, CA: Addison-Wesley.

Corbin, J. M., & Strauss, A. (1992a). A nursing model for chronic illness management based upon the trajectory framework. In P. Woog, (Ed.), *The chronic illness trajectory framework: The Corbin and Strauss nursing model* (pp. 9–28). New York: Springer.

Corbin, J. M., & Strauss, A. (1992b). Commentary. In P. Woog, (Ed.), *The chronic illness trajectory framework: The Corbin and Strauss nursing model* (pp. 97–102). New York: Springer.

Cox, T. (1993). *Cultural diversity in organizations: Theory, research and practice.* San Francisco: Berrett-Koehler.

Duncan, K. A. (1994). *Health information and health reform: Understanding the need for a national health information system.* San Francisco: Jossey-Bass.

Dunn, H. L. (1973). *High level wellness.* Arlington, VA: Beatty.

King, I. M. (1981). *A theory for nursing: Systems, concepts, process.* New York: Wiley.

King, I. M. (1987). *King's theory of goal attainment.* In R. R. Parse (Ed.), *Nursing science: Major paradigms, theories, and critiques* (pp. 107–113). Philadelphia: Saunders.

Lantz, L. M. (1989). Family culture and ethnicity. In P. J. Bomar (Ed.), (1989). *Nurses and family health promotion: Concepts, assessment, and interventions* (pp. 47–66). Philadelphia: Saunders.

Leininger, M. (1970). *Nursing and anthropology: Two worlds to blend.* New York: Wiley.

Leininger, M. M. (1991a). Selected culture care findings of diverse cultures using culture care theory and ethnomethods. In Leininger, M. M. (Ed.), *Culture care diversity and universality: A theory of nursing* (Pub. No. 15-2402) (pp. 345–371). New York: National League for Nursing.

Leininger, M. M. (1991b). The theory of culture care diversity and universality. In Leininger, M. M. (Ed.), *Culture care diversity and universality: A theory of nursing* (Pub. No. 15-2402) (pp. 5–68). New York: National League for Nursing.

Leininger, M. M. (1994). Transcultural nursing education: A worldwide imperative. *Nursing and Health Care, 15,* 254–257.

Lutjens, L. R. J. (1991). *Callista Roy: An adaptation model.* Newbury Park, CA: Sage.

Munhall, P. L., & Oiler, C. J. (1986). *Nursing research: A qualitative approach.* Norwalk, CT: Appleton-Century-Crofts.

Pender, N. J. (1996). *Health promotion in nursing practice* (3rd ed.). Stamford, CT: Appleton & Lange.

Pender, N. J. (1987). *Health promotion in nursing practice* (2nd ed.). Norwalk, CT: Appleton & Lange.

Strauss, A. L., & Glaser, B. G. (1975). *Chronic illness and the quality of life.* St. Louis: Mosby.

Strauss, A. L., Corbin, J., Fagerhaugh, S., Glaser, B. G., Maines, D., Suczek, B., & Wiener, C. L. (1984). *Chronic illness and the quality of life* (2nd ed.). St. Louis: Mosby.

U.S. Department of Health and Human Services, Public Health Service. (1992). *Healthy People 2000: Summary Report.* Boston: Jones & Bartlett.

Whall, A. L. (1987). A critique of Rogers framework. In R. R. Parse (Ed.). *Nursing science: Major paradigms, theories, and critiques* (pp. 147–158). Philadelphia: Saunders.

BIBLIOGRAPHY

Frankenburg, W. K., & Dodds, J. B. (1992). *Denver II training manual* (2nd ed.). Denver: Denver Developmental Materials.

Giger, J. N., & Davidhizar, R. E. (1995). *Transcultural nursing: Assessment and intervention* (2nd ed.). St. Louis: Mosby-Year Book.

Grothaus, K. L. (1996). Family dynamics and family therapy with Mexican Americans. *Journal of Psychosocial Nursing, 34*(2), 31–37.

Jensen, L., & Allen, M. (1993). Wellness: The dialectic of illness. *Image: Journal of Nursing Scholarship, 25,* 220–224.

Schrefer, S. (Ed.). (1994). *Quick reference to cultural assessment.* St. Louis: Mosby.

Section III

CRITICAL COMPONENTS OF PROFESSIONAL NURSING PRACTICE

Chapter 6

EFFECTIVE COMMUNICATION

Nancy Courts

CHAPTER OBJECTIVES

On completion of this chapter, the reader will be able to:

1. Apply communication models to verbal, nonverbal, and written situations.
2. Describe the type of communication skills needed in professional nursing practice.
3. Explain the techniques for effective communication.
4. Evaluate personal communication patterns used in practice with clients.
5. Examine cultural differences in communication patterns and preferences.

KEY TERMS

Communication
Intrapersonal
    Communication
Process
Transaction
Multidimensional
Helping Relationship
Source
Encoder

Message
Channel
Receiver
Decoder
Noise Factors
Feedback
Therapeutic
    Communication
Trust

Empathy
Congruence
Genuineness
Respect
Self-Awareness
Listen
Nonverbal
    Communication

C ommunication is inevitable. It occurs even as two strangers sit side by side on a bus, although neither says a word. Newborn babies respond to eye contact, touch, and the voice of the mother or caregiver. Indeed, without this communication babies develop "failure to thrive," and may even die. Learning to communicate, then, begins at birth and continues throughout life. Even those who are cognitively impaired and cannot understand spoken words respond to tone of voice and touch. Persons with sensory impairments, such as loss of hearing or vision, respond to nonverbal cues and identify affective messages. People who are alone participate in self-talk, which affects their bodies in a variety of ways, and to which others respond. It is impossible not to communicate.

Communication is a dynamic process involving both verbal and nonverbal techniques, written materials, and visual and auditory materials (videos, TV, radio, tape recorders). Like everyone else, nurses need to communicate when they perform their professional responsibilities (Johnson, 1994). Communications range from research presentations to persuasive presentations to obtain resources or as an advocate for new programs; from preparation of manuscripts for publication to preparation of learning materials, pamphlets, or videos for clients; and from group leadership of colleagues to leading patient and family support groups (Table 6–1). Group problem-solving and technical report preparation are also skills needed to enhance effectiveness.

Communication is the means of transmitting ideas, information, and feelings from one person to another as people reveal themselves (Kozier, Erb, Blais,

& Wilkinson, 1995; Kurz-Cringle, 1988). It is a reciprocal process in which the sender and the receiver of the message participate simultaneously (Taylor, Lillis, & LeMone, 1993). The way people send and receive messages (communicate) is influenced by past experiences, values, beliefs, knowledge, culture, education, and how they feel about themselves, the content of the message, and each other. Thus, the message the sender intended to send may not be the message the receiver actually received, making it important to assess and validate messages.

The intrapersonal component of the communication process controls what message is sent and how it is received. **Intrapersonal communication** is how one communicates with oneself, or self-talk (Farley, 1992). In fact, daily self-talk influences how one feels about oneself. For example, if a staff nurse has had an unpleasant encounter with the nurse manager, his or her self-talk will most likely be angry and self-comments about the manager derogatory. Further communications, with both the manager and others, will be influenced and shaped by this self-talk. The feelings generated may then be communicated to clients.

Effective communication requires a great deal of skill. Communication with clients is especially challenging and has been described as "a difficult and potentially stressful aspect of nursing" (Jarrett & Payne, 1995, p. 73). It takes maturity, skill, sensitivity, and time to communicate with patients. In addition, environmental issues, such as being too involved with tasks and procedures, and socialization issues, such as placing no value on talking with clients, interfere with nurse-patient communication. Therapeutic relationships, however, are an important part of nursing practice; nurses, therefore, need to continuously develop effective communication skills.

Nurses' workloads in acute care settings coupled with early discharge are challenges that affect nurse-client relationships. It does not, however, take long, uninterrupted periods of time to establish a therapeutic relationship for nurses experienced and skillful in communication techniques. Effective communication skills can be learned. This chapter identifies communication models, discusses essential ingredients of effective communication, considers forms of communication, and examines specific communication techniques.

COMMUNICATION MODELS

Communication models are helpful in understanding the process of communication. This section presents the basic assumptions and components of communication models as well as selected models.

TABLE 6–1. Definitions of Selected Work-Related Communication Skills

Presentational: oral reports to colleagues.

Public speaking: oral reports to the general public.

Technical writing: writing for colleagues.

Leadership: coordinating and/or delegating others' activities.

Small group discussion: participating with two or more persons, engaged in problem solving, decision making.

Listening: attending to others, recalling, and understanding others' messages.

Persuasion: convincing and motivating others.

Employment interviewing: gathering employment information.

Performance review: evaluating employees' performance.

Nonverbal: using appropriate body language.

Source: Johnson, J. R. (1994). The communication training needs of registered nurses. *Journal of Continuing Education in Nursing, 25*(5), 214, with permission.

Basic Assumptions of Communication Models

Communication models are based on the assumption that communication is a transactional, multidimensional process (Northhouse & Northhouse, 1992). The concept of **process** means an event is "dynamic, on-going, ever-changing, continuous" and without a beginning, end, or set sequence of events (Berlo, 1960, p. 34). Communication is a process with all parts affecting all other parts.

Communication is often pictured as one person talking to another to impart information or influence the person on a certain course of action. This linear model of communication does not adequately explain the communication process, since it does not include the multifaceted parts of the person sending or receiving the message or the reciprocal effects of the responses. For example, during the communication of A with B, the "physical, emotional, and social states of A and B may change" (Northhouse & Northhouse, 1992, p. 3). As B receives the message, filtered through values, beliefs, attitudes, social system, and culture, a response is transmitted to A, who then adapts his or her message based on interpretation of the response. Thus, communication is an ongoing, ever-changing, dynamic, continuous, and reciprocal process (Berlo, 1960; Northhouse & Northhouse, 1992; Taylor et al., 1993).

Messages are given and received simultaneously and are therefore, a **transaction** in which the giver of the message continuously reacts to the responses of the receiver, and vice versa. In other words, it is the relationship of the sender and receiver, and how they influence each other, that is important in the communication process (Northhouse & Northhouse, 1992). Nurses sensitive to patient cues shape their communication techniques to meet the needs of patients. For example, if patients want or need detailed information about their conditions, they are given many opportunities to learn, such as written material, videos, and one-on-one teaching. Those who are not interested may receive only written material, which they may or may not read.

Communication is **multidimensional** because people bring their unique values, beliefs, culture, knowledge, and past experiences to the communication, which is influenced by how each person feels about, himself or herself, the message, and the nature of the relationship. It is no wonder, then, that the messages senders believe they sent may not be the messages that are received. Through communication process interactions, human beings reveal themselves and respond to each other, establishing a relationship (Kurz-Cringle, 1988; Taylor et al., 1993). It is through this relationship that communication is shaped and enriched and outcomes are determined. A second component of communication, in addition to a relationship, is content (Watzlawick, Beavin, & Jackson, 1967).

The content dimension includes words and information, but it is the relationship that shapes how the message is given and received. With a caring relationship, "it is time for you to walk" is interpreted by the receiver as helpful, whereas in an adversarial relationship the message may be interpreted as an attempt to control the receiver's behavior. The meaning of the communication transaction emerges from both content and relationship, requiring attention to both. The relationship is probably a more powerful determinant of effective communication than the content of the message.

The nurse-client relationship is referred to as an interpersonal relationship, a therapeutic relationship, or a helping relationship. The **helping relationship** results from a nurse-client emotional bond based on mutual trust, respect, and acceptance, and is focused on the client's well-being. The helping relationship is dynamic, time-limited, and goal-oriented with unequal sharing; thus, it differs from a social relationship, which is spontaneous and mutual.

Basic Components of Communication Models

All communication requires a **source** (a purpose for the communication) and an **encoder** (person who translates) (Berlo, 1960). The source and encoder are the same person. The **message** (expression) includes the content and how it is transmitted plus the nonverbal or body language that accompanies the message. The **channel** is the medium chosen to convey the message; it may be sent to any of the receiver's five senses. The **receiver** (target of communication) is also known as a **decoder** (person who retranslates or decodes the message (Berlo, 1960). Decoding involves making sense of the sounds of the message and is influenced by roles, life situations, and environment (Purdy, 1991a) in addition to values, beliefs, attitudes, and feelings. The response, or feedback, is the verbal and nonverbal message that the receiver returns to the sender/encoder. **Noise factors** include a room that is too warm, a blaring TV, pain, or a receiver/decoder who is preoccupied, depressed, or disinterested.

In the process of communicating, encoders become decoders and decoders become encoders when they respond. The messages sent by the encoder are analyzed, interpreted, and related to the decoder's experiences and knowledge to determine their meaning. **Feedback** is used by the encoder to determine if the decoder received the message and accurately interpreted it.

Shannon-Weaver Model

A linear model, developed by Shannon and Weaver (1949), was one of the first communication models (Figure 6–1). In this model, the information source determines the message, which is transmitted via signals to the receiver, who interprets the message and determines its destination. The transmitter is the encoder of the message, and the receiver is the decoder (Shannon & Weaver, 1949). The concept of noise is unique to this model. Noise refers to a disturbance, such as environmental noise and psychological or perceptual distortion. The strength of this model is that it demonstrates a communication pathway; its weakness is that one-way communication does not depict reciprocal or transactional aspects of communication.

Source-Message-Channel-Receiver Model

Berlo's (1960) classic source-message-channel-receiver (SMCR) communication model depicts communication as a process (Figure 6–2). The SMCR model has a source, a message, a channel, and a receiver. The messages of the source depend on communication skills, attitudes, knowledge, social system, and culture. The messages with elements, structure, content, treatment, and code, are transmitted via sensory channels (seeing, hearing, touching, smelling, and tasting). The receiver interprets the messages through communication skills, attitudes, knowledge, social system, and culture (Northhouse & Northhouse, 1992). The strength of this model is that it clearly depicts the complexity of communication and portrays the influence of personal characteristics in sending and receiving messages. Its weakness is the lack of feedback.

Leary Model

Leary (1955) developed a reflexive model. This is a transactional, multidimensional model that stresses interactional and interpersonal relationships. Leary, a psychotherapist, designed this model based on observations of his own behavior with patients; that is, he observed that people "train" others to respond to them in ways that meet their needs. To illustrate, clients who prefer to be submissive act in ways that influence the message sender to assume a dominant approach. Conversely, those who prefer the dominant role condition others to behave submissively.

According to this model, all communication transactions can be viewed on two continua: dominance/submission and love/hate. Leary (1995) identified two rules that demonstrate how this model works. Rule one is that dominant or submissive behavior stimulates the opposite behavior in others. Rule two is that love or hate stimulate the same behavior in others. This model may be useful to nurses when they are teaching submissive clients to become advocates or working with unhappy, difficult patients.

Health Communication Model

These models provide the structure for the health communication model (HCM) presented by Northhouse and Northhouse (1992). The primary focus of the HCM is on relationships occurring in health-care settings (Figure 6–3). The model's three components are relationships, transactions, and contexts. It is applicable to any health-care professional, including nurses, physicians, social workers, health educators, pharmacists, and others.

Based on a systems perspective, the model includes the relationships with which nurses deal on a regular basis: nurse to client, nurse to other professional, nurse to significant other, and significant other to client. This model indicates the interdependence of these relationships. For example, how

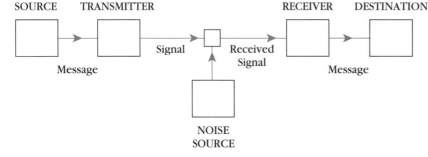

FIGURE 6-1. Shannon-Weaver model. (From Shannon, C. E., & Weaver, W. [1949]. *The mathematical theory of communication.* Champaign: University of Illinois Press, p. 72. Copyright 1949 by the Board of Trustees of the University of Illinois. Used with permission of the University of Illinois Press.)

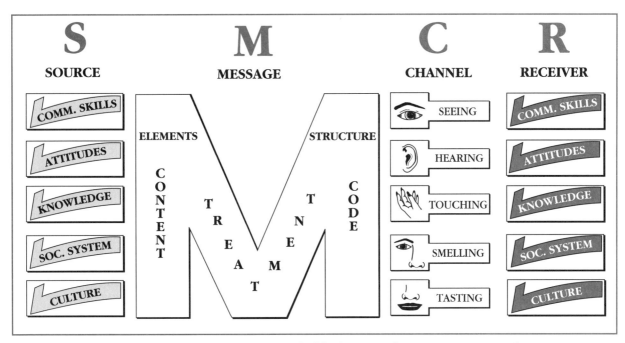

FIGURE 6-2. SMCR model. (From Berlo, D. K. [1960]. *The process of communication: An introduction to theory and practice.* New York: Holt, Rhinehart & Winston, p. 7, with permission.)

nurses communicate with other health-care providers influences the relationships of nurses with clients; likewise, how clients communicate with their social networks or significant others affect how they communicate with nurses (Northhouse & Northhouse, 1992). This model is particularly pertinent to nurses because it depicts the relationship clients have to significant others, a relationship that is often ignored in caring for clients.

Clients' personality characteristics, values, beliefs, and goals, plus their education, social networks, and ethnic and cultural experiences influence their interactions with nurses, other health professionals, and significant others. These same factors also influence nurses and other health professionals and shape their communication patterns. Therefore, three sets of individuals are involved in health communications: (1) professionals, (2) clients, and (3) significant others (Northhouse & Northhouse, 1992). The current changes in health care, with early discharge of clients with acute health problems, demands inclusion of family and significant others and enlarges

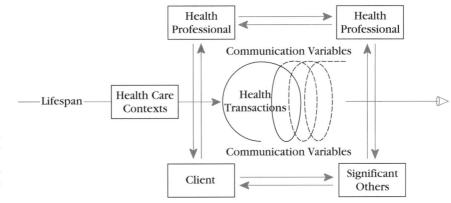

FIGURE 6-3. Health communication model. (Northhouse, P. G., & Northhouse, L. L. [1992]. *Health communication strategies for health professionals.* Norwalk, CT: Appleton & Lange, p. 16, with permission.)

the scope of the communication challenges of registered nurses.

The second major element of the HCM is transactions, that is, transactions between clients, significant others, and nurses (Northhouse & Northhouse, 1992). These transactions, both verbal and nonverbal, include the relationship components and the content of the health communication. Northhouse & Northhouse (1992) describe transactions as circles and spirals, illustrating that they are interactive and ongoing, occurring intermittently over the lifespan. The continuous feedback supports adjustment of health communication transactions to allow changes and message alterations. Health communication occurs over time and is ongoing, with changing variables and goals as clients and nurses learn and grow.

Contexts, the third major element in the model, are the settings in which the health communication occurs. These settings range from physicians' offices to hospital and outpatient settings, nursing homes, and clients' homes. The number of persons involved in the communication determines the complexity of the communication process. The number of interpersonal relationships increases with each additional person; therefore communication strategies for communication and teaching vary depending on the context.

The HMC is based on a systems perspective that provides a framework for health communication in a complex and changing health-care milieu. Thoughts, feelings, and attitudes, current roles, type of relationship (nurse-client, friend-friend), and personal history, including ethnic and cultural experiences, affect the accuracy with which messages are decoded.

ESSENTIAL INGREDIENTS OF EFFECTIVE COMMUNICATION

Trust, empathy, congruence, and positive regard have been identified as necessary for effective, therapeutic communication. Self-awareness and the ability to listen are basic and essential for effective communication that allows nurses to develop trusting relationships.

Variables in Therapeutic Communication

Therapeutic communication is a skill used "to help people overcome temporary stress, to get along with other people, to adjust to the unalterable, and to overcome psychological blocks which stand in the way of self-realization" (Ruesch, 1961,

p. 7). Some of the variables are trust, empathy, congruence, and respect.

Trust, a critical element of helping relationships, develops when clients feel that nurses accept and care about them. Trust is an essential part of the helping relationship that creates an environment in which clients are free to share and explore their feelings. It enables clients to depend on their nurses for qualities such as knowledge and integrity (Northhouse & Northhouse, 1992).

Empathy, the ability to "put oneself in the place of another and to see things" from the other's perspective (Patterson, 1985, p. 6), is essential for a therapeutic relationship (Olson & Iwasiw, 1989). Empathy is more than hearing the content of messages; empathy involves showing clients that nurses understand their plight. Nurses who empathize with clients and colleagues understand their experience and perspective. This understanding is then communicated to others verbally and nonverbally.

Verbal empathy involves the ability to listen and interpret another's statement, behavior, and feelings (Olson & Iwasiw, 1989). It accurately reflects what the client is experiencing. Verbal empathy is ongoing in a therapeutic nurse-client relationship. The empathic listener is able to "be with" clients in their world and sense what the experience is like for them (Mayeroff, 1971).

Empathic understanding of another's situation involves some risks. First, it may be difficult to understand the world from the view of clients with paraplegia or terminal illness, those who have been in jail, on welfare, in debt, and so forth (Wolvin & Coakley, 1988). By entering the world of clients with different conditions and lifestyles, nurses risk challenges to their values and beliefs, which then require reevaluation. There is also a risk of hearing something that one does not want to hear. Nurses can, however, develop empathy with their clients by identifying the feelings revealed by the sender and recalling situations in which they experienced similar feelings (Wolvin & Coakley, 1988).

Congruence is communicated when one's thoughts, feelings, and behavior are the same. Congruence is also known as **genuineness** (Patterson, 1985), which means that what is said is based on true feelings. It is not necessary to communicate every feeling or thought, but those that are communicated are based on what is real and true. The person who is genuine is nondefensive, spontaneous, and capable of self-disclosure (Patterson, 1985). Clients are intuitively sensitive and experience anxiety when nurses are incongruent. Clients are accepting when nurses are overwhelmed with too many clients, and will wait their turn, but they react negatively to nurses' nonverbal stress messages.

Respect, a nonpossessive caring, consists of "prizing, valuing, and liking" clients (Patterson, 1985, p. 59). Respect is communicated when the helper is able to listen in a genuine, nonjudgmental, and caring manner. It implies acceptance without demands or requirements to change. This can be especially challenging for nurses dealing with clients who do not participate in self-care. When nurses listen with empathy to clients, they increase their understanding of and respect for them.

Effective communication includes two additional necessary ingredients: self-awareness and listening. Being trustworthy, empathetic, congruent, and respectful depends on self-awareness. Effective communication depends on the ability to listen, a learned skill.

Self-awareness requires exploration of all aspects of one's thinking, feeling, and doing to develop personal and interpersonal knowledge and understanding (Burnard, 1992). Self-awareness is a gradual but continuous process of learning about how one thinks, feels, and behaves, with the goal of personal and interpersonal understanding so that one can learn "conscious use of the self" (Burnard, 1992, p. 180). Self-awareness begins with observation of what one is thinking and feeling while suspending judgment, interpretation, and understanding. Along with introspection, involvement with others and feedback from them are necessary since, introspection alone, without feedback, can be inaccurate and self-serving. Most people need some type of support and feedback for helping relationship to develop self-awareness (Kagen & Evans, 1995). A variety of approaches is available for developing self-awareness.

Self-awareness increases ego boundaries; that is, it allows one to differentiate between self and other (Burnard, 1992). It supports identification of problem ownership. Nurses with high levels of self-awareness are empathic and understanding of clients' problems; they are, at the same time, exquisitely aware that the problems "belong to" clients, who must ultimately resolve them. Without healthy self-awareness nurses can become emotionally enmeshed with clients' problems, losing the objectivity they need to be therapeutic and not recognizing client independence and autonomy.

Developmentally, the ability to **listen** is learned before the ability to speak (Purdy, 1991b). Listening, probably the most important communication skill, is critical for effective communication. A good listener focuses on the other person, without thoughts of self or even ideas about the content (Arnold, 1995). Listening and responding are complex cognitive, affective, and physiologic processes (Farley, 1992). Hearing sounds is a physiologic process, and the psychologic states of sender and receiver affect the cognitive interpretation of what is heard (Farley, 1992). Listening, an active process involving mind and body and verbal and nonverbal cues, allows nurses to be receptive to others' needs and concerns (Purdy, 1991b). Attending is the skill of focusing on the patient; it is a conscious process of being aware of what the other is saying or communicating (Burnard, 1992).

Burnard (1992) describes three zones of attending or attention (Figure 6–4). Zone 1 is consciously putting attention on something or someone outside of the self. Zone 2 is attention on one's thoughts and feelings, and Zone 3 involves fantasy. Zone 3 is self-focused, that is, what the nurse believes the client is saying. This is the zone of assumptions and interpretations. The danger of listening in Zone 3 is that the listener may well be wrong, and comments will leave the client feeling unheard, uncared for, and confused.

Listening with a focus on the client, with occasional moves to Zone 2, the domain of personal thoughts and feelings, allows clients to reveal who they are and what they need. It also allows nurses to maintain a therapeutic distance or appropriate ego boundaries, thus focusing on client problems without overidentifying. When nurses find themselves listening in Zone 3, it is important for them to take time for introspection and self-evaluation because personal problems, fatigue, and emotional distress interfere with listening. Self-awareness with self-evaluation enables nurses to deal constructively with their problems and free themselves to listen.

Listening or "hearing" another person includes attending to linguistic speech, paralinguistic speech, and nonverbal communication (Burnard, 1992). Linguistic speech includes the actual words, phrases, and metaphors used to relate feelings. Paralinguistic speech includes such speech components as accent, volume, pitch, and timing. Nonverbal communication is body language such as facial expressions, body position, gestures, and movements such as restlessness.

Listening, as attentive or active listening, thus entails all the senses, requires time, concentration, and energy, and includes verbal and nonverbal messages—their content as well as the feelings behind them. Active listening "is a dynamic process, whereby a person hears a message, decodes its meaning, and conveys an understanding about the meaning to the

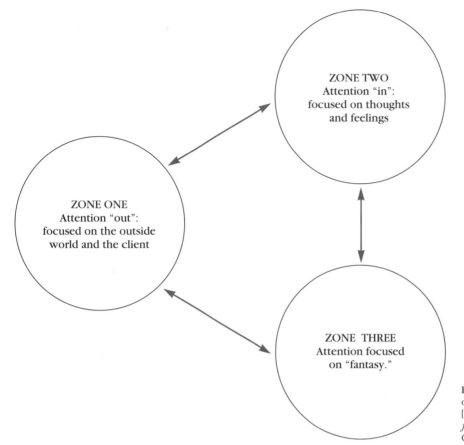

FIGURE 6-4. Three possible zones of attention. (From Burnard, P. [1992]. *Effective communication skills for health professionals*. New York: Chapman & Hall, with permission.)

sender" (Arnold, 1995, p. 202). It requires critical thinking and careful selection of responses based on previous conversations with the client. It is important to "quiet our inner voices" (Purdy, 1991a, p. 25) to listen. Active listening conveys caring.

Another way of looking at active listening is to think of it as "feeling listening" (Decker & Denney, 1992). Feeling listening involves the feelings behind the facts. It is the most important listening technique; without acknowledging feelings, we often lose messages. Using all of the senses, feeling listening conveys the acceptance and understanding of the listener to affirm others. Thus, an emotional connection is made.

Therapeutic listening, then, is nonjudgmental and also healing for clients and their families and colleagues (Purdy, 1991b). Listening with the other person as the focus enables the listener to be empathic or feel what the other is saying without judging or trying to change his or her behavior. This type of listening is quite different from collecting information for a client history. Understanding the illness in the cultural and biographical context of clients and their families demands that the nurse hear their story and focus on the meaning of the illness to them. Healing is supported by understanding the guilt, worries, lifestyle changes, and spiritual outcomes of the disease for clients and families. The meaning of the illness may be different for the client and family. Understanding the reactions of both clients and families thus allows nurses to support them as they "bridge the communication gap" and come to mutual understanding. This process not only prevents interpersonal crises but also allows clients and families to work cooperatively on solutions.

NONVERBAL FORMS OF COMMUNICATION

Nonverbal communication includes "all forms of human communication apart from verbal communication" (Jeffree, 1995, p. 145), that is, body language, tone of voice, eye contact, sounds, use of space, and touch (Northhouse & Northhouse, 1992). Often nonverbal communication discloses more about the feelings of clients than their verbal communication because it is less controlled. The ability to identify, interpret, and validate nonverbal symbols is a powerful skill for nurses. Likewise, the nonverbal communication of nurses is constantly being evaluated and interpreted by clients, so it is necessary for nurses to be aware of the messages they are sending.

Clear communication occurs when the verbal and the nonverbal messages are congruent. Nonverbal communication can be intentional or nonintentional (Northhouse & Northhouse, 1992). Intentional nonverbal communication occurs when body language and facial expressions match verbal content. A nurse who is teaching a cardiac client the dangers of a high-fat, high-sodium diet will adopt a serious facial expression that is congruent with the seriousness of the message. Nonintentional nonverbal communication is evident when nurses sound positive, but their facial expression and body language appear sad and they avoid eye contact. Indeed, when the biopsy report is due, clients often search the facial expressions of their caregivers for cues about results. Nurses need to be aware of their nonverbal communication since it is confusing when the nonverbal and the verbal messages are not congruent.

Nonverbal communication increases effective communication by (1) expressing feelings and emotions, (2) regulating interactions, (3) validating verbal messages, (4) maintaining self-image, and (5) maintaining relationships (Northhouse & Northhouse, 1992). First, nonverbal communication identifies feelings from joy and happiness to helplessness and hopelessness. Sensitive assessment and accurate identification of nonverbal messages encourage and support clients' discussion of feelings. They experience relief and understanding when their feelings are sensitively and accurately identified.

Second, nonverbal signals indicate when people wish to participate. The nonverbal communication of clients who answer in monosyllables while watching TV clearly indicates that they do not want to communicate. It may be that clients do not want to discuss the topic or that they are watching their favorite program and the timing is poor. Third, the nonverbal message is validated when the verbal and nonverbal are congruent. This is essential for effective communication. If the timing of the teaching is poor, communication validation permit the client and nurse to determine a mutually convenient time.

Fourth, clients maintain their self-image in a variety of nonverbal ways. Nonverbal cues may indicate a self-image of one who has some control over life. Nurses may be more successful with such patients if they allow them control and choices. For example, clients who have a self-image of being well-dressed and well-groomed appreciate nurses who help them maintain this self-image. Finally, nonverbal communication conveys relational messages including affection, control, and status (Northhouse & Northhouse, 1992). To illustrate, when clients and their families ask the nurse to join them in their meeting with the physician, they are communicating acceptance and status of the nurse as an important part of the team.

It is important to note that nonverbal cues have multiple meanings; no single cue (gesture, facial expression, or appearance) consistently reveals inner feelings (Northhouse & Northhouse, 1992). Nurses, therefore, must remember to verify with clients and others when they respond to nonverbal cues. To illustrate, a facial scowl can be interpreted as indigestion, anger, or discomfort. Interpretation includes the nurse's knowledge about the client plus validating with the client what the nurse interprets. One approach is to say, "Tell me if I'm wrong; are you feeling angry?" or, "You look as if something is bothering you." Both of these statements allow clients to express what they are feeling if they choose to do so.

Preverbal sounds are considered nonverbal communication. Preverbal sounds are moans and groans communicating physical or emotional pain; screams indicate a plea for help, and shouts may be joyful or sorrowful (Kurz-Cringle, 1988). Preverbal sounds are powerful and often create powerful feelings in others.

Dimensions of Nonverbal Communication

Nonverbal communication, "a complex and multifaceted phenomenon," can be divided into five categories: (1) kinesics, (2) proxemics, (3) paralinguistics, (4) touch, and (5) physical and environmental factors (Northhouse & Northhouse, 1992, p. 124).

Kinesics are behaviors of movement or body motion as nonverbal communication techniques (Northhouse & Northhouse, 1992; Pagano, Ragan, & Booton, 1992). Kinetic behaviors include gestures, facial expressions, and gaze. Because kinetic behaviors are culturally bound, nonverbal signals are not universal, much as verbal intonations can alter meanings of words (Pagano et al., 1992). Interpreting nonverbal signals requires skill and practice. Nonverbal communications must always be validated, to prevent miscommunications.

To complicate the process, clients may purposely present facial expressions that are incongruent with their feelings. A client may verbalize the presence of pain while smiling. Conversely, a client may deny pain while frowning or even crying. When verbal expressions and nonverbal communications are incongruent, the nonverbal communication is probably more trustworthy (Boggs, 1995). It is therefore necessary to evaluate communications holistically.

Proxemics is concerned with personal use of space or environment (Hall, 1963). Personal space, the invisible boundary surrounding a person, is fluid and changes with circumstances (Sullivan, 1995). Like kinetic behaviors, use of personal space varies from culture to culture and also between genders. On average, public space is defined as 12 feet, social space from 4 to 12 feet, personal space from 18 inches to 4 feet, and intimate space from 18 inches to body contact (Hall, 1963). Personal space provides "a sense of identity, security, and control" (Northhouse & Northhouse, 1992, p. 131).

Intimate contact is common as nurses provide physical care for clients, often without concern for clients' reactions or feelings. Sensitivity to personal space is shown by entering another's intimate space slowly and with permission, providing privacy and minimizing exposure, and using the minimum number of people for a procedure (Sullivan, 1995). Invasion of intimate space is less threatening to clients if they have a therapeutic relationship with the nurse; in situations in which procedures must be done, taking a few minutes to establish some rapport can reduce discomfort.

Paralinguistics, known also as paralanguage or vocalization, is the "oral delivery of a verbal message, expressed through tone of voice and inflection, sighing, or crying" (Boggs, 1995, p. 189). Sounds such as "ah" or "um" are voice sounds that influence message interpretation. Each person's voice is unique; indeed, people can be identified by their tape-recorded voices. Nurses need to be cognizant of what their voice pitch and intensity communicate to clients.

Touch is important to humans. It "expresses pleasure, reassurance, and comfort" (Vortherms, 1991). Touch is powerful when it communicates caring and helps establish rapport. Conversely, touch can communicate control, power, and authority as when one holds someone's hands to prevent interference with a procedure. Touch creates anxiety and discomfort in those who simply dislike being touched or do not understand the meaning of the touch.

Careful evaluation of cultural norms, family norms, and gender issues need to precede use of touch, since it affects the reactions of the one who touches and the one is touched. Touch can ease clients' sense of isolation and enhance relationships, but it can also be misinterpreted as imposing more intimacy than was intended. Nurses must therefore assess their relationship with clients along with cultural, familial, and gender issues before using touch as a therapeutic intervention.

Estabrooks (1989) describes three types of touch: caring, task, and protective. Caring touch is rooted in nurses' capacity to care. It subsumes comforting and encouraging touch. Encouraging touch includes affectionate hugs whereas comforting touch is hand holding or forehead stroking. Task touch is touch used in performing procedures, and it can be positively or negatively experienced by clients, depending on the approach of the nurse. Rough touch and controlling touch, even when necessary, are mainly experienced by clients as negative experiences. Protective touch includes protecting clients from hurting themselves, for example, by extubating themselves. Use of gloves, a form of protective touch, can create an emotional barrier.

Physical and environmental factors, such as furniture arrangement, lighting, noise, color, and room temperature, affect communication. In the acute care setting, most communication encounters occur in the treatment room, at the bedside, or in the hall. No matter where they occur, it is important to provide privacy and attentive listening. Communication is enhanced when nurses, clients, families, and other professionals arrange for a conference room. Arranging furniture to eliminate barriers between the nurse and others, sitting at eye level, and ensuring comfortable chairs while respecting personal space invite therapeutic communications. Arranging the environment in clients' homes is more challenging, but the same principles apply.

COMMUNICATION TECHNIQUES

Several factors influence effective communication. Preparation of self facilitates effective communication. Even a brief encounter can be powerful when nurses give undivided attention to clients who are hurting, confused, or lonely.

Timing. A nurse who is focused on the client may have unexpected opportunities to communicate. For example, while being given an intravenous medication, the client who is struggling with a problem or situation may give cues. This is the "teachable moment" or "window of opportunity." A comment such as "I will never see my son again" could indicate many concerns. A response of "Help me understand more about your concerns" lets clients know that they have been heard and allows them to talk a bit more. If the discussion will take more time than you have, set a time to return to talk about the specific topic.

Clients who are dealing with a difficult problem often test nurses to identify those who can listen to what they are saying without getting upset or judging them. For instance, clients who are dying or fear they are dying may mention death and observe the nurse's reaction. If the nurse changes the subject or becomes anxious, clients change the topic. Some nurses are uncomfortable when clients talk about such topics as death or sexual activity. It is, therefore, important to refer clients to the appropriate professional for support and counseling.

At times, clients or family members will tell nurses a great deal about themselves and their worries and problems, and they may not want to talk about them again. They may have needed to say it out loud or they may regret having mentioned it at all. Whatever their reason, it is clients who determine the content of communication. If clients or family members verbalize that they are going to hurt themselves or someone else, nurses must intervene. Confidentiality is not an issue in this situation.

Environment. Communication is enhanced by physical and environmental privacy. Since clients may be uncomfortable talking about personal concerns in an area where others can overhear, it is important to provide a private area where the interview will not be overheard or interrupted. Likewise, clients are uncomfortable overhearing professionals give personal and detailed information to other clients or families. Waiting rooms in both hospitals and physician offices are areas where clients often receive information about surgical or laboratory outcomes within hearing range of others. Not only does this violate confidentiality, it also concerns those who overhear. Unfortunately, this is a common problem but one that nurses can change as they serve as role models of good communication and manage client environments.

Provide an environment that is quiet and without interruptions. In the acute care or clinic setting it may be necessary to put a "do not disturb" sign on the door. Providing privacy in the home is more challenging. You may need to ask family members to leave the room. At other times you will want to communicate with family members in private. Rooms that are neither too cold nor too warm and clients and family members who are comfortable facilitate communication.

Preparing Yourself. When preparing for interviews, the first step is to observe yourself. Be relaxed and unhurried and prepare to spend the time you need for assessment. Remember, your nonverbal messages are powerful and may communicate more than verbal messages. It is important, therefore, to be congruent even as you assess the congruence of others.

First, sit at eye level. If the client is in bed, sit in a chair rather than standing over the client. Standing over people and looking down on them communicates that nurses have the power and does not invite sharing. When nurses sit beside clients, there is a sense of shared control as opposed to domination. Sitting in a chair also communicates that you have time and are not on your way out of the door.

Second, do not cross your arms since this communicates a closed and defensive attitude (Burnard, 1992). Third, leaning slightly toward clients encourages them to talk, thus increasing feelings of being understood. And finally, eye contact is important for most people. Remember that for some cultures eye contact is not as comfortable as in Western cultures. When appropriate, eye contact should be sustained while avoiding staring, which can be intimidating. Observe the eye contact of others and note when they look away or down.

During an interview, it is better to write only necessary information so that clients are not distracted; do not ask a series of questions that may make clients feel as if they are being interrogated (Pagano et al., 1992). Note nonverbal communications such as tears and body movements, twisting, turning, or hand wringing, which may indicate sadness and anxiety, and posture, such as lying in the fetal position, which can indicate pain or depression.

Assessment. Listen for themes (Arnold, 1995). Listening for themes includes identifying what clients are not saying. The following are some examples:

- "I'm worried about having a cardiac catheterization" may indicate that the client needs additional information about the procedure, or it may mean that the client is anxious and needs to talk.
- "I know that if I have a cardiac catheterization I will never get out of the hospital alive" changes the focus from a generalized worry to a specific concern about dying.
- "My wife needs me, and I wonder if I would be better off just to retire and be sedentary" introduces a relationship concern.

Listen carefully for the theme and assess accurately to respond in a therapeutic manner.

Comprehensive and objective assessment of communication style allows nurses to understand how their clients are coping (Arnold, 1995). Some cope by talking a great deal about what is happening to them, for example, while others withdraw and think; some give details and others omit significant information. To maintain or regain some control over what is happening to them, clients may be aggressive, complaining, abusive, or use humor inappropriately. Responding to the underlying feelings enables clients to focus more realistically on their concerns and supports their coping.

Questions or Statements

The ability of nurses to ask appropriate, effective questions enhances nurse-client relationships, provides important information for planning nursing care, and helps people explore and clarify their feelings, identify options, and evaluate consequences of their decisions. Use questions judiciously; that is, do not use questions "to manipulate, challenge and control" (Purdy, 1991a, p. 50). Skillful use of questions encourages clients to talk about themselves to explore and clarify what they are thinking and feeling, thus providing support. Questions are either open-ended or closed. Closed questions are those that can be answered with a "yes" or "no" or with specific information. Examples are "How old are you?"; "Where do you live?"; "Have you had this problem before?" Open-ended questions provide the opportunity to elaborate, and therefore provide more information (Burnard, 1992). They allow clients to express their interpretations of what is happening to them or in their lives. Examples are "Could you tell me a little more about that?"; "How did you feel when that happened?"; "How will your actions make the situation better?"

Open-ended questions are more effective in non-emergency clinical situations (Arnold, 1995). Only clients can identify their major concerns, and these may not be at all what nurses anticipate. Communication is blocked until major concerns are addressed. The focused question, closely related to open-ended questions, limits the parameters of the response and is used when a generalized description may be too vague to describe the client's personal experience (Arnold, 1995). Examples of focused questions are "Can you tell me more about your domestic situation?"; "Can you give me an example of when you felt you had no power or control?"

Leading questions, value-laden questions, and "why" questions tend to limit information gathering and leave people feeling judged or misjudged. For example, when nurses suspect that child abuse, spousal abuse, or elder abuse is occurring, collecting information becomes a challenge since most abusers are not prone to confessions. A leading question such as "Have you stopped beating your wife?" contains the assumption that the person is beating his wife and is difficult to answer without implicating oneself (Burnard, 1992). Value-laden questions, those that reflect the values of the interviewer, suggest what one should or should not do or feel. An example of a value-laden question is "Do you feel guilty about beating your wife?" The implication is that he should feel guilty about beating his wife. These types of questions should be avoided.

Finally, "why" questions imply a need to justify one's actions. This puts people on the defensive, especially since they are frequently unable to answer them. Instead of "why" questions, use open-ended questions that both support and allow exploration of feelings, thus increasing understanding.

Exploratory questions help clients look at alternative decisions and choices. This often helps them feel less like victims by identifying options and gaining some control over what is happening to them. These questions are asked "to encourage, to learn, not to confirm" what is already known (Purdy, 1991a, p. 52). Examples include questions such as "How will this therapy affect your family?"; "Have you thought about how your illness affects your daughter?"

The paraphrasing statement is often used to follow up on clarifying questions (Purdy, 1991a). Nurses paraphrase when they repeat what clients have said in their own words while keeping the meaning intact. Paraphrasing checks for accuracy while it gives clients an opportunity to correct any misunderstandings. It also helps clients as they hear what they are saying or feeling. It may also communicate to clients that the nurse is empathic and understanding (Purdy, 1991a). Paraphrasing is especially useful early in a relationship or when new data are introduced (Arnold, 1995).

Clarifying questions are those that seek additional information. It takes practice to ask clarifying questions that are not probing. Some examples of clarifying questions are "How did you feel when the doctor said that you did not qualify for the rehab unit?"; "What were you feeling as your spouse and the physician discussed your prognosis?"

The goals of supportive questions are to support

clients while helping them to explore the values and criteria used to make a decision and evaluate behavioral consequences (Purdy, 1991a). When asking supportive questions, it is important to be nonjudgmental and nondirective. The purpose is to help clients examine all angles of their decisions. Examples are "Do you feel that your choice of treatment is in the best interests of you and your family?"; "Have you examined the consequences of the alternative choices?"

Summarizing questions are generally used at the end of the interview. Nurses synthesize and interpret what they believe clients have said. Because these summaries contain interpretations, or what nurses think clients are saying, nurses must be especially skillful in asking these questions. An example of a summary question is "You have said that . . . Am I correct?" or "You believe your options include . . . Correct me if I'm wrong." It is important to base the summary question on what the client has said.

Additional communication techniques include restatement, reflection, reframing, validation, and the use of silence. Restatement of what the person has said can provide a sharper focus and may highlight a specific part of the communication (Arnold, 1995). This technique is especially helpful when clients overgeneralize, are repetitive in their comments, make irrational statements, or catastrophize. Restatement is a way to challenge what is said without challenging it directly. It is a useful technique when the subject matter is especially anxiety provoking (Kurz-Cringle, 1988). For example, when a client says "I feel so sad," a restatement "You are sad" communicates feedback that the message was heard and judgment was not passed. Do not use this technique too often or it loses its power.

Reflections are a way to focus on emotional aspects and help people see the relationship between content and emotions (Arnold, 1995). This technique can validate the universal experience of having conflicting emotions about an issue. Sensitivity to readiness to look at feelings and timing of the technique are vital to successful use of reflections. An example is "It sounds as if you feel angry or disappointed about the fact that your wife is not here."

Reframing is a cognitive process that is used when clients express distorted or irrational thoughts (Sundeen, Stuart, Rankin, & Cohen, 1989). The goal is to help clients change the way they view an experience. Reframing requires identification of an element in the situation that can be useful. An example is the client with a family history of cardiovascular disease who is unable to control his or her cholesterol levels. The statement "I'm a failure because no matter what I do my cholesterol level is high" might be reframed as "Your cholesterol levels demonstrate how well you take care of yourself considering your genetic history." Reframing can help clients put their thoughts and feelings into perspective and remove irrational guilt feelings.

Validation questions or comments are used to validate the message or information nurses hear or observe (Taylor et al., 1993). Validation is repeating what the client said. This technique is useful when the nurse has doubts or needs confirmation, but it should be used infrequently. Using this technique too often leads clients to wonder whether the nurse is listening. For example, a validation response to a client with chronic rheumatoid arthritis who has been crying might be "It is really hard wanting to do for your family but feeling too tired and having too much pain."

Silence is also a powerful intervention when used appropriately. Silence provides clients' time to think about what they have just said or want to say. It allows nurses time to assess their feelings, to foster acceptance and continued sharing. Silence is often comfortable but can increase the stress of both client and nurse. Preverbal sounds such as "Um" or gestures can communicate that the nurse is listening and waiting for the client to continue.

Nontherapeutic Communication

Just as a number of techniques support effective communication, a number of ways of relating are nontherapeutic. The most devastating nontherapeutic technique is failure to listen attentively, which is interpreted as lack of interest or caring (Sundeen et al., 1989). In addition, failure to explore and clarify to understand clients' feelings leave them feeling unvalued, uncared for, and lonely.

Nurses exert power and control in subtle ways. Talking in a loud voice, giving demands in the form of directions, and not providing people an opportunity to respond instigate feelings of powerlessness. Encouraging clients to agree to decisions that have already been made contributes to their feeling of lack of control. Persuasion by repetition, persistence, and questioning is a way of "forcing" clients, leaving them feeling coerced (Hewison, 1995). This is commonly done when clients do not want tests or procedures or have difficulty following the institutional routines.

Talking over or around clients, talking about them in their presence without involving them in the conversation, and talking to them as if they were children clearly identifies who is in charge and who has the power (Hewison, 1995). And finally, terms of endearment such as "dearie," "honey," or "granny" demean and strip clients of their identity and uniqueness as does the use of the first-person pronoun when you discuss activities.

Remember that some people do not want to discuss their problems with nurses (Jarrett & Payne, 1995). They may fear losing control and choose not to share, or may not want to upset the nurse or "tempt fate" by identifying unfavorable outcomes (Jarrett & Payne, 1995). They also may have a confidante and not need the nurse or choose to deal with their situations without expressing their feelings to nurses.

Gossiping about clients is nontherapeutic, inappropriate, and violates confidentiality. Clients should be discussed only with appropriate professional personnel and in areas where others cannot overhear.

Responses such as, "don't worry, everything will be all right," "you ought to be grateful that it is not worse," or "stop crying" are meant to be reassuring but are nontherapeutic and damaging. These statements discount what clients are feeling and stimulate guilt or anger. Nurses frequently respond in these ways because the clients' obvious discomfort makes them anxious. The responses are therefore likely for the nurse's benefit and not the clients'. Self-assessment is needed for nurses to identify what is making them uncomfortable.

Teaching and providing information is an important nursing intervention, but giving advice is nontherapeutic and stifles client-family decision-making (Sundeen et al., 1989). Giving advice may be viewed by clients as a promise or assurance that things will work out in a certain way. It is essential that you do not promise a particular outcome.

KEY POINTS

- Communication is a multidimensional process or transaction, involving verbal and nonverbal techniques, written, visual, and auditory materials.
- Communication is a reciprocal process in which sender and receiver participate simultaneously.
- Participants in effective communication include a source/encoder, who sends the message, and a receiver/decoder, who receives, interprets, and responds to the message.
- Effective communication is enhanced by the relationship that shapes how content is both given and received.
- Empathy is the ability to interpret and understand another person's experience.
- Genuineness or congruence occurs when one's thoughts, feelings, and behavior convey the same meaning.
- Self-awareness, the gradual and continuous process of understanding about how one thinks, feels, and behaves, increases ego boundaries.
- Listening includes attending to words, phrases, and metaphors and focusing attention on clients and families.
- Nonverbal communication is more powerful and revealing than the message's verbal content.
- Open-ended questions allow clients to reveal and discuss what is most important to them.
- It is more effective to avoid leading questions, value-laden questions, and "why" questions.
- Reframing is a powerful cognitive technique to expel distorted and irrational thinking.
- False reassurance is nontherapeutic and damaging to clients and families because it discounts feelings and stimulates guilt.

CHAPTER EXERCISES

1. Answer the question "Who am I" by listing words or phrases that describe yourself. Next, categorize the words or phrases as roles, personality, and so on. Give a person whom you trust, and with whom you are comfortable, your original list and ask for reactions to your descriptions. Discuss and compare your thoughts.

2. Ask three friends to go with you to a movie or theater and mingle with a large group. Have each describe what was seen and experienced. Respond to the following questions and share your answers:
   a. "How did I feel?"
   b. "What were the people doing and saying?"
   c. "What was the attitude or mood of the group?"
   d. "Was I comfortable?"

3. Keep a diary of your actions, verbal and nonverbal communications, and self-talk for a day. Try to stay focused. At the end of the day read and think about the day. Identify the areas where you could have been more effective. Would different self-talk evoke different attitudes? Were your nonverbal and verbal communications congruent? Is there a skill that you would like to practice?

4. Select a difficult person, colleague, or family member and listen to him or her without interrupting for 15 minutes. Focus on the person's feelings. At completion, identify his or her nonverbal communication and your nonverbal communication. Evaluate your feelings about the person before and after listening.

5. Video yourself doing interviews, and assess your verbal and nonverbal techniques. Evaluate the video to increase your awareness of your communication skills.

REFERENCES

Arnold, E. (1995). Developing therapeutic communication skills in the nurse-client relationship. In E. Arnold & K. U. Boggs (Eds.). *Interpersonal relationship: Professional communication skills for nurses* (2nd ed.) (pp. 198–232). Philadelphia: Saunders.

Berlo, D. K. (1960). *The process of communication: An introduction to theory and practice.* New York: Holt, Rinehart, & Winston.

Boggs, K. (1995). Communication styles. In E. Arnold & K. U. Boggs (Eds.). *Interpersonal relationship: Professional communication skills for nurses* (2nd ed.) (pp. 187–197). Philadelphia: Saunders.

Burnard, P. (1992). *Effective communication skills for health professionals.* New York: Chapman & Hall.

Decker, B., & Denney, J. (1992). *You've got to be heard to be believed.* New York: St. Martin's Press.

Estabrooks, C. A. (1989). Touch: A nursing strategy in the intensive care unit. *Heart and Lung, 18*(4), 392–401.

Farley, M. J. (1992). Thought and talk: The intrapersonal component of human communication. *American Operating Room Nurses' Journal, 56*(3), 481–484.

Hall, E. (1963). *Man's image in medicine and anthropology.* New York: International University Press.

Hewison, A. (1995). Nurses' power in interactions with patients. *Journal of Advanced Nursing, 21,* 75–82.

Jarrett, N., & Payne, S. (1995). A selective review of the literature on nurse-patient communication: Has the patient's contribution been neglected? *Journal of Advanced Nursing, 22,* 72–78.

Jeffree, P. (1995). *The practice nurse: Theory and practice* (2nd ed.). London: Chapman & Hall.

Johnson, J. R. (1994). The communication training needs of registered nurses. *Journal of Continuing Education in Nursing, 25*(5), 213–218.

Kagen, C., & Evans, J. (1995). *Professional interpersonal skills for nurses.* San Diego: Singular.

Kozier, B., Erb, B., Blais, K., & Wilkinson, J. M. (1995). *Fundamentals of nursing concepts, process, and practice* (5th ed.). New York: Addison-Wesley.

Kurz-Cringle, R. (1988). Communication. In J. B. Flynn & P. B. Heffron (Eds.). *Nursing from concept to practice* (2nd ed.) (pp. 307–328). Norwalk, CT: Appleton & Lange.

Leary, T. (1955). The theory and measurement methodology of interpersonal communication. *Psychiatry, 18,* 147–161.

Mayeroff, M. (1971). *On caring.* New York: Harper & Row.

Northhouse, P. G., & Northhouse, L. L. (1992). *Health communication strategies for health professionals* (2nd ed.). Norwalk, CT: Appleton & Lange.

Olson, J. K., & Iwasiw, C. L. (1989). Nurses, verbal empathy in four types of client situations. *The Canadian Journal of Nursing Research, 21*(2), 39–51.

Patterson, C. H. (1985). *The therapeutic relationship: Foundations for an eclectic psychotherapy.* Monterey, CA: Brooks/Cole.

Pagano, M. P., Ragan, S. L., & Booton, D. (1992). *Communication skills for professional nurses.* London: Sage.

Purdy, M. (1991a). Intrapersonal/interpersonal listening. In D. Borisoff & M. Purdy (Eds.). *Listening in everyday life* (pp. 21–58). New York: University Press of America.

Purdy, M. (1991b). What is listening? In D. Borisoff & M. Purdy (Eds.). *Listening in everyday life* (pp. 3–19). New York: University Press of America.

Ruesch, J. (1961). *Therapeutic communication.* New York: Norton.

Shannon, C. E., & Weaver, W. (1949). *The mathematical theory of communication.* Urbana: University of Illinois Press.

Sullivan, V. (1995). Bridges and barriers in the therapeutic rela-tionship. In E. Arnold & K. U. Boggs (Eds.). *Interpersonal relationship: Professional communication skills for nurses* (2nd ed.) (pp. 107–126). Philadelphia: Saunders.

Sundeen, S. J., Stuart, G. W., Rankin, E. A. D., & Cohen, S. A. (1989). *Nurse-client interaction: Implementing the nursing process.* St. Louis: Mosby.

Taylor, C., Lillis, C., & LeMone, P. (1993). *Fundamentals of nursing: The art and science of nursing care* (2nd ed.) (pp. 322–342). Philadelphia: Lippincott.

Vortherms, R. C. (1991). Clinically improving communication through touch. *Journal of Gerontological Nursing, 17*(5), 6–10.

Watzlawick, P., Beavin, J. H., & Jackson, D. D. (1967). *Pragmatics of human communication: A study of interactional patterns, pathologies, and paradoxes.* New York: Norton.

Wolvin, A., & Coakley, C. G. (1988). *Listening* (3rd ed.). Dubuque, IA: William C. Brown.

Chapter 7

CRITICAL THINKING

Rebecca Parrish
Genevieve M. Bartol

CHAPTER OBJECTIVES

On completion of
this chapter, the reader
will be able to:

1. Define concepts in the process of critical thinking.
2. Explain the identifying assumptions of critical thinking.
3. Discuss the judgments needed in clinical decision-making.
4. Apply the components of critical analysis to a given nursing practice situation.
5. Analyze problem-solving skills needed in nursing practice case studies.

KEY TERMS

Critical Thinking
Reflective Thinking
Reactive Thinking
Problem Identification
Data Collection
Hypothesis Testing

Induction
Deduction
Assumption
  Identification
Concept Formation

Interpretation of Data
Application of Principles
Interpretation of
  Feelings, Attitudes,
  and Values

W hat is critical thinking? What sort of images do the words bring to your mind? Do you visualize a person who finds fault with everyone and everything? Or do you visualize Rodin's famous sculpture of *The Thinker*? Perhaps it is something you do not care about or would rather not consider. You may see it as only the current craze of educators and the newest chapter title for nursing textbooks. Then again, you may have been taught that thinking should not be critical but inclusive, with all sides of an issue given equal weight. Perhaps you were taught that nice people are not critical. At this point you may want to get on with more practical matters, but hopefully you are curious enough to explore the term a bit more. This chapter gives you an opportunity to examine the authors' critical thinking.

Some suggest that critical thinking is just the latest buzzword (Cassel & Congleton, 1993). The proliferation of journal articles, monographs, essays, conference papers, and books devoted to exploring critical thinking testifies to the current interest but also suggests a closer look at the term is warranted. The denotative meanings of **critical** include "being related to criticism (the act of making judgments); based on or in accordance with the principles of criticism; characterized by careful analysis, and inclined to find fault" (Webster, 1979). **Thinking** is defined as a mental action, cognition, or judgment. (Webster, 1979). One may surmise that **critical thinking** is a special type of thinking designed for a specific purpose.

HISTORICAL PERSPECTIVE

The concept of critical thinking dates back at least to Socrates in ancient Greece. Dewey (1910; 1933) prompted educators to pay attention to how we think and to teach students how to think. Glaser's (1941) and Black's (1952) writings represent efforts to integrate clinical thinking into education (cited in Castle & Congleton, 1993). Paul (1990) reviewed the efforts to teach reasoning in the 1930s and the 1960s. McPeck (1990) pointed out that before 1980 few schools were concerned with teaching critical thinking, and even fewer theoretical analyses of the concept existed. According to McPeck, he had "to search disparate sources to find any sustained published discussions of critical thinking" (p. 1) when he researched the topic in 1979–80. In 1990, Facione gathered a panel of 48 educators and scholars, including leading figures in critical thinking theory to work toward a consensus on the role of

critical thinking in educational assessment and instruction. Facione and Facione (1996) reported that the expert researchers and theoreticians described critical thinking as "the purposeful, self-regulatory judgment which results in interpretation, analysis, evaluation and inference, as well as the explanation of the evidential, conceptual, methodological, criteriological, or contextural considerations on which that judgment was based" (p. 129). As you read this chapter, you will see that despite this consensual statement, the literature is replete with definitions and descriptions of critical thinking. Rubenfeld and Scheffer (1995) wrote an interactive textbook on critical thinking that uses Paul's description of critical thinking: "The art of thinking about your thinking while you are thinking in order to make your thinking better: more clear, more accurate and more defensible" (p. xi). It is in the spirit of this definition that we hope you will read this chapter.

CRITICAL THINKING IN NURSING

Nurses have long been taught to use the nursing process to guide their practice. The nursing process provides a structure for using knowledge and thinking to provide holistic care for individuals, families, groups, and communities. The process can be used with all theoretical frameworks and clients in all settings. Although its components may be expressed in slightly different ways, the nursing process is basically a problem-solving method that has served nurses well by helping them use empathic and intellectual processes with scientific knowledge to assess, diagnose, plan, implement, and evaluate nursing care and patient outcomes. When used appropriately, the nursing process involves critical thinking.

The increasing diversity and complexity of nursing practice and the exponential growth of knowledge requires nurses who can think critically. Nurses must master the reasoning skills needed to process growing volumes of information. When nurses assess patients, the data they gather needs to be organized into meaningful patterns. Responses to treatment and care need to be evaluated continuously to determine whether the nursing diagnosis was appropriate and the intended outcome achieved. Even one additional piece of information related to the patient may change the whole configuration and require redefinition of the problem. In nursing, situations change so rapidly that reliance on conventional methods, procedure manuals, or traditions to guide judgments about the appropriate nursing action required is insufficient.

Critical thinking requires attention to many factors. Complex legal, ethical, organizational, and professional factors are involved in seemingly simple decisions and require critical thinking skills. For example, nurses consider ethical factors (e.g., keeping patient information confidential) and scheduling factors (e.g., when to admit visitors) when they decide not to admit visitors to a unit between 10 A.M. and 12 noon because patients are participating in a support group in the commons room. Visitors passing by the commons room may compromise patient confidentiality.

Nurses make inferences, differentiate facts from opinions, evaluate the credibility of the sources of information, and make decisions, all of which are skills needed for critical thinking. Because each of these skills can be learned, at least to some extent, an individual's potential to become an effective critical thinker can be enhanced.

Critical thinking depends on knowledge. Nurses take courses in the biological and social sciences and the humanities to acquire a strong foundation on which to base their nursing judgments. Using information from one subject to shed light on another subject requires critical thinking skills. Since nurses deal holistically with human responses, they draw meaningful information from many other subject areas to understand data and plan effective interventions.

Conceptually, it may be argued that general critical thinking abilities enhance the ability to make good clinical judgments. Nurses can apply theoretical knowledge to specific clinical situations, thereby enhancing clinical judgment and decision-making skills. This ability to apply learning enables nurses to expand and modify existing knowledge to accommodate new situations as well as simplify or speed up the task of learning and performing in the new situation. For example, nurses use critical thinking when applying knowledge of physics (principles related to levers, fulcrums, and balance) and biology (anatomy) to transfer a patient from the bed to the chair safely. Because educational programs cannot provide students with all the information they need to deal with every nursing situation, students must learn to be critical thinkers.

DEFINITIONS OF CRITICAL THINKING

What is critical thinking? Some nursing educators would argue that it is really the same as the nursing process (Jones & Brown, 1993; Kintgen-Andrews, 1991; White, Beardslee, Peters, Supples, 1990;

Woods, 1993). Others insist that although the nursing process requires critical thinking, critical thinking is much more. It is generally maintained, however, that critical thinking is a valuable skill or set of skills capable of being learned and taught (Smith, 1990; Facione & Facione, 1996).

Critical thinking is often considered a special, even rare, skill. Because the characteristics of critical thinking match those of sound clinical judgments (Case, 1994), critical thinking is reviewed as a highly desirable skill. A review of the nursing literature indicates that there is no general agreement of what critical thinking is. Definitions abound in the nursing literature, Table 7–1 gives a sampling.

The definitions have common elements. Critical thinking is viewed as engaging in a purposeful cognitive activity directed toward establishing a belief or map of action. Each definition speaks to the need for a person to actively process and evaluate information, to validate existing knowledge, and to create new knowledge. Each echoes Dewey's (1933) urging to employ reflective thinking "of the kind that turns a subject over in the mind and giving it seri-

TABLE 7 – 1. Definitions and Descriptions of Critical Thinking

Definition	Source	Date
"The rational examination of ideas, inferences, assumptions, principles, arguments, conclusions, issues, statements, beliefs and actions" (p. 5).	Bandman & Bandman	1988
"Reflective and reasonable thinking about nursing problems without a single solution and is focused on deciding what to believe and do" (p. 352).	Kataoka-Yahiro & Saylor	1994
"A process and cognitive skill that functions in identifying and defining problems and opportunities for improvement; generating, examining and evaluating options; reaching conclusions and decisions; and creating and using criteria to evaluate decisions" (p. 101).	Case	1994
"Reasonable and reflective thinking that is focused on deciding what to believe or do" (p. 152).	Kingten-Andrews	1991

ous and consecutive consideration" (p. 3). All are consistent with Dewey's definition of **reflective thinking** as "active, persistent, and careful consideration of any belief or supposed form of knowledge in the light of the grounds that support it and the further conclusions to which it tends" (p. 9). All suggest using a "thought chain" (Dewey, 1993, p. 4) that aims at conclusions.

Different elements are also evident in the definitions and descriptions offered in the nursing literature. Some seem to equate critical thinking with reactive thinking (Kataoka-Yahiro & Saylor, 1994; Kintgen-Andrews, 1991). **Reactive thinking** implies a response to what is, and not to what may yet be. Most view critical thinking as a focused, rational analysis of existing knowledge with very specific steps (Bandman & Bandman, 1988; Kataoka-Yahiro & Saylor, 1994; Kintgen-Andrews, 1991). One refers to creating new knowledge (Case, 1994), while another implies that only existing knowledge is uncovered (Bandman & Bandman, 1988).

The discussion about critical thinking continues. Jones and Brown (1993) examine alternative views on critical thinking, arguing that it is "both a philosophical orientation toward thinking and a cognitive process characterized by reasoned judgment and reflective thinking" (p. 72). Woods (1993) insists on the importance of recognizing the role feelings and attitudes have in critical thinking.

The many definitions and descriptions suggest that consensus on the role of critical thinking in nursing has not been reached.

Descriptive Statements about Critical Thinking

The following statements gleaned from the literature and the authors' own thinking are an attempt to provide a fuller description of critical thinking:

- *Critical thinking is directed toward taking action.* Although it is often associated with scientific reasoning, which includes **problem identification, data collection,** and **hypothesis testing,** it is not limited to that activity. For example, critical thinking embraces thinking about how one thinks. Critical thinking also includes the affective processes of moral reasoning and development of values to guide decisions and actions (Woods, 1993).
- *Critical thinking presumes a disposition toward thinking analytically.* Uncritical acceptance of all data and statements is antithetical to critical thinking. An attitude that welcomes intellectual skepticism and honesty is essential.
- *Critical thinking assumes maturity.* Psychology reminds us that our thinking styles evolve as we grow and develop. We think concretely before we can think abstractly. The ability to think abstractly is requisite to critical thinking. We accept many beliefs as children, not because they are true but simply because an adult told us they were true. Only as we grow do we question and examine those beliefs. Moreover, experience enriches the store of knowledge we can bring to our thinking and provides us with material about which to think.
- *Critical thinking requires knowledge.* A broad educational foundation and a healthy intellectual curiosity are prerequisite. Nursing is sometimes described as a boundary discipline because nurses draw knowledge from so many other disciplines (Bartol, 1989). Moreover, the solid educational foundation needs to be informed by common sense and experience—by knowledge of self, for example, of one's own biases and limitations is necessary (Alfaro-Lefevre, 1994).
- *Critical thinking requires skills.* We need to know how to gather facts and data and how to evaluate the quality of each. We need to distinguish facts from opinions and to probe the assumptions behind a line of reasoning. We need to know how to draw inferences from facts and observations, evaluating them as tenable or not. Precision is key. We need to be aware of how our own experiences may influence our viewpoints and be open to those of others. Throughout the process, we need to suspend judgment until all the evidence is weighed. There are many ways to view a problem. The way we view a situation influences our proposed solutions.
- *Critical thinking, however, is more than a set of skills.* Syllogistic thinking, inductive and deductive reasoning, analysis, and synthesis are used, but other styles of thinking are also needed. According to Lonergan (1977), the imagination is the highest function of the intellect and precedes all other thinking activities. Certainly, critical thinking uses imagination. Using a metaphor such as a telephone system, a computer, or a holograph to describe a function of the brain, for example,

can provide additional insight into the process.

- *Critical thinking properly begins with doubt and uncertainty.* An attitude of humility, in the sense of recognizing that no one, including oneself, has all the answers or is immune to error, is essential.
- *Critical thinking also includes feelings.* Feelings are inseparable from all thinking and behavior. Feelings cannot be eliminated or viewed as an inconvenience that complicates the activity of critical thinking, but are an integral part of all we do.
- *Critical thinking frequently involves fault finding.* Questions, disagreements, and even arguments may be included in the process. Critical thinking always challenges the status quo. Criticism of one's own thinking is included.
- *Critical thinking considers the complexity and ambiguity of issues.* At the same time, critical thinking seeks to identify the essential elements and exclude whatever is irrelevant to the matter being considered. Commitment to excellence is crucial.
- *Critical thinking requires self-reflection.* When trying to solve complex problems, we need to monitor our approach to the problem and our reasoning process. An error in reasoning may be as serious a barrier to finding a solution as a miscalculation in determining a proper drug dose. We need to critique the process as well as the proposed solution. We need to check the reliability of the information and our interpretation of it. Perseverance is important.
- *Critical thinking requires an ability to collect and assess data relevant to the problem.* It is not enough to examine the existing data; we need to identify what data are missing. Knowing a fact is insufficient; we need to know how that fact was obtained and from where it was derived.
- *Critical thinking begins with identifying the problem and issues.* Valid conclusions cannot be drawn or appropriate action taken unless one knows what is to be considered.
- *Critical thinking is a contextual activity.* We must be aware of our own context and how it influences our thinking. Our social environment, past and present, may bias our thinking, and we must be aware of how this occurs and deal with it appropriately. We do not do our thinking in a vacuum.
- *Critical thinking is inseparable from language because it is applied to language and expressed through language* (Smith, 1990). Attention should be directed to the meaning of words and precision should be pursued.
- *Critical thinking is not always a self-conscious activity.* We may not be aware of when we are engaging in critical thinking, or even alert to its absence. Moreover, we often unconsciously work on problems and reach solutions without knowing precisely how we arrived until we reflect on the process.
- *Critical thinking is not an esoteric activity.* It is something everyone does to some degree at least some of the time. Certainly many nurses use critical thinking skills every time they approach a patient. Written guidelines, decision trees, algorithms, and critical pathways formalize the critical thinking process but cannot contain it wholly.
- *Critical thinking is not just reactive thinking.* Realizing you must confirm the data you have, examining it in a variety of ways, and collecting more data go beyond reacting.
- *Critical thinking is a habit that improves with proper use and withers with disuse.* In the beginning, we use structure to guide our practice. As we gain proficiency, structure diminishes, but we must continue practicing to improve or even maintain our ability to think critically.
- *Critical thinking is always about something.* It is conceptually impossible to think about nothing.
- *Thinking critically is a social, not simply a solitary, activity.* We expose our beliefs and actions, and the thinking that helped us arrive at those beliefs and actions, to the scrutiny of others. We invite this criticism in different ways, for example, by sharing with colleagues in a discussion or writing a report. We often need others to help us see our errors.
- *Critical thinking is creative.* We reach original solutions by drawing from past experience and making creative applications to new situations.

All these characteristics of critical thinking are present during the process of critical thinking. We may be more conscious of one particular characteristic at a specific point during the process, but the others remain in the background, influencing the outcome. All work together to promote critical thinking.

Measuring Critical Thinking

How does one know if one is thinking critically? Evaluation takes into account the purpose for which the information is gathered, and then a suitable technique is chosen. Many paper and pencil objective tests have been designed to measure generic competency in critical thinking, but not specifically in nursing. The Watson-Glaser Critical Thinking Appraisal (W-GCTA) and the Cornell Critical Thinking Tests, Level X and Z, are the most widely known and used (Norris & Ennis, 1989). The central aspects of critical thinking, **induction, deduction,** and **assumption identification,** are included in all three, but only the California Critical Thinking Inventory (Facione, Facione, & Sanchez, 1994) attempts to measure the disposition toward critical thinking. Probably the best way to increase your critical thinking ability is to think about how you are thinking and practice critical thinking.

Developing Critical Thinking Skills

Critical thinking skills can be developed. Nursing is a practice discipline. Knowledge gained in the classroom is applied in the clinical setting. Knowledge drawn from experience in the clinical setting informs the classroom. None of the knowledge in either setting is gained automatically. Information must be cultivated, organized, and conscientiously arranged by using critical thinking.

Nurses can develop a meaningful concept of information and material needed to practice nursing by using logical steps of the nursing process. Taba (Maleck, 1986) identifies four teaching phases necessary for developing critical thinking. Three phases—concept formation, interpretation of data, and application of principles—focus on the cognitive domain. The fourth phase speaks to the affective domain, including interpretation of feelings, attitudes, and values.

1. **Concept formation.** Concept formation is similar to the nursing process. First, the nurse needs to identify known data, determine common characteristics, and prioritized data.
2. **Interpretation of data.** Next, nurses are encouraged to differentiate between pieces of information, determine cause and effect relationships among variables, and extract meaning from what they have observed.

These first two logical phases or steps in thinking prepare nurses for the third phase:

3. **Application of principles.** Nurses analyze the nature of the problem or situation. It is important to note that nurses do not ask the analytic "why" questions until this application phase. The premature use of "why" questions produce deductive conclusions, rather than inductive alternatives. The question, "Why does an infection cause elevated temperature?" tends to lead to a rote response culled from classroom lectures or the textbook. Conversely, a thought-producing question such as, "What factors related to an elevated temperature suggest an infection?" encourages nurses to sift and combine cognitive knowledge to understand an important clinical concept. Only after defining the problem are nurses able to isolate the relationships among the data. Once these relationships are established, nurses can apply factual information to predict an outcome based on cognitive principles.

4. **Interpretation of feelings, attitudes, and values.** The fourth phase involves principles of interpersonal problem solving and analysis of values. This activity, though less concrete than the other three phases, is imperative for determining the nature of attitudes and perceptions developed through one's life experiences. For example, a nurse's concern about a rising temperature in a patient taking haloperidol (Haldol) may be provoked by a past experience with a patient who was taking the drug and developed neuroleptic malignant syndrome. At this point, the nurse needs to gather additional data to confirm or rule out the possibility that the rising temperature is a sign of malignant hyperthermia in the present patient, and not leap to a premature conclusion. Additionally, the nurse must be open to other possible explanations of the elevated temperature. Appropriate action is then taken, including gathering additional data when indicated.

These phases have been described in terms of steps, but they can occur almost simultaneously. Sequencing and pacing questions is essential in critical thinking. Sequencing questions is important because the processes of thought evolve from the simple to the complex. Just as programmed instruction follows a sequenced set of frames, clinical instruction should follow a carefully sequenced set of experiences and questions. As mentioned earlier, asking "why" questions prematurely would only bring premature closure. The principle of pacing allows nurses to match questions to their levels of readiness and cognitive ability. To accommodate pacing, nurses must pursue each question long enough to permit a variety of responses. In this way, they become active participants in the thinking process, and not simply vessels for facts.

A closer look at the nursing process shows that following it appropriately involves critical thinking. The five steps of the nursing process are assessment, diagnosis, planning, implementation, and evaluation. This process provides a framework for identifying and treating client problems. The nursing process is an ongoing and interactive cycle that results in flexible, individualized, and dynamic nursing care for all clients. Assessment is the foundation of the process and leads to the identification of both nursing diagnoses and collaborative problems. Nursing diagnosis provides the primary focus for developing client-specific individualization of client goals. The planning process allows for individualization of client goals and nursing care within the context of managed care guidelines. Implementation involves providing nursing actions to treat each diagnosis. Ongoing evaluation determines the degree of success in achieving the client's goals and the continued relevance of each nursing diagnosis and collaborative problem.

The implementation of the nursing process requires complex clinical and diagnostic knowledge and application of critical thinking skills. Learning and applying these skills is a continuing challenge for the nurse and requires much practice. If the nurse uses the diagnostic reasoning process appropriately, the result will be effective nursing interventions leading to desirable patient outcomes.

Nurses must be critical thinkers because of the nature of the discipline and their work. Nurses are frequently confronted with problem situations; critical thinking enables them to make sound decisions. During the course of a workday, nurses are required to make decisions of many kinds. These decisions often determine the well-being of patients and even their very survival, so it is essential that the decisions be sound. Critical thinking skills are needed to assess information and plan decisions. Nurses need good judgment, for example, to decide what they can manage and what should be referred to another health-care provider. Nurses deal with rapidly changing situations in stressful environments. Treatments and medications are modified frequently in response to a patient's condition. Routine behaviors are often inadequate to deal with the complex circumstances. Familiarity with the routine for giving medications, for example, does not necessarily help you intervene appropriately with a client who is afraid of injections. When unexpected complications arise, critical thinking ability helps nurses recognize important cues, respond quickly, and adapt interventions to meet specific needs.

Nurses use knowledge from other subjects and fields. Using insight from one subject to shed light on another subject requires critical thinking skills. Because nurses deal holistically with human responses, they must draw meaningful information from other subject areas to understand the meaning of client data and plan effective interventions. Nurses are required to take courses in the biological and social sciences and the humanities to acquire a strong foundation on which to build nursing knowledge and skills. Nurses need knowledge from neurophysiology, social sciences, psychology, and nutrition, for example, to effectively assist patients who are severely depressed.

Case studies offer us excellent opportunities to use critical thinking. The following case study (Figure 7–1) contains data about Mr. Jones, a patient admitted to the same-day surgery unit for repair of a right inguinal hernia. Test your ability to use critical thinking in determining the appropriate data to collect, assessment, nursing diagnosis, and interventions for the care of the patient and his family.

Clearly, critical thinking is used in every step of the nursing process as nurses collect, cluster, and analyze data and formulate nursing diagnoses (Table 7–2). Critical thinking enables the nurse to provide high-quality care that is appropriate, individualized, creative, sensitive, and comprehensive. In determining the appropriate care for Mr. Jones, it would be helpful for the nurse to organize her thoughts and actions by responding to the following critical thinking questions:

1. List the significant assessment findings:
   Objective:
   Subjective:
2. Cluster the significant assessment data by functional health patterns.
3. Using your own words, what general problem areas does Mr. Jones have?
4. Develop data clusters for each of the general problems identified in Question 3.
5. From the clustered data in Question 4, develop at least two diagnostic hypotheses using accepted nursing diagnosis labels.
6. Evaluate each of the diagnostic hypotheses by writing and comparing the definitions and applicable defining characteristics of each diagnosis.
7. Identify the priority nursing diagnosis. Explain your selection.
8. Write a complete nursing diagnosis statement for the choice you make.
9. Plan and implement appropriate nursing interventions.
10. Evaluate outcomes (Collier, McCash, & Bartram, 1996).

Health History and Range of Systems

Mr. Jones is a 45-year-old, married male, employed as a supervisor with Parrish Construction Company. He is accompanied by his wife to the Same Day Surgery Unit for presurgery assessment the day before his scheduled surgery. His breath smells of alcohol.

CHIEF CONCERN: "I need to get this surgery over with. We have a big job to do at work, and it will be my butt if it is not completed on schedule. I plan to cut down on my drinking. I know I drink too much sometimes, but it's because of the pain from this thing (patient points to area of hernia)."

HISTORY OF PRESENT ILLNESS: Mr. Jones was referred to Dr. Judge, a surgeon, by the nurse employed by the construction company. Mr. Jones had experienced periodic pain and swelling in his right groin area for at least 5 years and several times had seen the employee health physician, who told him he had a right inguinal hernia that should be repaired. He admits to experiencing decreased appetite and insomnia for the past 10 days.

Social and Family History

Mr. Jones' father died of cirrhosis at the age of 52 years. His mother is 80 years old and has a history of diabetes. Mr. Jones is the youngest of six children. One brother died at birth, another died at the age of 6 of a tumor, and a third brother was a heavy drinker. Two sisters are alive and well.

Mr. Jones has been married to his second wife for 9 years; they have no children. His second wife has three boys, aged 12, 14, 16 years, who live with her first husband and have no contact with Mr. and Mrs. Jones.

Mr. Jones has five children by his first marriage; all are alive and well, living with his first wife. He pays $50.00 a week for child support for each child. The children visit him every other weekend.

There is no family history of tuberculosis, hypertension, epilepsy, or emotional illness.

Review of Systems

GENERAL: No current change in weight and usually feels good, except when the hernia acts up.

SKIN: No symptoms.

EYES: He wears glasses for reading.

EARS: No symptoms.

NOSE: No symptoms.

MOUTH AND THROAT: Experiences recurrent episodes of hoarseness. Denies dysphagia.

NECK: No symptoms.

RESPIRATORY SYSTEM: Denies pain, dyspnea, palpitations, syncope, or edema.

GASTROINTESTINAL SYSTEM: Reports eating only three "good meals" during the past 10 days. Appetite is good when not drinking. Denies food intolerance, emesis, jaundice, flatulence, diarrhea, constipation, or melena.

GENITOURINARY SYSTEM: No symptoms.

NEUROLOGICAL: See History and Interview with Significant Other.

Physical Examination

Mr. Jones is a 47-year-old white male with a dark complexion and a ruddy face who appears chronically ill. He is mildly intoxicated and appears anxious. Weight is 136 pounds; 5'11": temperature is 98.8°F, pulse is 92, and regular respirations are 20 and unlabored; blood pressure is 160/90.

FIGURE 7-1. Case study.

SKIN: Well hydrated and without lesions.

HEAD: Normocephalic.

EYES: PERRLA. Vision corrected with glasses. Visual acuity decreased to 3 mm print at 18 in. on the left and 4 mm print at 18 in. on the right. Extraocular movements full; no nystagmus is noted. Visual fields are intact as tested per confrontation. Conjunctiva are slightly injected. Sclerae clear. Lenses are without opacities bilaterally. Funduscopic exam reveals the discs normally cupped, and no vascular changes bilaterally.

EARS: External ears symmetric, without lesions. Otic canal is clear. Tympanic membrane pearly gray bilaterally. Hearing is within normal limits per watch tick at 6 in.

MOUTH AND THROAT: Lips, tongue, and buccal mucosa are pink and moist. Teeth are brown, crooked. Gingiva are atrophic. No inflammation of posterior nasopharynx.

NOSE: Nasal septum in the midline. Nares are patent bilaterally. Sinuses not tender.

NECK: Full mobility and no significant lymphadenopathy. Thyroid not enlarged, without nodules.

CHEST: Bony thorax is without deformity or tenderness. Respiratory movement is full, and diaphragmatic excursion is adequate bilaterally. Lungs are clear to percussion and auscultation.

CARDIOVASCULAR: The PMI is in the fifth intercostal space of the LMCL. NSR without murmurs or gallops.

ABDOMEN: Abdomen is soft and flat. Bowel sounds are heard in four quadrants. Liver is descended 5 cm below the costal margin. No splenomegaly, tenderness, or mass. Surgical scar present in right lower quadrant.

GENITOURINARY: Normal male genitalia. No hernia palpated.

RECTAL: Internal and external hemorrhoids noted at 5 and 7 o'clock. Normal sphincter tone. Anal canal free of tenderness. Prostate is in the midline, firm without nodules, not enlarged.

EXTREMITIES AND BACK: Muscular development symmetrical. Normal in appearance, color, and temperature. Peripheral pulses palpable and symmetric. Free of varicosities or edema.

NEUROLOGICAL: Speech is slurred, sensorium somewhat cloudy. Cranial nerves II through XII are intact as tested per gross screen. Moderately tremulous. Biceps, triceps, brachioradialis, patella, and Achilles reflexes are symmetrical but brisk. Babinski's are down bilaterally.

Significant Laboratory Findings

Blood alcohol level: 0.29 U/L; Stool guiac: negative; ECG: Sinus tachycardia, otherwise WNL; Chest X-ray: No active chest disease; Coulter-S: Hgb 16.0 g/dL (H), HCT 48.2% (H), MCV 101 m^3 (H); CL 92 mEq/L (L); Uric acid 8.04 mg/dL (H), SGOT 90 U/L (H); Liver Panel: GGT 66 IU/L (H); and Urine: Bacteria 2+, WBC 8-12

Interview with Significant Other

According to Mrs. Jones, Mr. Jones works out of town from Monday morning to Thursday evening. When he returns home, he begins to drink. He does not drink during the work week. Mrs. Jones related the following incidents of the past 10 days, which occurred when her husband was intoxicated: ran all of the children out of the home into the rain, scuffled with brother-in-law, and brandished a shotgun after an argument. Mrs. Jones reports that she left her husband in June but returned to him about 4 weeks ago. She has never attended Al-Anon, but has reviewed information from the Alcoholism Information Center. This is the second marriage for Mrs. Jones; her first husband and her father were alcoholics as well.

Figure continued on following page

The nurse used critical thinking skills, appropriate interpersonal communication (see Chapter 6), and competent technical ability to develop a comprehensive database for Mr. Jones. Mr. Jones is the primary source of data and his physical condition, developmental level, and intellectual and emotional status determined the extent of information obtained from him. As the nurse talked with Mr. Jones and made observations, she drew on data derived from experiences with other clients and her knowledge base built on clinical experiences and reading. The nurse assessed Mr. Jones holistically and identified current and potential health needs and problem areas.

The nurse organized, synthesized, compared, and analyzed the data to establish the nursing diagnoses. Formulation of nursing diagnoses, as a diagnostic process, is a complex intellectual exercise that relies heavily on the nurse's critical thinking, clinical decision making, and interpersonal skills. The nursing diagnosis or diagnoses provided the framework for the next three nursing process steps: planning, implementation, and evaluation.

Planning includes priority setting of the nursing diagnoses, identification of Mr. Jones' goal and objectives, and establishing interventions with defined outcome criteria. After the planning stage, the nurse wrote the nursing care plan and began implementing nursing care. The delivery of the nursing care depends on the complexity and technical nature of the nursing care plan, the time and environmental limitations of the nurse, and the overall ability and condition of Mr. Jones. The evaluation phase of the nursing process begins with implementation because the nurse reviews the goal achievement and reassesses nursing actions as they are carried out.

As a result of this process, with data collected, the nurse determines that Mr. Jones needs the hernia repair and has multiple system disturbances associated with alcoholism. He has tremors due to withdrawal, poor nutrition, potential complications with anesthesia and surgery, potential abusive behavior related to loss of control, potential difficulties in parenting of adolescents related to disruption in family structure and poor role modeling, and potential alcoholism in three adolescent boys related to family history of alcohol problems. Engaging in the critical thinking process, the nurse continues to look for an increase in tremulousness or irritability. The nurse will notify the physician that Mr. Jones is in possible withdrawal; surgery may need to be postponed.

Because Mr. Jones shows evidence of poor nutrition related to excessive alcohol intake, alcohol consumption must be eliminated, with a corresponding increase in nutritious fluid and food intake. A high-protein diet will be needed to regenerate functional liver tissue and promote healing. A high-carbohydrate diet will be needed to sustain weight and spare the use of protein for cell building. Vitamin and mineral supplements will probably be needed to correct deficiencies. A low-fat diet is indicated because bile manufacturing is reduced with chronic drinking and fats are not easily digested.

FIGURE 7-1. Continued.

TABLE 7 – 2. Overview of Critical Thinking Throughout the Nursing Process

Nursing Process	Critical Thinking Skills	Nursing Process	Critical Thinking Skills
Assessment	Observing Distinguishing relevant from irrelevant data Distinguishing important from unimportant data Validating data Organizing data Categorizing data	*Planning*	Generalizing Transferring knowledge from one situation to another Developing evaluative criteria Hypothesizing
		Implementation	Applying knowledge Testing hypotheses
Analysis/diagnosis	Finding patterns and relationships Making inferences Stating the problem Suspending judgment	*Evaluation*	Deciding whether hypotheses are correct Making criterion-based evaluations and judgments

Source: Adapted from Wilkinson, J. M. (1996). *Nursing process: A critical thinking approach.* (2nd ed.). Redwood City, CA: Addison-Wesley, reprinted with permission.

KEY POINTS

- Critical thinking has been defined and described by many scholars.
- Critical thinking is multifaceted and involves a combination of logical, rhetorical, and philosophical skills and attitudes that promote the ability to determine what one should believe and do.
- Critical thinking is essential for professional nursing practice. The need for critical thinking in nursing has greatly increased with the diversity and complexity of nursing practice.

CHAPTER EXERCISES

1. Give an example from your clinical practice for each of the descriptive statements of critical thinking on pages 118 through 119.

2. Select a nursing issue, such as an open visiting policy in the surgical intensive care unit or family presence during a code, and engage in a debate with a peer.

3. Engage a peer in a discussion of selected problems you have identified at your place of work.

4. Analyze the problem-solving process you used to address the problem identified in Exercise 3.

5. Rewrite a case study from the patient's point of view. Repeat the exercise from a family member's point of view, the doctor's point of view, and the nurse's point of view. A short story such as *The Jilting of Granny Weatherall* by Katherine Ann Porter (1930) or *The Interior Castle* by Jean Stafford (1953) may be substituted for a case study.

6. Write an argument for a change in policy or to support a request for additional funds that can be presented in 10 minutes or less.

7. Select a health need, such as free access to a primary physician or nurse with questions about health, and prepare a fact sheet that could be presented to a legislator or an insurance provider to support the action you propose.

REFERENCES

Alfaro-Lefevre, R. (1994). *Applying nursing process: A step by step guide*. (3rd ed.). Philadelphia: Lippincott.

Ausubel, D. P. (1978). *Education psychology: A cognitive view*. New York: Holt, Reinhardt & Winston.

Bandman, E. L., & Bandman, B. (1988). *Critical thinking in nursing*. Norwalk, CT: Appleton & Lange.

Bartol, G. M. (1989). Creative literature: An aid to nursing practice. *Nursing & Health Care, 10,* 453–457.

Case, B. (1994). Walking around the elephant: A critical-thinking strategy for decision making. *The Journal of Continuing Education in Nursing, 25*(3), 101–109.

Cassel, J. F., & Congleton, R. J. (1993). *Critical thinking: An annotated bibliography*. Metuchen, NJ: Scarecrow Press.

Collier, I. C., McCash, K. E., & Bartram, J. M. (1996). *Writing nursing diagnosis*. St. Louis, MO: Mosby.

Dewey, J. (1910). *How we think*. Boston: D. C. Heath & Co.

Dewey, J. (1933). *How we think*. New York: D. C. Heath.

Facione, P. (project director). (1990). Critical thinking: a statement of expert consensus for purposes of educational assessment and instruction. *The Delphi Report: Research findings and recommendations prepared for the American Philosophical Association*. (ERIC Doc. No. ED 315 423). Washington: ERIC.

Facione, N. C., & Facione, P. A. (1996). Externalizing the critical thinking in knowledge development and clinical judgment. *Nursing Outlook, 44,* 129–136.

Facione, N. C., Facione, P. A., & Sanchez, C. A. (1994). Critical thinking disposition as a measure of competent clinical judgment: The development of the California Critical Thinking Disposition Inventory. *Journal of Nursing Education, 33,* 345–350.

Jones, S. A., & Brown, L. N. (1993). Alternative views on defining critical thinking through the nursing process. *Holistic Nursing Practice, 7*(3), 71–76.

Kataoka-Yahiro, M., & Saylor, C. (1994). A critical thinking model for nursing judgment. *Journal of Nursing Education, 33*(8), 351–356.

Kintgen-Andrews, J. (1991). Critical thinking and nursing education: perplexities and insights. *Journal of Nursing Education, 30,* 152–157.

Lonergan, B. (1977). *Insight, a study of human understanding*. New York: Harper & Row.

Maleck, C. J. (1986). A model for teaching critical thinking. *Nurse Educator, 11*(6), 20–23.

McPeck, J. E. (1990). *Teaching critical thinking*. New York: Routledge.

Norris, S. P., & Ennis, R. H. (1989). *Evaluating critical thinking*. Pacific Grove, CA: Midwest Press.

Paul, R. W. (1990). Critical thinking: Fundamental for a free society. *Educational Leadership, 41,* 4–14.

Porter, K. A. (1930). The Jilting of Granny Weatherall. In *Flowering Judas and other stories*. New York: Harcourt, Brace.

Rubenfeld, M. G., & Scheffer, B. K. (1995). *Critical thinking in nursing: An interactive approach*. Philadelphia: Lippincott.

Smith, F. (1990). *To think*. New York: Teachers College Press.

Stafford, J. (1953). The Interior Castle. In *The children are bored on Sunday*. New York: Harcourt, Brace.

Webster's new universal unabridged dictionary (1979). (2nd ed.). New York: Simon & Schuster.

White, N. E., Beardslee, N. Q., Peters, D., & Supples, J. M. (1990). Promoting critical thinking skills. *Nurse Educator, 15*(5), 16–19.

Wilkinson, J. M. (1996). *Nursing process: Critical thinking in action* (2nd ed.). Menlo Park, CA: Addison-Wesley.

Woods, J. H. (1993). Effective learning: One door to critical thinking. *Holistic Nursing Practice, 7*(3), 64–70.

BIBLIOGRAPHY

Benner, P., & Tanner, C. (1987). Clinical judgment: How expert nurses use intuition. *American Journal of Nursing, 87,* 23–31.

Birx, E. C. (1993). Critical thinking and theory-based practice. *Holistic Nursing Practice, 7*(3), 21–27.

Brigham, C. (1993). Nursing education and critical thinking: interplay of content and thinking. *Holistic Nursing Practice, 7*(3), 48–54.

Brookfield, S. D. (1991). *Understanding and facilitating adult learning*. San Francisco: Jossey-Bass.

Brookfield, S. D. (1991). *The skillful teacher*. San Francisco: Jossey-Bass.

Brookfield, S. D. (1993). On impostorship, cultural suicide, and other dangers: How nurses learn critical thinking. *The Journal of Continuing Education in Nursing, 24*(5), 197–205.

Brown, H. N., & Sorrell, J. M. (1993). Use of clinical journals to enhance critical thinking. *Nurse Educator, 18*(5), 16–19.

Case, B. (1995). Critical thinking: Challenging assumptions and imagining alternatives. *Dimensions of Critical Care Nursing, 14*(5), 274–279.

Duldt, B. W. (1994). Critical thinking. *Nurse Educator, 19*(6), 9–10.

Elias, M. J., & Kress, J. S. (1994). Social decision-making and life skills development: A critical thinking approach to health promotion in the middle school. *Journal of School Health, 64*(2), 62–66.

Fields, W. L., & Loveridge, C. (1988). Critical thinking and fatigue: How do nurses on 8 and 12 hour shifts compare? *Nursing Economics 6,* 189–191.

Fontaine, K. L., & Fletcher, J. S. (1994). Critical thinking. *Essentials of mental health nursing* (3rd ed.). Redwood City, CA: Addison-Wesley, 521–524.

Ford, J. S., & Profetto-McGrath, J. (1994). A model for critical thinking within the context of curriculum as praxis. *Journal of Nursing Education, 33,* 341–344.

Gillmore, V. L. (1993). Insight, initiative, and imagination in nursing administration. *Holistic Nursing Practice, 7*(3), 15–20.

Hartman, D. K. (1993). Critical thinking in psychiatric nursing in the decade of the brain. *Holistic Nursing Practice, 7*(3), 55–63.

Jenkins, H. M. (1985). Improving clinical decision-making in nursing. *Journal of Nursing Education, 24,* 242–243.

Jones, J. A. (1988). Clinical reasoning in nursing. *Journal of Advanced Nursing, 13,* 185–192.

Kemp, V. H. (1985). Concept analysis as a strategy for promoting critical thinking. *Journal of Nursing Education, 24*(9), 382–384.

Kramer, M. K. (1993). Concept clarification and critical thinking: Integrated processes. *Journal of Nursing Education, 32*(9), 406–414.

Lashley, M., & Wittstadt, R. (1993). Writing across the curriculum: An integrated curricular approach to developing critical thinking through writing. *Journal of Nursing Education, 32*(9), 422–424.

Lewis, J. B., & Eakes, G. G. (1992). The AIDS care dilemma: An exercise in critical thinking. *Journal of Nursing Education, 31,* 136–137.

McPeck, J. E. (1984). The evaluation of critical thinking programs: Dangers and dogmas. *Informal Logic 6*(2), 9–13.

Miller, M. A., & Malcolm, N. S. (1990). Critical thinking in the nursing curriculum. *Nursing and Health Care, 11,* 67–73.

Paul, R. (1992). *Critical thinking: What every person needs to survive in a rapidly changing world* (2nd ed.). Santa Rosa, CA: Foundation for Critical Thinking.

Pless, B. S., & Clayton, G. M. (1993). Clarifying the concept of critical thinking in nursing. *Journal of Nursing Education, 32,* 425–428.

Pond, E. F., Bradshaw, M. J., & Turner, S. L. (1991). Teaching strategies for critical thinking. *Nurse Educator, 16*(6), 18–22.

Reilly, D. E., & Oermann, M. H. (1992). Affective learning in the clinical setting. In Reilly, D. E., & Oermann, M. H. (Eds.). *Clinical teaching in nursing education.* (Publication 15-2471). New York: National League for Nursing.

Rew, L. (1988). Nurses' intuition. *Applied Nursing Research, 1*(1), 27–31.

Saarmann, L., Freitas, L., Rapps, J., & Riegel, B. (1992). The relationship of education to critical thinking ability and values among nurses: socialization into professional nursing. *Journal of Professional Nursing, 8*(1), 26–34.

Salmon, M. H. (1984). *Logic and critical thinking.* New York: Harcourt Brace Javanovich.

Schank, M. J. (1990). Wanted: Nurses with critical thinking skills. *The Journal of Continuing Education in Nursing, 21*(2), 86–89.

Snyder, M. (1994). Critical thinking (Letter to the editor). *The Journal of Continuing Education in Nursing, 25*(3), 100.

Snyder, M. (1993). Critical thinking: A foundation for consumer-focused care. *The Journal of Continuing Education in Nursing, 24*(5), 206–210.

Tanner, C. A. (1994). Provocative thoughts on critical thinking. *Journal of Nursing Education, 33*(8), 339.

Tanner, C. A. (1993). Thinking about critical thinking. *Journal of Nursing Education, 32*(3), 99–100.

Watson, G., & Glaser, E. (1980). *Watson-Glaser critical thinking appraisal.* San Antonio: Psychological Corporation.

Chapter 8

LEADERSHIP

Theresa M. Valiga
Sheila Grossman

CHAPTER OBJECTIVES

On completion of
this chapter, the reader
will be able to:

1. Differentiate between leadership and management.
2. Compare and contrast three leadership styles: democratic, authoritarian, and laissez-faire.
3. Distinguish among various theories of leadership: great man theory, traitist theory, situational theory, transformational theory, and leadership task theory.
4. Analyze the interdependence of leaders and followers.
5. Explain how each of the nine tasks of leadership, as outlined by Gardner, relate to nursing practice.
6. Analyze nursing practice situations in terms of the extent to which leadership was exercised.
7. Identify your own leadership abilities or potential leadership skills.

KEY TERMS

Leadership
Leadership Style
Authoritative Leaders
Laissez-faire Leaders
Democratic Leadership
Great Man Leadership
   Theory

Traitist Theories
Situational Leadership
   Theory
Transformational
   Leadership Theory

Leadership Tasks Theory
Internal Forces
External Forces
Managing

L eadership is a word that is often used, has tremendous appeal, and evokes images of greatness. When asked to think about individuals who have demonstrated leadership, agreement is likely about individuals like Martin Luther King, Mother Teresa, Gandhi, Jesus Christ, Eleanor Roosevelt, and even Florence Nightingale. But agreement is less likely about individuals such as Adolph Hitler, Richard Nixon, Candy Lightner, and Curtis Sliwa. And agreement is even less likely about the mother who, as a member of a local PTA, led the fight to increase parents' opportunities to meet with the school board when decisions affecting their children's health and well-being are made, or about the college-age student who spearheaded the establishment of a center for multiculturalism on a relatively homogeneous campus, or the staff nurse who mobilized her colleagues to change the governance structure on their unit.

Regardless of whether the name is known worldwide, in a particular region or circle of influence, or only in a local community, those who know the individual are likely to agree that what that person did was an example of leadership. In other words, we know leadership when we see it. But when we try to define, describe, and explain it to someone else, it becomes like chasing an elusive butterfly.

What is it about certain individuals that would lead one to conclude they are or were leaders? What is it about their character, their style, their manner of interacting with others, the goals for which they were striving that makes them leaders? What is it that sets them apart from ordinary citizens, mere politicians, and managers?

In this chapter, we explore the nature of leadership. We examine some of the hundreds of definitions of the phenomenon, explore selected leadership theories and leadership styles, analyze the concept of transformational leadership, look at leader/follower relations, analyze various components of leadership, and discuss the kind of leadership that will be needed, particularly by professional nurses, in the twenty-first century. Finally, we assert at the outset and conclusion that each of us has the potential to exercise leadership in our workplaces, professional organizations, and communities.

DEFINITIONS OF LEADERSHIP

Leadership has been studied extensively. As Bass (1990) notes, "there are almost as many different definitions of leadership as there are persons who

have attempted to define the concept" (p. 11). **Leadership** has been conceptualized as a set of traits, a role that needs to be played in any group, a particular position, an art, the exercise of influence, a form of persuasion, a power relation, and a way to attain goals (Bass, 1990). After analyzing 100 years of leadership research, VanFleet and Yukl (1989) concluded that "Where once we thought of leadership as a relatively simple construct, we now recognize that it is among the more complex social phenomena" (p. 66) in our world. In fact, Bennis and Nanus (1985) have noted that

> Decades of academic analysis have given us more than 350 definitions of leadership. Literally thousands of empirical investigations of leaders have been conducted in the last seventy-five years alone, but no clear and unequivocal understanding exists as to what distinguishes leaders from nonleaders, and perhaps more important, what distinguishes *effective* leaders from *ineffective* leaders. (p. 4)

In a critique of leadership studies undertaken over the years, Rost (1991) suggested that perhaps the reason we know so little about this phenomenon, even after so much analysis, is that these studies have missed the "essential nature of what leadership is, the process whereby leaders and followers relate to one another to achieve a purpose" (p. 4). Indeed, many of the studies of leadership have focused more on management styles or the person of the leader and ignored or minimized the role of followers in the "equation." Any exploration of leadership for the twenty-first century must attend to the interrelationship and interdependence between leaders and followers.

Although it is true that leaders "cause ripples," "rock the boat," "disturb the status quo," and take risks, they are effective as leaders only when those "ripples" inspire others to take action, make change, and realize goals. But since leadership is more an art than a science, there is no single or simple way to go about inspiring others; instead, the leader needs to use a number of styles to mobilize a group to achieve great things.

LEADERSHIP STYLES

Style can be thought of as the way in which something is done or said or as a particular form of behavior associated with an individual. **Leadership style** can be viewed as a set of behaviors that characterize individuals as they perform their leader role. These styles differ in terms of how power is distributed among those leading and those following, how decisions are made, and whose needs are of primary concern.

One's style reflects forces within oneself, the group, and the situation. Forces within the leader include her or his value system, expectations of self and others, prior experiences in a leadership role, self confidence, and tolerance for ambiguity and uncertainty.

Forces within members of the group include their need for independence, readiness for responsibility, commitment to a common goal, expectations about sharing in decision making, and ability to deal with the group task. Finally, one's style is also determined by forces within the situation, such as the traditions and values of the organization, its size and structure, the nature of the task at hand, the time available to accomplish a goal, and the history of the relationships among members of the group.

Depending on the mix of these factors, one's style can range from highly structured (i.e., authoritative), through moderately structured (or participative), to minimally structured (i.e., permissive). **Authoritative leaders** maintain strong control over the people in the group, give orders and expect others to obey, motivate others with fear, and dominate the group. With this style, work proceeds smoothly, productivity is often high, and procedures are well-defined; however, creativity, autonomy, and self-motivation are stifled, and the needs of group members go unrecognized.

Laissez-faire leaders, using a permissive, nondirective style are generally inactive and passive. In fact, one needs to question if they are leaders at all since they are not working actively to move the group forward. With this style, group members have a great deal of freedom and self-control; however, they can become disinterested and apathetic, goals may remain unclear, little if any feedback is likely to be given, and procedures are often confusing. This type of style is usually unproductive, inefficient, and unsatisfying.

Perhaps the most productive leadership style is that known as **democratic** or participative. This leader talks about "we" rather than "I," asks stimulating questions and makes suggestions rather than issuing commands, provides constructive criticism, and is egalitarian. The participative leader has confidence in the ability of the group members and actively stimulates and guides them to use their abilities to achieve the group's goals. In this situation, the leader and the followers are mutually responsive, communication is multidirectional, and any

member of the group is expected to assume the role of leader as the situation requires.

These different leadership styles are illustrated beautifully in the novel *Watership Down* (Adams, 1972). This is a story of a group of rabbits who, at the urging and insistence of one member, risk leaving their familiar warren to find a safer place to live. The "leader" of the rabbits' warren of origin, Threarah, is authoritarian in his style; he does not listen to advice, is very efficient, is closed to new ideas, does not adapt to new situations, and is removed from the needs of the followers. Similarly, in another warren, led by Woundwort, a totalitarian "regime" is ruled by fear and force; the lifestyle of all rabbits is totally controlled by others, no responsibility is given to members of the community, and the leader hungers for more and more power. Along the way, the rabbits encounter Cowslip's warren, which has no "chief rabbit" here, everyone does whatever he or she wants to do, there is no common goal, and the entire warren is rather passive, with little evident joy. Finally, in the community created by the rabbits who left the Sandleford Warren and are led by Hazel, the unique gifts of each member are recognized and used fully, and the group works together toward common goals. In addition, Hazel, the leader, seeks advice from others and encourages initiative, a sense of trust exists among members of the community, and because all group members are involved in making decisions they own their decisions.

In times of crisis, an authoritarian style may be the most appropriate one for a leader to use. When there is no time pressure to complete a task and the group is a mature one, the permissive style may be most effective. Likewise, when one is working to implement changes in a system, use of the participative style is apt to yield the best results. A key to effective leadership is to use the appropriate style at the right time and to be flexible enough to attend to the needs of the followers, use the talents of all group members, and meet the goals of the group. This approach reflects some of the more current theories of leadership.

THEORIES OF LEADERSHIP

Several theories look at the various types of leadership.

- **Great man leadership theory.** One of the earliest theories of leadership was the "great man" theory, which basically asserts that the individual who is born into the proper class and circumstance is the one to lead "the people." This theory, which was consistent with rule by monarchs, lacks relevance for more current, complex, democratic societies.

- **Traitist theories.** In an attempt to acknowledge that individuals born outside a royal lineage also provided leadership, theories were espoused to outline the ideal mix of traits or characteristics that make the most effective leader. Traits such as height, energy level, socioeconomic status, level of education, gender, decisiveness, and articulateness were related to effectiveness as a leader and offered some useful insights. Despite extensive research within this theoretical framework, however, no single mix of traits emerged to predict, determine or ensure who would be the best leader in a certain situation. In essence, these theories failed to acknowledge the role of the followers, the situation, or the task at hand in determining leader effectiveness, and they also have been shown to be of little help in understanding leadership in our ever-changing, unpredictable world.

- **Situational leadership theory.** These theories (e.g., the one proposed by Hersey & Blanchard, 1977) clearly recognized the significance of the environment or situation as a factor in the effectiveness of a leader. They asserted that the leader was the one who was in a position to initiate change when a situation was ready for change, and acknowledged that leadership is a dynamic process involving the interplay of the personalities and maturity levels of the leader and follower, the task to be accomplished, the goals to be attained, and the conditions within the environment.

- **Transformational leadership theory.** Perhaps one of the most contemporary leadership theories is that of transformational leadership (Barker, 1990, 1991; Barker & Young, 1994; Marriner-Tomey, 1993). This theory asserts that leadership is longer lasting and more far-reaching than had been thought previously. With this type of leadership, the leader engages the full person of each follower and transforms each to move beyond individual needs and interests toward higher-level concerns. The consciousness of the followers is raised, their aspirations are heightened, and they are intimately involved in determining the course of action for the group. The transformational leader operates out of a deeply held personal value system, is visionary, has strong convictions, and interacts significantly with followers to see that the vision is realized.

- **Leadership tasks theory.** Finally, among the more recent and scholarly approaches to explaining the universal, multidimensional, and complex phenomenon known as leadership is the work of John Gardner, a noted expert in the field. Gardner (1990) proposed a theory of the tasks of leadership that embodies the components of effective leadership. He asserts that individuals who consistently engage in these tasks are exercising true leadership and should be recognized for their contributions to their organizations, professions, and communities. Each of these tasks is explained and related to the practice of professional nursing.

COMPONENTS OF EFFECTIVE LEADERSHIP AND TASKS OF LEADERSHIP

Envisioning Goals. One of the most significant tasks of leadership is envisioning new goals and possibilities. In fact, leaders are often distinguished from nonleaders by their ability to see a different future, articulate that vision, communicate it to others in such a way that they accept it, and energize others to invest the energy needed to realize the vision and create the desired future.

Does it take special training or mystical insight to envision goals? Is this a leadership task reserved for only a few elite individuals? Of course not. Each and every one of us—if we care enough about our jobs, our professions, and our communities—has some idea of how things could be done better or how "our little corner of the world" could be a better place. The leader, however, is the person who *does* something with or about that dream. This is the leadership task of *envisioning goals.* Consider the example in Figure 8–1 illustrating this point.

Affirming Values. All groups and organizations are characterized by a set of values that may be clearly stated or implied from observed behaviors of members of the group. Those values may include such things as family-centered care, helping others develop to their fullest potential, or making the largest profit possible. The individuals who run organizations assume that members of the group accept the organization's values and act in concert with them.

It is all too clear, however, that explicitly stated values such as providing individualized, high-quality care, or respecting the dignity and worth of all indi-

Several RNs are working in a community health center that provides care to a poor, underserved, multicultural population. They frequently comment to one another how sad it is that women need to return to the center several times before they have all their family's health needs addressed, such as immunizations, dental care, GYN exams, and hypertension management. These nurses also recognize that after a while, the women fail to keep appointments because it is too difficult to get back and forth to the center.

While most of these nurses are well aware of a problem and acknowledge the serious implications of it, only one nurse begins to talk about a new approach to making appointments and scheduling visits. She envisions a "one stop shopping" arrangement where the family can come to the center on one day and everyone's needs can be addressed. This nurse begins to talk about this idea to the other nurses, her supervisor, and the center's director. She develops a proposal of how it can work; and she is willing to serve on a committee to work out the details. This nurse has envisioned a goal and exercised leadership.

FIGURE 8-1. Envisioning goals.

Nurses working in the local long-term care facility have always prided themselves on the caring environment they provide for residents and families. Elderly residents are respected, treated with dignity, and involved in their own care as much as possible. However, in recent months, one nurse notices that she and her colleagues seem to be spending more time complaining about their workloads, criticizing management, and "cutting corners" in their interactions with residents and families as a way to deal with the increased stresses they are feeling.

Rather than continuing to allow herself to be pulled in this direction, one nurse begins to reflect on why she has chosen to work in this kind of setting and what she finds rewarding about caring for the elderly. She then thinks about what is missing and how some of those basic values of respect and dignity seem to have eroded recently. This nurse exercises leadership when she begins to talk to her colleagues about what values they share related to caring for the elderly and how they can refocus their behaviors to reestablish that kind of commitment.

FIGURE 8-2. Affirming value.

viduals, often conflict with the values inferred from approved policies and ongoing practices, such as a drastic reduction in the size of the professional staff. The nurse who exercises leadership serves to remind group members of the values they share, as Figure 8–2 illustrates.

As Gardner (1990) noted, "values always decay over time, however, groups that keep their values alive do so not by escaping the processes of decay but by powerful processes of regeneration" (p. 13). Leaders, such as the nurse described in Figure 8–2, initiate and help sustain those "processes of regeneration" when they fulfill the task of leadership known as *affirming values*.

Motivating. Although it is critical that a leader envision new goals and help a group affirm the values underlying its existence, those tasks alone will not help organizations progress. A leader is nothing without followers, and if individuals are not motivated to choose to follow a leader, then little forward movement takes place. A leader cannot "go it alone." Thus, another important task of leadership is *motivating others*.

As individuals, we are motivated by **internal forces,** such as the desire to learn and grow or the satisfaction of knowing we did the very best we could in a situation, regardless of the outcome. We are also motivated by **external forces,** such as the praise we might receive from someone else, good grades, or a promotion. Both sources of motivation are valid, and both are important. It is the task of leadership to "unlock or channel" (Gardner, 1990, p. 14) the motives that drive individuals so that they can work to their fullest potential and help the group achieve its goals.

The nurse who tells her colleagues that their intervention in a difficult patient situation was highly effective or their contribution to a committee's work was valuable does much to motivate those colleagues to continue to strive toward excellence. Likewise, the nurse who openly shares his self-satisfaction after asserting himself at a staff meeting and influencing the group to make a significant decision also motivates himself and others to take risks in the future.

Nurses can motivate others by posting an article published by a colleague, sending a "good luck" card when a colleague decides to return to school, or "conspiring" with other nurses on the unit to name another member of the group "nurse of the week" after she cared for a very difficult patient. When one acts to inspire, encourage, and energize others, that person is fulfilling an important task of leadership, namely, *motivating*.

Managing. **Managing** is as much a part of effective leadership as the other tasks described because if one cannot manage a situation to "make things happen," visions will not be realized, and motivated individuals will soon become frustrated. According to Gardner (1990), the managing task of leadership involves a number of dimensions:

- Planning and setting priorities
- Creating processes and structures that will allow a vision to be realized
- Providing resources, delegating, and coordinating the group's activities
- Making decisions, even difficult ones

We often think that managing functions are the responsibility only of the person who holds some administrative position in an organization. Such persons do need good management skills, but the individual who is providing leadership within a group—and who may *not* be in any hierarchical position of authority—also needs to be able to plan, organize, delegate, and so on. This is the *managing* task of leaders, as illustrated in Figure 8–3.

Achieving a Workable Unity. There is no doubt that when a number of individuals come together in the context of complex organizations to face many difficult challenges, conflict is likely to arise. That conflict can come from differences in values, miscommunication or lack of communication, uncertainty, incompatible demands placed on individuals, competition for scarce resources, poorly defined responsibilities, change, and normal human drives for success, power, and recognition. Indeed, there is rarely only one source of conflict.

Conflict was traditionally viewed as bad and something to be avoided at any cost. The emphasis was on resolving or getting rid of conflict. More contemporary perspectives on conflict, however, acknowledge that it can be a healthy thing, provided it is not overwhelming. Moderate amounts of conflict serve as an incentive to develop, excel, change, and grow; thus, the role of the leader is to *manage* conflict but not necessarily *resolve* it.

One of the important tasks of leadership, therefore, is to serve as a unifying force within the group to achieve "some measure of cohesion and mutual tolerance" (Gardner, 1990, p. 16) so that the group can move forward to achieve its goals. The leader needs to try to minimize polarization and the formation of cliques by building teams and creating a sense of community among the group. The example in Figure 8–4 illustrates how a nurse can fulfill the leadership task of *achieving a workable unity*.

Several weeks ago, the staff on the oncology unit decided they wanted to do their own staffing, and the nurse manager of the unit agreed that they should pursue the idea. The nurses were excited about this new opportunity, and the nurse manager was pleased with the initiative shown by the staff. However, since the time this decision was made, no progress has occurred toward implementing this new model. Staff members thought that the nurse manager would guide them in making this change, and the nurse manager assumed that, since the idea came from and was enthusiastically endorsed by the staff, the nurses themselves were working on a plan to "make it happen."

As time went by, some nurses became discouraged and convinced themselves that the idea was not a good one after all. Other nurses became angry with the nurse manager, thinking she was "dragging her feet" in an attempt to sabotage the new model. Still others sat passively by, waiting for the nurse manager to tell the staff what to do and when and how to do it. But one nurse realized that if the group was to do its own staffing, several steps had to be taken to make that happen.

This nurse asked the hospital librarian to gather a few recent articles on self-staffing projects that had been implemented elsewhere, and she reviewed the notes on change from her senior leadership/management course. She then thought about the steps that needed to be taken on the unit and at higher levels of the hospital before their dream would become a reality, and she reflected on her own talents and those of her colleagues in an attempt to match everyone's strengths with the tasks that needed to be done. She then wrote this up in a 1–2 page "proposal," asked the nurse manager for time on the agenda of the next staff meeting to discuss it, presented the proposal to the group as a starting point, and succeeded in getting the group to implement self-staffing within the next two months. As a result of this nurse fulfilling the managing task of leadership, she emerged as a leader and helped her peers reach a much-desired goal.

FIGURE 8–3. Managing.

As the hospital in which they were employed underwent major reorganizations when it merged with several other health-care institutions, the nurses working in the medical area—both the inpatient units and the outpatient clinics—became more and more worried about the security of their jobs. They were less inclined to voice their concerns to one another for fear that they would be labeled as unhappy, uncooperative troublemakers and not team players. If they were so labeled, they might lose their jobs or their chances of promotion.

One seasoned nurse, who had experienced major changes many times in the past, was troubled by the lack of cooperation among her nursing peer group. She noticed that nurses were unwilling to help one another, rarely comforted one another when someone had a particularly difficult patient assignment, were quick to point out one another's faults, and seemed to make more of an effort to build alliances with physicians than with their fellow nurses. All of these, she concluded, were signs of the lack of unity and cohesion on the unit. She was concerned that, not only were the nurses dissatisfied with the work they were doing, but also the patient care might eventually suffer. Thus, she decided to try to do something to coalesce the group.

This nurse made an effort to compliment her colleagues on the work they were doing. She made a point to ask others for advice and suggestions on different patient situations, even though she was quite able to manage those situations on her own. She invited a colleague to sit down with her for coffee for a few minutes and took time to casually reflect on why she went into nursing and what keeps her excited about her job. She mused about the many times throughout her career when the autonomy and practice of nurses had been threatened, how the nurses always thought that the immediate crisis was going to be the one to sound their "death knell," and how the resilient nurses always came through stronger than ever.

This nurse also talked with the nurse manager about ways she could keep the staff better informed of the changes being made or considered to minimize rumors. She asked the nurse manager to allow time on a staff meeting agenda for discussion of concerns and to consider contacting the psych liaison nurse to meet with the staff. Finally, she agreed to be the first to talk at the staff meeting about the very real fears and concerns experienced by the nurses, thereby taking the risk of speaking up that she thought her colleagues might not be willing to take.

As a result of these small but focused actions by this seasoned nurse, the nurses on the unit started to open up to one another, work together more as a unit, and support one another—through discussion, humor, and other means—as changes continued to occur.

FIGURE 8-4. Achieving a workable unity.

Explaining. If individuals opt to follow a leader and work with that leader to achieve a goal or realize a vision, they need to understand what the goal is, what is being expected of them, and why they are being asked to do certain things. An important task of leadership, therefore, is *explaining* things to followers, teaching them, and being sure they are making an informed choice to follow in the first place. The nurse described in the situation illustrated in Figure 8–5 fulfills this task of leadership in an effective way.

This nurse manager explained, taught, and supported his staff, and he anticipated their needs and planned, in advance, to meet them or minimize their potentially negative effect. In essence, he exercised effective leadership in relation to the specific task of explaining. As Gardner (1990) noted, "Leaders teach" "Teaching and leading are distinguishable occupations, but every great leader is clearly teaching—and every great teacher is leading" (p. 18).

Serving as a Symbol. One of the most significant roles leaders play and one of the most important tasks they perform is serving as a symbol for the group they lead. In other words, when those outside the group observe, listen to, and interact with the leader, they see, hear, and experience all that the group is attempting to do or be.

For example, Martin Luther King preached nonviolence, and he acted in a nonviolent way when confronted with charges and challenges from others. Jesus Christ had a vision of a world where people loved and respected their fellow human beings, regardless of who they were or how much or little they had; He lived His life among the poor and persecuted, shared what He had with those in need, and held no king above any peasant. Likewise, Florence Nightingale asserted time and again that a healthy environment was critical to the recovery and well-being of the soldiers wounded in battle, and whenever she had the opportunity to speak to health officials, supervise a hospital, or write about the care of the ill, she was consistent in her message. No less can be expected of the nurse who is providing leadership in today's world. Consider the nurse who *serves as a symbol* described in Figure 8–6.

After extensive study and consultation, the nursing management team of the nearby rehabilitation center decided to institute computerized bedside charting throughout the institution within the next 6 months. The system has been selected, the infrastructure has been laid, the hardware has been ordered, and all nurse managers have been trained in the new system. The management team has outlined a plan for implementation, on a unit-by-unit basis, that begins in 1 month and ends 5 months later. All nurse managers have been directed to plan to bring their staff members "up to speed," and the heads of all other departments (e.g., Pharmacy, Medicine, Physical Therapy) have been directed to do the same.

Knowing that his unit will be among the first ones to go on line, that many of his staff members are not convinced that computerized bedside charting is "the way to go," and that many are not comfortable with computers in general, the nurse manager of one unit formulates a plan to prepare his staff appropriately. First, he arranges for some nurses from his graduate program classes who are in institutions that have recently implemented computerized charting to meet with his staff to talk about what the experience was like for them and how they "survived" it. The nurse manager also gathers a few articles about computers and their use in health care, and he shares these with the staff. He gains approval for his staff to go to the local university school of nursing to practice patient care documentation in their computer lab, and arranges schedules so they have the time to go. In addition, he plans time during several upcoming unit staff meetings to talk about the difficulty of dealing with change, the need for the new computer system, the benefits to patients and staff of such a system, and individuals' fears and concerns about their new responsibilities. Finally, he plans for ongoing resources and opportunities for the staff to raise questions, make suggestions, express fears, and receive support throughout the implementation process and until they feel comfortable with the new system.

FIGURE 8-5. Explaining.

Serving as a symbol means reflecting the group's values and collective identity in whatever one says and does. Admittedly, this is a serious responsibility for a leader to assume, but it is one that will make her more effective in helping a group achieve its goal.

Representing the Group. A leader must often serve as the spokesperson for the group, argue on its behalf, and represent its wishes and desires to others. We may conjure up an image of the corporate CEO or the President of the United States giving his or her "state of the union" address to an audience when we think of representing a group, but this leadership task occurs at all levels in all arenas, as Figure 8–7 illustrates.

This nurse provides us with an excellent example of the task of leadership that Gardner (1990) refers to as *representing the group*. She exhibits that "distinctive characteristic of the ablest leaders [namely, that she did not] shrink from external representation. [She saw] the long-term needs and goals of

Nurse educators teach students about the value of research, the need to base their practice on research findings, the importance of participating in professional organizations, and the significance of lifelong learning, among other things. Additionally, they expect students to internalize these values as they begin or pursue new directions in their professional nursing careers. How many of these educators, however, "practice what they preach" and serve as symbols of that kind of behavior?

Often the educator who is thought of as a leader by her students and her peers is the one who lives these values and integrates them into her teaching. The teacher who tells students what she learned from a conference, the book she read, or the research presentation she heard is conveying to students that she, too, needs to continue to learn. By supporting her class presentations with research findings and helping students identify gaps in our knowledge and areas in need of further study, the nurse educator is not merely *telling* students how important research is, she is *living* that value. Finally, the nurse educator who continually revises the teaching strategies she uses because the latest pedagogical research has shown a certain strategy to be effective in facilitating student learning demonstrates to students how one's practice needs to change continually in response to new knowledge.

FIGURE 8-6. Serving as a symbol.

The nurses who worked in the outpatient clinics at the medical center felt they were spending more time on paperwork and clerical duties than on patient care. They were angry, frustrated, and feeling abused.

One nurse in this group — who shared the feelings of anger and frustration — began to keep track of specific incidents that she and others experienced rather than just the vague, general complaints that were often expressed. She also made an effort to talk with her colleagues about what they saw as ways to avoid negative incidents and better use their professional expertise. When she had collected a number of such ideas, she shared them with her peers to validate whether her accountings were accurate and fair. She then asked the group if they wanted her to speak with the clinic director about their concerns and their suggested solutions, and she asked for their commitment to invest the time and energy needed to make changes in how the work got done if the clinic director challenged them with that charge.

With the support of her peers, this nurse made an appointment with the clinic director, calmly and rationally presented specific complaints, suggested reasonable and well-thought-out solutions to solving these problems, and suggested that the nursing staff prepare a more comprehensive proposal of ways to deal with these issues. The clinic director was so impressed by the nurse's approach and her ability to speak confidently on behalf of the entire group, that he enthusiastically supported the efforts of the staff to explore operational changes that would better use their expertise.

FIGURE 8-7. Representing the group.

[her] constituency in the broadest context, and [she acted] accordingly" (Gardner, 1990, p. 20).

Renewing. Finally, and perhaps most significantly, "leaders must foster the process of renewal" (Gardner, 1990, p. 21). They must constantly provide members of the group with new challenges, reinforce the importance of the goal toward which all are striving, encourage and help group members to reach their fullest potential, be willing to change the

A staff nurse who worked for the visiting nurse service that served an inner-city community was recently elected president of a local professional nursing organization. Based on her involvement in the organization to date, she had observed that in recent years, those who held office and served on committees repeated programs from previous years, "recycled" the same people from one position to another, and structured all meetings in the same way. Additionally, she noted that there was little, if any, reflection on the purpose of the organization or discussion of where the organization wanted to be in the next 5 to 10 years.

Because this nurse believed so strongly in the purposes of this organization and in the value of organizational work itself, she launched a personal campaign to revitalize the group during her term of office. She went back to the organization's mission statement and bylaws to note what its stated purpose and goals were. She then asked her friends, work colleagues, and members of the organization to share their ideas about what those goals might suggest in terms of programs and activities they could sponsor in the current health-care climate.

This nurse approached some of the new graduates who were working at her agency, and she spoke to the faculty member who had students at the agency for clinical experiences. In each instance, she extended an invitation to them to come to the next meeting of the organization and to consider joining the organization and serving on a committee.

She then reflected on the kinds of health care and patient care problems she saw in practice every day and read about in newspapers and professional journals, and she looked at all the flyers posted on the bulletin boards at work announcing conferences, programs, and community projects. This gave her a whole repertoire of possible program topics, speakers, and brochure formats.

Armed with these ideas, she approached the executive committee of the organization and presented them with a variety of ways to revitalize themselves. She was sure to acknowledge how the expertise of those on the executive committee matched some of the ideas suggested, recognize the valuable contributions made by members over the years, ensure the group that it did not have to take on many new things all at once, and commit her time and resources to work with others to "make it happen."

FIGURE 8-8. Renewing.

course of action when it no longer serves the intended purpose, and provide opportunities for members of the group to assume the role of leader. Such actions keep the group stimulated, excited, and energized. An illustration from the perspective of involvement in professional organizations (see Figure 8–8) helps illustrate the process of renewal and its positive impact on a group and an entire organization.

While the process of *renewal* should be a continuous one to keep a group alive and healthy, leaders often have to implement strategies to revitalize a group that has been allowed to stagnate, as was the case here. Once that renewal starts, however, the task of leadership may become keeping the energy focused and reasonably controlled.

NURSING LEADERSHIP FOR THE TWENTY-FIRST CENTURY

It is obvious from this discussion of the tasks of leadership that leadership and management are not the same phenomena. One hopes that an effective manager will also be a leader and carry out all nine tasks of leadership, but this is not always the case. One should not assume that everyone in a position of authority—a nurse manager, the vice president for nursing, the dean of a school of nursing, or the president of a professional organization—is automatically a leader.

By the same token, and perhaps more significantly, leadership is not limited to those in positions of authority, as a number of the examples showed. Each of us has the potential to exhibit leadership at various points in our professional careers, regardless of our title, position, or academic credentials. The only barrier to our exercising leadership is our own unwillingness to take on the challenge.

There is no doubt that leadership is hard work; it takes time and sustained energy, and the rewards for those efforts are often not immediate. But if nurses and nursing are to assume the kind of position in the health-care delivery system of the twenty-first century that we deserve and can manage, each of us must be willing to take on the risk of being a leader.

Nursing leaders for the twenty-first century will need a clear vision of what they want for their profession and for the individuals, families, and communities they serve. They must fight for excellence and be unwilling to accept mediocrity. They must be flexible, willing to change, and able to deal with uncertainty and ambiguity.

The nurses we will look to for leadership in the twenty-first century must be self-assured and self-confident but always open to new ideas and interested in growth and self-improvement. They must be collegial in their interactions with other nurses, acknowledge the strengths, capabilities, and achievements of others, mentor others, and help others take advantage of opportunities to facilitate their own growth.

If nursing is to be a powerful force in health care in the twenty-first century, we will need leaders who are articulate, whose actions are consistent with their words, who are competent and credible, and who can work collaboratively with an interdisciplinary team. Leaders will be needed who are visionary, can ignite followers to join in the effort to make visions real, and can sustain and continually challenge a group as it strives to implement change and face the challenges presented along the way.

Such leaders now exist within our educational programs, the ranks of staff nurses, professional organizations, and among colleagues in nursing education and nursing administration, nurse scientists, and nurse entrepreneurs. Each of us must incorporate the tasks of leadership into our professional practice repertoire and perform those tasks as needed. This kind of behavior on the part of many nurses will ensure the profession's strong future, and nursing will be a significant player in the health-care arena of the twenty-first century.

KEY POINTS

- Leadership is not the same as management, nor is it tied to a position of authority. Leadership is more an art than a science.
- The relationship between leaders and followers is interactive and mutually beneficial.
- A key to effective leadership is the use of an appropriate style at the right time and flexibility to attend to the needs of the followers, use the talents of the group members, and meet the goals of the group.

- Leadership style can be viewed as a set of behaviors that characterize individuals as they perform their leader role. These styles differ in terms of how power is distributed among those leading and those following, how decisions are made, and whose needs are of primary concern.
- There is no single widely accepted definition or theory of leadership. Leadership theories include the great man theory, traitist theory, situational theory, transformational theory, and leadership task theory.
- Leaders "cause ripples," "rock the boat," "disturb the status quo," and take risks.
- Leaders are visionary. They envision goals and possibilities.
- Leaders help a group reflect on their shared vision when they fulfill the leadership task known as affirming values.
- Leaders motivate others to work toward group goals. Motivation includes both internal and external forces that drive individuals to work toward their fullest potentials and help the group achieve its goals.
- Leadership involves managing situations to achieve goals including careful planning, creative processes, providing resources, and making decisions.
- Leaders help a group coalesce as a unified whole so that the group can move forward to achieve its goals.
- Effective leaders teach and explain to allow followers to make informed choices.
- Leaders serve as symbols and spokespersons for the group by reflecting the group's values and collective identity and representing the group.
- A group or organization must constantly be renewed to remain viable and strong.
- The role of the follower is critical, for without followers there can be no leaders.

CHAPTER EXERCISES

1. Think about a nurse in your workplace whom you think of as a leader. What makes that person a leader in your mind? Consider how that individual carries out the tasks of leadership outlined by Gardner.

2. Read about or watch a documentary about someone in history—Eleanor Roosevelt, Thomas Jefferson, Margaret Sanger, John F. Kennedy, Mother Teresa, Martin Luther King—who is often thought of as a leader. What did that person do that influences us to affix the label "leader" to him or her? Do you find evidence that the basis for such acknowledgment is warranted?

3. Write down your vision of the ideal situation where you work. Consider the following questions:
   - What do you see the nurses doing?
   - What patient care outcomes do you envision?
   - How are the nurses treated?
   - If this vision does not match the reality you face on a daily basis, how could you go about making it become reality? In other words, how could *you* provide leadership in your employment setting—like the nurses in the examples provided in this chapter did—to benefit patients and nurses?

4. Using Gardner's nine tasks of leadership, think about how well you "measure up." For those areas you see as strengths, what could you do to reinforce them? For those areas you think are not as well developed, what *specific* strategies could you employ to enhance your leadership abilities?

5. Read the children's story *The Little Engine That Could* (Piper, 1961), or Rudyard Kipling's poem "If." How do the little engine or "being a man" relate to leadership and the challenges inherent in the role of leader?

REFERENCES

Adams, R. (1972). *Watership down*. New York: Avon.

Barker, A. M. (1991). An emerging leadership paradigm: Transformational leadership. *Nursing & Health Care, 12*(4), 204–207.

Barker, A. M. (1990). *Transformational nursing leadership: A vision for the future*. Baltimore: Williams & Wilkins.

Barker, A. M., & Young, C. E. (1994). Transformational leadership: the feminist connection in postmodern organizations. *Holistic Nursing Practice, 9*(1), 16–17.

Bass, B. M. (1990). *Bass & Stogdill's handbook of leadership: Theory, research, and managerial applications* (3rd ed.). New York: The Free Press.

Bennis, W., & Nanus, B. (1985). *Leaders: The strategies for taking charge*. New York: Harper & Row.

Gardner, J. W. (1990). *On leadership*. New York: The Free Press.

Hersey, P., & Blanchard, K. (1977). *Management of organizational behavior: Utilizing human resources* (3rd ed.). Englewood Cliffs, NJ: Prentice-Hall.

Marriner-Tomey, A. (1993). *Transformational leadership in nursing*. St. Louis: Mosby.

Piper, W. (1961). *The little engine that could*. New York: Platt & Munk.

Rost, J. C. (1991). *Leadership for the twenty-first century*. Westport, CT: Praeger.

Van Fleet, D. D., & Yukl, G. A. (1989). A century of leadership research. In W. E. Rosenbach & R. L. Taylor (Eds.), *Contemporary issues in leadership* (2nd ed.) (pp. 65–94). Boulder, CO: Westview Press.

BIBLIOGRAPHY

Bennis, W. (1989). *On becoming a leader*. Reading, MA: Addison-Wesley.

Block, P. (1993). *Stewardship: Choosing service over self-interest*. San Francisco: Berrett-Koehler Publishers.

Bruderle, E. R. (1994). The arts and humanities: A creative approach to developing nurse leaders. *Holistic Nursing Practice, 9*(1), 68–74.

Burns, J. M. (1978). *Leadership*. New York: Harper Torchbooks.

Cassidy, V. R., & Kroll, C. J. (1994). Ethical aspects of transformational leadership. *Holistic Nursing Practice, 9*(1), 41–47.

DePree, M. (1989). *Leadership is an art*. New York: Dell Publishing.

DiRenzo, S. M. (1994). A challenge to nursing: Promoting followers as well as leaders. *Holistic Nursing Practice, 9*(1), 26–30.

Greenleaf, R. K. (1977). *Servant leadership: A journey into the nature of legitimate power and greatness*. New York: Paulist Press.

Kelley, R. E. (1992). *The power of followership: How to create leaders people want to follow and followers who lead themselves*. New York: Doubleday Currency.

Nanus, B. (1992). *Visionary leadership: Creating a compelling sense of direction for your organization*. San Francisco: Jossey-Bass.

Rosenbach, W. E., & Taylor, R. L. (Eds.). (1993). *Contemporary issues in leadership* (3rd ed.). Boulder, CO: Westview Press.

Rost, J. C. (1994). Leadership: A new conception. *Holistic Nursing Practice, 9*(1), 1–8.

Valiga, T. M. (1994). Leadership for the future. *Holistic Nursing Practice, 9*(1), 83–90.

Chapter 9

MANAGEMENT

Maureen Murphy-Ruocco

CHAPTER OBJECTIVES

On completion of this chapter, the reader will be able to:

1. Differentiate between management and leadership.
2. Analyze factors included in motivational, situational, contingency, and path-goal management theories.
3. Discuss the stressors and types of power used in selected managerial situations.
4. Describe skills needed for negotiation in a professional nursing practice dispute.
5. Examine the issues and skills needed to delegate to collegial or ancillary personnel.
6. Discuss techniques for the effective manager to use when dealing with difficult individuals and groups.

KEY TERMS

Management
Interpersonal Role
Informational Role
Decisional Role
Entrepreneurial Role
Motivational Theory
Maslow's Theory of
    Motivation
Theory X

Theory Y
Motivational Factors
Two-Factor Theory
Hygiene Factors
Motivational Factors
Theory Z
Situational Theory
Fiedler's Contingency
    Theory

Leader-Member
    Relationship
Task Structure
Position Power
Path-Goal Theory
Power
Negotiation
Delegation

Since the advent of the principals of scientific management, management and management theory have been marked by constant change. Many authors have defined management, but no one definition of management has been universally accepted. Several authors have defined management as follows:

"**Management** is the process of obtaining and organizing resources and of achieving objectives through other people. Management is dynamic rather than static" (Hellriegel & Slocum, 1989, p. 27).

"**Management** is the process of working with and through others to achieve organizational objectives in a changing environment" (Kreitner, 1992, p. 9).

"**Management** is assuming leadership in planning, directing, monitoring, recognition, development, and in the representation of staff members and administration when needed" (Tappen, 1995, p. 56).

"**Management** is the process of getting work done through others. Nursing management is the process of working through nursing staff members to provide care, cure and comfort to patients (Gillies, 1994, p. 1).

"**Management** refers to the activities needed to plan, organize, motivate, and control human and material resources needed to achieve desired outcomes" (Wise, 1995, p. 4).

MANAGEMENT PROCESS

The management process parallels the nursing process, including data gathering, problem identification, planning, implementation, and evaluation. The steps in the nursing process include gathering information about patients whereas the steps in the management process consist of gathering data about the institution, patients, staff, community, and the legal and budgetary constraints that affect the organization.

DIFFERENCES BETWEEN LEADERSHIP AND MANAGEMENT

Management should not be confused with leadership. According to Tappen (1995), "[a]n effective leader is one who is successful in attempts to influence others to work together in a productive and satisfying manner" (p. 31). Tappen (1995) further describes an effective leader as one who does the following:

- Is knowledgeable in leadership and in a professional field
- Is self-aware and uses self-awareness productively

- Possesses effective communication skills
- Encourages positive energy for leadership activities
- Defines clear, congruent, and meaningful goals
- Initiates action

Figure 9–1 lists the seven components of effective leadership. The most effective leader is one who is successful in all seven components. Tappen (1995) also describes seven components of effective management and concludes that "leadership is a prerequisite for effective management" and the first of its seven components (p. 56). The other components of effective management are planning, direction, monitoring, recognition, development, and representation. An effective manager is one who gets work done efficiently through others and does the following:

- Provides leadership to work group
- Engages in planning the work of the group
- Gives adequate direction to the work group
- Engages in monitoring the quality and productivity of the work performed
- Gives recognition and rewards for quality and productivity
- Encourages development of every member of the work team
- Provides representation of administration and staff in discussion and negotiations

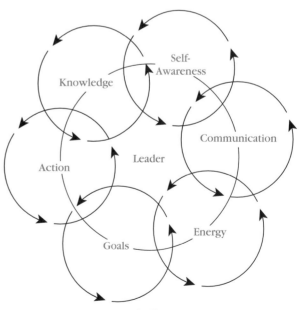

FIGURE 9-1. Components of effective leadership. (Tappen, R. [1995]. *Nursing leadership and management: Concepts and practice.* Philadelphia: F. A. Davis, p. 31.)

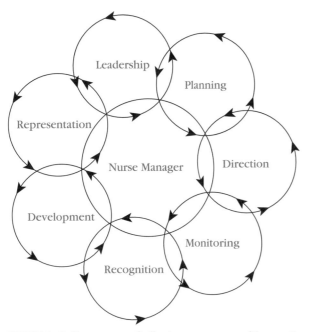

FIGURE 9–2. Components of effective management. (Tappen, R. [1995]. *Nursing leadership and management: Concepts and practice.* Philadelphia: F. A. Davis, p. 56.)

TABLE 9 – 1. Leaders and Managers: Similarities and Differences

Leaders	Managers
May or may not have official appointment to the position	Are appointed to the position
Have power and authority to enforce decisions as long as followers are willing to be led	Have power and authority to enforce decisions
Influence others toward goal setting, either formally or informally by modeling the way	Carry out predetermined policies, rules, and regulations
Are interested in risk taking and exploring new ideas	Maintain an orderly, controlled, rational, and equitable structure
Relate to people personally in an intuitive manner	Relate to people according to their roles by enabling others to act
Feel rewarded by personal achievements	Feel rewarded when fulfilling organizational mission or goals by fostering collaboration
May or may not be successful as a manager	Are managers as long as the appointment holds

Source: Douglass, L. M. (1996). *The effective nurse: Leader and manager.* (p. 8). St. Louis: Mosby, with permission.

Figure 9–2 describes the seven effective management skills. The most effective manager is one who is successful in all seven components. Thus, the components of effective leadership include adequate knowledge, self-awareness, effective communication, productive use of energy, clear, meaningful goal setting, and taking appropriate action (Tappen, 1995); the components of effective management include planning, directing, monitoring, using reward power, developing staff, and adequately representing both staff and administration (Tappen, 1995). Although the terms "leadership" and "management" are often used interchangeably, they actually refer to two distinct attributes. Some individuals in leadership or management positions possess both attributes; however, others do not. It is important to realize that leadership and management skills can be learned. As Drucker (1967) describes the differences, leadership and management both involve the process of influencing others, but management has the specific intention of getting individuals to perform and contribute to organizational goals. Management is a formal, official, designated position within the organization, whereas leadership is an unofficial achieved role assumed by a person at a given time. Management deals with the specific job classification, whereas leadership deals with an individual's characteristics in a particular situation.

Tappen (1995) summarizes the difference by describing management as an assigned role while leadership is an attained one. It is important to understand that, to be a good manager, one must be a good leader; however, to be a good leader one does not need to be a manager at all. In today's health-care market, nurse managers might want to combine the effective components of leadership and management to become the most effective leader-managers. This concept is described by Williamson (1986) in *The Leader-Manager*. Table 9–1 further summarizes the similarities and differences between leaders and managers.

FOUNDATION OF EFFECTIVE MANAGEMENT

Understanding the foundation of effective management is essential in developing one's own management style. Nurse managers must select the most appropriate theory for a given situation. The management process is a logical, rational process based on problem-solving principles (Huber, 1996).

Henri Fayol (1949), the "father of the management process," was associated with the universalist approach to management. His approach involved three important principles: authority, unity of command, and communication. Fayol's (1949) ideas translated into the functions of a manager to plan, organize, command, coordinate, and control. He believed that regardless of the organization in which he or she is employed, the manager is involved with these five functions.

FUNCTIONS OF A MANAGER

Mintzberg (1975) describes the functions of the manager differently. He stated that the manager fulfills four types of roles: interpersonal, informational, decisional, and entrepreneurial. The **interpersonal role** includes participating in ceremonial and leadership activities, and acting as a figurehead and liaison. The **informational role** includes informational power and accessing information to improve the productivity of work, as well as being a monitor, disseminator, and spokesperson. The **decisional role** includes making budgetary allocations, negotiating, and dealing with conflict in roles such as entrepreneur, disturbance handler, resource allocator, and negotiator. The **entrepreneurial role** involves being aware of new ideas and opportunities to improve the effectiveness and profitability of the organization. The manager's ability in each role is vital to the functioning of the organization. The work of Henri Fayol and Mintzberg laid the foundation for effective management. Fayol's approach conceptualizes the management process. Mintzberg's model conceptualizes the way managers think about their role. This model can be used to provide self-evaluation and examine and analyze managerial styles, behaviors, and roles (Huber, 1996).

MANAGEMENT THEORIES

Management theory began with Frederick Taylor, the "father of scientific management." Taylor was an engineer who applied his scientific management in the steel industry. His work and ideas spread throughout Europe and America through his books, *Shop Management* in 1911 and *The Principles of Scientific Management* in 1912 (cited in Locke, 1982). Management theory provides a framework for organizing thought, ideas, and experiences. Taylor conducted time and motion studies to determine how to get a task done in the shortest period of time. He was able to calculate how many employees were needed for a specific project. Once he determined the most efficient way to perform a task, he trained individuals to follow his method. He focused on how to increase the efficiency and productivity of each individual employee. Taylor introduced the concept of basing pay on one's rate of production. This helped reduce resistance to change while increasing production and profits. The scientific management approach "reduced time wasters, set performance standards, encouraged specialization and stressed the selection of the most qualified worker for a particular job" (Marriner-Tomey, 1996, p. 282). Today, you can see the influences of Taylor's work in the emphasis on cost-effectiveness, quality control, and productivity.

MOTIVATIONAL THEORIES

Motivational theory identifies and describes the forces that motivate individuals toward a goal. Tappen (1995) states that motivation stimulates satisfaction and productivity and eliminates factors that inhibit growth (p. 89). "Motivation is tapping into what we value, personally and professionally, and reinforcing those factors to achieve growth and movement toward our vision" (Wise, 1995, p. 9). The most successful manager is one who highly motivates individuals, thus enhancing their productivity.

Maslow's Hierarchy of Needs

Maslow's (1970) **theory of motivation** is based on the idea that some human needs are more basic than others. Maslow's hierarchy begins with the most basic physiologic needs, followed by the needs for safety and security, love and belonging, esteem, and, at the highest level, self-actualization. The theory is that the most basic needs must be at least partially satisfied for a person to have enough energy and motivation to work toward higher needs. This theory can be useful to managers by focusing attention on individuals' needs and recognizing that different people may have different needs at different times. This knowledge allows the manager to focus on helping people meet basic needs to gain the energy to work on higher-level needs.

McGregor's Theory X and Theory Y

McGregor (1960) makes many assumptions about motivation in *The Human Side of Enterprise*. He identifies two beliefs about human nature and describes how they lead to different approaches to leadership and management. Theory X is compared to the traditional idea of direction and control, whereas Theory Y involves integrating the individual goals with organizational goals. Thus, Theory X is the basis for effective management and Theory Y is the basis for management by objectives (Bernhard & Walsh, 1995). The principle underlying **Theory X** is that a traditional manager of bureaucratic organization operates under the assumption that individuals are lazy, unmotivated, dislike work, are not interested in organizations' goals, and avoid responsibility. These individuals will work only as hard as necessary to keep their jobs and must be told what needs to be done and how to accomplish a goal. Direction and control by the manager is necessary for these individuals to feel secure in their accomplishments. A system of rewards and punishments is used to motivate them. The individuals who obey the rules and regulations are rewarded, and those who disobey are reprimanded or fired.

McGregor questioned the validity of these assumptions and developed another set of assumptions called Theory Y, which assumes that Theory X is not true but is a result of a manager whose constant control leads to lack of motivation. **Theory Y** sees individuals as eager, motivated, enjoying and being rewarded by work, interested in organizational goals, and willing to accept responsibility appropriately. These individuals will complete their projects without constant supervision. The manager role in Theory Y is to provide guidance, support, and encouragement for individuals who are already creative, self-directed employees.

Herzberg's Hygiene and Motivational Theories

Herzberg (1966) proposes a two-factor theory. The **two-factor theory** separates the needs that affect an individual person's motivation to work into two factors: motivation and hygiene. The **hygiene factors,** or dissatisfiers, are factors a person needs to avoid pain and discomfort in the workplace. These factors include supervision, company policy, working conditions, status, job security, salary, and the effect on one's personal life. When these hygiene factors are not met the individual is dissatisfied. The **motivational factors,** or satisfiers, are factors that a person needs to grow to reach higher levels of performance. The motivational factors include achievement, recognition, work itself, responsibility, advancement, and growth. When these motivational factors are met, the individual is satisfied. The manager helps increase job performance by ensuring that both hygiene and motivational needs are met.

TABLE 9–2. Comparison of Maslow's, Herzberg's, and McGregor's Theories

Maslow	Herzberg	McGregor
Physiologic needs Safety needs	Hygiene factors	Theory X
Need to belong Esteem needs Need for self-actualization	Motivator	Theory Y

Source: Adapted from Kelly, J. (1980). *Organization behavior* (rev. ed.) (p. 220). Homewood, IL: Irwin, reprinted with permission.

As viewed in Maslow's theory, individuals who are highly motivated can tolerate some dissatisfaction, which provides some insight into Herzberg's theory. Hygiene factors can be motivators, but only when "hygiene factors are satisfied do satisfiers such as responsibility become motivators" (Marriner-Tomey, 1996, p. 341). Herzberg maintains that individuals given challenging work with responsibility will continue to be motivated employees.

Table 9–2 describes the relationship between Maslow's physiologic, safety, and love needs, Herzberg's hygiene factors, and the factors in McGregor's Theory X. Similarly, the esteem and self-actualization needs described by Maslow can be compared to Herzberg's motivators and McGregor's Theory Y.

Ouchi's Theory Z

Ouchi (1981) describes the Japanese style of managerial success as an alternative to American management style. The Japanese style focuses on developing more productive ways to motivate people. The theory focuses on collaborative management, which involves trusting employees and having them participate in decision making. Thus, Theory Z, like Theory Y, takes a humanistic approach.

ELEMENTS OF THEORY Z

The elements included in **Theory Z** are "collective values and decision making, long-term or lifetime employment, slower but more predictable promotions, indirect supervision and a holistic concern for employees" (Ouchi, 1981). The collective values and decision-making process is a democratic, participative style of decision making. The participation involves everyone affected by the decision. The goal is to reach full consensus of the group for a decision. The "consensus approach yields more creative decisions and more effective implementation than does individual decision making" (Ouchi, 1981, p. 43). Long-term or lifetime employment and slower predictable promotions are also important elements in Theory Z. The objective is to keep individuals moving within the same organization, promoting them after careful performance appraisals. This encourages long-term commitments and discourages people from trying to make themselves look good at the expense of others (Tappen, 1995, p. 92).

Indirect supervision is another element of Theory Z (Ouchi, 1981). Employees who are knowledgeable of the philosophy, goals, and objectives of the organization are accepted as part of the whole. Since they are part of the team, they do not need to be told what to do or what decision to make. Team members communicate with each other, producing a highly effective organization.

Caring behavior, described by Ouchi as holistic concern, is another element of Theory Z. Simply stated, the organization treats everyone fairly. This includes concern for the individual's well-being as a member of the organization as well as his or her well-being as a human being.

Other elements of Theory Z are trust, fairness, commitment, and loyalty to the organization. Theory Z helped create work groups that identify problems, explore solutions, and make decisions. These work groups, or *quality circles,* are disciplined operations committed to training individuals in group skills, in a step-step improvement process (Strader, 1987). Quality circles helped "increase worker productivity,

enhanced job satisfaction, and reduced turnover, in addition to solving identified problems" (Marriner-Tomey, 1996, p. 340). These work groups have been successful in the United States. However, Ouchi's style of management has lost influence as management theorists have come to realize that Japanese values, culture, and society are different from those of the United States. Many American organizations using Ouchi's style have been successful, but some theorists believe the success of this theory is unproven. Figure 9–3 illustrates Ouchi's Theory Z.

SITUATIONAL THEORIES

Situational theory is a "leadership approach based on the leader's self-understanding, understanding of the group affected by the situation, and comprehension of the situation itself" (Wise, 1995, p. 562). The manager must assess the size, complexity, and climate of the organization, the characteristics of the leader, the abilities of the staff, and the ability of the organization to adapt and react to change (Wise, 1995). This theory assumes that in a constantly changing environment managers may need to adapt their style of leadership. This approach also assumes that no one style of leadership is appropriate in all leadership situations. The environment plays a considerable role in the outcomes of all leadership and management events. Fiedler's contingency theory and House's path-goal theory are both situational theories.

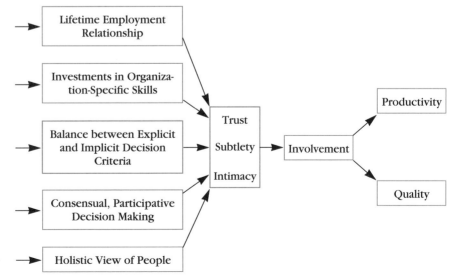

FIGURE 9-3. Theory Z model. (Shortell, S. M. [1982]. Theory implications and relevance for health care management. *Health Care Management,* 74, 9, with permission.)

Fiedler's Contingency Theory

Fiedler's contingency theory (1967) defines leadership as an interpersonal relationship in which power and influence are unevenly distributed so that one person is able to direct and control the actions and behaviors of others to a greater extent than they direct and control their actions and behaviors. Fiedler and Chemers (1974), from the University of Washington, have done extensive research on this leadership model. In their model, leaders may be appointed, elected, or emerging (Fiedler, 1967). They believe that the leader's characteristics are fixed and cannot be changed. A leader's style is either task-oriented or relationship-oriented. The leader is primarily responsible for getting the group to complete the task, and the group's productivity measures the leader's effectiveness. The measure of power and influence depends on three factors that make the situation favorable or unfavorable for the leader (Bernhard & Walsh, 1995, p. 85): the *leader-member relationship, task structure,* and *position power.*

SITUATIONAL FACTORS

The **leader-member relationship** is based on the amount of confidence, loyalty, trust, and acceptance a group has in the leader. The relationship is measured on a continuum from good to poor. Fiedler concludes that the better one's relationship with the staff, the easier it is to influence them. Figure 9–4 illustrates how Fiedler measured leadership effectiveness by a group-atmosphere scale and sociometric index of the least-preferred coworker (Fiedler, 1967). Fiedler suggests that those with high ratings are relationship-oriented leaders and those with low scores are task-oriented leaders. Relationship-oriented leaders perform best when there is no imminent issue or crisis. Task-oriented leaders perform best when a situation needs control (Wise, 1995).

Task structure is the degree to which a task can be defined and measured. Fiedler measured task structure by examining four criteria:

1. The extent to which the followers understand the goal
2. The extent to which the followers know who is responsible for what
3. The number of solutions to the situation
4. The number of best possible solutions

A nursing procedure may have high task structure, but a situation that involves human feelings and concerns may not have many solutions or a best solution, and thus may need low task structure (Marriner-Tomey, 1996, p. 272).

Position power refers to the power inherent in a position, and the organization's willingness to support that power. The leader influences the behavior of the staff through the use of legitimate reward and coercive power. Power runs along a continuum from strong to weak, indicating the individual's status in the organization. Douglass (1996) suggests that the leader should attempt to define a particular style of leadership that is appropriate for a given situation and then match the style and situation. The leadership style one uses in a given situation determines its effectiveness or ineffectiveness. In this model, the

The group is instructed to rate the least preferred co-workers on an eight point bipolar adjective scale as illustrated here. A high score gives a person a favorable or positive rating and a low score is an unfavorable or negative rating. Describe the atmosphere of your group by checking the following items:

	8 7 6 5 4 3 2 1	
1. Friendly	:__:__:__:__:__:__:__:__:	Unfriendly
2. Accepting	:__ __ __ __ __ __ __ __	Rejecting
3. Satisfying	:__:__:__:__:__:__:__:__:	Frustrating
4. Enthusiastic	:__ __ __ __ __ __ __ __	Unenthusiastic
5. Productive	:__:__:__:__:__:__:__:__:	Nonproductive
6. Warm	:__ __ __ __ __ __ __ __	Cold
7. Cooperative	:__:__:__:__:__:__:__:__:	Uncooperative
8. Supportive	:__ __ __ __ __ __ __ __	Hostile
9. Interesting	:__:__:__:__:__:__:__:__:	Boring
10. Successful	:__ __ __ __ __ __ __ __	Unsuccessful

FIGURE 9–4. Group atmosphere scale. (From Fiedler, F. E. [1967]. *A theory of leadership effectiveness.* New York: McGraw-Hill, with permission.)

most effective leader is one who assesses the situation and selects a manager whose style fits the situation. Fiedler and Chemer's model has contributed significantly to the management literature, but some questions still remain. Is the leadership style really fixed and rigid and why weren't more observations made of the interactions between the leadership style and the situation (Douglass, 1996, p. 26)? The most effective leader is one who can adapt his or her leadership style to a given situation.

Path-Goal Theory

House (1971) developed the **path-goal theory,** in which the leader facilitates task achievement by limiting obstacles to attaining a goal and rewarding the individual who completes tasks successfully (Marriner-Tomey, 1996).

Two behaviors that have positive influences on group satisfaction and productivity are *initiating structure* and *considerations* (Fleishman, 1973). Initiating structure is a behavioral dimension that shows a leader's concern with the work and goals of the organization. This includes defining roles, planning, assigning tasks, and encouraging productivity. Consideration is a behavioral dimension that shows a leader's concern for the individuals under his or her guidance. It includes the development of trust, caring behaviors, and encouragement of good communication skills (Fleishman & Harris, 1962).

INITIATING STRUCTURE

In House's (1971) path-goal theory, the leader initiates structure to facilitate the actions of others toward attaining goals. This structure includes planning, organizing, directing, and controlling activities. It helps increase motivation by decreasing role ambiguity. Leaders who structure activities usually have more productive work groups and get better performance evaluations (Marriner-Tomey, 1996).

CONSIDERATIONS

The leader uses consideration, such as removing an obstacle, to make goal attainment easier. These considerations include being warm and friendly, exhibiting caring behaviors, and removing obstacles that may be undesirable to staff. Research shows that group cohesiveness depends on both initiating structure and consideration (Bernhard & Walsh, 1995). Leaders who use behavioral dimensions, initiating structure, and considerations are the most effective leaders (Stogdill, 1974).

LEADERSHIP STYLE

House (1971) indicates that experienced individuals prefer a structured leader, while less experienced individuals prefer a considerate leader. Depending on a given situation, the leader may use "directive, supportive, participative, and achievement oriented styles" (Douglass, 1996, p. 26). The leader's behaviors affect the individual's and group's performance. Individual differences affect the individual's perception of leader behavior (Marriner-Tomey, 1996). The leader who can select the best style in a given situation produces the best outcomes, including higher job satisfaction and higher overall performance, with minimal grievances (Douglass, 1996).

POWER

Power is the "ability to change people's behavior whether they want it changed or not" (Tappen, 1995, p. 345). Power consists of a gentle or harsh force used to overcome resistance to a problem or issue. The original five conceptualizations of power developed by French and Raven (1959) identify legitimate, reward, coercive, expert, and referent power. These original sources relate mostly to an individual's power base. Other authors have identified sources that are specifically related to groups and organizations. Raven and Kruglanski (1975) and Hersey and Goldsmith (Hersey & Duldt, 1989) identify two sources of power: connection power and informational power. Liberatore and associates (1989) identify group decision-making power. Tappen (1995) identifies several other types of power, including physical strength, ability to harm, positional power, money, legal power, public recognition and support, expert power, power of an idea, strength in numbers, and control of access to resources. Marriner-Tomey (1996) also identifies reward, coercive, legitimate, referent, and expert power, and adds informal sources of power. Power is influence potential that enables a manager to gain control. The following are descriptions of the different types of power:

Legitimate power is given to a manager in the organizational hierarchy. Legitimate power is power of official position, which empowers the manager with the right to influence others. Empowerment gives an individual the authority, responsibility, and freedom to act on what he or she knows the confidence in his or her ability to succeed (Kramer & Schmalenberg, 1990).

Reward power comes from the ability to give something of value to an individual who has complied with the manager's request. Sources of this power include salary increases, promotion, special assignments, praise, public acknowledgment of accomplishments, and personal space (new office, designated parking space). Reward power is based on the ability to give individuals desired rewards (Huber, 1996, p. 386).

Coercive power comes from the ability to use the fear of punishment for noncompliance with the manager's wishes. The power includes the ability to deliver penalties if individuals do not comply with requests. Coercive power is the opposite of reward power. Sources of coercive power include salary cuts, undesirable assignments, reprimands, public embarrassment, and termination of employment.

Expert power comes from manager's possession of special knowledge, skills, and ability in a particular area. Expertise combines the knowledge, skill, and experience that help the manager influence the actions of others toward goal attainment. Managers with expertise get respect and compliance from their employees. A group may also give expert power to the manager by deferring to the manager because they trust his or her knowledge and expertise (Bernhard & Walsh, 1995).

Referent power comes from the manager's ability to influence others by charisma. The manager is admired and exerts influence over individuals because they want to emulate him or her. Referent power can be viewed as inspirational because the admired manager can influence others without offering them rewards or threaten punishments (Huber, 1996).

Legitimate, reward, and coercive forms of power are given to managers by the organization. Expert power and, to some degree, referent power are characteristics of the individual manager, and are usually not given by the organization. Expert power is gained through education and experience. Referent power is usually gained by learning how to deal with people. The most successful manager is one who uses many power sources to influence others. Table 9–3 lists other sources of power.

THE ART OF NEGOTIATION

The art of negotiation is one of the most important strategies that a nurse manager needs to learn. Smeltzer (1991) confirms that nurse administrators who use a scientific method of negotiation to augment their professional judgement and decision mak-

ing create a climate conducive to success. "**Negotiation** is a high-level management skill" (Marquis & Huston, 1994, p. 310). However, it is crucial that nurse managers not be intimidated by the process of negotiation. Negotiation is a strategy that is useful in avoiding head-on competition or a win-lose conflict outcome (Huber, 1996). Negotiation means compromise. Compromise is giving up something that you want. It can be successful if both parties give up something of equal value. Huber (1996) describes negotiation as a give-and-take exchange among persons aimed at resolving problems or conflicts in a way that is acceptable to all parties. Booth (1993) describes negotiation as a process that occurs when individuals reach an agreement with stated conditions and expectations as a resolution. Negotiation is used when individuals have strong or conflicting views and agreement, resolution, or compromise is needed. Smeltzer (1991) describes two types of negotiation: cooperative and competitive. In *cooperative negotiation,* everyone involved wins, and in *competitive negotiation,* only one party wins. If both parties in a situation want change, cooperative negotiation is likely to be used. However, if only one party wants a change, competitive negotiation is more likely. Negotiation is needed to resolve conflict.

The negotiation process is the back-and-forth communication that occurs when parties want to change their relationship. One of the most important factors in successful negotiation is the mutual trust between the parties involved and trust in the negotiating process. Information about the other party's needs can be a strategic power resource and helpful input for decision making (Huber, 1996). Negotiators who identify the needs of the other party put themselves in a better position to negotiate. The other party in the negotiation usually attempts to catch the negotiator offguard. Negotiators who have done their homework will not be caught by this tactic. The more information the negotiator has, the greater degree of bargaining power. There is a positive relationship between informational power and a successful negotiation.

Another important factor of successful negotiating is determining the climate in which the negotiation is going to take place. The climate surrounding a negotiation falls on a continuum from defensive to supportive. A defensive climate is one in which the interaction leads to feelings of superiority, and parties see the negotiator as controlling. In a supportive climate, the interaction is focused on the issues and is problem-centered.

It is important for a successful negotiator to have adequate information and good active listening and communication skills. A good negotiator will try to win

TABLE 9–3. Other Sources of Power

Type of Power	Definition
Connection power	Manager's ability to get accurate, reliable information because of the manager's connections with other powerful individuals. This type of power comes from networking and getting to know individuals in and out of the organization.
Informational power	Manager's ability to access information of value to others. A manager's control of the information he or she gives away is a major organizational power source (Kanter, 1979). Information can be a tremendous source of power in negotiating. The control of information contributes to a strong power base (Huber, 1996).
Group decision-making power	Manager's ability to create a group that can make decisions together and act as a unit. Unity of action is a powerful strategy in achieving goals (Huber, 1996). The larger the group, the harder it is for others to oppose them. Examples of groups that have decision-making power are the American Nurses Association and professional nurses' groups.
Physical strength	The use of physical force to change behavior. Using physical force in leadership is rarely appropriate. It is not an acceptable social norm, may be illegal, and can lead to violence (Tappen, 1995).
Money	Power of individuals or group who have control of financial assets. These individuals may have tremendous power because they can control workers' behavior. This power may be exerted to encourage workers to work hard if they want to increase their income or maintain their salary.
Legal power	Power that requires knowledge of law and legislation. Established laws can support change in the system. Using legal power can force a system to change.
Public recognition and support	Power related to receiving public approval and recognition. Many organizations have public relations departments to ensure public approval and support. Favorable public opinion usually increases the number of individuals who use the organization and financial contributions to the organization (Tappen, 1995). Favorable newspaper articles and letters of support for the organization can be tremendous sources of power.
Power of an idea	Power of an idea being heard. Ideas have the most power when they can be simply stated, easily remembered, and accepted by most members of the group (Tappen, 1995).
Strength in numbers	Power of the number of people who support an idea. An organized following is an important power strategy (Tappen 1995).
Control of access to resources	Power from controlling access to money, information, and communications. Organizations are not successful without access to money, information, and communication. Individuals who control access to these sources have an enormous power base (Tappen, 1995).
Informal sources of power	Power related to one's personal power. Individuals may have personal characteristics that make them reliable and credible. These characteristics include education, experience, drive, and decisiveness. Interpersonal relations can also increase one's personal power base. These relations can help an individual gain power of information (Marriner-Tomey, 1996).

as much as necessary to achieve the goals and objectives, lose as little as possible, and make the others feel the outcome of the negotiation was successful. The abilities to use appropriate negotiation strategies, provide closure, and follow up on the negotiation are essential for an effective negotiator (Marquis & Huston, 1996). Awareness of negotiating strategies enhances the nurse manager's role in choosing alternative solutions to problems or issues. Factors that lead to poor negotiating include inactive listening, inadequate information, and poor communication skills.

Learning the specific language of negotiating is also important for nurse managers. Laser (1981) defines five terms used in negotiating:

- Issues—What must be resolved
- Impasse—A situation in which an issue cannot be resolved to the satisfaction of both parties

- Deadlock or stalemate—When an agreement cannot be met at all
- Power—The ability to influence the other party
- Concession—Something given up to satisfy the other party to facilitate a settlement

The nurse manager must become familiar with these negotiating terms to be a successful negotiator. Laser (1991) also defines four negotiating strategies:

- Flinch—Drawing back at the initial proposal of the other parties. This reveals the uncertainty of the other parties and opens the negotiation process.
- Deadline—Deadlines are advisable for every negotiation and are negotiable.
- Concession—Something given to satisfy the other party to facilitate settlement.

▪ Nibble—A small extra requested after a settlement has been reached. The nibbler relies on the impatience of the negotiator to finalize the negotiation.

The nurse manager must learn these strategies for successful negotiating. Peter Block describes negotiation with allies and adversaries in his book *The Empowered Manager*. Following are the five types of characters involved in the negotiation process:

▪ Adversaries—People with whom we have low agreement and low trust
▪ Opponents—People whom we trust but disagree with on goals and objectives
▪ Allies—People with whom we have high agreement and high trust. They are truly our friends
▪ Bedfellows—People with whom we have high agreement but low trust. Information should not be freely shared because of the low trusting relationship
▪ Fence setters—People who do not take a stand for or against the issue

Steps in the negotiating process are (1) recognizing the tactic, (2) raising the issue explicitly, and, (3) questioning the legitimacy and desirability of the tactics (Marriner-Tomey, 1996). Trust, not agreement, is the major issue in negotiating. When we have principled negotiations with individuals with whom we more or less agree, trust builds the relationship and advances the negotiation (Marriner-Tomey, 1996).

THE ART OF DELEGATION

Delegation is the "transfer of responsibility of the performance of an activity from one individual to another, with the former retaining accountability of the outcome" (American Nurses Association, 1994, p. 11). Marquis and Huston (1994) have defined delegation as directing the performance of one or more individuals to accomplish organizational goals. Essentially, delegation is getting the work done through others. The delegator is the nurse manager who assigns the task or project. The delegate is the person who receives the task or project. Delegation is necessary for every manager. Delegation extends the manager's influence and capability by increasing what can be accomplished (Marquis & Huston, 1994). An effective manager empowers individuals to perform assigned tasks. One important aspect of delegation is that the delegate must have a clear understanding of expectations. Another important aspect is acceptance of responsibility and accountability for the project (Huber, 1996). Reasons for delegation are

described by Rowland and Rowland (1985) as assignment of routine tasks, assignment of tasks for which the manager does not have time, problem solving, changes in the manager's job emphasis, and capability building or empowering others.

Huber (1996) states that delegation is not the indiscriminate assignment of work, giving orders, or abdicating control or responsibility. The nurse manager's ability to apply the principles of delegation is essential to effective management.

Principles of Delegation

Delegation requires assessment of a person's or group's competency. Hansten (1991) identifies six principles of delegation:

1. Knowing yourself and members of your team well
2. Assessing strengths, weaknesses, job descriptions, the situation, and the skills of yourself and the team members
3. Understanding the state practice acts, practice limitations, and job descriptions
4. Knowing the job requirements
5. Keeping communication clear, complete, and constant
6. Evaluating the outcomes

Education, experience, empowerment, clear expectations, and willingness (Wise, 1995) are all factors that the nurse manager must consider before appropriate delegation can occur. Knowing the level of expertise of your staff is critical to successful delegation. It is the responsibility of the delegator to do an adequate assessment, which should include how long the individual will need supervision. The nurse manager's legal responsibility in making assignments is to delegate appropriate assignments and provide adequate supervision (Barter & Furmidge, 1994). Delegation involves giving responsibility, but how much authority is transferred with this responsibility is important to the delegate's ability to perform the task (Huber, 1996). Effective delegation requires the authority to accompany the responsibility (Huber, 1996). However, ultimate responsibility and accountability rest with the nurse manager, who is responsible for the outcome of the task or project. Delegation has many positive effects, including increased freedom, time, and efficiency to accomplish organization goals (Huber, 1996).

Process of Delegating

Huber (1996) describes four basic steps in the delegating process: (1) selecting a competent and capable person, (2) explaining the task and project outcome, (3) confering authority and means to do the job, and (4) keeping in contact and giving feedback. The process also includes giving a timetable and conference time to review the project to date and provide appropriate feedback. Establishing specific time frames helps keep the project on task and keeps the channels of communication between the delegator and the delegate open. The success of the delegation depends on two factors: clear communication and trust. When you delegate, you must trust the individual to whom you delegate a project. Many errors can occur in delegating. Marquis and Huston (1994) describe three:

1. *Underdelegation.* The manager does not delegate enough and is overworked and overwhelmed.
2. *Overdelegation.* The manager delegates because he or she is a poor time manager and delegates the work to others.
3. *Improper delegation.* Projects are not delegated to the right person at the right time or for the right reason.

Delegation can increase the manager's influence if projects are accomplished in a timely fashion. When goals are accomplished, subordinates feel a sense of ownership and satisfaction. For an organization to be successful, managers must delegate appropriately.

DEALING WITH DIFFICULT PEOPLE

One essential element a nurse manager should convey to his or her staff is the importance of knowing the institution's policies and procedures. The nurse manager's responsibility is to orient the staff to the policies and procedures and keep them updated accordingly. The staff's responsibility is to keep the knowledge current and review the policies and procedures as needed. All employees must receive a written copy of the employee handbook, which includes all policies and procedures. Policies that relate to disciplinary action and grievance procedures are extremely important for the employee to understand. These policies and procedures need to be well-defined and outlined.

Individuals have different values, needs, and expectations in the workplace. When these values, needs, and expectations do not match their goals, conflict usually occurs. Conflict can be defined as the internal discord that results from differences in the ideas, values, or beliefs of two or more people (Marquis & Huston, 1994). Conflict can be minor or major. Minor conflict is usually not important to any

of the parties. Major conflicts, however, are enormously important and can involve emotional, political, and financial issues (Tappen, 1995). Conflict may continue for hours, days, months, or even years. It can be manifested by competition, people glaring at one another, exchanges of angry words, or withdrawal (Douglass, 1996).

Negative behavior can reflect conflict. Nurse managers are challenged when they have to deal with individuals who display negative behaviors and attitudes. Mintzberg (1975) describes the manager as a disturbance handler. Disturbance handlers decide when, how, and where they will resolve the disturbance or problem or handle the difficult person. One's interpersonal managerial skills are tested in dealing with difficult people. After each interaction with a difficult person, the manager should assess his or her assets and deficits in the interaction. This assessment enables the manager to capitalize on strengths and learn from weaknesses. With every interaction we can learn new behaviors or strategies to deal with difficult people or situations. The manager's role is to identify the source of conflict and understand the friction points (Douglass, 1996, p. 226).

Lewis-Ford (1993) categorizes difficult people as follows:

- Exploders have temper tantrums.
- Bulldozers are condescending know-it-alls, who do not respect other people's judgment.
- Balloons range from braggarts to tyrants, they like to know what's going on.
- Sherman tankers are abusive, abrupt, and intimidating.
- Negative nabobs are naysayers and pessimists.
- Complainers are whiners who find a problem with everything.
- Clams use silence as weapon.
- Snipers use digs to take low shots at people. Hostiles are aggressive individuals.
- Stallers agree with plans, but then do not follow through (pp 36–38).

Lewis-Ford (1993) also describes a two-step management approach for dealing with difficult people. The *grand tactic,* the first approach, is used to maintain peace and dignity for all involved. Management strategies include calming down and gaining control; lowering your voice, which helps keep the environment calm; choosing your position on the subject; guarding your position, and never whining or crying.

Long-range strategies are the second approach. These strategies include categorizing difficult people to help you understand them, and validating your assessment with others, planning a strategy for each category of difficult person, and practicing the strategies, and thus, preparing yourself psychologically before you interact with these people. When the behaviors of difficult people are too destructive, discipline may be an appropriate approach.

Managers must acquire the necessary skills to fa-cilitate conflict resolution between individuals, as well as their own intrapersonal or interpersonal conflicts. A successful manager is one who has the participants leave feeling a sense of "self-worth because their views, feeling and behaviors were respected" (Douglass, 1996).

KEY POINTS

- Nursing management has been defined in several ways, but no single definition has been accepted by all.
- The terms "leadership" and "management" are often used interchangeably, but they actually refer to two different attributes of an individual.
- The six components of effective leadership are knowledge, self-awareness, clear communication, positive energy, having meaningful goals, and initiating action.
- The seven components of effective management are leadership, planning, directing, monitoring, recognition, development, and representation.
- Leadership and management skills can be learned through education and practice.
- Leadership is a prerequisite for effective management.
- Management is a formal, officially designated position.
- Leadership is an attained role; management is an assigned role.
- Henri Fayol's ideas identify the functions of a manager as planning, organizing, commanding, coordinating, and controlling.
- Mintzberg describes the manager as fulfilling four different roles: interpersonal, informational, decisional, and entrepreneurial.
- Frederick Taylor was the father of scientific management.
- The most successful manager is one who can highly motivate individuals, enhancing their productivity.
- Maslow's theory of motivation helps managers focus on meeting individuals' basic needs, providing the energy to work on their higher-level needs.
- McGregor describes Theory X and Theory Y—two approaches to leadership and management based on different principles.
- Herzberg describes a two-factor theory that deals with hygiene and motivation factors. The manager improves job performance by making sure hygiene and motivation factors are met.
- Ouchi's Theory Z is the Japanese form of participative management. The elements in Theory Z are collective decision making, long-term employment, predictable promotions, indirect supervision, and a concern for others.
- Situational theory assumes that a constantly changing environment requires managers to adapt their style of leadership accordingly.
- Fiedler and Chemers believe that the leader's characteristics are fixed and cannot change; thus, specific leaders should be matched to specific leadership situations.
- In path-goal theory, the most effective leader is one who uses behavioral dimensions, considerations, and initiating structure.
- Power is the ability to change people's behavior. Its use can be described as legitimate, reward, coercive, expert, and referent. Sources of power include connection power, informational power, group decision making, physical

strength, money, legal power, public recognition and support, power of an idea, strength in numbers, control of access to resources, and informal sources.

■ Negotiation is a high-level management skill needed to resolve conflict.

■ A successful negotiator has adequate information and uses active listening and good communication skills. The negotiator makes the other party feel the outcome of the negotiation was successful.

■ Trust is a major issue in the art of negotiating.

■ Delegation extends the manager's influence and ability to get work done through others.

■ The success of delegation depends on two factors: clear communication and trust.

■ Marquis and Huston (1994) describe three errors made in delegating: under-delegation, overdelegation, and improper delegation.

■ Managers are challenged in dealing with individuals who display negative behaviors and attitudes.

■ The manager's role in dealing with difficult people is to identify the source of negative behaviors and attitudes or conflict and develop a management approach to deal with these people.

■ All managers must develop skills to facilitate conflict resolution. If the behaviors of individuals are too destructive, discipline may be appropriate.

CHAPTER EXERCISES

1. Apply the seven components of effective management to a nursing practice situation.

2. Apply Mintzberg's four managerial roles to a situation that you have observed in practice.

3. Describe how Theories X, Y, and Z could be used in a nursing unit situation.

4. Analyze a nursing situation in which you need to use power. Debate this issue with a colleague as follows:
   ■ Choose sides in the power struggle.
   ■ Identify your opponent's power sources.
   ■ Role-play the position in the situation.
   ■ Analyze your power position.

5. Develop a scenario in which negotiation takes place to solve a nursing issue or situation.
   ■ Understand negotiating terms.
   ■ Identify negotiating strategies.
   ■ Identify five different characters in negotiating.

6. Develop a scenario for working with difficult people.
   ■ Identify the characteristics of a difficult person with whom you work.
   ■ Develop a strategy for dealing with this person.
   ■ Practice this strategy with a colleague who can role-play negative behaviors.

REFERENCES

American Nurses Association. (1994). *Registered professional nurses and unlicensed assistive personnel*. Washington, DC: American Nurses Association.

Barter, M., & Furmidge, M. L. (1994). Unlicensed assistive personnel: issues relating to delegation and supervision. *Journal of Nursing Administration, 24*(4), 36–40.

Bernhard, L., & Walsh, M. (1995) *Leadership. The key to the professionalization of nursing* (3rd ed.). St. Louis: Mosby-Year Book.

Block, P. (1987). *The empowered manager*. San Francisco: Jossey:Bass.

Booth, R. (1993). Dynamics of conflict and conflict management. In Mason, D., Talboot, S., & Leavitt, J., (Eds.). *Policy and politics for nurses: Action and change in the workplace, government, organizations, and community* (2nd ed.) (pp. 149–165). Philadelphia: Saunders.

Douglass, L. M. (1996). *The effective nurse— Leader and manager* (5th ed.). St. Louis: Mosby-Year Book.

Drucker, P. F. (1967). *The effective executive*. New York: Harper & Row.

Fayol, H. (trans.). (1949). *General and industrial management*, by C. Storrs. London: Pittman & Sons.

Fiedler, F. E. (1967). *A theory of leadership effectiveness*. New York: McGraw-Hill.

Fiedler, F. E., & Chemers, M. M. (1974). *Leadership and effective management*. New York: Scott, Foresman & Co.

Fleishman, E. A. (1973). Twenty years of consideration and structure. In Fleishman, E. A., & Hunt, J. G. (Eds.). *Current developments in the study of leadership*. (pp. 1–40). Carbondale: South Illinois University Press.

Fleishman, E. A., & Harris, E. F. (1962). Patterns of leadership behavior related to employee grievances and turnover. *Personnel Psychology, 15,* 43–56.

French, J., & Raven, B. (1959). The bases of social power. In Cartwright, D. (Ed.). *Studies in social powers*. (pp. 150–167). Ann Arbor: University of Michigan, Institute of Social Research.

Gillies, D. (1994). *Nursing management: A systems approach* (3rd ed.). Philadelphia: Saunders.

Hansten, R. I. (1991). Delegation: learning when and how to let go. *Nursing 91, 21*(2), 126–133.

Hellriegel, D., & Slocum, J. (1989). *Management*. New York: Addison-Wesley.

Hersey, P., & Blanchard, K. (1993). *Management of organizational behavior: Utilizing human resources* (6th ed.). Englewood Cliffs, NJ: Prentice-Hall.

Hersey, P., & Duldt, B. (1989). *Situational leadership in nursing*. Norwalk, CT: Appleton & Lange.

Herzberg, F. (1966). *Work and the nature of man*. Cleveland: World Publishing.

House, R. J. (1971). A path goal theory of leader effectiveness. *Administrative Science Quarterly 16*(3), 321.

Huber, D. (1996). *Leadership and nursing care management*. Philadelphia: Saunders.

Kanter, R. (1979). Power failure in management circuit. *Harvard Business Review 57*(4) 65–75.

Kramer, M., & Schmalenberg, C. (1990). Fundamental lessons in leadership. In Simendinger, E., Moore, T., & Kramer, M. (Eds.). *The successful nurse executive: A guide for every nurse manager*. (pp. 5–21). Ann Arbor, MI: Health Administration Press.

Kreitner, R. (1992). *Management*. Boston: Houghton Mifflin.

Laser, R. (1981). I win–you win negotiating. *Journal of Nursing Administration, 11*(11/12), 24–29.

Lewis-Ford (1993). Management techniques: Coping with difficult people. *Nursing Management, 24*(3) 36–38.

Liberatore, P., Brown-Williams, R., Brucker, J., Dukes, N., Kimmey, L., Pierre, J., Riegler, D., & Shearer-Pedu, K. (1989). A group approach to problem-solving. *Nursing Management, 20*(9), 68–72.

Locke, E. A. (1982). The ideas of Frederick W. Taylor: an evaluation. *Academy of Management Review, 7*(1), 14.

Marquis, B. L., and Huston, C. J. (1994). *Leadership roles and management functions: Theory and application*. Philadelphia: Lippincott.

Marriner-Tomey, A. (1996). *Nursing management and leadership*. St. Louis: Mosby-Year Book.

Maslow, A. H. (1970). *Motivation and personality*. (2nd ed.). New York: Harper & Row.

McGregor, D. (1960). *The human side of enterprise*. New York: McGraw-Hill.

Mintzberg, H. (1975). The manager's job: Folklore and fact. *Harvard Review, 53,* 49–61.

Ouchi, W. G. (1981). *How American business can meet the Japanese challenge*. Reading, MA: Addison-Wesley.

Raven, B., & Kruglanski, W. (1975). Conflict and power. In Swingle, P. (Ed). *The structure of conflict*. (pp. 177–219). New York: Academic Press.

Rowland, H. W., & Rowland, B. L. (1985). *Nursing administration handbook* (2nd ed.). Germantown, MD: Aspen Systems Corp.

Smeltzer, C. (1991). The art of negotiation: An everyday experience. *Journal of Nurse Administration 21*(7/8), 26–30.

Stogdill, R. M. (1974). *Handbook of leadership: A survey of theory and research*. New York: Free Press.

Strader, M. K. (1987). Adapting Theory Z to nursing management. *Nursing Management, 18* (4), 61–64.

Tappen, R. M. (1995). *Nursing leadership and management: Concepts and practice*. (3rd ed.). Philadelphia: Davis.

Taylor, F. W. (1911). *The principles of scientific management*. New York: Harper & Row.

Williamson, J. N. (1986). *The leader-manager*. New York: Wiley.

Wise, P. (1995). *Leading and managing in nursing*. St. Louis: Mosby.

BIBLIOGRAPHY

Drucker, P. F. (1974). *Management*. New York: Harper & Row.

Fiedler, F. E., & Garcia, J. E. (1987). *New approaches to effective leadership: cognitive resources and organizational performance*. New York: Wiley.

Herzberg, F. (1991). One more time: How do you motivate employees? In Ward, M. J., & Price, S. A. *Issues in nursing administration: selected readings*. St. Louis: Mosby-Year Book.

Herzberg, F., Mausner, B., & Snyderman, B. (1959). *The motivation to work* (2nd ed.). New York: Wiley.

Marriner-Tomey, A. (1993). *Transformation leadership in nursing*. St. Louis: Mosby.

Porter-O'Grady, T. (1992). Transformational leadership in an age of chaos. *Nursing Administration Quarterly, 17*(1), 17–24.

Sullivan, E. J., & Decker, P. J. (1995). *Effective management in nursing*. Menlo Park, CA: Addison-Wesley.

Wren, D. A. (1972). *The evolution of management thought*. New York: Ronald Press.

Chapter 10

ORGANIZATIONS

Rose Kearney Nunnery

CHAPTER OBJECTIVES

On completion of this chapter, the reader will be able to:

1. Apply systems theory to an organizational scenario.
2. Examine the structure, functions, goals, and culture of selected organizations.
3. Analyze the differences in goals and culture of different types of organizations.
4. Examine ways of communicating and negotiating in a health-care organization.
5. Examine the various roles for and skills of nurses in a health-care organization.

KEY TERMS

Organization
Goals and Values
Technical Subsystem
Psychosocial Subsystem
Structural Subsystem
Managerial Subsystem
Bureaucratic Structure

Adhocracies
Functional Structure
Product Structure
Matrix Organization
Centralization
Decentralization

Flat organizational
 Structure
Tall Organizational
 Structure
Organizational Functions
Organizational Culture

Max Weber (1947), the renowned German sociologist, described an organization in economic and social terms as "a system of purposive activity of a specified kind" (p. 151). An **organization** is simply an arrangement of human and material resources for some purpose, as in the creation of some institution or agency to meet a stated aim. Organizations range from the single-purpose association to multipurpose, monolithic institutions. They have been studied for years in an effort to improve on outputs as the intended mission or purpose. Organizations can be viewed in terms of their structure, function, and people. Most simply, they can be envisioned as the open system described in Chapter 4 with inputs, throughput or transformations, and outputs. But understanding organizations, especially health-care organizations, becomes more complex by the day as organizations expand, contract, and redefine themselves.

From a mechanistic viewpoint, Weiss and Gershon (1989) look at the operating process of a health-care organization with patients as the input; resources of the hospital, physicians, nurses, and medical equipment; direct output of healthy patients; and byproducts of treatment side effects. This is merely the image of a simple system described in Chapter 4. A more humanistic and systematic consideration of the organization is needed to fully understand the complexity of the modern health-care agency.

We examine how organizations are structured and how they function to meet their intended mission. But recall the metaparadigm of nursing: person, environment, health, and nursing. This provides us with a broader environmental and interpersonal vision than patients and health-care providers with equipment in an isolated hospital or agency. In an open system, we must further consider the culture of the organization within a larger society for congruent aims or goals. Communication and negotiation are important factors, as are the leadership and management concepts provided in the two previous chapters. Applying the concepts of contemporary nursing practice is vital for the operation of a successful organization and an effective health-care system.

ORGANIZATIONAL THEORY: ORGANIZATIONS AS SYSTEMS

Systems theory provides a useful perspective for viewing the internal and external influences with any organization. In fact, Bertalanffy (1968), who provided the foundations of general systems theory, stated that the basis of organizational theory is the premise that the only meaningful way to study an organization is as a system (p. 9).

In nursing, Clark (1994) uses systems theory to define organizations identifying three component systems of the organization: the social system, the operational system, and the administrative system. The social system represents people in terms of the organizational climate, communication channels, status and role structures, and decision making. The operational system contains the work structures and placement for human and material resources. Procedures and policies emerge from the administrative system to interrelate and direct the social and operational systems. More specific to nursing administration, Dienemann (1990) advocates the use of a systems model to understand organizations emphasizing the structure of the work and people and the formal and informal interaction process among work and people (p. 230). She further suggests that for analysis and use in their organization, nursing administrators select from one of four models: general systems, congruence, professional bureaucracy, and contingency. The actual selection of a particular systems model depends on the complexity and uniqueness of the organization. This requires careful assessment of the organization, examining its mission and goals, present structure, and the prevailing leadership and management styles being used to guide practice.

Health-care delivery systems are complex open environmental systems. The organization must be examined at the system level, with its component subsystems, as well as the macrosystem, which includes the client system as the consumer group. Agency administrative, policy, and operational structures internally influence and guide the system. The surrounding environmental system of the organization is the health-care arena that provides the professional, specialization, economic, and additional value structures for the organizational unit and its members. The broader social or macroenvironment reflects societal norms and values through the real and potential needs of health-care consumers. Direct or indirect linkages among all system parts are assumed to be essential for effectiveness and continuity. But let us look further at this complex system and the internal environment.

A useful perspective for viewing the intricacies of a health-care organization is to envision it as a system affected by other systems and within the larger health-care and societal systems (environmental suprasystem or macrosystem). Kast and Rosenzweig (1979) regard organizations as open, sociotechnical systems that structure and integrate human activities around various technologies (p. 108). This is particularly applicable to health-care organizations with their focus on people and the dynamic influence of technology. The organizational system in this model is further composed of five subsystems: goals and values, technical, psychosocial, structural, and managerial (Figure 10–1). The subsystems and their inherent internal forces can be described as follows.

Goals and values are implied in a statement of purpose or philosophy. This is the basis of the organization's existence. The institutional mission statement and original or revised incorporation papers contain valuable information on how people within the organization are viewed, as customers, staff members, and administrators. Humanistic versus mechanistic values will be apparent in these statements of mission, philosophy, and purpose.

The **technical subsystem** represents the knowledge and skills of the people providing service in the system as well as the physical resources. Specialized knowledge and expertise of professional and nonprofessional labor forces are represented in this subsystem. Physical resources include operating and investment capital, equipment, information systems, services, and tangible assets.

The **psychosocial subsystem** contains the interpersonal and interdisciplinary relationships unique to the organization. This includes role relationships, attitudes, and values of people and groups within the system. Examine the expected behaviors of each member of the organization and their interrelationships, in both formal and informal interactions. As we will later see, this can be further visualized as the organizational culture.

The **structural subsystem** is the institutional or agency design to accomplish the system's mission to provide the intended services. This structure may be complex or simple, centralized or decentralized, tall or flat. The structural subsystem also relates to the hierarchy or lines of authority, as demonstrated by

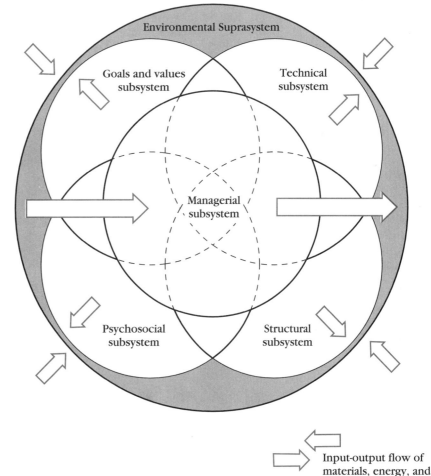

FIGURE 10-1. The organizational system. (From Kast, F. E., & Rosenzweig, J. E. [1979]. *Organization and management: A systems and contingency approach* [3rd ed.]. New York: McGraw-Hill. Reprinted with permission.)

Input-output flow of materials, energy, and information

the bureaucratic or organic structure. The system structure is described in formal documents and further interpreted in operation through informal sources, such as technical staff, to determine how tasks are actually accomplished in the organization.

The **managerial subsystem** includes the management style pervasive in the organization. This may be directed from the top-most governing board or corporate officers downward, as in a bureaucratic organization operating under Theory X. Alternatively, it may be more flexible and participatory, as in Theory Z organizations. Recall the differences between the mechanistic bureaucratic management style and the humanistic empowerment of individuals described in the previous chapter.

Once the subsystems are identifiable, move outward into the environmental layers of the open system, or the suprasystem. To understand the external environment, we must first reevaluate the organization's mission. As in any business, this provides us with market forces. Is a product being produced or a service being delivered, and to whom? Consider the differences between the environments of local organizations focused on a specific community versus national or multinational conglomerates. To understand an organization's initial environmental layer, focus first on the immediate output of the system. Suppose we are looking at a home care agency. These agencies provide home care within specific specialty parameters to an identified service area. In the environment, we initially have the local community with a specific geography, client population, health-care provider groups, payment streams, resources, and health-care needs. This local agency has additional environmental influences from state and federal regulatory bodies and agencies, professional disciplines, and the larger health-care system. But these factors generally have less influence than those affecting the larger health-care environment, which offers more services to a larger clientele.

Conversely, consider this larger health-care agency, such as a teaching hospital. This has a broader service menu and service area. We have to consider the geography, client population, health-care provider groups, payment streams, resources, and health-care needs across the state or perhaps across several states. Services may include not only acute and chronic care, but also day surgery, multispecialty clinics, research, and outreach programs. We have more care providers, including students, faculty, and visiting specialists from various health-care disciplines. There are more requirements and regulations from state and federal regulatory bodies and agencies and professional disciplines, just by virtue of the expanded services, funding streams,

and service expectations. Coordination with the broader health-care system must also be considered, as people come from and return to their local areas.

In an open system, all boundary influences must be identified and relationships evaluated. All external layers and interrelating systems are important factors in a true understanding of the influences on any particular system. These environmental influences have repercussions on the system and its component subsystems. External forces include inputs of energy, information, materials, and the myriad technologies received from the environment, transformed, and returned to the environment as outputs. Vecchio (1991) looks at three dimensions of the external organizational environment: (1) simplicity versus complexity, (2) static versus dynamic, and (3) environmental uncertainty (pp. 528–529).

The health-care environment can easily be seen as highly complex, dynamic, and uncertain. The issue of complexity has been well illustrated by Hall (1987), who notes that "there is a strong tendency for organizations to become more complex as their own activities and the environment around them becomes more complex" (p. 65). Changes are occurring rapidly. Change is influenced by consumers, technological advances, government, and third-party payers. The external forces in the broader environment provide inputs into the system and affect internal operations and resultant outputs, such as client outcomes. Health-care organizations must respond to external forces in a rapid, dynamic, and innovative manner. Knowles (1980) delineated the characteristics of dynamic or innovative organizations (Table 10–1), which are applicable to health-care organizations dealing with multiple and complex external forces. The differences between static and innovative organizations exist in organizational structure, atmosphere, philosophy, decision making, and communication. The humanistic philosophy, with its focus on the people in an organization who create, define, and fulfill organizational goals, is apparent in the description of an innovative organization. This brings us to examining the various structures of organizational systems.

ORGANIZATIONAL STRUCTURES

Mintzberg (1983b) has defined organizational structure as "the sum total of the ways in which its labor is divided into distinct tasks and then [how] coordination is achieved among these tasks" (p. 2). Generally, when we think of an *organizational structure,* we conceive of some type of hierarchy that tells us about positions or roles, responsibilities, status, channels of command or reporting relationships, and tasks to be

TABLE 10-1. Some Characteristics of Static Versus Innovative Organizations

	Static Organizations	Innovative Organizations
Structure	Rigid—much energy given to maintaining permanent departments, committees; reverence for tradition, constitution, and by-laws	Flexible—much use of temporary task forces; easy shifting of departmental lines; readiness to change constitution, depart from tradition
	Hierarchial—adherence to chain of command	Multiple linkages based on functional collaboration
	Roles defined narrowly	Roles defined broadly
	Property-bound	Property-mobile
Atmosphere	Task-centered, impersonal	People-centered, caring
	Cold, formal, reserved, suspicious	Warm, informal, intimate
		Trusting
Management philosophy and attitudes	Function of management is to control personnel through coercive power	Function of management is to release the energy of personnel; power is used supportively
	Cautious—low risk-taking	Experimental—high risk-taking
	Attitude toward errors: to be avoided	Attitude toward errors: to be learned from
	Emphasis on personnel selection	Emphasis on personnel development
	Self-sufficiency—closed system regarding sharing resources	Interdependency—open system regarding sharing resources
	Emphasis on conserving resources	Emphasis on developing and using resources
	Low tolerance for ambiguity	High tolerance for ambiguity
Decision making and policy making	High participation at top, low at bottom	Relevant participation by all those affected
	Clear distinction between policy making and policy execution	Collaborative policy making and policy execution
		Decision making by problem solving
	Decision making by legal mechanisms	Decisions treated as hypotheses to be tested
	Decisions treated as final	
Communication	Restricted flow—constipated	Open-flow—easy access
	One-way—downward	Multidirectional—up, down, sideways
	Feelings repressed or hidden	Feelings expressed

Source: Knowles, M. S. (1980). *The modern practice of adult education: From pedagogy to andragogy* (rev. ed.) Chicago: Follett, with permission.

accomplished. The picture that comes to mind is usually a bureaucratic structure with a multitude of "red tape" with which to contend. This is not always the case. The appropriateness of the structure depends on the organization's purposes (goals and values subsystem), the people in the organizational system (psychosocial subsystem), the skills and technology used or available (technical subsystem), how outcomes are best accomplished (managerial subsystem), and influences from the external environment(s). These system influences provide us with information on the size and complexity of the organization as the structural subsystem.

The structure demonstrates the relationships among an organization's components and presents us with its design. Looking at health-care organizations, we find two general structures: bureaucratic and organic. Mintzberg (1983b) places these two organizational designs at opposite ends of a continuum of standardization (Figure 10-2). This range provides us with a way of viewing organizational structures from the controlled, mechanistic, and standardized classic bureaucracy through a number of adaptations to the opposite extreme of a humanistic organization, which contains no standardized

Bureaucratic Structure	Organic Structure
High standardization of processes, outputs, and skills	Absence of standardization

FIGURE 10-2. Mintzberg's (1983b) continuum of standardization in organizations. (Adapted from Mintzberg, H. [1983]. *Structure in fives: Designing effective organizations.* Englewood Cliffs, NJ: Prentice-Hall, with permission.)

processes, outputs, or skills across the structure but an alternative design to meet the organization's intended mission. Health-care organizations generally fall somewhere between the two extremes, depending on their mission. Let us begin by reviewing the concepts inherent in a bureaucratic design.

Bureaucratic Organizational Structures

The most recognized and traditional organization is the **bureaucratic structure.** Classic works on bureaucratic structures were done by Max Weber and other sociologists. Weber (1864–1920), a German sociologist, provided the original bureaucratic model, with a high degree of efficiency and control. His work has been translated and interpreted frequently in research on organizations and organizational theory. Merton (1957) defined a bureaucratic organization as "a formal, rationally organized social structure involving clearly defined patterns of activity in which, ideally, every series of actions is functionally related to the purposes of the organization" (p. 195). This is a hierarchial structure with designated lines of authority and control. The mission of the organization is all-consuming. A bureaucracy is a mechanistic model focused on outcomes. Actions to meet the purposes and directives are taken in lower layers whereas policy making, authority, and control are primarily in the upper layers of the organization. Specific characteristics of a bureaucratic organization include the following:

1. A clear-cut division of labor
2. Differentiated controls and sanctions
3. Roles assigned based on qualifications and technical efficiency

4. Clearly stated rules and conformity to regulations
5. A premium is placed on precision, speed, expert control, continuity, discretion, and optimal returns on input
6. Strict devotion to regulations
7. Depersonalized relationships (Merton, 1957, pp. 195–196)

Examples of bureaucratic health-care organizations are depicted in Figures 10–3 and 10–4. In these illustrations, control flows downward from the hospital board through the chief operating officer (COO) or chief executive officer (CEO), who is appointed by the board and is responsible for the organization's missions, whether for-profit or not-for-profit. To accomplish these aims, the executive layer is responsible to the COO or CEO. The executives receive mandates from the board through the COO or CEO and decide on priorities, plan implementation, and regulations. Executives, in turn, direct their administrative staffs, and on down the line. Direction is given with policies and regulations, down the

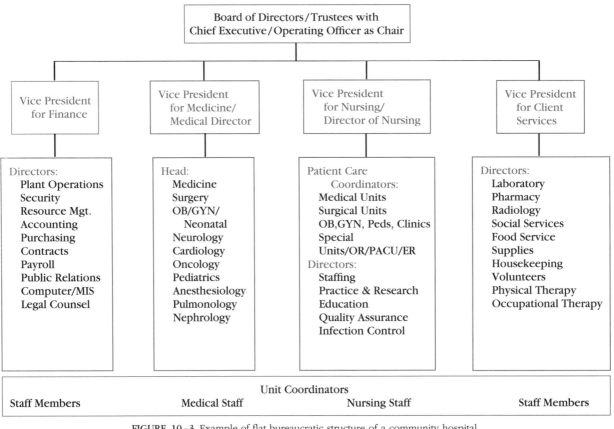

FIGURE 10-3. Example of flat bureaucratic structure of a community hospital.

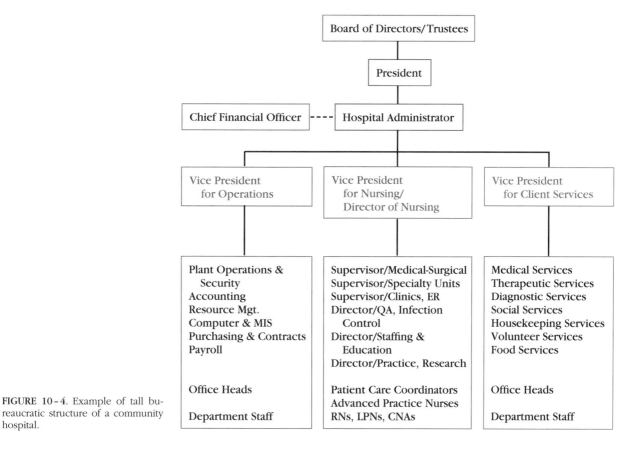

FIGURE 10-4. Example of tall bureaucratic structure of a community hospital.

line, to the worker with the least authority but who still has a precise role in carrying out the organizational mission.

A bureaucratic organization is structured, standardized, controlled, and in many instances, authoritarian. Written and unwritten policies and regulations are prevalent, as are specified channels of command. Efficiency and effectiveness in achieving the organizational mission are organizational values. Marriner-Tomey (1992) has identified the following principles for maximizing effectiveness in bureaucratic organizations:

1. Clear lines of authority and responsibility need to be present
2. A clear chain of command is needed with each person having one boss
3. Each person should have role clarity on authority, limitations, and responsibilities, preferably in writing, to reduce role ambiguity
4. Delegation should be done when there is sufficient competence and information for effective performance and decision making
5. Employees should have formal authority and

be held accountable for the responsibilities delegated to them
6. Coordination by one person is limited by the interdependency and complexity of the functions, services, and areas under their span of control
7. The organizational structure should be flexible enough for expansion and contraction when conditions change (pp. 113–116)

Bureaucratic organizational structures are seen in the older, traditional, and large authoritarian settings in which control and the ultimate mission of the institution are all-consuming. External influences should be predictable to obtain the most efficient functioning of the organization. Channels of command and productivity are important components of the system. But in recent years, a move toward more flexible and humanistic organizational structures, focusing on environmental influences along with employee involvement and job satisfaction for higher productivity, have led to a transformation to more innovative practices that are inconsistent with the bureaucratic design.

Organic Organizational Structures

Organic organizational structures, or **adhocracies,** have evolved to meet the needs of organizations composed of humans in dynamic and sometimes complex environmental settings. The term "adhocracy" implies that the structure is a design that has been developed to meet the organizational mission and specific goals. Hall (1987) described adhocracies as dynamic organizations in which the environment is unknown and the structure can change dramatically as events demand adjustment (p. 51). These organizations represent a movement from the standardized, mechanistic bureaucracies to humanistic forms arising out of behavioral organizational research and management theories. Mintzberg (1983b) proposed that this structure is the most useful in a complex and dynamic environment in which experts, managers, and staff from different disciplines cooperate on decentralized project teams to meet a system output goal innovatively. Several organic designs are seen in health-care organizations. The most prevalent organic or adhocratic designs are functional, product, and matrix forms.

A **functional structure,** like the bureaucracy, focuses on organizational outcomes but has control and responsibility spread horizontally across the system to meet specific organizational functions. Vecchio (1991) notes that "a functional form is especially appropriate when the most important needs of an organization are collaboration and expertise within a defined set of operations, when the environment is stable, and when only one or a few products is produced" (p. 513). A functional form can therefore be used in an organization with a specific function, such as a rehabilitative facility. The function of the rehabilitative care across specialty lines is the organization's purpose. The people in the organization have the decision-making authority for their services in the organization. Functional units are thus arranged in specialty areas, as illustrated in Figure 10–5.

The organization is designed to focus on the function of delivering rehabilitative care to the consumer. Two distinct functions are apparent in our example of this functional form: (1) finance and administration of the agency and (2) delivery of rehabilitative health care. An executive director or president oversees the organization with the assistance of two directors. The main organizational function of rehabilitative care delivery is structured as specialty units under the direction of the health-care director. Fragmentation and duplication of services across specialties limit this design. This becomes a more severe limitation as the organization grows in size and complexity for example, when services increase and the service area is enlarged. Vecchio (1991) has further described the disadvantages of the functional form as follows:

1. delays in response to changes in the organizational environments
2. less innovation and a limited vision of the organization's broader mission and goals
3. difficulty in coordination of services and activities across departments
4. difficulty in assessment of the contribution of individual departments when the focus is the functional outcome rather than the provider (p. 513)

A **product structure** is similar to the functional

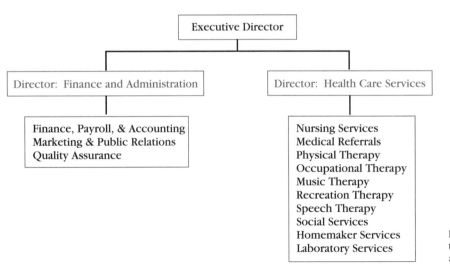

FIGURE 10–5. Example of a functional organization: rehabilitative agency.

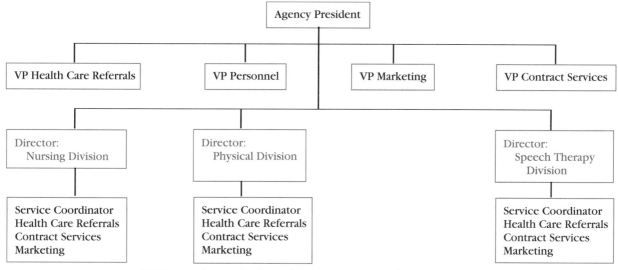

FIGURE 10-6. Example of a product form organization: home care agency.

structure except that the organization is focused on the product as the outcome, with people and processes being grouped accordingly. "The primary goals of a product structure are coordination among product lines and attention to consumer desires" (Vecchio, 1991, p. 514). Consider the example of a large home care agency (Figure 10-6). The product would be home care services, with attention being given to the needs and desires of the home care client. The product units would be organized in terms of nursing services, physical therapy, and speech therapy. Each unit has a director responsible to the president of the agency for the home care product. Vice presidents would be responsible to the president for general functions of health-care referrals, contractual services, personnel, and marketing. Product units would thus be arranged in specified areas (nursing, physical therapy, and speech therapy), with each being directed toward service coordination, referrals, contractual services, and marketing, to meet consumer needs, as illustrated in Figure 10-6.

The product form of structure works well with an organization whose services and marketing is directed at the consumer. This design is flexible in a dynamic or unstable environment, since consumer needs and satisfaction are of prime concern. Divisions are separated by product, whether that product be nursing care, physical therapy, or speech therapy. But duplication of services is an immediate problem, especially in health care where coordination of therapeutic regimes is vital for the consumer.

To address the need to coordinate consumer ser-

vices, another adhocratic design combines the functional and product forms. Multidimensional decision making and responsibility are the features of a **matrix organization.** In a health-care agency, this can refer to the product of state-of-the-art care and the function of provision of services to the client as the consumer. An example of the matrix design is an organization whose missions is directed at research and development and provision of care. Research managers in interdisciplinary areas such as aging, acute infectious processes, mental health, rehabilitation, and health promotion are apparent on one side of the matrix, with specialized health-care providers on the other side (Figure 10-7). People as leaders, managers, and workers, along with tangible resources in the environment, are all represented in the matrix cells.

Consider the example of home care for an elderly client following a hip fracture. Care for the client and the family along the continuum would move from acute care to short-term rehab to home care, with interdisciplinary care providers, including home care coordinators, therapists, and pertinent specialists, all contributing to the decision making and service provision based on resources and information on aging, mental health, rehabilitation, and health promotion factors. The complexity of this system is initially breathtaking. However, both functions and products must be considered in coordinating services needed by the client.

Vecchio (1991) provided an interesting view of this complexity: "given the continual reshuffling of human and material resources, a good way of de-

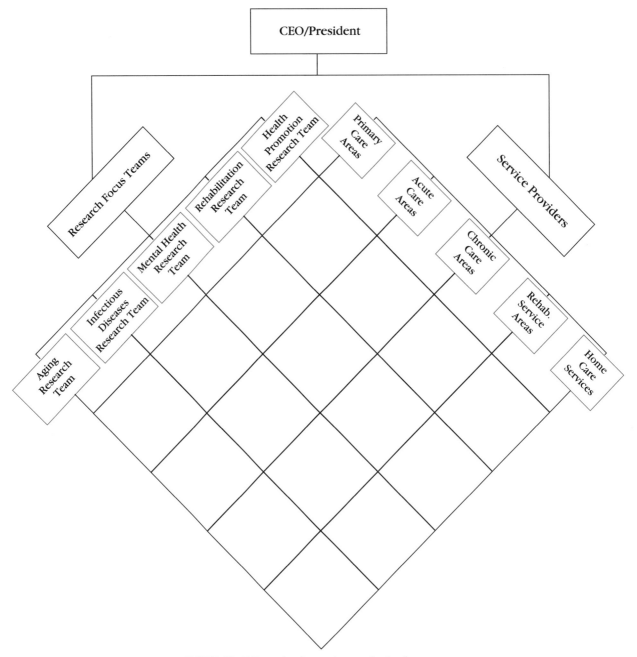

FIGURE 10-7. Example of a matrix organizational structure.

scribing the dynamics of the matrix design is with the three-dimensional analogy of a Rubik's cube" (p. 517). It is a collegial structure with an integrated functions and products that requires multilayered decisions. The number of people involved in the matrix for decisions varies. Larger organizations may involve only managers in the matrix, with traditional departmental structures evolving under each man-

ager. Smaller organizations, such as our earlier example of a home care agency, could realistically involve managers and providers in the matrix based on the scope of services (product) and resources (human and material as functions).

The matrix design promotes innovative practices as a result of a consumer focus in the context of current technology, emergent practice problems, research information, and specialty practice. Research and development issues are directed at current practice, with experts from each area represented for problem solving and decision making. This matrix design is seen more frequently in health settings with a dual focus, such as education and service or research and service. The complexity of the design and problems with integration of all appropriate people and resources are the main disadvantages of the matrix form. Vecchio (1991) describes its disadvantages more fully in the following areas:

1. Reporting and priorities are confusing because employees have more than one boss to whom to report.
2. Time-consuming meetings are required for communication and conflict resolution.
3. Performance evaluations, with more than one superior as an evaluator, are complex.
4. It is necessary and time-consuming to maintain a collegial and cooperative esprit de corps with sometimes conflicting priorities.

Coordination problems are a definite disadvantage of adhocratic designs. Experts and project teams or divisions are focused on innovation and targeting specific outcomes. This may represent only one piece of the mission of the organization. Thus, good communication and coordination are critical. But coordination problems are many times outweighed by the advantages of flexibility, innovation, and human involvement.

Structural Components for Decision Making and Management

Organizations are also categorized by how the components are arranged, as centralized or decentralized structures or flat or tall structures. *Centralized and decentralized organizational structures* relate to the lines of control and decision making within the organization. **Centralization** occurs when the span of control or management is in the classic bureaucratic style, governed from the top downward. Authority, control, and decision making occur in upper management, with less participation filtered down from the upper levels. Mintzberg (1983b) has described centralization as the tightest means of coordinating decision making in an organization, with decisions being made by one person and implemented through direct supervision (pp. 95–96). **Decentralization** distributes authority downward in an organization allowing decision making and control at local levels. Reasons suggested for decentralization are to establish a more collegial and participatory model, resulting in employee involvement, performance, and satisfaction. Vecchio (1991) de-

scribed difficulty in measuring decentralization but suggests that a good means of assessment is to "examine the dollar amount of expenses employees are permitted to incur without the prior approval of a supervisor: the larger the amount of latitude allowed employees on expenditures, the greater the extent of decentralization that can be inferred" (p. 501).

Organizations can also be described as having flat or tall structures, depending on the layers of differentiation for authority, decision making, and coordination. **Flat organizational structures** have a wide base and few layers or tiers for decision making and authority. Decisions, controls, and governance are widely spread across the organization in a horizontal differentiation. **Tall organizational structures** have more tiers and lines of command, with less local decision making at the lower levels. Tall organizations have more management levels, with lines of command resulting in a vertically differentiated hierarchial structure. Compare the organizational structures in Figures 10–3 and 10–4. Both are bureaucratic structures, but decisions and work functions are spread more widely across the organization in flat structures (see Figure 10–3).

Deciding whether a centralized or decentralized, tall or flat structure is best depends on the characteristics of the specific organization. As Vecchio (1991) points out, decentralization and flat structures tend to go together, and tall organizations are more centralized. Many organizations have changed from centralized, tall structures to encourage more employee involvement. But problems can arise when communication, coordination, and monitoring of activities in the organization demand integration for effective functioning. As in his continuum of organizational standardization (see Figure 10–2), Mintzberg (1983b) suggests that centralization and decentralization be viewed as opposite ends of a continuum rather than absolutes (p. 98). The degree of centralization or decentralization actually depend on the organizational size and structure, technology, people, and mission. These factors are considered in four of the organization's subsystems (structural, technical, psychosocial, and goals and values) as they interact with the managerial (fifth) subsystem to determine where decisions are best made.

ORGANIZATIONAL FUNCTIONS

Tappen (1995) differentiates between two types of **organizational functions:** (1) formal and informal goals, and (2) formal and informal levels of operation. These two functions represent the interaction between two organization subsystems, the goals and values subsystem and the technical subsystem.

The goals and values subsystem was described in the institutional mission and purposes statement as the basis for the organization's existence. But this becomes confusing when we consider specific goals for the organization. The mission statement is the overall purpose of the organization, including how this purpose is generally met. This includes whether the organization is a for-profit organization or a not-for-profit organization. Stock- or shareholders expect to see some return on their investment in a for-profit (or proprietary) organization, and this is reflected in organizational goals. Not-for-profit organizations receive funding from various sources, but there is no sense of ownership. In a not-for-profit organization, profits are generally reinvested in the organization to keep it financially competitive.

Once the mission is understood, the targets to achieve this mission become the issue. *Organizational goals* are specified for effective and efficient functioning. Mintzberg (1983a) has identified four types of goals that demonstrate intent and consistency of behavior in organizations: ideologic, formal, shared, and system. Ideologic goals relate to the values people in the organization share. This is the values component of the goals and values subsystem. An example of an ideologic goal in a health-care organization is access to and provision of high-quality health care for people of all ages. Formal goals are those authorized through the organizational hierarchy. This often relates to the desires of those with authority who have a power base in the organization. The role and function of advanced nurse practitioners in a health-care setting can be determined by officially authorizing or inhibiting such practice in a particular setting. Shared goals are those set and pursued by a particular group in the organization. Involvement of family members in caregiving is an example of a shared goal that a specialty group favors and implements in the organization. System goals are those set to maintain the system. Mintzberg (1983a) has identified system goals as survival, efficiency, control, and growth. System goals relate to continuity of the organization and contain a strong economic component. These survival system goals are driving many health-care organizations, in response to unstable economic times and managed care.

Organizations are now recognizing that goals that are too broad can deplete the resources and effectiveness of the intended outcomes and the system goals. We hear of companies and major industries streamlining and getting "back-to-basics." They seriously consider examining what they know best, and refining it and focusing, rather than diversifying. Linkages with other organizations that can better handle the diversifications may be more beneficial to both the organization and the consumer group.

This "back-to-basics" focus is now occurring more in health care. Back-to-basics is often referred to as specialization. Specialization frequently comes to mind as medical specialties become more discrete and product-centered. Clients are now heard to complain, "I now have four or five doctors rather than one, like I used to. I can't keep track of them all!" Knowledge and technology are too great for one person to know everything to the extent we would like or need to. As a result, we focus to a manageable area of knowledge and skill. The same can be said for organizations. Organizations are now directing their goals to what they do best and divesting themselves of multiple services. These multiple services can be costly in resources, human and material, and lead to negative system outcomes. It is advantageous to arrange linkages with organizations that can offer high-quality services more economically, efficiently, and effectively.

As the business community has returned to a focus on basic human values, diversification has declined. And health care is big business, as noted by Hart and Goeppele (1994):

> Hospital management groups now find themselves not only trying to manage a declining census but also trying to support a wide variety of business entities such as home health services, sports medicine, clinics, freestanding laboratories, skilled nursing facilities, preventative medicine programs for the elderly, and urgent care centers. To complicate matters further, the variety of services has been expanded to include joint ventures with the medical staff. The most evident danger in restructuring a hospital into a diversified multicorporate entity is the loss of focus on the major purpose of the diversification. Corporate reorganizations were originally designed to protect the hospital . . . and to keep [it] healthy and viable. Over a period of time, as a variety of diversified activities are started, management tends to become preoccupied with the process of building these allied businesses. (pp. 110–111)

Packard (1994) has illustrated the historical influences that have led to changes in hospitals and the health-care system in the past 30 years as follows:

1967–1972 Medicare extended care legislation and incentives

1973–1980   Revisions in extended care and specification of skilled nursing care facilities

1981–1986   Prospective payment system (PPS) for Medicare services.

1986–1994   Increased competition, with expansions in organizational missions as efforts are made to increase referral bases, open new revenue sources, and reduce hospital stays

Now we are faced with a restructuring of Medicare and Medicaid.

There are three basic reasons for the changes in health-care structures: environmental influences, changes in the provider system, and changes in consumer needs and demographics. First, external environmental influences have had a major impact on health-care organizations. Diagnostic-related groups (DRGs) and the prospective payment system (PPS) for health-care reimbursement and regulations have had a major impact. Second, specialization and changes in the health-care provider system have confused consumers and legislators. Disciplinary lines between health-care providers necessarily have some overlap as we implement cross-training and focus on humanistic and holistic values for persons and groups. Coordination and collaboration are important components of this issue. Third, changes in consumer needs must drive the system to provide health-care services. Today, we are faced with consumer needs related to increased longevity, chronicity, AIDS, personal involvement, and health promotion activities.

Health-care organizations are now seeing the wisdom of this lesson learned in industry. Not every community hospital needs to have every specialty service. Community hospitals can offer services that are complementary rather than duplicated, meager, and lacking quality. Regionalization can be accomplished by having maternal and infant or pediatric services in one agency and cardiac diagnosis, surgery, and rehabilitation in another. This prevents duplication and fosters quality. The population and the health service needs must drive the goals of the organization. A needs assessment provides the information for deciding on revisions of organizational goals. This brings us to specific operations of the organization and the available technology.

The technical subsystem was described as representing the knowledge and skills of the people providing services in the system, along with physical resources. This subsystem provides for the formal and informal *levels of operation* of the organization. Specialized knowledge and expertise of professionals and nonprofessionals are represented in formal and informal functions. Formal functions are those defined by the organizational structure. Compare the different functions for a unit manager in a vertical, bureaucratic organization with decision making in the upper levels of the hierarchy with those of the unit as a cost and decision center in a more horizontal adhocratic structure. This demonstrates a difference in formal operational functions. Informal functions facilitate goal accomplishment in most organizations. Informal functions include effective communication channels and how the organizational plans and tasks are actually accomplished in relation to the available resources.

Developing an appreciation of the formal and informal functions of the human and material resources in the technical subsystem is essential for understanding the operations of the organization. To do this, it is essential to be further aware of the human factor, or the people who comprise the system.

ORGANIZATIONAL CULTURE

The psychosocial subsystem of the organization is termed **organizational culture.** It is perceptible as the culmination of the norms, attitudes, and values related to the organizational mission accompanied by the expected behaviors of the people. Branum (1990) has described the organizational climate or culture as the atmosphere in which people work, including a composite of the attitudes, beliefs, and values of the group as well as the physical environment, interprofessional relations, and structure of the organization.

Scrutiny of the organizational climate can provide a sense of the prevailing degree of humanism present in the organization, in other words, how people are viewed as employees and consumers. New organizational values and behaviors have emerged as we redefine and recreate organizations for functioning in today's world. We have moved from the belief that humans in organizations are lazy and need direction and management of McGregor's (1967) Theory X. We are now in the age of humanism that emerged with the philosophies of Theory Y (McGregor, 1967) and Theory Z (Ouchi, 1981). This perspective moves to a positive view considering the importance of the people in the organization. Still, during times of cost-cutting, a humanistic perspective can quickly disappear when the focus turns to head counts or full-time equivalents (FTEs). Gaucher and Coffey (1993) differentiated between positive and negative organizational cultures as follows:

A positive culture is one in which employees experience pride in their work, where everyone is involved and committed to continuous improvement, where people freely help each other to achieve goals and have fun during the process. . . . [Whereas] in negative organizations people spend a lot of time guarding their turf and protecting themselves. (pp. 149–151)

Important clues on the involvement, satisfaction, and effectiveness of the people in the organization are reflected in both management styles and the behaviors and attitudes of those in the environment.

In health care, the organizational culture includes both the consumers and the providers in the agency. It is also influenced by the environments: the immediate institutional or agency environment as well as societal expectations and mandates. Barker (1992) proposes that health organizations are now based on the following positive beliefs:

1. Humans as workers are basically good with talents and skills, able to be trusted and capable of change
2. Using feelings and the intuition of people in addition to rational decision making is important
3. Conflict and risk-taking are used for the benefit of the organization.
4. Personnel evaluations include human growth and development, as opposed to sticking strictly to fixed job descriptions.
5. Collaboration and participatory management are encouraged rather than personal power and gamesmanship.
6. Movement is toward the semiautonomous work unit rather than the traditional bureaucratic structure.

As with any set of cultural expectations, the person is expected to enculturate and espouse the prevailing principles. Failure to enculturate results in being ostracized or terminated. Marriner-Tomey (1992) observed that these cultural expectations are the customary ways of thinking and behaving shared by all members of an organization, and they must be learned and adopted by newcomers before they can even be accepted in the agency (p. 144). Cox (1993) described this organizational socialization process as "conveying the organization's goals, norms, and preferred ways of doing things to members" (p. 164). An example of this is adopting and using a specific theory that guides the operation of the organization. At the most ideal level, if the nurse cannot view or provide care for clients in accordance with the specific model used at that agency,

such as Orem's self-care theory, the best remedy would be to seek employment at another agency more consistent with the nurse's own worldviews, for example, an agency that functions based on King's theory of goal attainment.

Cox (1993) applied six areas of behavior to cultural differences of people and groups in organizations:

1. Time and space, such as territoriality in work areas, and orientation to time as in rigid versus flexible schedules
2. Leadership style favoring institutional procedures versus emphasis on relationships and a democratic climate
3. Individualism, looking at personal goals and achievement, versus collectivism, which focuses on teamwork and attaining group goals
4. Competition versus cooperativeness in social interactions and task performance
5. Locus of control, as internal control over events and one's destiny versus external influences, and the concept of fate affecting life events
6. Communication styles related to confidence, speech anxiety, desire for discussion as sharing, and a sense of interpersonal trust (pp. 108–127)

The concepts of time and space, leadership, management, locus of control, and communication are particularly appropriate to understanding the people as individuals and groups in health-care organizations. Health-care personnel generally view time as highly fixed, with set schedules. But tight schedules are often problematic when emergencies or unanticipated delays occur as a function of human events and differences. A classic example is a client's appointment for same-day surgery. We expect them to appear on time, as scheduled, but then they wait in the reception area, answer many repeated questions, and wait for check-ins, assessments, and preparations, and then for the actual procedure, discharge, and recovery or recuperation from the experience and the health care problem. Time frames and perceptions vary for providers and clients, and diverge further among different cultural groups and subgroups.

Space is a highly personal concept. In health-care organizations, the importance to clients of touch, space, and territoriality must be considered in their comfort status, both physical and emotional. Chapter 4 illustrated the importance of touch as part of the health beliefs of selected cultural subgroups. For health-care providers, work space, privacy, and territoriality are important considerations in job performance. Individual space may be at a premium in the crowded physical plant of a hospital or clinic or an environment that favors open, shared work spaces. This may present either a comforting environment for an individual or group that favors interpersonal relations and cooperativeness or unsettling for an individualist who needs "quiet time" for greater creativity and job performance.

In Chapter 8, selected leadership styles were demonstrated. The cultural climate generally supports the predominant leadership style. But, differences have been demonstrated among genders and minority groups. Cox (1993) found that women and Mexican-Americans display a marked emphasis on relationships compared to the Anglo-American male leadership tradition of institutional procedures and task accomplishment. The leadership style is a major influence on the organizational culture or climate.

Closely related to leadership style is management focus, whether on individualism and achievement or on collectivism or teamwork and group goals. Management styles have an important influence here. Consider the differences in management with Theory X, focused on individual performance, versus Theory Z, which evolved from the Japanese business view and emphasizes collectivism and cooperation. The organizational focus on individualism or collectivism is apparent in promotion or evaluation structures. Administrative policies and procedures provide important clues to the organization's official position. However, subgroups or minority groups within the organization may create factions. These subgroups may set certain expectations for collectivism and cooperation in behavior or function. For example, the organization may be highly bureaucratic, with expectations and rewards valuing individual performance, competition, and task accomplishment; but if collectiveness and cooperation are the prevailing values in the nursing department, these values will be translated into accomplishing outcomes at the upper level of management.

Internal locus of control over life events is a prevailing value of Anglo-American culture and health-care system. We promote responsible behavior and health promotion activities. But, as with health beliefs, values of different cultures may conflict with those in the health-care system. Research has shown that external controlling factors are much stronger in Arab, Asian, African, and Latino minority and cultural groups (Cox, 1993). This has implications for health-care providers as well as clients in terms of motivation and confidence in life situations or work performance.

Communication of ideas and views is important in

all of the cultural differences described here. Being able to communicate with clients is quite different from having your ideas heard, considered, and implemented at the organizational level. Conveying yourself as an expert and as a colleague is necessary in both client and professional interactions within the organization. Whether by ensuring that all committee or group members have the opportunity to express their opinions or by making special efforts to demonstrate recognition and give credit for another's ideas, attention to cultural differences is important. It can make the most of the talents, abilities, and skills of the human resources in the organizational system.

In addition to understanding the people and groups in the organizational system, other factors provide information on the organizational culture and the operational climate. Based on research, Vecchio (1991) identified the following six central concepts for understanding the organizational culture:

1. Critical decisions of the entrepreneur or founding members
2. Guiding ideals and mission
3. Social structure
4. Norms and values
5. Remembered history and symbolism
6. Institutional arrangements (pp. 553–555)

Discovering the critical decisions made in founding the organization reveals the original intent for the organization and views for the future. Closely related to the founding decisions are the present guiding ideals and mission. The guiding ideals and mission relate to the service orientation. Consider the difference between not-for-profit and for-profit missions and the intended consumer groups. This could range from elected fee-for-service care in the for-profit setting to a not-for-profit agency focusing on health care to the indigent. The philosophy of the organization provides important information of the current ideals and mission. If revisions have been made over the years, it can be quite helpful to look back at old versions to determine whether the philosophy changed in response to environmental factors.

The social structure provides information on organizational structure, leadership, and management theories and strategies used. As the previous chapter showed, views of humans as clients and providers of services differ, and these differences are reflected in leadership and management styles.

The norms and values of the organization are basic beliefs, attitudes, and expected behaviors. They have been translated over time and are pervasive in organizational policies and procedures that continue to interpret the organizational design and function.

Remembered history and symbolism of the organization contribute additional information, for example, about an institution designed to provide hospital care countywide that has evolved into a regional referral and tertiary care center. Remembered traditions of personalized obstetrical care by a local woman's group may provide funding for a special prenatal program for indigent pregnant teenagers.

Finally, institutional arrangements and linkages such as consortia, cooperating, or referral agencies are frequently quite complex but provide essential information on organizational relationships and interrelationships. These facts are necessary for understanding the culture and influences on the organization within a system of health-care service providers.

COMMUNICATION UNIQUE TO ORGANIZATIONS

As Hall (1987) pointed out, communication is vital in complex, highly technological, and dynamic organizations that are people- and idea-oriented. This fits the characterization of the modern health-care organization. Communication in organizations depends on channels, technology, purpose, and people.

As was illustrated with organizational functions, the structure of the organization plays an important role in *communication channels*. Formal channels are easily apparent in highly bureaucratic structures, as dictated by the organization diagram. But the informal communication, or "grapevine" channels, are sometimes less evident and can be highly effective in such a structure. Consider the need for supplies in some areas of an agency. Ordering can easily be handled through the computerized entry system. But what if some urgently needed item is unavailable through the system? An informal channel may be employed to locate a supply from which the item may be "borrowed" and replaced as soon as the official order is received. The departmental secretary who has an informal chain of communication may be able to use his or her knowledge of these informal systems highly effectively in this procurement process.

Communication channels are important in relating subsystems to each other and to the total system. Recall our systems model, discussed earlier in this chapter, with the five subsystems: goals and values, technical, psychosocial, structural, and managerial.

Organizational goals and values must be translated, transmitted, and reinforced throughout the system to meet the institutional mission. The specialized knowledge, skills, and resources represented by the technical subsystem require excellent communication within the system and from external environments to be current and responsive to changes in the knowledge base and technology. Communication is the action component of the psychosocial subsystem of interpersonal and interdisciplinary roles, behaviors, and relationships in the organization system. The formal and informal communications and interactions that arise from this subsystem are the essence of the organizational culture. The structural subsystem provides the formal design, with its hierarchy or lines of authority, for the communication channels. Communications may be formally dictated in a linear manner by the bureaucratic structure, or they may be flexible and circular in adhocratic matrix designs. Informal communications must be identified to reveal the actual flow of information, decision making, and task accomplishment. Communicating information and expectations stems from the managerial subsystem within the organization's pervasive leadership and management styles. Evaluation of the appropriate channels is vital for effective functioning in the organizational setting.

In addition to the verbal and nonverbal interpersonal communication techniques discussed in Chapter 6, additional methods of communication are routinely, if not uniquely, used in organizations. Consider the *technology* available in organizational settings. We have computer networks, fiberoptics, and satellite technology. As we discuss in Chapter 23, computers manage information storage, inventory, and rapid retrieval, data processing, data analysis, and report generation. The information we compile and the method we use to transmit it varies by the nature of the communication channel we are using. For example, the general rule in an organization is to limit memos to one page or less and disperse them to the appropriate parties; however, the sender needs to consider the available and appropriate technology, such as interoffice paper copies or electronic mail. This leads us from the technology to the purpose of the communication and the people involved.

Considering the *purpose* of communication in an organization is indispensable. Whether we are involved in health teaching or transmitting physiologic findings, the method and receiver of the information are important. Clear, concise, and timely transmission of information is necessary for an effective process. This includes both the purpose of the information and the nature of the information. The time frame and ongoing evaluation are also factors in the initial communication phase, as well as in the feedback phase of the process.

Information can be sent or received verbally by telephone, telefax, or electronic mail, depending on sender's and receiver's access to and skill with the available technology. This involves not only the channels, technology, and purpose of the information, but also the *person, as the receiver* of the information. A classic problem in some organizational settings is fear of technology. Consider the use of electronic mail in organizations. The intent is to efficiently and rapidly deliver information to other individuals or group of individuals in the sender's network while reducing paper and administrative costs. But some people avoid this form of mail while others regularly check for messages. If the information is not sent correctly or received appropriately, the message is not communicated and the process is ineffective. Personal skills in verbal and written communication through specific techniques or technologies must be continually developed and refined. Evaluating the appropriate channels and preparing the information in the correct format are vital for effective communication in the organizational setting.

In essence, organizational communication can be thought of in a way similar to the five rights of administering medications. In organizational communications, these rights are (1) information or content, (2) communication channel, (3) format, including use of correct grammar, terms, and language, (4) level of understanding, and (5) technology. It is a professional responsibility to transmit a correct, credible, easily delivered message. The appropriate communication channel must be selected, using the appropriate chain of command to convey your message. The correct format is essential for decision making. One must decide whether to use an interdepartmental or a formal letter. The nature of the message dictates the format or type of communication. Correct grammar, terminology, and language are essential to presenting a professional image. Next, knowing the level of understanding of your intended audience is vital so that they can process the information. This means using the appropriate reading level and vocabulary. And finally, selecting the appropriate technology is important. Effective communication in organizational settings involves accurate attention to verbal, nonverbal, and written forms in professional and interpersonal relations and negotiations.

ORGANIZATIONS, HEALTH CARE, AND NURSING

In the past two decades, health-care organizations have undergone radical change and restructuring. Pettigrew, Ferlie, and McKee (1992) noted changes in health-care organizations from mesurement-oriented management styles, in the 1980s, to a focus on organizational cultures, in the 1990s, stressing quality-based values (p. 21). Conrad and Hoare (1994) observed that "the emphasis on vertical integration in the 1990s has supplanted the focus on horizontal integration that was so evident in the 1970s and early 1980s" in dealing with payment structures, market forces, integration of services, and consumer demands (pp. 1–2).

The systems theory fits well with changes going on in health-care organizations. But the focus is now on the openness and flexibility of the system boundaries, greater attention to environmental forces, and expanding relationships among organizations as the system becomes a macrosystem or multilayered suprasystem. Conrad and Hoare (1994) describe a three-step strategic adaptation process that is occurring in health-care organizations: (1) environmental assessment and strategy-making, (2) building and balancing systems and structures, and (3) strategy implementation and reassessment (p. 4). The first step directs special attention to external influences. The second step turns the focus to the organization, considering its human resources, information systems, and governance structures. Ongoing feedback and evaluation occur in Step 3. Professional nurses have major roles in all steps of the strategic adaptation process.

Administrative nursing positions in health-care systems have been expanded at all levels. In fact, director and supervisor roles, when still apparent in an organizational chart, have been greatly expanded. As we have seen in the chapters on leadership and management, nurses have major responsibility in health-care organizations. Nurses influence many colleagues, well beyond care providers in areas classified as treatment units. Nurse managers have a knowledge of people and influences of the environment on health-care needs. This is the domain of nursing. In addition to this, nurses are now well prepared in organizational theory, finance, and policy. They have entered the administrative arena as interdisciplinary care managers, coordinators, and leaders. Strategic planning, public relations, and cost containment have become essential skills. Nurses who have this knowledge have legitimate power in health-care organizations.

Max Weber (1947) defined power as "the probability that one actor in a social relationship will be in a position to carry out his own will despite resistance, regardless of the basis on which this probability rests" (p. 152). More specific to organizations, Mintzberg (1983a) defines power as "the capacity to effect (or affect) organizational outcomes" (p. 4). This latter definition has much relevance for professional nursing practice, since nurses are major players in health-care organizations and are positioned to effect or affect positive health-care outcomes. These outcomes can be viewed as outputs from the health-care system, such as clients with improved health status, whether for the conditions that brought them to the health-care system or another deficit identified during the professional relationship. Legitimate power is the authority to effect change within one's position. The professional relationship provides the opportunity for legitimate power, and many nurses now have legitimate power by virtue of their position, role, and expertise. Informal power is the assumption of one's will over a situation to achieve a goal without formal or "vested" authority.

Power was described in Chapter 9, in relation to management strategies. Mintzberg (1983a) identified the general bases of power through (1) control of resources, (2) control of a technical skill, (3) control of a body of knowledge, (4) exclusive rights or privileges to impose choices (legal prerogatives), and (5) access to people who have and can be relied on for the other four.

These power bases are applicable to professional nursing, especially in organizational settings. First, nurses have begun to demonstrate effective management of resources in decentralized and vertical organizations. They are being vested with responsibility especially with reference to decisions and resources needed for effective organizational functioning. Second, care of clients involves technical skills that must be performed or supervised by nurses. Third, as described in Chapter 3, nursing uses borrowed knowledge from other disciplines and has an evolving unique body of knowledge needed for the health of clients. The fourth base of power involves the legal prerogatives granted and implied under the practice acts, licensure, certification, and professional codes described in Chapter 1. And finally, nurses have access to colleagues, clients, and influential people who they rely on for access to the other bases of power because of their common concern for the health of individuals, families, communities, and groups in society.

Negotiation for power must first be related to the goals of the organization. Next is the utilization of the power bases. Nurses have the ability and responsibility to negotiate for legitimate power in organizations. Think back to the sources of power as control of resources, technical skills, and a body of knowledge along with legal prerogatives and access to key people. Nurses certainly have access to these power sources if developed and used. Change for the good of clients or the industry can be a result of applying these principles in health-care organizations. As we will see in the next chapter, professional nursing practice has an integral role in this process.

KEY POINTS

- An **organization** is simply an arrangement of human and material resources for some purpose, such as creating an institution or agency to meet a stated aim. Organizations can be viewed in terms of their structure, function, and people.
- A useful perspective for viewing the intricacies of a health-care organization is as a system affected by other systems and within the larger health-care and societal systems (environmental suprasystem).
- Kast and Rosenzweig (1979) regard organizations as open, sociotechnical systems that structure and integrate human activities around various technologies (p. 108). The organizational system in this model is further composed of five subsystems: goals and values, technical, psychosocial, structural, and managerial.

■ An *organizational structure* is the design of the organization, including the type of hierarchy that tells us about positions or roles, responsibilities, status, channels of command or reporting relationships, and tasks to be accomplished. The major organizational structures are bureaucratic and organic (adhocratic).

■ Specific characteristics of a **bureaucratic structure** include control, standardization, efficiency, conformity to rules and regulations, and clear lines of authority with depersonalized relationships.

■ **Adhocracies** have evolved to meet the needs of organizations composed of humans in dynamic and sometimes complex environmental settings. The term "adhocracy" implies that the structure is a design that has been developed to meet the organizational mission and specific goals. Examples of adhocratic designs include functional, product, and matrix forms.

■ *Centralized versus decentralized organizational structures* involve the lines of control and decision making within the organization. In a **centralized organization**, the span of control or management is in the classic bureaucratic style, with governance from the top downward (vertical). **Decentralization** distributes authority downward in an organization, with decision making and control at local levels. Decentralization creates a more human and participatory model, resulting in employee involvement, performance, and satisfaction.

■ **Organizational functions** include goals and operations to efficiently and effectively fulfill the mission of the organization. Ideologic, formal, shared, and system goals demonstrate intent and consistency of behavior in organizations (Mintzberg, 1983a). Organizational operations include formalized activities defined by the structure as well as informal functions for daily accomplishment of the organization's goals.

■ The **organizational culture** involves the culmination of the norms, attitudes, and values related to the organizational mission accompanied by the expected behaviors of people.

■ Communication in organizations depends on the channels, technology, purpose, and people. The organizational communication process can also be thought of as containing five "rights": (1) information or content, (2) communication channel, (3) format, including use of correct grammar, terms, and language, (4) level of understanding, and (5) technology.

■ Legitimate power is the authority to effect change within one's position. Power bases are built on control of resources, technical skills, and a body of knowledge as well as exclusive rights and access to other people with power.

CHAPTER EXERCISES

1. Apply systems theory to a health organization with which you are familiar. Describe the components as the various subsystem structures for this organization.

2. Obtain a copy of the organizational chart from a health-care agency. Describe the structure, functions, lines of decision making, communication patterns, and sources of power relative to the organizational mission.

3. Examine the structure, functions, and culture of a for-profit and a not-for-profit organization in your community. Contrast the organizations.

4. Examine the communication structures, channels, technology, purposes, and receivers of information in a local health-care organization.

5. Interview a member of the administrative team from a large health-care facility on the various positions held by nurses. Describe their roles, changes that have occurred, areas of legitimate power, and the skills professional nurses need in this setting.

REFERENCES

Barker, A. M. (1992). *Transformational leadership: A vision for the future* (Pub. No 15-2473). New York: National League for Nursing.

Bertalanffy, L. V. (1968). *General system theory: Foundations, development, applications.* New York: George Braziller.

Branum, Q. K. (1990). Assessing organizational climate. In Waltz, C. F., & Strickland, O. L. (Eds.). *Measurement of nursing outcomes. Vol. 3: Measuring clinical skills and professional development in education and practice* (pp. 259–278). New York: Springer.

Clark, C. C. (1994). *The nurse as group leader* (3rd ed.). New York: Springer.

Conrad, D. A., & Hoare, G. A. (Eds.). (1994). *Strategic alignment: Managing integrated health systems.* Ann Arbor, MI: AUPHA Press/Health Administration.

Cox, T. (1993). *Cultural diversity in organizations: Theory, research and practice.* San Francisco: Berrett-Koehler.

Dienemann, J. A. (1990). Organizations as open systems. In Dienemann, J. A. *Nursing administration: Strategic perspectives and application* (pp. 229–247). Norwalk, CT: Appleton & Lange.

Gaucher, E. J., & Coffey, R. J. (1993). *Total quality in healthcare: From theory to practice.* San Francisco: Jossey-Bass.

Hall, R. H. (1987). *Organizations: Structures, processes, and outcomes* (4th ed.). Englewood Cliffs, NJ: Prentice-Hall.

Hart, J. D., & Goeppele, M. A. (1994). Corporate restructuring: Phase II. In Conrad, D. A., & Hoare, G. A. (Eds.). *Strategic alignment: Managing integrated health systems* (pp. 109–123). Ann Arbor, MI: AUPHA Press/Health Administration.

Kast, F. E., & Rosenzweig, J. E. (1979). *Organization and management: A systems and contingency approach* (3rd ed.). New York: McGraw-Hill.

Knowles, M. S. (1980). *The modern practice of adult education: From pedagogy to andragogy* (rev. ed.). Chicago: Follett.

Marriner-Tomey, A. (1992). *Guide to nursing management* (4th ed.). St. Louis: Mosby-Year Book.

McGregor, D. (1967). *The professional manager.* New York: McGraw-Hill.

Merton, R. K. (1957). *Social theory and social structure* (rev ed.). Glencoe, IL: Free Press.

Mintzberg, H. (1983a). *Power in and around organizations.* Englewood Cliffs, NJ: Prentice-Hall.

Mintzberg, H. (1983b). *Structures in fives: Designing effective organizations.* Englewood Cliffs, NJ: Prentice-Hall.

Ouchi, W. G. (1981). *Theory Z: How American business can meet the Japanese challenge.* Reading, MA: Addison-Wesley.

Packard, N. J. (1994). Linkages between acute and long-term care services. In Conrad, D. A., & Hoare, G. A. (Eds.). *Strategic alignment: Managing integrated health systems.* (pp. 95–106). Ann Arbor, MI: AUPHA Press/Health Administration.

Pettigrew, A., Ferlie, E., & McKee, L. (1992). *Shaping strategic change: Making change in large organizations.* London: Sage.

Tappen, R. M. (1995). *Nursing leadership and management: Concepts and practice* (3rd ed.). Philadelphia: Davis.

Vecchio, R. P. (1991). *Organizational behavior* (2nd ed.). Chicago: Dryden Press.

Weber, M. (1947). The fundamental concepts of sociology (A. M. Anderson & T. Parsons, Trans.). In Parsons, T. (Ed.). *Max Weber: The theory of social and economic organization* (pp. 87–157). New York: Oxford University Press.

Weiss, H. J., & Gershon, M. E. (1989). *Production and operations management.* Boston: Allyn & Bacon.

BIBLIOGRAPHY

Hassard, J., & Parker, M. (1994). *Towards a new theory of organizations.* London: Routledge.

Lippitt, G. L. (1973). *Visualizing change: Model building and the change process.* La Jolla, CA: University Associates.

Rogers, E. M. (1983). *Diffusion of innovations* (3rd ed.). New York: Free Press.

Chapter 11

CHANGE

Rose Kearney Nunnery

CHAPTER OBJECTIVES

On completion of this chapter, the reader will be able to:

1. Differentiate among the theories of change proposed by Lewin, Lippitt, Havelock, and Rogers.
2. Apply the stages of unfreezing, moving, and refreezing to a client situation for managed change.
3. Given a practice situation, describe the roles and characteristics of an effective change agent.
4. Discuss differences needed in the change process for use with individuals, families, and groups.
5. Describe the process and strategies for effective organizational change.

KEY TERMS

Change
Planned Change
Change Agents
Restraining Forces

Driving Forces
Unfreezing
Moving
Refreezing

Internal Sources of Change
External Sources of Change

C hange is a part of normal daily life. We talk about changing our hair color, our attitude, someone else's mind, and so on. **Change** can be defined as a process that results in altered behavior of individuals or groups. It may be accidental or, as sometimes described, "change by drift" (Brooten, Hayman, & Naylor, 1988). This type of accidental, spontaneous, or haphazard change is caused by outside forces. On the other hand, **planned change** involves conscious effort toward some goal as a deliberate and collaborative process. Change is an integral and essential component of professional nursing practice.

In today's world, change must be viewed as the necessity for and impact on both the individual and the group. Consider the individual and a diet as a process of altering nutritional intake. The result (the change) is an increase or decrease in weight. A family crisis or a normal bout of depression may lead to weight change. Accidental change may be due to outside influences. The individual may have been eating chocolate. Gaining weight was not the intention, but it was easy, and the individual was hungry, or it made him or her feel better. In contrast, as a planned change process, the same individual may have gone to Weight Watchers. Improved nutrition and eating practices also influence other family members through food selections and meal preparation in the home, and even with friends and colleagues through the individual's example.

Change is also a daily occurrence in society. Think about the number of times you have read or heard of global relations, changes in political forces, and changes in health-care organizations.

In professional practice, we need to focus on the process of planned change, being proactive rather than reactive. Planned changes for persons or groups in the environment require structural shifts in an environmental system for improved functioning. Improved functioning involves new (changed) behaviors, attitudes, and relationships. As professional nurses, you are the movers and the shakers, or **change agents,** for people and health. Your role is to move for needed, planned change for individuals, families, community groups, and society. This will occur in individual practice as well as on an organizational level.

THEORIES OF CHANGE

Understanding the theories of change applicable to individuals, families, groups, and society is the first step in moving from being reactive to change to becoming proactive, and a major player in the process.

Chinn and Benne (1976) described major groups of change strategies based on three philosophies: (1) the empirical-rational nature of man; (2) normative-educative philosophy, based on human motivation and norms (attitudes, values, skills, and relationships); and (3) power-coercive philosophy, based on leadership and the application of power (p. 23). The change models by Havelock and Rogers reflect the empirical-rational philosophy whereas the normative-educative philosophy guides the models developed by Lewin and Lippitt (Chinn & Benne, 1976). These two philosophical orientations are consistent with the metaparadigm nursing concepts of person, environment, health, and nursing, focused on the nature of the person or the group in the context of the environment.

Lewin

The classic change theorist was Kurt Lewin. Lewin (1951) developed a model based on his Field theory, a method of analyzing causal relationships and building the scientific constructs for change (p. 45). The mathematical model in his theory merely indicates that human behavior is based on the person (or group) and his or her environment at that point in time. Lewin (1951) focused on social change, pointing out that "group life is never without change, merely differences in amount and type of change exist" (p. 199). In groups and organizations, multiple influences from individuals and their reactions to the environment cause group behaviors and norms. This Field theory proposes maintaining the status quo, or a state of equilibrium, when restraining forces and driving forces balance each other. To achieve change, the restraining forces must be weakened and the driving forces strengthened. Consider the illustration of change in Figure 11–1.

Restraining forces in society resist change and include norms, values, relations among people, morals, fears, perceived threats, and regulations. In essence, these restraining forces are the "old guard" that maintains the status quo. **Driving forces,** on the other hand, support change and include the desire to please or the desire for more novel, effective, efficient, or different activities. System imbalance becomes the impetus for change. The process involves weakening the restraining forces and strengthening the driving forces. To do this, Lewin proposed three aspects of permanent change: unfreezing, moving, and refreezing of group standards.

Unfreezing involves unequilibrium, discontent, and uneasiness. Lewin (1951) stated, "to break open the shell of complacency and self-righteousness it is

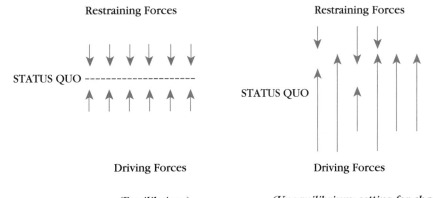

FIGURE 11-1. Illustration of restraining and driving forces in the change process.

(Equilibrium)   *(Unequilibrium; setting for change)*

sometimes necessary to bring about deliberately an emotional stir-up" (p. 229). The restraining and driving forces are identified, and comparisons are drawn between the ideal and the actual situation. To bring about change, participants are prepared for change (unfreezing) to make the need for change apparent and accepted. In many situations, making individuals uneasy and discontented with the environmental system is the initial step in the process. Malcontents want change while individuals satisfied and comfortable with the current state of affairs resist changes that will create unequilibrium. Activities are centered on unfreezing the existing equilibrium.

Moving occurs when the previous structure is rearranged and realistic goals are set. The system is moved to a new level of equilibrium. Choices must be made about accepting the change agent and the roles of the group members in the change process. At this stage, group decisions are preferable for moving toward permanent change. This represents the distribution of power among the group members to make them driving forces engaged in the process. The individual involved in the change process acts as a member of a group in which new social values and norms are being established.

A new status quo is established with **refreezing.** Lewin called this originally the "freezing" stage, but the idea of refreezing better describes the new level of equilibrium and reinforcement needed for the new patterns of behavior. The focus is on maintaining the goal achieved and highlighting the present benefits over past practices.

Consider Lewin's model with a client population. The individual with heart disease who is placed on a low-salt, low-fat diet has a teaching need to bring permanent change to his diet. You discover through interviews with the client and family members that the diet at home is highly seasoned and high in ani-

mal protein and fats. *Restraining forces* include cultural values, family traditions, individual and group (family) preferences in food selection and preparation, attitudes toward diet, foods, or food preparation, fears of further illness with changes in diet, attitudes toward restrictions on personal life style, and so on. Now consider each of these factors in relation to all members of the household and the client's work, recreation, and social environments. Think about the *driving forces:* fear of further illness without the dietary changes, respect for advice given, support network, educational presentations, role models, and so forth. *Unfreezing* involves the identification of the restraining and driving forces, motivating the client toward change, and assessing readiness for teaching. *Moving* consists of supporting a positive attitude toward change, and providing nutritional information including food selection, preparation, and presentation options. This is a time of goal setting with the client to bring changes that must occur after discharge, through a rehabilitation program, and life long. Valuable nursing theories to support nursing actions include King's Theory of Goal Attainment and Orem's Self-Care Agency. Supporting attitudinal and behavioral changes could occur through follow-up telephone service after discharge or interviews at clinic appointments. *Refreezing* would occur with the client's stabilization, evidenced through subjective reports (e.g., food diary), objective observations (e.g., health assessment), and laboratory studies in the rehabilitation phase. A similar application could be developed for group change using Lewin's field theory.

Lippitt

As an outgrowth and expansion of Lewin's theory, Lippitt (1973) pointed out that "if we want to under-

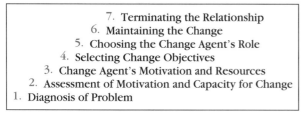

7. Terminating the Relationship
6. Maintaining the Change
5. Choosing the Change Agent's Role
4. Selecting Change Objectives
3. Change Agent's Motivation and Resources
2. Assessment of Motivation and Capacity for Change
1. Diagnosis of Problem

FIGURE 11-2. Lippitt's (1973) seven stages of planned change.

stand, explain, or predict change in human behavior, we need to take into account the person and his environment" (p. 3). To do this, he identified several complex factors of human behavior that must be considered: motivation, multiple causation, and overrationalized habits. Looking at both individual and organizational change, he further focused on the change agent and defined seven specific phases (Figure 11–2) within an idea similar to Lewin's change model. Thus, more specific activities were described that are still applicable to the three steps of unfreezing, moving, and refreezing.

Unfreezing. First, there is the need to collect data and *diagnose the problem* and the key people. The driving and restraining people, environmental, and organizational forces are identified, defined, and targeted. Second, the *motivation and resources* are assessed to identify the desire and capacity for change. This includes resistance and readiness of the people in the environment. In the third step, the *change agent's motivation,* commitment and resources must be assessed for the potential success of the change activity. The skills, efforts, and responsibilities are critical planning pieces in this phase of change.

Moving. Initially, *change objectives* must be selected considering activities for progressive change. Lippitt uses the leverage point concept as the starting point when receptivity for change is apparent and the objectives are initiated. Planning and evaluation are primary activities in this step. Then, following the development of an action plan with evaluation criteria, the *change agent and group roles* are selected and assigned. Acceptance and selection of an appropriate role is critical in defining the power, outcomes, and strategies of the change agent.

Refreezing. *Maintaining the change* occurs through ongoing training, communication, and support of the people in the environment. Communication by both driving and restraining forces advertises

the success of the change using actual evaluation results. In many cases, the loudest and most visible of the restraining forces become the change agent's greatest supporters when they accept the merits of the process with evaluation. How many times have you heard someone say, "I never thought it could be done but. . ." or "I was behind that all along but I did not want to show it"? Finally, *terminating the helping relationship* is necessary on the part of the change agent and major players for the change to become part of the people and the environment, and not just the activity of a select individual or group. Rather, it becomes the new norm of the people or the organization.

A major piece of Lippitt's (1973) model involves the roles for the professional change agent. He proposed four major roles for the change agent:

- Specialist
- Coordinator
- Fact finder and information link
- Consultant

Recall that in the moving phase of change, Lippitt views the selection of the appropriate role for the change agent as essential. As a *specialist,* the change agent is the expert in the environment on methods and strategies for change. As a *coordinator,* the change agent functions as manager planning, organizing, and coordinating efforts and programs for the change. The change agent as a *fact finder and information link* serves as a seeker, clarifier, synthesizer, reality-tester, and provider of information as well as a communications link among all participants in the system (Lippitt, 1973, pp. 60–61).

The *consultant* role is viewed as the most important role for the change agent, both inside the system and with external individuals, groups, and environments. In fact, as Figure 11–3 illustrates, Lippitt (1973) developed a model of eight specific activity roles within this consultant role: advocate, expert, trainer, alternative identifier, collaborator, process specialist, fact finder, and reflector (p. 63). The correct role for the change agent is presented along a continuum, depending on the people, the environment, and how much direction is needed from the agent to implement the change. As the advocate, the change agent as consultant is highly directive in leading the group toward change. Conversely, the change agent consultant is the least directive helping the group clarify and evaluate their efforts with the group as a reflector. The change agent must have knowledge, skill, and perseverance in the work-intensive process of change.

Consider, again, our example of the client who must change to a low-salt, low-fat diet. First, there is

DIRECTIVE CONSULTATION							
Position 1	Position 2	Position 3	Position 4	Position 5	Position 6	Position 7	Position 8
Advocate	Expert	Trainer	Alternative Identifier	Collaborator	Process Specialist	Fact Finder	Reflector
Persuades client as to proper approach	Gives expert advice to client	Develops training experiences to aid client	Provides alternative to client	Joins in problem solving	Assists client in problem-solving process	Serves to help client collect data	Serves as a catalytic agent for client in solving the problem
						V	V
						Nondirective consultation	

FIGURE 11-3. Multiple consulting approaches of change agent. (From Lippitt, G. L. [1973]. *Visualizing change: Model building and the change process.* LaJolla, CA: University Associates. Adapted from Lippitt, G. L., & Nadler, L. [August 1967]. Emerging roles of the Training Director. *Training and Development Journal,* 9. Permission granted by The Gordon Lippitt Foundation, Bethesda, Maryland.)

the need to collect data on meals, food preferences, and preparation at home to diagnose the problem and the key people involved at home, work, and social settings. The environmental forces identified as family, friends, cultural, and collegial (work or recreational) forces are identified, defined, and targeted. Second, the motivation, resistance, readiness, and resources of the client and his family are assessed to identify the desire and capacity for change in dietary habits. In the third step, your motivation, commitment, and resources must be realized as the nurse/change agent. Your skills, efforts, and responsibilities are critical in this planning phase. Lippitt's concept of leverage point occurs when the client and his family are receptive for change and the action plan is initiated with evaluation criteria. Your role as change agent is defined specific to the client and his needs. Consider the applicability of Orem's three modes of nursing, especially the supportive-educative mode, in relation to his continuum of consultant activities. Your role as change agent may alter rapidly as the client moves from the hospital setting to the home and clinic settings. Empowerment of the client and his significant others is critical for success in this type of change. And with the maintenance of the change in diet and health status that occurs through ongoing training in dietary management, communication, support, and reinforcement during the follow-up period, the client and family are moved into the termination phase, when the helping relationship is no longer necessary and the dietary changes have become part of the person and family in their environment.

Havelock

Havelock (1971) used a system and process model to depict an organization with major concepts of role, linkages, and communication for transfer and use of knowledge. Using the three major perspectives of problem-solving, research-development-diffusion, and social interaction, Havelock further examines the linkage process to view the broader system (Havelock & Havelock, 1973).

Building on Lewin's stages of change, Havelock added steps to the three stages highlighting communication and interpersonal activities in these steps:

- Perception of need
- Diagnosis of the problem
- Identification of the problem
- Devising a plan of action
- Gaining acceptance of the plan
- Stabilization
- Self-renewal (Havelock & Havelock, 1973).

Unfreezing. There is the *perception of a need* for a change in the system followed by *diagnosis and identification of the problem.* At this time, a reciprocal relationship develops between the user (client) system and a resource system. Linkages with needed resources before moving on the change occur in this initial stage. Havelock and Havelock (1973) stress that the problem-solver must be "meaningfully linked to outside resources" (p. 23).

Moving. Movement toward change in Step 2 requires *devising a plan of action* and *gaining accep-*

tance of the plan in the system. This is a stage of searching for a solution and applying that solution to the identified problem, using resource linkages in the environment.

Refreezing. In the final step, refreezing, stabilization and the need for self-renewal are specified. First, *stabilization* in the system is specified to sustain change (refreezing). Havelock describes *self-renewal* as being needed to sustain client system in the future. In essence, the values, goals, and activities of the system become the norm.

The importance of and roles for the change agent are also an important component of Havelock's model, which lists four roles for the change agent:

- Catalyst
- Solution giver
- Process helper
- Resource linker (Havelock & Havelock, 1973, p. 60)

These roles become increasingly complex. The catalyst serves as the impetus for change to the resource linker, who brings people, environments, and resources together at the subsystem, system, and macrosystem levels (Havelock & Havelock, 1973, pp. 60–64). For effective functioning within these roles, Havelock further developed a training program for preparing effective change agents.

Havelock's model can also be used with the example of dietary change for our client with heart disease. Communication and interpersonal activities are core ingredients in the nurse-client relationship. Identifying the need for altering dietary salt and fat relates to the client's medical condition. The personal, environmental, social, cultural, and dietary habits are assessed through interview, to define the problem. A reciprocal relationship between the client system and a resource system occurs through linkages, including meeting with a nutritionist for food selection and preparing options. Informational lists on cook books, restaurants, and community associations advocating healthy eating with low-fat, low-salt meals are provided. Using this model, the nurse encourages linkages with outside resources such as the American Heart Association, American Association of Critical Care Nurses, and collegial relationships with nutritionists, rehabilitation specialists, and cardiologists. The plan for dietary change is devised in collaboration with the client system and includes linkages with community resources acceptable to the client and his family. Linkages must be retained with the client after discharge in the home, clinic or rehabilitation setting. This follow-up is necessary for stabilizing the diet, given the client's physiologic and psychosocial system influences. The role of the nurse–change agent has moved from catalyst and solution giver, in the initial phase of problem identification, to process helper in the planning phase, and then resource linker. The changes in diet must become a part of the client's value system. The nurse–change agent then terminates the relationship with the client while linkages with external resources provide the client with self-renewal.

Rogers

As an outgrowth of the change model, Rogers developed the Diffusion of Innovations model. In 1971, Rogers and Shoemaker stated the following:

> Although it is true that we live more than ever before in an era of change, prevailing social structures often serve to hamper the diffusion of innovations. Our activities in education, agriculture, medicine, industry, and the like are often without the benefit of the most current research knowledge. The gap between what is actually known and what is effectively put to use needs to be closed. (p. 1)

This is no less true today, more than 25 years later. We live in a time of even greater social change. Our information superhighways can be more timely in the transfer of information, but we must understand the innovations adopted to bridge this gap. This model was used in nursing in the 1980s to promote research-based practice and is still appropriate today.

Rogers and Shoemaker (1971) focus on communication and view change as the effects of a new idea or innovation being adopted and put into use or rejected. Change may occur at the level of the individual, group, organization, or society. The model was first proposed with four major steps in the process of social change: knowledge, persuasion, decision, and confirmation (Rogers & Shoemaker, 1971, p. 25). Rogers (1983) then extended the Innovation-Diffusion process to five stages:

- Knowledge
- Persuasion
- Decision
- Implementation
- Confirmation

The interest and commitment of key people and policy makers are critical in this model.

Unfreezing. Developing a sequence of knowledge, persuasion, and decision making is the key activity in the unfreezing stage. To *develop knowledge,* key people and policy makers are introduced to the innovation to gain understanding. Then comes *persuasion* to develop attitudes on the innovation. Rogers (1983) uses persuasion to focus on the individual whose attitudes change, either positively or negatively toward the innovation, not on the external force that changes one's mind. The *decision* to adopt or reject an innovation is the bridge between the unfreezing and moving stages in Roger's model.

Moving. *Implementation* applies to the stage of moving. Revisions, potential adoption, or rejection of the innovation are included in this implementation phase.

Refreezing. Roger's fifth step, when the innovation changes from being novel to being part of the routine or norm, involves refreezing the equilibrium. This is defined as *confirmation,* in which reinforcement is sought and the key people and policy makers decide to maintain or discontinue the innovation. Rogers (1983) admits that the research evidence shows no clear distinction between the implementation and confirmation stages. This may be related to the idea of a flexible timespan between implementation and confirmation, when the process of refreezing for the innovation occurs. Rogers (1983) describes this final confirmatory stage as "routinization" of the innovation.

Throughout the entire process, five attributes determine the rate of adoption of an innovation by members of a social system:

- Relative advantage
- Compatibility
- Complexity
- Trialability
- Observability (Rogers & Shoemaker, 1971, p. 39; Rogers, 1983, pp. 238–240)

These attributes should be included in all evaluation plans and data on the change. Relative advantage is determined by comparing the innovation with what was done in the past. The advantage may be effectiveness as well as efficiency, and the process has been described as weighing economic advantages or the cost-effectiveness. Compatibility with the values, beliefs, and needs of the group is the second factor. The complexity (difficulty in use), trialability (experimental trials), and observability (visible evidence) are all considered in the implementation stage and have a direct effect on adoption, revision, or discontinuance of an innovation.

Rogers' model also highlights the roles of the change agent, which occur in the following sequence:

1. Develops the need for change
2. Establishes the relationship with the client system

3. Diagnoses the problems
4. Motivates the client system for change
5. Translates intent for change into the actions needed
6. Stabilizes change in system and "freezes" new behavior
7. Terminates the relationship (Rogers, 1983, pp. 315–317)

Like Lippitt, Rogers views the change agent as a professional, skilled in change for effective functioning in the role.

We take a slightly different approach with the application of Rogers' Innovation-Diffusion process model to our example of the client who needs to change his diet. You have found research studies on effective dietary compliance in cardiac rehabilitation. You now wish to bring this innovation into practice in your organization to use in client teaching programs. During the initial development of knowledge, key people and policy makers in nursing service and cardiology are introduced to the teaching program content and methods, along with the results from use with clients in other settings. Next, you need to persuade people of the effectiveness and applicability of this approach—the organization and its resources, as well as the client population. The decision to adopt or reject the new teaching program is made. If it is decided to try the teaching program with a client population, the phase of implementation is entered. The teaching program may be revised, adopted, or rejected, based on its specificity to the client group and the organization. If the teaching program is found to be applicable and advantageous, it is "confirmed" as the agency procedure or organizational norm. If the procedure is not adopted, the key people and policy makers must confirm the decision to discontinue the program.

The four models of change are illustrated in Table 11–1. Selecting an appropriate model to guide practice involves how you look at the world and what is most helpful in driving your skills as an agent in the change process. Moving from the theoretical stages of change to strategies for change brings the focus to the change agent.

CHANGE AGENTS

Our second step in becoming a major player in the change process is to develop greater understanding of the roles and attributes of a successful change agent. We have seen the importance of the change agent emerge in the models of Lippitt, Havelock, and Rogers. Table 11–2 illustrates the roles and ac-

TABLE 11 – 1. Comparison of the Stages of Change Represented in Theoretical Models

Theorist	Stages						
Lewin (1952) Force Field	[1] Unfreezing			[2] Moving		[3] Refreezing	
Lippitt (1973) Planned Change	[1] Diagnosis of problem	[2] Assessment of motivation and capacity for change	[3] Change agent's motivation and resources	[4] Selecting change objectives	[5] Choosing change agent's role	[6] Maintaining the change	[7] Terminating the relationship
Havelock (1973) Linkages	[1] Perception of need	[2] Diagnosis of the problem	[3] Identification of the problem	[4] Devising a plan of action	[5] Gaining acceptance of plan	[6] Stabilization	[7] Self-renewal
Rogers (1983) Innovation-Diffusion	[1] Knowledge	[2] Persuasion	[3] Decision	[4] Implementation		[5] Confirmation	

TABLE 1 1 – 2. Comparing the Roles for the Change Agent from the Different Theoretical Models

Stages of Change	Lippitt (1973)	Havelock (1973)	Rogers (1983)
Unfreezing	A specialist in the diagnosis and assessment of client system and change agent as • Information seeker • Clarifier • Synthesizer • Reality-tester • Provider • Problem-solver	A catalyst in the identification of needs, diagnoses, and all aspects of the problem within the roles of • Clarifier • Synthesizer • Reality-tester • Provider • Problem-solver	Range of roles from support to consultant for sharing knowledge, building persuasiveness, and leading the group toward decision making on the innovation through activities of • Needs identification • Establishment of professional relationship with client system • Diagnosis of problems • Motivation of client system
Moving	Communication link viewed within one of eight directive toward nondirective consultative roles • Advocate • Expert • Trainer • Alternative identifier • Collaborator • Process specialist • Fact-finder • Reflector	Solution giver and process helper as • Clarifier • Synthesizer • Reality-tester • Provider • Problem-solver	Range of roles from support to consultant to translate intent for change into the actions needed
Refreezing	Consultation for • Maintenance of the change • Termination of the relationship	Resource linker for stabilization and self-renewal as • Clarifier • Synthesizer • Reality-tester • Problem-solver	Range of roles from support to consultant for • Confirmation of change and stabilizing the adoption to prevent discontinuance reinforce of new behaviors • Termination of relationship

tivities of the change agent in these models. In Lewin's original model, change in humans is a function of the person and his or her environment at that point in time. Consider the roles of the change agent in the three general phases of change.

Unfreezing. Good interpersonal and assessment skills are needed to acquire data to weaken restraining forces and enhance driving forces in the present system, and both internal and external system forces must be considered. The change agent must then establish a climate that encourages and supports change. Needs assessment, diagnosis, and establishment of a professional relationship have consistently occurred during the unfreezing phase in all models. Now look at the similarity of this stage to the assessment and diagnosis activities of the nursing process.

In the nursing process, health assessment data are collected and problems are identified. Assessing the client's characteristics and current level of satisfaction with the health problem or condition are essential components of this activity. Diagnostic statements are developed following needs identification.

Asking questions and diagnosing the problem for changed client behaviors or responses, then, lead to the planning stage of the nursing process.

Moving. The change agent must assist the client group in setting and striving for clear, realistic goals. A good deal of the change agent's time and energy is needed during this phase for strategies to deal with those resisting change. Again, interpersonal and motivational skills are critical. The change agent needs to constantly assess and evaluate resistance, conflict, and motivation in the client system and maintain movement toward the goals and objectives of change.

As in the nursing process, the major activities of this moving phase are implementing plans, goals, and objectives and collecting evaluation data. Client data are analyzed, interpreted, and acted on. The nurse actively uses critical thinking, decision-making, interpersonal, and evaluation skills. These same skills are necessary to move toward change. This will probably be the most comfortable phase for the nurse functioning as a change agent because skills in this area are developed through nursing practice.

Refreezing. Providing rewards and reinforcement for the change is a major part of the change agent's role in the third stage. Evaluation data for reinforcement of change must be used as supportive evidence. Activities for the change agent during this stage are supportive, initially, but involvement decreases with the need to terminate and have the client system totally involved and responsible for the change without external change agent intervention.

In the nursing process, the nurse-patient relationship is terminated when objectives are achieved and nursing diagnoses are resolved. The nurse has prepared the person or family for this termination long before discharge orders are written or the person leaves the agency environment. Just as discharge planning starts with admission, this last stage must be planned for and worked toward during the entire change process, with the person, family, or group taking increasing responsibility for the new behaviors.

The interventions of a skilled change agent can make all the difference in the planned change process. Corey (1976) emphasized the concepts of enabling, understanding, and action, stating that "to be an effective change agent therefore, I should strive to enable myself and others to recognize forces in the environment, to understand the consequences of intervening among those forces, and to provide the necessary support to take planned action" (p. 273). More specifically, the skills of change agents include the following:

- Vision for the future and creativity
- Ability to look at a situation, narrowly and broadly (assessment skills)
- Good interpersonal skills, including those of communication, motivation, assertiveness, problem solving, and group process
- Flexibility and a willingness to consider alternative views
- Perseverance and a positive attitude
- Integrity and commitment
- Ability to manage conflict and resistance

CHANGE IN INDIVIDUALS, FAMILIES, AND GROUPS

As noted earlier, Chinn and Benne (1976) categorized change strategies into three major types: empirical-rational, normative-reeducative, and power-coercive. Power-coercive strategies are based on the application of power by legitimate authority. Nursing concerns are with the person or group and their empowerment for healthy behaviors or the creation of optimal health status. Applying power as "the authority" is inconsistent with empowering people. Altering practices, procedures, or the environment in organizations as a coercive change can occur by imposing major policy, but think of the upheaval this change creates. Coercive change may also be necessary in an emergency situation or when the person or family must have major assistance. The problem is that the change may not persist unless the person or group has internalized it in their value system.

The philosophical basis of nursing is consistent with the Empirical-Rational or the Normative-Reeducative strategies for change. The Empirical-Rational strategy assumes that people are rational and have a self interest in change. Power for the individual or group occurs through knowledge. The Normative-Reeducative approach is based on social norms and the person's interaction with the environment. The Normative-Reeducative philosophy can be viewed as empowerment with an emphasis on interpersonal skills. Both of these philosophical orientations are consistent with nursing, but their applicability differs based on the nursing model selected for practice. For example, King's Theory of Goal Attainment, Orem's General Theory of Nursing, and Roy's Adaptation model contain philosophical assumptions similar to the normative reeducative strategies, with the person viewed as a thinking, feeling, reacting being in the context of his or her environment.

Since nursing looks at both the person and interactions within the environment, several factors must be considered. These include resistance to change, empowerment or involvement of the client, and environmental or situational factors.

A major concern of the change agent is the person's or group's resistance to change. To handle this resistance, one must evaluate what makes people resist change. People are naturally threatened by change. Change involves the loss of "near and dears" held by a person or a group. This is a threat to their value system and a loss of the comfortable status quo. They feel vulnerable and insecure. Stress is created and must be managed. The need for or the activities involved in change may also be mistrusted or misunderstood. Another innately human characteristic is the fear of failure or being unable to perform the new activities or tasks. This creates more stress. Think about the first time you had the challenge of starting an intravenous infusion!

Resistance to change can be reduced by several techniques:

- Careful planning
- Allowing sufficient time

- Support and reinforcement
- Involving the person or group

Understanding the full impact of individual or group norms and planning for a change in attitudes can lead to changes in behavior. Recall the old adage, "fools rush in. . . ." Allowing sufficient time for the change to occur and persist is essential. A gradual move toward change is more effective than a radical move. The time needed depends on the physical, psychosocial, cultural, and attitudinal characteristics of the individual or group. Patience, persistence, perseverance, and creativity are essential traits of the change agent. Another strategy for decreasing resistance to change is good communication with key and resource people throughout the entire process. In addition, a good deal of support and reinforcement will be needed. This goes back to the need for excellent interpersonal skills, verbal and nonverbal, with both individuals and groups.

The involvement of the person or group is needed for lasting change. It is essential to build on their readiness, motivation, self-concept, abilities, and resources throughout the process. Involving people in planning and decision making both reduces resistance to change and creates empowerment. Strategies for involving people include education, training, socialization and persuasion, and facilitation. It would often be easier to make the change yourself as an external force, but the action by the client system is slower and more enduring. Note that education and training involve enlightenment and preparation rather than preaching. This creates the empowerment and sets the stage for a revision of the norm or value system.

Looking at the situation or environment is critical in the change process. First, one must understand the past or the personal history of the individual, family, or group. You include a past, personal, psychosocial, family, and environmental history in a health history. These are important basic items of information to obtain before doing the physical appraisal in any health assessment. The same thing is needed in the change process.

- What types of change has the person or group faced in the past? Information on experience and success with change is valuable to determine whether this person is a novice with change, has embraced change throughout life, or falls somewhere between these experiential extremes.
- How has the person or group handled change? Stress and coping factors will emerge with this information. You can then discover how to best motivate and support behaviors.

- What resources have been available or used in past change activities?
- What is the person's or group's perspective on the applicability of the resources in the environment to the present situation?

Human resources are included as support systems, which can be family, friends, colleagues, clergy, professionals, or even "ideal" role models. These resources may still help the person or group. If these are not available or appropriate, linking the person or group with similar resources may be effective. Remember, some people do well in support groups whereas others need more individualized support.

ORGANIZATIONAL CHANGE

To broaden the perspective from the individual, family, and community, we move to organizational change. Although organizations such as many small to medium-sized hospitals may operate as a community, both internal and external influences in contemporary health care are major considerations. Everyone within an organization has faced organizational change, from minor changes in policy to restructuring of services. Many have experienced or know a colleague who experienced a radical reorganization, with restructuring and managerial shifts, layoffs, or ownership changes. With organizational change comes tension and conflict as a natural function of stress on the system, its people, and their daily activities and interactions.

Vecchio (1991) has classified sources of organizational change as either internal or external:

- **Internal sources of change** are the traditional sources within the organization: management, personnel, and the values and culture of the environment or agency.
- **External sources of change** include suppliers of services and equipment, other health-care agencies and providers, clients, the current economic climate, the professional and nonprofessional labor force, regulatory agencies, and legal and ethical requirements for provision of quality health care.

Systems theory provides a useful perspective for viewing the internal and external forces of any organization. A health-care institution or agency is an open environmental system with great complexity. The organization must be considered in terms of the system with its component subsystems, as well as the macrosystem and client system. Internal influences come from agency administrative, policy, and operational factors guiding the system. The surrounding environmental system of the organization is the health-care arena, which provides the professional, specialization, reimbursement, and additional value structures for the organizational unit and its members. The broader social or macroenvironment reflects societal norms and values through the needs and potential needs of consumers of health care. Linkages among all system parts are assumed as necessary for effectiveness and continuity. But look further at this complex system and the internal environment.

When change is proposed for an agency or institutional system, an in-depth look at the organizational environment is needed. Recall that Kast and Rosenzweig (1979) view organizations as open, sociotechnical systems composed of five subsystems (see Chapter 10). Internal sources of change can arise from any one or some combination of these five subsystems. Consider the traditional health-care agency: the hospital. The subsystems and their associated internal forces can be described as follows:

- *Goals and values* for health care are specified for an organization as a purpose, philosophy, or mission statement. Valuable information on the internal forces is apparent with this organizational view of people, health, and medical care before translation into departmental or policy statements. Insight can also be obtained from the historical documents on how the institution evolved into a modern health-care organization.
- The *technical subsystem* represents the knowledge and skills of the health-care providers and physical resources in the system. Consider internal forces from the specific equipment, services, and expertise of professional and nonprofessional labor forces in the organizational setting.
- Interpersonal and interdisciplinary relationships are a component of the *psychosocial subsystem,* with role relationships, attitudes, and values of people and groups within the system. Nurses are expected to exhibit behaviors related to the roles of health-care provider, manager, teacher, researcher, and advocate and to collaborate with members of other health-care disciplines. Direction of nonprofessional and ancillary personnel is another important aspect in this subsystem.
- The *structural subsystem* is the organizational design to provide health-care services. In addition to considering organizational charts, position descriptions, and policy and procedure manuals, Kast and Rosenzweig (1979) advise looking further at informal sources to discover how tasks are accomplished in the organization. Valuable information on the organization's daily operations can be obtained from technical and clerical staff.
- The *managerial subsystem* includes the governing board and corporate officers. This organizational governance may include paid or volunteer board members, required institutional review boards, and the chief officers (executive, financial, medical, nursing, etc.).

Environmental influences are the next factors to consider in terms of impact on the system and its subsystems. External forces include inputs of energy, information, and materials received from the environment, transformed, and returned to the environment as outputs. One input into the hospital environment is the client system. The client enters the hospital with a health-care deficit and, through the care received while hospitalized (throughput), strives for a higher level of wellness as the intended outcome (output). But environmental influences add more complexity. External forces are the broader environment providing inputs into the system. But, as with any open system, the external forces affect internal operations, and an exchange of information is returned to the environment as outputs.

External forces have a major impact on the function of the traditional hospital. Suppliers to be considered include physicians, drug and equipment companies, volunteers, and educational facilities. Physicians supply patients. Drug and equipment companies compete for contracts, and organizations seek purchasing power with consortia or multiorganizational contracts. Volunteers provide valuable unsalaried transportation, recreational, and interpersonal services without which many hospitals could not survive. Educational suppliers provide additional health-care services in the present, with trainees as residents, interns, nurses, therapists, and other preparers of ancillary personnel as well as the future workforce. In addition, new staff members bring different ideas and methods into the system.

Customers are generally thought of as the client system: in-patients, same-day surgery, clinic patients. But the concept of customer can be seen more broadly to include community initiatives, educational programming, health contracts with business and industry, HMOs, and physician practice groups. Large corporate entities, intraorganizational agreements, health insurers, and second- and third-party payers are major service and economic influences on the client system. Federal legislation, state laws, local ordinances, regulatory bodies, court precedents, insurers, and professional organizations all have a legal impact on the hospital.

On a broader, macrosystem level consider changes predicted for the population. The increase in the elderly population, especially frail elders, has a great impact on services that will be needed from a health-care provider or agency. The national, state, and local economies, with their associated concerns about health-care financing, are other societal factors that have a profound impact on hospitals and health-care organizations. All these factors, individually and combined, influence how the hospital markets and cares for its customers and personnel and meets their organizational mandates and mission.

But let us return to the change process and activities in the phases of unfreezing, moving, and refreezing. During *unfreezing,* the major change activities include assessment, diagnosis, and establishment of a professional relationship. Assessment must involve an in-depth analysis and synthesis of both internal and external forces. As with individuals, families, and groups, methods for data collection include interviews and observation. But with a larger group of people, methods can include questionnaires or surveys for timely and, at times, confidential data collection.

Similar to the past and personal change history obtained on a smaller scale with the person, family, or group, an organizational history provides valuable insights. The organizational history can reveal information on development and problem resolution to this point. Methods for gathering an organizational history require not only skillful interviewing of key people, but also a careful review of records and documents of the organization.

Consider all environments, including the constraints, demands, and opportunities present. Resources in the environment, people and physical resources, provide major influences on any organizational change. Identifying the driving forces and individuals in the system is essential for building a base of support. External environments must be analyzed, especially population trends.

Diagnosis of problems becomes more complex as the volume of information and people increase. Whether the change agent is selected from within the organization or is an external consultant, a high level of skill will be needed to achieve organizational change. Clear understanding of both internal and external forces will be necessary, along with a good deal of fortitude to survive the experience.

The *moving* phase in organizational change involves developing strategies to match resources to constraints, demands, opportunities, and history as part of the planning process for change to proceed. Changes in goals and values must be reflected in organizational documents. Key work groups will be needed for decision making and policy formation. The technical subsystem will need training and educational programs to transmit knowledge of resources and to refine skills. A great deal of time and energy will be needed for the people. The psychosocial subsystem with role and status relations will require finesse and great sensitivity. Relating to the variable and altering readiness, resistance, and motivation of many individuals and groups will be quite a challenge. People must be actively incorporated and empowered in this decision making and implementation phase. Involvement of people in the organizational change process necessitates use of excellent leadership and skills in group dynamics, conflict management, and team building. This is especially true when the structural subsystem, how the work is accomplished, has undergone major revisions. Communication links with the managerial subsystem must be increased and reinforced as organizational members are included rather than alienated from key planners and controllers in the system. Minimizing people's stress and turmoil is a major function of the change agent in this phase.

A formalized evaluation plan must be in place and initiated in this moving phase. Data collection and feedback on the process communicating even small results is vital and must be ongoing. People in the system need to be continually aware of the result of their efforts. If indicated in the evaluation data, additional resources or linkages must be sought. This is the feedback loop that continues through the phase of refreezing and is essential to any successful organizational change. Evaluation data must be systematically recorded, analyzed, interpreted, and communicated. Evaluation data can be communicated through distribution of short reports, articles, or observations from various sources in newsletters and on bulletin boards, and in formal and informal discussion groups. Keeping the people on track and moving toward new organizational goals and norms requires stamina and a positive outlook despite the inevitable pitfalls and side-tracking that will occur.

Refreezing the change may take longer than anticipated in the multilevel organizational system. Establishing the change as the organizational norm will be related to the turmoil and differences that have arisen with the altered internal environment and the strength of external forces. Support and reinforcement are indispensable activities of the change agent, along with ongoing analysis, interpretation, and communication of the evaluation findings. The role will naturally become more consultative as termination approaches. At this point, the change should be a part of the expectations of the organization and its members. Ownership of the change is held by the people in the institutional or agency environment and not by key people or the change agent.

Consider the following example of organizational change, extending services from the traditional hospital into the community. Needs assessment, diagnosis of problems, and motivation in agency subsystems must occur in the unfreezing phase for organizational change. In addition to the traditional hospital, this may involve outpatient departments and clinics, home care agencies, rehabilitation or nursing home settings, HMOs, physician groups, and therapy group practices.

Internal restraining and driving forces are considerations in each of the five organizational subsystems proposed in the Kast and Rosenzweig model. Organizational goals and values for health care in the mission statement must change with the move from hospital to home, outpatient, or community care. The technical subsystem that represents the physical resources, knowledge, and skills of the health-care providers must now be broadened for in-home care, such as intravenous or other therapies requiring periodic skilled nursing care. The psychosocial subsystem will need extended interpersonal and interdisciplinary relations with a move into the community, and coordination of services, role relationships, attitudes, and values of people. Nursing roles of health-care provider, manager, teacher, researcher, and advocate are expanded to include service facilitator and coordinator. The structural system is enlarged, with agencies providing both inpatient and in-home or community services, or it becomes more flexible and interactive with other environments providing health-care services. The managerial subsystem is similarly broadened to include overseeing corporations, resulting in buying power, larger constituencies, and overriding governing boards. This translates into augmented goals and policies, comprehensive strategic plans, and more controls for all members of the organization including hospital, medical, or health-care corporations.

The external forces that drove the need for change include health-care needs of the client population, reimbursement policies, provider restrictions, and societal trends. Earlier hospital discharge and high-tech home care in the client system have

driven service providers from the traditional hospital setting into the community. A good deal of this has been secondary to the reimbursement and insurance restrictions. The phrase of discharge "quicker and sicker," has persisted to the present day. In addition, the background for escalation of nonprofit and for-profit home care agencies has been demonstrated nationwide.

Organizations will continue to change and evolve based on internal and external forces and the needs of the client system. Nurses have increasing responsibility in this area. They function as members of change teams, change agents, and developers of organizational systems. This will continue and expand as their skills in change are recognized and sought out. Remember the following steps regardless of the extent of the organizational change:

- *Always do your homework.* Be prepared with the information and knowledge of the organization. Spend the time and acquire the information and background needed before acting or reacting. Then proceed from a solid theoretical base. Understand the change process and all the steps. Review your talents for change strategies.
- *Know your restraining and driving forces.* Take the time to understand or, at the minimum, recognize the behaviors. Share information. Make both sides aware of the situation. Take more time to understand behavioral reactions. Cultivate the driving forces and become viewed as the champion for the cause. Use all your skills in interpersonal relationships and develop more!
- *Be sensitive to environments.* Increase your awareness of what is occurring in society and health care. Look beyond your immediate environment. Analyze internal and external forces. Imagine how your environment could be affected by these forces. Use intuition and insight as well as foresight. Be both inspired and inspiring.
- *Maintain a positive attitude and refuse to be diminished by negativity.* Negative colleagues and superiors will always be present. They are an environmental fact and hazard. But these restraining forces should not be or become your role models. Someone will always be readily available to tell you something has never or can never be done. If your "homework" background knowledge told you something different, become the agent of change instead of another restraining force. Have courage.
- *Be open and receptive to new ideas.* No matter

how you long to keep things as they are presently, be mindful that there may be a better way of doing things. Refuse to be limited by the present, and look to the future.

■ *Be open to new people.* Venture out of your discipline. View the situation as larger than nursing care. Look at the health-care arena. Make contacts with physicians, occupational therapists, physical therapists, and other professionals and nonprofessionals. Discuss. Debate. Interact. Try to recognize when turf issues arise, and negotiate based on facts and what will be best for the client system and the organization while maintaining the integrity of your profession.

■ *Involve others.* Try not to do it all yourself. Remember that the most successful and enduring changes occur when others are involved. The change has to become the norm and the expectation of the people in the environment.

■ *Refine skills.* Cultivate your change agent skills. Recall the skills and roles of the change agent. Continually develop and refine these skills. Make adaptations necessary for the people and the environments. Look at yourself as objectively as you look at others. If assistance or collaboration is needed, get it. Consider this as using resources and making linkages for effectiveness of the change agent.

■ *Reassess and evaluate.* Remember to continually evaluate activity and progress. Sufficient time for the change to occur and persist is a necessary component of organizational change. Recall Rogers' (1983) attributes in the diffusion of innovations, which determine the rate of adoption by members of a social system: relative advantage, compatibility, complexity, trialability, and observability. Include these attributes in your evaluation process.

■ *Persevere, persevere, persevere.* Have fortitude. Use resources to cope with your stress and frustration levels. Organizational change is not easy. Look for small gains as major steps in the process. Strive for the finish line, but do not look for accolades. Terminate the relationship as the organizational norm takes hold and the organization congratulates itself on the accomplishment.

Remember, the philosophical basis of nursing focuses on the health of people as individuals, families, groups, and society in a complex environment. In this role, nurses can be highly effective change agents.

KEY POINTS

■ The classic change model was developed by Lewin (1951), based on his Field theory. This model contained three phases in the change process: unfreezing, moving, and refreezing.

■ Building on Lewin's work, Lippitt (1973) considered human motivation, multiple causation, and habits. He defined seven specific phases in the change process: diagnosis of the problem, assessment of motivation and capacity for change, change agent's motivation and resources, selecting change objectives, choosing the change agent role, maintaining the change, and terminating the relationship. A focus on the change agent emerged with four specific roles and skills.

■ Havelock's change model contains the major concepts of role, linkages, and communication. This adds steps to the three stages of change, with heightened communication and interpersonal activities. Havelock & Havelock's (1973) seven steps in the change process are perception of the need, diagnosis of the problem, identification of the problem, devising a plan of action, gaining acceptance, stabilizing the plan, and self-renewal. Four different roles for the change agent are proposed with Havelock's model.

■ Rogers' (1983) Innovation-Diffusion process has a five-stage view of change: knowledge, persuasion, decision, implementation, and confirmation. Rogers also considers five factors that influence the rate of adoption of an innovation that may be used as evaluation criteria in the change process. Seven roles for the change agent are highlighted in this model of change.

- The roles and attributes of a skilled change agent are included in the models by Lippitt, Havelock, and Rogers. General roles for the change agent include assessor or evaluator, communicator, translator, encourager, mediator, and consultant.
- In relation to the activities in the nursing process, the phases of change are consistent with assessment, planning, implementation, and evaluation for resolving the problem or stabilizing the change.
- The skills in change agents include having a vision for the future and creativity, good assessment skills, good interpersonal skills, flexibility, perseverance and a positive attitude, integrity and commitment, the ability to manage conflict, and resistance.
- Strategies for reducing resistance to change include careful planning and timing, along with good communication and interpersonal skills.
- Empowerment or involvement of the client is needed for lasting change. Strategies for client involvement include education, training, socialization and persuasion, and facilitation.
- Environmental or situational factors relative to individuals, families, and groups provide additional information in the change process. Past experience, stress and coping factors, motivational clues, and resources are important data sought by the change agent.
- To view organizational change, look at internal and external forces with a multisystem approach. Internal sources of change include management, personnel, and the values inherent in the organization. External sources of change include suppliers, other agencies and health-care providers, clients, the economic climate, the labor force, regulatory agencies, and other guides or quality.
- Suggestions for people involved in organizational change include being knowledgeable about the organization, its restraining and driving forces, and the environments, maintaining a positive attitude and being receptive to new ideas and people, involving other people in the change, continuing to refine skills and reevaluating the situation, and persevering throughout the process.

CHAPTER EXERCISES

1. Two community hospitals located 6 miles apart are merging. Medical, surgical, and specialty services are being divided between the two agencies based on the resources available in each environment. Reorganization of a hospital has been mandated. As the nurse manager of a specialty unit, you must prepare your staff for expansion of their telemetry unit from 24 to 32 beds and plan for an entry of eight additional professional and ancillary staff from the other agency whose telemetry unit is being closed. Using concepts of organizational change and systems theory, describe the system with the inputs, throughput, outputs, and feedback using the following outline.

a. Describe all subsystems and surrounding environments.

b. Describe the following:

Inputs	*Throughput*	*Outputs*	*Feedback*
Knowledge	Resources	Alteration in inputs	Evaluation criteria
Skills	History	Desired outcomes	and methods:
Attitudes	Constraints	discussions	reports, observations
Regulations			

2. A newly appointed vice president for nursing of a 250-bed community hospital wants information on managed care presented to the medical and nursing staff members. You are hired to present your experiences with managed care and development and use of care maps. Use the diffusion of innovations model to describe how you, as a change agent, would approach Rogers' (1983) five phases of the process.

3. Use Lewin and one additional change theorist to explain the steps of the process for permanent change to assist a new 18-year-old single mother with a normal 7 lb, 9 oz full-term infant (AGA, Apgar 9) in developing parenting skills and health care, including prevention and health maintenance.

REFERENCES

Brooten, D. A., Hayman, L. L., & Naylor, M. D. (1988). *Leadership for change: An action guide for nurses* (2nd ed.). Philadelphia: Lippincott.

Chinn, R., & Benne, K. D. (1976). General strategies for effecting change in human systems. In W. G. Bennis, K. D. Benne, R. Chinn, & K. E. Corey (Eds.). *The planning of change* (3rd ed.). (pp. 22–45). New York: Holt, Rinehart & Winston.

Corey, K. E. (1976). Structures in the planning of community change: A personal construct. In W. G. Bennis, K. D. Benne, R. Chinn, & K. E. Corey (Eds.). *The planning of change* (3rd ed.). (pp. 265–275). New York: Holt, Rinehart & Winston.

Havelock, R. G. (1971). *Planning for innovation through dissemination and utilization of knowledge.* Ann Arbor: Institute for Social Research, University of Michigan.

Havelock, R. G., & Havelock, M. C. (1973). *Training for change agents: A guide to the design of training programs in education and other fields.* Ann Arbor: Institute for Social Research, University of Michigan.

Kast, F. E., & Rosenzweig, J. E. (1979). *Organization and management: A systems and contingency approach* (3rd ed.). New York: McGraw-Hill.

Lewin, K. (1951). *Field theory in social science.* New York: Harper & Row.

Lippitt, G. L. (1973). *Visualizing change: Model building and the change process.* LaJolla, CA: University Associates.

Lippitt, G. L., & Nadler, L. (1967, August). Emerging roles of the training director. *Training and Development Journal, 9.*

Rogers, E. M. (1983). *Diffusion of innovations* (3rd ed.). New York: Free Press.

Rogers, E. M., & Shoemaker, F. F. (1971). *Communication of innovations: A cross-cultural approach* (2nd ed.). New York: Free Press.

Vecchio, R. P. (1991). *Organizational behavior* (2nd ed.). Chicago: Dryden Press.

BIBLIOGRAPHY

Barker, A. M. *Transformational nursing leadership: A vision for the future* (Publication No. 15-2473). New York: National League for Nursing.

Clark, C. C. (1994). *The nurse as group leader* (3rd ed.). New York: Springer.

Duncan, K. A. (1994). *Health information and health reform: Understanding the need for a national health information system.* San Francisco: Jossey-Bass.

Fawcett, J. (1993). *Analysis and evaluation of nursing theories.* Philadelphia: Davis.

Hall, R. H. (1987). *Organizations: Structures, processes, & outcomes* (4th ed.). Englewood Cliffs, NJ: Prentice-Hall.

Hassard, J., & Parker, M. (1994). *Towards a new theory of organizations.* London: Routledge.

Marriner-Tomey, A. (1992). *A guide to nursing management* (4th ed.). St. Louis: Mosby-Year Book.

Parse, R. R. (1987). *Nursing science: Major paradigms, theories, and critiques.* Philadelphia: Saunders.

Pettigrew, A., Ferlie, E., & McKee, L. (1992). *Shaping strategic change: Making change in large organizations.* London: Sage.

Tappen, R. M. (1993). *Nursing leadership and management: Concepts and practice* (3rd ed.). Philadelphia: Davis.

Weiss, H. J., & Gershon, M. E. (1989). *Production and operations management.* Boston: Allyn & Bacon.

Chapter 12

TEACHING-LEARNING PROCESS

Rose Kearney Nunnery

CHAPTER OBJECTIVES

On completion of
this chapter, the reader
will be able to:

1. Discuss the components of teaching and learning.
2. Examine differences in the ways people learn.
3. Describe methods to assess learning readiness and motivation.
4. Propose different teaching methods for a variety of learning needs.
5. Devise a lesson plan on a topic that includes behavioral objectives, a content outline with appropriate teaching methods, and a plan for evaluating learner outcomes.

KEY TERMS

Behaviorist Perspective	Teaching	Learning Environment
Classical Conditioning	Learning	Cognitive Learning Styles
Operant Conditioning	Lesson Plan	Andragogy
Gestalt Theory	Affective Domain	Readiness
Cognitive Theories	Cognitive Domain	Motivation
Social Learning Theory	Psychomotor Domain	Behavioral Objectives
Humanism		

Teaching and learning are integral parts of contemporary nursing practice. Client or patient teaching has long been an expected nursing behavior. As a process, teaching and learning are much more than sharing and accepting information. Intricate parts of the process must be considered for effectiveness.

Consider the steps in the nursing process: assessment, diagnosis, outcome identification and planning, implementation, and evaluation. These steps are also applicable to the teaching and learning process. For assessment, think about both the learner and the teacher. These are more than simply the provider and receiver of information. Communication is a vital component in the teaching and learning process. It is a mutual process in which critical thinking is essential for both teacher and learner. Both teacher and learner obtain information, use reasoning skills, make analyses based on the data, and then move to decision making or problem solving on the learning need. The learner learns from the teacher—good, bad, or indifferent. But the teacher also gains awareness and skill from each interaction with learners. There is essential information we need to know for an effective teaching-learning process. Some of the following questions arise:

- What are the attributes of each individual teacher and learner?
- What are the learning needs of the learner?
- How do they learn?
- What is the readiness for and motivation to learning?
- What changes in behavior or attitude are perceived as being needed by both the teacher and the learner?
- What individual characteristics will enhance or inhibit learning?
- What are the teacher's teaching style and skills?
- What is the cognitive style of the learner?
- What environmental factors will enhance or inhibit learning?
- What activities and resources will enhance the learning?
- How can both the teacher and the learner evaluate the effectiveness of the learning process?

Assessing for a learning deficit or teaching need incorporates many factors. Notice that the concentration of the assessment is on the process of teaching and learning, not on specific content to be included in a presentation of information. Determining content is a discrete task performed later in the process, based on specific attributes and needs of the people and environment.

Next, developing behavioral objectives gives direction for a teaching plan and evaluation of the learning. Then teaching strategies, methods, and resources to meet the diagnosed learning need, with specific content, are planned and implemented. Finally, the outcomes of the process are evaluated. The evaluation component focuses on how the learner met the objectives and the specific outcome behaviors from the experience. Outcome objectives can be assessed by both the learner and the teacher. Evaluation is focused on the behavioral objectives specified for the learner earlier in the process. All of these considerations and more are important in the teaching-learning process addressed in this chapter.

THE TEACHING AND LEARNING PROCESS

Learning Theory

Educators have studied learning theories for many years to understand and improve on the teaching-learning process. There are several schools of learning theories. Major examples of these theories applicable to professional nursing practice include behaviorism, gestalt, social learning theory, and humanism.

In introductory psychology courses, classic stimulus-response conditioning and operant conditioning are taught, providing a **behaviorist perspective** on learning. Pavlov's pioneering research with dogs led to our understanding of **classical conditioning,** with the reflexive responses in behavior resulting from some stimulus. In classical conditioning we saw that the pairing of food (the unconditioned stimulus) with the sound of a bell as a neutral (conditioned) stimulus led to salivation in dogs as an unconditioned response—first, as an unconditioned response for the sight of the food, and ultimately, as a conditioned stimulus with the sound of a bell alone. Using classical conditioning with infants, John Watson provided further insight on learning with his focus on the environment and emotional responses. Watson was a true behaviorist, looking at the development of emotions of fear, love, and rage through classical conditioning and desensitization.

Use of classical conditioning in nursing practice is limited. One situation may be in teaching clients to intervene as needed to physiologic or emotional cues, auras, or triggers prior to an allergic, metabolic, or neural response. The individual with diabetes, a severe allergy, or epilepsy can be taught to perceive and associate early signs or symptoms that could lead to a larger physiologic reaction. Classical conditioning is useful for early intervention to circumvent the reaction chain. Reflexes are important in this scenario to ensure that the individual is in a safe environment that has the resources for prompt treatment. Another example is the use of distraction, focusing, and breathing in certain reflexive situations such as clients in labor, pain, and fear.

Operant conditioning provides further clues to learning, with a focus on purposive behaviors and the role of reinforcement. In Thorndike's Law of Effect, reinforcement of a behavior is more likely to lead to repetition of that behavior. B. F. Skinner's research with rats and reinforcers for learned behaviors provided much additional information. Operant conditioning is defined as "changing the rate of a response on the basis of the consequences that result from that response" (Gerow, 1992, p. 214). This introduced positive and negative reinforcers and reinforcement schedules to learning. The work of Skinner led to behavior modification programs and programmed instruction with shaping, reinforcement, and generalization of behavior.

Behavior modification programs are widely used in health care and education. They have been used effectively in certain nursing situations such as nutritional programs that require a lifelong change in behavior. In such situations, old patterns are broken, stimuli are introduced to effect positive outcomes, responses are generalized to specific dietary items, positive and negative reinforcement are applied, and behavior is shaped over time. Another example using behavioral techniques is adult clients who have urinary incontinence. One method of treatment includes bladder retraining with the components of education, scheduled voiding, and positive reinforcement (Urinary Incontinence Guideline Panel, 1992).

Other learning theories address additional human characteristics. Behaviorism focuses on observation and measurement of actions in response to some association or conditioning. Rigorous use of the scientific process in the laboratory setting was a major factor in this perspective. Dissatisfaction with the emphasis on conditioning and reinforcement led to the evolution of other perspectives, including gestalt theory, cognitive theories, social learning theory, and humanism. In these later perspectives, we see an increased focus on the human intellect and human emotions.

Gestalt theory focuses on meaning and thought with learning occurring through perception. In the German tradition, a "gestalt" is perception of a whole form rather than its component parts. More than 100 laws on this perspective evolved with the identification of major principles concerning the way we perceive objects related to organization, proximity, similarity, direction, simplicity, background, and closure. Gestalt theorists view learning as being based on perception of and completion of patterns. Patterns are perceived and reorganized by the person. In terms of learning, this perspective focuses on how the learner perceives the information and their environment. Kurt Lewin's Field theory and work on change (see Chapter 11) provide a major influence in this perspective. Lewin's Field theory emphasizes the importance of the environmental field. The perception of this environmental field by the person influences how that person, as a system, responds within the larger environmental system.

The classic principle in the Gestalt perspective is that the whole is not merely the sum of the parts. This principle is consistent with the holistic view of the person in professional nursing practice. Consider the importance we place on understanding how the person views the information to be learned. This involves teaching materials that are used in addition to perceptual values. Further consider the learning environment, and the importance we place on client teaching in an unrushed, private, and comfortable setting when teaching (or promoting change for) specific health practices.

Cognitive theories of learning focus on the intellect and the development of knowledge. Recall the example of Piaget's theory of cognitive development from Chapter 4. Schema were seen as patterns of thought or behavior that become more complex with the addition of more information. Assimilation was the acquisition of this information and incorporation into the individual's existing cognitive and behavioral structures. Accommodation is the change in the individual's cognitive and behavioral patterns based on the new information acquired. This acquisition of information is learning with the comprehension of concepts, memory, and analysis.

There are many different cognitive theories, and others evolving, with a focus on information processing. In nursing practice, use of cognitive theory is readily apparent with our focus on the level of cognitive development and acquisition of healthcare knowledge. We use principles of cognitive development to tailor a teaching plan to the client's level of development, whether an elderly diabetic client or a child. We are also concerned about the way they process information so we can tailor our teaching strategies to suit their learning style. In addition, the use of behavioral objectives with our clients provides a focus for developing cognitive skills moving from recall of knowledge to comprehension, application, analysis, and synthesis, as we will see later in discussing Bloom's (1956) taxonomy.

Cognitive learning through observation and imitation is the basis of Bandura's **Social Learning Theory.** Through the research of Bandura and his associates, aggressive and socialization behaviors of children were documented following observation of both symbolic and actual models. An important aspect of Bandura's work is the modeling of behavior with television and the effect of visualizing vicarious reinforcement and punishment for behavior. A humanistic rather than mechanistic orientation is apparent in this theoretical focus. Bandura (1977) explained the emphasis of vicarious, symbolic, and self-regulatory processes on how humans learn and influence their own destiny.

Nursing applications of this learning model are prevalent for the development of psychomotor skills in clients such as self-administration of medications, procedures, and treatments. We often demonstrate skills to clients in person and expect them to return the demonstration. We provide positive reinforcement in the coaching function during the process, saying "that's good," "that's the way," "what a nice job," and the like. We promote healthful practices with encouragement and the hopes for positive results as a reinforcement for the behavior. We show clients films or videotapes on a procedure in which they see modeling and positive and negative reinforcement through a case scenario. These nursing behaviors are based on social learning theory and focus on the individual in the environmental as a thinking, feeling, and reacting being.

Humanism is another major perspective on learning. In this perspective, the focus is totally on the person. Abraham Maslow and Carl Rogers were major influences on this learning theory. As Maslow (1971) stated,

> the humanistic goal . . . is ultimately the "self actualization" of a person, the becoming fully human, the development of the fullest height that the human species can stand up to or that the particular individual can come to. In a less technical way, it is helping the person to become the best that he is able to become. (p. 169)

The full range of human experiences are considered, as personally experienced and interpreted. As will be seen later in this chapter, Maslow's humanistic focus included motivation as a vital concern. Humanism is the basis of Carl Rogers' person-centered counseling. As described by his daughter, Rogers

"above all, valued the worth and dignity of the individual and trusted their capacity for self direction if given the proper environment" (Rogers & Freiberg, 1994, p. iii). Personal growth and autonomy are highlights of the humanistic perspective.

The humanistic perspective is consistent with the metaparadigm concepts of professional nursing. We focus on the person and assist in empowering him or her for health, whether an emerging state or to a higher level, therefore on the consumers of health care, advocating for their active involvement in the health promotion process. The environment should be considered in terms of the person and his or her unique environmental setting. Consider the promotion of a healthy lifestyle with cardiac rehabilitation clients. Self-direction and insight into personal beliefs, attitudes, lifestyle, and behaviors are fundamental to the learning process.

Given the variety of learning theories, application may involve selecting a more eclectic approach. Specific teaching guides involve our consideration of the person and the environment, given the particular health focus in contemporary nursing practice. Certain principles provide direction in this process.

Teaching and Learning Principles

The philosophical and theoretical structures of any discipline reflect how the teacher and learner are viewed. In nursing with our metaparadigm concepts of person, environment, health, and nursing, we view both the teacher and the learner as thinking, reasoning, active participants involved in the teaching-learning process. We believe individuals are influenced by and influence their environment. These environmental influences, including persons, events, and tangible surroundings, must be taken into account when any teaching behavior is considered as conditions affecting the learner as well as the teacher. In terms of health, teaching in nursing reflects information to promote or maintain the highest level of health attainable. The teacher's and the learner's definition of health and wellness influence physical, psychological, emotional, and spiritual health as personal determinants of behavior.

With this in mind, several other processes can be readily seen as inherent in the teaching-learning process, for example, communication and critical thinking. King (1986) has defined learning as an interactive process of "sensory perception, conceptualization, and critical thinking involving multiple experiences in which changes in concepts, skills, symbols, habits, and values can be evaluated in observable behaviors and inferred from behavioral manifestations" (p. 24). Although the teaching and learning process is an interactive process, its component parts must be considered.

Teaching is more than the transmission of information. The information must be received, understood, and evaluated by the learner. **Teaching** has been described as an interactive communication process containing three elements—communicator, message, and receiver—with a feedback mechanism (VanHoozer et al., 1987, p. 49). The professional nurse functions as teacher for consumers of health care and colleagues in a variety of settings. Benner (1984) has identified the teaching-coaching function of the expert nurse working with acutely ill patients. Broadening these characteristics of the expert could include the following:

1. Use timing to capture learning readiness and motivation.
2. Assist with integration of learning into lifestyle.
3. Demonstrate an understanding of client's own interpretation of the situation.
4. Provide interpretations of situations and rationales for new behaviors.
5. Show, through example, coaching behaviors in culturally sensitive issues (Benner, 1984, pp. 77–94).

These characteristics demonstrate the active roles of both teacher and learner in the process. Readiness and motivation must be present on the part of both the teacher and the learner during the process. The best teachers are those who truly believe in the information they are sharing and can communicate this. They provide the excitement, or at least some reinforcement, for the learner who wants to know more. The active role of the learner in the process is vital, since passive learning rarely results in persistent change in attitudes or behaviors. Along with this is the motivation of teacher and learner, as the teacher demonstrates an understanding of the learner's perspective on the subject or situation. Providing information is the traditional role of the teacher, but doing so in the context of the learner's reality helps provide a rationale for behavior changes. Finally, coaching through example, with sensitivity, is the essence of expert teaching and nursing.

Teaching is an interactive process not a unidirectional transmission of information. As Benner (1984) shows in her examples of expert nurses, we also learn from those we teach.

Learning is the perception and assimilation of the information presented to us in a variety of ways. Learning contains the following characteristics:

1. Perception of new information.

2. Initial reaction to the information.
3. Ability to recall or repeat the information (simple knowledge level)
4. Rejection or acceptance of the information (comprehension)
5. Use of the information in a similar situation (application)
6. Critical analysis of the information
7. Incorporation of the information into the value system
8. Use of the information in various situations and combinations (synthesis)

An increasing complexity emerges here as the learner moves from receiving and recalling information through comprehension, application, and synthesis of the knowledge acquired. We see this in the client who accepts information on breast self-examination, is able to perform the self-exam, does so on a monthly basis, teaches her daughter or mother the process, and is now investigating regular screening for colon cancer for herself and family members. This client has moved from simple knowledge to incorporating knowledge into the value system and behaviors of herself and other family members.

Learning can be enhanced with specific strategies or approaches with learners. Babcock and Miller (1994) identify the following 16 principles of learning:

- Focusing intensifies learning.
- Repetition enhances learning.
- Learner control increases learning.
- Active participation is necessary for learning.
- Individual styles vary.
- Organization promotes learning.
- Association is necessary to learning.
- Imitation is a method of learning.
- Motivation strengthens learning.
- Spacing new material facilitates learning.
- Recency influences retention.
- Primacy (first items) affects retention.
- Arousal influences attention.
- Accurate and prompt feedback enhances learning.
- Application in a variety of contexts broadens the generalization.
- Personal history shapes the perception of the experience. (pp. 45–48)

Each of these principles should be evident in a **lesson plan,** to increase the effectiveness of the presentation and the acquisition and application of knowledge.

Since learning is the acceptance and assimilation of information, it is incorporated into the learner's affective, cognitive, and psychomotor domains of knowledge and behavior. Note the difference reflected here between the knowledge and the demonstration of behaviors. We may "know" something, but either consciously or unconsciously decide not to demonstrate that behavior. For example, we may be on a low-fat diet but decide that ice cream is a part of the diet, ignoring the fat content!

A domain is merely a category, in this instance, either knowing something or demonstrating some behavior. There are three domains of learning or knowledge: affective, cognitive, and psychomotor.

The **affective domain** includes attitudes, feelings, and values; for example, how the client feels about the importance of or the positive effect on his life of the needed dietary change will influence whether he will make the change. Often, the nursing goal is to incorporate the value of the diet into the person's belief system. However, cultural influence, cultural differences in the individual, family, or group, and the nurse's professional influences can all either positively or negatively affect achieving this goal.

The **cognitive domain** involves knowledge and thought processes within the individual's intellectual ability. Using the same example of the client on the low-fat diet, the cognitive domain involves understanding the information received on nutrition, diet, health conditions, and indications, and more. The ability to conceptualize types of foods, gram counts, and dietary needs involves comprehension, application, and synthesis at an intellectual level before the actual behaviors are performed.

The **psychomotor domain** is the processing and demonstration of behaviors; the information has been intellectually processed, and the individual is displaying motor behaviors. To continue with the example, psychomotor skills are demonstrated by how he has performed on the changed diet, as seen in food diary reporting, preparing and ingesting appropriate foods, and even laboratory reports demonstrating bodily functions.

It is important to consider these three domains in the teaching-learning process. Behavioral objectives, teaching content and methods, and evaluation of learning are different for the three domains and should be distinct. Remember, to achieve a lasting change in observed behavior (psychomotor domain), the value of that change (affective domain) and the intellectual capacity to understand and process the information for behavioral changes (cognitive domain) must first be present. More attention is given to the affective, cognitive, and psychomotor domains in preparing and using behavioral objectives.

Consistent with the philosophical focus of nurs-

ing, the **learning environment** is important in any teaching or learning activity. Physical comfort as well as respect and acceptance of the learner are humanistic factors. The consumer of health care may also have physical, sensory, or psychological deficits that can interfere with comfort in the learning environment or in the teaching-learning process. Comfort measures should be validated with the client before and during the process. Physical comfort can include such things as the temperature of the room or the height or firmness of the chairs, in addition to specific effects from acute or chronic health problems. Sensory concerns include the extraneous sensory stimuli perceived by the teacher or learner in the learning environment, such as sounds, smells, and sights. In addition, the client may have sensory deficits that can interfere with learning or require more resources, such as visual or hearing problems. Psychological deficits including fear, problems with cognition, attention span, effects from medications, or worry can be major inhibitors to teaching and learning. Receptivity of the learner to new and different ideas is vital. Creative measures on the part of the teacher to provide for an environment conducive to learning are essential.

COGNITIVE LEARNING STYLES

The cognitive learning process, is a broad area that examines how meaning is perceived, evaluated, remembered, reinforced, and demonstrated. Piaget gave us information on childhood cognition through observations of his own and other children. The different stages of cognitive development are sensorimotor, preoperational thought, concrete operations, and formal operations. Piaget provided us with the concepts of assimilation and accommodation in cognitive development. Recall that assimilation is the acquisition and incorporation of new information into the individual's existing cognitive and behavioral structures. Accommodation is the change in the individual's cognitive and behavioral patterns based on this new information.

Investigation of cognition in relation to teaching and learning has moved from content to stylistic approaches with an increased emphasis on the structure of learning (Goldstein & Blackman, 1978). The American Association of School Administrators (1991) differentiates between learning styles and cognitive styles, defining learning style as a broader concept including affective, physiologic, and cognitive styles. **Cognitive learning styles** are the ways learners perceive, organize, use, and retain knowledge, including their sensory preferences, the importance of context for the learning, impulsive or reflective learning behaviors, and the need for diversity or consistency (American Association of School Administrators, 1991, p. 16). For example, consider the difference between field-dependent and field-independent cognitive styles. The learner who is field-dependent perceives the total field as a global picture and is more socially oriented. The field-independent learner is more analytic, more attuned to perception of the component parts of the field or environment, and takes a more impersonal approach to problem-solving. Learning activities may need to be adjusted for these two different learners. As Hiemstra and Sisco (1990) state, understanding differences in cognitive styles can help teachers and learners make more informed decisions about which learning activities will be useful or productive (p. 241).

Cognitive styles are further applied in cognitive mapping. Cognitive maps are a type of latent learning in which one has a mental representation of the situation or environment, but the behavior evidencing the learning may not be apparent until later (Gerow, 1992, p. 241). Joseph Hill has used testing procedures to develop individualized cognitive maps illustrating how students and teachers acquire and transmit meaning. Cognitive mapping of the individual learner looks at three areas: (1) use and understanding of symbols and their meanings, (2) cultural influences focused on relationships as an individual, through associates, or through family, and (3) reasoning with categories, differences, relationships, by all three, or deductively by logical proof (Hill & Nunney, 1971).

Teaching and learning strategies are thus developed to match the learner with the teaching resources most effective for their learning style or to develop strategies to adjust to the prevalent teaching style. For example, some learners are highly visual in the way they perceive information and derive meaning. In this situation, structured lectures with few visual aids is a less desirable learning environment than one enhanced by visual aids. Others learn better through the written word, by either reading or notetaking. Learners who are highly auditory in their learning preference derive greater meaning from just listening to the information.

Another consideration is change over time. Cognitive styles do not remain static over the individual's lifetime. Goldstein and Blackman (1978) reviewed research in this area and have noted differences in learning styles among children, college students, adults, and the elderly. Assessment data in this area

may be obtained from the client in a nursing interview rather than formal testing inventories used with larger groups. In essence, good assessment of the learner is vital to ensure the most effective teaching and efficient and enjoyable learning.

ADULT LEARNING THEORY

Most consumers of nursing care are adults: parents, couples, individual adult or aging clients, families, community groups and even professional peers. Learning in adults requires some adjustments on the part of the teacher to meet the different characteristics of learners. Adult learners differ from children in that they have past experiences, good and bad, with both teaching and learning.

Malcolm S. Knowles was a major force in adult learning in the United States, providing a theoretical model termed **andragogy.** Both formal and informal teaching and educational programs have differentiated between the learning needs of children and adults. The term "andragogical model" was borrowed from European education (Knowles, et al., 1985; 1990). Expanding the traditional pedagogical learning models used with children to incorporate learning characteristics and needs of adults, this is a developmental model in that the accumulated life experiences of adults gives them different teaching and learning needs from younger learners. In the pedagogical model, learners are generally dependent or passive, have little prior experiences to build on, and have external pressures from parents and others to learn something (Knowles et al., 1985, pp. 8–9). Adult learners are self-directing, have experiences that have shaped their identity, experience life events or a learning need that triggers their readiness to learn, have internal motivators, and demand an available, knowledgeable resource to assist them with practical problems and identified needs (Knowles et al., 1985).

The developmental experiences of adults have created different teaching and learning requirements. As Knowles (1985) has pointed out, adult learners often initially assume the comforting and passive learner roles of pedagogy; but then an inner conflict develops with their self-directing nature. The adult's ego system is based on his or her self-concept and accumulated knowledge and experiences whereas the child is gratified by impressing a parent, teacher, or peer. Knowles' developmental focus is further demonstrated with his identification of life problems by age group in early, middle, and later adult groups. He specified life problems in the areas of vocation and career, home and family life, personal development, enjoyment of leisure, health, and community living (Knowles, 1990). Health promotion and maintenance is a consistent theme of adult health problems throughout the age groups.

Teaching and learning skills in adults depend on both the physical and psychologic climate. Physical climate relates to the learning environment. The setup of the room should avoid the stilted lecture setting and promote comfort so that the learners can focus on learning needs and problem solving. Knowles emphasizes the need for adults to feel at ease in the learning environment. This is related to the psychological climate for the adult learner. Knowles (1985) identified seven characteristics of the psychological climate conducive to adult learning: mutual respect, collaborativeness, mutual trust, supportiveness, openness and authenticity, pleasure, and humanness (pp. 15–17). Knowles views the teacher as the catalyst and facilitator. A common thread running through teaching and learning strategies for adults is mutuality in diagnosing, planning, learning, and evaluating.

One key to successful teaching and learning in adults is active involvement throughout the process. Knowles (1980, 1985) has suggested adult learners should be involved in the planning, needs identification, development of learning objectives and contracts, and evaluation of their learning. Adults must be able to apply information to past experiences, self-identified or mutually agreed on learning needs, or some future desire or informational inquiry. Based on the work of Knowles, Vella (1994) has identified 12 principles for effective adult learning:

- Needs assessment: participation of the learners in naming what is to be learned
- Safety in the environment and the process
- A sound relationship between teacher and learner for learning and development
- Careful attention to sequence of content and reinforcement
- Praxis: action with reflexion or learning by doing
- Respect for learners as subjects in their own learning
- Cognitive, affective, and psychomotor aspects: ideas, feelings, actions
- Immediacy of the learning
- Clear roles and role development
- Teamwork: using small groups
- Engagement of the learners in what they are learning
- Accountability: how do they know they know? (pp. 3–4)

This brings us to the concept of lifelong learning. Lifelong learning, personal, or professional, is a frequently used term. We hear people say they continue to learn, so they continue to grow. Although this "growth" is rarely measurable, it can be better viewed personally as intellectual stimulation and remaining current in the world. We see this with seminars open to the public and in credit and noncredit courses available on health or other topics. Growth may also occur in one's profession or position. Continuing education to further one's knowledge or skill base is evident in the corporate and professional worlds. Personal and professional responsibility account for lifelong learning to a greater degree than mandatory or job requirements. The quest for knowledge, the rapid changes in today's world, and personal wellness are great motivators.

READINESS AND LEARNING

Readiness is an important concept in learning, regardless of the learner's chronological age. Readiness relates to developmental needs and tasks of individuals. Erikson (1963) described readiness as critical periods. Havighurst (1972), another developmental psychologist, refers to readiness as sensitive periods for learning, or the "teachable moment." For teaching to be effective and learning to take place, the readiness of the learner must be a prime consideration. A good example of this is the issue of compliance and noncompliance in the client group.

Compliance is an often misused and misunderstood concept. We talk about patients being noncompliant when they do not follow their discharge or health-care teaching. The reasons and background for the behavior in the client group must first be realized and understood, not assumed. Compliance is yielding to the desire of others, possibly as a result of threats or force. But as we saw in the change process, this does not bode well for a permanent change in behavior. Human behavioral change is more effective when one is personally involved in the process. This brings us to learning and the readiness to receive and accept information for a change in lifestyle. Consider the teenager on dialysis who carefully monitors his sodium intake after dialysis but fills up on fast food the day or morning before the scheduled dialysis. Is this truly noncompliance or developmental maneuvering with peer pressure and dietary restrictiveness? Now consider the adult cardiac client discussed in Chapter 11. Was noncompliance in sodium restriction due to a stubborn adherence to food preferences, culture, custom, or perhaps failed health teaching for change because of a failure to achieve learning readiness?

The learner must be willing to change and accept the learning need. When this occurs, the **readiness** for learning is apparent. This can be seen in terms of King's (1981) theory of goal attainment: both the nurse and the client must be focused on and sensitive to the same goal. Readiness for the learning and teaching is then present. Ultimately, the effectiveness of the teaching methods and content is evaluated on the basis of the learning that did or did not take place. Learning readiness contains the following factors: human motivation, understanding, and applicability or acceptability.

Motivation in humans is a manifestation of internal and external personal and environmental factors that cause people to respond to a situation in the way they do. Motivation has been classically viewed as needs, drives, and impulses causing behavior. One view of motivation in humans is Maslow's Theory of Human Motivation, based on the hierarchy of basic needs. Maslow (1954) suggested 16 propositions on human desires or motivation:

1. The individual is an integrated, organized whole.
2. Hunger is a specific physiologic drive, not a classic motivation paradigm.
3. Desire for something is often a means to another end, rather than the end itself.
4. Culture affects desires.
5. Multiple motivations are often present.
6. Motivation is a constant state, but fluctuating and complex.
7. Relationships among motivators must be considered.
8. Human drives are varied and are not mutually exclusive or isolated.
9. Fundamental goals and needs are the basis for classification of motives.
10. Care must be present when animal data are used to understand human motivation.
11. Motivation is affected by the individual's environment and culture.
12. Humans may display integrated or segmented responses in reactions.
13. Not all behavior or reactions are motivated by needs.
14. Humans are motivated by the conscious possibility of attainment.
15. The influence of reality on unconscious impulses must be considered.
16. Motivation theory includes both positive and negative cases (pp. 63–79).

These propositions imply a complex interrelationship in human motivation based on internal and external factors, as personally interpreted by the individual. Maslow's work indicates the hierarchy of human needs is based on motivation. But motivation is as intricate as the person, not merely inherent impulses and drives.

The concept of motivation, then, takes us to the person's interpretations of the situation. Readiness, thus, involves motivation and understanding. Understanding is the cognitive ability to perceive and intellectualize the content and consequences of information. This adds to the concept of motivation. Bandura (1977) defines this cognitively based motivation as how behavior is activated and maintained (p. 160). He believes that most actions are under anticipatory control, as humans use symbolic representation to envision future outcomes of behavior. How the person views these future consequences of behavior becomes the motivation to behave or proceed in the present. This relates well to health teaching in that the client can be motivated to learn with a realistic anticipation of the situation and consequences. This can be accomplished easily in the assessment phase with enlightenment through interview data, the diagnosis of the teaching and learning needs, and the development of behavioral objectives. During this process, motivation can be assessed and stimulated by the client as well as by the professional nurse.

The person's cognitive level is a component of understanding in that the content must be at the person's level of understanding. Piaget's theory of cognitive development describes the differences in learning levels between the sensorimotor infant developing object permanence and the older child able to learn abstract mathematical skills through formal operations. Information is available to the person at his or her cognitive level for processing and development of knowledge. The person may require concrete examples to envision future consequences or may be able to handle more abstract or even philosophical examples. A further consideration here is the client's state of health. Current physiologic or psychological functioning and medications may interfere with reasoning and understanding as well as the attention span. Readiness for health teaching in this instance may be at different levels, depending on physical and emotional functioning.

This brings us to a third component of readiness for the teaching-learning process: applicability and acceptability of the information. The person must perceive that the information is applicable to him or her, as an individual, a member of the family, or a member of a group. If the person denies that a health problem exists, he or she will not be ready for health teaching in that area. It is not perceived as personally applicable. Acceptability means that the information must be within the person's worldview. Cultural influences are important, since values and belief systems influence understanding and acceptability of information. The health problem and readiness must be seen in context of the individual's belief system. This is an important relationship, as we see in the health belief model. Cultural assessment data provide important information on the client's belief system to incorporate into the teaching and learning process.

WRITING BEHAVIORAL OBJECTIVES

The purpose of writing **behavioral objectives** is to provide a frame of reference for the intended outcomes of the teaching-learning activity for both the teacher and the learner. Reilly and Oermann (1990) define behavioral objectives as the intended action-oriented outcomes of an educational process, as either an individual experience or a program of study (p. 7). This provides us with a focus on learners and evaluation of their experiences with specific measures for behaviors. Behavioral objectives are the intended outcomes of the learners, not the teacher's goals for the activity.

Think of behavioral objectives in terms of the learner's who, what, where, when, and how. In viewing the individual components of behavioral objectives, consider those listed at the start of this chapter. Initially, there is the stem statement, "Upon completion of this chapter, the reader will be able to. . ." This provides the "who"—the reader of the chapter—and the "when"—after completion of the chapter. The "what" and "how" are the action-oriented outcomes that the learner will demonstrate in the listed behaviors. Behavioral objectives do not address all the content that will be ultimately included in the teaching plan—the specific "what" we wish to impart to the learner. Rather, the "what" in the behavioral objectives is the outcome we can evaluate after the teaching has occurred. Consider the chapter objectives to determine the "how" and "what" information.

1. *Discuss (how)* the components of teaching and learning (what).
2. *Examine (how)* differences in the ways people learn (what).
3. *Describe (how)* methods to assess learning readiness and motivation (what).
4. *Propose (how)* different teaching methods for a variety of learning needs (what).

5. *Devise (how)* a lesson plan on a topic that includes behavioral objectives, a content outline with appropriate teaching methods, and a plan for evaluating learner outcomes (what).

This example focuses on the learner at the end of the prescribed learning activity, with action verbs of discussing, examining, describing, proposing, and devising as their outcome ability—as "how" they should perform. The next focus is on the complexity you as the evaluator (whether learner or teacher) wish to see demonstrated at the end of the activity. This is the degree that can be measured, or the "where." This brings us to the type and complexity of the outcome behavior as the level of the learning domain.

When developing behavioral objectives, be sure to consider the domains of knowledge. Further, within each domain, there is a leveling process, or progress in attainment of increasing complex skills. Based on the work of Bloom and other teaching and learning theorists, Reilly and Oermann (1990) provide a useful summary for viewing taxonomy, or leveling, within the three domains.

In the affective domain, complexity progresses from receiving to responding, valuing, organizing values, and finally characterizing or standing for certain values transmitted. Consider a newly diagnosed diabetic. Acceptance of his or her condition is vital to developing long-range personal care skills. But this is a difficult domain to measure because values and attitudes are more difficult to assess than knowledge, that can be measured with a paper-and-pencil test of information recalled. Action verbs for evaluating "how" that can be used for the five affective domain levels include receiving, responding, valuing, organizing values, and characterizing or standing for. Still, this is a difficult domain of learning to evaluate. We must rely on the individual to honestly communicate his attitudes, feelings, and values in verbal and nonverbal behaviors.

In the cognitive domain, we first have the knowledge received through recall or recognition. Next, we proceed to comprehension and manipulation of the information. The final three levels of the cognitive domain are applying the information, evaluating and analyzing the information, and finally synthesizing for redesigning and applying the knowledge in other situations. Consider the five levels in the cognitive domain with the following action words in your behavioral objective for teaching a client about his or her condition.

1. *Knowledge* implies simply that the learner has perceived the information and can report it back to the teacher. Action verbs such as *iden-*

tifies, recalls, recognizes, and repeats are useful for behavioral objectives at this knowledge level of the cognitive domain.

2. At the next level, the learner demonstrates further understanding as *comprehension.* Action verbs for behavioral objectives at this level include *describes, defines, discusses, and distinguishes.*

3. The third level of the cognitive domain is *application,* demonstrating the ability to relate the learning to a situation. The following action verbs are appropriate for behavioral objectives for the learner's outcomes at this point: *applies, demonstrates, employs, and uses.*

4. Further critical thinking occurs at the next cognitive level of *analysis.* The learner steps back and analyzes the information objectively. Action verbs useful at this level of complexity include *assesses, appraises, critiques, and evaluates.*

5. *Synthesis* is the highest level of the cognitive domain, in which the learner manipulates the concepts from the learning in new combinations and situations. Action verbs addressing this level of complexity in the taxonomy include *creates, designs, devises, and generates.*

The psychomotor domain is perhaps the easiest domain for which to write objectives, but it requires observation or recording of skills attained. In the psychomotor domain, evidence of motor behaviors proceeds from simple to complex demonstration of skills; from imitation to manipulation, demonstration of precision, articulation or use, and competence in the skill (Reilly & Oermann, 1990). To evaluate the learner's outcome for the objective, the teacher and the learner must have some demonstrated evidence of the skill. For example, you have taught a newly diagnosed diabetic to self-administer insulin. As the teacher, you must be able to see how the learner-client has accomplished this task, beyond the simple return demonstration with saline injections as you observe. Action verbs reflecting the "what" the learner is demonstrating include *imitates, follows instructions, and repeats.*

At the next level of manipulation of the psychomotor skill, the learner demonstrates the entire procedure of proper injection of insulin, from filling the syringe to properly disposing of the needle. Action verbs reflecting the "what" the learner is demonstrating at this point include *carries out, follows the procedure, and practices.*

Precision of the psychomotor skill is demonstrated when the learner can perform the injection on schedule with a sense of comfort in his ability in the process, expressed with the phrase *"Demonstrates skill in the procedure."*

Articulation, or full use of the skill, is demonstrated as the diabetic is able to manage at home on insulin, including testing blood sugar and urine for additional needs during stressful periods. This is reflected in the phrase *"Uses results of blood sugar monitoring to regulate."*

The highest level of skill acquisition comes when the individual has a sense of competence and the skill has become a natural part of his or her routine; the individual can determine signs of hyperglycemia or hypoglycemia and self-test as naturally as dressing or bathing. The individual has incorporated the process sufficiently to spend a month traveling abroad with a sense of independence, comfort, and control in the process. Action terms reflecting this level include *independently monitors and effectively regulates administration of insulin.*

Selecting the appropriate level in each of these domains is the "where," or the level of complexity or the degree to which the learner is to demonstrate the outcome behavior. This really depends on the time frame for the learner, how long the teaching-learning process will last, perhaps similar objectives addressing different phases of the teaching-learning process, and when the evaluation component can reasonably occur. Reilly and Oermann (1990) view behavioral objectives as the "what" of an educational endeavor and evaluation as the "how" (p. 251). But since behavioral objectives are the intended action-oriented outcomes of an educational process, they contain all of the "who" (the learner), "when" (on completion of the learning activity), and "how" (the action verb) used to identify the "what" (the behavior) that the learner will demonstrate as the outcome, or "where" (at a specified point in the taxonomy), of learning. All of these are involved in the preparation for and the process of evaluation. Behavioral objectives are tools for teaching, learning, and evaluating. Evaluation data can provide useful feedback that the objective has been met or that repetition, reinforcement, or revision is needed. Specific evaluation strategies are covered later in this chapter.

DEVELOPING LESSON PLANS

Once the assessment of learners and teachers has been completed and the behavioral objectives to address the learning deficit have been developed, we must plan for the specific content and how it will be transmitted to the client group. Learning experiences and time frames are stated or referred to in the behavioral objectives. Content is more specified as the lesson plan evolves.

Initially, when you think of lesson plans, you may picture primary school teachers with their attendance books and plans or activities for the day. This is far from the content included in the professional nurse's lesson plan for a teaching activity. But the primary school teacher has some advantages over the nurse: a consistent audience of 25 to 35 7-year-old students and subject matter identified in the school curriculum guide. The nurse, on the other hand, has a variable audience of clients, with variable health and teaching needs. The nurse interacts not only with an individual or group of "student" client learners, but also, in many cases, with family members and community groups.

Babcock and Miller (1994) describe a client education lesson plan as consisting of the client, objectives, content, setting, strategies, materials, and the means of evaluation (p. 176). The assessment data obtained earlier in this process have been used to define and describe the client, including characteristics, attributes, learning assets and deficits, readiness, and specific needs to be addressed. This procedure is done with the client as an individual, family, or group to diagnose the learning needs and prepare for continuation of the process. Next, behavioral objectives were identified to guide the process and plan for the evaluation of outcomes. Now we must plan the content, teaching strategies and methods of delivery, learning resources, and specific evaluation procedures.

Traditional lesson plans, like the nursing care plan, are frequently prepared in a column format. The first column contains the behavioral objectives developed for the learning activity. Subsequent columns contain learning content, teaching strategies, perhaps teaching principles, learning resources, evaluation methods, and timing, which can all be easily viewed in relation to the behavioral objectives. A sample format is illustrated in Table 12–1. The learning content is the specific content outline designed to meet the objective. Teaching strategies relate to the objective and the specific content, including variations for the learning setting. Suggested learning resources and materials are proposed to enhance the teaching strategy and meet the learner's cognitive style, especially if a group or lecture presentation is appropriate for the general audience but may not meet the needs of individual learners. All of the lesson plan so far is the proposal for the teaching-learning activity. Before implementing it, one must specify evaluation methods along with a proposed time frame for the process. Implementation of the teaching-learning process can then proceed using the appropriate teaching and learning strategies identified in the lesson plan. Evaluation of the teaching-learning process is essential and designed to address the behavioral objectives at the level of the taxonomy specified for acquisition of affective, cognitive, and psychomotor behavior.

Consider the simple example of a 56-year-old white female outpatient with unstable hypertension without angina. She has come to the health clinic today after being denied health insurance last week because of the prepolicy examination requirement. Blood pressure measurements ranged from 210/105 to 185/100 on the two consecutive visits. She has had no serious illness or hospitalizations, but is leaving town in 5 weeks to visit family living abroad for a month. Today, daily antihypertensive medica-

TABLE 12–1. Sample Client Teaching Lesson Plan Format

Behavioral Objectives	Learning Content	Teaching Strategies	Learning Resources	Evaluation Methods	Time Frame

tion and a low-sodium diet were prescribed. The client has verbalized the need to lower her blood pressure for insurance purposes. She also reported that she has used a salt substitute for the past 3 days and has continued to play tennis three times a week. Her descriptions of nutritional intake indicate high dietary fat and sodium content in meals prepared at home and selected in restaurants. She volunteers much information about cooking for her family and her attendance of gourmet cooking classes at the local college because she wanted to watch the teacher and ask questions rather than just read the cookbooks.

The assessment data indicate a teaching deficit, learning readiness, and the motivation to adhere to a treatment plan within a confined time frame. You and the client determine that you will schedule individualized teaching sessions with her for her next four weekly visits. Behavioral objectives for this teaching-learning process might include the following:

1. Demonstrates food selection and food preparation techniques to maintain a low-sodium diet
2. Assesses blood pressure regularly
3. Uses Vasotec as prescribed, monitoring for side effects, adverse effects, and toxicity
4. Demonstrates maintenance of a low-sodium diet
5. Continues her exercise program
6. Reapplies for health insurance coverage

These behavioral objectives are in the cognitive and psychomotor domains.

The learning content, in the second column, addresses the behavioral objectives by teaching food selections, revisions needed with food preparation, periodic assessment of blood pressure, administering medication and monitoring for side effects and toxicity, and maintaining a healthy nutritional and exercise program. Teaching strategies are then selected for the individualized cognitive style of the client, using resources such as visual aids and written information to take home. Evaluation methods are proposed to address each of the behavioral objectives at the following four weekly visits, with the time frame for each activity specified.

TEACHING SKILLS AND METHODS

Teaching strategies are geared toward accomplishing the behavioral objectives in light of the audience. Selection is also based on how the content can best be delivered and addresses the affective, cognitive, and psychomotor domains of learning.

Teaching strategies generally include lecture presentations, demonstrations, discussions, modeling, role playing, individualized instruction, programmed instruction, computer-assisted instruction (CAI), other simulations, and group activities.

Selection of a teaching strategy, or some combination of teaching strategies, depends on the client. For presentation to a client group of 24, a lecture format followed by breaking out into four small groups to apply the lecture content may be quite appropriate for presenting information on child development and wellness practices. For a group of three new mothers on the postpartum unit, a lecture would be impersonal and less effective than a small group discussion on plans for returning home with their healthy neonates. In our example of the client with hypertension, individualized teaching would be most effective, since the client prefers the interaction with a teacher and has a limited time frame to accomplish the behavioral outcome objectives. The characteristics of the client group and their intended outcomes therefore, guide the selection of appropriate teaching strategies. For further information on selected strategies, refer to Table 12–2.

Enhancing the delivery of content and improving learning based on the cognitive style of the client require careful selection of learning resources. Teaching aids change as our available technology changes. In 1978, Guinee listed teaching aids as display boards (bulletin, magnetic, felt or flannel, chalk), projectors (overhead, micro), textbooks, models, equipment, specimens, exhibits, films, slides, filmstrips, audiotapes, and closed-circuit television. Some of these are still appropriate and readily available, but others have been displaced as our technology has grown to include videotapes, satellite program links, computer-assisted instruction and simulations, computer networks and bulletin boards, and more.

Teaching aids and instructional technology, such as audiovisual, computer applications, and case study simulations, are frequently used in client teaching situations to enhance the content and actively involve the learner in the teaching-learning process. Using the assessment data, consider how the client told you she or he best learned information in the past. When preparing for larger group presentations, think how smaller group activities or assignments will address the needs of learners who do not do their best in the large group setting. Remember, adults learn best when actively involved in the process. Think of ways to move the client from a passive to an active learning situation.

A major consideration is how to enhance the con-

TABLE 1 2 – 2. Teaching Strategies

Strategy	Advantage	Disadvantage
Lecture	Easier to organize and transfer large amount of information Predictable, quicker, more efficient, and useful for a large group Allows teacher control over material being presented Easy to focus material	Lacks opportunity for feedback Risk of information overload Sustaining interest may be difficult Difficult to tailor material for the group
Discussion	Allows for continual feedback, attitude development, and modification Flexible, able to be modified according to the motivation of the audience Able to identify confusion and resolve difficulties Serves as a vehicle for networking	Increases chance of getting off the focus Risk of discussion becoming pointless Allows participants to be dominant or passive Time-consuming
Demonstration	Activates many senses Clarifies the "whys" as a principle Commands interest Correlates theory with practice Allow for problem identification Helps learner received well-directed practice	Time-consuming Does not cover all aspects of cognitive learning
Modeling	Facilitates active learning By-passes defenses Effective with children	Ineffective without rapport Learning not always visible Risk for learner ambivalence
Programmed instruction	Allows learning at a self-directed pace Able to repeat sections at will Breaks down information into manageable increments Saves teacher time	Effectiveness depends on learner motivation Does not account for unplanned feedback, which can distance learner
Simulated environments, games, activities, and role playing	Greatest transfer of learning Facilitates learning of what is needed to cope with problem or environment Allows for practice that is most transferrable	Facilitates unpredictable occurrences May be threatening to learner Time-consuming Achievement of outcomes is difficult
Team teaching	Uses competencies of more than one teacher Allows for learning among the teachers Accentuates divergent points of view	Lacks continuity and internal consistency Requires more planning Group processing slower Eliminates teacher autonomy

Source: Babcock, D. E., & Miller, M. A. (1994). *Client education: Theory and practice* (1st ed.). St. Louis: Mosby. Reprinted with permission.

tent for the learner's own cognitive style. Some learners are highly perceptive in one or several senses in learning information. They may be highly visual, auditory, tactile, or perceptive in some combination of these senses. When you select teaching resources, consider whether the learners are highly visual and obtain and process information mainly through observation of the world around them. These learners do well with visual aids that enhance the content presented in the teaching strategy, such as films, videotapes, slides, charts, transparencies, posters, models, or photographs or with information presented through books, pamphlets, and handouts. Compare that style to the learner whose auditory sense is the most perceptive. Effective auditory

teaching aids include films, videotapes, audiotapes, and recordings with well-developed sound presentations. In addition, this learner may do well using a recorder to take notes and reinforce learning through review later. For the individual who prefers to touch and manipulate new information, plan for active involvement in the teaching and learning through demonstrations, models, and samples.

Another consideration is whether the learner prefers to be an individualist or to have other people in the learning environment for interaction and stimulation. Some people learn in a very individualistic way. They prefer to obtain information and then go their own way to process, analyze, and synthesize the material. Having a group discussion to evaluate and apply information directly after it is presented in a lecture is stressful to this individual, who needs time before he or she can share thoughts or apply the information. Alternatively, some learners enjoy interactions and learning in a stimulating group environment. A large, impersonal lecture is deadly boring to this learner, who thrives on group discussion to work on questions posed in a case study. But learners are generally not easy to classify; these characteristics can be combined over a wide range. Pure types are rare, and the challenge is to find those teaching strategies and resources that enhance the teaching content and promote learning. Resources for different cognitive styles are presented in Table 12–3.

In our example of the client with hypertension, we decided on individualized teaching since she prefers the interaction and has a limited time frame to accomplish the outcome objectives. Teaching aids in this case include short films and videotapes shown in the office during or before the teaching session, followed by discussion using charts and models. Pamphlets and handouts to take home for reinforcement and discussion with family and friends would also be useful.

In addition to client teaching, contemporary nursing practice includes collegial teaching and learning opportunities such as educational programs, lectures, demonstrations, group discussions, clinical conferences, case studies, clinical preceptorships, and grand rounds. The same steps are involved in this process as with assessment, diagnosis of learning needs, development of behavioral objectives, preparation of a lesson plan, selection of teaching strategies and resources, and evaluation. The difference generally lies in the size of the group, which can range from a one-to-one collegial or the unit staff to a large group of professionals from various

TABLE 12–3. Teaching Resources to Enhance the Cognitive Style of the Learner

Cognitive Style	Teaching Strategies	Teaching Resources
Highly visual	Small group lecture and discussion Role playing, simulations Modeling, demonstrations Programmed instruction Computer simulations	Films, videotapes, slides, charts, overhead projectors, posters, models, photographs, chalk/white/bulletin boards Books, pamphlets, prepared handouts, paper and pencils for notes, reading lists CAI with pictorials
Highly auditory	Lecture and discussion Role playing, simulations Modeling, demonstrations	Films, videotapes, recordings (audiotapes prepared or self-taped during teaching) CAI with auditory reinforcers
Highly tactile	Small group activities Individualized teaching Role playing, simulations Modeling, demonstrations Programmed instruction Computer simulations	Models, bulletin boards Books, pamphlets, prepared handouts CAI
Highly interpersonal	Small group lecture and discussion Role playing, simulations Modeling, demonstrations Programmed instruction Computer simulations	Films, videotapes, audiotapes, charts, posters, models, photographs, pamphlets CAI
Highly individualistic	Lecture Role playing, simulations Modeling, demonstrations Programmed instruction Computer simulations	Films, videotapes, audiotapes, slides, charts, overhead projectors, posters, models, photographs Books, pamphlets, prepared handouts, paper and pencils for notes, reading lists CAI

disciplines who are interested in the latest research and information on a selected topic. With the larger group, it is essential to assess the prevalent characteristics of the learner population. This includes the overall learning need that will become the topic for the presentation. Behavioral outcomes should address what the learners are expected to have gained as knowledge and skills at the end of the program or teaching session, since they will be the ones providing the evaluation data. Teaching strategies may include a team approach, especially for presentations across disciplines to foster the development of knowledge and collaboration. Although active learning in small groups is highly effective with professional colleagues, this may be the second breakout phase after the basic information has been presented in a lecture format. Highly effective learning resources in this case include films, videotapes, slides, charts, overhead projections, posters, models, photographs, boards, pamphlets, handouts, paper and pencils for notes, and reading lists. Following the program or presentation, the teacher or program coordinator receives completed evaluation forms from the program participants and then develops an overall analysis based on the evaluation data the participants provide.

EVALUATION OF OUTCOMES

Evaluating outcomes is a vital component of the teaching-learning process. It may be ongoing and lead to important information for revisions needed for effective teaching and learning. It can also provide valuable information for making adjustments in the process during the next offering. Although evaluation strategies focus on both the teaching and the learning that occurred, the primary focus is on the learner. Is the learner able to demonstrate the outcomes envisioned at the beginning of the process? As in the nursing process, the evaluation phase of the teaching-learning process is used to assess the effectiveness of the process and whether the client has resolved a knowledge deficit.

Clients are more difficult to evaluate than traditional student learners. Measurement of cognitive domain learning activities of students is easily done with paper-and-pencil tests assessing knowledge. In the client teaching situation, such tests are rarely used except in research or large group situations. Client evaluation can be complex, with problems related to timing, access, continuity, measurement, and other factors. In addition, recall that adult learn-

ers should be involved in evaluating their own learning. Normally, client evaluation is done with methods such as return demonstrations, observation, diaries, rating scales, and discussion, depending on the behavioral objectives.

Recall that we used different action verbs to address the three domains of learning and levels, or taxonomy, within each. Capturing evaluation data requires specificity in the behavioral outcome objective. The behavioral objectives are the intended action-oriented outcomes of an educational process and contain the "who" (the learner), the "when" (upon completion of the learning activity), and the "how" (the action verb) used to identify the "what" (the behavior) that the learner will demonstrate as the outcome "where" (at a specified point in the taxonomy) of learning. The objectives should indicate what you are looking at and how you are measuring the outcomes of the teaching-learning process.

The affective domain consists of attitudes, feelings, and values. Evaluation data should show how the learner progressed from receiving to internalizing the values mutually agreed on for the learning. In our prior example of a newly diagnosed diabetic, the teacher and the learner must be able to measure or see attitudinal or value changes through verbal and nonverbal behaviors. The action verbs in the affective domain included receiving, responding, valuing, organizing values, and characterizing or standing for specific values. We need the individual to communicate his attitudes, feelings, and values in verbal and nonverbal behaviors. Methods of evaluation in this area include interviews, discussions, and observations that demonstrate certain beliefs and values. Another means of evaluating affective learning is a diary in which the client can jot down feelings and problems that arise between teaching sessions. Analyzing the content of the diaries can provide useful information on the affective domain as well as knowledge gaps in the cognitive domain.

In the cognitive domain, knowledge builds from simple recall to comprehension, application, analysis, and synthesis of the information. Interviews and discussion with clients can be used to evaluate whether the learner can repeat or report back the information imparted by the teacher. For comprehension, the client describes, discusses, and distinguishes information during the interview. Application of the information can be evaluated as the client demonstrates and uses the information, providing specific examples of how this was done. Critical thinking and analysis take this one step further, as the client explains problems and difficulties that arose and steps taken to solve problems without the presence of the teacher. Synthesis of the information occurs when the learner manipulates the learning in new combinations and describes to the teacher how he or she effectively applied the information to a similar problem or situation. The learner has devised a new way of handling a situation based on information obtained in another area. Occasionally posttests are used in client teaching, but test anxiety is a major deterrent to their use for some clients. The most useful evaluation strategies for both teachers and client-learners for gauging cognitive learning are discussion, questioning, and allowing for description.

Evaluating client outcomes in the psychomotor domain is easiest through direct observation of skill attainment. At the simplest level of psychomotor skill attainment is the client's ability to imitate, as seen in a return demonstration. This allows one to assess understanding and the ability to perform a specific skill, such as testing one's blood sugar. But demonstration of a skill in a clinical setting can be artificial, since the client's own environment often has additional factors not present in the health-care agency, such as shared bathrooms or medication storage problems in a home with toddlers. Flow charts, diaries, and check sheets are easy for clients to use as reminders and reinforcers in the home, and they can then be discussed at the next clinic visit or teaching session interview. The level psychomotor skills can be assessed with a checklist or flow chart in terms of following instructions to proper scheduling, precision, and problem solving in the procedure. The client can be encouraged to note problems encountered and how they were handled, to demonstrate skills in both cognitive and psychomotor domains. This will provide evaluation data for both the client, as the learner, and the nurse, as the teacher.

In our example of the client with hypertension, we implemented an individualized teaching strategy within a limited time frame to accomplish the outcome objectives. Objectives were developed to address learning in the cognitive and psychomotor domains. One method of evaluation was for the client to maintain a diary, including daily food intake and exercise, and list daily blood pressure measurements, medications taken, and effects on a check sheet. This evaluation method provides visual data that address the initial five behavioral objectives agreed on by both the client and the nurse:

1. Demonstrates foods and food preparation techniques for maintaining a low-sodium diet
2. Assesses blood pressure regularly
3. Uses Vasotec as prescribed, monitoring for side effects, adverse effects, and toxicity
4. Demonstrates maintenance of a low-sodium diet
5. Continues her exercise program

At each of the four client visits or teaching sessions, the information in the diary is reviewed and discussed. When both the learner and the teacher are satisfied that these objectives have been met, control of the hypertension problem may be present. A health certificate can then be provided by the primary care provider so that the last objective, reapplication for health insurance coverage, can be attempted with an outlook for success. At the final teaching visit, the client and the nurse discuss the strategies and resources used during the 4-week process, to evaluate the teaching that took place.

In essence, behavioral objectives are a tool for teaching, learning, and evaluating. Evaluation data can provide useful feedback that the objective has been met or that repetition, reinforcement, or revision is needed. This brings us to the evaluation of teaching strategies. Teaching strategies, as methods and resources, should be evaluated by both the teacher and the learner. Discovering what worked and what may have worked better helps the learner view the process and reinforce the learning while sharing with the teacher methods that were successful and alternative strategies for the future. These things can be communicated in an interview or discussion with the client or on an evaluation form at the end of the process. Important factors here are encouragement and openness for honest and constructive evaluation data from both teacher and learner.

This brings us full circle in the teaching-learning process: from assessing the learner and learning needs, to awareness of learning readiness and cognitive styles, developing behavioral outcome objectives, developing the lesson plan, implementing the teaching strategies and using appropriate resources, to evaluate the process. The evaluation data may have returned the teacher and the learner to an earlier step for repetition, revisions, or reinforcement or provided evidence that the process had been completed and the learning deficit resolved. Knowledge of the process and its intricacies will make each teaching-learning experience effective, if not enjoyable, for both teacher and learner.

KEY POINTS

- There are several schools of learning theories. Major examples of these theories are behaviorism, gestalt, social learning theory, and humanism.
- Teaching is more than transmitting information. The information must be received, understood, and evaluated by the learner. **Teaching** has been described as an interactive communication process containing three elements: communicator, message, and receiver, with a feedback mechanism (Van-Hoozer et al., 1987, p. 49).
- Learning is the perception and assimilation of the information presented to us in a variety of ways.
- Characteristics of learning include
    Perception of new information
    Initial reaction to the information
    Ability to recall or repeat the information (knowledge)
    Rejection or acceptance of the information (comprehension)
    Use of the information in a similar situation (application)
    Critical analysis of the information
    Incorporation of the information into the value system
    Use of the information in various situations or combinations (synthesis)
- The three learning domains are
    Affective: attitudes, feelings, and values;
    Cognitive: knowledge and thought processes; and
    Psychomotor: demonstration of behaviors.
- Cognitive mapping of an individual learner's style looks at how information is interpreted, influences from others, and reasoning methods. Teaching and learning strategies can then be developed to match the learner's needs and resources.
- Andragogy is the model used to focus on the adult learner's characteristics of self-direction, experiential background, readiness triggers, internal motivation, and demand for knowledgeable resources.
- Teaching-learning skills depend on the physical and psychological climate for the adult learner. Physical climate is the environment. The seven characteristics of the psychological climate conducive to adult learning are mutual respect, collaborativeness, mutual trust, supportiveness, openness and authenticity, pleasure, and humanness (Knowles et al., 1985, pp. 15–17).
- Readiness occurs when the learner is willing to change and view the learning need. Learning readiness includes human motivation, understanding, and applicability or acceptability. Motivation in humans is a manifestation of internal and external personal and environmental factors that cause people to respond to a situation in the way they do. In addition, to achieve learning readiness, the person must perceive the information at his or her level of cognitive functioning, and it must be applicable to the person, as an individual, a member of the family, or a member of a group.
- The purpose of writing behavioral objectives is to provide a frame of reference for the intended outcomes of the teaching-learning activity for both the teacher and the learner. The focus of the objective is on the learner and the behavioral outcomes of the teaching-learning activity.
- A lesson plan is frequently prepared in a column format containing the following components: the behavioral objectives, content outline, teaching strategies, learning resources, evaluation methods, and timing.

■ Teaching strategies are geared toward accomplishing the behavioral objectives in light of the audience. Teaching strategies generally include lecture presentations, demonstrations, discussions, modeling, role playing, individualized instruction, programmed instruction, computer-assisted instruction (CAI), other simulations, and group activities.

■ Evaluating learning outcomes of the teaching-learning process is essential and designed to address the behavioral objectives at the taxonomic level specified for the acquisition of affective, cognitive, and psychomotor behaviors.

■ Teaching strategies as methods and resources are evaluated by both the teacher and the learner, to discover what worked and what could have worked better in a similar teaching-learning process. Evaluation of teaching strategies by the learner provides a further view of the process and reinforces the learning. It provides the teacher with data on methods that were successful and alternative strategies for future application.

CHAPTER EXERCISES

1. Select a client teaching topic and develop at least three behavioral objectives for the three learning domains. Include various levels of complexity in different domain objectives. Propose methods for evaluation of each objective.

2. Develop a lesson plan on a topic that includes behavioral objectives, a content outline with appropriate teaching methods, and a plan for evaluating learner outcomes.

3. Select a health promotion topic to present to a group of 30 clients. Describe the planning process, content for presentation, and evaluation methods.

4. Develop a staff conference as a seminar presentation on a clinical topic, with appropriate content for a unit staff of 10 RNs, 6 LPNs, and 15 CNAs. Present assessment data on the learners and ways to match cognitive styles and teaching strategies for the group.

5. Develop an interdisciplinary grand rounds program on a clinical topic of interest. Determine roles and content areas for representative presentations by nursing practice, nursing administration, medicine, appropriate therapies, and the consumer.

REFERENCES

American Association of School Administrators. (1991). *Learning styles: Putting research into common sense practice.* Arlington, VA: Author.

Babcock, D. E., & Miller, M. A. (1994). *Client education: Theory and practice.* St. Louis: Mosby.

Bandura, A. (1977). *Social learning theory.* Englewood Cliffs, NJ: Prentice-Hall.

Benner, P. (1984). *From novice to expert: Excellence and power in clinical nursing practice.* Menlo Park, CA: Addison-Wesley.

Bloom, B. S. (ed). (1956). *Taxonomy of educational objectives.* New York: Longman.

Erikson, E. H. (1963). *Childhood and society* (2nd ed.). New York: Norton.

Gerow, J. R. (1992). *Psychology: An introduction* (3rd ed.). New York: Harper Collins.

Goldstein, K. M., & Blackman, S. (1978). *Cognitive style: Five approaches and relevant research.* New York: Wiley.

Guinee, K. K. (1978). *Teaching and learning in nursing: A behavioral objectives approach.* New York: Macmillan.

Havighurst, R. J. (1972). *Developmental tasks and education* (3rd ed.). New York: David McKay.

Hiemstra, R., & Sisco, B. (1990). *Individualizing instruction:*

Making learning personal, empowering, and successful. San Francisco: Jossey-Bass.

Hill, J. E., & Nunney, D. N. (1971). *Personalizing educational programs utilizing cognitive style mapping: The educational sciences.* Bloomfield Hills, MI: Oakland Community College.

King, I. M. (1986). *Curriculum and instruction in nursing: Concepts and process.* Norwalk, CT: Appleton-Century-Crofts.

Knowles, M. S. (1990). *The adult learner: A neglected species* (4th ed.). Houston: Gulf.

Knowles, M. S. (1980). *The modern practice of adult education: From pedagogy to andragogy* (rev. ed.). Chicago, Follett.

Knowles, M. S., & associates (1985). *Andragogy in action.* San Francisco: Jossey-Bass.

Maslow, A. H. (1954). *Motivation and personality.* New York: Harper.

Maslow, A. H. (1971). *The farther reaches of the human mind.* New York: Viking Press.

Reilly, D. E., & Oermann, M. H. (1990). *Behavioral outcomes: Evaluation in nursing* (3rd ed.). New York: National League for Nursing.

Rogers, C., & Freiberg, H. J. (1994). *Freedom to learn* (3rd ed.). New York: Merrill/Macmillan.

Urinary Incontinence Guideline Panel. (1992). *Urinary incontinence in adults: Clinical practice guideline* (AHCPR Pub. No. 92-0038). Rockville, MD: Agency for Health Care Policy and Research, Public Health Service, Department of Health and Human Services.

VanHoozer, H. L., Bratton, B., Ostmoe, P., et al. (1987). *The teaching process: Theory and practice in nursing.* Norwalk, CT: Appleton-Century-Crofts.

Vella, J. (1994). *Learning to listen, learning to teach.* San Francisco: Jossey-Bass.

BIBLIOGRAPHY

Bevis, E. O. (1989). *Curriculum building in nursing: A process.* New York: National League for Nursing.

Crain, W. C. (1985). *Theories of development: Concepts and applications* (2nd ed.). Englewood Cliffs, NJ: Prentice-Hall.

DeYoung, S. (1990). *Teaching nursing.* Redwood City, CA: Addison-Wesley.

Edelman, C. L., & Mandle, C. L. (1990). *Health promotion throughout the lifespan* (2nd ed.). St. Louis: Mosby.

Fuszard, B. (1995). *Innovative teaching strategies in nursing* (2nd ed.). Gaithersburg, MD: Aspen.

Hunt, M. (1993). *The story of psychology.* New York: Doubleday.

Knox, A. B. (1993). *Strengthening adult and continuing education: A global perspective on synergistic leadership.* San Francisco: Jossey-Bass.

Lewin, K. (1951). *Field theory in social science.* New York: Harper & Row.

Long, D. G. (1990). *Learner managed learning: The key to lifelong learning and development.* New York: St. Martin's Press.

Rankin, S. H., & Stallings, K. D. (1990). *Patient education: Issues, principles, practices* (2nd ed.). Philadelphia: Lippincott.

Skinner, B. F. (1968). *The technology of teaching.* New York: Appleton-Century-Crofts.

Smith, R. M., & associates. (1990). *Learning to learn across the life span.* San Francisco: Jossey-Bass.

Whitman, N. J., Grahman, B. A., Gleit, C. J., & Boyd, M. D. (1992). *Teaching in nursing practice* (2nd ed.). Norwalk: Appleton & Lange.

Chapter 13

GROUP THEORY

Joanne Lavin
Rose Kearney Nunnery

CHAPTER OBJECTIVES

On completion of this chapter, the reader will be able to:

1. Describe different types of groups, including their characteristics and roles.
2. Differentiate between effective and ineffective groups.
3. Discuss the characteristics of an effective group leader.
4. Observe for effective functioning of leaders and members of selected groups.
5. Evaluate a group for effective functioning in meeting the group's common goals.

KEY TERMS

Group
Group Process
Group Structure
Formal Groups
Informal Groups
Group Composition
Homogenous Groups

Heterogenous Groups
Group Focus
Work Groups
Educational Groups
Therapeutic Groups
Effective Groups
Ineffective Groups

Functional Group Roles
Nonfunctional Group Roles
Interorganizational Groups
Intraorganizational Groups

G roup theory and the concepts of effective group processes are important components in professional nursing practice and require an understanding of the types of groups, their composition and functions, and the roles played by the members. As nurses, we need to develop skills to use as both leaders and members of various work and professional groups, as well as to apply a group format to intervene therapeutically with clients. Examining the structure and functioning of groups provides the knowledge and skills needed to accomplish these goals. A basic premise of group process is that people behave consistently; therefore, a group format can be an excellent tool for increasing awareness of how they communicate and interact with others.

GROUP PROCESS

A **group** consists of three or more individuals with some commonality, such as shared goals or interests. Living in society, we are members of many groups. Consider the different groups illustrated in Table 13–1. We are members of our family and school, work, professional, and social groups. Each type of group has a specific goal and membership. As nurses, we are involved as participants in work groups and interact with groups of clients in their health promo-

TABLE 13–1. Examples of Types of Groups

Group Types	Examples
Family	Nuclear family Extended family
Social	Classical music lovers group Chess club Computer club
Community	Parents-teachers association Garden club League of Women Voters
Work	Policy and procedure committee Budget committee Professional standards committee
Therapeutic	Insight-oriented psychotherapy Rational emotive therapy (RET) Recovery group
Support	Alcoholics Anonymous Overeaters Anonymous Encore
Professional	American Nurses Association American Association of Critical-Care Nurses American Psychiatric Nurses Association

tion activities. We use the principles of group process in all of these activities and to assist our clients in adapting to their illnesses. Some of these groups are structured loosely, with minimal rules, whereas others have clearly defined roles and limits. It is essential to understand group processes to function effectively as both an individual and a professional.

Group process is the dynamic interplay of interactions within and between groups of humans. At times, this interplay is directly observable, while at other times it is much less obvious, but nonetheless an important aspect of groups. It includes what is said and done in groups as well as how members interact with one another and the group leader. It cannot be objectively measured and is more than the sum of these parts. Recent literature reflects the use of group process by nurses in working with a wide variety of clients (Ambrose, 1989; Bonnivier, 1992; Hochberger & Fisher-James, 1992; Klose & Tinius, 1992; Koontz, Cox, & Hastings, 1991; Pearlman, 1993; Ripich, Moore, & Brennan, 1992).

GROUP CHARACTERISTICS

Groups can be classified according to structure, composition, leader and participant roles, and focus. A particular group often fits more than one classification, especially in terms of its roles. For example, the initial purpose of developing an HIV support group might be to provide the members with a sense of sharing and support. But this type of group often fills many other roles or functions, such as education regarding medications, traditional and nontraditional treatment programs, health-care providers; sharing of information about benefits, wills, and finances; and sharing of strategies for coping with HIV-related symptoms and managing daily life.

Group Structure

Groups may be differentiated by their **structure,** such as formal or informal groups. **Formal groups** are highly structured, with functions specified in job descriptions, contracts, policies, and procedures. Formal groups include the entire nursing staff or the professional standards committee. Each of these groups has particular requirements for membership and specific rules, procedures, and standards of practice. A professional group can also be viewed as a formal group with requirements for membership, rules that govern meetings, and specific member expectations. Examples of formal professional associations or groups, listed in Appendix A, are with the American Nurses Association and Sigma Theta Tau International. An advantage of structured groups is their conveyance of a clear understanding of roles and expectations. This same benefit may become a disadvantage, however, if the group is not open to change or modification. The heads of more structured groups tend to have greater power.

By contrast, **informal groups** are more loosely structured, at times disbanding or reconvening depending on the needs of the membership. Examples of informal groups are special interest groups and support groups. Informal groups benefit from some degree of flexibility in roles, expectations, and leadership or power from their structure.

Composition of Groups

Groups can also be differentiated by membership or composition. **Group composition** depends on the unique characteristics of the group members and their interactions toward their common purpose or goal. Memberships of some groups are homogenous while others are quite heterogenous.

Homogenous groups have a membership similar in some aspect, such as all female clients, depressed males, or female nurses employed in the intensive care units. A benefit of working with a homogenous group is the sense of shared connection that the members typically feel from the beginning. This may be expressed as "he can really understand me," "he has the same problem," or "she thinks the same way I do." What might be lost in such a group is diversity, and the concomitant breadth of experiences that accompanies this characteristic. Another aspect of working with a homogenous group is the ability to select a style appropriate to this population. An example is the use of reminiscence groups with elderly depressed clients (Clark & Vorst, 1994).

Heterogenous groups consist of a mix of individuals such as clients with various diagnoses or ages or a work group of both male and female nurses on acute care units. This type of group has a wider range of diversity and therefore usually a greater variety of opinions, beliefs, and hopefully, suggestions for new approaches. The leader may initially have to work harder to facilitate a sense of connection among members, but once established, this group functions similarly to a homogenous group.

Leader and Participant Roles

A third way to classify groups is in terms of the roles of the leader and participants. Some groups are led by a professional or board that is often responsible for determining the rules, establishing the structure, and determining the membership. This professionally led group is a formal group in which members cannot attend group at will, but must conform to the established norms. If they do not comply, they will no longer be members of the group. Membership in this type of formal group is through a contract, which establishes clear expectations for the leader and the participants. An example is an outpatient recovery group. Typically, a substance abuse counselor leads the group, initiates themes for discussion, and often sets criteria for members participation. This may include random urine testing to determine eligibility or requiring members to take Disulfiram (Antabuse) to join the group.

Other groups have informal leadership as well as rules for members. Peer support groups are an example of this type. Traditionally, the leadership is actually shared by members who are usually working on a common issue. Members are free to attend or not, depending on their own needs. Twelve-step groups such as Alcoholics Anonymous, Overeaters, and Codependents constitute this type. At times, the group may become engulfed in struggles for leadership, translated by some as power, which can compromise the group's effectiveness. An example is the election of a chairperson and secretary for the group. The politicking and election process can consume the members' attention and take the focus of the group off its intended mission, namely, remaining sober, eating healthy, or living independently. Another problem is advice-giving by some members who, by definition of a peer group, are not professionals and whose advice may be inappropriate or even harmful. Specific group roles are discussed later in this chapter.

Group Focus

Another way to classify groups is to consider their focus or approach. The **group focus** can be work-related, educational, therapeutic, or professional. Professional groups were described in Chapter 1, with their unique missions and membership requirements. These professional groups are generally formal, directed at professional issues and needs addressed in their mission statements.

Work groups are task oriented, focused on a particular work-related activity. An example of a work group is the nursing department budget committee, which focuses on the task of allocating the budget monies for the department. Many of us are members of a variety of work groups. Nurses on a particular unit comprise one group, while the nursing department as a whole is another functioning work group. Committees that meet monthly are probably commonly viewed as work groups. They may be convened ad hoc (as the need arises), or they may be more or less a permanent standing group, such as the nursing standards committee or the quality assurance committee. The membership changes over time, and the structure varies in terms of degree of formality. If the group is focusing on one specific issue, group members may be expected to fulfill assigned roles. At other times there may be a more informal, shifting assignment of roles, as occurs in monthly staff meetings on a particular unit. The attendance varies, depending on the schedule, client load, and issues involved.

Educational groups are frequently led by nurses to impart knowledge. The need is tremendous to educate clients about medications, lifestyle changes, and treatments, and nurses have traditionally assumed this role. Here the "life of the group" may actually be an individual session, if held in a clinic or institutional setting, or it may include a series of sessions. An example is a stress reduction class for clients diagnosed with hypertension, which is scheduled on a weekly basis in a clinic department. Membership and attendance, of necessity, vary depending on an individual's schedule but certainly offer an important adjunct in the health care of these individuals. Although the group is led by a professional, the structure is typically less formal and directed at the learning needs of the audience. Teaching and learning principles, discussed in Chapter 12, are important considerations along with the group process.

Therapeutic groups are varied in nature, depending on the specific treatment or clients' needs. Psychoanalysis is probably what typically comes to mind in considering the focus of group therapy. The focus is on assisting members to analyze issues and their antecedents and involves some degree of restructuring of one's personality in a psychoanalytic therapeutic group. The roots of this approach can be found in Freudian theory, and issues such as transference, defenses, and resistance are addressed. This group is led by a professional and is a formally structured group that typically specifies when members can join and when they can terminate from the group. Examples of clients in psychoanalytically focused groups are members with anxiety disorders. Client defenses may be challenged by the therapist who is trained in this approach. According to the ANA (1994) *Standards of Psychiatric–Mental Health Clinical Nursing Practice,* a nurse prepared at the master's level, with advanced certification as a clinical specialist or nurse practitioner, can lead this type of group. Additional types of therapeutic groups are described in Table 13–2.

SETTING UP A GROUP

To develop an effective group, whether professional, work-related, educational, or therapeutic, consider the following important circumstantial factors described by Zander (1994):

1. Conditions in the environment or in the lives of potential joiners are unsatisfactory or suggest an opportunity for desirable change.
2. Organizers conceive of a more satisfactory state of affairs.
3. Members believe they can achieve a more satisfactory state of affairs through activities of a group.
4. Conditions surrounding the unit encourage persons to establish a group and to take part in its activities. (pp. 9–10)

Each of these circumstances suggests that there is an identified need for a change and a commitment to the process.

Once the decision is made to form a new group, there are several issues involved in setting up or structuring the group. Arnold (1995) terms this the pregroup phase, in which activities include the following:

- Alignment of purpose and membership
- Creation of the appropriate environment
- Determination of appropriate group size (pp. 274–277).

The first consideration is the purpose for forming the group. This purpose must be clearly stated for specification of the membership. Next, once the intended membership is determined, members can be recruited and goals set for the group. The size of the group or membership must be appropriate to effectively address the group goals. A professional group requires a larger group to effect change than a work group. A work or therapy group becomes less effective when the group enlarges, becoming more heterogenous and unable to focus on the task or treatment aims. In some groups, the leader will also spend time interviewing potential members prior to the initial meeting. This serves as an orientation to the group as well as a way to determine whether the individual will "fit in."

Other factors to consider involve the basic setup issues:

- Where the group will meet
- Fees

TABLE 13-2. Group Foci and Appropriate Clients for Selected Therapeutic Groups

Group Approach	Purpose	Sample Clients
Cognitive therapy	Focus on the identification of irrational thoughts and beliefs and restructuring perceptions with the substitution of more effective thoughts and beliefs. This approach is based on cognitive theory, and usually involves homework assignments that assist the individual members in recognizing these thought patterns. This type of group is led by an experienced professional.	Depressed and anxious clients
Behavioral therapy	Based on the principle that since behavior is learned, ineffective behaviors can be unlearned, and replaced by more effective behaviors. Learning theories of behaviorism and social learning theory discussed in Chapter 12 provide the basis for some of these groups.	Personality disorder clients, e.g., abusive individuals
Task-oriented groups	Have a specific goal or focus as the objective. An example of a client task-oriented group is a social skills training group. The goal is for the clients to develop specific social skills, perhaps interacting in a group home.	Schizophrenic clients
Support	Developed to provide support to a particular population. They tend to be more homogenous in composition, and may be peer-led, as in Alcoholics Anonymous. There are also support groups for nurses employed in certain units, such as oncology. These groups are generally peer-led and highlight the need for supportive relationships.	Substance abuse, HIV/AIDS, or cancer clients
Psychodrama	A particular type of therapeutic group that involves an opportunity for catharsis to occur. A member identifies an issue, perhaps related to some significant relationship in her or his life, and the participants play out a role. Group members play roles other than themselves, which increases their understanding of others. The group leader is the director and helps to set the tone with music or other aids. This type of group is complex, intense, and the leader needs specific training in the techniques.	Personality disorder clients, e.g., abusive individuals
Therapeutic activity groups	Includes a wide array of art, music, dance, kinesitherapy, psychodrama, and many other techniques. There is usually a defined therapeutic goal, such as identifying feelings or communicating with others. It is professionally led, usually by a specialist in the particular area, and can be formal or not in terms of structure. Most inpatient psychiatric units have a structured program for the clients, including a variety of these groups.	Clients needing assistance with developing insight, coping, or socialization skills, and recreational interests

- Frequency and length of meetings
- Documentation needed for third-party payers or sponsoring organizations

The room, arrangement is another important factor for creating the appropriate environment. When setting up the room, consider the goals of the group and interactions needed among members. A large conference table and chairs may be needed for a work group, while placing chairs in a circle to allow individuals to make eye contact without the barrier of a table is imperative in many therapy groups. Neither of these arrangements is feasible or essential in an educational group.

Another issue for the setup of a group is determining whether there will be a single leader or coleaders. Proponents of two-leader groups cite the enhanced ability to examine dynamics, provide feedback, and manage absences of the leader. Those against this style look at the possibility of problems arising between these two individuals in terms of power, equality, and accountability, with the potential for splitting of the group members and resulting disastrous effects. The goal is to form a strong, viable group. Consider the attributes of a strong group:

- Free interaction among members
- Interdependence among members
- Members who want to remain members
- A group that has the power or potential to effect change (Zander, 1994)

Before initiating a group, a nurse should consider all of these concerns.

EFFECTIVE GROUPS

Effective groups are those that work toward the stated goals and whose members derive a sense of belonging and acceptance. How these outcomes can be accomplished requires a closer look at behaviors,

TABLE 13-3. Factors to Consider in
Evaluating Effectiveness of Groups

Goal attainment

Member participation

Cohesiveness

Decision making

Communication patterns

Attendance

Creativity

Power

strategies, and goals. In addition, organizations and third-party payers may determine their own criteria of effectiveness based on their particular goals. General factors to consider in determining effectiveness of any group are identified in Table 13-3.

Goal attainment is the initial and most important criterion in determining the effectiveness of any group. This is an evaluation of whether the intended task or goal was accomplished, especially in a work group. In a professional association, goal attainment is focused on the activities related to the organization's mission. In therapy groups, goal attainment relates to the focus of the group, such as gaining insight, awareness, skills, or supportive nurturing.

Member participation is another important criterion for assessing the effectiveness of a group. Consider whether all members are included in the discussions and what roles they are playing as group members. On the other hand, think about a situation in which an autocratic leader limits the members' ability to participate in the group discussions. In an effective group, there is evidence of belongingness, camaraderie, and acceptance.

Cohesiveness among the group members indicates that they are working together toward the group's common purpose or goal. If all members are not focused on the purpose, the original goal for which the group was formed will be difficult to attain, and strife will be present among the members. When a group lacks cohesiveness, disruptive roles are evident, interfering with goal attainment and member participation. To achieve cohesiveness, the group members must be refocused on the original intent for the group, with the leader and members supporting each other in their actions and demonstrating satisfaction with the common goal.

In an effective group, *decision making* must occur at the group level, with all members being involved in decisions rather than unilateral actions be-

ing taken by the leader or a disruptive member. A democratic leader, along with involved and cohesive members directed toward the common goal, usually signify effective group functioning. This indicates that the members agree on the common goal and are actively working as a group toward that goal.

The *communication patterns* among the members will provide valuable information on whether there is a common focus, respect, and decision making. Evaluate how the group decisions are made. The group leader should facilitate effective communication patterns, thus allowing all members to be heard and involved in the group process. In an effective group, members are actively involved in a mutual communication process rather than monopolizing the conversation and the focus of the group.

Attendance is regular and active in an effective group. Members are punctual and involved, energetically focused on the task or purpose of the group. When schedules are cleared and a group meeting is arranged in advance, members in an effective group honor their commitments to the meeting rather than managing excuses for not attending or demonstrating routine tardiness.

A high level of *creativity* among the members is another sign of an effective group. The group members are spontaneously generating novel ideas for solutions on the common problem. Brainstorming sessions are focused on the goals, and communication is encouraged, with all ideas and contributions from members considered in effective groups.

Typically, the leadership style in more effective groups is described as democratic and the interactions among the members as interdependent and collaborative. *Power* is distributed, based on the common purpose and abilities of the members to achieve their goal in an effective group. Power struggles disrupt group process, with members focusing inwardly rather than working collaboratively on the group aims.

Ineffective groups have low levels of productivity. These groups contain much strife, and members feel that they do not belong or that it is not safe for them to share their thoughts, ideas, or feelings. The group members demonstrate an uncaring attitude toward one another and have little spontaneous involvement or are reluctant participants. The members do not appear to trust one another, seem unwilling to take risks, and in work groups, rarely volunteer for or willingly accept assignments. The attendance may be uneven, with a high rate of dropouts and tardiness. The leadership style in less effective groups is often described as autocratic or laissez-faire, and the group interactions as independent and competitive.

It is also important to recognize that a group format is not appropriate for all individuals. First, quieter, more introverted people may not participate fully. Some individuals perceive others as more important. It is essential to consider both the individual members and the group purpose in evaluating the effectiveness of a group.

Groups are traditionally viewed as necessitating face to face meetings. This is changing. Computer and telecommunications have provided the means for *nontraditional groups,* with people connecting with others not in the same physical environment. The group is still focused with a common goal, and members interact with some leadership present to organize and maintain the group. For example, Ripich (1992) has described the ability of homebound clients to participate and interact with others through computers. These individuals, traditionally viewed as isolated, exchanged stories via postings and discussed issues and connected on the forum. Many nursing groups now have web sites on the Internet, and so comprise examples of students and professionals in groups using this medium. Again, consider the shared goals, participation, cohesiveness, decisions, communication content, and creativity of the individuals involved in analyzing a nontraditional group.

STAGES OF GROUP DEVELOPMENT

Understanding the expected stages of group development and how to purposefully facilitate groups during these stages is essential to nursing practice, as both a group member and leader. Like the developmental stages of individuals, groups go through predictable stages. An effective group leader must be aware of these stages and motivate members and modify approaches accordingly. Consider the descriptions of the stages of group development in Table 13–4.

We can use the traditional stages of the nurse-client relationship (*initial, working,* and *termination*), with the addition of the conflict and norming stages prior to the working phase, to better understand the process of group development. The stages of group development, along with expected goals and examples of appropriate nursing approaches, are illustrated in Table 13–5. Now, consider the five stages of group development: initial, conflict, norming, working, and termination.

In the *initial* or *forming* stage, the group is being

TABLE 13-4. Stages of Group Development

Tuckman (1965)	▪ Forming ▪ Storming ▪ Norming ▪ Performing ▪ Mourning or termination
Yalom (1985)	▪ Orientation ▪ Conflict ▪ Cohesion ▪ Working ▪ Termination
Arnold (1995)	▪ Forming ▪ Storming ▪ Norming ▪ Performing ▪ Adjourning

formed. The members are becoming acquainted with each other, the group, and the purpose and expectations. Arnold (1995) identifies the major group tasks during this forming stage as establishing the group contract, developing trust, and identification. The leader focuses on orienting the members

TABLE 13-5. Group Stages, Goals, and Nursing Techniques

Stage	Expected Goals	Nursing Techniques
Initial forming	Sense of trust	Making introductions Structuring of group Defining parameters and goals Encouraging the sense of group
Conflict storming	Sense of commitment	Encouraging verbalizations Allowing interactions and role development Handling confrontations and setting limits
Norming	Sense of purpose	Setting limits, rules, and expectations Encouraging group cohesion
Working performing	Sense of hope	Facilitating discussion Identifying themes and progress Refocusing, as needed Identifying processes
Termination adjournment	Sense of accomplishment	Summarizing and evaluating goals Facilitating transfer of knowledge and skills Supporting closure

and determining the structure in terms of time, duration, frequency, and the goals for the group. Cohesiveness of the group is enhanced by clearly stated goals and group norms. Work groups require an introduction, identification of goals and expectations, and orientation to the structure. Client groups also require this introduction and orientation information, but issues of confidentiality and personal disclosure are important considerations in their forming stage.

The next phase is the *conflict* or *storming* stage. This is the time when members become more comfortable with the group, but may be ambivalent about the need for the group and the intended aims. This can be demonstrated by "testing" the authority of the leader, skipping sessions, or coming late. These issues need to be dealt with openly and clearly so that the group can settle into the work of the group. This becomes the time of *norming,* with the identification of standards and expectations of behavior. Some level of discomfort or conflict is often expressed overtly or covertly, until the group becomes functional. All groups need this time to set norms as roles, rules, and structure.

The *working* or *performance* stage involves exactly that—performance of the work of the group. In this stage the leader becomes less involved in running the group. The members, themselves, decide what to discuss, how to address the goals, and to some degree, manage the group themselves. Cohesiveness and creativity should be demonstrated and encouraged. The leader's role is to refocus and clarify as needed, handle problems if they arise, and identify the process as it develops. This process may include members avoiding issues or repetitive reactions and behaviors. By bringing this out in the open, the participants can examine these issues and make changes. Some groups have established dates for each stage; others depend on the tasks and type of group. Another factor that depends on the particular group is whether members can join or leave at different times, or if all members must remain and terminate together.

Termination or *adjournment* is the formal ending of the group. How long this stage lasts depends on the type of group and its duration. The leader again assumes an active role at this stage. The goals are to assist the members in expressing what has been accomplished and preparing for closure. This can be an emotional stage, with some members striving for continual closeness in some therapeutic groups or the "relief" of the goal accomplished in selected work groups.

THE GROUP LEADER

As described in Chapter 8, leadership is an important component of professional nursing practice. Leadership is an essential consideration for the viability of any group. Factors that may influence the particular leadership style adopted by an individual will include the person's personality and skills, the purpose of the group, the characteristics of group, and the participants or members.

Traditional Leadership Styles

Traditional group leadership styles have been described as democratic, autocratic, and laissez-faire. Although each is discussed individually, group leaders often use a combination of styles or modify their style, depending on the group membership or the topic being discussed.

With a *democratic leadership style,* the leader shares the authority and decision-making tasks with members. A democratic leader seeks greater participation by, and feedback from, the group members. One of the benefits of this style is that it typically produces a greater sense of satisfaction among members. On the other hand, there may be some sacrificing by individual members to accomplish the goals. At some meetings, the need to have a consensus opinion may impede the progress of the group by limiting the discussion.

An *autocratic leadership style* is one in which the leader makes all pertinent decisions, informs members of the rules, and structures the sessions. An autocratic leader limits the group's interactions, which tend to be more unidirectional. This style can facilitate the group effectiveness and goal achievement because the expectations have been clearly delineated and actions controlled. However, it may make some members feel that they are disenfranchised and their opinions are not valued.

The *laissez-faire leadership style* is unstructured, allowing members a great deal of freedom and the ability to come and go at will. This style might also involve a changing of the leader from session to session. This can be effective with a highly functional, goal-directed population, but it may not work well with poorly focused or unmotivated groups.

Regardless of the leadership style, characteristics of an effective group leader include the ability to understand the dynamics of the group, listen attentively, focus on the goals, and facilitate the progress of the group. Again, effective communication and interpersonal skills are vital for an effective leader.

Leadership Skills

Consider the leadership skills necessary to successfully manage a group by analyzing its structure, member participation, communication, and goal attainment. One of the first tasks for the group leader is to establish a *structure* that will promote an effective working relationship. The leader needs to consider the differences between a work group and a therapeutic group when choosing an appropriate structure. The leader is also responsible for securing a meeting place, deciding the length and frequency of meetings, and determining the goals for this group. These goals must be clearly communicated to the members so that they can assume their roles. At times, goal determination may be delayed to allow members to participate in this area. The leader must also physically set up the room. As discussed earlier, the arrangement of the physical environment is crucial in some groups. Another critical task for the group leader at this point is to clearly orient the members to the group and its expectations and to allot sufficient time for the group to form before initiating work. The leader can accomplish this by ensuring that the interactions among the members during the initial period of forming remain on a superficial level while the members become acquainted. The leader may need to deliberately halt the communication of a member in a therapeutic group who engages in sharing too early by using the techniques of refocusing and changing the topic. The stages of forming, storming, and norming may be much briefer in a work group, but the leader must still ensure that there is some time for the members to settle in. This may be accomplished in one meeting, but some allowance for chit-chat, introductions, and getting to know one another is important, regardless of the group's focus.

The leader needs to ensure *participation* by all members. Group members must be allowed to participate during the group sessions. This can be accomplished in a variety of ways. Some groups have an around-the-table format, in which each person expresses feelings or opinions on the topic. Some leaders believe this is counterproductive to a free-flowing discussion and recommend a more open format in which members can share their feelings as they see appropriate. The actual format is less important than the realization that the leader needs to encourage the more introverted members, and may need to limit those who seem to monopolize the discussion. Techniques to discourage a group member who monopolizes a discussion include directly setting limits, mirroring back their comments, or interpreting this behavior. Techniques for encouraging active participation by the less verbal members include asking the group member directly, "How do you feel about . . .," or more indirectly, "Who haven't we heard from." In a work setting, confrontation by the other group members generally diminishes the problem of monopolizing behavior; however, the leader may need to directly ask less verbal members for their opinions.

Striving for *group cohesiveness* is another skill needed by the group leader. Coming together as a group, focused on the common goal or purpose, is reinforced by the effective group leader. Recall that Zander's (1994) characteristics of a strong group described members as depending on each other and wanting to remain members of the group. This cooperative and cohesive group spirit can occur and endure when the group leader provides the positive, supportive, and encouraging lead or model for the group. This group *esprit de corps* can be accomplished by focusing periodically on the progress of the group toward the goals and outlining the next steps agreed on in the group process. Conflict must be managed and creativity encouraged as appropriate to the focus of the group.

Leadership skills are essential to facilitate the group in its deliberation and discussion for *decision making*. Ensuring participation by all members, avoiding premature closure on the topic, and recognizing the recurring themes are important activities for an effective group leader. The leader can set the tone for the level of *communication*—that is, superficial or deep sharing—as well as set limits on appropriate and unacceptable styles. Techniques used by the leader include restatement, reflection, clarification, collaboration, and problem solving while always attempting to promote open communication among the members. These techniques are more fully described in Chapter 6. Another useful technique for the leader is role modeling for the group members how to *provide constructive feedback,* for example, saying "We need to allow others to contribute their ideas and finish their comments." In this way, the group leader is actually teaching the members effective communication skills. In work groups the members can often behaviorally modify negative behaviors of others by inattention and focusing on the task at hand.

Ineffective communication techniques the leader, as well as members, should avoid are giving advice, giving approval, blaming, and scapegoating. Giving advice is generally considered nontherapeutic. However, giving approval is also unhelpful to group members. Rather than express approval for an individual's efforts or successes, the leader can reflect back the accomplishment to the person or other members allowing them to express their feelings. Blaming is also rather easily identified as nontherapeutic and noneffective. Group leaders need to be vigilant not to inadvertently scapegoat an individual or allow group members to do so, especially in the case of problem members for their interruptions or other maladaptive behavior.

Group leaders must also remain vigilant for effective communication appropriate to the stages of the group's development. In the initial stage of a group, when members are anxious, one individual may be hyperverbal and repeatedly interrupt the discussion. In the working phase, a person may make multiple requests for reassurance that impedes the group discussion. In the termination phase, feelings of abandonment may cause some disruption by some members. The leader needs to recognize these dynamics and intervene appropriately, creating a safe, open, and productive environment for the group.

The leader can use the group format as a means of teaching effective communication skills such as how to listen, give and receive feedback, and express feelings. Most groups have rules regarding cross-talk and interrupting others. If an individual seems to have difficulty receiving messages, the leader can paraphrase or clarify the message. All of these activities are important leadership skills for effective group communication and dynamics.

Goal accomplishment has already been identified as the benchmark of success for groups. The leader is the facilitator for the members striving to work toward specific goals. Strategies to accomplish these goals begin with a clearly stated identification of the goals. Refocusing is a useful technique to return the group to its mission. Giving assignments, such as recording feelings for a time period or trying out a particular suggestion from the group, is another helpful measure. The use of assignments communicates the belief that members are capable and that change involves work on the part of the members. In a work group, members are given specific areas to work on or research, with the expectation that the group will reconvene to put these pieces together. Ultimately, the leader is responsible for ensuring that activities in the group remain focused on the common goals that were set for the group.

Another leadership activity focusing on effective communication and goal attainment involves facilitating closure. To provide for *group closure,* the leader needs to summarize at the end of each session as well as the official termination of the group. If the members enter and leave the group at various individual points, the leader may actually summarize at the start of each session to orient newer and longer-term members to the current status, goals, and tasks. This is also highly effective in educational groups, to reorient learners to prior content. Regardless of the focus of the group, periodic summarization and closure can be essential for the successful functioning for both the group and its members. Group members need an opportunity to acknowledge their accomplishments and express their feelings related to this endpoint.

ROLES OF GROUP MEMBERS

Group members demonstrate a variety of roles during particular meetings. These roles may be either functional or nonfunctional for the group process. They may remain similar or constant over the life of the group, or individuals may alter their role from meeting to meeting. It is vital for nurses to recognize the roles assumed in groups, and to purposefully interact when functioning in these settings. Consider the last unit meeting you attended. Think back to who led the group. Did anyone stall or disrupt the discussion? Were the topics discussed major issues on the unit or "pet peeves" of one individual? Did all members participate in the discussion? As the group leader, how could you have changed this meeting?

Functional group roles facilitate the group process and the ultimate effectiveness of the group, especially toward accomplishing a task or attaining the goal. In any type of group, members may play both functional and nonfunctional roles for various periods of time. For the effectiveness of the group process, the goal is for members to demonstrate predominantly functional group roles. For nursing work groups, Tappen (1995) differentiates between functional task roles (Table 13–6), which contribute to completion of the task, and functional group-building roles (Table 13–7), which support development and meet relational needs (pp. 245–246).

Observe these roles in any work group setting, such as a committee or unit meeting. Many functional task and group-building roles are demonstrated by the group leader. The leader may start out as the information giver and standard setter during the forming stage, but then function as an information seeker, gatekeeper, and encourager as the group process evolves in the working stage. The leader may also demonstrate the functional roles of coordinator, energizer, summarizer, and consensus taker to facilitate group process and attainment of the group goals. Effective communication techniques will be apparent when the leader serves in the roles of diagnoser or expressor. However, other group members will also serve in these roles as they become more active and progress toward the achievement of the group's goals. Observe who behaves as the procedural technician, assisting the leader in organizing the group and supplying needed equipment and materials. Examine who appears to be the more passive follower in the group, who cracks jokes as the tension reliever, and who records the actions and progress of the group.

Although these roles have been discussed mainly for the work setting, applications can be made for the

TABLE 13-6. Functional Task Roles

Initiator/ contributor	Makes suggestions and proposes new ideas, methods, or problem-solving approaches.
Information giver	Offers pertinent information from personal knowledge appropriate to the group topic or task.
Information seeker	Requests information or suggestions from other members appropriate to the group topic or task.
Opinion giver/ seeker	Offers or requests views, judgments, or feelings about the topic or suggestions under consideration by the group. Provides the opportunity for values clarification by the group members.
Disagreer	Identifies errors in statements made or proposes a different viewpoint.
Coordinator	Suggests relationships between the different suggestions or comments made by the group members.
Elaborator	Elaborates or expands on suggestions already made.
Energizer/catalyst	Stimulates the group into action toward the goals either by introducing certain issues or topics or by behavior.
Summarizer	Summarizes suggestions, actions, and accomplishments that have occurred in the group.
Procedural technician	Provides the technical tasks needed for the group functions, such as arrangement of the group, including any audiovisual equipment and work supplies.
Recorder	Takes notes to record the progress, suggestions, and decisions of the group.

Source: Adapted from Tappen, R. M. (1995). *Nursing leadership and management: Concepts and practice* (3rd ed.). Philadelphia: Davis. Reprinted with permission.

TABLE 13-7. Functional Group-Building Roles

Encourager	Encourages and praises accomplishments of the group and other group members.
Standard setter	Reinforces the standards or processes for effective group functioning.
Gatekeeper	Ensures that all members have contributed to the discussion and that the group is not being monopolized by the views of more verbal members.
Consensus taker	Seeks the weighting of group sentiments or consensus on the issues.
Diagnoser	Identifies barriers or blocks for group progress that are occurring.
Expresser	Restates or identifies and expresses the feelings of the group.
Tension reliever	Uses humor and mediation when group tensions rise and interfere with the group process and accomplishment of tasks.
Follower	Consents to whatever is proposed by others in the group. Demonstrates no active participation without great encouragement.

Source: Adapted from Tappen, R. M. (1995). *Nursing leadership and management: Concepts and practice* (3rd ed.). Philadelphia: Davis. Reprinted with permission.

professional, educational, and therapeutic group settings. In a professional group, observe the leadership roles shared by the officers, procedural technician roles by the aides or room monitors, and the standard setter role by the parliamentarian. In an educational group, consider the specific content and the size of the audience. Observe the roles taken by the teacher or facilitator, the people who are seated close to the teacher, the people in the back of the room, and the people who are asking most of the questions or who may be cracking jokes. In a therapy group, observe the particular role of the leader and how the members are facilitated to share their feelings and beliefs. Observe the members who verbalize supportive comments versus those who disagree or give further information about similar feelings.

These are functional roles that facilitate the group in achieving their common purpose and goals. At times group members will demonstrate nonfunctional roles when they interrupt the group process. An example can be seen with the individual who provides negative comments on whatever is proposed by others. However, a group can actually be mobilized to act in response to the unacceptable actions of one member, such as the individual who repeatedly comes late and then insists on being updated on what already occurred.

Nonfunctional roles are disruptive to group-building, task accomplishment, and progress toward goal attainment. Nonfunctional roles include dominator, monopolizer, blocker, aggressor, recognition seeker, follower, and victim.

- The *dominator* controls conversations, determines what will be discussed, and may control or intimidate other members. The dominator is often focused on his or her own needs. An example of the dominator in a work group is a unit coordinator at a quality assurance meeting who suggests the group focus on the number of requests for schedule changes. An example in a therapy group is a client who opens the group by suggesting that members discuss the upcoming holidays.

- The *monopolizer* seeks attention and demands that the group focus on him or her. He or she may repeatedly interrupt others, and perceive his or her issues and problems as the most important. A work group example is the nurse who goes on and on about how the unit is always left short staffed. In a therapeutic group, an example is a client who repeatedly interrupts and insists the group listen to his problem.

- The *blocker* interrupts the discussion, often focusing on another topic or personal concerns. Tappen (1995) describes this individual as making unconstructive and negative comments, or resisting beyond a reasonable point (p. 246). These individuals are evident in many work, educational, and therapeutic groups, often the ones that appear to be forced into membership in the group.

- The *aggressor* attacks during the discussion, with comments that may or may not be relevant to the discussion. Often this individual is focused inwardly on personal needs and demands to be heard, regardless of relevance to the discussion. In this process, other group members are criticized because they are not perceived as having the same insights or experiences as the aggressor. This individual is readily apparent in professional, work, educational, and therapy groups by the expression of hostile comments that interfere with the group process. At this point, signs of discomfort or counterattacks may be apparent among other group members.

- The *recognition seeker* consistently attempts to draw the group's attention to his or her personal beliefs, values, and concerns. This individual has the need to stand out among the group members and be heard, respected, and perhaps admired. This member actually sounds like the leader. Unfortunately, he or she often does this at the expense of working on personal issues.

- The *follower* passively consents to whatever is proposed by others in the group. This person adds little to the interactions and may not verbally participate without great encouragement. In either a work or a therapy group, this is the individual who sits quietly, and responds only when asked a direct question.

- The *victim* personalizes remarks of others and views others as aggressors. This individual interprets whatever the group is discussing as a personal threat or offense. In work and therapy groups this individual looks for pity or sympathy from other members and seems stuck at this point. In our work group example, this is the nurse who declares, "It's not all shifts that are short staffed. Mine is the one that's always short staffed with temps and you expect me to orient them and take care of everyone else!"

In every group there are individuals who take on these roles. The group leader must be sensitive to the behaviors presented but promote effective functioning of the group. Table 13–8 describes nonfunctional group roles and management strategies. Effective communication techniques and interpersonal skills are critical to success in group process.

TABLE 13–8. Sample Group Roles and Management Strategies

Role	Example	Nursing Action
Dominator	"Follow me"	Provide feedback and set limits Encourage listening to others
Monopolizer or blocker	"Me me me!"	Set limits Provide constructive feedback
Follower	"Don't ask me"	Direct question Verbalize the implied
Recognition seeker	"Yes me"	Make observations Support if positive effect Set limits if negative
Victim	"Poor me"	Empathy Refocus Direct question
Aggressor	"Listen to me"	Reflection Focus on feelings

INTERORGANIZATIONAL AND INTRAORGANIZATIONAL GROUPS

Our focus has been primarily on singular or small groups, such as professional, work, educational, and therapeutic groups. Groups exist in complex and multilayered systems and organizations. In an organizational system, groups may be differentiated as interorganizational or intraorganizational, depending on whether they coexist between or within an organization.

Interorganizational groups are those that occur between systems or organizations. These interorganizational groups may include the hospital and the community mental health center, the home health agency, or the various subgroups of a health department. Outpatient hospital groups and inpatient unit groups also fit this category. These groups are often highly structured, with functions specified in job descriptions and policies and procedures. Other examples of interorganizational groups are 12-step support groups and privately run group therapy. By contrast, these groups are more loosely structured.

Nurses are involved with and provide leadership for effective functioning between or among systems in interorganizational groups. Communication and interpersonal skills are valuable attributes of professional nurses in this process. Along with these skills, a full awareness of each system or organization and their interrelationships is needed. This involves an understanding of each organization's subsystems (goals and values, technical, psychosocial, structural, and managerial), as illustrated in Chapter 10. Consistent goals and values, complementary technical subsystems, and compatible psychosocial, structural, and managerial subsystems promote effective functioning. In addition, consider the environment in which the different organizations or systems exist. Nursing involvement in interorganizational groups is increasing as the complexity of health care and professional practice expand.

Intraorganizational groups are those that exist within a single, overall system or organization. The nursing department and the housekeeping department are intraorganizational groups within a hospital system. These groups are somewhat similar in terms of their structure, with specified roles, policies, and procedures. It is imperative for nurses to learn how to interact and negotiate effectively with these intraorganizational groups. An example is how to obtain needed supplies and services from the housekeeping department. How well this is accomplished often depends on the ability of members of each department to collaborate with the others. Within a therapeutic mental health setting, intraorganizational groups include the art therapy sessions, the recreational or occupational therapy groups, and the insight-oriented group therapy sessions. These latter examples, are less structured than the nursing and housekeeping departments. An art therapist therefore has more leeway in determining the when and how of individual sessions than a nursing director has in scheduling staff, which may be predetermined by client census and needs.

The additional complexity of any group, whether an interorganizational or intraorganizational work, professional, educational, or therapy group, demands the use of skills in observation, interpersonal communication, and group process that are essential characteristics of the involved professional nurse. These skills are tailored to the developmental stage of the group and the unique characteristics of the individual members. Professional nurses function as both members and leaders of such groups, and constant attention to these skills allow them to be integral components in effective groups in the profession and throughout the health-care delivery system.

Group process involves the communications, verbal and nonverbal, between and among members of the group. One can deliberately stimulate or provoke certain responses or assist individual members to recognize their behaviors and move toward change and the common goals of the particular group. Learning about these group characteristics will make the nurse an effective member and leader in all group situations.

KEY POINTS

- A **group** consists of three or more individuals with some commonality, such as shared goals or interests. Groups to consider in professional nursing practice include professional, work, educational, family, and therapeutic groups, each with specific goals and membership.
- **Group process** is described as the dynamic interplay of interactions within and between groups of humans. Three or more persons who share some commonality can be considered a group.

- Groups are classified according to structure (formal or informal), composition, leader and participant roles, and focus (professional, work, educational, and therapeutic).
- The composition of a group may be **homogenous,** with the group members sharing similar characteristics, or **heterogenous,** with a mix of individuals.
- The issues to be addressed in establishing a group are the need and objectives for change and basic setup activities, including specifying and aligning the group purpose with the intended membership and determining the appropriate environment and group size.
- **Effective groups** are able to accomplish their goals in a manner that allows all members to participate while ineffective groups become fragmented or dysfunctional.
- Group leaders structure the sessions to promote communication and participation by all members.
- Recent literature has identified innovative ways in which nurses have incorporated these group dynamics in a variety of nontraditional groups.
- Groups go through predictable developmental stages: forming, storming, norming, working, and adjourning. These stages are similar to the stages of therapeutic relationship with initial, working, and termination stages. The leader modifies her or his approach based on the particular stage.
- Traditional group leadership styles are democratic, autocratic, and laissez-faire. However, group leaders often use a combination of styles or modify their styles, depending on the group membership or topic being discussed.
- **Functional group roles** facilitate the group process and the ultimate effectiveness of the group and include both task and group-building roles. **Nonfunctional roles** are disruptive of the group-building, task accomplishment, and progress toward goal attainment; these include the roles of dominator, monopolizer, follower, catalyst, pacifier, and victim.
- Groups may be differential as **interorganizational** or **intraorganizational groups,** depending on whether they exist between organizational systems or within an organization.

CHAPTER EXERCISES

1. Select two of the following groups for comparison: professional, educational, work, and therapeutic. Contrast the following characteristics of the groups:
  - Structure
  - Composition
  - Leader and participant roles
  - Focus

2. Observe the members of the next departmental committee or nursing group you attend.
  - Determine whether the group leader is the designated leader or a member who has assumed this role?
  - Describe the roles other members have assumed. Are these group roles different from these individuals' interactions in other settings?
  - Evaluate whether the members appear satisfied with the group's outcomes.
  - Evaluate whether this group or committee meets the characteristics of an effective group.

3. Select a type of group you would like to lead. Set up objectives, format, structure, and membership characteristics for the group. Determine how often and where it would meet, and the duration of meetings. Establish outcome criteria to evaluate effectiveness. Determine the style of leadership that will work best in this group. Discuss how you would develop the needed strategies to effectively manage this group.

4. Attend a community support group. Following the group meeting, describe the following:
  ▪ Format, leadership, and participation of members.
  ▪ Differences between the support group and another therapeutic group you have attended or led
  ▪ Differences between the support group and work groups where you were a member
  Evaluate the effectiveness of the support group you attended.

REFERENCES

Ambrose, J. (1989). Joining therapeutic groups for change. *Journal of Psychosocial Nursing, 27*(11), 28–32.

American Nurses Association. (1994). *Statement on psychiatric–mental health clinical nursing practice and standards of psychiatric–mental health nursing practice* (Publication No. PMH-12). Washington, DC: American Nurses Publishing.

Arnold, E. (1995). Communicating in groups. In E. Arnold, & K. Boggs. *Interpersonal Relationships: Professional Communication Skills for Nurses* (2nd ed.) (pp. 259–294). Philadelphia: Saunders.

Bonnivier, J. (1992). A peer supervision group: Put countertransference to work. *Journal of Psychosocial Nursing and Mental Health Services, 30*(5), 5–8.

Clark, W. G., & Vorst, V. R. (1994). Group therapy with chronically depressed geriatric patients. *Journal of Psychosocial Nursing and Mental Health Services, 32*(5), 9–13, 44–45.

Hochberger, J. M., & Fisher-James, L. (1992). A discharge group for chronically mentally ill: Easing the way. *Journal of Psychosocial Nursing and Mental Health Services, 30*(4), 25–31.

Klose, P., & Tinius, T. (1992). Confidence builders: A self-esteem group at an inpatient psychiatric hospital. *Journal of Psychosocial Nursing and Mental Health Services, 30*(7), 5–9, 37–38.

Koontz, E., Cox, D., & Hastings, S. (1991). Implementing a short term family support group. *Journal of Psychosocial Nursing, 29*(5), 5–8, 10, 38–39.

Pearlman, I. (1993). Group psychotherapy with the elderly. *Journal of Psychosocial Nursing and Mental Health Services, 31*(7), 7–10, 32–33.

Ripich, S., Moore, S. M., & Brennan, P. F. (1992). A new nursing medium: Computer networks for group intervention. *Journal of Psychosocial Nursing, 30*(6), 15–20.

Tappan, R. M. (1995). *Nursing leadership and management: Concepts and practice* (3rd ed.). Philadelphia: Davis.

Tuckman, B. (1965). Developmental sequence in small groups. *Psychological Bulletin, 63* 384–387.

Yalom, I. (1985). *Theory and practice of group psychotherapy* (3rd ed.). New York: Basic Books.

Zander, A. (1994). *Making groups effective* (2nd ed.). San Francisco: Jossey-Bass.

BIBLIOGRAPHY

Agapetus, L. (1994). Yalom's model applied to an outpatient better breathers group. *Journal of Psychosocial Nursing and Mental Health Services, 32*(12), 11–12, 26.

Berne, E. (1963). *The structure and dynamics of organizations and groups*. New York: Grove Press.

Brennan, P. F., Moore, S. M., & Smyth, K. A. (1995). The effects of a special computer network on caregivers of persons with Alzheimer's disease. *Nursing Research, 44*, 166–172.

Clark, C. C. (1995). *The nurse as group leader* (3rd ed.). New York: Springer.

Miller, C., Eisner, W., & Allport, C. (1994). Creative coping: A cognitive-behavioral group for borderline personality disorder. *Archives in Psychiatric Nursing, 8*(4) 280–285.

Robinson, G. M., & Pinkney, A. A. (1992). Transition from the hospital to the community: Small group program. *Journal of Psychosocial Nursing and Mental Health Services, 30*(5), 33–36.

Staples, N. R., & Schwartz, M. (1990). Anorexia nervosa support group: Providing traditional support. *Journal of Psychosocial Nursing and Mental Health Services, 28*(2), 6–8, 10, 36–37.

Section IV

PROVIDING CARE

Chapter 14

NURSING PROCESS

Phyllis B. Heffron

CHAPTER OBJECTIVES

On completion of
this chapter, the reader
will be able to:

1. Discuss the steps of the nursing process.
2. Given sample assessment data, propose appropriate nursing diagnoses.
3. For the planning phase, differentiate between behavioral objectives, goals, and outcome criteria.
4. Distinguish implementation activities that are client-focused as opposed to provider-focused.
5. For a given nursing process situation, formulate evaluation strategies that are measurable with indicators for documentation.

KEY TERMS

Nursing Process
Assessment
Client Database
Primary Data Source
Secondary Data Sources
Objective Data
Subjective Data
Health History

Physical Examination
Nursing Diagnosis
NANDA
PES Format
Planning
Client Goals
Long-Term Goal
Short-Term Goal

Behavioral Objective
Outcome Criteria
Nursing Care Plan
Nursing Actions
Nursing Intervention
   Classification (NIC)
Implementation
Evaluation

The **nursing process** is a systematic framework that offers a specific and organized method for delivering nursing care. Through a series of specific steps, the nursing process provides the nurse with a structured way to identify client needs, formulate nursing diagnoses, plan nursing actions, and evaluate the extent to which the process has benefited the client. It helps nurses organize and challenge their thinking as they administer nursing care.

The nursing process, derived from the scientific method of problem solving, is a cyclical, open-ended process that allows for flexibility and refinement. It is an ongoing process, particularly when the nurse has more than one opportunity for client interaction, such as during a hospitalization or over time in a home care situation. In practice, the nursing process is applicable in any health-care setting and can be tailored to fit various nursing theories and situations. There are five steps in the nursing process: *assessment, nursing diagnosis, planning, implementation,* and *evaluation.* Table 14–1 lists the five steps, with an introductory description of each.

Although the steps of the nursing process can ideally unfold in the logical order presented in Table 14–1, the nurse may move in and out of the steps in a slightly different order, depending on the clinical situation. For example, in emergency nursing when there is no time for pondering a nursing diagnosis or planning care, the nurse takes immediate action to alleviate a symptom or sign after an instantaneous assessment. Later, when the patient has stabilized, the nurse can go back to refine the assessment and proceed in a more in-depth fashion to complete the nursing process. To the novice nurse, or the nurse who is reentering nursing having never used the nursing process in practice, this step by step procedure may seem cumbersome and awkward. It may appear impossible to both think about and actively care for clients at the same time. With practice and more familiarity with the five steps, the actual "hands on" use of the nursing process becomes instinctive. It becomes so customary and usual that experienced nurses can use it without a continually focused conscious awareness.

Historically, nurses have used various approaches to organize the way nursing care is given to clients. Before the mid-1960s and the formal introduction of the nursing process, nursing care most commonly reflected standardized procedures based on doctor's orders or medical diagnoses. When describing independent nursing actions, nurses tended to rely on traditional ways of doing things, and were likely to

TABLE 14–1. Steps of The Nursing Process

Assessment

Assessment is the ongoing process of systematically collecting *relevant* client information for the purpose of identifying nursing diagnoses and planning nursing care. Assessment data come from various sources and are organized into a format called the client database.

Nursing Diagnosis

A nursing diagnosis is a statement the nurse makes about an actual or potential nursing care need of a client. A nursing diagnosis is derived through a process of clinical decision making, based on the analysis and integration of information from the database.

Planning

Planning is the phase of the nursing process in which the nurse determines a plan of action and chooses nursing interventions (nursing actions) to resolve actual and potential nursing diagnoses or otherwise move the client toward a state of optimal health and wellness. Planning deliberations include weighing priorities, setting client goals and objectives based on suggested nursing interventions, and designing an individualized nursing care plan.

Implementation

Implementation is the action phase of the nursing process, focusing on carrying out nursing interventions according to the plan of care. The viability of the nursing care plan is tested during this phase. Additional activities that characterize this phase include validating and refining the care plan, documenting nursing actions, and revising or adding new assessment data to the client database.

Evaluation

This phase of the nursing process allows for evaluation of the client's response to the delivery of nursing care. Nursing actions are measured in terms of the achievement of desired outcomes specified in the care plan. The evaluation phase is ongoing and assists in refining the plan of care and guiding the nurse's response to new assessment data.

cite intuition as their reason rather than scientific method. In addition, nurses did not function in as many diverse and expanded roles as they do today, and they were not expected to make or be accountable for the in-depth and independent assessments now common in nursing practice.

The actual term "nursing process" appeared in the nursing literature several times around midcentury (Peplau, 1952; Hall, 1955; Johnson, 1959; Orlando, 1961), but it was not until 1967 that it was formally introduced as a recommended tool for nursing practice. Helen Yura and Mary Walsh, nursing faculty at The Catholic University of America in Washington, D.C., pioneered its use in the first edition of their classic textbook, *The Nursing Process* (Yura &

Walsh, 1967). Nursing was in the midst of a number of changes during this time, as nursing leaders were recognizing the critical need for legal and ethical accountability of nursing practice, hospital quality assurance programs were being strengthened, and the increase in nursing knowledge was expanding the scope of nursing roles.

The concept of the nursing process gradually and steadily proved successful, first in theory and then in practice, as it was adopted by schools of nursing and health-care institutions alike. At this time the nursing process consisted of only four steps, because the term "nursing diagnosis" was not yet commonly used in the practice. In 1980 the American Nurses' Association published a document (ANA, 1980) that defined nursing as "the diagnosis and treatment of human responses to actual or potential health problems" (p. 9). This document, along with the growing influence of the North American Nursing Diagnosis Association (NANDA), paved the way for the nursing process to be described in terms of a five-step process, with "nursing diagnosis" as the second step after assessment. Nurses began to see the many advantages of proceeding in a deliberate fashion, *with intention,* rather than intuitively. The nursing process could not only be used productively in practice, but it could be combined with other nursing theories to establish a database for future research purposes.

Over the years the nursing process has continued to evolve as nursing has strengthened its professional base and responded to many societal changes and massive transformations in the health-care system. Today, consumers of health care are more sophisticated and more knowledgeable about the kind of care they receive and can play a major role in decision making. Increasingly, there is a demand for legal and ethical accountability by nurses, both of which the nursing process can provide a sound framework for. Accrediting agencies and national nursing organizations have incorporated the use of nursing process data into standards for care and accountability (Spradley & Allender, 1996). With the advent of diagnostic-related groups (DRGs) as a part of Medicare's prospective payment system, nursing has been challenged to deliver hospital-based nursing care to sicker patients with shorter hospital stays. In light of this, the nursing process, particularly care planning and documentation, has been credited as a major influence in delivering high-quality care and helping to reconcile cost-containment with quality care (Holloway, 1993). Overall, changes in health care and nursing management that have enhanced the use of the nursing process

include the increased scientific base for nursing knowledge, the proliferation of nursing research, role expansion and increased scope of nursing practice, rise in health-care technologies, and expanded use of nursing diagnosis (Koldjeski, 1993).

The nursing process begins with contact between a nurse and a client or between a nurse and another source of information about that client, such as the written medical record, a relative, or another health-care provider. This contact provides the entree into assessment, the beginning step of the nursing process.

ASSESSMENT

The purpose of assessment is to identify and obtain data about the client that will be needed to diagnose obvious client problems, identify potential health problems or risks, and affirm wellness. In other words, assessment is organized information gathering with a therapeutic purpose (Riehl & Roy, 1974). **Assessment** involves specific activities of gathering, substantiating, and communicating data that, together, provide a comprehensive view of a person's health status. The assessment phase incorporates all the data gathered from the nursing history and the physical examination, and is the cornerstone on which all other nursing process activities depend. It can be likened to a power or energy source that drives the process.

From a nursing perspective, the term "nursing assessment" implies a comprehensive and holistic approach in which the physiologic, psychological, sociocultural, and spiritual dimensions of the person are integrated. This attention to multiple dimensions of an individual is what distinguishes the health assessment performed by the nurse from health assessments performed by other members of the health team. Assessment is a part of each activity the nurse does for and with the client. It can be done all at once, in a complete assessment on admission to a hospital, or as a partial assessment in the emergency room or intensive care setting. In the hospital setting, it is customary for a patient to receive an admission nursing assessment that is refined and updated as necessary; in this situation the process may include assessment for discharge planning, and it continues throughout the hospitalization. In an outpatient setting, a nurse practitioner may be doing a comprehensive assessment for an employment physical, and the process may begin and end in less than an hour. A home care nurse may focus his or her assessment on a new symptom the client reports during a visit, and will integrate this information with past assessment data. Not all nursing assessments look alike, partly because of these diverse clinical situations and settings, but also because each nurse brings a unique set of skills and abilities to the assessment process.

A number of generic guidelines and ways of looking at assessment help nurses in any setting understand and organize their actions in the data-gathering process. These include types of data, sources of data, methods of data collection, and the importance of organizing and documenting data. It is also important to keep in mind that the potential for collecting data from a single human being is enormous, given the complexities and life experiences of individuals. The challenge for the nurse is to develop expertise for collecting *relevant* data, a process that requires critical thinking skills, highly developed interpersonal communication, and competent technical ability.

A comprehensive assessment begins with taking the health history and performing the physical examination, the results of which form the client database. The **client database** is composed of all the information gathered about the client, and this information comes from several sources: the client, other health-care providers (including written medical records), the client's family, and sometimes close friends. Sources of data can be categorized into primary and secondary data sources.

The individual client is the **primary data source.** The client's physical condition, developmental level, and intellectual and emotional status determine the extent of information that can be obtained during the encounter. Whenever possible, the client is encouraged to take an active part in the assessment process. If the client is unable to provide information and validate findings, the family or significant other person may assume the role of primary data source.

Secondary data sources include medical records, family members, other health-care providers, predesigned care plans, the professional literature, and nursing experience. Whenever they are available, written secondary sources of information are particularly useful to review before visiting the client for the history interview and examination. Particularly in the hospital situation, clients are subjected to many questions, examinations, and requests for information by a variety of health-care workers. Much of this information is overlapping, and care should be taken not to repeat questions whose answers are readily apparent in the health record. When information is transferred to the nursing assessment from written sources, it is usually

mentioned during the interview so that the client is aware of what information is already known to the nurse. As the nurse talks with the client and makes observations, she is also aware of data derived from experiences with other clients and information derived from continuing education and the professional literature. This type of data is constantly being applied and validated as the client database takes form; it can be visualized as a thread woven in and out of the data-gathering process.

Another important way of looking at assessment data is as objective versus subjective data. **Objective data** are measurable in some way and are determined by the nurse through listening, observing, feeling, smelling, or manipulating. Examples of objective data are such things as hemoglobin test results, skin temperature, pulse rate, blood pressure, and acidotic breath smell. **Subjective data** are data that only the client can experience and relate to the nurse. These data are perceived ONLY by the client and cannot be objectively measured, verified, or described by another person. Examples of subjective data are vertigo, nausea, pain, and feelings of depression, happiness, or security.

The **health history** is usually the beginning of the assessment process, and it is implemented both formally and informally. Typically this is done at the time of hospital admission or on the first home visit. Formally, the nurse conducts an interview with the client and asks questions according to a predesigned format or a theory-based outline. A commonly used format is based on the medical model, in which the questions are organized according to body systems and geared specifically toward uncovering physiologic abnormalities. Rooted in the medical profession, the medical model views people as physiologic systems, and health is narrowly defined as the absence of signs and symptoms of disease. The focus in this model is the relief of the signs and symptoms of disease and elimination of dysfunction and pain. Nurses and other health professionals have used the medical model as a base model for many years, in some instances adding categories such as health behaviors, lifestyle profiles, and nutritional data. As nursing has grown professionally and introduced nursing theories and research-based knowledge, nurse authors of history formats have either abandoned the medical model approach or greatly modified it to create a broader, holistic focus. The focus of a nursing-oriented history is to look at the entire person and identify current or potential health needs amenable to nursing interventions. In this process specific problem areas are identified, including medical conditions. The nursing history seeks to identify relationships between behaviors and look for patterns of behaviors or occurrences. A widely used format, based on a nursing model, is Gordon's functional health patterns (Gordon, 1991). In contrast to the medical model, which categorizes history questions by body systems, Gordon has organized a framework of 11 functional health patterns; each pattern is designed to reflect a pattern of behaviors that fit together naturally. Table 14–2 compares categories for grouping history questions from these two models.

A complete health history, regardless of format, ideally includes the following sections: biographical information, statement of the client's words regarding why he or she is seeking care, present health and illness status, past health history, current health information, family health history, review of systems (physical, psychosocial, and functional), developmental data, and nutritional data (Barkauskas, Stoltenberg-Allen, Baumann, & Darling-Fisher, 1994). Informally, the nurse continues to gather historical data as she or he converses with the client while performing the physical examination and giving nursing care.

The **physical examination** typically follows the health history. It is an orderly process in which the nurse evaluates the client using the sensory skills of sight, hearing, touch, and smell. Data-gathering and measurement tools such as the stethoscope, thermometer, otoscope, and tuning fork are used for this activity. Examination techniques used by the nurse include inspection, percussion, auscultation, and palpation. Table 14–3 provides an overview of the assessment techniques of physical examination.

As with health history, preprinted physical examination formats may be used, depending on the organization or health-care institution the nurse is associated with. In government agencies such as the Armed Services, for example, standard forms must be used. Independent nursing practitioners may have developed their own format or modified an existing one. Also, as with the health history, the depth of the physical assessment is carried out in accordance with the client situation and purpose of the assessment. A nurse midwife or specialty nurse practitioner would possess selected physical examination skills that other nurses would not. A "head to toe" physical examination is required for a yearly health appraisal, whereas a modified examination is appropriate if a client has identified a focused and specific health complaint. Other factors that define the type or length of the physical examination include time limitations, age, severity of illness, and emotional status.

During the assessment phase of the nursing process, the beginning of the trust relationship between nurse and client is established. During this

TABLE 14–2. Comparing Two Models for History Format

Medical Model Categories

History of present illness	Cardiovascular
Family disease history	Musculoskeletal
Infectious diseases/immunizations	Endocrine
Eye, ear, nose, and throat	Reproductive
Dermatology/allergy	Genitourinary
Dental	Gastrointestinal
Neuropsychiatric	Hematopoietic
Respiratory	

Functional Health Patterns (Gordon, 1987; & Carpenito, 1991)

Health perception–health management
  Growth and development, health maintenance, compliance behavior
  Health-seeking behaviors and high-risk behaviors

Coping–stress tolerance
  Adjustment and coping behavior, posttrauma responses
  Risk behaviors for suicide, self-harm, and violence

Value–belief
  Beliefs and ideas about health and illness, medicine, and treatment
  Cultural issues, religion, and spiritual life

Cognitive–perceptual
  Sensory perceptions (e.g., pain), cognitive patterns (e.g., knowledge deficits and general thought processes)

Role relationship
  Communication patterns and behaviors (e.g., verbal impairments, grieving, and trust); human relationships (e.g., with family, significant others, parent–child, and social); patterns of love, belonging, intimacy

Self concept
  Patterns of self-concept (e.g., well-being, powerlessness, body image, self-esteem, and identity); feeling states (e.g., anxiety and fear)

Elimination
  Bowel and bladder functioning, perspiration patterns

Nutrition–metabolic
  Patterns of food and fluid intake, fluid balance, body temperature regulation, breast feeding, risk for infection, tissue integrity

Sleep–rest
  Patterns of sleep, rest, and relaxation

Activity tolerance–exercise
  Exercise and activity level, cardiac output and tissue perfusion, mobility, self-care ability for activities of daily living

Sexuality pattern
  Gender role identity, satisfaction with sexuality patterns, reproductive history

initial contact, it is crucial to set a tone that communicates unconditional respect for the individual and commitment to a caring and holistic framework for care giving. Chapter 6 provides information on the use of *therapeutic communication* skills, in which

TABLE 14-3. Techniques of Physical Examination

Inspection

Inspection is the skill of seeking physical, bodily signs by observing the client. Accurate inspection depends on the knowledge of the examiner, the "trained eye." General inspection refers to observation of the body as a whole, and in local inspection the examiner focuses on a single anatomic region. Inspection is sometimes aided by the use of tools such as a flashlight, tongue depressor, otoscope, or speculum.

Palpation

Palpation is the act of feeling with the hands through the sense of touch to determine temperature, texture, vibration, position, size, shape, movement, and location of skin surfaces, organs, or masses. The fingers, palms, or backs of the hands are used, depending on the type of palpation being done. Nurses learn to perform four types of palpation: light, deep, ballottement, and fluid wave.

Percussion

Percussion is a method of examination in which the surface of the body is struck in a rapid tapping motion to emit sound vibrations that vary in quality with the density of the underlying tissue. The vibration is both felt and heard by the examiner. Percussion is used to determine the borders of various organs, detect the collection of fluid or air in body spaces, and check for tissue tenderness.

Auscultation

Auscultation is the act of listening with a stethoscope to hear body sounds and obtain physical signs. Nurses use a stethoscope to listen to sounds emanating from the flow of blood through the heart and blood vessels, and to the flow of air through the lungs and gastrointestinal tract.

planned deliberate communication techniques assist in building a trusting nurse-patient relationship. Setting the tone and ensuring this type of professional relationship allow for the nurse to be recognized as a reliable and credible resource for the client. This, in turn, strongly influences the ability of the nurse to be successful in accomplishing the remaining steps of the nursing process.

Last but not least, a final and critical component of assessment is documentation of the data in the client health record. Documentation has five purposes: establishing a mechanism for communication, facilitating the delivery of quality care, providing a mechanism for evaluating care, establishing a permanent legal record, and providing a source of data for research (Iyer, Taptich, & Bernocchi-Losey, 1995). The data-collection tool may be a paper format or it may be computerized. In most instances, these forms become part of the legal medical record and it is important that they provide a crystal clear description of the relevant data. New assessment data are added over time, and ideally, the record re-

flects an ever-changing and up-to-date picture of the client's health status at any given time.

NURSING DIAGNOSIS

Once the client database has been established, the nurse draws from it nursing diagnoses, the second phase of the nursing process. At this point, assessment data are organized, synthesized, compared, and analyzed. A **nursing diagnosis** is a statement the nurse makes about an actual or potential nursing care need of a client. Nursing diagnosis is both a process and a product—the process being *to diagnose* or the act of *diagnosing,* and the product referring to the final statement of the nursing diagnosis. With this focus, the diagnostic process is a complex intellectual exercise that draws heavily on the nurse's critical thinking, clinical decision making, and interpersonal skills. The formulation of the nursing diagnosis is the framework for all activities in the next three nursing process steps: planning, implementation, and evaluation.

Historically, the term *"nursing diagnosis"* did not always exist in nursing vocabulary. Instead, the terms "nursing needs" and "nursing problems" were most commonly used before 1973. In 1973 the first national conference on the classification of nursing diagnoses was initiated by Gebbie and Lavin (1975). This conference set the stage for nursing diagnosis to become an accepted term for use by nurses and, in time, to become solidly known as the second step of the nursing process. In 1982 the group of nurses that continued to meet from this first conference organized themselves into the North American Nursing Diagnosis Association, known as **NANDA.** NANDA has met at least annually since that time, and they continually define, classify, and describe nursing diagnoses, using a standardized nomenclature. With each conference they publish the latest list of accepted nursing diagnoses. Although practicing nurses are not obligated to use the exact wording of the NANDA diagnosis list, many health-care institutions and nursing groups promote its usage because it allows for accountability and a common communication.

The diagnostic process begins with data analysis or data processing. The nurse studies the data and begins to classify them, make interpretations, and validate those interpretations. An example of classification is the functional health patterns portrayed in Table 14-2. Using this framework, for example, a home health nurse is reviewing a statement made by her client that "no one really wants to talk to a person who has cancer." After validating this statement with the client, who further stated she "thought her illness made her unattractive as a person," the nurse began to see a pattern emerge in the Self-Concept Functional Health Pattern. Interpreting the data means assigning meaning to it and beginning to identify actual and potential client problems as well as client strengths. Using nursing knowledge and nursing experience, the nurse separates relevant data from irrelevant data, identifies gaps in the data, and looks for patterns. Client data are compared to norms and standards of such things as growth and development, disease-specific behaviors, or expectations (Creasia & Parker, 1991). In the preceding example, had the client been a young teenager, the concern about self-concept would be even greater. Although the cognitive process of interpreting data and making clinical decisions is complex, the nurse develops an ability to think quickly and accurately as she or he draws on knowledge, experience, and familiarity with client situations.

The next step in the diagnostic process is identifying and formulating the nursing diagnostic statement. There are a number of ways to state nursing diagnoses using different systems. One way is according to NANDA guidelines, using the NANDA taxonomy. The NANDA taxonomy is a listing of nine human response patterns that serve as a framework for organizing the diagnoses (NANDA, 1992). These nine patterns reflect how individuals interact with the environment and respond to particular states of health and illness. Table 14–4 lists these patterns with examples of human responses correlating to each pattern. When NANDA publishes their updated list of nursing diagnoses periodically, they are grouped under these nine classifications as well as alphabetically.

Using this taxonomy, the nursing diagnosis is formulated by two statements joined by the term "related to." The first statement reflects a human response, such as a feeling of pain (pattern nine of the taxonomy), and the second statement reflects factors that contribute to the presence of that response, such as a brain injury. Using these two examples, the nursing diagnosis would be *pain related to burn injury*. A number of helpful reference books are devoted to nursing diagnosis and list NANDA diagnoses in easy to read and find formats (see Bibliography).

A similar method to use as a guide in writing a nursing diagnosis is known as the **PES format** (P = problem, E = etiology, S = signs and symptoms). The problem is a clear description of the client's actual or potential health status or problem. It depicts the client's condition and helps establish a diagnostic category.

TABLE 14–4. NANDA (1992) Taxonomy of Human Response Patterns for Nursing Diagnoses

Pattern 1—Exchanging	Involves mutual giving and receiving, e.g., fluid exchange
Pattern 2—Communicating	Involves sending verbal messages
Pattern 3—Relating	Involves establishing bonds, e.g., social exchange, parenting roles, and relationships
Pattern 4—Valuing	Involves assigning worth, e.g., belief patterns, spirituality
Pattern 5—Choosing	Involves setting alternatives, e.g., coping mechanisms, decision making
Pattern 6—Moving	Involves activity, e.g., physical mobility, daily activities
Pattern 7—Perceiving	Involves receiving and comprehending information, e.g., self-concept
Pattern 8—Knowing	Involves comprehending knowledge, e.g., exhibiting understanding
Pattern 9—Feeling	Involves subjective awareness of information, e.g., pain, anxiety

> *P   Example of problem:* the client has an ineffective breathing problem.

The etiology of the problem identifies any environmental, sociological, spiritual, psychological, or physiologic factors related to or the probable cause of the problem.

> *E   Example of etiology:* the client has an incision on her chest wall that causes painful breathing.

The signs and symptoms include those objective and subjective factors that define characteristics of the problem or provide supportive evidence that a pattern exists.

> *S   Example of signs and symptoms:* the client takes frequent, shallow breaths and has rales in both lungs. She states "breathing hurts."

When diagnoses using the PES format, the problem and etiology are also connected by the phrase "related to." Thus, *ineffectual breathing pattern related to surgical incision on chest wall* would be a proper nursing diagnosis in this case.

PLANNING

Planning, as the third step of the nursing process, is directed toward identifying nursing actions or nursing interventions required to prevent, reduce, or eliminate the nursing diagnoses identified during the diagnostic phase. Specifically, planning includes priority setting of the nursing diagnoses, identifying client goals and objectives, and selecting action strategies with defined outcome criteria. The planning stage ends with the completion of the written nursing care plan, often characterized as the blueprint for action.

There are a number of ways to set priorities among multiple nursing diagnoses. The first task is to identify the most important problem that needs to be resolved and rank any others below it as high, medium, and low. The nurse's clinical judgment in this task is influenced by the acuity of the situation (e.g., life-threatening events), preventive factors (e.g., stabilizing a potentially fractured limb), individual client wishes regarding priority (e.g., take care of my pain first), and a host of other factors related to time, space, availability of resources, and environmental forces. Theoretical frameworks such as Maslow's Hierarchy of Needs (Maslow, 1970) can also be helpful in setting priorities. Using this particular framework, a nurse working with a young single-parent family may need to place financial assistance, child care, and employment concerns in a higher priority than concerns about chronic colds, obesity, and immunizations. After receiving counseling and nurse-initiated referrals to social services and other community resources, the family may later be able to devote a higher priority to nutritional planning and clinic visits. Because priorities can constantly change as the client's health status changes, the task of setting priorities is dynamic and challenges the nurse to reassess and reorder the priorities as necessary.

Establishing client goals and objectives related to each nursing diagnosis is the next component of the planning phase. **Client goals** are broad guidelines that direct the overall action strategies that will be necessary to carry out the nursing interventions in the implementation phase. Goals communicate the purpose of the nursing care plan to other caregivers and assist the client in understanding and feeling a sense of achievement as goals are met. Goals can be long-term or short-term. **Long-term goals** direct nursing care over time and are broader than short-term goals. In the hospital setting, long-term goals are those goals that may not be achieved before discharge and will most likely require continued attention in the future, and **short-term goals** are those achieved more quickly, perhaps as precursors to long-term goals or facilitating movement to another level of care (Doenges & Moorhouse, 1992). Short-term goals are particularly applicable to acute care or unstable and rapidly changing client's conditions. An example of a long-term goal is "client maintains body weight within suggested range," and an example of a short-term goal is "client demonstrates the correct method for crutch walking within 72 hours."

After goals are formed, the next step in planning care is to state desired outcomes in specific and measurable terms. These outcomes can be stated as behavioral objectives and listed under each client goal, as appropriate. A **behavioral objective** measures the client's progress and describes desirable, observable behaviors (Billings, Jeffries, & Kammer, 1989). Following is an example of a behavioral objective: "the client will verbalize four side effects of diuretics." In general, there is at least one goal for every nursing diagnosis, and several behavioral objectives under each goal. Further, outcome criteria may be formulated as separate statements at this time. **Outcome criteria** are written, measurable standards with time frames used to determine the client's response to nursing interventions. An example is "the client is able to correctly perform injection technique within 48 hours of instruction." They are developed in the planning phase and used specifically during the evaluation phase of the nursing process. Kozier, Erb, and Blais (1995) offer a helpful hint regarding writing outcome criteria. They suggest the nurse needs to ask two questions: (1) How will the client look or behave if the desired goal is reached?, and (2) What must the client do and how well must the client do it before the goal is attained? Table 14–5 illustrates a nursing diagnosis example showing how client goals and behavioral objectives proceed through the writing of outcome criteria. Formats for stating client goals, client objectives, and outcome criteria vary. It is possible, for example, to just state client goals with outcome criteria attached. Using the example in Table 14–5, the

TABLE 14–5. Example of a Nursing Care Plan Entry: Relationship of Nursing Diagnosis, Goals, Objectives, and Outcome Criteria

Nursing diagnosis	Sleep deprivation is related to hospitalization.
Client goal	Client will reestablish normal sleeping pattern.
Behavioral objectives	Client sleeps 6 hr undisturbed within 24 hr.
	Client will resume afternoon nap and usual sleep pattern within 48 hr.
Outcome criteria	Client is sleeping 6 to 8 hr without prolonged periods of wakening.
	Client states he or she has resumed normal nighttime sleeping pattern along with normal afternoon nap routine.

client goal could be phrased as "Client will reestablish normal sleeping pattern as evidenced by (a) uninterrupted sleeping for 6 hours attained within a 24-hour period, and (b) a resumption of normal sleeping pattern within 48 hours."

Important points to remember, regardless of terminology or format, are to state desired outcomes in behavioral terms, differentiate clearly between client behaviors and nursing behaviors, and attach an expected time of achievement to each outcome. Differentiating between client behaviors and nursing behaviors is becoming increasingly important as hospital stays are shorter and more nursing care takes place in the home setting. Clients at home are often taught how to carry out procedures that would be done exclusively by nurses in the hospital. Generally, nursing behaviors are endeavors by the nurse to assist the client in performing activities for himself or herself, or to teach, counsel, or support.

The format of the **nursing care plan** should flow from the goals identified for each nursing diagnosis. Care plan formats are usually tailored to fit an individual health-care institution and can be a paper copy kept in a chart or kardex or be stored in a computer and used online. Customarily, columns or "boxes" have header labels for *Nursing Diagnosis, Goals, Objectives, Outcome Criteria,* and *Nursing Interventions.* It is helpful to complete the nursing care plan as each task in the planning phase is decided on. In this way, the goals, objectives, and outcome criteria can be visualized to facilitate choosing the nursing interventions.

Nursing actions are strategies designed to assist the client in achieving the behavioral objectives and specified outcomes related to each nursing diagnosis. Examples of nursing actions are administering a medication, teaching a client to use crutches, and reassuring a client preoperatively. For the purposes of this chapter, the terms "nursing intervention" and "nursing actions" are used interchangeably. The process of developing individualized actions or interventions is a critical responsibility of the professional nurse and involves scientifically based critical thinking, hypothesizing situations, and collaborating with others on the health-care team. Factors nurses consider when choosing nursing actions include the following:

- The scientific knowledge base supporting the intervention and current nursing research findings
- Nursing standards related to the intervention
- Examination of alternative nursing actions
- Comparison of chosen intervention to standard care plan

- Consultation with client, client's family, and other members of the health-care team
- Current literature regarding the chosen intervention
- Consideration of human variables such as age, sex, sociocultural background, level of growth, and development

Additionally, Atkinson and Murray (1990) have suggested the following questions as helpful in planning interventions:

- Are the nursing actions safe for the client?
- Are the nursing actions congruent with other therapies?
- Are the nursing actions selected *most likely* to develop the behavior described in the outcome statement?
- Are the nursing actions realistic for the client, the ability and availability of staff, and available equipment?
- Are the nursing actions agreeable to the client and compatible with personal beliefs, values, and goals?

Another valuable resource that specifically assists nurses in selecting and documenting nursing actions during the planning phase is the **Nursing Interventions Classification (NIC).** NIC is a comprehensive listing of standardized nursing interventions developed by a nursing research team at the University of Iowa College of Nursing. The NIC researchers have systematically categorized, standardized, and described everything nurses do involving the care of clients. NIC interventions describe both direct and indirect nursing activities and are organized in a taxonomy that can be indexed alphabetically or by classes, in six domains. Contrasted with NANDA, which classifies nursing diagnoses, NIC identifies and classifies nursing behaviors and activities. NIC interventions are the result of the nursing diagnosis. The latest edition of the NIC textbook contains more than 400 uniquely coded nursing interventions that have been linked to NANDA nursing diagnoses (McCloskey & Bulechek, 1996).

NIC entries include the full range of nursing interventions, from general practice and specialty areas, and interventions include physiologic and psychosocial, illness treatment and prevention, and health promotion. In NIC, each nursing intervention has three parts: (1) the name or "label," (2) the definition of the concept, and (3) actions or defining activities that must be performed to implement the activity. A reference list of related readings is also provided for each intervention. A unique number code is assigned to each intervention and linked to specific NANDA diagnoses. The NIC interventions do not have to be used with NANDA diagnoses, but for nurses who use NANDA, the linkage list facilitates the use of NIC.

An example of the use of an NIC intervention label can be illustrated using the nursing care plan example in Table 14–5. The nursing diagnosis, sleep deprivation related to hospitalization, can be linked to the NIC taxonomy in the following way:

Step I   Review the NIC taxonomy and determine the general area of *sleep* comes under Domain 1: Physiological—Basic. Under Domain 1, sleep is further specified under Class F: Self-Care: Facilitation.

Step II   Continue filtering down through the NIC taxonomy and review the interventions listed under Self-Care: Facilitation. *Sleep Enhancement* is listed as Intervention #1850.

Step III   Go the Intervention #1850. The label for this intervention is *Sleep Enhancement* and the definition is stated as "facilitation of regular sleep/wake cycles." There are 24 activities listed for this intervention and six references.

For an even quicker way to link NANDA diagnoses and NIC interventions, refer to the second edition of *Iowa Intervention Project: Nursing Interventions Classification (NIC)* (McCloskey & Bulechek, 1996, pp. 605–706). Appendix B identifies the NIC interventions according to the NANDA-approved list of nursing diagnoses for 1996. In the preceding example of sleep deprivation, the corresponding NANDA nursing diagnosis is *Sleep Pattern Disturbance*. Looking at the text under this diagnosis, there are several interventions for problem resolution, including *Sleep Enhancement*. This, in turn, refers the reader to Intervention #1850, as well as others to consider.

The NIC project is ongoing, and one of its activities involves working with various nursing specialty groups to make certain all nursing activities are included and any new interventions are categorized and added to the list. The NIC taxonomy and a complete listing of the current NIC intervention labels are provided in Appendix B.

IMPLEMENTATION

Implementation begins on completion of the nursing care plan. The purpose of implementation is to carry out the nursing actions specified in the care plan, and the goal is to achieve the expected outcomes. **Implementation** is the actual delivery of the nursing care phase of the nursing process. The client is always the recipient of nursing care activities, but these activities may be client-focused or provider-focused. Client-focused activities are those in which the client performs alone or with minimal help, and provider-focused actions are those carried out by the nurse on the client's behalf. The exact course of action necessarily depends on the complexity and technical nature of the nursing care plan, the time and environmental limitations of the nurse, and the overall ability and condition of the client. Examples of client-focused activities are active exercises done at specified intervals, a client keeping a diary of foods eaten, or a sitz bath taken at home twice a day. Examples of provider-focused activities are administration of intravenous medications, urethral catheterization, and passive exercises done by a nurse or physical therapist.

The nursing care plan gives direction to nursing actions, but the one-to-one interface between nurse and client may pose new or changed directions. For example, new priorities may emerge at this time, warranting reassessing and replanning. The focus here is on action, and this action is intellectual, interpersonal, and technical in nature (Yura & Walsh, 1988). An occupational health nurse may plan a caring activity with a recently widowed employee by scheduling a series of counseling sessions on a weekly basis. During implementation of one of these sessions, the nurse assesses signs of suicidal behavior. She immediately rearranges her plan of action, seeks more data, and intervenes appropriately to a crisis situation. The importance of nursing judgment comes into play as the nurse figures out what to do with data, what additional data are needed, what the data mean, and whether a new diagnosis is evident, warranting a new plan of action (Yura & Walsh, 1988).

Types of nursing actions have been described by Kozier, Erb, Blais, and Wilkinson (1995) as independent, dependent, and collaborative. An independent nursing action or strategy is an activity that the nurse undertakes based on nursing knowledge and skills. The nurse is fully accountable for both deciding on and initiating the independent action. Dependent nursing actions stem from physicians orders and are activities that are under a physician's supervision or based on a written routine. Dependent nursing actions are usually related to the medical diagnosis, and the nurse carries out related nursing activities as appropriate. Collaborative nursing actions involve other members of the health-care team and are sometimes referred to as interdependent nursing actions. Interdependent actions are selected after consulting with another health professional, such as a physician or physical therapist.

One common example of this is when the nurse carries out orders written by a physician in a protocol. The protocol establishes what the nurse may do, and under what circumstances it may be done. This type of order permits a nurse to take immediate action in a circumstance without consulting a physician (Chitty, 1993).

Following the implementation of nursing actions, it is imperative that a description of what was done be documented in the client record (medical record, hospital chart, etc.). Numerous formats and types of recordkeeping vary among health-care settings. It is important that documentation of nursing actions reflect the terminology found in the nursing care plan and give clear, accurate accounts of care related to client goals and outcome criteria.

EVALUATION

The final step in the sequence of the nursing process is evaluation. **Evaluation** involves two related areas: reviewing goal achievement and reassessing nursing actions. Reviewing goal achievement requires taking a look at actual client outcomes and determining how well they match the expected outcomes written in the nursing care plan. This type of evaluation is ensured when the steps of the nursing process are well documented and planned; that is, the specification of client goals and outcome criteria serve as a built-in evaluation tool. The plan of care, specifically the nursing actions, are evaluated periodically to update and make certain the plan reflects the current status of the client. The ongoing nursing care must reflect the changing health status of the client, any medical treatment changes, environmental fluctuations, and the overall changing needs of the client and family (Atkinson & Murray, 1990).

When looking at specific client goals and the attached desired outcomes, the nurse first validates the outcomes with the client, if possible. A school health nurse has planned care for a group of junior high students who are learning to develop healthy eating behaviors. To assist in evaluating the stated outcomes (e.g., being able to identify foods low in fat, listing snack alternatives, describing a balanced diet), the nurse administers a written questionnaire addressing these topics. In this way, the outcomes can be evaluated for each client. Then, through direct observation of the client, examination of relevant written reports, and possible consultation with other health-care givers, the nurse makes a judgment about the stated desired outcomes and documents this in the client record. In the preceding example, the school nurse may further evaluate outcomes by talking to the families of the clients and directly observing the clients for behavioral changes. Documentation reflects whether the goal was met fully, partially, or not at all. Additionally, the documentation includes a reference to any timespan stated in the outcome criteria and describes the client behavior in terms of how it is referred to in the goal statement.

Evaluating the plan of care provides a clear illustration of the cyclical nature of the nursing process. At this time, the client database is updated and the nursing diagnoses are reviewed for relevancy and accuracy. As goals are met and problems solved, some of the nursing diagnoses can be removed or their focus changed. Those goals that are not met are reviewed, and a new data-collection effort is begun. The plan of care is then revised as necessary.

KEY POINTS

- The term "nursing process" became well accepted by the profession in the years following the 1967 publishing of *The Nursing Process* by Yura and Walsh. Initially, it consisted of four steps (assessment, planning, implementation, and evaluation), and during the early 1980s, nursing diagnosis became accepted as the second step.
- The nursing process, an organized systematic framework for the delivery of nursing care, has become an important tool beyond the provision of a sound methodology to guide nurses as they work with clients. It has influenced, and greatly improved, the documentation, researchability, accountability, and communication about what nurses do, how they do it, and what results are achieved. In the current climate of expanded roles in nursing, high technology in health care, and vast reform efforts to contain costs, the nursing process remains an important constant in the nursing profession.

- Assessment is the first step of the nursing process, and it is focused on gathering relevant health-care information about the client. This information is organized into a client database that serves as a primary resource for understanding the client's health status and formulating nursing diagnoses.

- The nursing history and the physical examination are typical tools nurses use to gather client data for assessment purposes. The nursing history is conducted by either a formal interview process or an informal questioning during care giving. The physical examination is conducted by the nurse as she or he uses the techniques of observation, percussion, auscultation, and palpation.

- This database is composed of all the information gathered about the client during assessment. It includes information that comes directly from the client, from written medical records, and from all other sources.

- In health assessment, the client is considered the primary source of data. These data include direct information the client verbalizes and direct observations and measurements the nurse carries out.

- Sources of client information other than that directly from the client are known as secondary. Examples of secondary data sources are medical records, lab reports, and information derived from family members.

- Objective data are data that can be measured against some standard such as skin temperature, red blood cell count, and pulse rate.

- Subjective data are data that only the client can experience and report to the nurse. Examples are feelings of dizziness, pain, or nausea.

- The health history is a body of client data obtained by the nurse through interviewing and asking the client questions. The history is organized through a format that includes all relevant aspects of the client health status.

- The physical examination is that part of the assessment in which the nurse examines the client and obtains data through inspection, palpation, percussion, and auscultation.

- A nursing diagnosis is a statement the nurse makes about a client's actual or potential nursing care need. The diagnosis is made by analyzing the assessment data and making clinical decisions about the meaning and interrelationships of the data.

- The North American Nursing Diagnosis Association (NANDA) is an organization devoted to the development of a taxonomy of nursing diagnoses. NANDA works continually to develop new diagnoses and refine and update the currently acceptable diagnoses. A NANDA-accepted list of nursing diagnoses is published about every 2 years.

- PES stands for problem, etiology, and signs and symptoms. It is a method to guide the nurse in writing a nursing diagnosis.

- The Nursing Intervention Classification (NIC) is a comprehensive listing of standardized nursing interventions organized into a taxonomy, indexed both alphabetically and by specific domains and classes. NIC is an ongoing project by nurse researchers that attempts to include all nursing behaviors and activities that nurses can describe. NIC interventions can be linked to NANDA diagnoses, to facilitate documentation and accountability for nursing.

- The focus of planning is on identifying those nursing actions necessary to resolve or eliminate the nursing diagnoses. Planning includes writing client goals, behavioral objectives, and outcome criteria. These components are organized into a format called the nursing care plan, which guides the delivery of nursing care.

- Goals are broad guidelines that direct the overall nursing strategies in a nursing care plan.
- A short-term goal is one stated in very specific terms, that can usually be accomplished in a relatively short time. Short-term goals are common in the hospital setting, where the client's health status is continually changing. An example is: *client will demonstrate the correct method for crutch walking within 72 hours.*
- A long-term goal directs nursing care over time, perhaps indefinitely. An example is: *client will continue to maintain body weight within suggested guidelines.*
- A behavioral objective is a suggested measurement of the client's progress, stated in specific behavioral terms that can be clearly described. An example is: *the client will verbalize four side effects of diuretics.*
- Outcome criteria are written, measurable standards with specific timeframes for accomplishment that will determine client response to selected nursing actions. An example is: *client is able to correctly perform injection technique within 48 hours of instruction.*
- The nurse draws on the total nursing knowledge base and uses critical thinking skills in choosing nursing actions. Examples of considerations include research rationale, adherence to nursing standards, safety, looking at other viable options, cultural and age-related variables, and overall client acceptance.
- The nursing care plan is a documented record (computerized or paper copy) that lists the nursing diagnoses along with the goals, objectives, and outcome criteria attached to each diagnosis. This document specifies and communicates what the individualized plan of care is for the client.
- The nursing actions specified in the nursing care plan are carried out during implementation. Nursing actions may be client-focused or nurse-focused, depending on the task at hand and the ability or desire of the client to be involved in the activity.
- Nursing actions can be classified as independent (based solely on nursing knowledge and undertaken with nursing authority), dependent (stemming from physician's orders), and collaborative (based on consultation with another health provider and decided on mutually).
- Evaluation involves reviewing goal achievement and reassessing nursing actions. Actual client outcomes are identified through observation and talking with the client and other providers. These outcomes are compared to the expected outcomes written as outcome criteria in the nursing care plan.

CHAPTER EXERCISES

1. Choose any 4 of the 11 categories in Gordon's functional health patterns and propose several questions under each that could be used to elicit history data from a client. Then try out these questions on a friend or classmate and gather some data. Next, evaluate the quantity and quality of data you were able to obtain. Did your questions give you useful information? Why or why not?

2. Pick a health-care institution, preferably one you are familiar with such as your workplace. Observe how the nursing process is used in this institution.

Do the nursing personnel seem knowledgeable about it? How can you tell? What suggestions do you have for better utilization of the nursing process in this institution?

3. Interview a friend or classmate about a health problem he or she has recently experienced. This may involve a recent visit to a physician, clinic, or other health facility, or it may be a perceived problem that has not been evaluated by a health provider. Attempt to formulate nursing diagnoses from the data you receive, and write them according to the PES format, using NANDA terminology.

4. Mr. Sebastian was referred to the Mainstreet Nursing Agency by Dr. Nocando. The physician had diagnosed Mr. Sebastian with diabetes type II and requested the nursing agency to (1) instruct the client on measuring his blood sugar (fasting A.M. and 2 hours post evening meal), (2) talk with him about limiting sweets and carbohydrates, (3) help him establish a daily exercise regimen, and (4) educate him in general about his condition. Mr. Sebastian is relatively healthy other than his diabetes, and is not overweight. He is 68 years old and lives by himself. With this information, construct a nursing plan for the agency nurse to use. Include nursing diagnoses, goals, behavioral objectives, and outcome criteria.

REFERENCES

American Nurses' Association (1980). *Nursing: a social policy statement.* (Publication No. NP-63 35M). Kansas City: ANA, p. 9.

Atkinson, L. D., & Murray, M. E. (1990). *Understanding the nursing process* (4th ed.). New York: Pergammon Press.

Barkauskas, V. H., Stoltenberg-Allen, K., Baumann, L. C., & Darling-Fisher, C. (1994). *Health and physical assessment.* St. Louis: Mosby-Yearbook.

Billings, D. M., Jeffries, P. R., & Kammer, C. H. (1989). *RN to BSN review and challenge tests.* Philadelphia: Lippincott.

Carpenito, J. C. (1991). *Nursing care plans and documentation.* Philadelphia: Lippincott.

Chitty, K. K. (1993). *Professional nursing concepts and challenges.* Philadelphia: Saunders.

Creasia, J. L., & Parker, B. (1991). *Conceptual foundations of professional practice.* St. Louis: Mosby-Year Book.

Doenges, M. E., & Moorhouse, M. F. (1992). *Application of nursing process and nursing diagnosis, an interactive text.* Philadelphia: Davis.

Gebbie, K., & Lavin, M. A. (Eds.). (1975). *Classification of nursing diagnosis: Proceedings of the first national conference.* St. Louis: Mosby.

Gordon, M. (1991). *Manual of nursing diagnosis.* St. Louis: Mosby-Year Book.

Hall, L. (1955). Quality of nursing care. Address at meeting of Department of Baccalaureate and Higher Degree Programs, New Jersey League for Nursing, Feb. 7, 1955, Seton Hall University, Newark, NJ.

Holloway, N. M. (1993). *Medical surgical care planning.* (2nd ed.). Springhouse, PA: Springhouse Corp.

Iyer, P. W., Taptich, B. J., & Bernocchi-Losey, D. (1995). *Nursing process and nursing diagnosis* (3rd ed.). Philadelphia: Saunders.

Johnson, D. E. (1959). Philosophy of nursing. *Nursing Outlook, 7,* 198.

Koldjeski, D. A. (1993). A restructured nursing process model. *Nurse Educator, 18* (4), 33–38.

Kozier, B., Erb, G., Blais, K., & Wilkinson, J. M. (1995). *Fundamentals of nursing: Concepts, process and practice* (5th ed.). Redwood City, CA: Addison-Wesley Nursing.

Maslow, A. (1970). *Motivation and personality* (2nd ed.). New York: Harper & Row.

McCloskey, J. C., & Buleche, G. M. (Eds.). (1996). *Nursing interventions classification (NIC)* (2nd ed.). St. Louis: Mosby-Year Book.

NANDA (1992). *NANDA Nursing diagnosis: Definitions and Classification 1992–1993* (pp. 6–9). Philadelphia: North American Nursing Diagnosis Association.

Orlando, I. J. (1961). *The dynamic nurse-patient relationship.* New York: Putnam.

Peplau, H. (1952). *Interpersonal relations in nursing.* New York: Putnam.

Riehl, J. P. & Roy, C. (1974). *Conceptual models for nursing practice.* New York: Appleton-Century-Crofts.

Spradley, B. W., & Allender, J. A. (1996). *Community health nursing: Concepts and practice* (4th ed.). Philadelphia: Lippincott-Raven.

Yura, H., & Walsh, M. (1967). *The nursing process.* Norwalk, CT: Appleton-Century-Crofts.

Yura, H., & Walsh, M. (1988). *The nursing process.* (5th ed.). Norwalk, CT: Appleton Lange.

BIBLIOGRAPHY

Ackley, B. J., & Ladwig, G. (1995). *Nursing diagnosis handbook: A guide to planning care* (2nd ed.). St. Louis: Mosby-Year Book.

Carpenito, L. J. (1995). *Nursing care plans and documentation, nursing diagnoses and collaborative problems* (2nd ed.). Philadelphia: Lippincott.

Carpenito, L. J. (1995). *Nursing diagnosis, application to clinical practice.* Philadelphia: Lippincott.

Morton, P. G. (1993). *Health assessment in nursing* (2nd ed.). Philadelphia: Davis.

Nursing Intervention Classification (NIC) List Serve. (The NIC List Serve is an electronic message system to communicate with others about NIC. Readers who have access to the Internet and want to join the NIC List Serve can send an e-mail message to william-donahue@iowa.edu.)

Chapter 15

MANAGING AND PROVIDING CARE

Vicki L. Buchda

CHAPTER OBJECTIVES

On completion of
this chapter, the reader
will be able to:

1. Discuss the issues impacting on health-care planning and providing for clients and groups of clients.
2. Describe the evolution and current concerns of nursing care delivery systems.
3. Contrast the different models of nursing care delivery.
4. Design a critical pathway for a client with a selected health problem.
5. Describe the documentation system and the taxonomy needed for selected care delivery systems.

KEY TERMS

Value
Cost-effective
Outcomes of Care
Differentiated Nursing
  Practice

Team Nursing
Primary Nursing
Case Management
Managed Care

Care Map
Nursing Minimum Data
  Set

As health care has experienced rapid and dramatic changes in financing, reimbursement, technology, and lengths of stay and increased numbers of aging and chronically ill individuals over the past several years, care management and delivery systems have evolved. Because nurses have provided most of the client care in recent history, nursing care delivery is frequently targeted for redesign and restructuring to meet these demands. Redesign and restructuring can have positive impacts on quality, outcomes, and cost-effectiveness. This is possible if the care to be delivered is clearly articulated and matched with an appropriate delivery system.

ORGANIZING CARE

Driving Forces

Although economics drives health-care reform, and therefore has the greatest impact on how American health care is organized and delivered (Porter-O'Grady & Wilson, 1995), the movement from the industrial age, with its Newtonian physics and linear relationships, to quantum mechanics has had major implications as well. In this new age, the focus is once again on the whole, not just the parts, and integration is a key component. Work is also viewed differently, with less emphasis on process and a greater focus on outcomes. These factors influence the kind of care that is delivered, and nursing care delivery models define how care is delivered.

Ultimately, care is planned, organized, and provided to meet the needs of clients, nurses, and the department or organization. Several important themes emerge in defining the kind of care needed in the new age: client-focused, cost-effective, and outcome-oriented.

CLIENT-FOCUSED CARE

As providers of care, nurses recognize the need to shape a system focused on and organized around consumers: the client, the family, and the community (Smith, 1994). This is a shift in philosophy from the past resulting, in part, from the shift from the industrial model to the new age. This change is influencing many aspects of our care delivery systems, beginning with nurses' approaches to clients and their care. With clients as the center of all activities, the focus is no longer on the nursing needs of a client, but on client needs. This is a fundamental change for nurses who traditionally saw themselves

as the center of all client care, with care from other disciplines providing assistance. For example, nurses were previously socialized to believe that the physical therapist walked a client for nursing, not as a contribution to client care. Today an interdisciplinary plan of care is developed and implemented for each client, with goals and interventions mutually agreed on by the care providers and client.

This shift in values not only drives how the client is viewed, but also influences department organization. Historically, hospital structure services were organized around functions for the convenience of the staff. In the new client-focused paradigm, it is logical to organize and deliver care based on the client's needs. Based on this philosophy, some organizations are focusing all care and services on the client as much as possible. As a result, some models are restructuring and redesigning roles so that, for example, the admitting department admits the client at the bedside. Some departments may be totally decentralized. The housekeeping department may be eliminated, with the work being completed by personnel who now report to nurses. These are a few examples of how the shift in focus from provider needs to the client is changing the organization of care.

VALUE

A second theme that is driving how care is organized is value. Consumers and payers are demanding value in health care. In health care, **value** includes two essential components: cost and quality (Arford & Allred, 1995). Understanding this concept is vital because "survival in a reformed healthcare industry will require nurses to articulate their value—i.e., nurses must demonstrate how they contribute to improving the quality of desired patient outcomes and reducing costs" (Arford & Allred, 1995, p. 64). Nurses are in a position to demonstrate their contribution to client outcomes, and plan and deliver cost-effective care.

Accomplishing this involves, in part, matching needs with resources, so that the most cost-effective care provider is delivering the care. **Cost-effective** analysis examines the relationship between the cost to provide the service and the outcomes (Arford & Allred, 1995). Less expensive substitutes for professional nurses (referred to by some as "cheaper doers") therefore may not be cost-effective if outcomes are poor. However, using professional nurses to perform tasks that could be delegated is not cost-effective either. Decisions about who should do what are best based on the knowledge and skill sets needed to deliver the care.

OUTCOMES

One of the greatest and most important challenges in all of these shifts is to clearly demonstrate the contributions of nurses to **outcomes of care.** This is important because nurses are an integral part of the health-care system, but value can be demonstrated only by defining the link between the quality of nursing care delivered and client outcomes. In addition, only by understanding the link between nursing care and client outcomes can we measure the impact of changing care delivery systems (American Nurses Association, 1995). Finally, nurses need to define their contributions in the complex care delivered to ensure that their contributions will continue to be recognized as care becomes even more highly integrated with other interdisciplinary team members.

This poses some challenges for nurses who have followed routines for years. Taking and documenting vital signs, for example, is a firmly entrenched practice usually based on routine. Nurses are being asked to examine such practices for their contribution to the outcome. If no link to a positive outcome can be established, the practice should be dropped.

Various studies and projects are being conducted to explore nurses' contributions to the outcomes of care. Some of the challenges to demonstrating nurses' contributions to the outcomes of care are the lack of national databases or agreement on the language to be used. This is further discussed in the section on taxonomies.

A project reported recently in a publication by the American Nurses Association (ANA) explored many of the links between nursing care and client outcomes in acute care by identifying quality indicators (ANA, 1995). This "report card"–type study identified 21 nursing quality indicators that have strong conceptual ties to quality nursing care. Although the study could not link all of the indicators to quality nursing care, the report emphasized the importance of such report cards and identified areas, through a review of current research and literature, where nursing is making a contribution. A review of other similar report card–type studies is also included in the publication (ANA, 1995, Appendix A). The report serves as a springboard for other studies, including a similar project in the state of Arizona (AzNA, 1996).

Roles and Role Delineation

PROFESSIONAL NURSING IN THE CURRENT SYSTEM

In further exploring the organization of care, the role of professional nurses must be considered. The importance of understanding the contributions nurses make to client care outcomes has already been emphasized, but it leads to the question of what nurses really do in organizing and providing care.

McCloskey (1995) describes two roles for the nurse: provider of care and manager of the care environment. As the provider of care, nurses deliver direct and indirect care on two levels: for individual clients and for groups of clients. Direct care is defined as those interventions "performed through interaction with the patient(s)" (McCloskey, 1995). Indirect care is performed on behalf of the client to support the direct care interventions. An example of indirect care is communication with other interdisciplinary team members.

In addition to being the provider of care, nurses have several levels of management responsibilities. At the client care level, nurses' care management responsibilities include organizing, directing, and coordinating the care of each client and groups of clients. Nurses are ultimately accountable for the overall outcomes of care. The responsibility for matching needs with resources, as described earlier, is another aspect of this role. This may include talking with payers, including insurance companies, and negotiating for client services.

In addition, nurses have management responsibilities for the client care unit or department in which care is planned, organized, integrated, and delivered to groups of clients. This includes delegating and supervising other personnel and unit operations, such as staffing and scheduling. This aspect of the management role varies with the delivery system, but the trend is toward flatter organizations, with direct care providers assuming more of the traditional management roles in the department.

INTERDISCIPLINARY CARE DELIVERY

In the current system, nurses work closely with other interdisciplinary team members, such as social workers, rehabilitation services, and nutrition services. The contributions of each of these highly skilled team members is coordinated and integrated into the plan of care for clients by professional nurses. In the future, as new-age ideas are implemented in practice, care will be delivered to clients by groups of care providers working in highly integrated teams. Cost and quality will continue to be emphasized, and the team will be held accountable for the outcomes of the care delivered.

Interdisciplinary teams, working collaboratively to deliver care, support cost-effectiveness because the right person with the right skills is delivering the service. This is an important step in matching needs with resources. Many current redesign and restructuring programs are taking other steps to evaluate both the care a client receives and the functions that need to occur for the unit to operate and to add other workers to perform tasks that do not have to be performed by a nurse. Depending on the care delivery model, these workers may be other nurses, nursing assistants, or unlicensed personnel. Historically, nursing has delegated certain tasks, such as the housekeeping functions of bedmaking and emptying trash. In the current system, however, some of these tasks are still being performed by nurses, for various reasons. This use of nursing time is not efficient or cost-effective.

The development of highly integrated interdisciplinary teams is necessary, but not without problems. Some of the issues that need to be addressed are defining contributions to care, territoriality, and the shift in power.

As discussed earlier, defining the contributions to care by the various providers is one of the greatest challenges facing health-care providers. It is an important step in the process, however, because the setting (e.g., intensive care unit, home health, or the whole communities) and the needs of the clients determine the logical providers and coordinator of care. This may lead to concerns about turf; for example, nurses may give up some responsibilities to social workers, and physicians to nurses. Some may view this shift in accountability and power as threatening, but ultimately the integration will strengthen the team.

INTRADISCIPLINARY ROLE DELINEATION

The concepts of matching needs with resources, and care providers with the knowledge and skills that best match client needs, may seem simplistic. The examples provided differentiate between nurses and other professionals, and between nurses and support personnel such as nurses' assistants and housekeepers. Another step in the drive to articulate contributions to care and cost-effectiveness, however, is requiring nursing to closely examine its own knowledge and skill sets.

In the current environment, most nurses are employed by hospitals, and most job descriptions for registered nurses define one set of performance expectations to fulfill the role, regardless of educational preparation. With these blended job descriptions, some nurses' knowledge and skills are being underutilized and others are being asked to perform at higher levels than they were prepared for. To be seen as efficient and cost-effective in the future, nursing needs differentiated nursing competencies, and nurses can no longer be viewed as "all things to all people." A joint report by the American Association of Colleges of Nursing (AACN), American Organization of Nurse Executives (AONE), and National Organization for Associate Degree Nursing details current efforts in differentiated practice and offers recommendations for the future (AACN, 1995).

Levels of nursing practice is a concept first introduced by the American Nurses Association (ANA) in 1965, and **differentiated nursing practice** has been a goal of nursing professionals for a decade (AACN, 1995). It was recognized at that time that nurses possess a variety of skill sets, depending on educational preparation and experiential learning, and clients and the profession would benefit from differentiating the practice. The development of models using differentiated practice in care delivery was minimal during the 1980s, because of the nursing shortage. During that critical time resources were funneled into preparing more nurses. More recently, however, many hospitals have developed pure or transitional models (Milton, 1992).

There are two types of differentiated practice: education-based practice, which is delineated according to educational credentials, and assessment-based, which incorporates both education and experiential learning. A major strength of both models is valuing the contributions of all team members, regardless of educational preparation.

One model of differentiated practice that defines roles by educational preparation was reported by Primm (1986). This model defines major and minor components of nursing practice, and these various components are assigned according to the nurses' educational preparation.

Technical nurses care for clients and are responsible for meeting identified care goals in a specified work period and within structured health care settings that provide policies and procedures and nursing experts for consultation and support. In addition to the responsibilities defined for technical nurses, professional nurses care for families and communities from the time of admission to postdischarge, in structured and unstructured settings and in situations that may not have policies and procedures, but require independent nursing decisions (Primm, 1986). In such models, the contributions of all nurses are valued and pave the way for better delineation of outcomes with clearer job descriptions and expectations. Implementing such a model has been shown to increase efficiency and cost-effectiveness because it "places the highest-quality, lowest-cost provider next to the client" (JONA, 1995).

Currently, the most sophisticated model of differentiated practice is at Sioux Valley Hospital, Sioux Falls, South Dakota (AACN, 1995). Roles for nurses with associate degrees, bachelor's degrees, and master's degrees are delineated within a case management model, and cost-effectiveness and quality outcomes have been demonstrated (Koerner & Karpiuk, 1994). In addition, the hospital provides a site for nursing students from BSN and ADN programs to learn differentiated clinical practice in the real world (AACN, 1995).

DELIVERING CARE

Current Concerns of Care Delivery Systems

Nursing care delivery systems are undergoing tremendous restructuring to meet the changing needs of clients, nurses, and the organization. To be effective, the nursing care delivery system must be consistent with the mission, vision, and values of the care providers, the department, and the organization (Kayuha, 1996). The system also works best when it is consistent with the unit or organizational culture (Milton, 1992).

Some of the current concerns of care delivery systems include the content of care, which focuses on client needs, is cost-effective, and is outcome oriented. The care delivery system needs to ensure that needs are appropriately matched to resources, quality care that contributes to the outcome is delivered, and documentation is streamlined to capture the essential elements of care and client outcomes.

A comprehensive model also involves having the right caregivers available to provide care, and is therefore linked to nurse staffing systems. Various acuity systems have been developed and implemented; in efforts to classify or categorize clients by needs to ensure the right caregivers are available. It is beyond the scope of this chapter to discuss staffing and scheduling systems, but these assist in the process of planning and evaluating models of care delivery.

Models of Care Delivery

Care delivery models have evolved through the years to meet the demands and challenges of the health-care arena. Many factors influenced the models of care delivery existing today. This section of-

fers a brief review of generic care delivery models. In-depth discussions of various delivery models are provided in other sources (Mayer, Madden, & Lawrenz, 1990; Nursing Clinics of North America, 1992; Walker, 1991; Walker et al., 1991). Although care delivery models have undergone many changes, their underlying objectives are to "assess the patient, identify the nursing needs of the patient during hospitalization, and provide the nursing care necessary until the patient is discharged" (Lyon, 1993).

CASE METHOD

The case method was one of the earliest models of care delivery. A nurse was assigned to provide complete care for a client or group of clients for a defined period of time, usually 8 hours. Sometimes referred to as private-duty nursing, this method was inefficient because one nurse provided all care to the client (Cohen & Cesta, 1993; Poulin, 1985).

FUNCTIONAL

Functional nursing evolved next, improving on the case method of assignments by using a variety of caregivers to complete the tasks (Cohen & Cesta, 1993). Within this model tasks were allocated, and one nurse gave all medications, another performed all treatments, and other caregivers gave all baths. Although a variety of caregivers participated in client care delivery, this model has been criticized because it emphasizes task completion over client needs, resulting in fragmentation and unmet needs (Thomas & Bond, 1991).

TEAM

Team nursing emerged after World War II, when there was a shortage of nurses and other personnel were recruited to deliver care (Lyon, 1993). In the team model, other health-care workers—some licensed, such as a licensed practical nurse, and some unlicensed, such as aides and orderlies—delivered care under the supervision of a registered nurse. The team was led by a team leader, who delegated the tasks and activities and provided some direct care. Team nursing provided an advantage over functional nursing by providing professional nurses to more clients, increasing continuity of care, and freeing professional nurses from performing nonprofessional tasks (Cohen & Cesta, 1993).

Team nursing has inherent problems, however; it results in fragmented care, complex channels of communication, and shared responsibility with lack of accountability (Manthey, 1980). Care is fragmented by being divided into components delegated to appropriate caregivers, resulting in clients being cared for by at least three people during an 8-hour shift (registered nurse, licensed practical nurse, and nursing assistant) with a total of 24 caregivers in a day. Communication is also complex; the caregivers report to the team leader, who relays the information to the next shift team leader. In some cases, the team leader reports to a charge nurse, who relays the information to another charge nurse, who passes it on to the team leader. The information is subject to interpretation by each person in the chain. Responsibility and accountability are major issues in team nursing. The nursing care plan, for example, is supposed to be completed and updated routinely, usually daily. The team leader has this responsibility, as does the next shift team leader. What is not completed on one shift is completed on the next shift. According to Manthey (1980), shared responsibility equals no responsibility, and activities such as completing care plans are not carried out consistently.

PRIMARY

Primary nursing evolved to meet the needs that were not addressed in the team nursing system. Manthey (1980) described primary nursing as a delivery system designed to "rehumanize" hospital care through decentralized decision making; responsibility for one client's care, 24 hours a day, is allocated to a primary nurse who actually provides the care whenever possible. Because one nurse has the responsibility, accountability, and authority to assess clients needs, develop a plan of care, and evaluate the clients' responses to the plan of care, a therapeutic relationship can be established between the nurse and the client (Mathews & Kamikawa, 1994; Wilkinson, 1994). The primary nursing model recognizes the contributions of various care team members but relies heavily on registered nurses, not only for care planning, but also for delivery of care.

OTHER MODELS

The nursing shortage of the 1980s, the cost of an all-professional staff, and other issues led some hospitals to examine variations on primary nursing. Nurses routinely work 12-hour shifts in some hospitals, which creates an obstacle to implementing primary nursing. One nursing unit changed from team nursing, for many of the reasons already discussed,

to a modified primary nursing delivery system, called Personalized Total Patient Care, to gain some of the benefits of primary nursing with 12-hour shifts (Altman, 1993). Another unit piloted a model called Primary Team Nursing, which incorporated the best features of functional, team, and primary nursing (Hyams-Franklin, Rowe-Gilliespie, Harper, & Johnson, 1993). Many other variations of these models also exist.

Case Management

The forces in health care today have made it necessary to develop care delivery systems that go beyond the industrial model, in which task completion and outputs are emphasized, to integrated systems that include mechanisms to define the links between nursing care and outcomes, facilitating demonstration of cost-effectiveness. In evaluating care delivery systems, many institutions have implemented the case management model because it helps organize care around the client and is in concert with interdisciplinary and intradisciplinary differentiated practice. Because this model addresses many concerns previously identified, it is discussed here is some depth. Entire texts have been written about case management, however, and you are encouraged to refer to these and other sources for further information (Cohen, 1996; Cohen & Cesta, 1993; Powell, 1996).

Case management is not a new concept. Nurses and members of other disciplines have been providing case management for clients for many years. Community public health programs have had case management services since the 1900s (Lyon, 1993). Behavioral health nurses have been using many of the concepts in the community since the 1960s. Case management received more attention from other areas of health care, including acute care settings, when insurance companies began using the model. Now it is one of the most frequently used care models in the country (American Hospital Association, 1990).

Case management is care delivery model focused on the client that promotes continuity and cost-effectiveness, recognizes the contributions of the members of the interdisciplinary team, and allows for differentiation of practice within the nursing profession. There are many definitions of case management. Bower (1992) described case management as a "paradoxically simple yet complex concept" (p. 3). Simply stated, case management refers to "patient focused strategies to coordinate care" (Bower, 1992, p. 2). Case management has also been defined as "an approach that focuses on the coordination, integration, and direct delivery of patient services, and places internal controls on the resources used for care" (Cohen & Cesta, 1993). The purposes of case management are to ensure cost effectiveness, quality, and continuity of care.

Case management is often confused with other concepts, including **managed care,** because the terms are frequently used interchangeably, and because the historical development is similar (Cohen & Cesta, 1993). Chapter 20 presents an in-depth discussion of managed care plans and financing. A brief overview of managed care is included here to help you differentiate it from case management.

Kaiser developed the first managed care plan in the 1930s, to avoid the need for the employees of his ship building company to worry about health care as the country prepared for war. Prevention and early intervention were emphasized with the idea that fewer dollars would be spent than if one waited until an illness had progressed (Himali, 1995). Managed care plans today are financed by collecting a set dollar amount per enrollee per month. The managed care plan contracts with care providers, including physicians, hospitals, and home health agencies, to provide the needed care. The contract between provider and managed care company usually includes incentives to keep the client (or enrollee) well and to use services cost-effectively.

The similarity between managed care and case management is in the control of services, or matching needs with resources. Powell (1996) differentiates between the two concepts in this way: managed care is systems-oriented, and case management is people-oriented, negotiating the managed care system.

Provision of Case Management Services. Case management services may be provided on several levels. The entity with the most risk for expensive care and treatment of the client typically provides case management services. Managed care providers or insurance companies may provide case management services in an attempt to promote wellness and prevent hospitalization, because hospital care is usually the most costly kind of care. The hospital may also provide case management services once clients are admitted, because contracts are usually for a designated amount of money, either per day or for the entire period of hospitalization (e.g., with DRGs), and the incentive is for hospitals to provide care as cost-effectively as possible.

Case management can be provided in a variety of settings. Lyon (1993) delineates three categories of case management in health-care settings: hospital-based case management, case management across the health-care continuum, and community case management.

Hospital-Based Case Management. Hospital-based case management began with the introduction of the prospective payment system in 1983 (Lyon, 1993). Since then, professional nurses have been responsible for clients' lengths of stay and for matching needs with resources.

The case management care delivery model can be implemented in a way that addresses some of the issues identified earlier; the care clients receive is provided by the caregivers with the right knowledge and skills, in the right setting for the intensity, amount of services or care needed, and severity of illness. The role of case managers is to facilitate and integrate the contributions of the interdisciplinary team. The case manager's role also lends itself to intradisciplinary differentiation. For these reasons, this model facilitates cost-effective, quality care.

The role of case manager is carried out differently in different models. Case managers, for example, can be staff nurses who, with some additional training and education, incorporate case management activities into the planning and provision of care on a daily basis. Some organizations have designated case managers for groups of clients within the walls of the institution. Others have case managers who follow clients within the hospital, but also follow select groups of clients through the continuum of care. Some organizations assign case managers to a unit or units with clients who have common diagnoses, while others assign case managers to follow clients through the course of the hospital stay. Each model has advantages and disadvantages, and no one model is right for every organization. Some organizations even use case managers differently within the setting, depending on the client type and other identified needs. For example, one case manager in a hospital may be unit based while another is population based, crossing units.

The case management system can be used with a variety of nursing care delivery systems, including primary, team, functional, or combinations of these systems (Lyon, 1993). If it is used with one of these client care delivery systems, it can be overlayed onto the existing structure, or the entire system can be reengineered. Another strength of the case management system is that it can be used with differentiated care models. As discussed earlier, differentiated care delivery matches the needs of the client to the caregiver with the appropriate knowledge and skills.

At Sioux Valley Hospital, practice is differentiated for registered nurses, and case management competencies are defined. The nurses are in either associate or primary nurse job descriptions, based on educational preparation and competencies. Associate nurses provide direct care to clients based on associate degree competencies and implement the plan as defined by the critical pathway. Approximately 60 percent of clients have few complications during their hospital stay and are cared for by an associate nurse. Primary nurses, whose role is based on baccalaureate degree competencies, oversee the client's plan of care for an episode, usually from preadmission to postdischarge. They oversee medical and nursing orders that extend beyond the critical pathway. They are accountable for a timely, well-prepared discharge, and occasionally provide home health for patients with complex conditions. Approximately 30 percent of clients require the care of a primary nurse (AACN, 1995; Koerner & Karpiuk, 1994).

Sioux Valley Hospital has also defined a case management role for the clinical nurse specialist or nurse practitioner with master's degree preparation. These nurses manage select groups of clients, defined as frequently admitted to the hospital and incurring high costs, across the continuum, in all settings and across a client's lifetime. About 10 percent of clients are cared for by advanced practice nurses (AACN, 1995; Koerner & Karpiuk, 1994).

The role of case managers is to facilitate matching needs to resources through a systematic process. As discussed earlier, matching needs with resources is an important component in quality and cost-effectiveness. The steps in the process vary with the overall model used within the organization; however, there are some common functions. The following is an example of a model in an acute care setting in which a nurse case manager is responsible for a group of clients. This description is included to provide some concrete ideas about the role and how to go about matching needs with resources.

Process of Matching Needs with Resources.
There are several levels of complexity in planning and organizing care in case management models. Case managers prioritize for groups of clients, and then address the needs of individual clients. As a part of their role, nurse case managers evaluate practice patterns for appropriateness, timeliness, and medical necessity. A systematic process is used to address over- and underutilization of resources, in-efficiencies, and delays. Care and services are coordinated and integrated.

The following steps are presented sequentially, but they do not have to be carried out in this order.

1. The process used to organize a day or caseload involves reviewing payer status of the clients. Clients who are members of certain health plans, such as capitated plans, may be evaluated first, because the case manager often communicates with payers about the clients' status and anticipated length of stay. Health plans frequently need to "authorize" admissions and continued stays.

2. The case manager prioritizes review of medical records. This may be accomplished by talking with other members of the health-care team and responding to potential problems they identify, or answering referrals from other sources.

3. Clients are evaluated, usually daily, based on some criteria for appropriateness of service level. This can be accomplished by applying criteria such as intensity of service and severity of illness. This is key in matching needs with resources, because some levels of care, such as intensive care are very costly to the organization. If the client no longer meets intensity or severity criteria for the intensive care unit, the case manager facilitates transfer to an appropriate level of care. Sometimes the case manager may determine that the resources needed are too intense for a particular unit and recommend transfer to a higher level of care. The cost to quality equation is always considered.

4. Throughout the day, the case manager communicates with various payers.

5. The case manager also focuses on individual clients, evaluating what the client needs now, what needs are anticipated, and what resources are available, and works through any obstacles to achieve the best outcome.

6. The case manager assists the team in developing and implementing the plan. This involves communicating with nurses, other members of the interdisciplinary team, and the client and family.

7. The case manager also has responsibilities in evaluating the case management process, including productivity indicators, quality and outcome indicators, and financial information tracking.

8. The evaluation information is used to change practice, including matching the care provider who has the knowledge, skills, and abilities

with the care to be given and documentation. The case manager usually facilitates development of clinical pathways.

These are examples of the kinds of activities case managers are involved in daily. The knowledge, skills, and abilities required for this role include excellent communication skills, analytical skills, and clinical knowledge.

Although in the process described previously the case manager is the person carrying out the role functions delineated, nurses with various levels of educational preparation and experience participate in this process. For example, the nurse providing direct care to the client may be most knowledgeable about the client's clinical course. Although the case manager may be the most appropriate person (based on knowledge, skills, and abilities) to approach a physician about moving a client to another level of care, other nurses can assist in identifying those patients who do not meet criteria for the current level of care.

Case Management Across the Continuum. Case management services can be episodic, usually initiated and completed during a hospital stay, as described in the previous section, or they can continue as the client moves back into the community. Some models that include services across the continuum report improvement in the quality of care and cost reduction (Koerner & Karpiuk, 1994; Lamb & Huggins, 1990). At Sioux Valley Hospital, which uses differentiated case management, more than $500,000 was saved in a 6-month period through the case management of 35 complex patients (AACN, 1995).

Case Management in the Community. Some case management programs are community based and begin after clients are discharged from the hospital. These services are provided by nurses and other members of the interdisciplinary team. Clients are assessed, counseled, reminded of appointments for follow-up, and referred to other professionals as needed. These services are frequently provided for behavioral health clients, who are reintegrating into the community.

CARE MAPS

Many case management concepts have been discussed, and advantages of the system have been identified. Some of the strategies, such as integrating and coordinating services and tracking outcomes, are not easy to implement. Tools are available, however, to facilitate the processes discussed. One of the tools for supporting this process is a document, developed to define the care for a particular client type, commonly referred to as a **care map,** or critical pathway. Figure 15–1 illustrates a sample critical pathway.

Care maps are important tools to map client care and expected outcomes through an acute episode of illness (Gibson, 1996). They define not only care, but outcomes as well, and encourage identification of variances so that new interventions can be planned.

Care maps are different from nursing care plans, which focus on individual differences, because they define the most usual care for a client type, and focus on the similarities of clients. Care maps also allow for documentation of care provided and comparison of clients' actual status with predefined outcomes.

Typical care maps identify the care that clients receive during a specific time frame, along with expected outcomes. Continuity of care providers is not always possible, but continuity of care is possible if a detailed map is available. Care maps are developed by interdisciplinary teams through a systematic process. Some maps extend across the continuum and follow the client into the community, but most are designed for the acute care period. The processes used to develop the actual care map may vary somewhat, but the basics are essentially the same.

The process of developing a care map includes identifying a client group with like diagnoses and outcomes, identifying the interdisciplinary team members who provide care, reviewing current practices and applicable standards from all involved disciplines, and mapping out the care provided and expected outcomes for defined time frames. The format of the care map varies from organization to organization, but most list the discipline and the expectations of care with time frames and expected outcomes. The time frames are usually in daily increments, but they may be in hourly or even 15 minute increments, for example, during the first hour that a client presents with an acute myocardial infarction. The care map for hip replacement may be in daily increments, with expected outcomes defined for each day.

Depending on the philosophy of the organization, care maps may represent physician's orders. Other organizations use them as tools for anticipating the next steps in care. Nurses working in an area other than their area of expertise could use the map to anticipate and plan care for a specific client that day.

Categories	15 – 30 min	1 – 4 hr
Assessments and Evaluations	• Identify appropriate attending physician • Nursing cardiopulmonary assessments • Continuous cardiac rhythm monitoring • $\overline{q}$ 15 min. BP monitoring • Pulse oximetry • Transfer to CCU or Cath Lab by 60 minutes	• Nursing assessment by standards • Vital signs per standards • Continuous cardiac rhythm monitoring • Continuous noninvasive BP monitoring • Pulse oximetry • Weight • Strict I & Os
Consult	• Cardiologist after EKG, if applicable	• "Consult cardiac rehab"
Tests	• ECG • pCXR • Chem 16, CBC, PT/PTT _____ (time drawn) • CK and CKMB q 8 hrs. × 3 _____ (time drawn)	• ECG postthrombolytics × 90 min or when pain free • Test all stools for guaiac if on heparin infusion
Medications/ Infusions	• O_2 _____ L/min • IV access (Cobain to all IV sites) • ASA • NTG s.l. prn chest pain IV MS prn chest pain • Consider IV NTG (for persistent pain/pulmonary edema) • IV heparin infusion • Beta blockers • Thrombolytics _____ (if indicated)	• Complete TPA infusion • Continue heparin infusion • IV NTG if chest pain persists • NTG s.l. prn chest pain • O_2 if $SaO_2 < 94\%$ • Tylenol for headache • Antianxiety agent if indicated • Stool softener
Nutrition	• NPO (sips with meds)	• Clear liquids
Activity	• Bedrest	• Bedrest, commode with assistance
Education	• Review plan of care • Early reporting of chest pain, SOB, diaphoresis, hypotension, decreased level of consciousness, etc.	• Early reporting of angina • Orient to environment, plan of care, current therapy • Cardiac cath/PTCA teaching, if indicated
Clinical Outcome	• Items above • Reduction or pain control • Emotional support to patient and family	• Items above • Pain relief by second hour • ECG improvement by second hour

Physician Signature: _____

Clinical pathways do not represent a standard of care. They are guidelines for consideration, which may be modified to the individual needs.

INITIALS/SIGNATURES: _____

_____

FIGURE 15 – 1. Definition of Acute MI: Chest Pain, ST Elevation, Cardiac Enzyme Positive (Optional). Del E. Webb Memorial Hospital Acute Myocardial Infarction Clinical Pathway.

Defined expected outcomes are important in identifying contributions to care and cost-effectiveness. Variances from care maps, in either the care clients are to receive or achieving outcomes within the specified time frames, can be tracked and analyzed. Process issues can be resolved through a process improvement team.

Care maps are powerful tools that are useful in defining care, client outcomes, time frames, and the responsibilities of interdisciplinary team members. Variances from the map and other data are shared with the members of the team, and opportunities for improvement are identified.

The task of developing a care map can be overwhelming to a nurse who has not participated in the process. Some organizations have a prescribed

Categories	4 – 24 hr	24 – 48 hr
Assessments and Evaluations	• Nursing assessment by standards • Vital signs by standards • Continuous cardiac rhythm monitoring • Continuous noninvasive BP monitoring • Pulse oximetry	• Nursing assessment by standards • Vital signs by standards • Discontinue continuous noninvasive BP monitoring, if stable • D/C pulse oximetry if not on supplemental O_2
Consult	• Dietary	• "Cardiac rehab," dietary, PT
Tests	• PTT by protocol if on heparin infusion • Schedule echo for 36–48 hr from ED presentation per physician • ECG as clinically indicated • Test all stool for guaiac • Schedule cardiac cath per physician	• PTT by protocol if heparin infusion • H & H, platelets at 24 and 48 hr if on heparin • Echo by 48th hour per physician • Schedule cardiac cath per physician, if not done previously • Stools (guaiac)
Medications/ Infusion	• Continue heparin infusion • NTG if already infusing • NTG s.l. if prn chest pain • IV MS prn chest pain • O_2 if $SaO_2 < 94\%$ • Tylenol for headache • Stool softener • IV access • Antianxiety prn • Oral beta blockers if indicated	• ASA • Heparin infusion • Beta blockers • D/C IV NTG if no chest pain • NTG s.l. prn chest pain • D/C O_2 if $SaO_2 > 94\%$ • IV access
Nutrition	• Cardiac diet	• Cardiac diet
Activity	• Bedrest and commode with assistance; may dangle	• Up ad lib
Education	• Update on therapy and course	• Cardiac anatomy and physiology, normal structure and function, coronary artery circulation, atherosclerosis • Angina • MI healing process • Supplemental educational films • Smoking cessation • Risk factor modification
Clinical Outcome	• Dysrhythmia control • Resolution of chest pain • Adequate oxygenation • Unchanged neuro status • Controlled anxiety/fear • Hemodynamic stability • Injection sites without bleeding	• No angina • No heart failure • Lungs clear • No sustained dysrhythmia • Hemodynamic stability • Understanding of diagnosis and treatment plan • Injection sites without bleeding

FIGURE 15-1. *Continued.*

method for developing care maps. This can be very formal, involving the interdisciplinary team, a prescribed format, and sets of parameters. The initial development of a care map can start simply with chart reviews of clients with similar diagnoses. Often the medical records department can provide lists of names of clients who were discharged with similar diagnoses. These patients names can be further categorized by physician, to identify that physician's practice pattern. A group of charts is reviewed, and practice patterns are identified. The patterns can be categorized by activities and outcomes. Having

Categories	48–80 hr	80–96 hr
Assessments and Evaluations	• Nursing assessment by standards • Vital signs by standards • D/C continuous cardiac rhythm monitoring by 48 hr if no sustained arrhythmias • Transfer to telemetry unit	• Nursing assessment by standards • Vital signs by standards
Consult	• "Referral for phase II cardiac rehab"	
Tests	• ECG if clinically indicated • Schedule stress test if no cardiac cath	• Stress test if scheduled
Medications/ Infusions	• ASA • Beta blockers • NTG s.l. prn chest pain • D/C heparin infusion if no angina • Ace inhibitors if LVEF < 0.4	• ASA • Beta blockers • Ace inhibitors if LVEF < 0.4 • NTG s.l. prn chest pain
Nutrition	• Cardiac diet	• Cardiac diet/NPO if stress test
Activity	• OOB ad lib	• Discharge
Education	• Cardiac anatomy and physiology, normal structure and function, coronary artery circulation, atherosclerosis • Angina • MI healing process • Supplemental educational films • Smoking cessation • Risk factor modification • Energy conservation/sexual activity	• Activity on discharge • When to call physician if problems • Medication review • What to do if chest pain • Follow-up on smoking cessation • Follow-up on risk factor modification
Clinical Outcome	• No angina • No heart failure • Lungs clear • No sustained dysrhythmia • Hemodynamic stability • Understanding of diagnosis and treatment plan • Injection sites without bleeding	• Items above

FIGURE 15-1. *Continued.*

members of the interdisciplinary team present for the chart reviews is helpful but costly because of the amount of time invested. After usual practice is identified, the interdisciplinary team is brought together to determine whether all essential elements are represented and reach general agreement with the information. Opportunities for improvement are often identified immediately; for example, scheduling a test a day earlier could decrease the client's length of stay by a day. Some teams develop care maps by simply putting all of the essential care and expected outcomes into the map, without doing chart reviews. Involving all interdisciplinary team members, including the physician, is essential for the success of care maps.

DOCUMENTATION

The shift in care delivery systems has also contributed to a shift in the focus of nursing documentation. In the functional model, documenting task completion was the focus. As the movement into team nursing increased continuity of care, a system was needed to support the documentation of the plan of care. The nursing care plan was emphasized and even required by the Joint Commission on Accreditation of Hospitals and Healthcare Organizations (JCAHO) (Cohen & Cesta, 1993). The nursing care plan was also emphasized in primary nursing.

The change in paradigm from a focus on care

providers (nurses) to one on clients as care recipients has shifted our use of language in documentation. Client databases (not nursing admission forms) are now completed on admission, and client or patient care plans (not *nursing* care plans) are developed.

As the reimbursement structure continues to change, the emphasis on documentation will change. For example, under a reimbursement structure in which the provider or health-care institution is reimbursed based on charges, it is extremely important to document all supplies and equipment used through a systematic process. Some plans will not reimburse for the use of a specialized bed, such as a low air loss bed, without daily documentation of the client using the bed. Infusion of every liter of intravenous solution needs to be documented, or the plan can refuse to pay for the solution, even though it was charged to the client. Reimbursement can be denied for an entire hospital stay if administration of an antibiotic was not documented. This kind of documentation is also important in traditional quality management monitoring and risk management.

TAXONOMIES

Ultimately, as discussed earlier, nurses will be asked to identify what they do and what they contribute to care (Barry-Walker, Bulechek, & McCloskey, 1994). This will require collection of essential nursing information by implementing classification systems for nursing diagnoses, interventions, and outcomes.

One goal the profession is working toward is to implement the uniform collection of essential nursing information, known as the **Nursing Minimum Data Set** (NMDS) (Moorhead, McCloskey, & Bulechek, 1993). This database will provide large data sets, not just 30 or 40 samples allowing nursing data to be compared across populations, to complement information from other professionals. Implementation of the NMDS depends on having a standardized language for four essential components: nursing diagnosis, nursing interventions, nursing outcomes, and nursing intensity (Delaney & Moorhead, 1995).

Classification of client problems has been available for two decades through the North American Nursing Diagnosis Association (NANDA, 1992) and as a components of the Omaha System. These two systems are very different; NANDA's approach is very broad, and the Omaha System focuses on community health (Delaney & Moorhead, 1995).

Three classifications for nursing interventions have been developed: the Omaha System, the Home Healthcare Classification, and the Nursing Interventions Classification (NIC). Work began on the most comprehensive classification, NIC, in 1987. Since the initial work was published in 1992, research has continued; a taxonomy has been constructed, validated, and coded; validation surveys have been completed; and interventions have been added. The interventions have also been linked to nursing diagnosis (McCloskey & Bulechek, 1996). The next phase is to implement NIC clinically. The challenge in the clinical setting is to document both professional knowledge (for research and statistical purposes), and care delivered (for legal and reimbursement purposes). In the future the plan will link the interventions with outcomes (McCloskey & Bulechek, 1996).

A standardized language for nursing outcomes is being developed by a research team at the University of Iowa. The Nursing Outcome Classification (NOC) will include outcome labels, label definitions, and indicators for each outcome (Delaney & Moorhead, 1995).

The fourth component NMDS requires is standardized language for nursing intensity. Nursing intensity is difficult to define, and even more difficult to measure. Nursing needs to be able to document the resources required to provide client care and achieve defined outcomes. This standardized language is still needed (Delaney & Moorhead, 1995). Without this language, determining the true cost of care will be difficult, and making it cost-effective will be even more difficult.

While it is extremely important to capture nursing's contribution to care and outcomes, it is also important to remember that as we move to highly integrated interdisciplinary teams, we may not be able to use language that belongs exclusively to nursing, such as nursing diagnosis. As integrated documentation is developed, and all professionals rely more heavily on communication in records, language that everyone can use is required.

Managing and providing care is extremely complex. Many of the economically driven changes in health care will continue to have a great impact on nurses. The concepts discussed in this chapter provide information to help practicing nurses understand the current situation enough to ask pertinent questions in evaluating care delivery systems and realize the importance of capturing nursing's contribution to care and outcomes.

KEY POINTS

- ■ Health-care planning and provision is changing dramatically as a result of economics and the shift from the industrial age to the quantum age.
- ■ Cost and quality are the two essential components in the care that is provided.
- ■ The economic forces and philosophical shifts experienced today are encouraging nurses to demonstrate their contributions to client outcomes.
- ■ Roles of the interdisciplinary and intradisciplinary care providers need to be differentiated by knowledge, skills, and abilities and contributions to client outcomes.
- ■ Various care delivery models, such as team and primary nursing, are currently used to organize the delivery of care. Models need to address the needs of the organization, match the organization's culture and values, and consider the content of care delivered.
- ■ Case management is one care delivery model that addresses many of the current concerns of care delivery systems. Care maps are tools that assist in achieving the goals of case management.
- ■ Documentation, an essential component of care, is changing as care delivery systems and charge or reimbursement systems change.
- ■ Nursing is developing taxonomies to assist in identifying what nurses do and what they contribute to care. The Nursing Minimum Data Set will assist nurses in the uniform collection of essential nursing information.

CHAPTER EXERCISES

1. Analyze the care delivery system on a client care unit. What model is in place? Are responsibilities differentiated according to knowledge, skills, and abilities?

2. Identify a group of clients with a common diagnosis or problem. Develop a care map for that client type.

3. Compare and contrast case management and managed care.

REFERENCES

Altman G. D. (1993). Adjusting primary nursing to 12 hour shifts. *Nursing Management, 24*(2), 80–82.

American Association of Colleges of Nursing. (1995). *A model for differentiated nursing practice*. Washington, DC: American Association of Colleges of Nursing.

American Hospital Association. (1990). *Report of the hospital nursing personnel survey — 1990*. Chicago: American Hospital Association.

American Nurses Association. (1995). *Nursing report card for acute care*. Washington, DC: American Nurses Publishing.

Arford, P. H., & Allred, C. A. (1995). Value = quality + cost. *Journal of Nursing Administration, 25*(9), 64–69.

AzNA awarded report card grant. (1996, May). *Arizona Nurse,* 3.

Barry-Walker, J., Bulechek, G., & McCloskey, J. C. (1994). A description of medical-surgical nursing. *MEDSURG Nursing, 3*(4), 261–268.

Bower, K. A. (1992). *Case management by nurses*. Washington, DC: American Nurses Publishing.

Cohen, E. L. (1996). *Nurse case management in the 21st century*. St. Louis: Mosby.

Cohen, E. L., & Cesta, T. G. (1993). *Nursing case management: From concept to evolution*. St. Louis: Mosby.

Daly, J. M., Mass, M., & Buckwalter, K. (1995, August). Use of standardized nursing diagnosis and interventions in long-term care. *Journal of Gerontological Nursing, 21*(8), 29–36.

Delaney, C., & Moorhead, S. (1995). The nursing minimum data set, standardized language, and health care quality. *Journal of Nursing Care Quality, 10*(1), 16–30.

Differentiated nursing practice in all care settings. (1995). *Journal of Nursing Administration, 7*(8), 5–6.

Gibson, S. J. (1996). Differentiated practice within and beyond the hospital walls. In E. L. Cohen (Ed.), *Nurse case management in the 21st century*. (pp. 222–244). St. Louis: Mosby–Year Book.

Himali, U. (1995, June). Managed care: Does the promise meet the potential? *American Nurse, 27*(4), 1, 14, 16.

Hyams-Franklin, E. M., Rowe-Gillespie, P., Harper, A., & Johnson, V. (1993). Primary team nursing: The 90s model. *Nursing Management, 24*(6), 50–52.

Kayuha, A. A. (1996). Organizational systems. In C. Loveridge & S. Cummings *Nursing management in the new paradigm* (pp. 24–57). Gaithersburg, MD: Aspen.

Koerner, J. G., & Karpiuk, K. L. (Eds.). (1994). *Implementing differentiated nursing practice: Transformation by design.* Gaithersburg, MD: Aspen.

Lamb, G. S., & Huggins, D. (1990). The professional nursing network. In G. G. Mayer, M. J. Madden, & E. Lawrenz (Eds.), *Patient care delivery models* (pp. 169–184). Rockville, MD: Aspen.

Lyon, J. C. (1993). Models of nursing care delivery and case management: Clarification of terms. *Nursing Economics, 11*(3), 163–169.

Manthey, M. (1980). *The practice of primary nursing.* Boston: Blackwell.

Mathews, B. P., & Kamikawa, C. (1994). Primary nursing. *Nursing Administration Quarterly, 19*(1), 48–50.

Mayer, G. G., Madden, M. J., & Lawrenz, E. (Eds.). (1990). *Patient care delivery models.* Rockville, MD: Aspen.

McCloskey, J. C. (1995). Recognizing the management role of all nurses. *Nursing and Healthcare: Perspectives on Community, 16*(6), 307–308.

McCloskey, J. C., & Bulechek, G. M. (Eds.). (1996). *Nursing interventions classification (NIC)* (2nd ed.). St. Louis: Mosby.

Milton, D. (1992). The evaluation of new nursing structures in single or multifacility systems. In C. Wilson (Ed.). *Building new nursing organizations: Visions and realities* (pp. 187–208). Gaithersburg, MD: Aspen.

Moorhead, S. A., McCloskey, J. C., Bulechek, G. M. (1993). Nursing interventions classification: A comparison with the Omaha system and the home healthcare classification. *Journal of Nursing Administration, 23*(10), 23–29.

North American Nursing Diagnosis Association. (1992). *NANDA nursing diagnosis: Definition and Classification 1992.* St. Louis: North American Nursing Diagnosis Association.

NCNA. (1992). *Nursing Clinics of North America* 1(27).

Porter-O'Grady, T., & Wilson, C. K. (1995). *The leadership revolution in healthcare: Altering systems, changing behaviors.* Gaithersburg, MD: Aspen.

Poulin, M. (1985). Configuration of nursing practice. In American Nurses Association (Ed.). *Issues in professional nursing practice* (pp. 1–14). Kansas City: American Nurses Association.

Powell, S. K. (1996). *Nursing case management.* Philadelphia: Lippincott-Raven.

Primm, P. L. (1986). Entry into practice: competency statements for BSNs and ADNs. *Nursing Outlook, 34*(3), 135–137.

Smith, G. (1994). The paradox of collaboration. *Nursing and Health Care, 15*(7), 338–339.

Thomas, L. H., & Bond, S. (1991). Outcomes of primary nursing: the case of primary nursing. *International Journal of Nursing Studies, 28*(4), 291–314.

Walker, P. H. Dollars and sense in health reform: Interdisciplinary practice and community nursing centers. *Nursing Administration Quarterly, 19*(1), 1–11.

Walker, D. D., Jones, S. L., Yamauchi, S. S., Lima, C., Archer, S., Mathews, B. P., Harris, M., Kamikawa, C., Irvine, N., Lanier, J. et al. (1994). The Queen's Medical Center Honolulu, Hawaii. *Nursing Administration Quarterly, 19*(1), 33–65.

Wilkinson, R. A. (1994). A more autonomous and independent role: Primary nursing versus patient allocation. *Professional Nurse, 9*(10), 680–684.

Chapter 16

RESEARCH AS A BASIS FOR PRACTICE

Rose Kearney Nunnery

CHAPTER OBJECTIVES

On completion of this chapter, the reader will be able to:

1. Define basic terminology used in nursing research.
2. Describe legal and ethical considerations applicable to nursing research.
3. Explain the importance of research for the profession of nursing.
4. Describe different ways to participate in nursing research.
5. Identify barriers to the application and conduct of clinical research in nursing.
6. Prepare a basic critique of a published nursing research study.

KEY TERMS

Research	Empirical Research	Research Design
Ethical Codes	Qualitative Research	Operational Definition
Basic Human Rights	Research Utilization	Variables
Beneficence	Research Critique	Sampling
Full Disclosure	Research Problem	Instruments
Self-determination	Literature Review	Descriptive Statistics
Privacy and Confidentiality	Hypotheses	Inferential Statistics
Minimal Risk		

R esearch has been defined as a "systematic, controlled, empirical and critical investigation of natural phenomena guided by theory and hypotheses about the presumed relations among such phenomena" (Kerlinger, 1986, p. 10). Given this definition, research is still viewed by some as an academic exercise. But it is much more than this in nursing. The purposes of research are to describe, explain, predict, and control phenomena and provide information for future use by a discipline in practice or for expansion of the knowledge base.

Research supports our knowledge base and answers questions of clinical concern. It provides sound information on which to base practice. We need both seekers and users of the information in practice to develop knowledge. Clinicians in the practice setting have the questions. These questions must be refined and studied for nurse researchers to come up with solutions to health-care practice problems.

A vital issue is the need for reliable and valid research on questions of clinical concern for decision making and change. Speaking for health-care reform, Duncan (1994) describes the need for outcomes research through clinical trials, studies using existing records, and metaanalysis using the results of several prior studies as the data for a larger unit of analysis (pp. 74–75). In nursing, research must be directed at interventions over which nursing has control so that the knowledge developed can lead to needed change. Current knowledge and practice must be based on research data rather than intuition, tradition, or past practice. This is the essence of research as the basis for professional nursing practice.

NURSING RESEARCH FOCUS

Nursing research began with Florence Nightingale and her identification of environmental influences on health and illness. In her classic *Notes on Nursing* (1859), she identified factors that influence health and wellness, supporting them with observational accounts, statistics, and deductive reasoning. Following her landmark efforts, nursing research limited to research on nurses and nursing education was often conducted by researchers who were not nurses. Then in the mid-twentieth century, graduate nursing programs began to proliferate as did nurses' involvement in research studies, often on nurses and delivery of nursing services. The introduction of the journal *Nursing Research* in 1952 provided a specific channel to disseminate research findings to other nurses.

During the second half of the twentieth century, the number of graduate and baccalaureate nursing programs grew. Content on research became prevalent in baccalaureate nursing curricula during the 1970s and early 1980s. Graduate student enrollments increased with the growth in doctoral programs in 1980s. Research findings were used to develop and refine conceptual and theoretical models. More nurses were now doing research, and the ANA Cabinet on Nursing Research identified research expectations by level of education in 1981. The primary focus of research changed during this time from educational programs and methods to the focus of nursing: people as patients, clients, and members of society. Support has grown for research as we see the needs to investigate the domain of nursing, test theories and interventions, and demonstrate efficacy and efficiency of nursing actions.

The establishment of the National Center for Nursing Research (NCNR) as part of the National Institutes of Health (NIH) in April 1986, under the Health Research Extension Act of 1985 (PL99-158), demonstrated the importance of research for and by the profession. In 1993, the National Institute for Nursing Research (NINR) was established from the former divisional and center status, with fiscal year appropriations from Congress growing, thus further demonstrating the importance of generating knowledge in nursing. The stated mission of the NINR is "to promote and support research and research training in universities, hospitals and research centers across the country and also to conduct research with other scientific disciplines at NIH" (NINR, 1993). Extramural research programs for the NINR concern (1) health promotion and disease prevention, (2) acute and chronic illness, and (3) nursing systems.

Research proposals are highly competitive at NINR, more so than in many other areas of NIH. Research proposals are reviewed by a panel of experts and scored based on the consistency with the mission of NINR and the merit of the research project. In addition, since there is much competition, selected research priorities receive a percentage of the funding as preference areas are identified. During the initial phase of NINR initiatives, research priorities were specified for investigations (Table 16–1). Following a November 1992 conference with 53 top nursing scientists, the research priorities for 1995 through 1999 changed to specific areas targeted by year. Note the comparison of these research initiatives displayed in Table 16–1. Highly evident in the

TABLE 16-1. Funding Preferences of the National
Institute of Nursing Research

Time Frame	Funding Preference
1992–1994	Low birthweight (mothers and infants)
	HIV infection (prevention and care)
	Long-term care (older adults)
	Symptom management: pain
	Nursing informatics (to enhance patient care)
	Health promotion for older children and
	adolescents
	Technology dependency across the lifespan
1995–1999	
1995	Community-based nursing models
1996	Effectiveness of nursing interventions in HIV and
	AIDS
1997	Cognitive impairment
1998	Living with chronic illness
1999	Biobehavioral factors related to
	immunocompetence

Source: NINR (1993). *National Institute for Nursing Research, National Institute of Health* (pp. 1–2). Bethesda, MD: National Institute of Nursing Research with permission.

descriptions of these priorities are testing nursing interventions that promote health behaviors in individuals or population groups. The clinical focus of these priorities is on providing care for people with highly visible health needs, emphasizing the person or group in need of nursing care.

Nursing research is further supported in the position statement of the American Association of Colleges of Nursing (AACN, 1990). This organization of member schools with baccalaureate and graduate programs believes that "as the discipline of nursing has moved into the mainstream of academia, the depth and breadth of nursing research has increased . . . [with] the purpose of nursing research to test, refine, and advance the knowledge on which improved education, clinical judgment, and cost-effective, safe, ethical nursing care rest" (AACN, 1990, p. 1). This has implications for the baccalaureate-prepared nurse in the identification of research problems, the support of ongoing research, and the use of applicable findings in practice. Sigma Theta Tau, the International Honor Society for Nursing, for some time has recognized the importance of generating and using research. The purposes of this honor society include encouraging scholarly and creative work. This is applicable to both the conduct and utilization of research. Scholarship involves discovery, integration, application, and teaching. Utilizing and communicating research in nursing

practice projects and conferences have been focuses of Sigma Theta Tau International. The organization also supports research investigations generating nursing knowledge through competitive extramural grants for researchers, as does the American Foundation of Nursing. Again, nurses have a major responsibility in identifying research problems, supporting ongoing research, and using applicable findings in practice along with continued learning in this area of scholarly nursing practice. An additional responsibility in professional nursing practice is protecting the rights of research subjects.

LEGAL AND ETHICAL CONSIDERATIONS

The rights of people in research have been of great concern to ethicists, legislators, and professionals and have led to **ethical codes** and guidelines for the protection of research subjects. History has provided much of the impetus for our professional codes and federal regulations. During World War II, experiments noted for the unethical treatment of subjects include the Nazi medical experiments and Japanese concentration camp experiments on human subjects. As a result, international ethical codes evolved. In 1949, the Nuremberg Code set standards for involving human subjects in research, with guidelines for consent, protections, risks and benefits, and qualifications of researchers. The Declaration of Helsinki (1990) in 1964, and revised in 1975 and 1989, provided guidelines on therapeutic and nontherapeutic research, along with the requirement for the disclosure of risks and potential benefits and obtaining written consent for participation as a research subject.

In the United States, the Tuskegee syphilis study on sharecroppers, the Jewish Chronic Disease Hospital study with oncology patients, and the Willowbrook hepatitis study with children as late as the early 1970s were further examples of unethical treatment of research subjects. In the quest for knowledge, researchers failed to consider the basic human rights of these subjects. U.S. Federal Regulations have evolved from the original guidelines of the former Department of Health, Education and Welfare, with the National Research Act in 1974. This law specified the composition and authority of institutional review boards (IRBs). IRBs were now mandated as oversight bodies to ensure protection of research subjects, especially for research projects seeking federal funding.

The Belmont Report (1979) was the outcome of a

National Commission for the Protection of Human Subjects of Biomedical and Behavioral Research from the National Research Act. This commission was charged with identifying principles and developing guidelines. Their report specified boundaries between practice and research. Basic ethical principles were reinforced highlighting respect for persons and defining the principles of beneficence (doing no harm, with maximum benefits and minimal risks) and justice (fairness relative to one's share, need, effort, contribution, and merit). Specific applications that resulted from the Belmont Report (1979) included the following: (1) guidelines on informed consent, including provision of information and ensuring comprehension and voluntariness; (2) assessment of risks and benefits; and (3) selection of subjects. The Belmont Report provided the basis for federal laws, including the recent federal codes on the Protection of Human Subjects in 1983 and 1991.

All activities involving humans as subjects must provide for the safety, health, and welfare of every individual. Subjects do not abdicate rights with their participation in a research study. Four **basic human rights** must be ensured for research subjects. These principles speak to ethical considerations and human rights:

1. **Beneficence (Do no harm)**
2. **Full Disclosure**
3. **Self-determination**
4. **Privacy and confidentiality**

The "do no harm" concept includes careful consideration of the risk-benefit ratio with any research project. Keep in mind that **minimal risk** has been defined in the code for the Protection of Human Subjects (1991) as "the probability and magnitude of harm or discomfort anticipated in the research are not greater in and of themselves than those encountered in daily life or during the performance of routine physical or psychological examinations or tests" (p. 6). Full disclosure of information and self-determination by potential subjects are necessary conditions for informed consent. In addition, subjects' rights to privacy and confidentiality must be ensured throughout the process. As protections for these four rights, the guidelines must be considered by researchers and their respective IRBs (Table 16–2).

As with other areas of nursing practice, legal and ethical considerations are deliberated with any research activity. These issues occur in the planning, implementation, analysis, and reporting stages for a research endeavor. In the proposal or planning stage of any research study, the researcher must consider the rights of the subjects and the ethical nature of the study. When a researcher defines the

TABLE 16–2. Federal Guidelines for the Protection of Human Subjects in Research Analysis, and Dissemination of the Findings

Principle	Guidelines
Risks to subjects are minimized (do no harm)	Using procedures that are consistent with sound research design and which do not expose subjects to unnecessary risk
	When appropriate, using procedures already being performed on the subjects for diagnostic or treatment purposes
	Risks are reasonable in relation to anticipated benefits and the importance of the knowledge that may reasonably be expected
	Risks/benefits are related to the research, not additional therapies subjects would receive even if not participating in this study
	Do not consider long-range effects of applying knowledge gained in research
Selection of subjects is equitable	Consider research purposes and setting
	Special considerations are made for vulnerable populations of children, prisoners, pregnant women, mentally disabled persons, or economically or educationally disadvantaged persons
	Additional safeguards are in place when some or all of the subjects are likely to be vulnerable to coercion or undue influence to protect the rights and welfare of these subjects
Informed consent	Must be sought from each prospective subject or the subject's legally authorized representative
	Will be appropriately documented
Safety	The research plan makes adequate provision for monitoring the data collected to ensure safety
Privacy	Adequate provisions to protect the privacy of subjects and maintain confidentiality of data

Source: 45 Code of Federal Regulations (CFR), 1991, with permission.

problem and purpose of the research, the significance of the problem for the body of knowledge and ethical issues associated with the proposed investigation are vital considerations.

Once the basic research plan is developed, an IRB committee must review and approve the start of the study. In the past, many IRBs were called human subjects committees, but strict federal guidelines for review by an IRB must be adhered to, especially in agencies seeking funding for research. Human subjects' rights of full disclosure, self-determination (informed consent), privacy and confidentiality, and safety (not to be harmed) must be ensured. The research proposal, with statements of the problem and purpose or significance, literature support, theory and definitions, specific research questions or hypotheses, design, and sampling plans along with how the data will be collected and analyzed, must be approved for use with human subjects. The researcher submits a proposal to an IRB for approval or exemption to proceed to the next step of data collection. During this stage of implementing the research project, the investigator must adhere to the procedures specified for data collection and analysis. Evaluation is done throughout the project to ensure that subjects are not placed at risk and that the integrity and confidentiality of the data are maintained during collection, analysis, and dissemination of the findings.

In addition to basic ethical principles, federal, state, local and institutional regulations, the American Nurses' Association (ANA) has specified human rights guidelines for nurses in research. These guidelines address the rights of both subjects and professionals (Table 16–3). As with the federal rules, the nursing guidelines address the basic human rights of research subjects, including freedom from harm, informed consent, and preservation of privacy. In addition, the rights and responsibilities of nurses are evident in the professional code. For example, the ANA (1985) points out that informed consent "applies not only to subjects per se but also to workers who are expected, as part of their daily work, to implement activities that potentially or actually carry risk for others or have uncertain outcomes" (p. 5). This demonstrates that professionals in a practice setting must be aware of any ongoing research and its associated risks to both subjects and participants. And nurses have both the right and the responsibility to participate in research. Participation of nurses should be evident, for example, as members of research teams and IRBS. Active participation also occurs through support and assistance to others involved in research for the advancement of knowledge and enhancement of professional practice. The process of research with human subjects

TABLE 16–3. ANA (1985) Human Rights Guidelines for Nurses in Clinical and Other Research

Principle	Guidelines
Right to freedom of injury	Degree of risk must be estimated and specified from intrinsic risk Prospective subjects must be given all relevant information prior to their consent to participate Nurses should be particularly vigilant to the potential for exploitation of vulnerable groups
Right to privacy and dignity	Research proposals, instruments, protocols, and techniques must be specified in advance and discussed with subjects and other participants in the research
Right to anonymity	Safeguards must be in place so that subjects experience no physical, psychological, or social disadvantages during the study or as a result of dissemination of its findings Prior consent must be obtained whenever the study may risk the subjects' anonymity or confidentiality Special safeguards to ensure subject confidentiality must be in place if the data from the study will not remain under the control of the investigator
Subjects	All individuals, including patients, outpatients, donors, informants, volunteers, and those included in identified vulnerable population groups Research involving subjects from vulnerable population groups must be justified by the benefits to them or others in similar situations and be mindful of the consent guidelines
Advancement of knowledge and the public good	Nurses are obligated to support the accrual of knowledge that broadens the base of nursing practice and the delivery of nursing services Qualified nurse scientists are a resource who need support and encouragement
IRBs	Their prime responsibility is safeguarding the rights of human subjects Nursing representatives should be members of the group
Informed consent	Free and voluntary consent for participation following consideration of the following information: ■ an explanation of the study, procedures involved, and their purpose; ■ a description of risks (physical, comfort, dignity, privacy, and confidentiality); ■ a description of benefits (personal and for development of new knowledge); ■ alternative procedures available ■ understanding of the ability to withdraw at any time without jeopardy; ■ answers to any additional questions that may arise; ■ if any concealment of information is required to maintain the integrity of the study, a subsequent period of debriefing should be provided to disclose the information with the rationale for concealment

must be diligent and benefit subjects and participants through acquisition of new knowledge.

PROCESS OF NURSING RESEARCH

The actual research process is generally thought of as the "scientific method." However, this can be misleading when one considers the different types of research. To understand the basics of nursing research, first think about the scientific method as a systematic process for answering a question or testing a hypothesis. One problem emerges: this is easier done in a controlled laboratory setting, dealing with variables such as chemicals, than in a natural setting dealing with people, well or ill, who need nursing interventions. Burns and Grove (1993) state that research is "diligent, systematic inquiry or investigation to validate and refine existing knowledge and generate new knowledge," and must be consistent with the philosophical orientation and theories of the discipline (p. 3). With this in mind, it is easiest to begin with empirical research using quantitative methods.

First, consider the steps with research. **Empirical research** is based on the strict rules of the scientific method. It is based on the philosophical perspective of positivism. With this perspective, the focus is on an observable, measurable, and predictable world. It is guided by a controlled set of steps that one goes through to observe something or test a hypothesis. It is a deductive and linear method with the following steps:

1. identification of the problem,
2. statement of the purpose,
3. review of the literature,
4. description of theoretical framework,
5. definition of terms,
6. statement of hypothesis(es),
7. selection of the research design, population, and the sample,
8. collection of data,
9. analysis and interpretation of data, and
10. presentation of findings and recommendations.

Using this empirical approach, the researcher may return to a prior step in the planning stage, for example, to refine the problem after the review of the literature, but will still go through all successive steps in a systematic and controlled manner to maintain the integrity of the process. Once the plans for the study are finalized, strict research protocols are adhered to with quantitative methods, to reduce threats to the validity of the study. Although some of the steps may be combined, nurse researchers using quantitative methods engage in the same process to describe, explain, predict, and control phenomena of concern to nursing. The following is a review of the research process. For specific information on each step of this process, refer to a nursing research textbook.

In the initial step of problem identification, the researchers specify what they are interested in studying. This is the "what" that will be done as the study progresses. For example, a specific nursing intervention is compared with a traditional nursing intervention for a selected group of clients. Next, the reason they are interested in this problem, or the purpose of the research, is specified. At this time, the significance of the problem for the body of knowledge and ethical issues associated with the proposed investigation are considerations. This is the "why" the researchers want to investigate the new intervention, for example, to effectively increase the health awareness or healthy behaviors of the client group.

The researchers next go to the literature to "discover" what is known on the topics: the interventions, the client group, cultural factors, useful theoretical bases (for example, self-care), and what problems have been studied in the area. This provides the current information known on the topic. This is a time-intensive process that requires absorbing a great deal of information for the planning stage for the project. Manual and computerized literature searches are done, followed by careful critique and assimilation of the information. Next, the researchers specify the philosophical orientation that will guide the research, the theoretical framework. Defining terms and variables specific to the study emerge from the theoretical framework, as do specific research questions that will be addressed or hypotheses (predictions) the study will test.

So far we have the basic idea for the investigation, but the researchers must select a design or plan for the study that is appropriate for the problem in light of the theoretical framework. Once the appropriate design has been selected, the researchers must define the population, those individuals or groups to whom the findings will be applicable or generalizable. Researchers know that not all the people from this intent of applicability can be studied, so they must study a select group of the population: the sample. The researchers' decision about the type and the size of the sample is based on the research design, the theoretical framework, research purpose, and research problem. It all relates back in a linear manner, but the goals in sampling are to limit bias and statistical error and be representative of the population.

The researchers now have the basic plan for their investigations, but no one has been studied yet. The rights of human subjects must be considered and protected. At this point the researcher submits a proposal to an IRB for approval or exemption to proceed to the next step of data collection. Once IRB approval has been given, the researcher is ready to begin collecting data.

Plans for data collection and analysis have already been made in the research proposal and are strictly adhered to. The design that was proposed must be followed when data are collected. The researcher cannot decide to replace interviews that were planned with a questionnaire. Perhaps it would be better, but that would be another study, starting at step one! Data must be orderly and systematically collected and recorded before analysis and decision making begin.

Measurement issues are of prime concern. The type of data collected and the measurement instruments are, again, determined before the study is started, based on the research problem, literature review, theoretical basis, research questions or hypotheses, research design, and sampling method. Issues of reliability (consistency of measurement) and validity (measuring the variable of interest properly) are considered by the researcher based on prior methodologic studies, use in similar research, or a pilot study. Polit and Hungler (1991) describe a pilot study as a small-scale version or a "trial run" before the actual larger study (p. 651). Measurements may be self-reported, in writing, by the subjects in the sample (tests, questionnaires, diaries, etc.) or require taping or note-taking in personal or telephone interviews. Measurements can also be observations of behavior (ability to perform a skill, like a dressing change), responses by subjects on a scale (such as a Likert scale), physiologic measures (such as BP, ECG, EEG, O_2 saturation), review of records, and a number of other types of measurement methods specific to some study designs. Research protocols are strictly adhered to, using the identical and detailed process with each research subject. Scripts are used to read instructions to subjects to ensure that each subject has been given the same information for the data collection process.

Once all subjects have been investigated and all data are collected, the researcher moves into the analysis stage. The analysis provides information to answer the research questions or support or refute the hypotheses. The analysis stage seems to be the most threatening to the research novice. Keep in mind that the research depends on a good analysis of the data so that reliable, valid information is made available on the topic. The most important decisions for this stage were made before the study was started, with the selection of the correct statistical tests. In addition, computers or statisticians can easily perform calculations. Try to see this stage as one of discovery and understanding how the data provide answers to the research questions or hypotheses. Reading analysis sections of research articles becomes easier and easier for the research novice. The findings are reported for each research question or hypothesis very objectively. The results of the descriptive statistics (such as frequencies, means, standard deviations, correlations) are reported to characterize the sample. Appropriate inferential statistics are used to generalize to the population (such as t-test, analysis of variance, correlations, and multivariate analysis), based on the type of measurement scale, sample size, and the assumption of a normal distribution. From the point of reporting the statistics, the researcher then interprets the meaning and implications relative to the stated research questions or hypotheses. Recommendations for use of the findings and further research are then presented in the research report.

Disseminating the findings to others is the final responsibility of the researcher as part of the particular study. The findings can be disseminated locally, regionally, and nationally through presentations or publications. It is vital that the information be shared with others. If the findings are important and point to a need for change, practicing nurses must have the opportunity to implement the information, if appropriate to their practice settings. Further research is also needed. If the findings were not significant or indifferent, then further research is needed, perhaps further specification of the problem, better measurement instruments, or a different environment or sample. If the research findings were negative, the new intervention was less effective. Still more research may be needed if there were problems with reliability and validity. If a safety issue emerged during the research, a subject would have been withdrawn from the study or the study stopped. Still, it is necessary for others to know all situations to make use of good information or avoid problem areas.

The research process with qualitative research methods is somewhat different. These methods are inductive and theory-generating research. **Qualitative research** is used to generate theory to explore, describe, and illuminate phenomena. Wilson (1989) has described the philosophical basis of qualitative research as symbolic interactionism. This perspective focuses on the meaning and interpretation of experiences to understand some phenomena. Types of research classified as qualitative include ethnography, field studies, grounded theory, historical, analytic induction, and phenomenology. Data collection methods mainly include naturalistic observation (hence the term "field studies") as well as on-site interviewing. Some researchers describe the data that emerge from this research as "information rich," since you begin a study with a need to understand from the perspective of people in the environment. You are not limiting the data collection to a few variables. Rather, you are trying to have the people in their environment describe the phenomena; you then classify concepts, identify themes, and generate theory. This is why some also see it as a "humanistic" form of research, discovering people and their unique experiences.

Using a qualitative perspective, the linear steps of the process are not the procedure. The researcher must still complete the initial process of developing the project, with identification of a "problem" of a little understood area of phenomena, and the statement of purpose as an inquiry for "discovery" of the phenomena. The review of the literature looks at what is known, which is often tangential, since little may be known before the research "uncovers" the phenomena. The theory will evolve from this research, rather than be driven by it, as are the terminology and future study hypotheses that use quantitative methods for theory testing. The process of IRB approval is still required prior to data collection, for the protection of human subjects.

Qualitative methods have different inquiry forms and processes. Data collection and analysis are driven by the particular qualitative method. Reliability and validity issues can be difficult with this form of research, and investigators frequently use triangulation of data to provide valid results. Triangulation involves the use of multiple data sources, complementary investigations, or theoretical perspectives to increase the data's validity. Dissemination of the findings through presentations and publication is the final step in the process, along with identification of future areas for inquiry.

Whether quantitative or qualitative research methods are selected depends on the phenomena of interest and the purpose of the research. For example, the researcher may select or use qualitative methods to investigate health beliefs of a particular cultural group whereas, quantitative methods will be used to test a new intervention designed to enhance the functional independence of older adults with a limitation in mobility. Regardless of the methods selected to address the need for information on the problem, the research must respect the individual or group in the quest for knowledge.

RESEARCH UTILIZATION

Recently, we have seen a concentration on the use of research findings in practice, or research-based practice. **Research utilization** has been described as the use of research findings to define new practices and the use of research methods to assist in implementing new practices with accuracy and evaluating their impact on patients and staff (Crane, 1985, p. 262). This addresses an accountability issue for the profession, and the direction of nursing research on clinical issues for improved patient outcomes and creative care in a time when resources are stretched beyond unimaginable limits.

Research roles of the baccalaureate-prepared nurse are utilization, participation in and support of investigations, and problem identification. A major movement for research-based nursing practice began in the 1970s. The WICHE Project (Western Interstate Commission for Higher Education) was a 6-year project funded by the Department of Health, Education, and Welfare (HEW) between 1971 and 1975. It focused on both the conduct of research projects and the utilization of research findings. The initial thrust of the project was to support collaborative research endeavors followed by a focus on using research findings in practice (Lindeman & Krueger, 1977). The second federally funded activity was the CURN Project (Conduct and Utilization of Research in Nursing) in Michigan between 1975 and 1981. This project focused on use in the hospital setting of the knowledge from research already available. Finding the information and the applicability to the practice setting were the skills of concern. This led to the development of guidelines and specific protocols for research-based nursing interventions. Videotapes illustrating the process became available.

Currently, we are seeing a positive view of research. Since the 1970s, an increasing number of journals are dedicated to publishing research findings. Specialty journals now include special columns or research features. Professional conferences, both general and specialty, now provide more research presentations as special and concurrent offerings. These sessions are well attended, particularly as the clinician's comfort level with terminology and the thirst for the most current information increase. A focus on research has also emerged in certification examinations.

In 1981, the ANA Cabinet for Nursing Research developed guidelines for involvement in research based on level of nursing education. In these guidelines, the graduate with doctoral preparation is seen as providing leadership on investigations, in applying theory, and in developing methods to generate knowledge for the discipline. With an expertise in specialty practice, the master's-prepared nurse is the facilitator for using research findings and conducting investigations. Associate degree and baccalaureate nursing graduates are research consumers. Baccalaureate graduates are also responsible for identifying researchable problems and findings from prior research on which to base practice. Research-based practice is fundamental to contemporary nursing, providing a firm foundation for nursing interventions. Proficiency in critiquing research lies at the core of professional practice behavior.

RESEARCH CRITIQUE

Given the steps and process of research, consider the process of critiquing a research study. A **research critique** is an objective analysis of a published research report. The reader must critically consider all components of the report, including problem, purpose, supporting literature, theoretical framework, definitions, study questions or hypotheses, design, population and sample, data collection methods and procedures, analysis, and interpretation of findings. Table 16–4 shows the areas to be addressed in a research critique. The ultimate goal of a research critique is to evaluate applicability of appropriate scientific findings to one's own professional practice and knowledge base.

Thoughtful critique is based on critical thinking skills used to address the steps of the research process. When publishing research reports, authors must provide the essential information gained from the study within the given space. This can create a challenge for the reader attempting to glean the vital information for a critique. A published research report is frequently organized into the following sections: abstract, introduction, review of literature, theoretical framework, methods, results, discussion, and references.

Preliminary information provides valuable information for the reader. First, the title of the study should clearly reflect the problem area and capture the reader's interest. Information on the researcher includes their background and qualifications in the

practice area and for conducting the research study. The abstract briefly reviews the problem, purpose, methodology, findings, and conclusions, summarizing the content and also capturing the reader's attention. Next comes the introduction to the research report.

The opening paragraphs outline background of the problem, including its purpose and significance to nursing and the care of clients. The **research problem** is the central question, which the research has been designed to answer. It is the "what" that is being done in the study to describe, explain, predict, or control some phenomenon of concern to nursing. The research problem contains the major variables and the population of concern to the researcher. The author may also identify specific research aims in this introductory section.

Next, a review of literature pertinent to the research problem is provided. The **literature review** is a report and comparison of all pertinent prior investigations on the topic, variables of interest, theoretical models, and methods used. Unlike the library research done for a paper, a research literature review concentrates on primary references. A primary literature source is the actual report of an investigation or development of an instrument or theory, written by the researcher or theorist. This eliminates the chance of error in interpretation that could occur through analyses by others or loss of the context of the original work. The literature review should provide a critical appraisal and synthesis of what is already known on the topic. Thus, the literature review supports the study and how the investigation proposes to contribute to the existing body of nursing knowledge.

The *theoretical framework* may be described in a separate section or included with the literature review. As was discussed in Chapters 3 and 4, a theoretical framework or model is the way the researcher views the concepts and their interrelationships; it may be described in words or displayed symbolically. This underlying view drives the research in describing, explaining, predicting, or controlling the phenomena.

At this point, the researcher may present specific questions to address in the study or hypotheses to be tested. Specific research questions must flow from, and relate back to, the main research problem or purpose. **Hypotheses** are predictions about the variables that the investigation is testing with a subject group. Hypotheses may be null (statistical), predicting no relationship; conversely, the researcher may state research (alternative) hypotheses that do predict a difference and, in some cases, the direction of the difference (increase, decrease, greater,

TABLE 16-4. Guidelines for the Critique of a Published Nursing Research Study

Study Content	Questions to Address in a Research Critique
Title and abstract	Is it of interest and applicable to practice?

Introduction
  Problem
  Purpose
  Significance
  Aims
	What was the stated research problem for the study?
	Did the stated problem clearly reflect the main issue addressed in the investigation?
	What was the purpose of the research study?
	Were any aims stated for the investigation?
	How is the problem significant to the knowledge base of nursing and the care of clients?

Literature review	What was said about previously known information on the topic? How were the sources reviewed important to the present study? What variables were reviewed? Were mostly primary sources used in the review? Did the authors present a critical analysis and comparison of prior studies? Were strengths and weaknesses of prior studies identified? Did the review provide rationale for the present study?
Theoretical framework	Was the theoretical framework described clearly with appropriate reference citations? Was the framework a nursing model or a theory from a related discipline? Would a nursing model have been more appropriate as a guide for this study? Does the framework make sense as a guide for the study?
Specific questions or hypotheses	Were the research questions or hypotheses clearly stated? Did they reflect the research problem or purpose? Were they consistent with the theoretical framework? What variables will be investigated?
Methods Research design	What, where, with whom, and exactly how was the research done? Was an experimental or nonexperimental design used? What independent, dependent, and confounding variables were identified? How were the variables defined? Did the researcher identify special controls used in the study?
Ethics	How were subjects' rights protected?
Sampling	What sampling method was used for the subjects? Was the sampling method appropriate for the study framework and design? What were the descriptive characteristics of the subjects? To what population did the researcher wish to generalize the study results? Was the sample group representative of this population?
Data collection	What data collection methods were used? What research instruments were used? What was the reliability and validity of the instruments?
Results/analysis	How were the data analyzed? Was this appropriate for the design and research methods used? Were appropriate statistics used to describe the characteristics of the sample and answer the research questions? Were answers provided for all the research questions? Were results given for each of the hypotheses? Were appropriate statistics used to test the hypotheses? What information was presented in figures and tables?
Discussion Conclusions	What conclusions were presented? Did the conclusions make sense? Were the conclusions consistent with the theoretical framework? Did the study lend further support to the theory used? Were the conclusions based on actual data obtained from the study? What limitations were described by the researcher? What additional limitations can be identified? Can the conclusions from the sample be generalized to the population?
Recommendations	What were the practice recommendations? What were the teaching (client or professional) recommendations? What were the recommendations for nursing administration? What recommendations were made for subsequent research on the topic?

less). Both null and research hypotheses can be either simple (stating a prediction between two variables) or complex (stating a difference between more than two variables). Hypothesis testing used inferential statistics, inferring from the sample to make generalizations about the population. Both research questions and hypotheses must be consistent with the framework that provides the theoretical guidance for the investigation. The variables to be investigated should be readily apparent in either the stated research questions or hypotheses.

The next major section in a published research report describes the methodology or methods. This section includes information on the research design, research subjects including ethical considerations and sampling, and data collection and procedures used. The **research design** is the overall blueprint for the study. The design includes the setting for the study, the subjects (sample group), the experimental or nonexperimental treatment or grouping methods, the data collection methods, and procedures or protocol. The research design is selected to address the variables of concern to answer the research questions or test the hypotheses. Study designs may be experimental or nonexperimental. Experimental designs are true experimental, quasi-experiments, and preexperiments, with varying degrees of control, manipulation, and randomization. Nonexperimental study designs may be used to answer the research questions with less human subject involvement or intervention; these designs include ex post facto, correlational, survey, case study, needs assessment, secondary analysis, and evaluation studies. Additional designs you may see in the literature are methodologic (studies on research tools or instruments) and metaanalysis, which uses many prior studies to determine the overall effect. The design must "fit" the research problem, purpose, and theoretical framework.

The researcher provides definitions for all major variables included in the study. Both theoretical and operational definitions may be provided in the introduction or the review of the literature. Theoretical, or in some cases conceptual, definitions are the general description of a term, that is, the term as defined in a specific theoretical framework or the dictionary. Researchers must provide operational definitions of the major variables of interest, especially when quantitative research methods are used. An **operational definition** is the description specific to the use of the variable in the study. It is precisely what the researchers are looking at and how they are measuring it. Consider the term "stethoscope." Every nurse knows it is an acoustical instrument used to measure heart rate apically or blood pres-

sure peripherally. But the type of stethoscope must be specified in the operational definition: bell-diaphragm combination, electronic, pediatric? The specification ensures controls in quantitative methods, describing exactly what the researcher used and enabling others to reproduce the study results given a similar set of circumstances.

Generally, the researcher provides operational definitions of the study variables in the section on methodology. **Variables** are concepts and constructs defined and manipulated, controlled, or measured in a research study. *Independent variables* are variables manipulated by the researcher, such as the cause, treatment, or difference between the groups (such as the type of dressing used, Telfa versus Tegaderm). *Dependent variables* are the outcome variables that the researcher is measuring and analyzing. The researcher wishes to see if the change in the independent variable (type of dressing) caused a difference in the dependent variable (healing time or bacterial colony count). *Uncontrolled or confounding variables* (such as nutritional status) must also be considered since they can produce extraneous and unwanted effects on the dependent variable (healing time). The researcher often attempts to control the extraneous effects by selecting a population or study procedures that meet specific criteria, to decrease the chance of the unwanted influences. In the methods section, special attention is given to the descriptions of the subjects. Ultimately, this allows the readers to determine the applicability to practice with their specific client group. Ethical considerations specific to the sample should also be described. Sampling methods are then identified.

Sampling is the use of a subset (sample) of the population as a feasible group to study, ultimately generalizing the findings to the population. The *population* is the total group to which the researcher wishes the results of the research to be generalized. For example, not all cardiac patients in a rehabilitation program can be interviewed in person. Yet the researcher would like the study results to be applicable to all patients similar to the subjects interviewed in the study, so that the information will add to the body of nursing knowledge. Samples may be selected by probability (based on statistical chance of selection) or nonprobability sampling. Types of probability samples include random, systematic, stratified, and cluster. Nonprobability samples include convenience, purposive, snowball, quota, and expert samples. Each type of sample has advantages and disadvantages that must be considered. At this point, look for the sample size. Smaller sample sizes are associated with qualitative methods. On the other hand, minimum sample sizes are necessary with some statistical procedures in quantitative methods and analysis.

Specific *research methods* are described as data collection procedures. Data are the measures or responses obtained from the subjects in the study. Analyzed data become information. Research methods may be quantitative or qualitative. *Quantitative methods* focus on numerical data that can be obtained from subjects using any one or a combination of measurement instruments. *Qualitative methods* focus on information gathered from individuals and groups, often in their natural environment, to explore their unique qualities in-depth and generate theory on a little known topic or construct. The different research methods can use similar or different instruments to obtain or measure data.

Instruments are the measurement tools for collecting data. They include paper-and-pencil instruments (such as questionnaires, diaries, or scales), biophysiologic instruments (such as a stethoscope, sphygmomanometer, pulse oximetry, ECG, or EEG), interview guides, video and audiotapes, and others depending on the specific investigation and variables. Important considerations for use of any instrument, including an observer as data collector, are the reliability and validity of the measurement. Researchers report the reliability and validity tests before they discuss the findings of their study.

Instrument reliability means that the instrument provides consistent measurement. The instrument measures the variable consistently over time. The need for instrument reliability is apparent in examples of a calibrated scale that reliably provides a reading of the client's weight or the test that consistently estimates the client's stress level. The types of instrument reliability that you will see reported in studies include test-retest (stability of the measure over time), internal consistency or alpha (statistical measure on items or parts of a test), equivalent forms of tests, and interrater (as equivalence among data collectors).

Instrument validity means the instrument measures what it is intended to measure, such as body surface area and not weight. Types of instrument validity include content, construct, and criterion-related. A panel of experts may assess the content validity of an instrument, ensuring that it adequately addresses the variable or area of interest. *Construct validity* is described with prior research on the instrument and may be reported as findings from a factor analysis or other statistical test. Criterion-related validity is important when the variable cannot be measured directly, such as family and visitor contacts, cards and gifts, and discussions (as another criterion) to discover social support for a study on the psychosocial stress of the hospitalized client.

Once the data collection methods have been described, the researcher describes methods used to analyze the data and reports the results in the findings or results section. Methods for analysis of the data are based on the specified research methods and the type of data involved. For numerical data, statistics are used in the analysis of quantitative research methods. **Descriptive statistics** are used to summarize and describe data through graphic displays of the information (percentages and frequency counts), measures of central tendency (means, medians, modes), and measures of dispersion (ranges, variances, and standard deviations). **Inferential statistics** are used to test hypotheses, make predictions, and infer from the sample (statistic) to the population (parameter). Depending on the variables, data, and sample size and distribution, inferential statistics include nonparametric tests (chi square, Spearman rho, median test) and parametric tests (*t*-test, ANOVA, Pearson r). The results are reported for each research question or hypothesis in an objective manner, for example, the result of the statistical test used to test each hypothesis.

Finally, the researcher presents his or her interpretation of the results in a discussion section. Conclusions should be consistent with the theoretical framework used to guide the study. The discussion also includes the researcher's identification of limitations and recommendations for using the findings in practice, teaching, administration, and further research.

At this point, the reader must determine the applicability of the results to the individual practice area. A research critique is an objective assessment, based on the information presented in the report against some criterion, such as the critique questions. The subjective evaluation for use of the findings in one's own practice area is done after the objective critique of the value of the study's process and results. If the critique is positive, you must decide whether the results are applicable in your practice area. If so, it is a professional responsibility to implement information found to be beneficial to clients, rather than continuing practice based on tradition instead of fact and efficacy.

Reading professional journals and keeping abreast of current knowledge is essential in contemporary nursing practice. Critique skills of the nurse is an integral part of this. Access to quality journals and the depth of reading must also be considered. Look carefully at the professional journals to which you subscribe and the journals that are available at your work site. Do they contain research reports? If so, are you reading research studies as well as the narrative and practice articles? Consider the four levels of reading: elementary reading, systematic skimming, analytic reading, and comparative reading (Wilson, 1989). At what level are you reading? Critiquing a research article is at the level of analytic reading rather than merely looking for articles of interest to your practice area. Make time, on a consistent basis, to look for and evaluate research in the professional literature.

Once you have obtained the information from the professional literature, the issue is implementation and sharing. Are you sharing the information with colleagues? This can be done informally among nurses or formally presented at a unit conference. Having access to a "user-friendly" database or library is essential for acquiring information on a clinical issue. Investigate what is available in your environment. The availability of "brown bag lunches" or participation in a journal club focused on research studies are ways of making this activity more enjoyable and rewarding.

Obtaining new information is the intended aim of attending a clinical conference, whether or not continuing education units are required for relicensure or recertification. Quality of programs and significance of the topics to your practice area must be considered. Selecting research-based concurrent sessions is a good way to hear current research information. Attendance at grand rounds in an institution committed to research is also a valuable experience. Research questions specific to nursing or interdisciplinary collaboration may become available. Your work setting may have a nursing or interdisciplinary research committee. Participating on a research committee can be a challenging and rewarding experience. Nurses can collaborate on different stages of the research process. In addition, the practice problems specific to your setting can emerge, be developed, and investigated when professionals start the discussion and raise the issues. It can be quite a stimulating as well as a fun experience.

ELIMINATING BARRIERS TO APPLICATION OF CLINICAL RESEARCH

Barriers to nursing research should be diminished or removed to further professional practice. Such barriers include real and perceived lack of educational preparation, administrative support, resources, and time. In this time of diminishing resources, the use of the most reliable and accurate information is crucial. This is research-based practice. Trial-and-error strategies waste valuable resources. We need an increasing sense of professional commitment to research-based practice.

Negative attitudes toward research or researchers need to be replaced with greater collaboration among clinicians, researchers, administrators, and educators. Clinicians have firsthand awareness of problem areas but must be assisted in: (1) accessing the current knowledge base, (2) looking at problems in the domain of nursing that address the need for improved client outcomes, (3) having the professional commitment to go the extra mile and take time to get involved with research activities, and (4) receiving some form of recognition for their efforts. The support and encouragement of the chief nurse administrator or executive is a must. This will ensure that the organizational climate, resources, and philosophy of practice are present in the practice setting. Moving to research-based practice will not be an easy transition without a dynamic person spearheading the process. Clinicians must keep an open mind and make a professional commitment to identify research problems and search the current knowledge base for information. Researchers must collaborate with clinicians to address nursing questions and avoid "researchese," thus providing clear practice implications in publications and presentations. Educators must also assist in the development of critique and research skills.

Commitment must be made to the ongoing nature of all research activities and interest maintained. Our knowledge base has been evolving since the time of Nightingale and before. It will constantly evolve because of the nature of the information and our focus on people in a dynamic environment. Our scientific base is still in its infancy, and we need more extensive research generalizable to and support for nursing as a major player in health-care issues. We need more replications to add reliability and validity to instruments and information. Constant updating and modification of any protocol is needed as more information becomes available. Gaining critique skills and learning the language of research are components of this process.

KEY POINTS

- **Research** is a process for generating scientific knowledge and utilizing the knowledge on which to base practice. Using nursing research is a vital professional attribute and a responsibility.

- Nursing research began with Florence Nightingale and has become vital to both professionals and consumers in investigating the domain of nursing, testing theories and interventions, and demonstrating the efficacy and efficiency of nursing actions.

- Highly evident in the research priorities of the National Center for Nursing Research is testing of nursing interventions that promote health behaviors in individuals or population groups.

- Ethical considerations in research must include the four basic human rights:
    1. Do no harm (beneficence)
    2. Full disclosure
    3. Self-determination
    4. Privacy and confidentiality

- A professional nurse should be an active consumer of nursing research, promoting use of current and valid scientific knowledge and identifying the questions to be addressed in further research. Professional accountability demands that one read the literature, attend educational sessions, use critique skills, and participate in investigations.

- Empirical research is based on the strict rules of the scientific method, with the following steps:
    1. identification of the problem,
    2. statement of the purpose,
    3. review of the literature,
    4. description of theoretical framework,
    5. definition of terms,
    6. statement of hypothesis,
    7. selection of the research design, population, and the sample,
    8. collection of data,
    9. analysis and interpretation of data, and
    10. presentation of findings and recommendations.

- Research-based practice, or **research utilization,** has been described as the use of research findings and methods to define and implement new practices and evaluate the effects of the revisions in practice.

- A **research critique** is an objective analysis of a published research report. The reader must critically consider all components of the report, including problem, purpose, literature support, theoretical framework, definitions, study questions or hypotheses, design, population and sample, data collection methods and procedures, analysis, and interpretation of findings. The ultimate goal of a research critique is to consider applicability of appropriate scientific findings to one's own professional practice and knowledge base.

- A **research problem** is the main issue or central question that the researcher addresses in the investigation. Specific research questions or hypotheses flow from the main research problem.

- The **literature review** is a report and comparison of all pertinent prior investigations on the topic, variables of interest, theoretical models, and methods used. The researcher focuses on primary sources for a critical appraisal and synthesis of what is known presently.

- **Variables** are concepts and constructs defined and manipulated, controlled, or measured in a research study. Independent variables are manipulated by the researcher, such as the cause, treatment of, or difference between the groups. Dependent variables are the outcome variables that the researcher is measuring and analyzing.
- **Hypotheses** are predictions about the variables that the researcher is testing with a subject group. Hypothesis testing uses inferential statistics to infer from the sample and make generalizations about the population. The **research design** is the overall blueprint and methods for the study.
- **Research methods** may be quantitative or qualitative. Quantitative methods focus on numerical data that can be obtained from subjects through any one or a combination of measurement instruments. Qualitative methods focus on information gathered from individuals and groups, often in their natural environment, to explore in depth their unique qualities and generate theory on a little known topic or construct.
- **Sampling** is the use of a subset (sample) of the population as a feasible group to study and ultimately generalize findings to the population.
- **Instruments** are the measurement tools for collecting data. Important considerations for use of any instrument are the reliability and validity of the measurement.
- **Statistics** are used in analyzing quantitative research methods. Descriptive statistics are used to summarize and describe data. Inferential statistics are used to test hypotheses, make predictions, and infer from the sample to the population.

CHAPTER EXERCISES

1. Critique a nursing research article. First, locate a current research article that pertains to your clinical practice area. Try to select an article that has subheadings such as theoretical framework or hypotheses, literature review, sample, findings, and discussion. Develop an objective critique of the study using the guidelines presented in this chapter. Discuss the applicability of this research to your practice setting and the potential for using the findings.

2. Describe research activities that are present in your practice setting.

3. Develop a plan to encourage or promote research-based practice in your nursing practice environment. Select a clinical protocol or problem. Use the following six phases of the research utilization process to organize your plan: (a) identification of clinical problems and access to research bases; (b) evaluation of the knowledge and the potential for application in the organization, along with policy and cost determinants; (c) planning for implementation and evaluation of the innovation; (d) clinical trial and evaluation; (e) decisions to adopt, modify or reject innovations based on evaluation; and (f) if adopted, planning for extension to other units (Horsley, Crane, and Bingle, 1978). Incorporate concepts from the change process to describe who will be involved in the process and how the change will be implemented. Finally, identify evaluation criteria.

REFERENCES

American Association of Colleges of Nursing (AACN). (1990, March). *Position statement: Nursing research*. Washington, DC: AACN.

American Nurses' Association Commission on Nursing Research. (1981). *Guidelines for the investigative function of nurses*. Kansas City, MO: American Nurses' Association.

American Nurses' Association. (1985). *Human rights guidelines for nurses in clinical and other research* (Pub. No. D-46 3M 9/87R). Kansas City, MO: American Nurses' Association.

Belmont Report: Ethical principles and guidelines for the protection of human subjects of research. 79 Fed. Reg. 12065 (1979).

Burns, N., & Grove, S. K. (1993). *The practice of nursing research: Conduct, critique, & utilization* (2nd ed.). Philadelphia: Saunders.

Crane, J. (1985). Research utilization: Theoretical perspectives. *Western Journal of Nursing Research, 7,* 261–268.

Declaration of Helsinki. (1990). Recommendations guiding physicians in biomedical research involving human subjects. *Bulletin of Pan American Health Organization, 24*(4), 606–609.

Duncan, K. A. (1994). *Health information and health reform: Understanding the need for a national health information system.* San Francisco: Jossey-Bass.

Horsley, J. A., Crane, J., & Bingle, J. D. (1978). Research utilization as an organizational process. *Journal of Nursing Administration, 8*(7), 4–6.

Kerlinger, F. N. (1986). *Foundations of behavioral research* (3rd ed.). New York: Holt, Rinehart and Winston.

Lindeman, C. A., & Krueger, J. C. (1977). Increasing the quality, quantity, and use of nursing research. *Nursing Outlook, 25,* 450–454.

National Institute for Nursing Research. (1993). *National Institute for Nursing Research, National Institute of Health*. Bethesda, MD: National Institutes of Health.

Nightingale, F. (1859). *Notes on nursing*. (reprint) Philadelphia: Lippincott.

Polit, D. F., & Hungler, B. P. (1991). *Nursing research: Principles and methods* (4th ed.). Philadelphia: Lippincott.

Protection of Human Subjects. 45 C.F.R. § 46 (1991).

Wilson, H. S. (1989). *Research in nursing* (2nd ed.). Redwood City, CA: Addison-Wesley.

BIBLIOGRAPHY

Betz, C. L., Poster, E., Randell, B., & Omery, A. (1990). Nursing research productivity in clinical settings. *Nursing Outlook, 38,* 180–183.

Bircumshaw, D. (1990). The utilization of research findings in clinical nursing practice. *Journal of Advanced Nursing, 15,* 1272–1280.

Burns, N., & Grove, S. K. (1995). *Understanding nursing research.* Philadelphia: Saunders.

Fawcett, J. (1984). Hallmarks of success in nursing research. *Advances in Nursing Science, 7*(1), 1–11.

Fawcett, J. (1992). *Relationships of theory and research* (2nd ed.). Philadelphia: Davis.

Fitzpatrick, J. J., & Stevenson, J. S. (1995). *Annual review of nursing research. Volume 13: Focus on key social and health issues.* New York: Springer.

Goode, C. J., Lovett, M. K., Hayes, J. E., & Butcher, L. A. (1990). Use of research-based knowledge in clinical practice. In C. A. Lindeman & M. McAthie (Ed.), *Readings in nursing trends and issues* (pp. 190–198). Springhouse, PA: Springhouse.

Haller, K. B., Reynolds, M. A., & Horsley, J. A. (1990). Developing research-based innovation protocols: Process, criteria, and issues. In C. A. Lindeman & M. McAthie (Ed.), *Readings in nursing trends and issues* (pp. 169–176). Springhouse, PA: Springhouse.

Horn Video Productions. (1987). *Using research in clinical nursing practice* (Video No. 187). (Available from Horn Video Productions, 607 West Second Street, Ida Grove, IA 51445.)

Horn Video Productions. (1989). *Research utilization: A process of organizational change* (Video No. 289). (Available from Horn Video Productions, 607 West Second Street, Ida Grove, IA 51445.)

Horn Video Productions. (1991). *Reading and critiquing a research report* (Video No. 391). (Available from Horn Video Productions, 607 West Second Street, Ida Grove, IA 51445.)

Knafl, K. A., Hagle, M. E., Bevis, M. E., Faux, S. A., & Kirchhoff, K. T. (1989). How researchers and administrators view the role of the clinical nurse researcher. *Journal of Advanced Nursing, 11,* 583–592.

Larson, E. (1989). Using the CURN Project to teach research utilization in a baccalaureate program. *Western Journal of Nursing Research, 11,* 593–599.

Lindeman, C. A. (1990). Research in practice: The role of the staff nurse. In C. A. Lindeman & M. McAthie (Ed.), *Readings in nursing trends and issues* (pp. 166–168). Springhouse, PA: Springhouse.

Munhall, P. L., & Boyd, C. O. (1993). *Nursing research: A qualitative perspective* (2nd ed.) (Publication No. 19-2535). New York: National League for Nursing.

Munro, B. H., & Page, E. B. (1993). *Statistical methods for health care research* (2nd ed.). Philadelphia: Lippincott.

National Center for Nursing Research. (1990). *National Center for Nursing Research, National Institute of Health*. Bethesda, MD: National Institutes of Health.

Nieswiadomy, R. M. (1992). *Foundations of nursing research* (2nd ed.). Norwalk, CT: Appleton & Lange.

Polit, D. F., & Hungler, P. (1994). *Nursing research: Principles and methods* (5th ed.). Philadelphia: Lippincott.

Porter, E. J. (1989). The qualitative-quantitative dualism. *Image: Journal of Nursing Scholarship, 21,* 98–102.

Ramos, M. C. (1989). Some ethical implications of qualitative research. *Research in Nursing & Health, 12,* 57–63.

Shott, S. (1990). *Statistics for health professionals.* Philadelphia: Saunders.

Stetler, C. B. (1985). Research utilization: Defining the concept. *Image: Journal of Nursing Scholarship, 17,* 40–44.

Streubert, H. J., & Carpenter, D. R. (1994). *Qualitative research in nursing: Advancing the humanistic imperative.* Philadelphia: Lippincott.

Tanner, C. A. (1990). Evaluating research for use in practice: Guidelines for the clinician. In C. A. Lindeman & M. McAthie (Ed.), *Readings in nursing trends and issues* (pp. 158–165). Springhouse, PA: Springhouse.

Vaughn-Wrobel, B. C. (1994). Reflections on research in nursing. *Reflections, 18*(3), 2.

Wilson, H. S., & Hutchinson, S. A. (1996). *The consumer's guide to nursing research: Exercises, learning activities, tools, and resources.* Albany, NY: Delmar.

Wilson-Barnett, J., Corner, J., & DeCarle, B. (1990). Integrating nursing research and practice—the role of the researcher as teacher. *Journal of Advanced Nursing, 15,* 621–625.

Chapter 17

THE POLITICALLY ACTIVE NURSE

Kathleen Winter

CHAPTER OBJECTIVES

On completion of
this chapter, the reader
will be able to:

1. Explain why it is important for nurses to understand and become involved in the political process.
2. List four levels of political involvement.
3. Describe the basic structure of government.
4. Discuss how a bill becomes a law.
5. Identify the major committees at the federal level that influence health policy.
6. Identify four points at which nurses can influence a bill.
7. Discuss the role of professional associations, nursing networks, and coalitions in influencing health policy decisions.

KEY TERMS

Politics
Laws
Nurse Practice Acts
Political Involvement

Lobbying
Policital Action
    Committees

Political Nursing
    Networks
Coalition

If nursing is to take its rightful place in setting health policy, nurses must know about the issues, understand the political system, and participate in it. (Goldwater & Zusy, 1990)

Politics means influencing—specifically, influencing the allocation of scarce resources (Mason, Talbott, & Leavitt, 1993). Nurses have become increasingly interested in public policy, realizing that both their personal lives and their professional activities are significantly influenced by government policy and programs. "Many nurses have become aware that health policy directly affects how they are educated, where they practice, and how they are reimbursed" (Goldwater & Zusy, 1990).

The potential of health-care reform in our country has shown the impact that even "proposed" legislative action can have. When President Clinton placed health-care reform on the national agenda, it was expected that a comprehensive national health-care law would be passed, possibly even a national health insurance program (single-payer plan) similar to that in Canada. Special interest groups mobilized to oppose such sweeping changes in the system. Hospitals and health-care agencies also reacted to the anticipated legislation, causing some dramatic changes in health-care delivery. Hospitals down-sized or "rightsized," laying off nurses or instituting hiring freezes, even before any laws or regulations were passed. Mergers occurred between rival hospitals and insurers, causing more than 4000 workers to lose their jobs in just one city alone. Physicians were also affected by these mergers, and some have sold their practices to hospitals and become employees rather than private practitioners.

REGULATING NURSING PRACTICE

Nursing practice and education are regulated directly and indirectly by both state and federal laws and nurse practice acts.

Laws

Laws are regulations enacted and enforced by federal or state legislators or regulatory agencies or set by court judgments, based on the U.S. Constitution. They govern behavior and relationships with others in society. Table 17–1 lists the types of laws. Consider the impact of laws that have been passed and their effect on nursing. When the federal government established and instituted diagnosis-related groups (DRGs) as a payment program for Medicare reimbursement, hospital patients began to be discharged from hospitals "sicker and quicker." Although this law applied only to Medicare clients, it

TABLE 17 – 1. Types of Law

Constitutional law	Specific guarantees granted by the U.S. Constitution
Statutory law	Formal laws enacted by federal, state, and local legislative branches of government
Administrative law	Laws created by administrative agencies under the direction of the executive branch of government
Common law	Laws created by judicial decisions. Judgments create a precedent by which future decisions are made. This is the most common source of law for malpractice.

set a precedent that other insurance carriers followed. The implications of this single act significantly reduced the availability of hospital jobs for nurses.

Laws also work to create opportunities and jobs for nurses. Many states have passed laws allowing some nurses to be directly reimbursed by clients or insurance carriers. Legislation varies from state to state, but advanced practice nurses, particularly nurse anesthetists, nurse practitioners, and nurse midwives, are most frequently covered. These laws have helped increase the autonomy of nurses and have set the stage for more nurses to enter into advanced practice. At present more than 100,000 advanced practice nurses—nurses with education and clinical experience beyond the 2 to 4 years of basic nursing education—are providing essential primary care services as certified nurse midwives, nurse practitioners, and clinical nurse specialists (ANA, 1994).

Laws that affect practice can be passed with the support of nursing, to address a particular need. For instance, some states have passed laws to allow registered nurses to pronounce death. The following example illustrates why these laws were needed.

Mrs. Smith, an elderly woman who had a terminal illness, died peacefully at home surrounded by her family. When the family was unable to reach the physician or funeral director, however, they had no choice but to call the paramedic unit serving their area. When the paramedics arrived, approximately 3 hours after Smith's death, they were required by law to initiate cardiopulmonary resuscitation (CPR) and to transport her to the nearest emergency department several miles from the family home. This situation was emotionally disturbing to the family but it was also costly with the paramedics' time, the ambulance, and emergency room fees.

Situations like this can prompt a nurse or a nursing group to approach a legislator for support in introducing a bill to rectify the problem. For instance, Pennsylvania nurses, particularly those working in home care, hospice, and long-term care, pushed for legislation that would permit them to release deceased persons to funeral directors, to prevent the situation described here. The bill was signed into law in 1992 (PNA, 1991).

State laws or regulations may also impact on nursing education. In North Dakota, for example, the baccalaureate degree has been designated as the minimal requirement for entry into professional nursing practice. This requirement was the result of passage of a law; however, regulations promulgated by a state board of nursing may also affect education and practice and, if passed, hold the force of law.

Nurse Practice Acts

Nurse practice acts are developed by each state to define the scope of practice, establish the requirements for licensure and entry into practice, create and empower a board of nursing to oversee licensees, and identify grounds for disciplinary action. Based in state law, they are meant to protect the public. Nurse practice acts can be revised or completely eliminated through a single legislative action (Table 17–2).

TABLE 17- 2. Nurse Practice Acts

The nurse practice act in each state provides nurses with the right to practice and delimits the parameters of professional practice. Most state practice acts contain basically the same major components, including reason for the law, definition of nursing, requirements for licensure, grounds for revocation of a license, provisions for persons licensed in other states, creation of a board for nurse examiners, responsibilities of the board, and penalties for practicing without a license (Kelly, 1991). The requirements in these categories vary from state to state. Because each state law differs, it is important for nurses to know about the law regulating their practice. Copies of the law can be obtained from the individual state nurses' association or from the state agency responsible for distributing laws.

Appointments to a state board of nursing are frequently political. It is therefore important to know the composition of one's respective state boards and to have a voice in selecting candidates to serve on the board. Because regulatory changes made by a state board have the same force as law, it is important to remain aware of the activities of the state board of nursing that regulates nursing practice within each state. Nurses are often unaware that changes are even being proposed until it is too late to influence them.

LEVELS OF POLITICAL INVOLVEMENT

There is nothing magical about political involvement. It is a task for which nurses, through their education, are prepared. Attempting to effect political change is similar to attempting to teach patients about changing their ineffective health habits. It requires using critical thinking skills in the political arena. Nurses must ask how and where they can make a difference and how they can become involved in the process. Not every nurse may choose to run for political office, but each nurse can make a contribution. It is vital that nurses use their voices and individual power to empower nurses and nursing.

Political involvement is not restricted to creating laws and government policies. Nurses can influence change: the workplace, government, professional organizations, and community (the encompassing sphere). Table 17–3 shows how nurses can become politically involved.

Workplace

The workplace is a significant political arena for nurses to exert influence, particularly regarding creation of optimal working conditions and promoting decision making that ensures high-quality patient

TABLE 17- 3. How Nurses Can Become
Politically Involved

1. Register to vote or, if registered, encourage others to become registered.

2. Learn who your legislators and other elected or appointed officials are at local, state, and national levels. (A phone call to the League of Women voters or your county elections office will provide this much-needed information. For listings of local officials, call your city or town clerk.) Be aware of the composition of your state board of nursing, and its influence on policy decisions affecting the profession.

3. Meet your legislators in their home district, even if only to pick up information and become acquainted with the staff. (Legislators want to hear the concerns of their nurse constituents, and most will regard you as the credible professional that you are. Establishing personal relationships is an important step in building rapport.)

4. Call or write to elected officials or legislators on issues important to nursing and health. Remember, you are the expert when it comes to nursing and patient care.

5. Be informed about legislation and policy decisions that have important consequences for the nursing profession and healthcare recipients.

6. Join and become involved in the professional nursing organizations.

care. Nurses are also more likely to be heard, and to be listened to, if they are involved and are known to the people they are trying to influence. To be influential, nurses must take an active role in institutional decision making, either at the unit level or by volunteering to serve on various hospital or agency committees, and they must remain current with the trends and issues in health care and the latest research related to health care to be able to present factual data and contribute to policy decisions. Serving as committee members, nurses have the opportunity to learn about and contribute to the legislative process. To be a positive force for change, nurses must be assertive in making their opinions known. This is most easily done by fostering good interpersonal relationships and learning as much as possible about the views of coworkers and those in positions of higher authority.

Government

The principles of politics that can be learned at the institutional levels can be used to influence change in other areas. It is imperative for nurses to become involved in issues directly affecting their work, their profession, and their personal lives at all levels. At the government levels, nurses must recognize that they are experts in delivering health care; they must teach legislators, who are not experts, the effect that laws have on the patient and health-care delivery. Establishing a personal relationship with a legislator is a vital part of this political process (Table 17–4). Legislators recognize that nurses have expertise on the unique needs of clients (who are also their constituents) and of health-care delivery. The input of nurses is vital to legislators because few of them have a health-care background. In fact, their only experience may be from being a patient or knowledge gained from a relative or friend who is a health professional. If these views are negative, the interests of nursing may not be served. Nurses can influence policy at the federal, state, and local levels.

FEDERAL LEVEL

Nursing organizations, such as the American Nurses Association (ANA), are most active at the federal level, lobbying for laws that favor nursing practice and better delivery of health care. At the federal level, nurses' influence can help promote or defeat legislation or help maintain funding for particular

TABLE 17-4. Tips for Talking to Legislators

- Before meeting with the legislator, get to know as much as possible about his or her party affiliation, voting record, committee assignments, and, if possible, beliefs about the nursing profession.
- Schedule a meeting for at least 15 to 30 minutes.
- If the legislator is not available, meet with a staff member who has a working knowledge of the issues you want to discuss.
- Be prepared to explain what nursing does, your philosophy of care delivery, and the impact of pending laws on care delivery.
- Investigate both sides of the issues you want to discuss.
- Use examples from your practice to illustrate the points you are making.
- If possible, be prepared to offer specific requests or solutions.
- If the legislator indicates he or she will support your position, ask for help in reaching other legislators.
- Send a follow-up thank you note for the time spent and restate your position.

purposes, such as nursing education. At this level of government, it is especially important for nursing organizations to speak with a unified voice in presenting their nursing concerns. Although specialty groups may have their own particular needs, dissention among groups within the same profession can be detrimental to the cause because it diminishes the groups' power and credibility. Nurses should remain knowledgeable about the positions set forth by the professional organizations on issues that are likely to come before the Congress, should learn who the key legislators and their assistants are and should communicate regularly about matters of concern.

STATE LEVEL

State nursing organizations tend to be active at the state level. Individual nurses can be involved with these organizations to support the goals of the organizations. At the state level, nurses have successfully lobbied to enact legislation that allows them to bill insurance companies directly for the care they provide. To get legislation enacted, individual nurses or a nursing organization can introduce legislation and seek a sponsor and cosponsors. Once the legislation is introduced, nurses must lobby legislatures to provide information on how passage on the bill will benefit the legislator's constituents.

During 1995, approximately 45 nurses served in state legislatures, and one nurse served at the federal level. Although it is rare to find health-care professionals serving in elected positions, things are beginning to change. The number of physicians running for public office has increased dramatically, for example, since President Clinton introduced health-care reform to the national agenda. Seeing nurses elected to leadership positions and appointed to serve on boards at the state government level is becoming more common, but there is a great need to increase the numbers who are willing and prepared to serve in these roles. Often it is through involvement at the local level that nurses gain experience to move on to state level positions.

Nurses can also be involved at the local level. For instance, nurses may choose to run for elected positions on the school board or local regulating boards. Others may attend meetings to voice their concerns. Changes in local policy can have a dramatic effect on the health and welfare of the community. Nurses need to be involved in these decisions, because they understand that what goes on in the community influences the health of the residents.

Professional Organizations

Every nurse should consider belonging to one of the major professional organizations. These organizations provide collective efforts to analyze policy and its effect on the profession and health-care delivery, and they can potentially mount more effective campaigns to influence policy. For instance, state nurses' associations often publish a legislative bulletin or summary of bills in their publications, and many specialty groups also have government relations committees that publish information on current nursing issues. Nurses who belong to the national organizations can become involved in the local chapters, and then at the national level. (See Chapter 1 for more information on professional organizations and Appendix A for a list.)

Community

In the community, nurses can identify potential health hazards that require attention of the local officials or businesspersons, such as intervening in the case of pollution.

STRUCTURE AND FUNCTION OF GOVERNMENT

To participate most effectively in the political process, it is essential to understand the structure of government at each level. Because government structures may vary across the country, become familiar with your particular local governing body.

County government generally takes one of the following forms: board of supervisors, elected board of commissioners, county executive or county manager, or mixed county board (Majewski, 1993). City government forms include mayor-council, council-manager, mayor-manager, and commissioners. Towns, boroughs, and villages also have a variety of elected officials similar to those of county government. School districts may also be regarded as governmental units, if their budgets are not tied to a municipal budget (Majewski, 1993).

Each branch of government plays a significant role in the development and implementation of health policy. The federal government and most state governments have three branches: the legislative, executive, and judicial. At the federal level, the executive branch includes the president, the cabinet governmental departments, and regulatory agencies. The executive branch is responsible for the administration of government and its laws. Additionally, the president sets the legislative agenda for Congress and a budget for the nation. The legislative branch includes the two houses of Congress and is responsible for lawmaking, representation, and administrative oversight (such as, overseeing the agencies of the executive branch and providing their funding). The judicial branch includes the Supreme Court, which interprets the law.

Although nurses are most often involved with the legislative branch of government, the executive branch can also be of great importance to nursing and health care. The president's budget influences the monies available for health care and nursing education, and the agenda set by the president determines what programs have a high priority for the administration. The president can also recommend legislation and approve or veto legislation passed by Congress. It is also in the executive branch that appointments to government departments, volunteer boards, or committees are made. The Congress of the United States receives its mandate from the U.S. Constitution. The Congress is bicameral, meaning that it is composed of two bodies: the Senate and the House of Representatives (Table 17–5).

State government structures are similar to those de-

TABLE 17-5. U.S. Congress

	Senate	House of Representatives
Number	100 senators (2 from each state) equal representation	Congresspersons (435 members)* Representation based on population of each state per U.S. Census Bureau
Terms	Elected for term of 6 years	Elected for term of 2 years
Reelection	Every 2 years, one-third of senators face reelection	Entire membership is up for reelection every 2 years
Qualifications	30 years of age Citizen of United States for 9 years Resident of the state represented when elected	25 years of age Citizen of United States for 7 years Resident of the state represented when elected

*The House also includes delegates from the District of Columbia, Guam, the Virgin Islands, and American Samoa, and the resident commissioner from Puerto Rico.

scribed at the federal level and also derive their powers from the U.S. Constitution. In some states, members of the state board of nursing, or other important health commissions, are appointed by the governor. As with the president, the governor can sign legislation into law and use the power of the veto.

HOW LAWS ARE MADE

The idea for a law may originate with an individual concerned citizen, a professional group such as the ANA or the National League for Nursing (NLN), a legislator, or the executive branch (the president or governor). The bill is authored or sponsored by either a representative or a senator, who introduces it after it is written in suitable legislative language by the legislative counsel of either the House or the Senate. At the federal level, bills are referred to full committee and generally, because of the enormous number of bills introduced, to a subcommittee. It is within the committee structures that most of the work of Congress takes place. Committee action is perhaps the most important phase of the congressional process, for this is where proposed measures are given the most intensive consideration and people have an opportunity to be heard. The subcom-

mittee studies the issue carefully, holds hearings, and reports back to the full committee with recommendations. There are numerous standing committees in the House and Senate, as well as several select committees and standing joint committees. Each committee has jurisdiction over certain subjects, and often has two or more subcommittees. In the U.S. Congress, the committees with greatest jurisdiction over health matters and their subcommittees are the following:

- *House Ways and Means Committee:* Social Security and Medicare (Subcommittee on Health)
- *House Commerce Committee:* health legislation including Medicaid (Subcommittee on Health and the Environment)
- *Senate Finance Committee:* Medicare and Medicaid (Subcommittee on Health)
- *Senate Labor and Human Resources Committee:* health legislation in general; also works cooperatively with Senate Finance Committee in considering issues involving Medicare and Medicaid
- *House and Senate Appropriations Committee:* authorizes all money necessary to implement action proposed in a bill (subcommittees for Labor, Education, and Health and Human Services)

As a result of full committee hearings, several things may happen to a bill:

- It may be reported out of committee favorably, and be scheduled for debate by the full House or Senate.
- It may be reported out favorably, but with amendments.
- It may be reported out unfavorably, or killed outright.

After a bill has been reported out of a House committee (with the exception of ways and means or appropriations committees) it goes to the Rules Committee, which schedules bills and determines how much time will be spent on debate and whether or not amendments will be allowed. In the Senate, bills go on the Senate calendar, at which time the majority leadership determines when a bill will be debated. After a bill is debated, possibly amended, and passed by one chamber, it is sent to the other chamber, where it goes through the same procedure. If the bill passes both the House and the Senate without any changes, it is sent to the president for his signature.

If the House and Senate pass different versions of a bill, however, the two bills are sent to a conference committee, composed of members appointed by both the House and the Senate. This committee seeks to resolve differences between the two bills; if the differences cannot be resolved, the bill dies in committee. If the conference committee reaches agreement on a bill, it goes back to the House and Senate for passage. At this juncture, the bill must be voted up or down, because no further amendments are accepted. If the bill is approved in both houses, it then goes to the president. If the president signs the bill, it becomes a law. If vetoed, it is sent back to the House and Senate. To override the veto, a two-thirds vote by both chambers is required.

Clearly, the passage of a law is a long and difficult process. This is often quite frustrating for "action-oriented" nurses who are used to seeing immediate outcomes, forming plans, and making things happen. Nevertheless, nurses can and do play a significant role at several points in the legislative process (Figure 17–1).

Nurses can influence the introduction of a bill as private citizens or as members of a professional organization. They can provide information to assist in drafting the bill and work to gather support from members of Congress on the proposed legislation. During committee or subcommittee hearings, nurses may provide testimony to inform committee members about their position. Nurses may also actively work to influence (lobby) the views of congressional members, both in their home district and in Washington, D.C. (or the state capitol). Finally, they may attempt to influence the president or governor to either sign or veto the legislation, using telegrams, letters, and phone calls.

After a law is passed, it is assigned to the appropriate department of the executive branch of government, which begins the process of regulation. The regulation-writing process includes studying the law and drafting and publishing regulations for implementation. Again, nurses can influence these regulations by writing letters to the regulatory agency or by speaking at public hearings. Clearly, nurses can do a great deal to help shape public health policy. If we fail to become involved in this process, however, others will simply determine policy for us.

GAINING SKILL IN POLITICS

To become politically astute, you will need to understand the political process and know that, although you may not always be satisfied with the

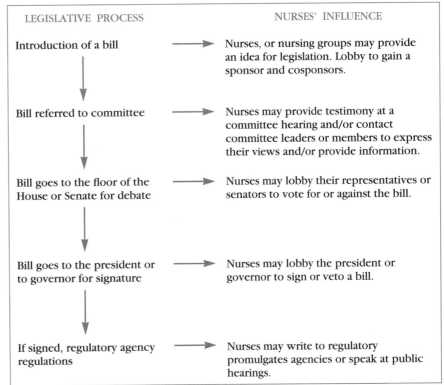

LEGISLATIVE PROCESS	NURSES' INFLUENCE
Introduction of a bill	Nurses, or nursing groups may provide an idea for legislation. Lobby to gain a sponsor and cosponsors.
Bill referred to committee	Nurses may provide testimony at a committee hearing and/or contact committee leaders or members to express their views and/or provide information.
Bill goes to the floor of the House or Senate for debate	Nurses may lobby their representatives or senators to vote for or against the bill.
Bill goes to the president or to governor for signature	Nurses may lobby the president or governor to sign or veto a bill.
If signed, regulatory agency regulations	Nurses may write to regulatory promulgates agencies or speak at public hearings.

FIGURE 17–1. How nurses may make an impact on the federal and legislative process.

way the system works, you can work to make significant changes (Winter, 1991).

Chalich and Smith in 1992 offered a model for individual political development that encourages grassroots involvement in local issues. As a nurse-activist herself, Chalich contends that involvement in partisan politics may be desirable, but grassroots efforts may be more fulfilling and should certainly not be discounted. This model is an activity-oriented ladder, including activities at four distinct levels:

Rung 1—Civic Involvement. Children's sports, PTA, neighborhood improvement group

Rung 2—Advocacy. Writing letters to public officials and newspapers and making organized visits to officials on local issues

Rung 3—Organizing. Independent organizing on local issues, incorporation of single-issue citizens' groups, and networking with similarly situated citizen's groups

Rung 4—Long-term power welding. Campaigning for oneself or another, local government planning, and agenda setting

To be involved in the political process, nurses must know and understand the issues. Issues are generally presented in the editorial sections of newspapers; most newspapers also have a political watch section, which reports the results of any significant votes at the state and federal levels. The ANA newspaper, *The American Nurse,* is an excellent source of information on issues of concern to the profession. In addition, the *American Journal of Nursing* "Newsline" feature and *Nursing and Health Care's* "Washington Focus" are excellent, easily readable sources of information. *Capitol Update,* the ANA legislative newsletter for nurses, reports on the activities of its nurse lobbyists and on significant issues in Congress and regulatory agencies. This publication requires a subscription but is available in most nursing school and hospital libraries.

State nurses' associations and many specialty nursing groups also publish newsletters or legislative bulletins. Many of these are free to members but may be sent only when requested. *Action alerts* may also be sent to inform members of nursing organizations of vital issues and the actions nurses need to take.

COMMUNICATING WITH LEGISLATORS

To effectively influence policy, nurses must establish a relationship with legislators and their legislative aides whenever possible. These officials are elected to serve. They expect constituents to inform them of their ideas and concerns. Many elected officials have little, if any, background in health-care matters. A nurse's offer to serve as a personal resource is therefore frequently welcomed by the legislator and his or her staff. This is particularly true at the local and state levels, where legislators may not have extensive staff to serve as aides for legislation involving health-care concerns. Writing a letter or stopping by a legislator's office to introduce oneself as a constituent and nurse and asking to be notified as matters related to health care arise (or volunteering as an information resource when needed) is a good way to become known and increase nursing's visibility.

Lobbying

Sometimes communications with legislators take the form of lobbying. **Lobbying** may be defined as attempting to persuade someone (usually a legislator or legislative aide) of the rightness of one's cause or to influence legislation. It is an art of communication, an area in which nurses are highly skilled. Lobbying methods include letter writing, face-to-face communication, telephone calls, mailgrams, telegrams, e-mail, letters to the editor, and providing testimony (verbal or written). Table 17–6 provides guidelines for letter writing.

Effective lobbying requires both persuasive and negotiating skills. Before you begin any lobbying effort, it is vital to gather all pertinent facts. In politics, getting the facts and laying the groundwork are analogous to developing a nursing care plan. Before visiting or writing a legislator, gather facts, delineate the problem or concern you wish to discuss, and develop a plan to articulate your concerns. Determine a method for evaluating your effectiveness.

To visit the legislator's office, set up an appointment in advance. At the federal level, the meeting may be with the legislative aide who is responsible for assisting in developing position statements and offering committee amendments for the legislator.

Be prepared to show that others support your position. When one person speaks, legislators may listen, but when many people voice the same concern, legislators are much more likely to pay attention.

Professional Organizations

Nurses have always had a great deal of potential power (by virtue of numbers), but have just begun to use this power collectively. This is one important reason to join professional nursing organizations.

TABLE 17–6. Guidelines for Letter Writing

1. Write on your personal stationery if expressing your own views.

2. A handwritten letter is acceptable, and often preferred, provided it is legible.

3. Be certain that your name and address are on both the letter and envelope.

4. Identify yourself as a nurse or nursing student.

5. A legislator is referred to as "The Honorable" on the envelope and inside address (The Honorable Jane Doe) and as "Dear Senator" or "Dear Representative" in the salutation.

6. Limit your letter to one subject.

7. Identify the specific issue or request. Include the bill number (e.g., H.R. 19) or Senate Bill 25 (S. 25), if known, or the intent of the bill.

8. Be brief. Limit your letter to one page, if possible; two at the most.

9. Be specific. Provide facts and figures to support your views or give anecdotal data on how your clients or families have been or may be affected. (Let them know what you want—vote for or against—oppose or support certain amendments.)

10. Emphasize needs or the positive or negative impact of proposed legislation and what the proposed legislation will mean to the legislator's constituents in terms of health care.

11. Be polite and reasonable. A positive-sounding letter is usually an effective tool even when you are asking your legislator to oppose a piece of legislation.

12. Write to thank legislators who supported your wishes or who have supported nurses in some manner.

Letters will reach legislators if addressed as follows:

FEDERAL LEVEL
The Honorable _____
United States Senate
Washington, DC 20510

The Honorable _____
House of Representatives
Washington DC 20310

If you know the room number and building, the correspondence will arrive faster.
You can call the official's local office to obtain this information.
To write to the President of the United States:

The Honorable _____
President of the United States
Washington, DC 20500

Only through unified efforts will nurses be seen as a powerful group and have their voices recognized in the policy arena.

Through the efforts of nursing organizations, professional nurse lobbyists have recently increased their visibility on capitol hill and in state legislatures (Goldwater & Zusy, 1990). The ANA has several nurse lobbyists working at the federal level, and a significant number of their constituent state organizations (SNAs) also hire professional lobbyists. Money from dues-paying members allows such services to be offered to the profession.

Although ANA has the largest governmental affairs office, many other national nursing organizations also have professional lobbyists, and some nurses lobby for businesses that have health-care interests (Goldwater & Zusy, 1990). The legislative or political arm of the ANA is known as the Department of Governmental Affairs. In addition to its lobbying activities, it promulgates legislative and regulatory initiatives for each session of Congress. This department also contains the political action unit, made up of the grassroots lobbying network that functions through the activities of congressional district coordinators and Senate coordinators, and the ANA political action committee (ANA-PAC).

Political Action Committees

It is a political reality that legislators are more likely to see and listen to a group of people who have contributed to their campaign through **political action committees** (PACs). The ANA formed a PAC to create power and influence for the nursing profession. Nurses who contribute to ANA-PAC donate because they want access to the policy makers who will advance nursing practice and promote quality client care in the legislative arena. The PAC raises money from voluntary contributions (dues money may not be used for this purpose) to support candidates and officeholders who are concerned about nursing issues. As Curtis and Lumpkin (1993) pointed out:

> PACs and lobbyists serve different functions. Lobbyists persuade public officials to work for legislation that nurses consider important. Primarily they try to convince those already serving in public office. PACs work to influence the outcome of elections. By endorsing candidates and contributing time and money, nurses can help elect to office and keep in place public officials who support their point of view. (pp. 562–576)

A distinction must be made between "special interest" and "monied interest" PACs. The latter type has received adverse publicity because of the large sums of money given to legislators by groups who influence an issue by donating money. A recent example of this inflated PAC spending is the millions of dollars insurance companies gave to members of Congress as health-care reform was being debated. Their lobbying goal was to further the financial needs of the companies whereas the ANA was lobbying Congress for a universal health-care program to benefit all citizens.

Special interest PACs are organized according to conservative or liberal ideologies or by trade associations (e.g., labor, teachers', environmental, and women's groups). These groups represent an egalitarian society participating in the most current democratic process: contributing to political action committees. Voluntary financial donations to political campaigns require rigid reporting and disclosure procedures and cannot be taken out of the members' dues or the association's treasury. The money given to PACs is required by law to be kept in a separate account.

Political Nursing Networks

Various nursing and other grassroots networks have been established to lobby in support of the legislative goals and objectives of the state nurses' associations. These groups are referred to as **political nursing networks.** In Pennsylvania, the Pennsylvania Political Nursing Network (PPNN), as a part of the Government Relations Committee of the Pennsylvania Nursing Association (PNA), encourages nurses throughout the state to participate in the political process by serving as key contacts for their own legislators. These nurses have an opportunity to practice lobbying skills and to educate legislators about nursing issues. The membership of the network, illustrated in Figure 17–2, shows the channels of communication to be used when nurses need to respond to a key issue. One of the challenges with such a network is recruiting and maintaining contacts for each legislator or legislative district. Other nursing networks may include nursing groups from a variety of settings as well as clinical specialty groups.

The Arizona Nursing Network, established in 1978, is an example of such a network. Bagwell (1984), who was responsible for its design, stated its basic functions as follows:
1. to disseminate information and educate nurses about health legislation,
2. to increase the political awareness of nurses,
3. to encourage nurses to participate in the legislative process, and
4. to promote and support the advancement of nursing through the legislative process.

These functions still apply today. As nurses (and nursing organizations) have become more sophisticated and have moved into a new age of technology, however, networks are also changing. The N-STAT, for example, was formed as ANA's grassroots rapid action network to send a strong message to Congress about the need for health-care reform.

Coalitions

Coalitions often result from networking. When one organization or group does not have sufficient power to make its voice heard, it may join with others who subscribe to similar goals. A **coalition** can be described as a temporary alliance of distinct groups or factions acting together in support of a common goal. A united front on a common issue increases the effectiveness of the group's work. In many cases, economic, environmental, and political restraints have brought together individuals and groups in collaboration: pooling personal, organizational, and financial resources.

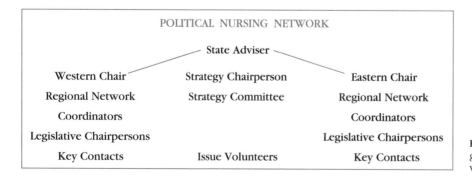

FIGURE 17-2. Example of the organization of a political nursing network.

KEY POINTS

- Nurses have become increasingly interested in public policy, realizing that both their personal lives and their professional activities are significantly influenced by government policy and programs.
- Laws are regulations that are enacted and enforced by federal or state legislators or administrative agencies or set by court judgments.
- Nurse practice acts are developed by each state to define the scope of practice, establish the requirements for licensure and entry into practice, create and empower a board of nursing to oversee licensees, and identify grounds for disciplinary action.
- Political involvement is not restricted to creating laws and government policies. Nurses can influence change in the workplace, government, professional organizations, and community.
- In the U.S. Congress, the committees with the greatest jurisdiction over health matters are the House Ways and Means Committee, House Commerce Committee, Senate Finance Committee, Senate Labor and Human Resources Committee, and House and Senate Appropriations Committee.
- Lobbying may be defined as attempting to persuade someone of the rightness of one's cause or to influence a legislator.
- Legislators are most likely to see and listen to persons who have contributed to their election campaigns through a political action committee.
- Political nursing networks are grassroots groups of nurses established to provide lobbying efforts to support legislative goals and objectives of the state nurses' associations.

CHAPTER EXERCISES

1. Locate the names and addresses of your state and federal senators and representatives.

2. Obtain a copy of your state nurse practice act.

3. Select a current issue of concern and develop an action plan to present your views to a legislator.

4. Write a letter to a legislator outlining your concerns over a major health-care issue.

REFERENCES

American Nurses Association. (1994). *Nursing facts.* Washington, DC: American Nurses Publishing.

Bagwell, M. M. (1984). The politics of nursing. In V. Schoolcraft (Ed.), *Nursing in the community.* New York: Wiley.

Chalich, T., & Smith, L. (1992). Nursing at the grassroots. *Nursing Health Care 13,* 242–244.

Curtis, B., & Lumpkin, B. (1993). Political action committees. In D. Mason, S. Talbott, J. Leavitt (Eds.), *Policy and politics for nurses.* Philadelphia: Saunders.

Goldwater, M., & Lloyd Zusy, M. J. (1990). *Prescription for nurses: Effective political action.* St. Louis: Mosby-Year Book.

Kelly, L. (1991). *Dimensions of professional nursing.* New York: Pergamon Press.

Majewski, J. (1993). Local government. In D. Mason, S. Talbott, J. Leavitt (Eds.), *Policy and politics for nurses.* Philadelphia: Saunders.

Mason, D., Talbott, S., & Leavitt, J. (Eds.) (1993). *Policy and politics for nurses: Action and change in the workplace, government, organizations, and community.* Philadelphia: Saunders.

N-STAT (Nurses Strategic Action Team): Program report. (1994). *Victory in key committee.* Washington, DC: American Nurses Association.

Pennsylvania Nurses Association. (1991). Action plan to mobilize PNA nurses. *Legislative Bulletin.* Philadelphia: PNA Publishing.

Winter, K. (1991). Educating nurses in political process: A growing need. *Continuing Education in Nursing 22,* 143–146.

BIBLIOGRAPHY

Abdellah, F. G. (1991). *Nursing's role in the future: A case for health policy decision making*. A Case For Monograph Series. Indianapolis: Sigma Theta Tau International Center Nursing Press.

Aburdene, P., & Naisbitt, J. (1993). *Megatrends for women: From liberation to leadership*. New York: Fawcett Columbine.

Sharp, N. (1994). All politics is local: And other rules. *Nursing Management 25*, 22–25.

Section V

MOVING HEALTH CARE INTO THE TWENTY-FIRST CENTURY

Chapter 18

HEALTH-CARE AGENDA AND REFORM

Sister Rosemary Donley

CHAPTER OBJECTIVES

On completion of this chapter, the reader will be able to:

1. Discuss the current health-care issues under debate at the federal, state, and local levels.
2. Describe the influence of market forces on health-care reform.
3. Contrast the managed competition with other payment systems of health-care financing.
4. Discuss the future issues that may lead to change in the health-care system.

KEY TERMS

Acute Care and High Technology
Disease-Based Framework
Primary Care
Fee-for-Service
Diagnostic-Related Grouping (DRG)
Flat-Rate Payment

Capitation Payment
Health Maintenance Organizations (HMOs)
Power and Money
Manpower Training
Graduate Nursing Education

Deregulation
Price Control
Competition
Universal Health Insurance
Managed Care
Networks

Over the second half of the twentieth century, the health-care agenda has developed and matured. In this chapter, the evolution of the health-care system, the health-care environment, payment plans developed before President Clinton introduced his health-care reform plan, and the reform program and its aftermath are discussed. The American health-care agenda weaves together a very complex set of concepts describing a system designed to ensure that people who need health care receive it in the appropriate setting from a trained health-care professional at reasonable cost. The agenda also introduces variables of industrial organization and the regulation and promotion of systems and services (Moran, 1995). Because every person in the United States eventually will need preventative, therapeutic, or restorative health care, health care is a private as well as a public matter.

THE EVOLUTION OF THE AMERICAN HEALTH-CARE SYSTEM

Acute and High-Tech Care

Historically, health care evolved as a plan to provide and finance the treatment of acute illness (Ayres, 1996). However, it was also a program to prevent illness by encouraging practices designed to improve the safety and cleanliness of the environment and to encourage healthy lifestyles and personal behavior. This health-care agenda also encompassed the maintenance or restoration of health after periods of acute illness (OASH, 1979). Although American health care has been presented as a continuum ranging from healthy living to prevention to rehabilitation, a study of health-care practice does not support this claim (Marczynski-Music, 1994). It shows an oscillation between the ancient myths of Hygeia and Asclepius (Dubois, 1959). Because the pendulum always seemed to swing toward the god of healing, investment in **acute care and high technology** medicine became the distinguishing mark of health care in America.

Research into the causes and treatment of disease has also been given a high priority in the United States. Most of this research activity is carried out at the National Institutes of Health and in academic health centers and schools of medicine and the health professions with their affiliated teaching hospitals (Kronenfeld & Whicker, 1984). Because acute care involves high technology and the use of drugs, medical devices, and diagnostic equipment, however, the business community is also engaged in biomedical research and technology transfer (Estes, Harrington, & Davis, 1994). As the postwar health-care agenda unfolded, acute care hospitals dominated the landscape, providing specialized settings where high-technology diagnosis, treatment, and research could be carried out and monitored. Acute care was sustained by a research partnership among government, universities, hospitals, and businesses.

Because so many resources had been focused on acute care, preventive care, primary care, and restorative care have received less attention (Institute of Medicine, 1988). They also derived what little status they had from their relationship to acute care practice. Prevention was defined within this acute care lexicon as actions to eliminate disease (Milio, 1981; Gruenberg, 1977). Attention to preventive health care of children meant the endorsement of childhood immunization programs (Richmond, 1977; Mowery & Mitchell, 1995). Within the elderly population, it was directed at warding off pneumonia and other respiratory illnesses by administering pneumonia vaccine and flu shots. Medicalization, to borrow a term from Renée Fox (1977), shaped the design and delivery of preventive health-care practices. Consequently, personal, community, and environmental influences on health were mostly overlooked. A **disease-based framework** set the parameters of diagnosis, therapy, and payment. It also discouraged the use, or even the testing, of any methodology or therapy that was not within the standard medical regime (Eisenberg, 1977). It is not surprising, given the dominance of medical ideology, that scientific reports about the human genome project describe defective genetic structures associated with disease. Seeking the cause and treatment of diseases such as AIDS further illustrates the thrust of preventive research at the National Institutes of Health. Historically, those who envisioned nonmedical approaches to preventive health care were not taken seriously by their colleagues, who saw prevention only in relationship to acute care. These health-oriented innovators, including nurses, were labeled alternative therapists, collaborative therapists, or sometimes quacks (Lyng, 1990). Their research projects were not funded, and their articles were rejected by peer-reviewed journals.

Primary care was also given a lesser place in the acute care constellation. Viewed as a precursor to acute care, **primary care** was given attention when it was oriented to the discovery of conditions amenable to therapy. In most primary care settings, angina triggered referrals, a serial angiography, and usually treatment with angioplasty or revascularization of the heart, even in the aged (Rogers, von

Dohlen, & Frank, 1991; Leape, 1992; Titus, Chelsky, Mundall, Bryan, & Spear, 1993; Wennberg, Kellett, et al., 1996). Patients were routinely screened for cancers for which some form of therapy existed (Czaja, McFall, Warnecke, Ford, & Kaluzny, 1994). Physicians or nurse practitioners who took a less aggressive approach to primary care were not perceived to be on the cutting edge. They did not enhance the referral game, and hospitals and specialty practice groups gave them low marks. Primary care physicians did not make as much money as their technologically driven colleagues (Mitkae, 1995). Because most hospital and ambulatory care nurses were salaried, their incomes were more affected by their occupational status than their practice decisions. The literature synthesized by Mittelstadt (1993) reflects almost half a century of struggle for direct reimbursement of nurses. Nurses who worked in ambulatory practices or on the general medical and surgical floors of hospitals were not at the top of the nursing hierarchy. Their colleagues considered them to be second-tier practitioners and bestowed more prestige on acute care nurses in specialty care units (Shames, 1993). Primary care practitioners, those who practiced on the fringes of acute care medicine, and nurses were not invited to health-care policy tables.

Health maintenance, rehabilitation, long-term, subacute, and extended care are other elements of the health-care spectrum that have been neglected because acute care dominated the health-care agenda. These health services received even less attention than prevention and primary care because, in the acute care worldview, maintenance, rehab, and long-term and subacute care are offered when treatment fails (Fins, 1993). A health-care system focused on acute care and intensive treatment has little interest in providing support for people who have reached their therapeutic limits or who do not respond to the extant therapy (Shames, 1993). The minimal research interest in subacute care has focused on aged persons suspected of having Alzheimer's disease. Interestingly, too, private insurance coverage for the care of persons placed in long-term care categories was limited, leaving most people to rely on Medicaid (Vladek, 1985). The health-care agenda that developed and prospered in the United States after the Second World War was a system of acute care medicine.

Financing Health Care

The second component of the American tradition in health care is its **fee-for-service** financing system, which blends public and private insurance and payments (Ayres, 1996). This system is unique because other first-world countries provide their citizens government-supported health insurance (Levit, Lazenby, Cowan, & Letsch, 1994). Much thought has been given to the American style of health-care financing and the various strategies to adjust it. In fact, the cost of health care has become a national preoccupation that, at times, has distracted policy makers and health-care professionals from evaluating the appropriateness, quality, and effectiveness of the care being given and received. The distinctions between medical practice and commerce have become blurred (Relman, 1992). Health-care financing has dominated conversations because Americans spend more money than any other country of the world on health care—14 percent of the gross national product (Marczynski-Music, 1994). The rate of spending for health care has also grown more rapidly than any other sector of the American economy, and conventional efforts to hold the line on health-care expenditures have failed (Reinhardt, 1986). Everyone is affected by health-care inflation. Ordinary citizens, employers, and federal and state governments find that the rate of growth of health-care costs, or the costs themselves, have limited their other economic choices (Marczynski-Music, 1994). The financing of health care has also attracted public and private attention, however, because of its link to American capitalism. In America, health care is more than an altruistic or political program for the sick. Health care offers investment opportunities, capital construction programs, and a variety of jobs. Last year, it accounted for 884 billion dollars, one-seventh of the economic activity in the country (Ayres, 1996).

Consequently, it is important for all health professionals to understand health-care financing and to distinguish among the methods of payment for health care, the persons who actually pay for it, and the services that are purchased with the health-care dollar. Three dominant payment patterns have emerged as the health insurance industry developed in this country: fee-for-service, flat-rate payment, and capitation payment. Traditionally, hospital payments have been calculated from an aggregation of the costs of a hospital day, whereas doctors have billed patients after each episode of medical care. These per diem hospital costs and fees for service were based on the charges for care a patient received each day (Ayres, 1996). Certain days—the day of surgery, the day of delivery, or the day spent in intensive care—were more expensive than others. Per diem charges were the standard in the hospital industry until 1983, when Congress adopted a different methodology to pay the hospital bills of its Medicare enrollees (Wagner, 1985). The new federal method of calculating hospital bills, which was widely copied by other payers, does not use the number or characteristics of the day of care as the basic unit of measurement. It employs a clinical measure, a **diagnostic-related grouping (DRG).** The DRG is a construct that bundles and then groups into categories the diagnoses requiring a similar pattern of resource allocation. For purposes of payment, all the diagnoses that fit under a particular DRG are considered to be the same. DRGs are then used to predict resource allocations. Hospitals are given a particular payment rate for each DRG. For example, if DRG 34 has a value of 3 days and $1000, the hospital would be paid $1000 for treating any patient whose diagnosis placed his or her case in this diagnostic-related grouping. Because DRGs pay a **flat-rate payment,** reimbursement is not influenced or increased (with such exceptions as surgery, age, and outlier status) by the quantity or range of diagnostic or therapeutic interventions, or by the number of days of hospital care (Shaffer, 1984). If the patient's particular diagnostic and treatment protocol or the number of days in the hospital consume more resources than are covered by the DRG payment, the hospital must absorb these costs. In direct contrast to after-the-fact, cost-based reimbursement, which had been the payment standard for decades, DRGs set prearranged financial brackets around payment for in-patient hospital care. In the mid-1980s DRGs replaced the cost per patient day as the building block of the health-care payment structure.

Capitation is another form of financing health care. Although a **capitation payment** is also a flat rate, it is derived differently from the DRG. With this method, named for its unit of payment, a payment is made for each person in a particular group. It has been used predominately by **health maintenance organizations (HMO)** (Battistella, 1978). The prototypes of HMOs entered the health-care marketplace emphasizing prevention and primary care. Their strategy was to improve the well-being of their clients and reduce health care costs by emphasizing prevention and separating payment from care delivery. Companies who enrolled their employees in HMOs made flat-rate payments, which entitled their workers and dependents to a wide range of wellness services and care for acute illnesses for a fixed price. People did not have to be ill to benefit from their health insurance plan. The cost of their health plan was determined by the size of the en-rolled group (head count), the assessment of the health status and risk of group members, and the costs in the local health-care market (Kronenfeld & Whicker, 1984). Successful HMOs enrolled a relatively healthy population, engaged them in health practices and preventive strategies, and treated the early stages of illness. When this business plan worked, the health status of HMO enrollees improved, and the company had an inexpensive health insurance plan to sell to businesses. Although HMOs have not changed considerably since the early days of the Nixon presidency, they have been agents of change (Morrison & Luft, 1990).

Rising Costs and Payors

Although hospitals have experienced some alternative payment patterns over the years, the payment of solo and group practice physicians has been based on the relatively stable and increasingly lucrative fee-for-service payments (Hanft, 1985). The federal government recently tried to reduce the escalating medical service fees and correct the historical distortion of payments across medical specialty lines (Physician Payment Review Commission, 1992). The Medicare fee schedule for physicians was also designed to discourage use of the more costly high-tech procedures and offer income incentives to encourage medical students to elect the more cognitive (and less technologically focused) medical career pathways (Kaufman, Naughton, Osterweis, & Rubin, 1991).

The most interesting dimension of the health-care financing agenda is not payment methods. It concerns power and decision making—who pays the health-care bill, who makes treatment decisions, and who receives and benefits from health care, especially high-tech health care. Because access to health care in the United States has been correlated with having health-care insurance, payment and questions about access to care usually become discussions about who has health insurance and who pays for it. Sixty percent of the insured population in the United States have insurance as an employee benefit (Source Book, 1991). Unlike western Europe, where health insurance is part of a social welfare system for citizens, the United States provides health insurance as a work-related fringe benefit. In line with the capitalistic thrust of the American health-care system, the health insurance industry is privately owned and managed. For many years, health insurance was synonymous with the program of a nonprofit group, Blue Cross. Today, health insurance is a for-profit venture. In 1992, at the beginning of the Clinton administration, an estimated 1800 firms were doing health insurance business in the country (Greenberg, 1992).

In 1965, the federal government joined the health insurance world when Congress enacted Medicare and Medicaid. These programs provided health insurance to two distinct populations, the elderly (persons over 65 years of age and the totally and permanently disabled), and the poor (persons who were disadvantaged because of the job link that had been forged with health insurance). Americans with health insurance fall into two categories, workers and their dependents and persons eligible for a government entitlement program. Because of this arrangement, employers and federal and state governments pay most of the health-care bills. Although some people pay for acute health-care services, most personal payments are for long-term care, copayments, and therapies not included in the benefit structure, notably medicine and eye glasses (Marczynski-Music, 1994).

Insurance companies, who came to be called third parties, were in an uncomfortable position as health-care costs escalated. The retrospective cost-based payment system rendered them fiscally impotent because they, and the employers who paid the major share of insurance premiums, were outside the clinical decision-making paradigm. Because health-care payments were made after an audit of health services, the other parties, patients and providers had no incentives to limit access or use or even to select less costly protocols. Some large purchasers, especially the federal government, exerted pressure to lower costs through regulation of utilization and reductions in the reimbursement rates. Private insurers negotiated lower hospital rates for their plan members when they insured a significant population in the geographic area. These discounts were based on the prevailing and customary rates, however, which were set in the medical and hospital marketplace. In the mid-1980s, migration to a flat-rate (DRG) prospective payment for Medicare beneficiaries put care providers at financial risk for overutilization and spending for the first time.

Power and money are the essence of the health-care financing agenda. Traditionally, those who controlled the allocation of health resources were separated from those who paid for them. Most of the control was in the hands of physicians, whose orders generated about 80 percent of health-care expenditures (Berndtson, 1986). Any effort to lessen medical control of health-care decision making met with resistance from the medical and hospital community, whose incomes were based on fee-for-ser-vice practice (Braverman, 1978). Control was also in the hands of persons with health insurance (Center for Health Economics Research, 1993). The old Blue Cross plans, which were the standard in the industry, and Medicare, which copied the Blue Cross payment model, gave patients almost unlimited choice of physicians and health-care settings (Ayres, 1996). Patients could see a specialist or a general practitioner, and the system allowed persons to overutilize a wide spectrum of diagnostic and therapeutic interventions (Halvorsen, 1993). The high expectations for the benefits of high-technology medicine encouraged everyone to "pull out all the stops" when they became ill. Persons without health insurance or with inadequate coverage were at greatest risk in the traditional system (Rowland, Lyons, Salganicoff, & Land, 1994). However, they had little ability to improve their status. Their problems were brought to public attention when the number of uninsured persons increased and more uninsured people sought treatment in hospitals (Lewin, 1985). Malpractice claims and the cost of malpractice insurance did not encourage prudent allocation of medical resources, because the standard of care required the use of high technology (Ziengenfuss & Perlman, 1989). Uninsured persons also expected high-technology medicine. When the bills of the uninsured became the responsibility of hospitals, who found it increasingly more difficult to pass on the costs of uncompensated care to insurance companies, the cost of high-technology treatment, especially for the uninsured, entered the public agenda (Reinhardt, 1986). Financiers and policy makers began to rethink their commitment to technology and to examine outcomes as well as costs of care (Rivlin, Cutler, & Nichols, 1994).

Health-Care Workforce

Manpower training was a major thrust of the health-care agenda. Beginning in the 1950s, education for the health professions grew more rapidly than general higher education (Fox, 1996). By the 1980s states were spending five times more for a student in an academic health center than for students in other programs in research universities (Millett, 1982). Fitzhugh Mullan (letter to author Fox, December 1994) former Assistant Surgeon General and director of the Bureau of Health Professions, has labeled this process the "medicalization of work force policy." Most analysts admit that the financial stakes of preparing health-care professionals for acute care practice have grown beyond anyone's expectations. The postgraduate training of physician specialists has been supported by Medicare's payments to hospitals under the Graduate Medical Education program (GME) of Medicare, part A. It has also been nourished by the extramural programs of the National Institutes of Health, and more recently by the Indirect Medical Education (IME) section of Medicare's prospective payment 1983 legislation. As a result of this investment, the United States has educated more specialist physicians than any other country of the world (COGME, 1992). Six out of 10 practicing doctors in the United States and 4 out of 10 doctors in other first-world countries are specialists (Ayres, 1996).

Nursing education developed differently in the postwar period, expanding to meet the demands of the acute health-care agenda. Its growth was stimulated by nursing education legislation in the 1950s, which became Title VIII of the Public Health Service Act and, to a lesser degree, by Medicare's GME (Helms & Anderson, 1993; Edwardson, 1996). Title VIII encouraged all nursing programs (2-year associate degree, 4-year baccalaureate, and 3-year hospital) to prepare nurses for public health and other national priorities. Because Medicare could direct its GME funds only to hospitals, Medicare funding, which was so significant in graduate medical education, supported only diploma programs in nursing. The graduate education of nurses was not assisted by the GME program. However, the more significant divergence between medical and nursing manpower policy was related to medicine's ability to achieve consensus around its educational mission. Lack of agreement about preprofessional nursing education, a schism deeply rooted in ideology, tradition, and economics, divided nursing, exhausted its leadership, and weakened it as a professional and political force. Because the marketplace did not differentiate among graduates of 2-, 3-, and 4-year nursing programs, it was hard to convince the public that the conflict in nursing around "entry into professional nursing practice" was related to quality of care rather than professional self-interest (DeBack, 1990). Although most nurses are now educated in community and senior colleges, hospitals continue to be very influential in the education and practice of nurses (Secretary's Commission on Nursing, 1988; Aiken, 1989). Viewed from the perspective of the health-care agenda, nursing kept the acute care delivery system viable by producing a steady stream of nurses to staff the nation's hospitals at modest cost.

Graduate nursing education was characterized by three trends in the preparation of educators and administrators, clinical specialists, and practitioners. In the early 1960s, the question turned on whether nurses should be educated as teachers, administrators, or clinical specialists. The development of high-technology medicine, the emergence of acute care hospitals, and Medicare, itself, then created a demand for nurses who were able to provide, manage, and direct the care of critically ill people (Hawkins & Thibodeau, 1993). Most graduate programs responded to the market and prepared clinical specialists to work as clinicians, consultants, patient educators, and staff developers (Clifford, 1992). The preparation of teachers and administrators received minor emphasis. Clinical specialists established organizations, certification programs, and journals to establish their credentials as advanced practice nurses (Hixton, 1996). The third curriculum initiative began in the late 1960s in Colorado. There, Silver and Ford pioneered a program to educate nurse practitioners to assume clinical responsibility for primary care of children (Ford & Silver, 1967). A parallel program to prepare physician assistants was begun at Duke by Dr. Stead in 1965 (Sadler, Sadler, & Bliss, 1972). These programs were attractive to people who sought autonomy in practice. In the late 1970s and early 1980s, when the cost of health and medical care came to dominate health-care debates, nurse practitioners and physician assistants were looked on as high-quality, low-cost health-care providers (U.S. Congress, OTA, 1986). By the mid-1980s nurse practitioner programs (adult, pediatric, womens' health, psychiatric mental health, geriatric) had become so popular that it became impossible to differentiate the preparation of the clinical specialist from that of the practitioner (Page & Arena, 1994; Gillis, 1966; Elder & Bullough, 1990).

In summary, the health-care agenda that developed after the Second World War evoked a sense of satisfaction, pride, and some complacency. Sustained by institutions, research, private and public financing, and an aggressive health manpower program, it fueled the economy and produced a health-care system that was the envy of the world.

SETTING THE STAGE FOR CHANGE

What happened? When did professional and private concerns about health care cause a shift in the health-care agenda? This section explores the 1980s and the Reagan–Bush presidency, which set the stage for the reform initiative. When Ronald Reagan assumed the presidency, he initiated a new era of government that he promised would restore power to the people, give more authority to local government, stimulate a competitive economy, and reduce taxes. Although the implementation of the Republican vision of a new federalism extended far beyond health care, President Reagan inherited costly health entitlement programs, Medicare and Medicaid. The analytic framework of access, quality of care, and cost, which had guided public policy since the New Deal, had produced marginal effects and few new strategies. Its recurring themes—to pass a national health insurance program and lower health care costs—had become a mantra. National health insurance was always just around the corner, and rearranging the benefit structures of the entitlement programs and regulating payments for care produced no real reduction in cost (Skocpol, 1993). Reagan's predecessors, Nixon, Ford, and Carter, had tried price controls and regulation. Neither of these strategies lowered the spiraling health-care costs (Feldman, 1988). During the Reagan era, deregulation, price control, and competition became the tools of cost reduction.

Early in his first term, Reagan's advisers proposed **deregulation** legislation to withdraw federal authority and funding from a wide spectrum of public health programs for mothers, children, the mentally ill, and persons who abused alcohol and drugs. They identified 25 categorical programs, spread across separate authorizations in the Public Health Act, and eventually clustered 21 of them into four block grants: primary care (one program), maternal child health (seven programs), preventive health and services (eight programs), alcohol, drug abuse, and mental health (five programs) (Feder, Holahan, Bovbjerg, & Hadley, 1982). In line with the Republican commitment to return authority to local government, this legislation transferred these block grants to the states, who were free to select and administer health services at the local level (OBRA, 1981). States were bound by fewer regulations and were given federal grants to support the programs they identified. The result was less regulation, less federal spending (a 25 percent reduction), and fewer community-based public health programs and clinics to serve the poor (Feder et al., 1982).

The next major health initiative to come from the Reagan White House addressed Medicare and its formula for payment to hospitals. As the block grant program diminished federal programmatic and fiscal authority under the Public Health Service Act, prospective payment legislation amended Title 18 of the Social Security Act and changed the way the federal government pays its Medicare bills (TEFRA, 1982). As was noted earlier, this financing scheme substituted a disease classification system for fee-for-service model and effectively put hospitals on a budget by paying a prospectively set flat rate based on the disease's classification within a DRG. This formula exerted a type of **price control** on health-care payments.

The Reagan presidency encouraged **competition** and challenged business to invest in the care delivery side of the health industry. It also stimulated hospitals, physicians, and investors to compete for health-care dollars. In the investor-owned sectors, mergers and acquisitions took place as for-profit health-care chains found community and specialized hospitals. Vertically and horizontally integrated health systems replaced independent hospitals. The voluntary health-care sector also embraced pro-competitive principles, forming their own health-care systems in much the same way as their for-profit colleagues (Hull, 1993). Home and ambulatory care, seeded by venture capital, expanded to provide services to patients now being treated in the community because of Medicare's DRG program. New insurance companies entered the health-care marketplace. These companies controlled utilization of services and assumed an aggressive posture in negotiating rates with hospitals and diagnostic centers. Acute care hospitals were disoriented. They had less funding from Medicare, sicker patients in their inpatient services, significant competition from commercial laboratories and ambulatory care centers, and shortened hospital stays (Rogers, Draper, et al., 1990). Their former allies in Blue Cross won discounts on payments for their enrollees. Hospitals had less money, more patients with no or inadequate insurance, and more difficulty shifting costs among insurers. The health-care landscape was unbalanced and ready for reform.

HEALTH-CARE REFORM

Even with the chaos in the provider and insurer communities, health care did not seem a likely issue in the 1992 presidential campaign. What happened to change this? Policy wonks recall 1991 and the special election to fill the seat of Senator John Heinz of Pennsylvania. During the campaign, which pitted former attorney general Elliott Richardson against a relatively unknown candidate, Harrison Wofford, a provocative public service announcement was issued beyond the boundaries of Pennsylvania (Ayres, 1996). Wofford explained that a person accused of a crime had the right to be represented by legal counsel, but an ordinary citizen had no comparable right to health care. He then asked the citizens of Pennsylvania for an opinion: would they most likely need a doctor or an attorney during their lifetime? If they expected to need a doctor, they were advised to vote for him. Wofford was elected and health became a political hot button. Health care then became a major issue in the Clinton campaign.

Universal Health Insurance Proposal

Once elected, Clinton proposed a dramatic agenda. Before a joint session of Congress and a live television audience he announced his intent to radically change health care (President's Health Security Plan, 1993). He asked his wife, Hilary Rodham Clinton, to provide the leadership and direction for this initiative. Reform was launched. In his speech to Congress, President Clinton linked his proposal for **universal health insurance** with citizenship and grounded it on six principles: security, simplicity, savings, choice, quality, and responsibility (Clinton, 1993). The term "responsibility" was later changed to "accountability." These terms will be used interchangeably. His proposal sought to correct some of the problems of the old health-care agenda and also introduced some new ideas. In ensured universal access to health insurance and promised everyone a health insurance card. President Clinton envisioned a system in which "every American would receive a health care security card that will guarantee a comprehensive package of benefits over the course of an entire lifetime" (Clinton, 1993). The insurance program would require only one form, eliminating the bureaucracy that consumes 25 cents of every health-care dollar. Health insurance purchasing cooperatives (HIPC) would serve as brokers to help individuals and companies select the best plans for themselves and their employees. These cooperatives, derived from the mircoeconomic principles espoused by Enthoven (1993), would bargain, on behalf of a large group of subscribers, with provider organizations for the best premium rates and assess the quality of health-care programs and providers. More important, they would issue report cards so that average Americans could judge the quality of their health-care package. Armed with this knowledge of cost and benefit, people could then choose their own plan of health care from a venue including a basic HMO option, a preferred provider program, and a fee-for-service offering.

The philosophy underlying the Clinton health-care program also balanced health care as a right with health care as a personal and professional responsibility. Individuals were expected to live healthy lives and seek preventive and primary care. Professionals were advised to practice prudently

and to recognize the finiteness of health care commons. There was also an appeal to a communitarian ethic and a plea to think of the common good when making personal health-care decisions. President Clinton reminded Congress "we are all in this together and we all have to be a part of the system. . . . Responsibility (Accountability) in our health care system isn't just about them. . . . It's about each of us" (Clinton, 1993).

President Clinton and his advisers had more difficulty explaining the financing and payment for the plan. Although President Clinton insisted that his health insurance proposal would save money, everyone wondered about the actual cost of his proposal and how it would be paid (Wilensky, 1993). One consistent theme was that savings would be achieved by moving the health-care agenda away from acute care, high technology, and fee-for-service medicine. **Managed care** was to be the vehicle for transforming care delivery and lowering health-care costs. The Clintons also said that the new health purchasing cooperatives would reduce payments for care because the HIPCs would negotiate with networks and systems of care delivery, not with individual providers. As time went on, the cost-effectiveness of managed care became an important part of the reform agenda because it removed the problematic separation of patient, provider, and payer and integrated clinical and financing decisions into the administration of the health-care plan. In contrast with fee-for-service payments, managed care strategies encouraged the use of less costly preventive and primary care services. Managed care assumed responsibility for the care of "a covered life," not just for an episode of illness. The Clintons explained that payment for health-care premiums would remain relatively stable because employers and the government would continue to pay the major share of the health-care bill. However, the fine print in the protocol said that all employers would be required by law to pay health-care premiums for their employees. Individuals would also pick up more of the premium tab if they chose a health-care plan that offered more choices or benefits than the basic health-care package, the HMO option.

As President Clinton's plan for health-care reform was debated in Washington and around the country, the principles of security and savings commanded most attention. It became obvious that people feared the loss or diminishment of their health insurance. Employees, especially those with histories of illness, liked the health insurance card because they worried about getting new insurance when they changed or lost jobs. People with serious illness or developmental disabilities also endorsed this idea because they knew the insurance industry tried to avoid the financial risk of providing coverage to chronically ill people. However, there were parts of the plan that were not popular (Gaylin, 1993). For example, people disagreed about how costs should be shared by the government, the employer, and the person to be insured. What came to be called the "employer mandate" was particularly troublesome to small business because, under the proposed legislation, they would be required to offer health insurance to their workers and to pay 80 percent of the premiums.

There were also questions about the benefit package and the balance between the government's and the private sector's engagement in the administration and management of the program. The insurance industry was understandably concerned about the fate of the 1800 health-care insurance companies and their employees if there were purchasing cooperatives and everyone used one insurance claim form. Although choice was promoted as a value undergirding the plan, the American Medical Association warned that people would not be free to choose a personal physician and that the therapeutic choices of physicians would be curtailed by managed care contracts. As the debate continued, it was clear that everyone wanted health insurance to be portable, accessible, and affordable. However, as the spring turned to the summer of 1994, it was not as clear that the Clinton health-care reform plan had captured the minds and hearts of the American people. By summer 1994, hope for the passage of any health-care reform bill had diminished (Disch, 1996).

Marketplace Reforms

Still, the health-care reform agenda did not die on the floor of Congress with the Clinton health-care plan. While Congress and the public were debating the merits of the reform proposals, the health-care industry was preparing for change. The marketplace targeted cost as well as the acute care delivery and financing systems. The reform debate brought new life to managed care companies and stimulated them to extend their programs beyond the West coast. Managed care, which the Clintons had talked about, became a reality on Wall Street and in local communities. Network, market, and system development became the key works in the dialogue over the health insurance of the future.

Development of health-care **networks** was the most striking phenomenon of the postreform movement, because it changed the configuration of local acute care landscapes. Capitalizing on the media attention given to health-care reform, managed care firms promised future enrollees lower costs, access to a health-care network, and a set of health-care benefits that emphasized primary care but included acute care (Leatherman & Chase, 1994). As managed care gained a presence in more local health insurance markets, the leadership in hospitals faced the oversupply of acute care hospital beds and began to downsize. They also scrambled to lower their operating costs and integrate their services. Small community hospitals and specialized hospitals, especially hospitals linked to academic health centers, joined together to create their own networks. Across the United States, hospitals merged, unified, consolidated, and partnered (Estes, Harrington, & Davis, 1994). Hospitals that could not withstand the competitive pressure were bought or closed. These patterns occurred in investor owned and secular and religious voluntary hospital sector.

As managed care firms tightened controls on the use of acute care hospitals and directed patients from hospitals to community-based care, the length of hospital stay fell and acuity levels rose (Hull, 1993). Shortened hospital stays, which began with the 1983 Prospective Payment amendments to Medicare, became normative in the industry. As hospital occupancy continued to decrease, managed care firms negotiated services across a broader care network. Managed care companies bought or entered into contract relationships with laboratories, ambulatory surgical centers, free-standing diagnostic facilities, home care agencies, rehab and subacute care centers, and general practice physicians and nurses. New networks were built around community-based structures. The acute care hospital, which was the sun of the old health-care agenda, moved back in the galaxy. In environments where managed care networks were strong, hospitalization and high-technology medicine were the therapies of last resort. In the world of managed care, a hospital occupancy rate of 30 percent was good news to the stockholders. It was bad news to hospital nurses because empty beds meant fewer jobs (Weil & Stack, 1993).

Obviously, the loss of status of high-technology medicine and the diminished role of acute care hospitals have had an impact on jobs, research, education, clinical training, patient care, and cash flow. For people who had built their lives and careers around the acute care agenda, the wave of change was chaotic and at times overwhelming. Interestingly, the influence of managed care was experienced differently in various parts of the country. Pennsylvania, Florida, Minnesota, California, Wisconsin, Oregon, and Massachusetts led the way in advancing the new health-care agenda (Gold, 1991). Other communities were slow to join the managed care revolution. Because of the different rates of innovation and acceptance of managed care, some locales coped with hospital networks, others saw the growth of community-based systems of care, and still others watched the merger of traditional insurance firms and managed care companies. Somewhere in the United States each of these events was taking place.

The second wave of change in the health-care communities did not affect caregivers as directly as network development. Its target audience was the approximately 1800 insurance companies. This phase engaged insurance firms in competition with each other over control of local health insurance markets. The same problem of oversupply that slowed the efficiency of acute care hospitals eventually troubled the insurance community. Because network development had gathered free-standing hospitals, ambulatory centers, laboratories, and solo practitioners into provider networks, the marketplace required fewer insurance firms. There were, after all, only so many people in any given market who could buy health insurance, and the membership base is a major factor in negotiating lower premiums. To adjust for the oversupply of health-care insurance firms, and in the true style of American capitalism, insurance companies bought or merged with their competitors. Illustrative of this process was Aetna's recent purchase of U.S. Health Care, a large and successful managed care company based in Philadelphia (Kertesz, 1996). This acquisition gave the new conglomerate a distinct advantage in the Philadelphia market, because after the consolidation, it had size, capital, a nationally recognized name and reputation, and a sophisticated medical management system.

However, the effect of market reorganization was not evident just on Wall Street. As insurance companies consolidated, merged, or just disappeared, people whose care was managed by a company caught in reorganization experienced a shift in benefits, financing plans, and provider and community networks. Reorganization in the health insurance community has been particularly hard for the chronically ill. Most of these persons are not in a position to benefit from appreciation of a particular insurance company's stock after sale, merger, or consolidation. They do, however, have to establish a relationship with a new primary care provider and adjust to a new practice style (Baker, 1966). Providers face similar difficulties; each managed care group has its own set of rules and protocols controlling utilization, physician case load, and ability to participate in a health-care plan (Auerbach, 1996; Berndtson, 1986).

Ongoing Debate

Most people will look back on the postreform era as a time of chaos and confusion. The fulcrum of change has been the aggressive management of use of health-care resources and a dramatic reorganization of the flow of health-care dollars. These same market forces are being used to control other parts of the health-care agenda, biomedical research, the education of the health-care workforce, and the development of a community-based care system. There are dire predictions in the science literature about the demise of the biomedical research enterprise and concern that erratic funding, privatization, and commercialization of the research endeavor will weaken the scientific community and discourage people from careers in biomedical research. The stimulus for this anxiety is the government's reluctance to support other science, the National Science Foundation (NSF) and the National Endowment for the Humanities (NEH), the financial attacks on graduate medical education and high-technology medicine, and congressional threats to decrease funding for the National Institute of Health (NIH) (Marshall, 1995). In the case of professional education, there seems to be little coordinated planning for training the health-care workforce. As more private health insurance, state Medicaid programs, and military health care embrace a cost-cutting frenzy on their way to being managed, no one is stepping forward to pay a fair share of the costs of graduate medical education, the clinical education of physicians, nurses, physician assistants, and allied health workers in community-based settings, or clinical research. Leaders from the professions have echoed or denied the Pew Commission's findings about medical education, and their proposal to upgrade the education and credentialing of nurses (Sabatino, 1991; O'Neil, 1992; deTornyay, 1992). However, no coherent educational policy has been articulated by the academic community. The leadership from the professions is also disappointing. For some, there is a mindless endorsement of the medical–industrial blueprint so feared by Paul Starr (1983). Other leaders have already cast off their professional and altruistic garments and are well on their way to becoming managed care entrepreneurs. Yet another group is anguishing over the assault to their identities and incomes. Their reactions, described in the business typology of ELVN (exit, loyalty, voice, and neglect), have caused some to wonder if the professions, especially medicine, will lose their positions of power and influence and join the working class (Lachman & Noy, 1966; Navarro, 1988). During this vacuum of professional advocacy in behalf of patients, market forces lower payments for graduate medical education and create financial incentives to reduce health-care utilization and costs, with no serious concern for the effect of these actions. The professions are silent or self-serving, and no one is speaking clearly for patient care or advocating for a system to educate health professionals for community-based practice.

Health care in the United States has been a unique partnership among business, the professions, and government. Where is the government that launched the health-care reform process? Most state governments have turned to cost controls, rate setting, and regulation to deal with health-care costs and the growing number of uninsured. State governments have more or less successfully crafted their own plans to manage Medicaid (Patel, 1966; Meyer, 1995), and some state legislatures have made it illegal for managed care companies to mandate that new mothers and babies be discharged within 24 hours. Shortly before the Democrats convened in Chicago for their August 1996 convention, President Clinton signed a remnant of his health-care reform package, a bill that would make health insurance portable and assure persons with chronic or serious illness that they would not be eliminated from the insurance ranks (Skidmore, 1996; Vanderbilt & Abood, 1996). Welfare reform, another bill signed on the way to Chicago, will also have an impact on health care of the poor, especially single mothers and their children (Moynihan, 1996).

Because the health-care agenda is changing so rapidly, it is premature to compare the emerging managed care system with the acute care, fee-for-service medicine of the past. No one knows if managed care will improve health-care delivery, enhance health-care outcomes, or even save money. The rhetoric that heralds the new health-care agenda uses the language of business, not of health care. It does not seem to be concerned with access to care, and quality of care is expressed more as a marketing concept than a professional goal. The poor and the underinsured seem particularly vulnerable as the health-care market becomes more competitive and focused on cost reduction. Joseph Califano (1994), the Secretary of Health, Education, and Welfare in the Carter administration, may have been right when he characterized health-care reform as an effort to redistribute wealth rather than health care. As the agenda changes, it is incumbent on the professions to exert leadership on behalf of the sick and to enter the policy dialogue with proposals emphasizing quality of care as much as cost reduction.

KEY POINTS

- The American health-care agenda weaves together a complex set of concepts for systems designed to ensure that people in need of care will receive it in the appropriate setting from a trained health-care professional at reasonable cost.
- Health care is a public as well as a private matter, because every person in the United States will need preventive, therapeutic, or restorative health care.
- Acute care with high technology and fee-for-service financing were the main components in the early design of the health-care system, with a disease-based framework that set the parameters for diagnosis, therapy, and payment.
- At times, a preoccupation with the cost of health care has distracted policy makers and health-care professionals from evaluating the appropriateness, quality, and effectiveness of the care given and received.
- The three dominant payment patterns for health care that emerged as the insurance industry developed in this country are fee-for-service, flat-rate payment, and capitation payment.

- The DRG is a construct that bundles and then groups into categories the medical diagnoses that require a similar pattern of resource allocation as a flat-rate payment system.
- HMOs use a capitation payment system in that the cost of the health plan is determined by the head count (size of the group enrolled), their health status and risks, and the local market costs.
- Because access to health care in the United States has been correlated with having health-care insurance, payment and access questions usually become discussions about who has health insurance and who pays for the care.
- Power and money are the essence of the health-care financing agenda.
- The health-care agenda has had major effects on manpower training and specialized medicine.
- Graduate nursing education has been characterized by three trends: the preparation of educators and administrators, clinical specialists, and practitioners.
- During the Reagan era, deregulation, price control, and competition became the tools of cost reduction.
- In 1993, President Clinton proposed universal health insurance grounded in the six principles of security, simplicity, savings, choice, quality, and accountability.
- In the Clinton reform proposal, managed care was to be the vehicle for transforming health-care delivery to lower health-care costs.
- In the managed care marketplace, network, market, and system development have become key words in the dialogue about health insurance. The development of health-care provider networks has changed the configuration of local acute care service environments and insurers.
- The rhetoric heralding the new health-care agenda uses the language of business rather than health care, leaving the poor and underinsured particularly vulnerable.

CHAPTER EXERCISES

1. Discuss the health-care issues of cost controls, rate setting, and regulation that have been debated at your state and local levels during the past year.

2. Identify the health-care market forces in your local community.

3. Identify organizational changes that have occurred in an acute care agency in your community. Apply the concept of managed competition to these changes.

4. Identify the acute care and managed care providers in your local community. Interview a representative from one of each of these health-care providers and discuss how they view services in the future.

REFERENCES

Aiken, L. H. (1989). The hospital nursing shortage: A paradox of increasing supply and increasing vacancy rates. *Western Journal of Medicine, 151*(1), 87–92.

Auerbach, S. (1996, June 14). Humana Inc. to pull out of Washington. *Washington Post.*

Ayres, S. M. (1996). *Health care in the United States: The facts and the choices.* Chicago: American Library Association.

Baker, R. (1996, June 1). Harry! Louise! You lied. *New York Times.*

Battistella, R. M. (1978). Inconsistencies and contradiction of health policy in the United States. In R. M. Battistella & T. G. Rundall (Eds.), *Health care policy in a changing environment* (pp. 2–21). Berkeley, CA: McCutchan Publishing.

Berndtson, K. (1986). Managers and physicians come head to

head over cost control. *Healthcare Financial Management, 40*(9), 22–24, 28–29.

Braverman, J. (1978). *Crisis in health care*. Washington, DC: Acropolis Books.

Califano, J. (1994, February 10). Health care reform: The special interests and the trillion dollar cookie jar. *Washington Post*.

Center for Health Economics Research. (1993). *Access to health care: Key indicators for policy*. Princeton, NJ: Robert Wood Johnson Foundation.

Clifford, J. C. (1992). Fostering professional nursing practice in hospitals: The experience of Boston's Beth Israel Hospital. In L. H. Aiken & C. N. Fagin (Eds.), *Charting nursing's future: Agenda for the 1990s* (pp. 87–97). Philadelphia: Lippincott.

Clinton, B. (September 23, 1993). The system is badly broken: It is time to fix it. *USA Today*.

COGME (Council on Graduate Medical Education). (1992). *Third report: Improving access to health care through physician workforce reform directions for the 21st century*. Rockville, MD: COGME, U.S. Department of Health and Human Services.

Czaja, R., McFall, S. L., Warnecke, R. B., Ford, L., & Kaluzny, A. D. (1994). Preferences of community physicians for cancer screening guidelines. *Annals of Internal Medicine, 120*(7), 602–608.

DeBack, V. (1990). Debate, entry into practice. In J. C. McCloskey & H. K. Grace (Eds.), *Current issues in nursing* (pp. 119–123). St. Louis: Mosby-Year Book.

deTornyay, R. (1992). Reconsidering nursing education: The report of the Pew Health Professions Commission. *Journal of Nursing Education, 31*(7), 296–301.

Disch, L. (1996, Spring). Publicity stunt participation and sound bit polemics: The health care debate. *Journal of Health Politics, Policy and Law, 21*(1), 3–33.

Dubois, R. (1959). *Mirage of health*. New York: Harper.

Edwardson, S. R. (1996). Financing nursing education in an era of managed care. *N&HC: Perspectives on Community, 17*(4), 180–184.

Eisenberg, L. (1977). The search for care. In J. H. Knowles (Ed.), *Doing better and feeling worse* (pp. 235–246). New York: Norton.

Elder, R. G., & Bullough, B. (1990). Nurse practitioners and clinical nurse specialists: Are the roles merging? *Clinical Nurse Specialist, 4*(2), 78–84.

Enthoven, A. C. (1993). The history and principles of managed competition. *Health Affair Supplement*, 24–48.

Estes, C. L., Harrington, C., & Davis, S. (1994). The medical-industrial complex. In C. Harrington & C. Estes (Eds.), *Health policy and nursing* (pp. 54–69). Boston: Jones and Bartlett.

Feder, J., Holahan, J., Bovbjerg, J., & Hadley, J. (1982). Health. In J. L. Palmer & I. V. Sawhill (Eds.), *The Reagan experiment* (pp. 271–305). Washington, DC: The Urban Institute.

Feldman, R. D. (1988). Health care: The tyranny of the budget. In D. Boaz (Ed.), *Assessing the Reagan years* (pp. 1–14). Washington, DC: The Cato Institute.

Fins, J. J. (1993, April 5). An acute care response to chronic care: The American perspective. *Cas-Lek-Cesk 132*(7), 197–199.

Ford, L. C., & Silver, H. K. (1967). The expanded role of the nurse in child care. *Nursing Outlook, 15*, 43–45.

Fox, D. M. (1996). The political history of health workforce policy. In M. Osterweis, C. J. McLaughlin, H. R. Manalsse, & C. L. Hopper (Eds.), *The U.S. health workforce: Power, politics, and policy* (pp. 31–46). Washington, DC: Association of American Health Centers.

Fox, R. C. (Winter, 1977). The medicalization and demedicalization of American society. *Daedalus*, 9–22.

Gaylin, W. (October, 1993). Faculty diagnosis: Why Clinton's health-care plan won't cure what ails us. *Harper's Magazine*, 57–64.

Gillis, C. L. (1966). Education for advanced practice nursing. In J. V. Hickey, R. M. Ouimette, & S. L. Venegoni, *Advanced practice nursing* (pp. 22–32). Philadelphia: Lippincott.

Gold, M. R. (1991). HMO's and managed care. *Health Affairs, 10*(4), 189–219.

Greenberg, W. (1992, December). Fewer insurers can improve competition. *Business & Health 14*, 55–56.

Gruenberg, E. M. (1977, Winter). The failures of success. *Milbank Memorial Fund Quarterly: Health and Society, 55*(1), 3–24.

Halvorsen, G. C. (1993). *Strong medicine*. New York: Random House.

Hanft, R. S. (1985). Physicians and hospitals: Changing dynamics. In M. E. Lewin (Ed.), *The health policy agenda* (pp. 99–114). Washington, DC: The American Enterprise Institute.

Hawkins, J. W., & Thibodeau, J. A. (1993). Advanced practice roles: Nurse's practitioner/clinical nurse specialist. In J. W. Hawkins & J. A. Thibodeau (Eds.), *The advanced practitioner. Current practice issues* (3rd ed.) (pp. 1–41). New York: Tiresias Press.

Helms, L., & Anderson, M. (1993). Medicare and the financing of nursing education: Implications of Board of Trustees vs. Sullivan. *Journal of Professional Nursing, 9*, 139–147.

Hixton, M. E. (1966). Professional development: Socialization in advanced practice nursing. In J. V. Hickey, R. M. Ouimette, & S. L. Venegoni, *Advanced practice nursing* (pp. 33–53). Philadelphia: Lippincott.

Hull, K., & The American Hospital Association. (1993). *Hospital trends: Hospital statistics, 1992-93 edition*. Chicago: The American Hospital Association.

Institute of Medicine. (1988). *The future of public health*. Washington, DC: National Academy Press.

Kaufman, R., Naughton, J., Osterweis, M., & Rubin, E. (1991). *Health current issues and the care public policy debate delivery*. Washington, DC: Association of American Health Centers.

Kertesz, L. (1996). Aetna deal signals provider squeeze. *Modern Healthcare, 26*(15), 2–3.

Kronenfeld, J. J., & Whicker, M. L. (1984). *U.S. national health policy: An analysis of the federal role*. New York: Praeger.

Lachman, R., & Noy, S. (June, 1966). Reactions of salaried physicians to hospital decline. *Health Services Research, 31*(2), 172–190.

Leape, L. L. (1992). Unnecessary surgery. *Annual Review of Public Health, 13*, 363–383.

Leatherman, S., & Chase, D. (1994). Using report cards to grade health plan quality. *Journal of American Health Care Policy, 4*(11), 32–40.

Levit, K. R., Lazenby, H. C., Cowan, C. A., & Letsch, S. W. (1994). National health expenses. In C. Harrington & C. Estes (Eds.), *Health policy and nursing* (pp. 14–27). Boston: Jones and Bartlett.

Lewin, M. E. (1985). Financing care for the poor and uninsured: An overview. In M. E. Lewin (Ed.), *The health policy agenda* (pp. 115–126). Washington, DC: The American Enterprise Institute.

Lyng, S. (1990). *Holistic health and biomedical medicine: A counter system analysis*. New York: State University of New York.

Marczynski-Music, K. K. (1994). *Health care solutions*. San Francisco: Jossey-Bass Publishers.

Marshall, E. (July 14, 1995). Heavy weather ahead for clinical research. *Science, 269*(5221), 158.

Meyer, H. (1995, January 23). Quality problems could spell trouble for Medicaid HMOs. *American Medical News, 23*(30), 7.

Milio, N. (1981). *Promoting health through public policy*. Philadelphia: Davis.

Millett, J. D. (1982). *Conflict in higher education: State govern-

ment coordination vs. institutional independence. San Francisco: Jossey-Bass.

Mitkae, M. (1995, August 14). Experts not sure why pay for specialists is increasing. *American Medical News, 38*(30), 9.

Mittelstadt, P. C. (1993). Federal reimbursement of advanced practice nurses' services empowers the profession. *Nurse Practitioner, 18*(1), 43, 47–49.

Moran, M. (1995, Fall). Three faces of the health care state. *Journal of Health Politics, Policy and Law, 20*(3), 767–781.

Morrison, E. M., & Luft, H. S. (1990). Health maintenance organization environments in the 1980's and beyond. *Health Care Financing Review, 12*(1), 81–90.

Mowery, D. C., & Mitchell, V. (1995, Winter). Improving the reliability of the U.S. vaccine supply: An evolution of alternatives. *Journal of Health Politics, Policy and Law, 20*(4), 973–1000.

Moynihan, D. P. (1996, August 4). When principle is at issue. *Washington Post.*

Navarro, V. (1988). Professional dominance or proletarianization?: Neither. *Milbank Quarterly, 66*(Suppl 2), 57–75.

OASH (Office of the Assistant Secretary for Health and Surgeon General). (1979). *Healthy People. The Surgeon General's report on health promotion and disease prevention.* Washington, DC: U.S. Government Printing Office.

Omnibus Budget Reconciliation Act (OBRA) of 1981. (1981). Washington, DC: U.S. Government Printing Office.

O'Neil, E. H. (1992). Education as part of the health care solution. Strategies from the Pew Health Professions Commission. *Journal of the American Medical Association, 268*(9), 1146–1148.

Page, N. E., & Arena, D. M. (1994, Winter). Rethinking the merger of the clinical nurse specialist and the nurse practitioner roles. *Image: Journal of Nursing Scholarship, 26*(4), 315–318.

Patel, K. (1996). Medicaid: Perspectives from the states. *Journal of Health and Social Policy, 7*(3), 1–20.

Physician Payment Review Commission. (1992). *Medicare physicians payment: Report to Congress.* Washington, DC: The Commission.

President's health security plan: The Clinton blueprint. (1993). New York: Random House.

Reinhardt, U. E. (1986). Uncompensated hospital care. In E. A. Sloan, J. F. Blumstein, & J. M. Perrin (Eds.), *Uncompensated hospital care: Rights and responsibilities* (pp. 1–14). Baltimore: Johns Hopkins University Press.

Relman, A. S. (1992). What market values are doing to medicine. *The Atlantic Monthly, 269,* 99–106.

Richmond, J. B. (1977). The needs of children. In J. H. Knowles *Doing better and feeling worse* (pp. 247–259). New York: Norton.

Rivlin, A. M., Cutler, D. M., & Nichols, L. M. (1994, Spring). Financing estimating, and economic effects. *Health Affairs, 13,* 30–48.

Rogers, W. B., von Dohlen, T. W., & Frank, M. J. (1991, August). Management of coronary heart disease in the elderly. *Clinical Cardiology, 14*(8), 635–642.

Rogers, W. H., Draper, D., Kahn, K. L., Keeler, E. B., Rubenstin, L. V., Kosecoff, J., & Brook, R. H. (1990). Quality of care before and after implementation of the DRG-based prospective payment system. *Journal of the American Medical Association, 264*(15), 1989–1994.

Rowland, D., Lyons, B., Salganicoff, A., & Land, P. (1994). A profile of the uninsured in America. *Health Affairs, 13,* 283–287.

Sabatino, F. (1991). Training of health care professionals must change, says Pew Commission director. *Hospitals, 65*(4), 50, 52.

Sadler, A. M., Sadler, B. L., & Bliss, A. A. (1972). *The physician's assistant—today and tomorrow.* New Haven, CT: Yale University School of Medicine.

Secretary's commission on nursing: Final report. (1988). Washington, DC: U.S. Department of Health and Human Services.

Shaffer, F. A. (1984). A history of prospective payment. In R. P. Caterinicchio (Ed.), *DRGs: What they are and how to survive them* (pp. 9–57). NJ: Slack Inc.

Shames, K. H. (1993). *The Nightingale conspiracy: Nursing comes to power in the 21st century.* Montclair, NJ: Enlightenment Press.

Skidmore, D. (1996, August 19). Understanding the Kassebaum–Kennedy health coverage bill. *Washington Post.*

Skocpol, T. (1993). Is the time finally ripe? Health insurance reform in the 1990's. *Journal of Health Policy, Politics and Law, 18*(3), 531–550.

Source book of health insurance data. (1991). New York: Health Insurance Institute.

Starr, P. (1983). *The social transformation of American medicine.* New York: Basic Books.

Tax Equity and Fiscal Responsibility Act of 1982 (TEFRA). Washington, DC: U.S. Government Printing Office.

Titus, B. G., Chelsky, R., Mundall, S. L., Bryan, G. K., & Spear, E. M. (1994). Coronary angioplasty practice in the United States. *Circulation, 89*(1), 508.

U.S. Congress, Office of Technology Assessment (1986). *Nurse practitioners, physicians' assistants, and certified nurse-midwives: Policy analysis.* Washington, DC: OTA.

Vanderbilt, M. W., & Abood, S. A. (Eds.). (1996, August 19). Health insurance reform approved. *Capital Update, 14*(15), 1–2.

Vladek, B. C. (1985). The static dynamics of long term care policy. In M. E. Lewin (Ed.), *The health policy agenda* (pp. 115–126). Washington, DC: The American Enterprise Institute.

Wagner, J. L. (1985). DRGs and other payment groupings: The impact on medical practice and technology. In M. E. Lewin (Ed.), *The health policy agenda* (pp. 85–98). Washington, DC: The American Enterprise Institute.

Weil, T., & Stack, M. (1993). Health reform—Its potential impact on hospital nursing service. *Nursing Economic$, 11*(4), 200–206.

Wennberg, D. E., Kellett, M. A., Dickens, J. D., Dickens, J. D., Jr., Malenka, D. J., Kellson, L. M., & Keller, R. B. (1996, April 17). *Journal of the American Medical Association, 275*(15), 1161–1164.

Wilensky, G. (1993). Clinton's tooth-fairy financing. *Journal of American Health Policy, 3*(6), 14–19.

Ziengenfuss, J. T., & Perlman, H. (1989). Decreasing medical malpractice: Toward an organizational systems approach. *Health Care Management Review, 14*(4), 67–75.

BIBLIOGRAPHY

Aiken, L. H., & Fagin, C. N. (1991). *Charting nursing's future: Agenda for the 1990s.* Philadelphia: Lippincott.

Boaz, D. (Ed.). (1982). *Assessing the Reagan years.* Washington, DC: Acropolis Books.

Braverman, J. (1978). *Crisis in health care.* Washington, DC: Acropolis Books.

Dubois, R. (1978). *Mirage of Health.* New York: Harper.

Estes, C. L., Harrington, C., & Davis, S. (1994). *Health policy and nursing.* Boston: Jones and Bartlett.

Feder, J., Holahan, J., Bovbjerg, J., & Hadley, J. (Eds.). (1982). *The Reagan experiment.* Washington, DC: The Urban Institute.

Hickey, J. V., Ouimette, R. M., & Venegoni, S. L. (Eds.). (1996). *Advanced Practice Nursing*. Philadelphia: Lippincott.

Kaufmann, R., Naughton, J., Osterweis, M., & Rubin, E. (Eds.). (1991). *Health current issues and the care public policy debate delivery*. Washington, DC: Association of American Health Centers.

Knowles, J. H. (Ed.). (1977). *Doing better and feeling worse*. New York: Norton.

Lewin, M. E. (Ed.). (1985). Financing care for the poor and uninsured: An overview. *The health policy agenda*. Washington, DC: The American Enterprise Institute.

McCloskey, J. C., & Grace, H. K. (Eds.). (1990). *Current issues in nursing*. St. Louis: Mosby-Year Book.

Osterweis, M., McLaughlin, C. J., Manalsse, H. R., & Hopper, C. L. (1996). *The U.S. health workforce: Power, politics, and policy*. Washington, DC: Association of American Health Care Centers.

Chapter 19

OUR AGING POPULATION

Rose Kearney Nunnery

CHAPTER OBJECTIVES

On completion of this chapter, the reader will be able to:

1. Describe the trends and terminology relative to our aging population.
2. Discuss the demographic characteristics of the aging population.
3. Identify the major health problems of aging adults and health promotion activities.
4. Evaluate the needs of aging adults and their impact on the individual, the family, and society.
5. Describe the professional area of gerontological nursing practice.

KEY TERMS

Ageism	Able Elderly	Psychological Theories
Gerontophobia	Geriatrics	Medical Theories
Senescence	Gerontology	Successful Aging
Senility	Gerontological Nursing	Usual Aging
Aged	Demography	Pathological Aging
Senior Citizen	Biological Theories	Disability
Elderly	Sociological Theories	Chronicity
Frail Elderly		

T he nation's population profile is changing. Although we remain a youth-oriented society, the aging of the baby boomers will have a profound impact on the demographics and the health needs of the population. We now see that movement in the direction of healthy behaviors and prevention are vital for individuals, families, and society.

The percentage of the population aged 65 years and older has been steadily increasing. Proportional changes went from 4 percent in 1900 to 12.4 percent in 1988, with predictions for 13 percent and 22 percent in 2000 and 2030, respectively (U.S. Department of Health and Human Services [USDHHS], Public Health Service [PHS], 1992, p. 23). This is often referred to as the "graying of the population" as the post-World War II baby boomers age. The Department of Health and Human Services, PHS (1992) has supported a prediction that the "most rapid population increase over the next decade will be among those over 85 years of age" (p. 23). In fact, the 85 year and older population has already increased over 500 percent in the past 40 years, from 577,000 in 1950 to 3.1 million in 1990 (Beers & Youdovin, 1993, p. 4). It is projected that by 2050, 33 percent of the population will be over 65 years and 5 percent (16 million people) over 85 years. Still differences among ethnic and cultural groups exist.

What we now see is chronic illness rather than acute illness as the major morbidity factor in aging adults. Approximately one-third of people hospitalized are over 65 years of age. Even though the length of hospital stays is decreasing, those over 65 years need a great proportion of our health-care resources, both in and out of the acute care setting. In 1989, the average length of stay for people over 65 years was 8.9 days versus the 5.3-day stay for those under 65 years of age (AARP, 1991). Personal expenditures for health care also increase with chronicity. In 1987, per capita personal health-care total expenditures for all persons 65 years and older were $5360, but for persons 85 years and older the expenditures were almost double, at $9178 (Taeuber, 1993, pp. 3–20). These expenditures were significantly higher than a decade earlier, even when adjustments for the value of the dollar are made.

In *Healthy People 2000* three general goals were stated as national health promotion and disease prevention objectives. The first goal was to "increase the span of healthy life for Americans" (USDHHS, 1992, p. 6). The term "healthy life" relates not only to longevity but also to functional independence of the aging adult. Though life expectancies for both men (79.8 years) and women (83.7 years) have greatly increased, the 12 years of functional health and independence after age 65 is less than the average 16.4 remaining years of life (USDHHS, 1992, p. 23). The difference is the loss of independence in activities in daily life and increasing chronic diseases and dependence on others for health and routine care. Aging adults received special age-related attention in the report, with a discussion of activities to prevent disability and promote independent functioning. Healthy behaviors include smoking cessation, good nutrition, reduction of sodium intake and body weight, reduction in social isolation, regular physical activity, and availability of primary health-care services.

A gentleman I know proposed referring to the aged as the "chronologically challenged" to address challenges lying ahead in life and possible accomplishments. This truly characterizes those who are successful and positive in aging—what we hope for ourselves in the near or distant future. This chapter presents an overview of aging and the population of aging adults with implications for health care. Concerns of both the aging population and the health-care industry are discussed.

HISTORICAL ASPECTS

It is important to look at how aging has become an increasingly important consideration in our population and to the health-care system. In colonial times, elders were revered because they were the land holders until death. But their lifespan was short, with less than 2 percent of the population surviving to age 65. The causes of mortality were mainly communicable diseases, infections, epidemics, and wars. In this agrarian society, with extended family units, people continued to hunt, plant, and work. Planning for retirement was not in the scheme of things until after the American Revolution, in the late 1700s, when the first mandatory retirement laws passed (Chenitz, Stone, & Salisbury, 1991, p. 4).

At the turn of the twentieth century, life expectancy was 47 years of age. Causes of death were still communicable diseases, infections, epidemics, and wars. World War I, the Depression, and World War II occurred during the first 50 years of the 1900s. Then social programs started to emerge, and public focus on the needs of aging adults increased (Table 19–1).

In 1935, the Social Security Act was intended to guarantee each working person a minimum retirement income (Swisher, 1990, p. 124). Presently, approximately 45 million people collect Social Security

TABLE 19-1. Programs Focusing on Aging Adults

1935	Social Security Act
1958	Association of Retired Person's (AARP) founded
1961	First White House Conference on Aging leading to the enactment of the Older Americans Act (OAA) in 1965
1965	Medicare established
1971	Second White House Conference on Aging leading to the inclusion of the nutrition program in the OAA as Title III-C
1981	Third White House Conference on Aging leading to streamlined services of the OAA
1983	Amendments to the Social Security Act and Medicare program with the start of diagnostic-related groups (DRGs)
1986–1990	Omnibus Reconciliation Acts (OBRA) of 1986, 1987, 1989, and 1990
1995	Fourth White House Conference on Aging

benefits as retirees, disabled persons, or dependents of a current or deceased beneficiary (USDHHS, Social Security Administration, 1994, p. 5).

This was also the time when nursing home care began to emerge. In the middle of the twentieth century, care of the aged moved from being provided by family members or poor houses to old age homes, boarding houses, and public hospitals. Minimal standards and licensing for nursing homes by the states existed in the 1940s. Then, in 1965, Medicare was established as Title XVIII of the Social Security Act Amendments, to cover a portion of basic medical expenses.

In 1961, the first White House Conference on the Aging (WHCoA) was convened as a national meeting with representatives from federal, state, and local governments as well as professionals and nonprofessionals working for the needs of the aging. The WHCoA is held each decade under the direction of the Secretary of Health and Human Services.

The Older American's Act (OAA) was an outgrowth of the 1961 WHCoA, enacted in 1965, and continually reauthorized. This legislation was created as a social program to address isolation and loneliness of older Americans, regardless of their social or economic status. It evolved further to address other social problems. Prime concerns for aging Americans have included the areas of health, housing, economic needs, social needs, access to services, legal and employment assistance, retirement, and community services. Each subsequent WHCoA has led to improved services for aging adults

through the OAA. The latest revision of this law occurred in 1992 (P.L. 102–375), with seven "titles" or sections (Table 19–2).

The implementation of diagnostic-related groups (DRGs) began in 1983 through amendments to the Social Security Act and the Medicare program. The resultant prospective payment method was a prelude to major changes in our health-care system, with concentration on in-patient lengths of stay, necessary procedures and tests, and a move back to care in the community and home settings. Although DRGs started with federal health-care programs, second-party payers and insurers placed additional limits on coverage with this step in an attempt to control health-care costs. The national Agency for Health Care Policy and Research (AHCPR, 1994) has reported that, based on data from 1980 to 1987, the average length of hospital stays for the 20 most common DRGs, regardless of age, declined from 10 to 52 percent, from 6.06 days in 1980 to 5.18 days in 1985. And we see lengths of stay continue to decline as cost controls become a major consideration.

In the late 1980s the Omnibus Reconciliation Acts (OBRA) further focused on the health and care of the aging. We started to see a financial impact from this legislation that provided for amendments to the Social Security Act, especially concerning Medicare and Medicaid payment provisions. OBRA 1989 (P.L.

TABLE 19-2. Provisions in the 1992 Older Americans Act (P.L. 102-375)

Title I	Objectives and definitions
Title II	How the legislation will be administered and interact with other federal agencies, offices, and policy makers
Title III	State and community programs on aging are legislated. Provisions on managed in-home and community-based long-term care, program development, advocacy and outreach efforts for the needs of minority populations, supportive and nutrition programs, including congregate meal, home-delivered meals and school-based meals for older volunteers, and multigenerational programs are included in this section.
Title IV	Training, research, and discretionary projects
Title V	Community service employment projects for Older Americans
Title VI	Grants programs for Native Americans, including Indian and Hawaiian Native Americans
Title VII	Addresses vulnerable Older Americans, especially for the prevention of abuse, neglect, and exploitation, including legal assistance, outreach, counseling, and assistance programs

101-239) included requirements for nursing homes on residents' rights, facility safety, and certification in addition to financial payments. Classification and reimbursement for rural hospitals, providers, and community care were important elements in this legislation. Critical economic appraisal of social programs is constantly occurring at both the federal and state levels. Changes in Medicare and Medicaid were of prime concern in the 104th Congress on the aging population who need health-care services.

The political power of this growing aging population has great influence. The success and influence of groups like the American Association of Retired Persons (AARP) is a testimony to what good organization and political activism can accomplish. The AARP (1991), which has grown to 33 million members, serves the needs of aging persons through legislative advocacy, research, programs, publications, and local community services. In addition, a cooperative arrangement between the U.S. Public Health Service and the AARP was formed to stimulate programs for aging people as an at-risk special population based on the priorities of *Healthy People 2000* (Office of Disease Prevention and Health Promotion, PHS, no date).

A formal WHCoA was delayed from 1991 until May 1995. Convening of the 1995 WHCoA was mandated in the 1992 amendments of the OAA. State and local meetings for grassroots information on the needs of older Americans were held before the national conference. Forty-five resolutions were then presented in the Final Report in 1996. The top five resolutions concerned the following:

- Preservation of Social Security
- Reauthorization and preservation of the Older Americans Act
- Preservation of Medicaid
- Alzheimer research
- Ensuring the future of Medicare (WHCoA, 1996, p. 124).

Resolution 10 was focused on health behaviors of responsibility, prevention, wellness, and self-care as "assuming personal responsibility for the state of one's health" (WHCoA, 1996, p. 61). Throughout the next decade, the conference committee, president, and legislators will address concerns raised about the health and well-being of aging Americans.

BASIC TERMINOLOGY IN AGING

Terminology specific to the aging population is a consideration, especially to avoid stereotypes and promote positive views of aging. Negative views on

TABLE 19 – 3. Negative Terms Associated with Aging

Ageism	Discrimination against persons of a certain age group.
Gerontophobia	The veneration of youth that we often see in commercials and advertisements. Age is seen as a disability or a social problem.
Senescence	The time when the biological system is vulnerable to disease and death. This may be used as a negative term, when it it said that someone is in "his senescence" meaning dotage or second childhood. But the term "senescence" merely means the last stages of the aging process, since we actually are aging from birth or the point of viability.
Senility	Used erroneously and negatively, referring to older adults. The loss of orientation and mental facilities may be due to one of the dementias, as a progressive process, or it may be reversible and due to polypharmacy or drug interactions. Care and adequate descriptors are essential to avoid stereotypes associated with this state.

aging are typified by terms defined in Table 19–3. Actual terms used to identify those 65 years of age and older vary. Some individuals object to specific terms. One gentleman told me that he objected highly to the term "senior citizen." He preferred to be described a person or a senior or a citizen. But he felt he should not be labeled as a senior citizen, as something different, merely because he had turned 65 years of age. Table 19–4 lists terms used to categorize the aging adult.

Those specializing in the aging population use different terminology as well. Consider the disciplinary differences among the following definitions.

- **Geriatrics.** The discipline of medicine focusing on the diseases and disabilities of older people.
- **Gerontology.** The study of normal aging and the problems of aging persons, which is multidisciplinary in nature.
- **Gerontological nursing.** Focusing on the responses of aging individuals to actual or potential health problems, not merely the disease.
- **Demography.** The statistical study of human populations, especially with reference to size and density, distribution, and vital statistics.

THEORIES OF AGING

Research has evolved in several disciplines, all proposing different theories on aging. No agreement on any one specific theory has emerged. Research

TABLE 19–4. Descriptive Terms Used to
Characterize Aging Adults

Aged	A nondescriptive term, since it simply means old age. But the 4-year-old is aged compared with the infant, and chronological age is more descriptive in a pediatric population than in an aging population, as we will see when considering functional abilities.
Senior citizen	Generally used to characterize people over 65 years. Often it is also associated with retirement or special discounts in retail stores. Generally, this label has more positive nature unless you meet the aging person who finds the term offensive.
Elderly	Individuals are generally thought of as 65 years and older. But this is merely chronological age. Further categories have evolved as: Young-old—65 to 74 years Middle-old—75 to 84 years Old-old—85 years and older To deal with some of this age bias, additional terms have been tried, based on functional abilities, in an attempt to be more descriptive and positive.
Frail elderly	Used to represent functional ability as medically ill or incapacitated much of the time, such as many individuals formally placed in the old-old category.
Able elderly	Those aging individuals who function in the community with little or no assistance.

continues and our knowledge of the aging process grows with biological, sociological, psychological, longevity, medical, and nursing theories on aging.

The **biological theories** focus on the functional capacity of cells, cell division, and organ systems. They address genetics, immunology, connective tissues, free radicals, stresses from "wear and tear," and neuroendocrine and neurochemical factors. One of the popular theories at present is the free radical theory, which proposes introduction of antioxidants to slow down the aging process by binding to free radicals and neutralizing them.

Sociological theories focus on roles and behaviors in society, including such theories as disengagement, activity, subculture, age stratification, and person–environmental fit. Much of the research in this discipline took place from 1950 through the 1970s. The more recent theories look at the unique effects of the environment and roles that are experienced by specific age groups with their unique histories. For example, the person's life history and reaction to the world will be different if they experienced the

Depression as a child versus the Viet Nam War. Specific research on roles and behaviors continues.

Psychological theories of aging target human behavior and adaptation. Included in this group of theories are those on human needs (Maslow) and development (e.g., Havighurst, Erikson, and Peck). Havighurst's research and theories were applicable to the areas of both sociology and psychology. His developmental tasks of later maturity can be useful in planning wellness initiatives. Erikson (1963) described the positive aspect of his final stage of ego integrity versus despair as "the acceptance of one's one and only life cycle as something that it had to be and that, by necessity, permitted of no substitutions" (p. 268). However, Erikson broadened some of the limitations with acceptance of one's life and impending death in this final stage after he entered this stage himself. Fostering this sense of self-worth and dignity is a challenge for all health professionals working with frail elders in the health-care system.

Related to the aging, Peck (1968) believed that Erikson's eighth stage was too broad and contained different adjustments in later life. He proposed three stages for "old age": ego differentiation versus work role preoccupation, body transcendence versus body preoccupation, and ego transcendence versus ego preoccupation. Peck (1968) further believed that, since people go through these stages at different rates, the developmental criteria rather than chronological age should be the main consideration. This has implications for a focus on the individual's functional health, both psychological and physical.

Theories on longevity look at the life expectancy in a cohort or age-related group for specific factors that yield increased lifespan. Various factors have been proposed (Ebersole & Hess, 1994; Rose, 1991; Rowe & Kahn, 1987). Longevity factors that have some research support include genetics, gender, environment, physical activity, alcohol consumption, sexual activity, nutrition, social factors including economics, marital status, and family, religious beliefs, purpose in life, and even laughter.

Medical theories on aging highlight disease-related factors on physiologic functioning of the person. They include the Single-Organ Theory, with disease- and death-related failure of a vital body organ. There are also senescence theories that include research on causes of death and why some people survive the same symptomatology in middle age that causes death in an older person. The life expectancy and functional health theory looks at quality of life issues, with activities of daily living (ADLs) as a measure of health. The concept of functional health defines active life expectancy for individuals after age 65 as 16.4 years while there is an average of only 12 years of functional independence in the lifespan after age 65. (USDHHS, 1992, p. 23).

The Functional Consequences Theory is a **nursing theory** (Miller, 1990) in which age-related changes are seen as progressive, irreversible, and inevitable. Add to these age-related factors the risk factors that occur in the aging population. These risk factors are physiologic, psychological, and environmental forces that can accelerate aging but they are reversible. They include diseases, medications, environment, lifestyle, support systems, attitudes, knowledge deficits, and psychosocial circumstances (Miller, 1990, p. 55). The goals of nursing in this theory include good assessment and diagnosis of both age-related changes and risk factors to provide interventions that produce positive consequences such as the highest performance and the lowest dependency in the individual.

Aging has also been classified as successful, usual, and pathologic (Rowe & Kahn, 1987).

In **successful aging,** there is an interaction between the individual's genes and environment, both being positive. Positive genetic characteristics and positive environmental factors result in no serious detriment in functioning from the middle twenties until the early seventies. Minimal measurable changes in functioning are seen with these as the energetic and functional "survivors" in aging. They have no genetic diseases, but they represent only about 5 to 10 percent of the population. These individuals are the aging "stars" we aspire to be like—those active, energetic, and involved elders we revere, admire, or respect.

Usual aging occurs in the vast majority of individuals. We see an interaction between the person's genetic endowment and environment. A neutral or negative environment has positive or neutral genes. This raises concern for the reversible risk factors that occur with aging. The gene–environment interaction leads to obvious functional limitations, but the limitations are not serious enough to affect ADLs as long as the person makes compromises and adaptations. An example is the person whose mobility is limited but adjusts to this and is still able to live independently without assistance in daily life. For example, in a Canadian study published by the Minister of National Health and Welfare (1993), at least one-third of people over 65 years reported an activity limitation but were still living in the community and coping very to fairly well with the limitation. With successful aging, we may also see genetic diseases, but again, adaptations are made that do not significantly interfere with independent daily functioning.

At the opposite extreme is **pathological aging.** Here we see a negative interaction between genetic and environmental factors. Some combination of negative or neutral influences arise from both the individual's genes and the environment. We often see clinical evidence of genetic diseases in these aging individuals. This genetic-environmental interaction leads to serious functional limitations for the individual, such as being unable to take care of hygiene or personal needs, seriously affecting ADLs and sometimes the ability to sustain life. These functional limitations require substantial intervention, for example, in an extended-care setting.

DEMOGRAPHICS AND AGING AMERICANS

Aging adults represent a growing segment of our population. In 1990, the population over 65 years was 31.1 million (12.5 percent) with women outnumbering men three to two (Taeuber, 1993). We are now also seeing a great increase in the 85 years and older population as well as in aging adults who are members of minority groups. As these population proportions increase even more in the next century, we will need to consider further individual differences, needs of age groups, cultural and ethnic trends, and changing family patterns.

Intergenerational issues will involve more than children, parents, grandparents, and perhaps great-grandparents. Consider the complexity of a family with two or three older adult groups, those in their middle to late sixties, eighties, and hundreds, as well as the family members under age 60. The concern also arises as to who will be the caregiver for the frail older adult. Will the 80-year-old be caring for a frail spouse as well as a 99-year-old mother, or will the 60-year-old be caring for both the 80-year-old parents and the 99-year-old grandmother? Recall that women outnumber men three to two, but the ratio for those 65 to 69 years old is presently only five to four whereas women 85 and older outnumber men five to two (Taeuber, 1993, pp. 2–8).

Living Arrangements

Living arrangements are an important factor for aging adults. Most aging adults live in the community, usually with spouses or alone. Atchley (1991) reports that the proportion of aging adults who live with family members other than a spouse, most frequently adult offspring, increased with age from 10 percent between 65 and 74 years to 20.1 percent at

85 years and older (p. 34). Physical frailty, chronicity, and death of the spouse are important factors in this 85 year and older age group. The proportion of people over 65 who are living in nursing homes is less than 5 percent.

Decisions on living arrangements should include considerations for optimal promotion of functional independence and health. Opportunities for social interactions and access to resources and caregivers, when needed, are vital considerations.

Various housing options are considered by aging adults. In our more mobile society, being tied to a homestead may no longer be preferable, especially for urban and younger aging adults. Retirement planning may include relocating to a more temperate climate or closer to children. Instead of the large family homestead, smaller detached homes, condominiums and townhouses, retirement communities, continuing care communities, assisted-living apartments, senior homes, and group homes are options, depending on needs, affordability, and accessibility. In addition, a frail elder may relocate again to live with a child or other relative following the death of the spouse, sale of the retirement home, and increasing loss of functional independence.

Age-Related Changes

Characteristics of aging adults are as varied as the individuals themselves. Aging adults come with years of unique experiences that have molded their psychosocial profile. Physically and physiologically, aging adults also differ in development and progression of age-related changes. Aging is progressive and irreversible, but the manner in which these changes occur is variable. Appearance changes and motor activities slow down. But things do not stop without some pathology. Aging adults are more susceptible to disease and environmental factors. Maintaining homeostasis is more difficult.

Age-related changes occur in biological systems. Skin becomes less elastic. Sweat glands, temperature receptors, pigment, and subcutaneous fat decrease. This makes the aging adults more susceptible to temperature extremes, cold or hot, and sunlight.

Other senses adapt to aging as well. Visual and hearing acuity diminish. Adaptation of the lens and ocular muscles decreases with a decrease in depth perception. Glare and driving at night become stressful, especially if the aging person looks at oncoming headlights. The home environment needs to be well illuminated, but with nonglare lights. For example, reducing the glare with fluorescent lights can also reduce the chance of accidents, especially

falls. Print may need to be larger and bolder. Eye exams are very important. The loss of the drivers' license may be devastating to an aging person, even if his or her driving is limited. Failure to pass the eye exam may even be a result of using no glasses or ones that were woefully inadequate.

Changes in level of consciousness or delirium are not normal signs of aging. Neurologic changes do occur, but may be indicative of an underlying pathology or drug interaction. These possibilities should always be investigated further with referrals. Time rather than loss should be your first thought: It may take a little more time to remember something, but that doesn't mean that the memory is lost!

Muscle mass and strength decrease, and joints may be stiff with arthritis. Muscle mass may be replaced with connective tissue. Osteoporosis occurs with calcium losses and hormonal changes, and worsens with inactivity. Low-impact, isometric, and routine exercise can prevent further immobility and loss of function.

Digestion and slower motility is improved with smaller meals. Food may taste and smell bland. Herbs and seasoning can be used, but caution must be taken with preparations that have a hidden sodium content. Meals must be attractively displayed, well timed, and easy to digest.

Sexuality and sexual intercourse continue, but adaptation may be needed as well, such as more time for arousal, excitement and foreplay or lubrication for vaginal dryness or to assist in foreplay. Impotence needs to be evaluated for pathology or possible drug side effects. Counseling, erectile aids, reduction in alcohol consumption, and changes in medications are all possible treatments. Options are available to aging persons of both genders, and sexual activity need not stop because of advancing age. More problems may arise in availability of partners, and the issue of intimacy must be stressed.

MAJOR HEALTH PROBLEMS OF AGING ADULTS

Chronic illness and frailty are primary concerns of both aging adults and health-care professionals. Eight diseases common to aging include osteoporosis, diabetes, stroke, depression, arthritis, Alzheimer's disease, cancer, and cardiovascular disease (Beers & Youdovin, 1993, p. 5). The difference between chronicity and disability must be considered. **Disability** is the inability to do something because of a physical or mental impairment. Frailty has been identified as a major cause for disability and the need for long-term care (National Institute on Aging, 1991). On the other hand, **chronicity** is related to duration or recurrence of a condition. The individual may have a chronic condition but, with healthy behaviors, can limit, delay, or prevent disability. Hence, health promotion behaviors and empowerment of the individual are essential for taking charge of one's own life.

Beers and Youdovin (1993) report that early detection and treatment are effective for a substantial proportion of the 15 most prevalent conditions in the over-65 population: arthritis, hypertension, heart disease, hearing loss, vision loss, influenza, injuries, orthopedic impairment, cataracts, chronic sinusitis, depression, cancer, diabetes, urinary incontinence, and varicose veins (p. 9). Unlike the irreversible normal changes of aging, risk factors can be reduced and in some cases eliminated.

Risks in aging adults include physical, environmental, psychosocial, and chemical factors. Physical risks affect the biological system and relate physiologic function. Examples of physical risks are limitations in flexibility that can lead to falls or vision changes resulting in automobile accidents. Environmental risks can be natural or artificial. Natural environmental risks include ultraviolet radiation and weather extremes. Examples of artificial or man-made environmental risks are air quality, hazards in housing, and poor maintenance of equipment or the environment. Psychosocial risks are a part of everyday life, whether isolated or active. Stress levels with illness of self, family members, or friends take an increasing toll on the individual. An inward focus on problems and the ego may make the aging person more isolated and egocentric. Consider some specific risk factors that commonly affect many aging adults and create conditions that interfere with activity.

Arthritis

Arthritis is the most frequently reported chronic health condition in aging adults, especially among women and African-Americans (Taeuber, 1993, pp. 3–11). Rheumatoid arthritis is characterized by joint inflammation, stiffness, and limitation in movement, frequently with discomfort and pain. Osteoarthritis involves degenerative changes in the cartilage of the articulation joints, resulting in joint limitation, possibly with pain and spur formation. Osteoarthritis is the most frequent type of arthritis with over 5.4 million Americans over 75 years of age having severe limitations in function (National Institute on Aging, 1991, p. 9). The effects on joints of either rheuma-

toid arthritis or osteoarthritis can severely limit mobility and functional independence. Further consequences can be a decline in the social network and mental stimulation and attitudes. The importance of safe medication practices, comfort measures, and exercise programs should be part of any teaching program or public service program on arthritis because of its prevalence in the aging population.

Hypertension and Heart Disease

Hypertension and heart disease are major health problems in the population of aging adults. Although the incidence of mortality related to coronary heart disease has declined in aging adults, heart disease is the major cause of death (Taeuber, 1993). Many factors are contributory, including longevity and the condition of this major muscle. A national panel has predicted that, since the incidence of heart failure rises after age 65, the prevalence will increase as the proportion of aging adults increases (Konstam, Dracup, Baker, et al., 1994, p. 1). The importance of teaching and support, with identification of symptoms, smoking cessation, sodium restriction, appropriate weight, and medication regimen are vital in this area. In addition, *Healthy People 2000* points to the association of increased levels of physical activity with a reduced incidence of coronary heart disease and hypertension (USDHHS, 1992, p. 24).

Influenza

Influenza can rapidly lead to respiratory compromise, but prevention activities can limit incidence and complications. In fact, it has been estimated that although more than 80 percent of influenza-related deaths occur in people 65 years and older, fewer than one-third of aging Americans receive vaccinations (Beers & Youdovin, 1993, p. 9). Health promotion activities should include information on vaccinations for influenza. In addition, if the aging adult has predisposing debilitating or chronic conditions, such as emphysema, he or she should be encouraged to discuss the advisability of receiving the pneumonia vaccine with a health-care provider. Risk also occurs by virtue of being active and involved. In crowded social settings such as bingo halls, the risk of transmission of respiratory infections can increase for the aging person, who may have a weakened immune system or chronic respiratory or cardiac problems. Good judgment and immunizations are important prevention activities in the cold and flu season.

Injuries

Accidents and injuries are major causes of both morbidity and mortality in aging adults. Accident prevention programs and environmental assessments are as important for aging adults as they are for the infant and toddler. The individual's functional abilities can predispose him or her to accidents. Stiffness, instability, and limited flexibility can lead to falls. As mentioned, uncorrected visual changes, altered behaviors, or assistive devices may lead to motor vehicle accidents. Aging adults must become more attuned to environmental hazards, functional limitations, driving hazards, and resources available to them.

Depression

As in other age groups, depression in aging adults can be caused by a variety of factors. But unlike in other age groups, it can also be confused with delirium and dementia. Certain nonpsychotropic drugs and preexistent medical conditions can cause symptoms of depression in the elderly (Depression Guideline Panel, 1993a). Depression is a risk factor in aging adults; untreated it can lead to a host of other problems. As the national Depression Guideline Panel (1993b) points out:

> the consequences of unrecognized and untreated depression in the elderly include increased health services utilization, longer hospital stays, poor treatment compliance, and increased morbidity and mortality from medical illness and suicide [while] the costs of treatment are relatively modest and can be minimized by careful monitoring of the patient's clinical status. (p. 99)

Alzheimer's Disease

The dementias and Alzheimer's disease are major fears in the aging population, and major concerns in family and health-care financing. Alzheimer's disease is now the fourth major cause of death in the aging adults and has major emotional, physical, and financial consequences for the family caregiver. Although the Alzheimer's disease is but one form of dementia, the three phases of the disease, on average, occur over a 10-year period. The care, safety, and emotional needs of the person can jeopardize the health and abilities of the caregiving family member unless acceptable resources and support systems are available.

Cancer

In 1992, the National Institute on Aging reported that "more than half of all cancer patients are over age 65" (p. 32). The type and location of cancer can be related to a variety of factors, known and unknown. One thing we can see from the biological theories of aging: genetic errors can accumulate with aging, and these may turn into cancer cells. Quality of life issues must be addressed for the various types of cancer and treatments selected, for example, in the individual with prostrate cancer and impotency.

Pain management is another issue of particular concern with the older cancer client. The Management of Cancer Pain Guidelines Panel (Jacox, Carr, Payne, et al., 1994), addressing aging adults as a special population, indicated that they "are at risk for undertreatment of pain because of underestimation of their sensitivity to pain, the expectation that they will tolerate pain well, and misconceptions about their ability to benefit from the use opioids" (p. 22). In guidelines for clinicians, this national panel identified eight assessment and treatment issues specific to aging clients:

- Multiple chronic diseases, complex medication regimens, and sources of pain
- Visual, hearing, motor, and cognitive impairments requiring simple and frequent assessments of pain
- Nonsteroidal anti-inflammatory drug (NSAID) side effects, especially gastric toxicity
- Higher peak opioid effectiveness and longer duration of pain relief
- Caution in initial dose, titration, and monitoring of patient-controlled analgesia
- Alternative routes of administration appropriate for client abilities
- Postoperative pain control and frequent reassessment
- Change of setting, such as from hospital to home or nursing home (Jacox et al., 1994, p. 22).

Sensory Losses

Hearing and vision losses occur with advanced age. Presbycusis, or hearing loss in aging, occurs with high frequency sounds. This may be due to environmental factors such as continual exposure to high frequency sounds or background noise. We may see more of this with the aging of the baby boomers. In addition, the accumulation of cerumen in the ear canals may be ignored, dampening sound and mimicking a true hearing loss. Ototoxic medications can also create permanent hearing losses. A good history is needed to investigate all these factors.

Visual losses occur with changes in eye structures causing problems with visual acuity and accommodation. The aging person is also more sensitive to variable illumination levels and glare. The most frequent visual loss is macular degeneration. This results in loss of central vision. In most cases, the cause of the degeneration is unknown, but early detection and treatment can prevent loss of vision. Cataracts are another cause of visual loss that frequently occur in aging adults. Risk factors for the development of cataracts vary, and research is ongoing. The national Cataract Management Guideline Panel (1993) identifies the following risks factors: ultraviolet B radiation, diabetes, drugs, smoking, diarrhea, alcohol, and antioxidant vitamins. Although much of the research is inconclusive, the incidence of cataracts in the aging adults may be reduced by greater use of sunglasses, limited alcohol consumption, and smoking cessation.

Urinary Incontinence

Although it is prevalent in the aging adult population, urinary incontinence is not a normal age-related change. The Urinary Incontinence Guideline Panel (1992) has indicated that the incidence of urinary incontinence for noninstitutionalized people over age 60 is 15 to 30 percent, and over 50 percent for nursing home residents (pp. 3–4). Incontinence can be caused by a variety of physiologic, chemical, and psychological risk factors. Incontinence can often be eliminated by eliminating the risk factors, such as certain medications. Specific exercises may also be recommended to increase muscle tone. Achieving urinary continence can also increase individuals' self-esteem and social network as they feel more comfortable and self-confident in social interactions.

Polypharmacy

Polypharmacy is a major concern and includes over-the-counter (OTC) as well as prescribed medications. Aging adults may have more than one physician to whom they may not give all their medication history because they feel rushed or sense they should not ask questions, or for a number of other reasons. In addition, prescriptions are expensive, consuming a large part of many aging adults' budgets. They may not purchase the medication because of the cost or save some for future use. Edu-

cation and careful monitoring of both prescribed and OTC medications are essential. Pharmacies may provide information on the prescribed medications, but the print may be small, light, or difficult to understand for the aging adult. This information may also not take into account other prescribed or routinely taken OTC medications that could cause interactions, potentiation, or adverse side effects in combination.

NEEDS OF AGING ADULTS

The major needs of aging adults can easily be viewed in relation to longevity factors, especially Maslow's hierarchy of needs. As mentioned, longevity factors with some research support include genetics, gender, environment, physical activity, alcohol consumption, sexual activity, nutrition, social factors such as economics, marital status, and family, religious beliefs, purpose in life, and laughter. Positive behaviors must be directed at promoting and maintaining health and functional independence, and reducing risk factors. Another piece of this is the need for access by the aging adult to affordable health care, including transportation, cost, and acceptability of the provider to the person.

According to Maslow (1970), the *physiologic drives* include the need to maintain homeostasis as well as meeting the physiologic needs of hunger, sleep and rest, activity and exercise, sexual gratification, sensory pleasure, and maternal responses. Before moving to higher level needs, the aging person must have relative satisfaction in these needs. Nutrition and physical fitness are important considerations. Maintaining an adequate nutritional status can become difficult when aging adults have problems with dentures, finances, transportation, food preparation abilities, and social isolation. Meeting the physiologic hunger drive is very different from meeting nutritional requirements. In addition, research supports the need for physical activity to maintain mobility and functional independence. *Healthy People 2000* (1992) stressed the need for physical activity and indicated that increased levels of exercise by older Americans were associated with decreased incidence of heart disease, diabetes, colon cancer, depression, and osteoporotic fractures. Sensuality and sexuality are other basic needs of aging adults. Sensuality must also be emphasized when, because of advancing age, difficulties arise with correctable, modifiable or irreversible physical conditions. In addition, with increasing age and longevity differences between genders, there are many more older women in an age group than there are older men.

The *safety needs* are at the next level of the hierarchy. Both physical and emotional safety must be achieved. These are important basic needs for aging adults in their living environment. A major factor here is the prevention of accidents. Falling and automobile accidents are the most common causes of fatalities in aging people. It has been noted that 210,000 older people have serious fractures due to falls annually, with 20 percent resulting in death within 12 months (National Institute on Aging, 1992, p. 3). In addition, consider the disability that can result from nonfatal accidents, such as hip fractures due to falls. Accident prevention is important in both promoting and maintaining health. This becomes difficult with sensory losses, impaired mobility, and medications that cause many accidents. Creating a safe environment is as important for the aging population as for infants and young children. Their living environment may not be accidentproof but should be assessed frequently and maintained. This is a vital part of any individual or family counseling. Motor vehicle accidents can be reduced with good judgment. As the National Institute on Aging (1992) recommends, impaired vision and slower reaction times can be mediated, in many cases, by avoiding night driving, limiting the number of hours on the road, and exercising additional caution in traffic and inclement weather (p. 3).

Love and belonging needs are frequently overlooked, and make the aging adult vulnerable to depressive symptoms. Coping with losses of family members, friends, pets, and a sense of usefulness in life are major threats to the aging adult's ego system. Another consideration is the adequacy of human contact and interactions such as intimacy and sexuality. As *Healthy People 2000* (1992) illustrates, social isolation is a risk factor in aging adults, often resulting in depression and attributing to the high rate of suicide in men aged 65 to 74 years. Attachments and involvement with other people are essential. These needs are challenged with continual losses and, in some cases, the isolation resulting with loss of functional abilities, impairments preventing independent mobility, and even isolation in the home during severe weather. An important piece of the Older Americans Act is the nutritional program. Congregate meals in senior centers increase the aging adult's social contacts as well as feelings of inclusion. For aging adults unable to participate in the congregate meal program, home-delivered meals may be available. The driver who delivers meals to a home-bound aging adult may be the only human contact in a 24-hour period. Caring about someone, for someone, and by someone are important considerations with aging adults.

This caring brings us to the next level of basic needs. *Esteem needs* involve having a sense of dignity and usefulness in life. This includes quality of life considerations. What is the quality of the aging adult's life? Do aging adults have a sense of self-worth through involvement with family, work, recreation, volunteerism, pets, and civic groups? Think about the factors that have been associated with longevity, and the risk with social isolation. Empowerment of the aging person is another important consideration in esteem needs. Maslow (1970) stated that "satisfaction of the self-esteem need leads to feelings of self-confidence, worth, strength, capability, and adequacy, and of being useful and necessary in the world" (p. 45). Positive aspects of esteem come with a sense of self-worth, empowerment, and competency in daily life, including physical and financial stability. Careful preparations for retirement with financial planning is a component of self-esteem that is now receiving more attention. The negative aspects of self-esteem needs may be reflected in the depressed, and perhaps suicidal, aging adult.

Self-actualization equates closely with Erikson's sense of ego integrity. Maslow (1970) defined self-actualization as "the full use and exploitation of talents, capacities, potentialities, etc., such [that] people seem to be fulfilling themselves and to be doing the best that they are capable of doing" (p. 150). A dear friend and very wise gentleman once declared, "I would rather wear out than rust out." This gentleman is not only wise, but a true example of a self-actualized aging adult. Involved aging adults who focus on others and the next goal or plan are self-actualized individuals, whether they are active in the community of their assisted living environment or in the broader society.

FAMILY NEEDS AND ISSUES

Given the proportion of aging adults living in the community and projections for population increases, especially in the 85 years and older group, family needs are a major issue in health promotion and care activities. Much can be found in the literature about family decisions for nursing home placement and the "sandwich generation" of caregivers. The fact is that caring for a frail older adult takes a major toll on the caregiver and the family. The role reversal between generations in caring for a parent with

Alzheimer's or deciding to place a parent in a nursing home in conflict with a promise can exact an emotional toll. The physical toll on the caregiver can be enormous considering the physical care a disabled family member needs while the caregiver continues maintaining other family, childrearing, social, work, and personal obligations. The concept of respite care, to give the caregiver a break, is ideal but not always available, affordable, or even emotionally acceptable. Regardless, the caregiver will need some form of respite, and this must be determined, sought, and used regularly. Family leave can now be obtained from employers, but all conditions should be carefully understood before a request is submitted and any agreement is reached. Placement in long-term care facilities or nursing homes might be necessary, and the caregiver and family supported throughout the process. But alternative options might be more acceptable such as adult day care, home care aides, or informal care providers. All of these should be discussed and weighed by the family with good support from family, friends, and health-care providers.

SOCIETAL NEEDS AND ISSUES

Public policy issues include the availability and allocation of health-care resources for aging adults as well as the use of these resources. Some people contend that aging adults are using the vast majority of the health-care resources with their chronic health problems. Yet prevention of these health problems in the current baby boomers should be the focus.

Health-care legislation and financing for aging adults is seen mainly through the Social Security amendments and budget reconciliation acts which include Medicare and Medicaid funding. With Medicaid, the role, legislation, and funding levels fall within the domain of the state of residence. But what about part-time residents who spend half the year in a state in which they do not claim primary residence? What about the issue of reverse migration of frail aging adults who, after years of retirement in a satisfactory condition, lose a spouse and become increasingly frail and move back to be cared for by their children? Their affluence was spent somewhere else, but when they move near the children, this community must address the financing of chronic health care and increasing frailty. Similar situations can have great impact on society and health-care resources. Regulatory agencies for health-care institutions also have a vital role in assessment, surveillance, and policy formation to ensure dignity and quality of life for aging adults who are consumers, patients, or residents.

An area of concern at the individual, family, and societal levels is elder abuse. This includes physical neglect or violence, verbal abuse, psychological or emotional abuse, financial exploitation, and sexual abuse. It may be intended or unintended, in active or passive actions on the part of the abuser. Those aging individuals most at risk are the frail elderly who are functionally impaired and depend on others. They may be in dysfunctional family situations but fear being alone more than the abuse or neglect they are experiencing. Assessment, reporting, educating, and counseling are responsibilities of health-care providers and members of society.

GERONTOLOGICAL NURSING PRACTICE

As defined, gerontological nursing practice focuses on the responses of aging individuals to actual or potential health problems. Health and health problems for this heterogeneous and unique group of individuals are the major concerns of this nursing specialty area. The emergence of gerontological nursing has been a twentieth-century phenomenon with initial publications, research, and divisional status in the American Nurses Association (ANA). Official recognition of gerontological nursing as a specialty area began in 1970, with periodic revision of standards of practice as professional nursing evolved (Table 19–5). In 1974, ANA certification for gerontological nursing started, followed by an increase in nursing textbooks and publications dedicated to the specialty area.

As a result of a W. K. Kellogg Foundation Project, further nursing competencies in gerontological nursing were specified. This project was the work of three nursing groups: The National League for Nurs-

TABLE 19 – 5. Evolution of ANA Standards for Gerontological Nursing Practice

1970	*ANA Standards on Geriatric Nursing Practice*
1973, 1976	Revisions to the original standards
1981	*ANA Scope of Gerontological Nursing Practice*
1987	*ANA Standards and Scope of Gerontological Nursing Practice*
1995	*ANA Scope and Standards of Gerontological Nursing Practice*

ing (NLN), The Community College–Nursing Home Partnership, and the Georgetown University School of Nursing (1992). Competencies identified were specific and consistent with the 1987 ANA Standards and Scope of Practice. These competencies were based on educational level—associate degree (ADN), baccalaureate (BSN), and master's (MSN). Competencies for ADN graduates were best taught in nursing homes and included technical skills in resident assessment, rehabilitation, and management. For BSN and MSN graduates, competencies were leveled by educational preparation and described under professional practice and nursing process. BSN graduate professional practice competencies included theory and research-based direct care, management, assessment, planning, intervention, and evaluation skills. Professional competencies for the MSN graduate were directed at advanced specialty practice.

Also in 1990, Johnson and Connelly reported the findings from a federal study on the status of professional and educational issues in gerontological nursing. Four areas of concern were raised on gerontological nursing:

- Variable and indistinct content in undergraduate education
- No specific content required on licensure exams
- Lack of prepared faculty and clinical role models
- Inadequate response within the profession to supply and demand qualified Gerontological nurses (Johnson & Connelly, 1990, p. v).

Given the demographic indicators for our population, and considering their emergent health-care needs, recommendations were made for consistent inclusion of gerontological nursing content in nursing program curricula. The intention of this recommendation was to provide quality health care to aging adults by nurses "based on [current] scientific knowledge and ethical standards" (Johnson & Connelly, 1990, p. 10).

The most recent standards of gerontological nursing practice were revised in 1995 as the *Scope and Standards of Gerontological Nursing Practice* (ANA, 1995). The standards for gerontological nursing care are presented with rationales for each phase of the nursing process, in assessment, diagnosis, outcome evaluation, planning, implementation, and evaluation. Eight standards of gerontological nursing performance are also described to guide specialty practice in the following areas:

- Quality of care
- Performance appraisal
- Education
- Collegiality
- Ethics
- Collaboration
- Research
- Resource utilization (ANA, 1995).

To demonstrate accountability within gerontological nursing practice, criteria designed to allow for measurement are provided, as in performance appraisals.

The scope of gerontological nursing practice highlights the concepts of health promotion, health maintenance, disease prevention, and self-care (ANA, 1995, p. 3). Identification of the differences in preparation and responsibilities of basic and advanced gerontological nursing practice are described. The basic nurse is a professional with a baccalaureate in nursing and expertise in gerontological nursing practice and responsibilities in "direct care, management and development of professional and other nursing personnel, and evaluation of care and services for aging persons" (ANA, 1995, p. 8). Specific knowledge and skills are described, focusing on use of the nursing process with aging persons and their families, advocacy, professional development, and participation in interdisciplinary health care.

Advanced gerontological nursing practice occurs at the specialist level. Preparation for practice includes the minimum of a master's degree as a clinical nurse specialist or nurse practitioner, preferably with a concentration in gerontological nursing (ANA, 1995, p. 9). The ANA Standards of Practice for advanced practice in gerontological nursing describe these specialists as "experts in providing, directing, and delegating the care of aging persons, and they support other practitioners in a variety of settings" (ANA, 1995, p. 9). Specialty roles include practice, education, research, consultation, and administration. Collaboration with other professionals within nursing and in other health professions is a major emphasis in advanced gerontological nursing practice.

For advanced practice, the ANA identifies the appropriate credential as national certification as a specialist in gerontological nursing. Advanced practice is defined in the individual state's practice act. Generally, advanced practice is based on master's education in the specialty area and national or state certification. In 1994, of the 102,928 nurses certified by the ANA, 10,282 were certified in gerontological nursing, 601 were certified as clinical specialists (CNS) in gerontological nursing, and 1698 were certified as gerontological nurse practitioners (ANA,

1995, p. 4). Beginning in 1992, eligibility requirements for the CNS in gerontological nursing include a master's or higher degree in nursing, preferably in gerontological nursing, along with postmaster's and current practice requirements. Education, currency in practice, and norms set by specialists are increasingly a component of professional nursing practice. The specialists in gerontological nursing serve the needs and promote a healthy future for aging adults, their families and caregivers, and society.

KEY POINTS

- Proportional increases in aging adults are predicted, with the greatest increase in the 85 years and older group. Women presently account for a large proportion of this group, outnumbering men 5 to 2. Predictions include an increase in minority groups represented in our aging population.
- The 1995 White House Conference on the Aging will yield future initiatives for the aging in the next decade, with adoption of the resolutions.
- Various terms are used to describe older adults. Negative views on aging are typified by the terms "ageism," "gerontophobia," "senescence," and "senility." Other terms may not truly characterize the aging adult, such as "aged," "senior citizen," and "elderly." Further categories have evolved: young-old (65 to 74 years), middle-old (75 to 84 years), and old-old (85 years and older). Additional terms have been based on functional abilities in an attempt to be more descriptive and positive, such as frail elderly versus able elderly.
- Disciplinary differences exist among geriatrics, gerontology, and gerontological nursing. Gerontological nursing focuses on the responses of aging individuals to actual or potential health problems, not merely the disease.
- Disciplinary research is ongoing on the theories of aging, with an increasing focus on functional abilities of aging adults.
- The demographics of the aging population shows a proportional growth with vital issues related to health status, intergenerational and environmental factors, and individual differences and changes.
- Chronic illnesses and increasing frailty account for the major causes of morbidity in aging adults. These include osteoporosis, diabetes, stroke, depression, arthritis, Alzheimer's, cancer, and cardiovascular disease. Arthritis, sensory losses, influenza, injuries, orthopedic impairment, cataracts, chronic sinusitis, and urinary incontinence are other common chronic conditions that affect the functional health of aging adults.
- Risks factors in aging adults include physical, environmental, psychosocial, and chemical factors. These risks commonly affect many aging adults, creating conditions that interfere with activity. Health promotion activities are vital in this area to maintain functional ability and reduce the incidence of frailty and disability.
- Maslow's hierarchy provides a useful framework for viewing the needs of aging adults. Health promotion activities should address the aging adult's needs as physiological drives, safety, love and belonging, esteem, and self-actualization.
- With increases in longevity as well as frailty in aging adults, family issues include intergenerational living arrangements, caregiving, and emotional needs.
- Broadening the view from the individual and family, major societal issues include public policy, allocation of resources, and health-care financing.
- Gerontological nursing practice has evolved into a distinct specialty area with standards for care and certification options. Basic gerontological nursing practice is guided by the nursing process focusing on the special needs of aging adults. Advanced gerontological nursing practice occurs at the specialist level, with roles in practice, education, research, consultation, and administration.

CHAPTER EXERCISES

1. Contact your local area agency on aging. Describe the resources available to aging adults in your county, area, and state.

2. Interview one individual from each of the following age groups: 60 to 69, 70 to 79, 80 to 89, 90+. Try to include both genders and individuals with different states of wellness. Describe their perspective of health and experiences with aging.

3. Examine the personal and group attitudes on aging in your community. Identify stereotypes of the aging that are apparent in your environment, and describe ways that these could be changed.

4. Identify health promotion programs and resources in your community that apply to older adults. Next, identify health-care services appropriate for health problems in older adults.

REFERENCES

Agency for Health Care Policy and Research. (1994). Hospital discharge rates and lengths of stay for specific medical conditions, 1980–1985. *Intramural Research Highlights* (AHCPR Publication No. 94-0133). Rockville, MD: Department of Health and Human Services, Public Health Service, AHCPR.

American Association of Retired Persons. (1991). *A profile of older Americans* (AARP Publication No. PF3049 1291 D996). Washington, DC: AARP.

American Nurses Association. (1995). *Scope and standards of gerontological nursing practice* (Pub. No. GE-12 7.5M 6/95). Washington, DC: American Nurses Publishing.

American Nurses' Association. (1987). *Standards and scope of gerontological nursing practice* (Pub. No. GE-12 10M 1/88). Kansas City, MO: ANA.

American Nurses' Association. (1981). *A statement on the scope of gerontological nursing practice*. Kansas City, MO: ANA.

American Nurses Credentialing Center. (1995). *1995 Certification catalog*. Washington, DC: ANCC.

Atchley, R. C. (1991). *Social forces and aging: An introduction to social gerontology* (6th ed.). Belmont, CA: Wadsworth.

Beers, M., & Youdovin, S. W. (1993). *The healthy aging imperative*. West Point, PA: Merck Public Affairs Department.

Cataract Management Guideline Panel. (1993). *Cataract in adults: Management of functional impairment. Clinical practice guideline No. 4* (AHCPR Pub. No. 93-0542). Rockville, MD: Agency for Health Care Policy and Research, Public Health Service, Department of Health and Human Services.

Chenitz, W. C., Stone, J. T., & Salisbury, S. A. (1991). *Clinical gerontological nursing: A guide to advanced practice*. Philadelphia: Saunders.

Depression Guideline Panel. (1993a). *Depression in primary care: Volume I. Detection and diagnosis. Clinical practice guideline No. 5* (AHCPR Pub. No. 93-0550). Rockville, MD: Agency for Health Care Policy and Research, Public Health Service, Department of Health and Human Services.

Depression Guideline Panel. (1993). *Depression in primary care: Volume 2. Treatment of major depression. Clinical practice guideline No. 5* (AHCPR Pub. No. 93-0551). Rockville, MD: Agency for Health Care Policy and Research, Public Health Service, Department of Health and Human Services.

Ebersole, P., & Hess, P. (1994). *Toward health aging: Human needs and nursing response* (4th ed.). St. Louis: Mosby.

Erikson, E. H. (1963). *Childhood and society* (2nd ed.). New York: Norton.

Havighurst, R. J. (1972). *Developmental tasks and education* (3rd ed.). New York: David McKay.

Jacox, A., Carr, D. B., Payne, R., et al. (1994). *Management of cancer pain: Adults. Quick reference guide for clinicians. No. 9.* (AHCPH Publication No. 94-0593). Rockville, MD: Agency for Health Care Policy and Research, Department of Health and Human Services.

Johnson, M. A., Connelly, J. R. (1990). *Nursing and gerontology: Status report*. Washington, DC: Association for Gerontology in Higher Education.

Konstam, M., Dracup, K., Baker, D., et al. (1994). *Heart failure: Evaluation and care of patients with left-ventricular systolic dysfunction. Clinical practice guideline No. 11* (AHCPR Pub. No. 94-0612). Rockville, MD: Agency for Health Care Policy and Research, Public Health Service, Department of Health and Human Services.

Maslow, A. H. (1970). *Motivation and personality* (2nd ed.). New York: Harper & Row.

Miller, C. A. (1990). *Nursing care of older adults: Theory and Practice*. Glenview, IL: Scott, Foresman/Little, Brown Higher Education.

Minister of National Health and Welfare. (1993). *Ageing and independence. Overview of a national survey* (Publication No. H88-3/13-1993E). Ottawa, Canada: Minister of Supply and Services.

National Institute on Aging. (1991). *Physical frailty: A reducible barrier to independence for older Americans. Report to Congress* (NIH Publication No. 91-397). Washington, DC: Department of Health and Human Services, Public Health Service, National Institutes of Health.

National Institute on Aging. (1992). *Who? What? Where? Resources for women's health and aging* (NIH Publication No. 91-323). Washington, DC: Department of Health and Human Services, Public Health Service, National Institutes of Health.

National League for Nursing, Community College-Nursing Home Partnership, & Georgetown University School of Nursing.

(1992). *Gerontology in the nursing curriculum* (Special report). New York: NLN.

Office of Disease Prevention and Health Promotion, PHS. (no date). National health promotion and disease prevention objectives. *Fact sheet: Healthy people 2000.* Washington: Department of Health and Human Services, Public Health Service, ODPHP. (Available from Coordinator, ODPHP, Room 2132, 330 C Street SW, Washington, DC 20201.)

Older Americans Act (OAA) Amendments of 1992. Pub. L. No. 102-375, 9/30/92.

Omnibus Budget Reconciliation Act (OBRA) of 1989. Pub. L. No. 101-239, 12/13/89.

Peck, R. C. (1968). Psychological developments in the second half of life. In B. L. Neugarten (Ed.), *Middle age and aging: A reader in social psychology* (pp. 88–92). Chicago: University of Chicago Press.

Rose, M. R. (1991). *Evolutionary biology of aging.* New York: Oxford.

Rowe, J. W., & Kahn, R. L. (1987). Human aging: Usual and successful. *Science, 237,* 143–149.

Swisher, K. (Ed.). (1990). *The elderly—opposing viewpoints.* San Diego: Greenhaven Press.

Taeuber, C. (1993). *Sixty-five plus in America. Current population reports. Special reports.* (Dept. of Commerce Publication No. P23-178RV). Washington, DC: U.S. Government Printing Office.

U.S. Department of Health and Human Services, Public Health Service. (1992). *Healthy people 2000: Summary report.* Boston: Jones & Bartlett.

U.S. Department of Health and Human Services, Social Security Administration. (1994). *Understanding Social Security* (Pub. No. ICN 454930). Baltimore, MD: USDHHS.

Urinary Incontinence Guideline Panel. (1992). *Urinary incontinence in adults: Clinical practice guideline* (AHCPR Pub. No. 92-0038). Rockville, MD: Agency for Health Care Policy and Research, Public Health Service, Department of Health and Human Services.

White House Conference on Aging (WHCoA). (1996). *1995 White House Conference on Aging executive summary: The road to an aging policy for the 21st century.* Washington, DC: WHCoA.

BIBLIOGRAPHY

Baines, E. M. (Ed.). (1991). *Perspectives on gerontological nursing.* Newbury Park, CA: Sage.

Burke, M., & Sherman, S. (Ed.). (1993). *Gerontological nursing: Issues and opportunities for the twenty-first century* (Pub. No. 14-2510). New York: National League for Nursing.

Bernstein, C., & Bernstein, H. (1991). *Aging, sex, and DNA repair.* San Diego: Academic Press.

Birren, J. E., & Bengtson, V. L. (Eds.). (1988). *Emergent theories of aging.* New York: Springer.

Cox, B. J., & Waller, L. L. (1991). *Bridging the communication gap with the elderly: Practical strategies for caregivers* (Pub. No. F4-130104). Chicago: American Hospital Association.

Gale, B. J., & Steffl, B. M. (1992). The long-term care dilemma: What nurses need to know about Medicare. *Nursing & Health Care, 13,* 34–41.

Jacox, A., Carr, D. B., Payne, R., et al. (1994). *Management of cancer pain. Clinical practice guideline No. 9* (AHCPR Publication No. 94-0592). Rockville, MD: Agency for Health Care Policy and Research, Public Health Service, Department of Health and Human Services.

Kuhlman, G. J., Wilson, H. S., Hutchinson, S. A., & Wallhagen, M. (1991). Alzheimer's disease and family caregiving: Critical synthesis of the literature and research agenda. *Nursing Research, 40,* 331–337.

Lang, N. M., Kraegel, J. M., Rantz, M. J., & Krejci, J. W. (1991). *Quality of health care for older people in America: A review of nursing studies* (Pub. No. GE-13 2M 8/91R). Washington, DC: ANA.

Mitty, E. L. (Ed.). (1992). *Quality imperatives in long-term care: The elusive agenda.* New York: National League for Nursing.

National Institute on Aging. (1991). *What is your aging IQ?* (USDHHS Publication No. 281-837/40019). Washington, DC: U.S. Government Printing Office.

National Osteoporosis Foundation, & University of Connecticut Health/Osteoporosis Center. (1991). *Boning up on osteoporosis: A guide to prevention and treatment* (Publication No. MIA-8011). East Hanover, NJ: Sandoz.

Ory, M. G., Abeles, R. P., & Lipman, P. D. (Eds.). (1992). *Aging, health, and behavior.* Newbury Park, CA: Sage.

Chapter 20

HEALTH-CARE ECONOMICS

Kathy Malloch

CHAPTER OBJECTIVES

On completion of this chapter, the reader will be able to:

1. Discuss the basic economic concepts of demand, supply, and price, as they apply to the health-care system.
2. Examine factors in the varied payment systems for health-care consumers.
3. Compare the health-care provider's location of service and cost factors.
4. Discuss financial management and budgeting for health-care providers.
5. Describe the key factors needed in short-term planning in a health-care organization.
6. Examine the components of strategic planning for health-care providers.

KEY TERMS

Economic Theory
Economics
Health-Care Economics
Demand
Supply
Price
Consumer Access to Health-Care Services
Provider-Driven System
Market-Driven System
Retrospective or Reimbursement Payment System
Prospective Payment System (PPS)

Prospective Pricing System
Diagnosis-Related Groups (DRG)
Health-Care Plans
Capitation
Managed Care Programs
Health Maintenance Organization (HMO)
Preferred Provider Organization (PPO)
Independent Physician Association (IPA)
Physician Hospital Organization (PHO)

Tax Equity and Fiscal Responsibility Act (TERFA)
Continuity of Care
Third-Party Payer
Level of Care
Peer Review Organizations (PROs)
Standard of Care
Patient Classification Systems
Nursing Productivity
Budgeting
Strategic Planning

T oday, even more than in previous years, it is essential for all nurses to understand the basic concepts of economic theory and its relevance to today's health-care system and the practice of nursing. Historically, nurses have not focused on the cost of care and methods of payment for care provided. Traditional nursing education programs have not incorporated economic courses into academic requirements and, in fact, have discouraged nurses from being involved in the cost and payment systems for health-care services. For many nurses and other providers as well, the economics of health-care strongly resembles a foreign language.

Significant changes in the health-care system, specifically the transformation from a provider-driven system to a market-driven system, requires nurses to learn the language and concepts of economics to provide effective care. Nurses, as the single largest group of providers of care and stewards of the organization's resources, are challenged not only to understand the concepts of a market-driven system, but also to defend the value of the type and amount of patient care provided and its relationship to patient outcomes. This chapter presents a broad survey of current health-care concepts and practices from an economic perspective. It is left to the nurse to explore further concepts of interest and integrate this information with other environmental and behavior theories to health-care services.

Many of the terms are selected from Slee and Slee's 1994 publication, *Health-Care Reform Terms*. This is an era of pervasive creativity; creativity abounds in the development of systems and payment structures to meet the health needs of patients, providers, and insurers. New labels and structures emerging in the health-care system may appear revolutionary or confusing, but the basic concepts of demand for health-care services will always be present. The need for a supply of health-care providers to meet these demands will always exist, as well as a concern about the price of the service (Table 20–1).

DEMAND FOR HEALTH CARE

The **demand** for health care includes consumer needs and expectations for illness cure, supportive care, preventive care, and health promotion services and is directly influenced by the individual consumer's conceptualization of health, cultural values, income, education, and access to services. The demand for health-care services is complex; it is multidimensional, subjective, and varies depending on the context.

The economic perspective of health recognizes

TABLE 20–1. Understanding Economic Concepts

Understanding the basic concepts of economics is especially important for nurses as the system continues its transformation from a provider-driven system to a market-driven system. In this rapidly changing environment, knowledge of economic basic concepts will assist nurses in responding quickly and effectively to changes in the market. Review the following definitions of terms essential to understanding the economics of health care.

Economic theory	A type of organizational environmental theory including the study of structures and policies of organizations that support rational decision making and efficient allocation of human and material resources to effectively achieve organizational goals
Economics	The study of the allocation of scarce resources among competing wants (Fuchs, 1993)
Health-care economics	A branch of economics dealing with the provision of health-care services, their delivery, and their use, with special attention to quantifying the demands for such services, the costs of such services and their delivery, and the benefits obtained
Demand	Consumer desire and means to purchase goods, or the amount of goods purchased at a specific price
Supply	Quantity of a commodity that is in the market and available for purchase at a particular price
Price	Sum or amount of money or its equivalent for which anything is bought, sold, or offered for sale

that individuals make trade-offs between health and other goals, and the valuation of health is necessary for the allocation of scarce resources. Economists approach the valuation of human life in two ways, discounted future earnings and willingness to pay. Discounted future earnings are based on estimated costs of various illnesses as the sum of direct expenditures for medical care, the foregone earnings attributable to morbidity, plus the cost of premature death, which is assumed to be equal to the present value of future earnings. Willingness to pay is defined as the amount of money an individual would require (pay) in exchange for an increase (decrease) in the risk of death (Fuchs, 1993).

The complexity is further complicated by the fact that there is no universally held conceptualization of what health means to consumers. According to Fuchs (1993), there is no completely objective, invariant ordering across individuals or populations with respect to health. Conceptualizations of health vary widely, based on criteria such as life expectancy, capacity for work, need for medical care, or ability to perform a variety of personal and social functions. The wide variation in conceptualizations of health impedes the potential for the establishing public policy that can be consistently implemented and financed. In fact, the wide variations are reflected in the continuing inability of health-care reform efforts to develop and finance a national health plan.

The demand for health-care services is also influenced by consumer access to health-care services. **Consumer access to health-care services,** the ability of the individual to physically get to and use health-care facilities, is influenced by geographic proximity of health-care services, eligibility for (access to) insurance benefits, income level, geographic location, and individual values. Urban medical centers tend to concentrate technology and providers, whereas rural areas often have a scarcity of primary health-care providers and minimal technologic support. Some individuals with income above a certain level are not eligible for state-funded coverage but cannot afford private insurance. Access to health care has been a central topic of discussion in many of the national health-care reform proposals.

In a **provider-driven system,** demand is controlled by the provider. In the provider-driven system, providers (health-care providers, health-care institutions) "prescribe" and furnish those services they consider to be appropriate. This approach is intended to meet the needs of consumers as determined by providers, rather than to meet the demand of the purchasers of care.

In contrast, a **market-driven system** responds to the demands of the market or the purchaser of goods. In this system, the purchaser of the goods, or the one paying for the service, is the customer but may not necessarily be the consumer or patient. The market-driven system supports the emergence of competitive health-care delivery plans that seek to attract customers by offering more of what customers want—amenities as well as services and competitive prices. It is important to note that consumers are better educated and want a more active part in the management of their care.

SUPPLY OF HEALTH CARE

Given the complexity of the demand for health care, the supply of these services is equally complex and multifocal. The **supply** of health-care services refers to the products, services, and facilities providing health care and is also based on the prevailing values of health and the goals of traditional medicine, namely, the cure of disease. The supply of health care is affected by the geographic location of providers and consumers, availability of health-care facilities, consumer income, consumer and provider cultural values, and availability of providers.

In a provider-driven system, the location of services, types of providers, and technology available are controlled by the dominant providers, physicians and hospitals. Provider education support, provider location, and types of services offered are identified primarily by the provider and secondarily by market factors. Provider category (physician, nurse practitioner, nurse midwife, physician assistant, and nonlicensed assistant) is determined primarily on the basis of available reimbursement.

In a market-driven system, the provider's level of education and the location and types of services provided are determined by the needs and location of consumers, rather than the needs and location of providers. Technology is funded and provided on the basis of consumer need rather than the availability of a skilled provider. Available interventions and procedures may extend beyond traditional allopathic and osteopathic medicine to include homeopathic remedies, energy therapies, or massage therapies if these are desired by the consumers. Approximately 34 percent of consumers are using nontraditional health-care therapies to meet their health-care needs in addition to treatment for the same condition from a medical doctor (Eisenberg et al., 1993).

Types of health-care providers used in a market-driven system is based on achieving the highest quality at the lowest cost. The use of physician extenders (nurse practitioners, nurse midwives, and physician assistants) and nurse extenders (nursing assistants, patient care technicians) is encouraged in the market-driven system to achieve these quality and cost goals.

PRICE FOR HEALTH CARE

Price is a fundamental variable in economic models affected by changes in the supply of and demand for goods. Applying economic concepts to health is difficult, as individual perspectives of health range from perceiving health as *priceless* to perceiving it as a *commodity*—an article of trade or commerce, something of use, advantage, or value.

In a provider-driven system, price is based on the

cost of the service, identification of the breakeven point, and selection of a predetermined profit level that the market will bear. Before prospective payment systems were introduced, care was delivered, insurance companies were billed, and payment was made to institutions. Indifference to cost was encouraged by the fact that customers paid through a third party, the insurer. All costs incurred were reimbursed.

In a market-driven system, pricing begins with the price rather than the product. A price is determined, and then the provider determines what costs can be incurred to produce the service. For nursing, the institution's reimbursement expectations are identified, and then the amount of care that can be provided within these limits is designed and provided. Market-driven nursing care represents a radical change for nurses who have been educated to identify and meet all health-care needs at each patient encounter.

Blancett and Flarey (1995) note that health-care costs continue to grow at more than 3 percent annually and are approaching 15 percent of the gross national product. Consumers are universally opposed to these spiraling costs and are demanding quality health-care services in a competitive model. Major economic and societal changes taking place in the United States will prevent any possibility of returning to unlimited financing for health care. These include the aging population, increasing cultural diversity, technological advancements in information systems, and patient care equipment.

Examining the demand, supply, and price of health care from an economic perspective provides useful information in understanding the myriad radical changes occurring in the market. Although most economists have argued for greater reliance on market mechanisms and less on regulation, the intricate web of social, political, and economic considerations tends to preclude a pure laissez-faire approach to health (Fuchs, 1993). Changes will dramatically alter the number and types of providers needed to provide health-care services.

Economic concepts have been applied to health care only relatively recently. Before 1960, few studies or publications were related to the systematic application of economic concepts and methods to the health-care field (Fuchs, 1993). The economic perspective provides a powerful framework for analysis, but analysis and decision making must also take into account the unique characteristics of the health-care market, consumer values, knowledge levels, and personal motivations. Economist John Maynard Keynes noted that the theory of economics

does not furnish a body of settled conclusions that are immediately applicable to policy. Economic theory is a method rather than a doctrine, an apparatus of the mind or a technique of thinking to help us draw correct conclusions (Fuchs, 1993).

PAYMENT SYSTEMS

There are two broad categories of payment types in health-care today, retrospective and prospective systems (Table 20–2). **Retrospective or reimbursement payment systems** provide payment for the cost of service, after it is provided, equal to the provider's expenses in providing the given service. **Prospective payment systems** (PPS) provide a predetermined payment for a designated period of time or a specific situation for an individual patient. When the price is predetermined but not prepaid, the more accurate term is **prospective pricing system.** Prospective payment implies that a predetermined amount is prepaid. Specific programs in the

TABLE 20–2. Comparing Payment Systems

Retrospective Payment Models	Prospective Payment Models
▪ Allows providers maximum control of services to the consumer	▪ Applied only to inpatient activities within hospitals, not provider services
▪ No preapproval needed for services	▪ Preapproval required for hospitalization
▪ Services provided are unbundled	▪ Patients are classified into categories, such as diagnosis-related groups (DRGs), and a predetermined price is allowed for the "package of care" provided in the hospital
▪ No hospital length of stay limits	
▪ No required location of services	
▪ No restrictions on the amount and type of diagnostic procedures, pharmaceuticals, or interventional procedures.	▪ Hospital can keep the entire amount of payment, even if the patient did not stay in the hospital the allotted number of days. If the care costs the hospital more than the allowable price, the hospital has to absorb the difference
▪ Payments made to providers equal the cost of providing service	
▪ Costs related to care delivery, including the cost of products, services, salaries, construction, unreimbursed care, and capital equipment, passed on to the consumer, most often government and insurance companies	▪ Services are bundled

prospective model are sponsored by both the federal government and private sector organizations.

Retrospective Payment Models

Retrospective models, also known as "fee-for-service" models, allow providers' maximum control of services provided to the consumer. Preapproval for services is usually not required in this model. No limits are put on the length of stay in the hospital, the location of the services, and the amount and type of diagnostic procedures, pharmaceuticals, or interventional procedures. Services are typically *unbundled*, and a fee is generated for each service or procedure provided. Payment to a hospital or other provider is an amount equal to the provider's expense in providing the given service. Costs related to care delivery, including the cost of products, services, salaries, construction, unreimbursed care, and capital equipment, are passed on to the consumer, most often government and insurance companies.

Prospective Payment Models

Prospective payment and pricing models have emerged in response to concerns about access to care for the elderly and spiraling health-care costs.

The Medicare program, a federally sponsored program for individuals age 65 years and over and others entitled to Social Security benefits, is an example of a prospective pricing model. In 1982, Medicare transitioned to a prospective payment (more accurately, a prospective pricing) system (PPS) based on a hospital classification system developed at Yale University and supported by federal grant monies.

In the Medicare program, patients are classified into categories, **diagnosis-related groups (DRGs)**, and a predetermined price is allowed for the "package of care" provided in the hospital. DRGs emerged as a hospital patient classification system in 1982, as a result of federal grants and research at Yale University. Services are grouped, or *bundled*, by DRG into a package for economic reasons. If the hospital can provide the services for less than the DRG price, it can keep the difference; if the care costs the hospital more than the allowable price, the hospital has to absorb the difference. More than 450 DRGs have been identified on the basis of the principle diagnosis, use of the operating room, age, comorbidity, and complications.

At present, the PPS is applied only to inpatient activities within hospitals, not provider services. The PPS adopted by Medicare, and used by other payers, is the most widespread example of prospective pricing. Private sector prospective systems are gaining in popularity and have been implemented in a variety of models. A brief review of current health-care plans includes capitated programs, managed care programs, health maintenance organizations, preferred provider organizations, independent physician associations, and physician hospital organizations. **Health-care plans** are organized services to provide stipulated medical, hospital, and related services to individuals under a prepayment plan.

Capitation models are a type of prospective payment plan in which a set periodic payment per person cared for (per capita) is made to the physician or health-care system contractually responsible for rendering care. The provider (physician or hospital) is paid a predetermined amount for health-care services provided each patient during a given period of time. The period of time for coverage is specifically outlined, and usually extends across all health-care locations. Capitation models are also referred to as risk plans because the plan offering prepaid care for a given fee or premium is "at risk" to provide the care with the premium funds available or to find the money elsewhere.

Managed care programs, in which arrangement is made for health care by an intermediary between the consumer and provider, are gaining in popularity. Managed care programs are also known as prepaid health plans. In this model, the intermediary has the authority to place restraints on how and from whom the patient may obtain health services in a given situation.

A **health maintenance organization (HMO)** is a type of managed care organization that offers prepaid care for a given fee or premium and is "at risk" for that care; that is, the HMO must provide the care from the premium funds available or find the money elsewhere. The HMO agrees to provide all needed medical and hospital care for a fixed, predetermined fee. HMOs typically have a closed panel of physicians and other providers, along with either their own hospital or allocated beds in one or more hospitals. Preapproval is required from the plan for both the services and the location of the service. Payment for services is included in the monthly member fee; individual procedure costs are bundled into this monthly member allocation.

Preferred provider organizations (PPOs) are designed to compete with HMOs and other delivery systems. A PPO involves a contract between health-care providers (both professional and institutional) and organizations such as employers and third-party administrators under which the PPO agrees to provide health-care services to a defined population for predetermined fixed fees. The PPO differs from an HMO in that the PPO physicians are paid on a fee-for-service basis rather than salary or capitation; providers are not at risk to provide the defined care.

Independent physician associations (IPAs) are different from HMOs and PPOs. This type of health-care provider organization is composed of physicians, who maintain their own practices but agree to furnish services to patients who have signed up for a prepayment plan.

A **physician health organization (PHO)** is a formalized relationship between physicians and hospitals in which a single organization, the PHO, contracts with a purchaser to provide physician, hospital, and other health-care services under a single contract for a single negotiated capitation fee.

Another type of prospective model is based on guidelines established by the **Tax Equity and Fiscal Responsibility Act (TEFRA)** of 1982. Specific care units in hospitals are based on the TEFRA guidelines. Payment is based on an established target amount for Medicare beneficiaries receiving services in the inpatient unit (e.g., acute rehabilitation, psychiatric, skilled nursing). The target amount, set in the base year of operation for the unit, equals the hospital's allowable per case operating costs (costs for routine services—nursing services and room and board—ancillary services, and special care unit services). Payment is determined by the relationship of a hospital's costs to a ceiling based on a target rate of increase in operating costs per case. The target is increased annually by a specific formula, that is, the market basket index plus one percentage point.

Using the TEFRA reimbursement plan, providers work to provide services within the allowed target and identified incentives above or below the target. Based on TEFRA guidelines a hospital that incurs allowable costs per case below its target amount will be paid its costs plus a bonus of the lesser of 5 percent of the target amount of 50 percent of the difference between actual costs and the target amount. It is important to note that, although the TEFRA guidelines are complex, the intent is the same as other managed care efforts—to contain health-care costs.

Prospective models are gaining in popularity and have emerged in several forms in an effort to control costs and manage quality. Variations on these two models will continue to emerge until optimal models for health-care quality and cost are identified. Nurses do not necessarily need to become contracting experts, but they must understand contract incentives, allowable referrals, contract protocols, and nonallowable services. Nurses need to work closely with contracting experts and provide the essential clinical information required to support quality patient care and achieve desired outcomes.

LOCATION OF HEALTH-CARE SERVICE

The location of health-care services has assumed increasing importance in the provision of health-care services. To achieve the goal of providing the highest quality of care at the lowest cost and increasing access to care, the cost of each setting is being carefully scrutinized. Goals of continuity of care and integration of services also guide the selection of service location. **Continuity of care** is the degree to which the care of a patient is continuous, from the onset of illness to completion. Continuous care may involve movement from facility to facility depending on the level of care required.

Third-party payers, who neither receive nor give the care but provide payment, are forcing a shift of care delivery away from the acute care setting, which is most costly, into subacute facilities, outpatient centers, and the home. According to Blancett and Flarey (1995), clinic services will be the second largest delivery system of care. Hospitals will become triage centers with the primary objective of making rapid diagnoses and stabilizing patients. All but the most complex surgeries will be performed in free-standing, outpatient surgery centers. Predictions for the future (Cerne, 1994) include a 50 percent decrease in the demand for inpatient hospital use as we know it today.

Levels of care and facilities that provide the care are specifically defined in Medicare, Medicaid, and other payment programs, as well as under statutes and regulations of various states. In general, **level of care** refers to the amount, intensity, and kind of professional nursing care required for a patient to achieve the desired medical and nursing care objectives. There is increasing pressure to provide services in the most cost-effective location and to have all locations conveniently available for consumers. To be cost-effective, the location and service must be provided at a reasonable cost, which is not necessarily the lowest cost but one that meets the needs of the purchaser.

Health-care networks, HMOs and PHOs, will require providers to offer a full continuum of services to patient populations. Patients need an identifiable network of fully integrated services that are coordinated at multiple levels to support healing and promote health. Achieving a full continuum of services is a challenge for current health-care organizations, which have typically focused only on acute, skilled, or home care services. Managed care programs are seeking the full range of locations and services that consumers need.

Managed care plans attempt to contract for the majority of services offered by an organization, and subcontract or "carve out" and pass on the risk for services not provided such as psychiatric services, outpatient pharmacy services, and durable medical equipment. The practice of carving out specific services or specific high-risk individuals is sometimes questionable and may be illegal. Carving out services may fragment health-care services that were initially intended to be integrated. Increasingly, efforts are being made to "carve in" these services, giving the organization maximum control of the premium dollars and quality of services provided.

The excess capacity in acute care hospitals presents opportunities to develop alternative accommodations to meet consumer needs. Conversion of acute beds to subacute beds and skilled nursing beds is occurring in many hospitals. Subacute units offer care at a level between acute and skilled nursing. The amount and level of nursing staff is decreased, and the amount of medications, laboratory tests, and medical imaging studies are also less than those provided in the acute setting. Payment is successively lower for each lower level of care.

COMPETITION, MARKETING, AND REGULATION

Although health-care providers are no strangers to regulations, the need for marketing services and development of competitive practices are relatively new. In fact, marketing and advertising have been shunned by health-care workers as being unprofessional and, in some professions, unethical.

A provider-driven market does not emphasize competition, but rather deliberately limits it as a result of public and private policy. Without competition, sellers with monopoly power or buyers with monopsony power can manipulate supply, demand, and price at the expense of customers or their suppliers, with results that are neither efficient nor equitable (Fuchs, 1993).

In a market-driven system, competition is fundamental to achieving the highest quality at the lowest cost. Competition implies several conditions for effectiveness; (a) a large number of buyers and sellers, no one of whom is big enough to significantly influence the market price, (b) no collusion among the buyers or sellers to fix prices or quantities, (c)

relatively free and easy entry into the market by new buyers or sellers, (d) no governmentally imposed restraints on prices or quantities, and (e) reasonably good information about price and quality available to buyers and sellers (Fuchs, 1993).

In the provider-driven system, the health-care industry as a whole did not rely on, or need, competition or marketing to attract patients. Today, institutions compete in many ways for patients or consumers, and nursing cannot be left out of this process. In a competitive, market-driven model, consumers are presented with many choices for health-care services. Information is presented in brochures and advertisements that influence the evaluation of alternatives and the final purchase decision. Postpurchase behavior is based on the level of satisfaction or dissatisfaction with the service consumers have experienced. Repeat use of the service is influenced by all of these factors, but most significantly by actual health-care experiences, of which nurses are the primary influences. Nurses' behaviors typically satisfy consumers, but in a market-driven competitive model, nurses are expected to exceed expectations to ensure return business. Marketing the institution and the division's nursing services is the responsibility of not only the nurse executive, but all nurses employed by the institution.

Regulation of health care is a significant factor in the provision of services. Multiple agencies and organizations oversee the activities of health-care organizations from consumer, employer, and provider perspectives. Licensure and reimbursement require compliance with regulations established by federal and state governments, such as those of the Health Care Financing Administration (HCFA), the Occupation of Health and Safety Act (OSHA), the Centers for Disease Control (CDC), by private organizations, and by the Joint Commission on Accreditation of Health Care Organizations, to name a few.

A specific example of health-care regulation is **peer review organizations (PROs).** PROs are set up as part of the prospective payment system to carry out certain review functions under HCFA contract. PROs are third parties, external to and independent of the hospital. Their duties include determining whether the medical records of Medicare patients support the diagnoses and procedures stated in the claims submitted; determining whether a changing pattern of care in a hospital, as reflected in its claims, represents an actual change in the kinds of patients and treatments, or is a result of fictitious claims submission and reporting systems; reviewing the medical necessity of DRG outliers; and attempting to achieve certain performance changes in hospitals within the jurisdiction of the PRO. Failure to meet the standards set by HCFA can result in loss of Medicare payments or loss of approval as a Medicare provider.

PROVIDING THE CARE

A market-driven system requires an expanded perspective for all health-care workers including nurses. First and foremost is the recognition of the business nature of health care. Providing health care is a business process, a collection of activities that takes one or more kinds of inputs and creates an output of value to the customer (Hammer & Champy, 1993). Patient outcomes are the output of the health-care system.

Given the intense competition in health care, nurses are challenged to integrate the organization's mission and margin goals into daily care practices. Allocation of resources needs to be consistent with the priorities and mission of the organization. People need to know the overall goals and directions of the organization on which the budget is based and how to use this information in daily work activities. In addition, health-care consumers expect providers to practice within accepted standards of care. **Standards of care** are developed from a consensus of experts, based on specific research and expert experience. Standards of care represent the principles and practices accepted by a health-care profession to be applied under ordinary circumstances.

With declining resources, nurses need to provide only the essential services known to have positive impacts on patient outcomes. Careful examination of current practices for effectiveness and performance by personnel with the appropriate skill levels requires constant attention. It is no longer acceptable or affordable for licensed personnel to provide basic hygiene care, nor is it acceptable or affordable for licensed personnel to delegate the planning and assessment of patient care to nonlicensed personnel, if appropriate quality and cost outcomes are to be achieved.

Staff nurses are in an excellent position to directly affect both the quality and cost of services provided. Several strategies and tools are available to assist nurses in assessing, monitoring, and evaluating patient care: patient classification systems, productivity monitors, and use of research findings.

Patient classification systems have been used in patient care settings to identify the amount of time required by patients. Traditional classification systems are limited by their focus on time and physical tasks. Also, most classification systems focus on measuring what is provided, not what is required. Although not perfect, classification systems do provide normative information related to the physical tasks needed for a particular type of patient. Recognizing that all patients are not the same, even though they may be assigned the same DRG, nurses are required to use patient classification information and incorporate additional information that affects the process of providing care. For instance, the skill of the nurse, complexity of the procedures, family dynamics, difficulty of the procedures on the specific patient, and interruptions in work flow are constant factors, but are not traditionally identified in patient acuity indicators. Interruptions in work flow, such as physician rounds, patient readiness, and visitors, are seldom incorporated into the plan for care though they occur regularly. Classification systems have yet to incorporate the complex dimensions of the exponential impact of the complex interactions of multiple diagnoses, patients' cognitive abilities, and the impact of ethical challenges on the provision of care. Nurses are challenged to clearly articulate and document the realities of providing care and to match patient needs with available resources and then communicate this information to those contracting with managed care programs. Using a meaningful patient assessment and identifying the problems to be addressed are necessary for care to be effective and efficient. Clinical pathways, or identified steps and procedures that should be carried out for diagnostic evaluation and management of the given diagnosis, are useful tools for those patients without identified comorbidity.

Indicators used by PROs or managed care plans, such as Intensity of Service/Severity of Illness (IS/SI) criteria to justify admission and continuing stays, need to be identified and incorporated into shift report and daily documentation. Using traditional documentation goals and incorporating managed care indicators will facilitate chart review and reduce denials from third-party payers for services.

Productivity monitoring serves to identify progress, and the nature and quantity of the output. Most managers would agree that improving productivity is central to the success and survival of health-care facilities. Nursing is labor intensive and requires continual evaluation and monitoring of both the level of care provider type and amount of service provided. Direct relationships between services provided to patient outcomes need to be identified in a market-driven system.

Nursing productivity, or the ratio between input and output or measures of work accomplished per level of resources applied, is typically monitored bi-weekly. Productivity increases if the ratio of input falls in relation to the measure of output or if the measure of output increases in relation to the input. Staff need to not only be cognizant of the need for productivity, but also encouraged to seek new ways for being productive. Careful use of skills at the appropriate level, standardization whenever possible, and streamlining of routine patterns of care are approaches that increase productivity.

Coordination of care and effective use of resources are optimized by using a form of case management in which specific formalized efforts are made to coordinate and manage care. One such model, the clinical nurse specialist/case manager (CNS/CM) model (Malloch, 1996) assigns the responsibility for coordinating patient services as well as communicating with payers and monitoring the cost and quality of services provided, to the clinical expert (CNS). The CNS/CM is positioned to directly affect the use of financial resources and to guide staff nurses in understanding and practicing in a managed care environment.

Outcomes research and research utilization are important processes in the competitive market-driven system, serving to assist providers in identifying valid and reliable practices to minimize the need for trial-and-error and intuitive guess methods of patient care. Selection of patient care procedures, delivery systems, and patient education materials needs to be based on valid and reliable research data to ensure optimal use of resources. Publications of the Agency for Health Care Policy and Research provide information on several common practices such as postoperative pain management, pressure ulcer care, and smoking cessation, which are identified by review of the literature, supportive studies, and published reliability and validity.

Redefining realistic expectations is critical not only to nurses, but also to all key members of the organization. There is pressure to adapt traditional quality of care standards to significantly more demanding cost of care standards. Therefore, resources need to be reallocated collaboratively, with key members clearly identifying the anticipated outcomes of changes based on reliable information and research data.

FINANCIAL MANAGEMENT AND BUDGETING

Basic financial information is essential to making appropriate decisions about the use of resources. Knowledge of the concepts of financial manage-ment and budgeting processes can improve nurses' abilities to make decisions that positively affect organizational effectiveness. It is no longer appropriate for nurses to be disconnected from the financial processes of the organization in light of their unique ability to impact the use of resources, and ultimately the financial outcomes of the organization.

Nurses are newly challenged to integrate the constraints of the organization's financial resources with patient care. Tending to economics is a special kind of caring that secures the organization's ability to support human care as it is expressed by nurses (Ray, 1989). Knowledgeable nurses can recognize the realities of human care and economics and integrate them into a system in which the goals of patient care and organizational survival are mutually supportive.

First and foremost, nurses are required to demonstrate fiscal accountability for their own practice while providing quality care. Nurses are also challenged to participate in designing and implementing delivery systems that are cost-effective, provide input into decisions of the organization, and continually suggest and implement more efficient ways of providing care to achieve the optimal efficiencies of cost and quality. Table 20–3 defines essential financial management terms.

TABLE 20–3. Understanding Financial Management

Term	Definition
Financial management	The body of knowledge and activities involved in obtaining funds that the institution needs, optimizing the use of those funds to support operations, and ensuring that outcomes are in line with goals
Accounting	The art of collecting, summarizing, analyzing, reporting, and interpreting information about the institution in monetary terms
Information services	A service group that collects data affecting finance, such as census, patient days, admissions and discharges, visits to clinics, and procedures performed
Budget	A financial description of the activities of the department; can be considered a quantitative expression of a plan of action that provides a basis for directing and assessing the performance of individuals and subunits within organizations

Financial Management

Several functions are managed within most financial departments, including accounting, reimbursement, data processing, and patient financial services. Each function provides specific information to assist in the preparing, monitoring, and evaluating of the budget.

Traditional accounting services control payroll, accounts payable, cash control, and taxes. Reimbursement and fiscal projects deal with the impact of external regulation on finance, for example, providing administration of Medicare and Medicaid interactions with other third-party payers such as Blue Cross, Blue Shield, and major medical coverage plans, and handling the cost reports such external agencies require for reimbursement. Changes taking place in reimbursement designs make it essential for institutions to have accurate data on what costs are actually incurred by individual patients and separate departments.

Information services collect data that affect finance, such as census, patient days, admissions and discharges, visits to clinics, and procedures performed. Patient financial services handle patient billing, credit and collection of fees, and the cashier function.

Budgeting

The **budgeting** process incorporates planning for the acquisition, allocation, and utilization of financial resources. Personnel, supplies, and capital are the major categories in the budget. The process of budgeting enhances sound judgment, it does not replace it. Competence in financial management requires skills and behaviors that establish the control and effective use of budgetary resources, personnel, capital, and supplies.

The product of nursing is a service whose costs are difficult to extract. Traditionally, nursing costs are included in a daily room rate, bundled with services such as food service and housekeeping. Nevertheless, knowledge of the real costs of nursing is critical in the budgeting process. Nurses need to know what level of funding is needed for different levels of care. Direct nursing cost, supplies, and indirect costs are included in this calculation. Indirect costs include the cost of nursing administration, nursing education, and orientation of new staff members. Budgets that support long-term strategies for building essential recruitment, retention, and staff development programs must be factored into the financial plans of the institution.

Labor, supplies, and capital are three basic cate-gories included in the nursing budget. Labor costs account for the largest portion, whereas supplies and capital are much less in most cases. Supplies include the products and equipment needed to provide the service. Capital includes major items defined by a certain minimum cost and expected lifespan of the item.

The actual costs attributed to nursing services are important in specifically identifying what nursing contributes to the care provided. Determining the amount and type of services provided by nurses is critical in the contracting process. Generating charges for specific billing and revenue production may be outdated in the era of capitated and prospective reimbursement systems, but it still applies in noncapitated agreements.

The nurse executive needs to translate the desired components of nursing practice and the chosen delivery system into logical requests for staff and other resources into the language of the fiscal officer, or more appropriately the nurse executive needs to communicate with the fiscal officer to develop common ground between clinical needs and fiscal responsibilities. The process should not be adversarial, but rather an interaction in which each discipline increases its understanding of the other to meet organizational goals. The budgeting process must assume a Socratic interaction among managers and staff, reducing the need for game playing in the system and power struggles.

A major challenge in the budgeting process is to develop a plan that includes payment from both retrospective and prospective systems. Each payment system requires different monitoring indicators. Providers are ultimately challenged in the market-driven system to understand and respond to the demand, supply, and price factors of each payer type.

Many organizations are fortunate to receive significant support from local foundations and, although the funds are never guaranteed on a predictable basis, anticipation of and planning for the use of these funds can greatly support the budgeting process. Donations from donors are often specified for certain uses in an organization, providing additional dollars to offset current expenditures.

The final budget for each year guides the organization. Regular monitoring of performance at least every 2 weeks is essential for success. Analyzing variances from budget includes the review of statistical reports, analysis of daily staffing expenditures, analysis of monthly performance, trends in performance by time of the year, trends in providers and payer activity, trends in patient types, and cost per unit of service.

PLANNING AND EVALUATION: EFFICIENCY VERSUS EFFICACY

Incorporating the economic perspectives of demand, supply, and price into health-care delivery systems provides important information to plan for the future and evaluate results. **Strategic planning** is fundamental for organizational survival. The process is applied to determine the goals and objectives of an organization, evaluate markets and competition, and identify environmental issues that are likely to impact on the organization. Analyses of both the organization and the environment are components of a strategic plan. Strategic planning tends to focus on the major, but not all, environmental issues.

Selecting key indicators to measure organizational effectiveness requires integration of market demand and organizational mission. The goals of consumers, providers, and the organization goals need to be met for success in a market-driven system. The outcomes of an organization are seldom clear and definitive. The organization's performance is affected by its multiple outputs—products and services—and the relative importance of each, the values different people put on different outputs, and the difficulty of measuring quantity and quality (Charnes & Schaefer, 1983).

The definition of quality health care is complex and varies with health beliefs, cultural values, and available resources. Quality can be defined as the degree of conformity to accepted principles and practices (standards), the degree of fitness for the patient's needs, and the degree to which achievable outcomes (results) are attained, consonant with the appropriate allocation of resources (Slee & Slee, 1994).

Indicators of quality are both subjective and objective; quality has different dimensions and subsequently different definitions. Dimensions involve access to health care, appropriateness of treatments, safety, continuity of care, and effectiveness of care. Each perspective provides information about our complex health-care system.

Health-care reform efforts have heightened the need for objective measures of health-care quality. The government is increasing public disclosure of morbidity and mortality rates as well as data from facility inspections and physician malpractice and licensure actions (Blancett & Flarey, 1995). Although individual institutions monitor many measures for internal review, most measures or indicators are not compiled by a centralized source of standards across institutions (ANA, 1995; Alsever, Ritchey, & Lima, 1995).

Current efforts to develop comparative indicators that can be shared across institutions and with consumers have resulted in the "report card phenomenon." A *report card* is a summary of information of doctor and hospital performance and consumer satisfaction designed for consumers/patients and health-care buyers. Health plan providers, employer groups, and care providers have initiated several collaborative efforts to formulate report cards that identify and measure the quality of patient care. Examples of report cards are the Maryland Hospital Association Health Indicator project. American Nurses Association Report Card for Acute Care, the Health Plan Employer Data and Information Set (HEDIS 2.0), and the U.S. News and World Report America's Best Hospitals Exclusive rankings. These reports include cost benchmarks as well as selected quality indicators, but the results have been hampered by serious gaps in information and lack of standard indicators.

Historical measures of efficiency and cost-effectiveness must be translated into new indicators for capitated models. Ongoing programs to assess patient satisfaction need to identify appropriate indicators of satisfaction and correlations to continuing use of facility services. Functional status, physiologic status, symptom management, and safety will continue but will now be specifically related to patient outcomes. New quality indicators for providers and plan managers also need to be developed. Timeliness, reporting, and cost-effectiveness will receive increasing scrutiny.

Traditionally, financial performance in health care is evaluated on the basis of ratios of profitability, liquidity, capital structure, asset efficiency, and other factors that do not fit into these categories. These ratios, in total, provide a more comprehensive picture of the financial position of the hospital. The Almanac of Hospital Financial and Operating Indicators (Cleverley, 1995), is published annually, including more than 150 indicators related to these categories collected from audited financial statements, strategic operating indicator data submitted by hospitals, and Medicare cost reports.

New measures of financial performance for prospective capitated payments will need to be developed in the context of all payments received by the organization. The increasing trend of allocating resources based on the number of enrolled members per month and the number of days (inpatient and skilled nursing) per thousand member days requires new systems and processes to identify, allocate, and measure costs.

PLANNING FOR THE FUTURE

As we approach the twenty-first century, nurses need to be acutely aware of the economic dimensions of providing health-care services and bottom-line considerations of the organization. Registered nurses, responsible for developing plans of care, using research, using equipment, and recommending staffing changes, need to know if changes are cost-effective and must be able to support these decisions with economic as well as clinical data (Dieter, 1996). Nurses must initiate challenges to our current systems to ensure long-term effectiveness.

Further, active participation in local, state, and federal policy making is important for all health-care providers. Issues of access, accountability, rationing, and financing of health care are still not settled to the satisfaction of most individuals. The notion of national health insurance based on citizenship rather than employment is an option. Discussions, debate, and reform proposals will continue until the majority of consumer demands are met. The opportunity remains for all providers to actively participate in the continuing development of national health-care policy.

KEY POINTS

- The health-care system is changing from a provider-driven to a market-driven system, and this change has major implications for nursing.
- Demand, supply, and price are three basic factors in any system providing a product or service.
- Nurses, as the largest single group of patient care providers, are ideally positioned to influence quality, cost, satisfaction, and return business for health-care facilities.
- Retrospective and prospective payment systems are the two basic types of payment systems, and each has multiple variations.
- In a provider-driven market, competition is not emphasized, but rather is deliberately limited by public and private policy. In a market-driven system, competition is fundamental to achieving the highest quality at the lowest cost.
- Peer review organizations are third parties, external to and independent of the hospital. They review the medical records of Medicare patients to ensure that they support the diagnoses and procedures stated in the claims submitted; to determine whether a changing pattern of care in a hospital, as reflected in its claims, represents an actual change in the kinds of patients or their treatment; to review the medical necessity of DRG outliers; and to attempt to achieve certain changes in performance of hospitals within their jurisdiction.
- Standards of care are developed from a consensus of experts, are based on specific research and expert experience, and represent the principles and practices accepted by a health-care profession as expected under ordinary circumstances.
- Patient classification systems have been used in patient care settings to identify the amount of time required by patients.
- Nursing productivity, or the ratio between input and output or measures of work accomplished per level of resources applied, is typically monitored biweekly.
- The budgeting process incorporates planning for the acquisition, allocation, and utilization of financial resources. Personnel, supplies, and capital are the major categories in the budget.
- Strategic planning is a process applied in determining the goals and objectives of an organization, evaluating markets and competition, and identifying the environmental issues likely to impact on the organization.

CHAPTER EXERCISES

1. Examine the current patient classification system in your organization, and make recommendations to include the concepts discussed in this chapter, such as indicators found in report cards, continuity of care, and demand and supply of staff.

2. Obtain a statistical and financial report from your current work unit, and identify those items that nurses can affect, such as supplies, labor costs, overtime hours, patient days, and location of services.

3. Discuss the implications of a 25 percent decrease in demand for services in acute care and a 25 percent increase in home care services in a specific organization, that is, providers, consumers, operating expenses and so forth.

REFERENCES

Alsever, J. D., Ritchey, T., & Lima, N. P. (1995). Developing a hospital report card to demonstrate value in healthcare. *Journal of Healthcare Quality, 17*(1), 19–25.

American Nurses Association. (1995). *Nursing report card for acute care*. Washington, DC: American Nurses Publishing.

Blancett, S. S., & Flarey, D. L. (1995). *Reengineering nursing and health care: The handbook for organizational transformation*. Gaithersburg, MD: Aspen.

Cerne, R. (1994). Shaping up for capitation. *Hospital Health Networks, 68*(7), 28–37.

Cleverley, W. O. (1995). *The 1995 almanac of hospital financial and operating indicators*. Columbus, OH: Center for Healthcare Industry Performance Studies.

Charnes, M. P., & Schaefer, M. J. (1983). *Health care organizations: A model for management*. Englewood Cliffs, NJ: Prentice-Hall.

Dieter, D. C. (1996). Cost effectiveness and quality nursing care. *CNS, 10*(3), 153.

Eisenberg, D. M., Kessler, R. C., Foster, C., Norlock, F. E., Calkins, D. R., & Delbanco, T. L. (1993). Unconventional medicine in the United States: Prevalence, costs and patterns of use. *New England Journal of Medicine, 328*(4), 246–252.

Fuchs, V. R. (1993). *The future of health policy*. Cambridge, MA: Harvard Press.

Hammer, M., & Champy, J. (1993). *Reengineering the corporation: A manifesto for business revolution*. New York: Harper Business.

Malloch, K. M. (1996). Managed care and changing nurse practice. *Aspen's Advisor for Nurse Executives, 11*(9), 5–6.

Ray, M. A. (1989). The theory of bureaucratic caring for nursing practice in the organizational culture. *Nursing Administration Quarterly, 13*(2), 31–42.

Slee, V. N., & Slee, D. A. (1994). *Health care reform terms* (2nd ed.). St. Paul: Tringa Press.

Chapter 21

QUALITY CARE

Francoise Dunefsky

CHAPTER OBJECTIVES

On completion of this chapter, the reader will be able to:

1. Discuss roles for the consumer and professional in quality appraisal in health-care settings.
2. Differentiate among terms used to assess and promote quality in health-care settings.
3. Identify quality improvement factors to be considered at the unit, organizational, and system levels.
4. Describe the steps in the process of continuous quality improvement and total quality management.
5. Discuss the role of regulatory agencies in quality evaluation in health-care settings.

KEY TERMS

Quality	Benchmarking	Top-Down Flow Chart
Outcome	Quality Assurance	Cause and Effect
Total Quality	Process Teams	Diagram
Management (TQM)	Variation	Pareto Diagram
Continuous Quality		
Improvement (CQI)		

Recent rapid changes have forced many health-care systems and providers to focus on quality. Largely, finances are driving this change. Quality is necessary to stay in the game. Institutions are attempting to understand principles before used only in certain industrial sectors. Many have become believers, some have attempted to incorporate basic principles and standards promoted by regulators, and others believe they have just wasted resources on yet another fad.

Societal forces are shifting the health-care paradigm from a paternalistic model of delivering care and services to one that responds to customer demands. Yet to be resolved is how society and the health-care system deal with issues of access, cost, and quality. With a professional commitment to patients, a professional domain of delivering and coordinating care, and roots in the psychosocial and physical sciences, nursing is poised to play an important role in the ongoing development and implementation of the change.

The dictionary defines **quality** as character with respect to fineness or grade of excellence. In health care, it is defined as being free of mistakes or perfect relative to process. The standard of perfection or one hundred percent compliance was focused within. The current quality movement defines quality as meeting customer needs, focusing on the **outcome,** from the customer's perspective.

Health-care providers have consistently looked at clinical care as the measure for quality. Traditionally, the qualifications of clinicians, state of the art technology, and errorless episodic interventions that cure illness or "do no harm" were considered indices of quality. When we ask how customers perceive quality, a more complex picture began to evolve. The consumer assumes the traditional indicators, but equally important are timely, courteous, and respectful treatment, easy access to caregivers, unfragmented care delivery, reasonable costs, and the ability to maneuver the system without too many obstacles.

HISTORICAL PERSPECTIVES

Human societies have always wished for excellence. Professional associations such as guilds and inspection by consumers are century-old methods used in this quest for quality. The societal values, however, are changing the context in which it is evaluated.

Pre–World War II health-care delivery in the United States was mostly a cottage industry. The wealthy and fortunate rural populations relied on services delivered by individuals in the home. The poor and urban working classes were sent to hospitals in critical circumstances or died at home. A sudden growth in technology, treatment modalities, and the building of hospitals stimulated by the Hill-Burton Act, began the corporatization of health-care delivery. Extensive development of policies, procedures, standards of practice, and professional disciplines ensued. It took 20 years before the industrial model of reliance on departmental inspection and supervisory audits became an official part of the fabric of health care. Several forces, including the state and federal government, accelerated this growth.

During the early 1970s, formalized measurement of clinical performance and outcomes began. Organizations such as the Joint Commission of Accreditation of Healthcare Organizations (JCAHO), professional review organizations (PROs), and some state health departments played major roles in the initial movement. Retrospective audits, investigation of problems, and indicator measurements were all attempts to discover less-than-acceptable performance by individuals, disciplines, or departments. The objective was to discover the guilty parties, implement a corrective action plan, and monitor its effectiveness through ongoing measurement. Quality was assumed to be a result of the performance of individuals or groups of individuals. The corrective action plans used education, disciplinary action, and increased resources such as technology and staffing as their tools.

A gradual quality paradigm shift began in the second half of the 1980s. Other industries, purchasing health care for their employees at rapidly increasing costs, challenged the health-care sector to provide "more" and "better" for "less." The Japanese were successfully invading the American marketplace, partly because of quality methodologies developed by Deming, Juran, and others. Deming had convinced the Japanese government and industrial machine that they should focus on quality rather than price and cost. Knowing this would take time and commitment, they infused their business with the beliefs that work is performed by interdependent teams, individuals want to do a good job, and mass inspection and fear do not automatically result in quality. Juran proposed the notion that by planning for quality one avoids multiple trial-and-error situations and costly rework. Quality could be cost-effective. Improvement required ever higher goals for quality. Reliance on systems analysis and statistical methods and techniques produced better quality products than supervision and inspection of individual human behaviors.

Over the next 10 years it was recognized that care is delivered by individuals who function as members of cross-functional and interdisciplinary teams and that individuals and teams are tools for, rather than objects of, improvement. Recently, a body of scientific knowledge has begun to emerge testing the new theories that care is supported by environmental, managerial, support, and governance structures, and that ensuring accepted clinical outcomes is not enough to meet customer needs.

Many individuals and organizations have contributed to the quality journey over the past 25 years. The Agenda for Change at the Joint Commission of Accreditation of Health Care Organizations (JCAHO) and Donald Berwick, MD, and his group at the Institute for Health Care Improvement deserve recognition as driving forces in implementing new quality care models.

THEORETICAL MODELS FOR QUALITY

Quality improvement models have come from industry. Some have been adapted for health care, but all share the common theme of using the scientific process.

Deming's Principles for Transformation

W. Edward Deming was the first to seriously challenge the managerial notion that quality and increased productivity are incompatible. In his research developing the 14 Points for Management (1982, 1986), he took the new radical approach of listening to those who actually did the work (Table 21–1). Deming contends that the model can be applied anywhere, including service industries and in divisions, rather than entire, companies. Nursing leaders at all levels of the organization can apply the principles in their quest to implement quality care. The more pervasive the quality culture in the organization, the easier the model application becomes. However, the absence of executive leadership in this area must be considered an obstacle to rather than an explanation for lack of action.

THE 14 POINTS FOR MANAGEMENT

1. *Create constancy of purpose for improvement of product and service.* Innovation is the foundation for the future. It requires a belief that there is a future and an unshakable commitment to quality and productiv-

TABLE 21–1. Deming's 14 Points

1. Create constancy of purpose for improvement of product and service
2. Adopt the new philosophy
3. Cease dependence on mass inspection
4. End the practice of awarding business on the basis of price tag alone
5. Improve constantly and forever the system of production and service
6. Institute training
7. Adopt and institute leadership
8. Drive out fear
9. Break down barriers between staff areas
10. Eliminate slogans and targets in the workplace that urge increased productivity
11. Eliminate numerical quotas for the workplace and management
12. Remove barriers that rob people of pride in workmanship
13. Encourage education and self-improvement for everyone
14. Take action to accomplish the transformation

Source: Adapted from Deming, W. E. (1982, 1986) *Out of the Crisis.* Cambridge: Massachusetts Institute of Technology, with permission.

ity. Resources must be put into education and research so we can constantly improve. The aim is to meet our mission, and serve our customers or we will not stay in business. We must deal with day-to-day problems without getting stuck in them. Many nurse managers fail to plan their resources, energy, and time to deal with the future. Working better, not harder, to plan new services, meeting our customers' needs, and training and retraining personnel help deal with required change.

2. *Adopt the new philosophy.* Do not accept existing levels of mistakes or staff not adequately prepared to perform. Become the change agent that meets the challenge. Propose, develop, and implement improvements in systems and services.

3. *Cease dependence on mass inspection.* Inspection is too late to improve quality. Quality comes from improvement in production processes. Tools such as 100 percent case review do not improve care, are time-consuming, and require resources that could be better spent in improving design or systems. Constant measuring of incomplete records, medication errors, or

delays, in and of themselves, will not improve the delivery of care.

4. *End the practice of awarding business on the basis of price tag alone.* The nurse manager has a responsibility to include total cost when recommending the purchase of goods or services. This includes not only the upfront price, but all the costs of disposables and maintenance, amount of vendor support provided, ease of training in use, labor costs, and cross-functional use. It is a managerial responsibility to make well-prepared, comprehensive recommendations to the executive team. Deming believes that limiting the suppliers we deal with and establishing long-term relationships with vendors create interdependency that assists in the demand for and achievement of quality.

5. *Improve constantly and forever the system of production and service.* Quality must be built in during design to avoid costly rework. Teamwork is essential in this process, especially in service industries such as health care in which we totally rely on interdependent, cross-disciplinary teams to deliver the care that is our product. As our customers' needs and available resources change, we are obliged to improve existing systems. Reductions in length of stay, shifts in delivery of care along the continuum, and changing demographics all require us to seek opportunities to "do it better." It is no longer acceptable to think "we always did it this way and it worked."

6. *Institute training.* Learning must be lifelong and pervasive. The principles of adult learning, and an appreciation of the fact that different people learn by different methods, apply at all layers of the organization, regardless of length of employment. All must understand the institution's mission, values, customer needs, and expectations. What the assignment is, what is acceptable work, and how we prepare people all need to be defined. For the manager, this includes knowing which processes are assigned and understanding variations in these processes. We must become learning organizations.

7. *Adopt and institute leadership.* The job of management is leadership, namely, vision and communication of that vision, not supervision. The assignment is to work on quality of service, design for quality, and deliver an actual product. This requires the leader to understand the work supervised and remove barriers preventing the staff from doing their work.

8. *Drive out fear.* Fear of reprisal, fear to admit mistakes, fear of not having the needed new knowledge, or fear of not meeting the deadlines or quotas interfere with seeing opportunities for improvement. The study of complaints may give a biased picture of quality in an organization. Errors, complaints, or areas that appear out of control must be analyzed for opportunities to improve.

9. *Break down barriers between staff areas.* This has proven especially difficult in health care, where the struggle to establish distinct professional domains fostered accountability, review, and disciplinary actions within professions. The emergence of matrix organizations, patient care departments, cross-training, and decentralization of services will assist in implementing patient care teams focused on the patient rather than the profession. Simultaneously, this will create a new challenge to ensure that no one can hide behind or dominate the team. All professional groups and all departments are responsible for quality.

10. *Eliminate slogans and targets in the workplace that urge increased productivity.* The assumption that one can improve quality and productivity by trying harder does not take into account that most problems come from systems, rather than individuals. The role of management is to improve the system and remove causes detected as a result of sound statistical methods.

11. *Eliminate numerical quotas for the workforce and management.* Quotas assume that the target is correct, not too high or too low, and that everyone can attain it. They have a negative effect on pride in workmanship. Productivity should be studied, analyzed, and understood. Everyone should know what to do and how to do it. A sustained requirement for all to participate in setting goals and figuring out how to reach them is needed.

12. *Remove barriers that rob people of pride in workmanship.* Make clear what the job is and what the expectations are. Improving the system to make it easier for people to

work well will make them feel important and invest of themselves in the organization, reducing turnover and absenteeism.

13. *Encourage education and self-improvement for everyone.* Study and development should focus not only on the immediate needs of the organization or department. Develop the organization and its members for the future as well as the present.

14. *Take action to accomplish the transformation.* The leaders must adopt the new philosophy with pride. It must be explained often and well to a critical number of individuals. Everyone in the organization must be asked to participate. This requires substantial and sustained commitment and energy.

Deming also recognized obstacles to the transformation. The desire to achieve instant results by hiring a consultant, the supposition that solving problems creates transformation, the beliefs that one can simply transfer a system from another organization, that the quality department takes care of quality, or that your problems are different, and poor understanding of statistical methods can all create difficulties during the transformation.

More serious blocks, referred to as deadly diseases because of their severity and resistance to eradication, include lack of constancy of purpose, emphasis on short-term profits, evaluation of performance without long-term improvement in mind, mobility of management, and management by numbers only.

When considering applying the principles for transformation, the nurse needs to acknowledge realities in the organization. Annual performance review, existing merit systems, strict organizational and professional hierarchies, and focus on monthly budget fluctuations may be mandated. The general principles of constancy of purpose, the focus on improvement, creating a learning environment, reducing fear, and removing barriers to pride in workmanship can be adopted by anyone in any setting.

JURAN TRILOGY

Dr. Joseph Juran (1989) defines quality as fitness for use. This definition assumes both freedom from defects and the multiple elements required to meet the total needs of a customer. Freedom from defect is measured by frequency of deficiencies over the opportunity for deficiency. The freedom from defect does not guarantee that this is the product the cus-

---

TABLE 21–2. Juran Trilogy

A. *Quality planning*
   1. Determine who the customers are.
   2. Determine the needs of the customer.
   3. Develop product features that respond to the customer's needs.
   4. Develop processes that are able to produce these product features.
   5. Transfer the resulting plans to the operating forces.

B. *Quality control*
   1. Evaluate actual quality performance.
   2. Compare actual performance to quality goals.
   3. Act on the difference.

C. *Quality improvement*
   1. Establish an infrastructure.
   2. Identify needs for improvement.
   3. Establish project teams for each project.
   4. Provide the teams with resources, motivation, and training.

Source: Adapted from Juran, J. M. (1989). *Juran on leadership for quality.* New York: The Free Press, with permission.

---

tomer wants. That requires that the product is something the customer needs and has features that are important to that customer. The patient assumes we can deliver the care without errors. Waiting time, ease of access, and cleanliness may be crucial factors when a patient chooses us.

The Juran trilogy uses the three managerial processes of planning, control, and improvement (Table 21–2). The trilogy's proposed procedural steps and tools are special and unique.

Quality Planning

Planning for programs or services requires that quality be built into them. Five distinct steps are followed:

1. Determine who the customers of the program or service are. They can be external customers, internal customers, or both. In health care, patients, families, and payers are all external customers. Departments and providers are internal customers of each other. Nursing receives services from dietary or medical records, and those departments in turn are customers of nursing. Independent medical staff members are often considered both internal and external customers because of their ability to choose the institution and their influence and provision of services within the institution.

2. Determine the customers' need. Surveys, focus groups, individual patient interviews,

complaint reviews, and market analysis can be used to determine what our customers want from us.
3. Develop product features that respond to the customer's needs. Services outside traditional business hours, including weekend day surgery, diagnostics early and late in the day, and respite care, are but a few possible examples.
4. Develop processes that can produce those product features.
5. Transfer the resulting plans to the operating forces.

For example, while teaching breast self-examination at a customer-friendly breast clinic, a nurse hears patients express concerns about the time it takes to receive mammography results. In response to complaints, the nurse, working with the department and a local women's group, initiates a formal survey of women who presently use the center and women who do not. The survey results revealed that women want results within 24 hours and the ability to self refer. As a result, the services at the center are redesigned to incorporate these features. An expanded license for self-referral is applied for and obtained, and policies, procedures, and standards are instituted to ensure that the improved services are implemented and monitored.

Quality Control

The three steps of quality control are as follows:
1. Evaluating actual quality performance. This requires knowledge of statistical methods of measurement and analysis.
2. Comparing actual performance to quality goals.
3. Acting on the difference. This assumes understanding of common and special cause variation. Variation is part of any process, and constant reaction to it may destabilize an otherwise stable process.

Quality Improvement

Raising performance to unprecedented levels requires four steps:
1. Establishing the infrastructure needed to secure ongoing quality improvement. The infrastructure, which may include a quality council, departmental teams, and assigned roles, ensures that quality improvement is included in the way business is done.

2. Identifying specific needs for improvement. Data from quality control, feedback from customers, and goals of the organization help in deciding what needs to be improved and what needs to be prioritized.
3. Establishing a project team for each project. Responsibility must be clearly defined. This includes the objective for improvement and measures of success.
4. Providing resources, motivation, and training for the teams to diagnose causes of lesser quality, stimulate a remedy, and establish controls to hold the gains in improvements.

Juran's work has shown that most of the potential for eliminating errors and improving the system does not lie with changing workers. The 85/15 rule, as it is now commonly called, states that 85 percent of problems can be corrected only by changing systems.

Both Deming and Juran have provided the foundation for today's quality movement in industry and health care. The JCAHO Agenda for Change helped in the transition from quality assurance to quality improvement.

JACHO 10-STEP MODEL FOR MONITORING AND EVALUATION

Dr. O'Leary at the Joint Commission (1991) takes the position that improvement requires effective monitoring, and effective monitoring requires good indicators.

The monitoring and evaluation process has been revised over time, but the 10 steps remain part of the foundation on which much of quality activities are based. The process requires identifying the most important aspects of care for a particular organization or division, selecting indicators that reflect these aspects, taking opportunities to improve care, taking action, and evaluating the effectiveness of that action. Dimensions of performance (JCAHO, 1995) include what is done and how well it is done. Doing the right thing includes efficacy and appropriateness. Doing it well involves availability, timeliness, effectiveness, continuity, safety, efficiency, and providing services with respect and caring.

Step 1: Assign Responsibility

The leaders in the organization are responsible for fostering quality improvement and setting priorities for assessment and improvement. Leaders are defined as the leadership of the board, the executive team (including the nurse executive), the leaders of the medical staff, and department directors. This has implications for nurse managers and other leaders in the nursing staff, because they now have direct responsibility for quality.

Step 2: Delineate Scope of Care and Service

The scope of care of the organization or service must be defined before going on to the next step. We are not all things to all people and need to put our energies into the mission and vision we have agreed on. Who the patients and other customers we serve are, and what we do for them, need to be clear.

Step 3: Identify Important Aspects of Care and Service

What are the key functions that warrant ongoing monitoring? Which functions need prioritization? The key functions in an outpatient area are often different from those in bedded units, as are those from services that focus on prevention, and acute or chronic illness. Timeliness as a dimension of care may vary based on a particular department's scope of service. It will be defined quite differently in an emergency department than in a chronic rehabilitation unit.

Step 4: Identify Indicators

Interdisciplinary teams develop and select indicators for those aspects of care that have been prioritized. As an example, turnaround time for lab results could be an indicator selected to reflect timeliness in an emergency department.

Step 5: Establish a means to Trigger Evaluation

The team selects at what level and time evaluations will be triggered. Determining thresholds that are not met after quarterly reviews is an example of how to implement evaluation. Reviewing within 24 hours every unexpected return to the surgical suite, during the same admission, is another.

Step 6: Collect and Organize Data

Defining data sources and methodology for collection, the actual data collection, and organization are all parts of this process. More often than not, too much peripheral information is collected, which actually interferes with meaningful organization of data, is labor intensive, and interferes with the next step.

Step 7: Initiate Evaluation

Once it is determined that further evaluation needs to occur, other feedback may be taken into consideration. Intensive evaluation should be performed by teams.

Step 8: Take Action to Improve

Actions include changes in the system, education, designation of clear authority and accountability, development of standards, and more.

Step 9: Assess the Effectiveness of the Actions

Whether the action improved the care or service and whether it sustained improvement are questions to be answered when evaluating effectiveness.

Step 10: Communicate Results to Relevant Individuals and Groups

Dissemination of conclusions, actions, and results to those affected and to the leaders is necessary. This may occur through team presentations, committee structures, and department or division meetings.

The 10-step model has been used successfully in both the traditional scope of quality assurance and quality improvement. The steps have remained the same, but the focus from within departments to processes, the level of accountability, the understanding and application of statistical methodologies, and the role of leadership have evolved significantly. Organizational leaders can no longer delegate responsibility to the quality department. Hiding behind professional or departmental boundaries is not acceptable. Leaders of boards, executive and management teams, and the medical staff are all being held accountable for delivering quality care.

TOTAL QUALITY MANAGEMENT AND CONTINUOUS QUALITY IMPROVEMENT IN HEALTH CARE

To survive and thrive requires a formal, organized way of focusing on the community we serve. *Doing the right things right* requires a tested methodology. Not every community has the same needs or the same resources.

Total quality management (TQM) and **continuous quality improvement (CQI)** have been used interchangeably. The term "total quality management" is mostly linked with industrial models. Continuous quality improvement has received wide acceptance in health care. Since the underpinnings remain the same, the health-care terminology of CQI is used throughout the remainder of this chapter.

The basic concept of continuous quality improvement is an ongoing process that is never finished that far surpasses the goals of catching up to competition or to preestablished goals. Quality is defined as meeting the needs of external and internal customers. Improvements can be large scale or incremental. **Benchmarking,** the process of comparing to the best in the industry, and innovation in how we meet customer's needs are involved in improvement. Innovation requires willingness to take risks and ability to think in new ways.

The strategy for implementing a new organization, namely, one that thinks and performs in the new paradigm, requires a shift in focus from ourselves toward those we serve. We must become customer minded. This requires a new culture to become pervasive in the organization. The leadership is responsible for creating vision, setting priorities for improvement, and supporting the focus on external and internal customers. Learning teamwork is essential. One needs to recognize that care is delivered by teams, is complex, involving many steps, and has blurred boundaries. The techniques employed in CQI include quality planning, assessment, improvement, and a focus on process and customers. Quality is no longer a separate job, delegated to a department or to certain times of the day; rather it is the real job. It requires that all members of the organization be empowered to complete their assignment well and affect appropriate change.

Transition from Quality Assurance to Continuous Quality Improvement

The traditional model of **quality assurance,** relying on inspection to catch "bad apples" and on correcting individual performances, has already evolved in many institutions. To assume that the journey through quality assurance was wasted fails to recognize that many of the tools used in quality improvement are still used in quality assurance, and the journey helped define what constitutes quality care. However, there are many differences. CQI is widely recognized as being broader in scope, involving the leadership and many more people, and blurring boundaries. The expectation of perfection is gone, but the search for excellence is essential.

It is important to understand that the evaluation of individual performance must continue. Standards for hiring competent members of the team are more important than ever. Results of individual performance should be looked at for trends across shifts, units, and departments. Findings can be used for staff and leadership development. Individual competence remains a professional obligation to all patients. Professional ethics require the same diligence when dealing with incompetent practitioners. The shift from individual to team does not change our standards or our accountability to those we serve.

Department or unit-based quality programs remain valuable and should not be demolished. They are an important vehicle for teaching the concepts of CQI and provide needed mechanisms for ongoing measurement and applying standards. They also recognize that much improvement requires no large teams, but can occur at the unit level.

Risk management evaluates the legal standards and their application to the delivery of patient care, the environment of care, and other services and functions. Similarly to quality assurance, it relies on inspection; however, the focus is on how to best protect the assets of the organization against liability. Table 21–3 highlights the differences and similarities among quality improvement, quality assurance, and risk management.

PUTTING A CQI STRUCTURE IN PLACE

It is now widely accepted that quality journeys are lengthy and costly. They require a well-developed structure and plan to connect the vision with the implementation. Getting started always requires education in the basic principles. Since CQI is, first and foremost, a management philosophy, the leaders must be the first educated in the principles and the first to buy in to the methodologies before others follow.

The actual mechanisms of setting up the program are beyond the scope of this chapter. Creating a

TABLE 21–3. Comparing Quality Improvement, Quality Assurance, and Risk Management

Quality Improvement	Quality Assurance	Risk Management
Broad in scope Organizational leadership designs and set priorities	Based at unit or departmental level Often uses separate department	Often separate department looks at legally acceptable level of care or service
Purpose is improvement	Compares against standards	
Focus is on customers	Focus is on the organization	Focus is on preventing loss
Uses problems as opportunities for improvement	Continuous ongoing monitoring identifies problems (Inspection)	Continuous ongoing monitoring (Inspection)
Focus is on the system as whole	Focus is on individual performance	Focus is on protecting organization's assets

structure usually involves a quality council and designation of a CQI coach. The coach functions as the facilitator, educator, and expert in tools and techniques. Ownership of quality belongs to everyone.

The function of the council is to create integration, prioritize efforts, allocate resources, develop a learning organization, and charter cross-functional teams. Since this is a major change project, all the principles of planned change apply. The journey is usually expected to take between 3 and 5 years, depending on the resources available and the readiness for change. One needs to assess where one is, what the driving and restraining forces are, and how best to use them. Learning will become a lifelong endeavor and part of the mission. Leaders and followers alike need to internalize the new beliefs and learn to use the new techniques and tools. The principles of adult learning should not be ignored. Many organizations fail in the quest to implement the new quality organization because the efforts are all focused on the beginning of the journey. *Just-in-time learning* tends to eliminate the feeling that this may be another managerial gimmick gone awry. Another common mistake is failure to prioritize efforts. Quality costs money, especially in the time and effort of human resources, and few organizations can afford to attempt to improve on all fronts at once. Having real successes as early as possible is also important. Some institutions prioritize based on populations served or product lines. Some concentrate their efforts on longstanding problems, whereas others ask their customers what they want. Recognize up front that it may be difficult to involve the medical staff, but since the scientific process is part of their psyche, the tools and techniques of CQI will seem familiar. Involving physicians early assists in achieving interdisciplinary success and credibility for the CQI beliefs and models. Setbacks will occur; accept them. Create a system that is as simple as possible. Explain how it works and where the boundaries are. Do not abdicate professional responsibilities. Know when to use external change agents.

Process Teams

Not all improvement projects require a process team. If the project or problem crosses functions and disciplines, and cannot be resolved in the day-to-day operations, a team is usually necessary.

Process teams need to be carefully chosen to represent those involved or affected by the process. If the team is very large, it may mean you have chosen too big a project, and you may need to break the project into steps.

How, then, does one choose an improvement project? Listen to your customers. Repeat complaints or requests for a particular service may require action. The evening charge nurse in a nonsectarian hospital receives ongoing requests for pastoral services from patients and their families. Each request requires multiple phone calls, and often results in delays. The nurse recognizes that she or he or the department cannot address this problem alone. It involves not only the hospital, but the community as well. The nurse develops a proposal for a process team. Other methods for selecting or recognizing processes to be improved include asking the people in the process, reviewing existing reports, and recognizing excess complexity or long delays.

Process teams require resources. Because resource allocation is a leadership function, many organizations will require the development of a proposal and the subsequent approval by the quality council. Despite the organization's standards, all teams should develop an opportunity statement (what is wrong or needs improving), define the expected output of the project, and include measures of success. Members of the team include, at a minimum, a team leader who is invested in the process, a facilitator who brings CQI skills, and a recorder or minute taker. Depending on the skills and information systems available, analytical and statistical support may be necessary.

Because process teams are groups, they will need to go through the stages of group development. Forming, storming, norming, performing, and since process teams dissolve, adjourning must all occur. All teams must mature to perform. It is important to recognize that anxiety, testing of boundaries, competition for control, and minimal completion of work are part of the early stages. Early cohesiveness and work does not start until the norming stage. Peak performance and "team" belongs to the performing step. Many teams also struggle with the adjourning phase, namely, meeting the final deadlines and dissolving of the group.

The process team needs to adopt a model or method for doing its work. This model is usually organizationwide. There is value in choosing one model, because it minimizes relearning and allows different teams to communicate easily. Some common models are the Juran quality improvement project model (1989), Deming's PDCA cycle (1982, 1986), and the IMPROVE process of Earnst and Young (1990).

UNDERSTANDING VARIATION

Variation is part of any process. People, equipment, supplies, procedures, techniques, and inaccuracies in the data all contribute to variation in data from an otherwise stable process. *Common-cause variation* is the ongoing, minute variations that are part of nature. *Special-cause variation* is much larger and can be more easily pinpointed to one of the preceding contributors through statistical methods such as run charts and control charts. These charts can monitor processes because, even though individual data points may be unpredictable, over time a fluctuating pattern will emerge. The normal pattern is bell-shaped, meaning that most points are near the center. As a manager of a process, it is important to know when to react to particular data or situations, and when it is necessary to improve the entire process. You have monitored medication errors on your unit for many months. When you calculate the number of errors over the number of doses administered, a percentage ranging between 0.01 and 0.02 percent emerges. This is probably the common-cause type of variation. You may want to compare that level against other institutions of similar type or size in your region, to evaluate whether this is an acceptable error rate. For the first time ever, you see a rise to 0.03 percent. It would be wise to further analyze the data before taking action or deciding to wait. Are all the errors of the same type, attributable to a few individuals, or have new systems been introduced? Constant tinkering with systems, without understanding what the causes of the variation are, destabilizes the process. Understanding variation is important. Common-cause variation requires an answer to the question: "Is this level acceptable when looked at over time?". Special-cause variation needs careful evaluation to identify the cause and take appropriate, focused intervention.

Tools and Techniques Commonly Used in Quality Improvement

An entire body of knowledge has been created in the area of valid techniques to be used when improving quality. Innovation requires team techniques such as brainstorming, boarding, decision matrices, multivoting, management of conflict, and quality communication.

Quality improvement (QI) tools can usually be divided into three categories: those used for process description, those used for data collection, and those used for data analysis. Many excellent texts provide further assistance in this area. The ultimate purpose of all the QI tools is to have data that can be used and translated into information.

Tools for process description include flow charts that describe the process in detail, from beginning to end, as accurately as possible. It is a picture of the movement of information, the people, or the materials. The **top-down flow chart** (Figure 21–1) takes the major steps in the process, writes them in a horizontal sequence, and shows the substeps to be taken under each step. Flow charts show the rework that gets done, the number of substeps or complexity in each area, the number of hand-offs between individuals and departments, and when subteams need to be formed from a particular process team. A too detailed flow chart makes focusing difficult and discourages progress or action.

The **cause and effect diagram** (Figure 21–2), also called the fishbone or Ishikawa diagram, helps identify the root causes of a problem. Typical categories are equipment, personnel, method, materials, and environment. The main arrow points toward the problem or desired result. It is important to remember that cause and effect diagrams only point toward possible causes, and more data will need to be collected to identify the root causes. Cause and effect diagrams are most effective after the process has been described, because flow charts help identify what must be included.

Tools for data collection include asking the right

STEP 1 → STEP 2 → STEP 3 → STEP 4

Substeps	Substeps	Substeps	Substeps
....	....	....	....
....	....	....	....
....	....	....	....
....	....	....	....

FIGURE 21‑1. Top-down flowchart.

questions, data sheets, check sheets, surveys, focus groups, interviews, and more. Much data are collected that turn out to be useless because the question asked was wrong, too broad, or poorly formulated. Data sheets and check sheets are both used to record data (Figure 21–3). They differ in that data sheets require further analysis. Ordinarily a data sheet is completed for each occurrence or event in the study. The data are subsequently aggregated, and sorted according to categories of interest. Check sheets are used to record multiple events by simply putting a mark in the appropriate box. The best check sheets are those that are easy to use, do not require much interpretation, and visually display the data. An example in which either tool could be used is a study of the delivery time of medications to a patient care unit. In the first situation, every time a medication is taken from the pharmacy, the runner initiates a new data sheet. At the end of the study all the sheets are gathered and analyzed. In the second case, the runner could calculate the time it took to deliver the drug and check the appropriate time box on the check sheet. There are obvious advantages and disadvantages to both tools. Data sheets tend to be more accurate because only one particular event is recorded. Check sheets quickly display trends as they occur, without requiring a sometimes lengthy analysis. Data sheets and check sheets shouldbe tested before projectwide work is undertaken so that improvements can be made and only useful data are collected. Surveys are a tool to get input from large groups. The response rate and the specificity of the question impact on the usefulness and quality of the information obtained. Focus groups and individual interviews are time-consuming and expensive, may require the use of experienced interviewers, but they provide the ability to ask open-ended questions and probe deeper, if necessary.

Tools for data analysis include those that compare among categories, such as bar and pi charts and the **Pareto diagram** (Figure 21–4), and those that analyze data within a category, such as numerical and graphic summaries. The Pareto principle, sometimes called the 80/20 rule, was applied to management by Juran. It identifies the few sources of problems that contribute to most of the effect. By ranking problems on a bar graph in descending order, from left to right, Pareto charts focus attention on the most common problems and

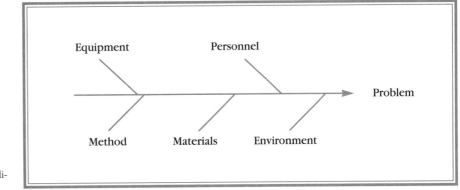

FIGURE 21‑2. Cause and effect diagram.

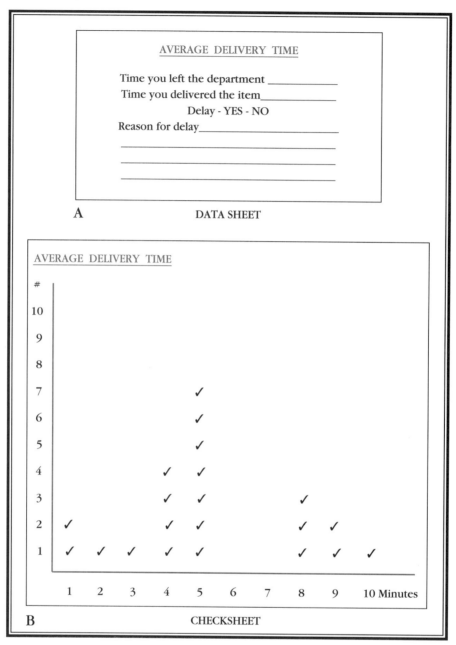

FIGURE 21-3. Average delivery time.

often build consensus on where attention and effort should be focused.

Analysis of a particular category can include numerical summaries such as average, median, mode, and standard deviation. Graphic summaries include line graphs, histograms, scatter diagrams, and control charts. Graphic summaries are especially valuable when working in diverse groups. They provide pictorial display of data, possible analysis and interpretation of patterns, relationships between vari-

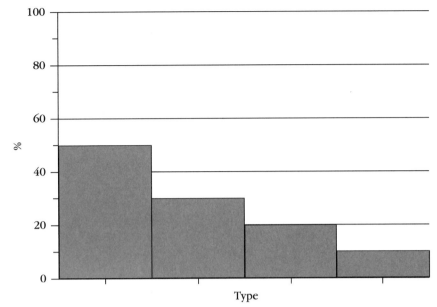

FIGURE 21-4. Pareto diagram.

ables, and the ability to distinguish between common and special cause variation.

The novice in quality improvement tools and techniques may need assistance from the CQI coach, or further study of these techniques.

RELATIONSHIP OF CQI TO DELIVERY REDESIGN

The rapid changes in health care previously discussed have also required delivery redesign. At a minimum, we have a professional obligation to ensure how we deliver care is evaluated along the continuum. We would fail in our professional obligation if we got stuck in anger because of a seemingly endless focus on costs. We must prudently manage resources to be able to provide the most benefit to the largest number of patients possible. It may no longer be possible or desirable to provide all care in traditional institutional settings. We may not be able to afford a predominantly registered nursing staff. We may need to bring services to the patient rather than the patient to the services. We may need to develop new delivery models that optimize the role of the professional nurse, delegate tasks, and meet the needs of our customers.

Case management and work redesign are presently being used across the country for delivery redesign. The Case Management Society of America

(CMSA) (1994) defines case management as "a collaborative process which assesses, plans, implements, coordinates, monitors, and evaluates options and services to meet an individual's health needs through communication and available resources to promote quality, cost effective outcomes." Critical pathways are tools commonly used in this process. Brainstorming, data-driven decision making, consensus seeking, process flow charting, evaluation of costs, and satisfaction are all tools used in case management as well as in the new quality model. Work redesign also requires quality to be built in up front. Professionals need to actively participate in this evolving course. Reliance on inspection and control will not ensure delivery of quality care. Simultaneously, we cannot insist on doing it the old way. The parameters set by the Robert Wood Johnson University Hospital PROACT model (Tonges, 1989) for work redesign include reaching comprehensive patient outcomes (including patient satisfaction) and contributing to staff satisfaction, retention, and productivity and to the financial integrity of the organization. Once again, there appears to be a natural fit between the tenets of CQI, its tools, and techniques.

CQI IN THE MANAGED CARE WORLD

Managed care has recently received much favor as a methodology for controlling escalating health-care costs. Buyers of managed care, such as employers and state and federal governments, have something to say about quality of, access to, choice, and satisfaction with services rendered to those for whom they pay. The more competitive the environment becomes, the more important demonstrated quality will become, to differentiate between one contract or provider and another. The managed care industry is already developing nationally accepted outcomes and indicators. Report cards on customer satisfaction with individual providers and organizations have gained popularity recently. Nursing must take an aggressive professional role in ensuring that the care delivery data reflect direct nursing care delivery, coordination provided by nursing, patient and family teaching, and nursing management along the continuum of care delivery.

ONGOING ROLE FOR REGULATORY AGENCIES

Agencies such as the JCAHO, the PROs, and state and federal government will continue to play a significant role in the assurance that quality care is delivered. Many of the organizations have already begun to assist in collecting benchmarking information. The JCAHO, in particular, is acting as an external change agent with regard to guaranteeing that all providers accept and implement the new paradigm. The hospital associations are assisting their members in dealing with uniform responses to the report cards required by many managed care contracts. Regulators and providers alike are struggling with the implementation of significant change regarding the delivery of quality care.

KEY POINTS

- Rapid changes in health care have prompted a new way of business.
- Purchasers require "more" and "better" for "less."
- Reliance on inspection and control against preestablished standards, the traditional quality assurance model, although of ongoing value, is no longer sufficient.
- Quality models, such as Deming's principles for transformation, the Juran trilogy, and JCAHO's 10-step model, provide an excellent foundation for improving quality of care.
- Quality is not only the result of correcting problems, but requires ongoing improvement.
- Quality journeys require vision, a plan to turn that vision into reality, and a well-developed structure to ensure implementation.
- Most problems lie within systems, not individuals.
- To improve quality, you must improve the system.
- Specific knowledge tools and techniques are required to create a new quality. They include cross-functional teamwork, lifelong learning, and process improvement.
- Process teams are required for those improvement activities that cross functions and disciplines and cannot be resolved in the day-to-day operations.
- Variation is part of all processes. It requires statistical analysis before actions that may destabilize the process are taken.
- Benchmarking is the process of comparing to the best practices in the industry.
- Tools for improvement can be divided in three categories: those used for process description, such as flow charts and cause and effect diagrams, those used for data collection, such as data and check sheets, and those used for data analysis, such as bar and pi charts and the Pareto diagram.
- Continuous quality improvement is not a separate management tool. It is a way of doing business.

CHAPTER EXERCISE

You are the nurse manager of an ambulatory day surgery unit. Recently, you have seen a sudden rise in the number of patients coming through the unit. Simultaneously, patients, physicians, and other providers have started to complain about long delays during pretesting, access to booking times, and transportation to diagnostic testing.

1. Compare using a process team versus attempting to fix the problem through a staff meeting within your unit.

2. Describe how you would analyze the process.

3. Explain which tools are appropriate in this case.

REFERENCES

Case Management Society of America, CMSA Proposes Standards. (1994). *The Case Manager* 5, No. 1.

Deming, W. E. (1982, 1986). *Out of Crisis.* Cambridge: Massachusetts Institute of Technology.

The Earnst and Young Quality Improvement Consulting Group. (1990). *Total quality, an executive guide for the nineties.* Homewood, IL: Business One Irwin.

Joint Commission on Accreditation of Healthcare Organizations. (1995). *1996 Comprehensive accreditation manual for hospitals.* Oakbrook Terrace, IL: Joint Commission on Accreditation of Healthcare Organizations.

Joint Commission on Accreditation of Healthcare Organizations. (1991). *An introduction to quality improvement in health care.* Oakbrook Terrace, IL: Joint Commission on Accreditation of Healthcare Organizations.

Juran, J. M. (1989). *Juran on leadership for quality, an executive handbook.* New York: Free Press.

Tonges, M. C. (1989). Redesigning hospital nursing practice: The professionally advanced care team (pro-ACT) model: part 2. *Journal of Nursing Administration, 19*(8), 19–22.

BIBLIOGRAPHY

Berwick, D. M., Godfrey, A. B., & Roessner, J. (1990). *Curing health care, new strategies for quality improvement.* San Francisco: Jossey-Bass.

Flarey, D. L. (1995). *Redesigning nursing care delivery, transforming our future.* Philadelphia: Lippincott.

Gale, F. (Ed.). (1994). *Tales of pursuit of quality in health care.* Tampa, FL: American College of Physician Executives.

Juran, J. M. (1988). *Juran on planning for quality.* New York: Free Press.

Satinsky, M. A. (1995). *An executive guide to case management strategies.* Chicago: American Hospital Publishing.

Schroeder, P. (1994). *Improving quality and performance, concepts, programs, and techniques.* St. Louis: Mosby-Year Book.

Spears, L. (Ed.). (1995). *Reflections on leadership.* New York: Wiley.

Chapter 22

NURSING IN THE COMMUNITY

Troy W. Bradshaw

CHAPTER OBJECTIVES

On completion of this chapter, the reader will be able to:

1. Examine the trends in community health care and community health nursing.
2. Discuss differences with care for the client, family, and group in the community.
3. Identify issues when the community is the client for health care.
4. Contrast urban and rural community health-care needs and resources.
5. Evaluate the progress made to date on the *Health Communities 2000* objectives.

KEY TERMS

Public Health Nursing
Community Health
   Nursing
Primary Prevention
Secondary Prevention

Tertiary Prevention
Rural Health
   Clinics (RHCs)
Community Health
   Center (CHC) Program

Migrant Health Centers
   (MHC) Program
Telemedicine
Environmental Health

An increasing number of nurses are shifting their employment from acute care to community settings (Brooks, 1995, p. 145). It therefore behooves today's professional nurse to understand the nature of nursing practice in the community.

One of the distinctive features of baccalaureate nursing programs in the United States is that they provide formal preparation in community health nursing. Courses in community health nursing are not usually included in associate degree programs. Although many associate degree programs are now including community-based experiences in their curricula because of the decreasing availability of acute care clinical experiences and shifting of employment settings, this is not the same as community health nursing preparation at the baccalaureate level.

So, what exactly is community health nursing? A prominent community health nurse educator addressed this question two decades ago and concluded that "Many nurses in both education and service seem to be in a conceptual and semantic muddle about the nature of community nursing practice: What it is or should be, whether it constitutes or should constitute a specialty, and—if it is a specialty—how it is distinct from other specialties" (Williams, 1977, p. 250).

This statement is probably as true today as when it was written. Debate and confusion regarding community health nursing practice have not been resolved, despite "official" definitions and statements. Differences in the literature revolve primarily around the appropriate level of intervention, the proper client focus, and the required educational preparation. These and other issues are examined later in this chapter. First, though, a brief overview of the early history of community health nursing will aid us in understanding how we arrived where we are today.

HISTORY OF COMMUNITY HEALTH NURSING

The first organized community nursing activities began with religious and other charitable groups providing home care for the sick. These groups, largely untrained caregivers, were active in both Europe and the United States prior to the mid-1800s, especially among the poor. However, it was not until the latter part of the nineteenth century that the stage was truly set for the development of professional community health nursing (Clark, 1996, pp. 20–22; Smith, 1995, pp. 34–35; Spradley & Allender, 1996, pp. 71–73).

A series of events created by a changing society helped pave the way for the development of community health nursing. In the early nineteenth century, Europe and the United States were witnessing the Industrial Revolution. Many people moved from farms and crowded into cities to work in factories. This influx resulted in sanitation problems and the spread of communicable disease. By the mid-1800s, sanitary reform was underway on both sides of the Atlantic. The emerging germ theory was later confirmed in the 1870s with the discovery of bacteria. This discovery added momentum to the sanitary reform movement and accelerated public health efforts (Clark, 1996, p. 20; Smith, 1995, pp. 38–39). Such was the environment that profoundly influenced the work of early community health nurses.

In 1859, William Rathbone, a wealthy philanthropist, established a district nursing organization in Liverpool, England. The community was divided into districts, hence the term "district nursing." Rathbone soon realized that more trained nurses were needed and, in 1861, turned to Florence Nightingale for assistance. With her help, Rathbone was able to open a nurses' training school in Liverpool. During the following two decades, district nursing organizations became well established in England and began making their appearance in the United States (Clark, 1996, p. 21; Smith, 1995, p. 72). Between 1865 and 1894, Florence Nightingale significantly influenced nursing outside of hospitals through her writings on organization and management of nursing services, sanitation, poverty, and social reform (Monteiro, 1985). Another of Nightingale's major contributions, often not fully appreciated by nurses, was her visionary and impressive use of biostatistics to bring about health reform (Swanson, 1993, pp. 21–26).

Frances Root is generally considered to be the first professional community health nurse in the United States. A nursing graduate of Bellevue Hospital, she was employed in 1877 by the Women's Board of the New York City Mission to provide home nursing care to the sick poor (Clark, 1996, p. 21; Smith, 1995, p. 35; Spradley & Allender, 1996, p. 72; Swanson, 1993, p. 31).

In 1893, Lillian Wald and Mary Brewster established the Henry Street Settlement House on New York City's Lower East Side to provide nursing and welfare services to the impoverished immigrant population. This organization was for forerunner of the Visiting Nurse Association of New York City, and is considered the first true community health nursing agency in the United States. Nurses of the Henry Street Settlement, like the district nurses who preceded them, mingled health education and disease prevention with home care of the sick (Clark,

1996, p. 22; Spradley & Allender, 1996, p. 74; Swanson, 1993, p. 31).

Wald and Brewster quickly recognized that individual nursing care was not enough; social, economic, and environmental influences on health and illness also needed to be addressed. Wald coined the term **"public health nursing"** to describe this expanded nursing role (Buhler-Wilkerson, 1993). More than 70 years later, the term **"community health nursing"** was adopted. These two terms will be contrasted later, but for now they are used interchangeably.

During the first decade of the twentieth century, public health nurses began specializing. Subsequent growth of public health nursing was tremendous. Unfortunately, by the end of the second decade organizations employing public health nurses constituted a hodge-podge of uncoordinated voluntary and governmental agencies. Conflict and rivalry between the private and public sectors of the health-care system emerged. Voluntary agencies and private physicians feared loss of income to the public agencies. Consequently, health departments were prevented from providing any sort of medical care services lest they infringe on the practices of private physicians. The activities of nurses in public health departments became largely limited to disease prevention, whereas nurses in voluntary agencies provided home care for the sick (Buhler-Wilkerson, 1993, pp. 1781–1783). This dichotomy prevailed until the advent of Medicare and Medicaid legislation in 1965 (Smith, 1995, p. 44). Subsequently, the nursing focus in many health departments shifted from disease prevention and health promotion to illness care.

ROLES, PRIORITIES, AND INTERVENTION STRATEGIES

Many nurses whose orientation is to clinical nursing or inpatient settings may have only a vague or stereotyped idea of the roles, functions, and activities of nurses in community practice. The RN contemplating a move into community practice or facing his or her first course in community health nursing may therefore have several questions: What do community health nurses actually do? What are their responsibilities and priorities? What intervention strategies do they use? Who are their clients?

Assuming for the moment that community health nursing is a specialty, these questions are difficult to address comprehensively in a brief discussion. **Community health nursing** cannot be as readily described as most other nursing specialties. It crosses many traditional boundaries. It is not, for example, limited to a particular age group, medical diagnostic category, or narrow set of specialized skills. Although its clients may include individuals and families, community health nursing may have a group or even an entire community as a client. Clients may be well or ill. Their health risk or health problem may be either physical or psychosocial in nature. Finally, conceptual differences and confusion superimposed on a rapidly changing health-care system add to the difficulty of concisely describing contemporary community or public health nursing.

Several factors determine the roles, activities, and intervention strategies of an individual community health nurse, but three factors are paramount:

1. the mission, philosophy, and priorities of the employing agency,
2. the level of prevention at which intervention is aimed, and
3. the definition of client.

The first factor usually drives the other two. The mission, philosophy, and priorities of a private agency may be quite different from those of an official governmental agency. The level of funding influences how well the agency is able to implement its priorities. Priorities, of course, should be based on identified health needs in the community.

The second factor that determines the community health nurse's duties is the agency's level of prevention focus. As was discussed in Chapter 5, prevention is an important concept for all disciplines in community health. Leavell and Clark (1965) identified three levels of prevention in their history of disease: primary prevention, secondary prevention, and tertiary prevention. **Primary prevention** includes interventions to prevent disease from occurring. **Secondary prevention** involves early detection and treatment of an existing health problem. **Tertiary prevention** seeks to correct a health problem, limit disability, and provide rehabilitation to maintain or restore function.

Opinions regarding the levels of preventive intervention most appropriate for community health nurses are conflicting. Currently, they may be involved in all three levels of prevention. However, a nursing focus on illness does not address causes of disease (Edelman & Mandle, 1994, p. 20). According to one author, "We must now encourage and facilitate the entire nursing profession's shift from focusing primarily upon secondary and tertiary prevention, individual and disease-oriented arenas to include community health promotion processes" (Baldwin, 1995, p. 162).

Historically, community health nurses have played

a key role in primary prevention efforts. For more than 100 years they have been involved in health promotion and disease prevention (Smith, 1995, pp. 37–39). Over the past several years, these traditional services have suffered under the Medicare and Medicaid amendments because they are not reimbursable (Kenyon et al., 1990). Primarily because of the need for revenue, official agencies (e.g., health departments) have been compelled for more than two decades to provide more direct clinical services. Consequently, many public health nurses have taken on a role that is more illness-oriented than preventive (Salmon, 1993, p. 1674; Clark, 1996, p. 27). But public health agencies may soon no longer be required to provide primary care services (Josten et al., 1995, p. 38). Such a change might be desirable from the standpoint of allowing health departments to focus on their core roles. On the other hand, public health nursing resources may be in jeopardy if these nurses are now viewed only as providers of personal care (Salmon, 1993; Zerwekh, 1993). Several major cities are already seeing public health nursing positions being eliminated by budget cuts, and personal health services are being contracted with private companies (Brider, 1996, p. 72). There is clearly a need for community health nurses, especially those in public health agencies, to renew and strengthen their role in primary prevention.

In 1990, the U.S. Department of Health and Human Services (USDHHS) published the landmark document *Healthy People 2000: National Health Promotion and Disease Prevention Objectives*. Based on previously published objectives, this document established specific national health objectives organized under 22 priority areas. Many of these objectives target selected age groups. In 1991, *Healthy Communities 2000: Model Standards* (American Public Health Association) was published to assist planners in adapting the *Healthy People 2000* objectives to the needs and resources of individual communities. The *Healthy People 2000* objectives are reprinted in the document, accompanied by model standards, which provide flexible practical guidance for achieving the objectives. Blanks are included in the objectives and standards to allow planners to tailor them to their communities. Indicators are provided for measuring achievement of the objectives and standards (pp. xxx–xxi).

While national public health policy does seem to be moving more toward a health promotion orientation (Clark, 1996, p. 27), it remains to be seen how well this policy will be embraced by society and the health-care system. Positive outcomes of preventive activities take time, "are difficult to demonstrate and therefore, are vulnerable to budget cuts" (USDHHS, 1995, p. 146). Primary prevention of disease makes good economic sense. But it is not nearly as glamorous, exciting, or lucrative for providers and medical suppliers as treating disease with high technology.

A third factor that shapes the community health nurse's role is the definition of "client." As previously stated, the community health nurse's client may be an individual, a family, a group, or a community. Table 22–1 illustrates examples of nursing interventions at each of the three levels for different types of clients.

Community health nursing has addressed the needs of each of these clients in varying degrees throughout its history. Although it initially focused heavily on individuals in their homes, the family context was not ignored. Friedman (1992) states that "family-centered practice has been promulgated by community health nursing since its inception" (p. 5). Yet some of community health nursing's most notable early accomplishments were made from the perspective of groups and communities as clients (e.g., Florence Nightingale and Lillian Wald).

Muecke (1984) compared definitions of community health nursing from publications of the American Nurses Association (ANA, 1980) and the American Public Health Association (APHA, 1980). She noted that the ANA definition focuses on nursing care of individuals and families, with equal emphasis on all three levels of prevention. The APHA definition, by contrast, focuses on the community as a whole and emphasizes primary prevention.

In a rapidly changing health-care environment, several authors are calling for a greater focus on populations, with the community as the client. For example, Swanson and Albrecht (1993), in the preface to their text, state that, "Since 1983, community health nurse educators at national conferences have acknowledged a need for greater emphasis in the baccalaureate curriculum on a community and aggregate focus rather than on the current family theory and family caseload focus" (p. xii).

The previously mentioned warning that public health nurses must be recognized as more than personal care providers (Salmon, 1993; Zerwekh, 1993) implies a need to move away from an individual focus. Baldwin (1995), also previously cited, obviously advocates a community or population focus, along with primary prevention. Berkowitz (1995), referring to problems such as substance abuse and teen pregnancy, emphasizes that "These population issues are difficult to solve on a case-by-case basis, but they do respond to community intervention" (p. 40). Swanson and Albrecht (1993, p. xi) refute the com-

TABLE 22–1. Example of levels of Prevention and Clients Served in Community

	Level of Prevention		
Definition of Client Served	**Primary (Health Promotion and Specific Prevention)**	**Secondary (Early Diagnosis and Treatment)**	**Tertiary (Limitation of Disability and Rehabilitation)**
Individual	Dietary teaching during pregnancy Immunization	HIV testing Screening for cervical cancer	Teaching new client with diabetes how to administer insulin Exercise therapy after stroke Skin care for incontinent patient
Family (two or more individuals bound by kinship, law, or living arrangement and with common emotional ties and obligations)	Education regarding smoking, dental care, or nutritional counseling Adequate housing	Dental examinations Tuberculin testing for family at risk	Mental health counseling or referral for family in crisis, e.g., grieving, experiencing a divorce Dietary instructions and monitoring for family with overweight members
Group or aggregate (interacting persons with a common purpose or purposes)	Birthing classes for pregnant teenage mothers AIDS and other sexually transmitted disease education for high school students	Vision screening of first-grade class Mammography van for screening of women in a low-income neighborhood Hearing tests at a senior center	Group counseling for grade-school children with asthma Swim therapy for physically disabled elders at a senior center Alcoholics Anonymous and other self-help groups
Community and populations (aggregate of people sharing space over time within a social system; population groups or aggregates with power relations and common needs and purposes)	Fluoride water supplementation Environmental sanitation Removal of environmental hazards	Organized screening programs for communities, such as health fairs VDRL screening for marriage license applicants in a city Lead screening for children by school district	Mental health services for military veterans Shelter and relocation centers for fire or earthquake victims Emergency medical services Community mental health services for chronically mentally ill Home care services for chronically ill

Source: Swanson, J., & Albrecht, M. (1993). *Community health nursing: Promoting the health of aggregates.* Philadelphia: Saunders. Reprinted with permission.

monly held viewpoint that communities and populations should be the primary unit of care only for community health nurses with graduate preparation.

Individual clinical and personal care services are, and will continue to be, important components of the health-care system. However, they must be put in proper perspective. Care of individual clients is the focus of basic nursing education programs, and this concept is ingrained in most nurses. But community health nurses must be able to see the larger health-care picture and move beyond this orientation. All health needs cannot be met on an individual basis, nor can they be met by attending only to those who present themselves for health care (Salmon, 1994, p. 236).

A frequently repeated criticism of recent health reform proposals is that most focus only on access to and financing of medical care and clinical services. Of course, these issues need to be addressed, but so do the complex social and environmental causes of disease. To do this requires a population orientation.

COMMUNITY HEALTH NURSING VERSUS PUBLIC HEALTH NURSING

Community health nursing has been closely associated with public health for most of the past 100 years. As noted in the historical narrative at the beginning of this chapter, Lillian Wald coined the term "public health nursing" in 1893 (Buhler-Wilkerson, 1993). It was not until more recent times that the term "community health nursing" came into vogue.

> While public health nurses continued their work in public health, by the late 1960s and early 1970s many nurses, not necessarily practicing public health, were based in the community. . . . To provide a label that encompassed all nurses in the community, the American Nurses Association and others called them community health nurses. This and other events led to confusion about the nature of community health nursing as a specialty practice. (Spradley & Allender, 1996, p. 75)

Community health nursing is frequently described in the literature as a synthesis of nursing and public health. This description is included in definitions published by both the American Nurses Association (ANA, 1980) and the American Public Health Association (APHA, 1980). The ANA uses the term "community health nursing" whereas the APHA uses the older term "public health nursing." In the spring of 1996, the APHA adopted a new definition statement on public health nursing (Wallinder, White, & Salveson, 1996, p. 81). At the time this chapter was prepared, however, the new statement had not yet been disseminated.

In 1984, a Consensus Conference on the Essentials of Public Health Nursing and Practice was held by the Division of Nursing, Bureau of Professions of the U.S. Department of Health and Human Services (1985). Participants in this conference concluded that *community health nursing* is a broad term that includes not only public health nurses, but all nurses working in a community setting. Formal preparation in public health nursing was not considered a prerequisite. Apparently the Consensus Conference participants did not endorse the concept of community health nursing being a synthesis of nursing and public health.

So the debate about the nature of community nursing practice continues. Burbach and Brown (1988), for example, argue that the growing field of home health nursing must be clearly distinguished from community health nursing. This distinction may become more apparent now that certification is offered in home health care by the American Nurses Credentialing Center. Others argue that public health nursing must not be used synonymously with community health nursing (Josten et al., 1995, p. 40). The confusion and debate regarding the terms "public health nursing" and "community health nursing" are not merely a semantic problem. They may well affect the role nurses will be allowed to play in future health care.

Although the important contributions of nurses were recognized by public health leaders in the 1920s (Smith, 1995, p. 38), they were scarcely mentioned in the 1988 report *The Future of Public Health* (Salmon, 1989; Ward, 1989). Has nursing's influence in public health waned over the years because of a lack of clarity regarding the public health nurse's role? Or is the diminished influence due to nurses being viewed only as personal caregivers? Both of these factors are probably significant, but the antecedent factor may be nursing education's failure to synthesize nursing and public health.

Several years ago, Salmon (1989) exhorted nursing education to reevaluate how it prepares nurses for public health leadership roles. Comparing the values and theoretical perspective of nursing with those of public health, she examined how this dichotomy affects public health nursing education. She noted that nursing is oriented to individuals and families, whereas public health is oriented to society at large. Nursing's primary focus is sick care, whereas public health seeks to prevent health problems. Salmon portrayed nursing education as parochial, with an emphasis on uniformity, whereas public health education is interdisciplinary and more diverse. She further asserted that public health content has been overshadowed and diluted by nursing content in most nursing programs—even in graduate-level community health nursing programs. Thus, a supposed nurse specialist is often ill-prepared in the basic public health sciences. Salmon indicated that few nursing faculty are actually prepared to teach public health nursing and, if they are, their expertise is often not valued by nursing education. By the same token, she noted that preparation in community health nursing is less valued in the public health field than a public health degree. Salmon advocates interdisciplinary education as one remedy. Josten and coworkers (1995) echo these sentiments regarding deficiencies in public health nursing education, particularly at the graduate level. They emphasize that epidemiology and other essential public health content are necessary to prepare leaders in public health nursing. They clearly distinguish between graduate education in community health nursing and in public health nursing, and they strongly advocate interdisciplinary education for public health nurses. In their opinion, public health nursing graduate programs should be associated with a school of public health to achieve the necessary collaboration.

Thus, nursing education is presented with a challenge to improve its preparation of nurses for public health practice and leadership. The preceding discussion regarding the need for interdisciplinary education should not be construed as nursing "selling out" to another profession. "This may come as a shock but public health is not a 'profession.' Public health is a 'goal' achieved through multidisciplinary teams composed of numerous professions, including physicians, nurses, lawyers, engineers, statisticians, molecular biologists, sociologists, and economists" (Sommer, 1995, p. 659). If nurses are to play a significant role in achieving the goal of public health, they must be educated in public health sciences.

RURAL VERSUS URBAN SETTINGS

There is no single definition of "rural." It is defined in several ways in the literature. This lack of a uniform definition is of concern because it impedes research and policy making. Most definitions are based on population or population density of an area, and approximately one-fourth of Americans are considered to be rural residents. But population density is not the only factor to consider in assessing access to health care. Transportation and required travel time may affect access for both urban and rural populations (Bushy, 1995, pp. 821–822).

It is important to be aware that the large majority of rural residents are not farmers. For those who are, agriculture is a dangerous occupation with great risk of injury and illness, even for children living on farms. But nonagricultural occupational hazards are becoming more important in rural areas (Hanson, 1996, pp. 625, 633).

"Little is known about rural residents in general, and even less is known about subgroups within the major culture in either rural or urban areas. . . . The various terms used to understand rural residency are relative in nature" (Bushy, 1995, p. 823). Rural communities may share some features, but they are not all the same. For example, characteristics and problems of rural residents in south Georgia may be quite different from those of rural residents in Montana or Iowa.

The rural health literature addresses a variety of problems. However, two recurring concerns seem to predominate: chronic illness (particularly in the elderly) and inadequate prenatal care. Chronic illness is prevalent in rural populations, and management of these illnesses is an important part of the rural community health nurse's role (Bushy, 1995, p. 823;

Hanson, 1996, p. 628). The poverty level in rural areas is much greater than in urban areas (Lund, 1993, p. 646). Rural residency and poverty are two important variables associated with inadequate prenatal care (Miller et al., 1996, pp. 6–18).

The U.S. Office of Technology Assessment (1990) has compared selected preventive behaviors and risk exposures of metropolitan residents with nonmetropolitan residents. The comparison indicates that nonmetropolitan residents engage less in preventive behaviors and more in risk exposure behaviors than metropolitan residents. Yet the incidence of cancer is higher for urban areas than for rural areas (Clark, 1996, p. 1016). This may be related to urban environmental pollution levels.

Delivery of health-care services in rural communities is heavily influenced by the availability, accessibility, and acceptability of services. Rural communities have fewer health-care resources. Distance, lack of communication, and other problems may hamper access. Acceptability of services may be limited by the clients' health-care beliefs and practices or other factors. Furthermore, most health-care providers have had little or no exposure to rural clients during their professional education (Bushy, 1995, p. 827).

The challenges of the community health nurse's practice can also be described within the context of availability, accessibility, and acceptability. For example, the rural community health nurse may well be the only health professional in the community, working with very limited resources. Hanson (1996, p. 628) notes that the community health nurse may even be a regular provider of emergency care. He or she may have to travel long distances, perhaps over rough terrain, to reach clients. In this situation, a four-wheel drive vehicle and a cellular telephone are tremendous assets. Rural residents tend to be religiously and politically conservative, self-sufficient, and wary of outsiders (especially urbanites). Thus, the community health nurse cannot expect to eagerly rush into a rural community with good intentions and gain immediate acceptance. Building rapport with residents of a rural community takes time; respect for their values and beliefs is imperative. In other words, the nurse must be culturally sensitive. A further challenge is presented when the rural residents are also members of an ethnic group that is different from that of the nurse. The rural community health nurse must beware of assuming that these clients (and their problems) are the same as those of their urban counterparts. Their ruralism may be as significant as their ethnic identity.

Under Public Law 95-210, **rural health clinics (RHCs)** have been established to provide primary care services for residents of medically underserved areas. Federal legislation has also created the **Community Health Center (CHC) program** and the **Migrant Health Centers (MHC) program** to provide primary care for medically underserved rural populations. Agencies receiving funding under the CHC program must provide diagnostic, preventive health, transportation, and emergency medical services. The MHC program is similar to the CHC program, but is limited to migrant farm workers and their families. Under both the CHC and the MHC programs, appropriate supplemental services may also be provided (Bushy, 1995, pp. 829, 831).

Federal reimbursement policy is a major issue for those in rural health care. Urban health-care providers are reimbursed by Medicare at a higher rate than rural providers. The National Rural Health Association (NHRA) ("NHRA adopts agenda," 1996) opposes this disparity and other inequities in the Medicare reimbursement schedule. Congdon and Magilvy (1995) found that an increasing paperwork burden, associated primarily with government reimbursement restrictions, was largely responsible for rural nurses leaving home health care. They also point out that home health-care delivery costs per client are higher in rural areas because of low volume and increased travel time.

The use of telecommunications technology in health care, or **telemedicine,** has greatly increased in recent years. It is being used extensively in some states (e.g., Texas) to enhance care of rural residents. For example, a specialist at an urban medical center can consult on a patient in a remote rural area via television and computers. Telemedicine has tremendous potential, but it is not without problems. Issues such as reimbursement, liability, and licensure (when state borders are crossed) must be addressed (Zetzman, 1995). Nevertheless, the interest and growth in telecommunications technology is evident in the literature. The NRHA ("NRHA Adopts Agenda," 1996) has encouraged the Department of Health and Human Services to expand Medicare payment for telemedicine services. Telemedicine and the strategic placement of community health nurses are suggested possibilities for providing continuity of care for rural clients who live at great distances from the hospital (Gibson, 1996, p. 232).

Clearly, rural practice presents several major challenges for community health nurses that are not usually found in an urban setting. However, "there has never been a more important time in history for rural health care" (Maxfield, 1996). For the nurse who wants more autonomy and truly desires to make a difference in people's health, rural community health nursing has much to offer.

THEORETICAL APPROACHES IN COMMUNITY HEALTH NURSING

A sound theoretical foundation provides direction and focus for nursing assessments and interventions. Unfortunately, the theoretical foundation of community health nursing is not yet as well developed as the theoretical foundation of clinical nursing. Most theoretical models in nursing focus on the individual client and lack an adequate aggregate perspective (Butterfield, 1993, pp. 68–70; Clark, 1996, pp. 878–879).

This brief discussion is not intended to describe or analyze the work of nursing theorists, but rather to examine theoretical approaches broadly, as they relate to community health nursing. (See Chapters 3, 4, and 5 for a more comprehensive discussion of the theoretical basis of nursing practice.)

There is no consensus among textbook authors regarding the best theoretical approach for community health nursing. Cookfair (1991) focuses on Neuman's work, although the author acknowledges several other theorists she believes have contributed to the development of community health nursing (p. 17). Smith (1995) states that "many concepts from the different nursing theories are applicable to nursing with families and communities" (p. 10). It is unclear to what extent she considers the work of the various theorists applicable to these aggregates. Clark (1996, p. 880) maintains that the theoretical models of Orem, Roy, Johnson, Neuman, and others are adaptable to families and communities, although they were developed for use with individuals. She thoroughly supports this assertion with examples, devoting an entire chapter to the topic (pp. 879–910). However, Clark uses her own model (the epidemiologic prevention process model) as the framework for her textbook (p. xxviii).

Butterfield (1993) is more critical of using individual-oriented nursing theories in community health nursing. She says that, "Unless a given theory is broad enough in scope to address health and determinants of health from a population perspective, it will be of limited use to community health nurses" (p. 70). She contrasts approaches that focus on individuals and their health behaviors with those focusing on populations and sociopolitical or environmental forces affecting health. This contrast provides community health nurses with a format for reviewing and evaluating theoretical approaches. Orem's theory and the health belief model are cited as examples of the former approach and are deemed too limited to adequately address population-based health problems (Butterfield, 1993, pp. 70–72, 74). Butterfield presents Milio's framework for prevention and application of critical social theory as examples of the latter approach. Both focus on health and illness in a social context and emphasize society's influence on health problems (pp. 75–77). Butterfield does not entirely discount the value of individual-oriented approaches, but she is concerned that nurses may inappropriately use them to address population-based health problems (p. 68).

At this point the nurse may be somewhat confused and uncertain about selecting an appropriate theoretical approach for community health nursing. The experts have obvious differences of opinion. Although this may be frustrating for the novice, conflicting viewpoints can stimulate critical thinking. Some guidelines are provided to facilitate this process and give encouragement.

One must remember that no theoretical approach is sacred. Theories and conceptual models are simply tools. As with all tools, the user must know their purpose and be comfortable with them. Familiarity with several theoretical approaches will provide the nurse with more options. Which particular approach is selected depends on personal preference, agency policy, and the nature of the client's problem. One of the individual-oriented nursing theoretical models may be suitable for the community health nurse working at the individual client level. However, the nurse working at the population level should consider evaluating a proposed approach with Butterfield's (1993, p. 71) review format. As an alternative, Clark's (1996, pp. 879–910) examples may provide the best guidance for adapting selected individual-oriented nursing models to aggregates.

This author's personal experience in the practice and teaching of community health nursing supports a preference for Clark's (1996, pp. 118–119) epidemiologic prevention process model. This model incorporates an epidemiologic perspective, the three levels of prevention, and the nursing process. It is broad enough to be used at all client levels, and health determinants can be addressed from a population perspective. Unlike most other nursing models, it was developed for community health nursing and therefore does not have to be "adapted." The epidemiologic prevention process model reflects the essence of community health nursing, and most baccalaureate nursing students can learn to use it with minimal difficulty.

THE FUTURE OF COMMUNITY HEALTH NURSING

Several authors have expressed concern about the future of community health nursing and the direction it should take. Some of these concerns and factors that are likely to have an impact on community health nursing's future have already been mentioned.

Although no one can predict the future with certainty, being attuned to changes in the world can provide a framework for making prudent decisions. To prepare for the future, nurses must be aware of political, social, and economic changes and how they affect national health-care priorities. Over a decade ago, Andreoli and Musser (1985) described five trends they believed would most affect nursing's future:

1. An increasing elderly population,
2. Rising costs of health care,
3. A physician surplus,
4. Increasing importance of health promotion and self-care, and
5. An increase in technology.

These trends are still applicable, especially for community health nurses. Most are not likely to change soon, and they should be given careful attention by all nurses.

Community health nurses, unlike many acute care nurses, have not previously been strongly oriented toward technology in health care. But biomedical and communication technology offer many ways for community health nurses to do their work more effectively and efficiently. Expanding technology is certain to be an important part of the future for community health nursing.

The importance of the environment in relation to health has been recognized for many years. Several diseases have been linked to environmental factors, including various forms of cancer and reproductive dysfunctions. Breast cancer is a critical concern, and research is underway to evaluate possible environmental risk factors (USDHHS, 1995, p. 80).

> In terms of impact, the environment may be the single most important determinant of health in the very near future. It is also the determinant about which nurses perhaps know the least. The nursing literature on environmental health and the role of public and community health nurses is alarmingly sparse. (Salmon, 1994, p. 237)

Neufer (1994, p. 156) finds it surprising that community health nursing and the nursing literature have devoted so little attention to environmental health. She points to Florence Nightingale's concern for environmental health and her emphasis on the environment in nursing education. Neufer asserts that community health nurses must address more than the traditional patient environment or home safety. They must also be active in environmental health issues that affect the community. Tiedje and

Wood (1995) believe that the environmental health role of community health nurses has been evolving for several years, and they suggest strategies for expanding this role.

Environmental health issues relate to a broad range of hazards, although many people think only in limited terms such as toxic chemicals or pollution. These, along with hazardous waste control, water and food quality, radiation, and other issues, are appropriate areas for community health nursing intervention. In a broad sense, communicable disease may also be considered an environmental hazard. Of much concern at present are human immunodeficiency virus (HIV) infection, hepatitis, tuberculosis, and childhood communicable diseases. The national health objectives for the year 2000 USDHHS 1990) specifically include each of these (although not under the category of environmental health). The community health nurse has an important role in preventing and controlling communicable diseases. If their incidence is not curtailed, communicable diseases are likely to have an even greater impact on community health nursing practice in the future.

Rapid global travel and emerging microbes are increasing the communicable disease threat. Travel (especially overseas) may expose people to both familiar and unfamiliar communicable diseases and, perhaps, several other environmental hazards. Compared to the United States, other countries may have no or less stringent environmental and health protection regulations. The infected traveler may return home before even developing signs of illness. If the disease is unfamiliar to the physician, diagnosis could be delayed, increasing opportunity for the disease to spread. With more global travel, U.S. healthcare personnel are already seeing several cases of unfamiliar "exotic" infectious diseases previously associated only with remote parts of the world.

While potential health problems related to global travel should be of concern to the community or public health nurse now, problems related to space travel may have to be considered in the future. As far-fetched as it seems, space travel may someday become as common as air travel is now. There may even be "space communities" or other unforeseen settings with health problems. That "someday" may arrive sooner than we expect. "The future will belong to those nurses who develop skills and behaviors to meet health care trends" (Andreoli & Musser, 1985, p. 51).

KEY POINTS

- Nursing jobs are increasingly shifting from acute care settings to community settings.
- There is considerable confusion and debate regarding the term "community health nursing."
- Modern community health nursing is considered to have begun with district nursing in England, during the latter part of the nineteenth century.
- Early community health nursing was strongly influenced by events of the Industrial Revolution.
- Two prominent figures in the early development of community health nursing were Florence Nightingale (England) and Lillian Wald (U.S.). Wald coined the term "public health nursing."
- Public health nursing's historic role in health promotion and disease prevention was diminished after the advent of Medicare, when personal care services increased.
- Public health policy seems to be shifting more toward health promotion and primary prevention. Several community health nursing leaders are advocating a shift in focus from secondary and tertiary prevention to primary prevention, along with a greater focus on community and population clients.
- Some authors believe that public health nursing must be clearly distinguished from other types of community nursing. Public health nursing leadership requires educational preparation in both nursing and the public health sciences.
- Community health nursing in rural areas is quite different from that in urban areas. Most rural residents are no longer farmers.

- Federal legislation has established rural health clinics, the Community Health Center Program, and the Migrant Health Centers Program to provide primary care to medically underserved rural populations.
- Telecommunications technology (telemedicine) is expected to play a prominent role in the future of rural health care.
- Most theoretical models in nursing were developed for use with individuals. Any model should be carefully evaluated before it is applied to population-based health problems.
- The future of community or public health nursing is uncertain. Planning for the future requires an awareness of current and emerging health-care trends.
- Environmental health is increasingly being recognized as an important health determinant. Community health nurses need to increase their knowledge, skills, and involvement in this area.

CHAPTER EXERCISES

1. Identify several community-based settings in which registered nurses are employed in your community. In which settings could the nurses be considered "community health nurses"? Why?

2. Identify services provided by the school nurses in your community. Do you consider these "community health nursing" services? Why or why not? If not, what services could school nurses offer that could more appropriately be considered "community health nursing" services?

3. Contact your local public health department's nursing office. Do nurses provide direct primary care to individuals? Are the types of nursing services provided likely to change within the next 3 years?

4. Survey the faculty in your nursing program. Do any hold a public health degree (e.g., MPH or Dr PH)?

5. Brainstorm with your classmates. Think of as many potential health problems as possible related to mass space travel or living in "space stations."

REFERENCES

American Nurses' Association (ANA). (1980). *A conceptual model of community health nursing.* Washington, DC: ANA.

American Public Health Association (APHA). (1980). *The definition and role of public health nursing in the delivery of health care.* Washington, DC: APHA.

American Public Health Association. (1991). *Healthy communities 2000: Model standards: Guidelines for community attainment of the year 2000 objectives.* Washington, DC: APHA.

Andreoli, K. G., & Musser, L. A. (1985). Trends that may affect nursing's future. *Nursing and Health Care, 6*(1), 47–51.

Baldwin, J. H. (1995). Are we implementing community health promotion in nursing? *Public Health Nursing, 12,* 159–164.

Berkowitz, B. (1995). Improving our health by improving our system: Transitions in public health. *Family & Community Health, 18*(3), 37–44.

Brider, P. (1996). AJN newsline. *American Journal of Nursing, 96*(6), 72.

Brooks, C. A. (1995). Healthcare organizations. In P. S. Yoder Wise (Ed.), *Leading and managing in nursing* (pp. 130–149). St. Louis: Mosby.

Buhler-Wilkerson, K. (1993). Bringing care to the people: Lillian Wald's legacy to public health nursing. *American Journal of Public Health, 83,* 1778–1786.

Burbach, C. A., & Brown, B. E. (1988). Community health and home health nursing: Keeping the concepts clear. *Nursing & Health Care, 9*(2), 97–100.

Bushy, A. (1995). Rural health. In C. Smith & F. Maurer (Eds.), *Community health nursing: Theory and practice* (pp. 820–847). Philadelphia: Saunders.

Butterfield, P. G. (1993). Thinking upstream: Conceptualizing health from a population perspective. In J. M. Swanson & M.

Albrecht, *Community health nursing: Promoting the health of aggregates* (pp. 67–78). Philadelphia: Saunders.

Clark, M. J. (1996). *Nursing in the community* (2nd ed.). Norwalk, CT: Appleton & Lange.

Congdon, J. G., & Magilvy, J. K. (1995). The changing spirit of rural community nursing: Documentation burden. *Public Health Nursing, 12,* 18–24.

Cookfair, J. M. (1991). *Nursing process and practice in the community.* St. Louis: Mosby-Year Book.

Edelman, C. L., & Mandle, C. L. (1994). *Health promotion throughout the lifespan* (3rd ed.). St. Louis: Mosby.

Friedman, M. M. (1992). *Family nursing: Theory and practice* (3rd ed.). Norwalk, CT: Appleton & Lange.

Gibson, S. J. (1996). Differentiated practice within and beyond the hospital walls. In E. L. Cohen (Ed.), *Nurse case management in the 21st century.* St. Louis: Mosby.

Hanson, C. M. (1996). Care of clients in rural settings. In M. J. Clark (Ed.), *Nursing in the community* (pp. 625–643). Norwalk, CT: Appleton & Lange.

Josten, L., Clarke, P. N., Ostwald, S., Stoskopf, C., & Shannon, M. D. (1995). Public health nursing education: Back to the future for public health sciences. *Family & Community Health, 18*(1), 36–48.

Kenyon, V., Smith, E., Jefty, L., Bell, M., McNeil, J., & Martaus, T. (1990). Clinical competencies for community health nursing. *Public Health Nursing, 7,* 33–39.

Leavell, H. R., & Clark, E. G. (1965). *Preventive medicine for the doctor in his community* (3rd ed.). New York: McGraw-Hill.

Lund, C. O. (1993). Rural health. In J. Swanson & M. Albrecht (Eds.), *Community health nursing: Promoting the health of aggregates.* Philadelphia: Saunders.

Maxfield, M. (1996). Leading the way for rural health. *Rural health focus—Newsletter of the Texas Rural Health Association, 7,* 1–2.

Miller, M. K., Clarke, L. L., Albrecht, S. L., & Farmer, F. L. (1996). The interactive effects of race and ethnicity and mother's residence on the adequacy of prenatal care. *Journal of Rural Health, 12*(1), 6–18.

Monteiro, L. A. (1985). Florence Nightingale on public health nursing. *American Journal of Public Health, 75,* 181–186.

Muecke, M. A. (1984). Community health diagnosis in nursing. *Public Health Nursing, 1*(1), 23–35.

Neufer, L. (1994). The role of the community health nurse in environmental health. *Public Health Nursing, 11,* 155–162.

NRHA adopts 1996 legislative agenda. (1996, March/April). *Rural Health FYI, 18,* 10–13.

Salmon, M. E. (1989). Public health nursing: The neglected specialty. *Nursing Outlook, 37,* 226–229.

Salmon, M. E. (1993). Editorial: Public health nursing—the opportunity of a century. *American Journal of Public Health, 83,* 1674–1675.

Salmon, M. E. (1994). Leadership for change in public and community health nursing. In J. McCloskey & H. Grace (Eds.), *Current issues in nursing* (4th ed.) (pp. 233–240). St. Louis: Mosby.

Smith, C. M. (1995). Origins and future of community health nursing. In C. Smith & F. Maurer (Eds.), *Community health nursing: Theory and practice* (pp. 30–52). Philadelphia: Saunders.

Sommer, A. (1995). Viewpoint on public health's future. *Public Health Reports, 110,* 657–661.

Spradley, B. W., & Allender, J. A. (1996). *Community health nursing: Concepts and practice* (4th ed.). Philadelphia: Lippincott.

Swanson, J. M. (1993). Historical factors: Community health nursing in context. In J. Swanson & M. Albrecht (Eds.), *Community health nursing: Promoting the health of aggregates* (pp. 13–39). Philadelphia: Saunders.

Swanson, J. M., & Albrecht, M. (1993). *Community health nursing: Promoting the health of aggregates.* Philadelphia: Saunders.

Tiedje, L. B., & Wood, J. (1995). Sensitizing nurses for a changing environmental health role. *Public Health Nursing, 12,* 359–365.

U. S. Department of Health and Human Services (USDHHS). (1985). *Consensus conference on the essentials of public health nursing and practice: Report of the conference.* Rockville, MD: USDHHS.

U. S. Department of Health and Human Services (USDHHS), Public Health Service (1990). *Healthy people 2000: National health promotion and disease prevention objectives.* Washington, DC: U. S. Government Printing Office.

U. S. Department of Health and Human Services (USDHHS), Public Health Service (1995). *Healthy people 2000 midcourse review and 1995 revisions.* Washington, DC: U. S. Government Printing Office.

U. S. Office of Technology Assessment (1990). *Health care in rural America* (Publication No. 052-003-01205-7). Washington, DC: U. S. Government Printing Office.

Wallinder, J., White, C., & Salveson, C. (1996). New definitions. *Public Health Nursing, 13,* 81–82.

Ward, D. (1989). Public health nursing and the future of public health. *Public Health Nursing, 6,* 163–168.

Williams, C. A. (1977). Community health nursing—what is it? *Nursing Outlook, 25,* 250–254.

Zerwekh, J. V. (1993). Commentary: Going to the people—public health nursing today and tomorrow. *American Journal of Public Health, 83,* 1676–1678.

Zetzman, M. R. (1995). Telemedicine, POTS and PANS technology and rural health care in Texas. *Texas Journal of Rural Health, xiv* (2nd quarter), 1–4.

BIBLIOGRAPHY

Lancaster, W. (1995). Is there a future for public health? *Family & Community Health, 18*(3), 1–8.

Lee, H. J. (1993). Health perceptions of middle, "new middle," and older rural adults. *Family & Community Health, 16*(1), 19–27.

Lundeen, S. P. (1994). Community nursing centers: Implications for health care reform. In J. McClookey and H. Grace (Eds.), *Current issues in nursing* (pp. 382–387). St. Louis: Mosby.

Reverby, S. M. (1993). Editorial: From Lillian Wald to Hillary Rodham Clinton: What will happen to public health nursing? *American Journal of Public Health, 83,* 1662–1663.

Williams, C. A. (1995). Beyond the Institute of Medicine report: A critical analysis and public health forecast. *Family & Community Health, 18*(1), 12–23.

Chapter 23

NURSING INFORMATICS AND HEALTH MANAGEMENT INFORMATION SYSTEMS

Cassy D. Pollack

CHAPTER OBJECTIVES

On completion of this chapter, the reader will be able to:

1. Define the specialty practice of nursing informatics and the integration of that role within the nursing services of a health-care institution.
2. Define the basic terminology used in nursing informatics.
3. Describe the relationship between nursing informatics and health management information systems.
4. Describe nursing computer and informatics applications used in clinical practice, education, and research.
5. Identify opportunities for interdisciplinary collaboration from an informatics perspective.
6. Describe nursing career opportunities in informatics.

KEY TERMS

Nursing Informatics	Health Management	Nursing Minimum Data
Patient	Information Systems	Set (NMDS)
Client	Computerized Patient	Free-Net
Datum (Data)	Record (CPR)	

A new area of nursing specialization, **nursing informatics,** is most commonly described by Graves and Corcoran's (1989) definition. They define the specialty as "a combination of computer science, information science and nursing science designed to assist in the management and processing of nursing data, information and knowledge to support the practice of nursing and the delivery of nursing care" (p. 227).

The American Nurses Association's (ANA) *Standards of Practice for Nursing Informatics* (American Nurses Association, 1995) incorporated this definition in the development of six comprehensive standards designed to guide informatics practice. These standards include the analysis, design, development, modification, implementation, evaluation, or maintenance of information-handling technologies that do the following:

1. collect patient and client data to support the practice of nursing,
2. use patient and client data to support decision-making,
3. provide for identification of outcomes for patients and clients,
4. develop plans for achieving identified outcomes,
5. document implementation of the plans, and
6. provide for outcome measurement and evaluation (pp. 3–8).

The language used in nursing informatics frequently differentiates between patients and clients. A **patient** is anyone who directly *receives* care, whereas a **client** is anyone who *makes use* of the nursing informatics efforts. Clients include administrators, clinicians, educators, and researchers. In examining the standards of practice, what becomes readily apparent is the broad scope of activities incorporated in an informatics practice.

Certification for this nursing specialty is available through the American Nurses Credentialing Center (Table 23–1).

NURSING INFORMATICS ROLES

The primary interest in nursing informatics is to expand our comprehension of how data, information, and knowledge are used within nursing practice. Experts in nursing informatics focus their efforts on the science of information and knowledge acquisition and the design and evaluation of the systems that process and provide data and information (Graves & Corcoran, 1989; National Center for Nursing Research, 1993). The actual work of informatics

TABLE 23 – 1. Nursing Informatics Certification

The American Nurses Credentialing Center (ANCC) recently began offering certification in the specialty of nursing informatics. The examination encompasses eight main topical areas:

- Systems analysis and design
- System implementation and support
- System testing and evaluation
- Human factors
- Computer technology
- Information/data base management
- Professional practice/trends and issues
- Theories

Source: American Nurses Credentialing Center. (1995). Informatics Nurse Certification Catalog. (p. 5). Washington, DC: ANCC, with permission.

specialists varies across settings, based on organizational needs and the practice interests of the individual. The common element in all functions within the informatics practice is the transformation of data to information, and ultimately to knowledge that supports and advances nursing practice.

Within care delivery institutions such as hospitals, nursing homes, and home health agencies, the nursing informatics specialist could be involved with both the tasks of nursing and improvement of the quality of care. Task-related activities include staffing and scheduling systems, standardization and automation of care plans, and implementation of systems to document the delivery of care. Improvement in the delivery of nursing care includes the refinement of information systems for quality assurance, development of mechanisms to support clinical decisions, and methods of adjusting risk across defined patient groups (Grobe, 1994).

Nursing informatics applications in academic settings encompass the use of technology to assist in teaching, research related to the impact of technology on learning, and the development of new technologies to advance the educational process. As information-age students seek innovative methods of enhancing learning, colleges and universities have become more focused on providing technological support for teaching and learning by incorporating sophisticated computer applications into program and course requirements. Examples of technology used in the classroom are computer-assisted instruction (CAI), teleconferencing, long-distance learning, interactive videodisc simulations, virtual learning, and CD-ROM applications (Hodson, Hanson, & Brigham, 1994; Jones, Skiba, & Phillips, 1994).

The Virtual Hospital (Galvin, 1994) is a complex

application of informatics in the educational setting. This medical multimedia textbook takes full advantage of high-speed computer technology. The user sits at a computer terminal, reads a document, and clicks with a mouse onto icons embedded in the text. These icons are seamlessly constructed links to off-site databases that bring to the screen digitalized audio and visual material. It is an impressive demonstration that allows users to read about the diagnosis of a pulmonary embolism and then see the chest x-ray, CAT scan, and bronchoscope as active videos, and watch open-heart surgical removal of a large embolus. This type of technology, accessible from anywhere in the world at any time of day, offers an entirely new approach to medical and nursing education, featuring diagnostic work from a distance, support for geographically isolated practitioners, and teaching materials available to anyone.

Tools such as these will eventually change how nurses teach, deliver, and communicate nursing care. Nursing students will soon be able to open a file on their home computer and (by clicking on certain icons) view videos of complex procedures, listen to heart sounds, and compare actual radiologic and other diagnostic imagery. This technology is currently awaiting application. Its organizational implications are tremendous. Some institutions may choose to downsize the personnel component of continuing education departments and increase access to this type of resource. Updating professional skills for those residing in isolated areas and requesting expert consultation from clinicians in distant geographic areas are two more applications for this technology.

TRANSFORMATION OF DATA TO INFORMATION AND KNOWLEDGE

The transformation of data to information and knowledge is an important informatics concept. A **datum** (**data** is the plural form) is a value placed on a variable. It exists without meaning or explanation. An example is the weight of a child. The value of the weight, such as 62 pounds, is the datum for the weight. This value has little meaning until it is put into some context along with other data. For instance, if the child were 3 years old, the weight might have one interpretation, but for a 10-year-old child, 62 pounds would mean something very different. Age and weight may not be enough data to offer much information. You also may want to know the child's height, which would allow you to better understand the weight's significance. Data viewed in association with each other provide meaning through the *information* that was not previously available or understood.

Knowledge arises from using information, often from combined sources, to determine new meanings, make new discoveries, or expand understandings. For example, patient diagnoses are reached by transforming combined laboratory data, radiology data, symptomology, and other information into a whole, the outcome of which is knowledge.

Informatics nurses seek to create new knowledge by working first with data and then with information. As stated in the ANA standards, this includes the "identifying, naming, organizing, grouping, collecting, processing, analyzing, storing, retrieving, communicating, transforming, or managing data or information" (ANA, 1995, p. 1). Informatics specialists do not work in isolation. All of their work is intended to support, promote, and advance the delivery of nursing care. Indeed, an informatics nurse is someone who has a specialty practice in nursing, not simply a computer expert who happens to be working on a nursing-related problem.

Some elements of nursing informatics are important for all nurses to understand. The data that are used arise from the processes involved in care delivery. Employing a clinical analogy, it is important for all nurses who provide direct care to have some understanding of diabetes, yet we still use nurse specialists in diabetes to support and promote the care of diabetic patients. Nursing does not function in exclusion of the other clinical, administrative, and managerial health professionals. Nor does nursing informatics exist independently of the larger health information management systems that hospitals, clinics, home health agencies, nursing homes, and health maintenance organizations depend on to manage their various functions.

HEALTH MANAGEMENT INFORMATION SYSTEMS

Management information systems produce and process data so that users can retrieve those data in a manner that creates pertinent managerial information. Both Tan (1995) and Hannah, Ball, and Edwards (1994) differentiate between health management information systems and general management information systems. **Health management information systems** include very specific data and information within the domain of health care. General management information systems include much of the same data and information, however, they lack the unique applications and communication links health-care institutions require.

In the past, management information systems were designed for specific functional units and remained independent of each other. For instance, the admitting, discharging, and transferring system would not have communicated with the laboratory system, or the nursing information systems may have had little or no communication with the financial system. Today's information systems are moving toward a more open design, able to move data among and between various functions and departments to reduce duplication and redundancy within an organization for enhanced efficiency. Bakker (1994) lists five ways to consider the concept of "open design":

- Communicate with other systems
- Extract data for external use
- Import data from external systems into the database
- Use different hardware platforms to run the system
- Accept additional modules from another vendor (p. xxvii)

In addition, as systems become more integrated, opportunities for shared research, joint quality assurance efforts, and a wider range of reporting capabilities become increasingly available.

Tan's (1995) eight elements of a health information management system all concern the acquisition, verification, storage, classification, update, computation, retrieval, and presentation of data, and they show remarkable similarity to the general functions for nursing informatics listed in the ANA Standards (ANA, 1995).

The specific management information needs of health-care institutions differ based on their mode of health-care delivery, third-party payer requirements, accrediting or licensing organizations, and internal reporting protocols. An acute care facility that manages an inpatient facility, an emergency room, operating suites, extensive clinical laboratories, and a large pharmacy is going to have different data and information needs from those of a visiting nurse agency. Currently no one health management information system fits all organizations. This is a significant barrier in developing a uniform patient record, merging patient information across institutions, and functioning in a managed care environment.

Information systems that support nursing must be capable of full integration within the institution health management system, yet also offer nursing the necessary tools to effectively deliver and manage nursing care. Mills (1995) offers a detailed

checklist of issues to consider when selecting, designing, or installing a nursing information system. Examples of such issues or considerations are system capabilities for order entry, updating and managing orders, producing bills or interfacing with billing activities, managing procedures, flexible data entry, patient scheduling, patient care planning, infection control, patient requirements, and nurse staffing and scheduling. The ease with which such a system can be queried is important in making opportunities for quality assurance, quality improvement, and research activities readily available.

Nursing informatics experts are important within a health management information system, as are experts in medical informatics, dental informatics, and pharmacy informatics. They provide the link between understanding the institution's data needs and uses and the needs and uses of data specific to nursing. Many opportunities exist for nurses interested in informatics to participate in programs offered by the National League for Nursing's Council for Nursing Informatics, the American Medical Informatics Association's Nursing Working Group, and the International Medical Informatics Association's Special Interest Group for Nursing. In addition, there are numerous local nursing informatics groups. Newbold and Jaffe (1995) offer an excellent listing of electronic nursing informatics resources for those who may wish to explore "online" contacts and information.

COMPUTERIZED PATIENT RECORDS

An interesting challenge emerging in the development and implementation of health management information systems is the increased need for patient-related information to be communicated and shared across organizations. When patients are referred for home care following hospital discharge, the referral forms are often faxed to the home care agency. Or, if patients are transferred from one hospital to another, the medical record is photocopied or summarized for the receiving institution. The influx of managed care organizations has greatly contributed to the demand for the transmission of health care data. The quality of information that could be used to provide care to those patients would be enhanced by access to the entire previous record, or even to all of the health records maintained over time for that individual.

A major national effort to develop a **computerized patient record (CPR)** has been underway for a number of years, with particular success realized by selected institutions. The CPR is an electronic version of the patient record. The intentions are to increase the ability to share patient-specific information and to create a permanent lifelong health record. The Institute of Medicine (IOM) produced an extensive report on the importance of developing a CPR built on a set of standards shared by all involved parties in both the private and public sectors (Dick & Steen, 1991). It is envisioned that CPRs will not only help in delivery of patient care, but also serve as a link between administrative, bibliographic, clinical knowledge, and research databases. Ultimately, the CPR could become the central element for the entire health management information system (Dick & Steen, 1991; 1992).

Creating a CPR is far more difficult than may at first be apparent. Standardized language, data collection, record format, access, confidentiality, and other ethical issues are but a few of the barriers still impeding the widespread development and use of the CPR. To have a CPR that can be shared across institutions, data must be collected and coded in a similar fashion.

McHugh (1992) raises similar issues in discussing the slow development of the CPR, and adds specific concerns related to nursing. Nursing has never had a common language or taxonomy that all members of the profession agree on as the best choice for depicting and documenting the delivery of nursing care. Extensive international research is currently being conducted to determine a language through which nursing can uniformly describe, capture, and report on nursing care.

NURSING DATA

Nursing uses not only medical terminology but also language unique to nursing practice. The development of nursing taxonomies and agreement about the best approach for describing nursing have long been debated in the profession. The **Nursing Minimum Data Set (NMDS)** developed by Werley and her colleagues (1988) has been supported by the ANA Steering Committee on Databases to Support Council Nursing Practice as the basic set of elements necessary to collect data on nursing practice. This recommendation was passed as a resolution in the 1990 ANA House of Delegates (McCormick et al., 1994). The 16 elements in the NMDS are divided into nursing care items, patient demographic items, and service items. The nursing care items include nursing diagnosis, nursing intervention, nursing outcome, and intensity of nursing care. The patient demographic items include personal identification, date of birth, gender, race and ethnicity, and zip code. The service items include a unique facility or service agency number, a unique health record number for the patient, a unique number of the principal registered nurse provider, admission date, discharge date, discharge disposition, expected payer, and a unique health record number of the patient (Werley & Lang, 1988). All but six of these data elements (the nursing-specific ones and the unique health record number of the patient) are currently captured by the Uniform Hospital Discharge Data Set required of acute care facilities (Ozbolt, Fruchtnight, & Hayden, 1994).

To institute data collection for the NMDS, a nursing language or classification system needs to be in place. The Division of Nursing, the National Institute for Nursing Research (NINR), the Health Care Financing Administration (HCFA), and the National Library of Medicine all support four nursing nomenclatures and recommend that all national databases include them. These are the North American Nursing Diagnosis Association (NANDA), the Omaha System: Applications for Community Health Nursing, the Home Health Care Classification System, and the Nursing Intervention Classification System (McCormick et al., 1994).

Systems for measuring and documenting nursing outcomes and the intensity of nursing practice are not yet well developed. Given the holistic nature of nursing and the complex manner in which nursing care is rendered, it is difficult to capture this work in a form that can be reduced to single data elements to be standardized, reliably measured, and transferred across settings (Graves & Corcoran, 1989). These are some of the challenges facing researchers in nursing informatics.

ADDITIONAL COMPUTER APPLICATIONS

Examples of unique applications for computers and informatics are described in the following text. They certainly do not represent the extent of innovative programs and projects now underway, but are only meant to offer a sampling of the exciting efforts conducted within a nursing informatics framework.

Both Cleveland, Ohio, and Denver, Colorado, have free-nets set up for anyone who wishes access (Skiba & Mirque, 1994). The **free-net** is a computer network of local services established on a citywide basis. The format is modeled on a town, with a school building, a hospital or clinic, a town hall, and other typical city buildings. One electronically "enters" these buildings and can obtain information, leave messages and opinions, ask questions, or join groups. There are support groups on just about any health concern, and both free-nets offer an "ask the nurse" type of forum. These free-nets are supported by public and private dollars, with no charge to the users. Anyone can log on as a guest to any free-net in the world. There are approximately 30 free-nets across the globe, which have the potential of creating a different form of nursing services than have previously been available. They are also becoming rich sources of data for various nursing research efforts. In 1987, the School of Nursing at the Colorado Health Sciences Center implemented an electronic bulletin board called NurseLink, which is connected to the Denver Free-Net. The center uses NurseLink as a tool for disseminating nursing research to local clinical sites (Skiba & Mirque, 1994).

Another innovative application is AIDSNET, a computerized AIDS support network developed by the Decker School of Nursing in Binghamton, New York (Parietti & Atav, 1994). This network provides nursing consultation, social support, and case management to persons who are either HIV positive or have AIDS. Designed as a bulletin board system, AIDSNET is available 24 hours a day, 7 days a week, at no charge to the users. Analysis of the postings shows users to be seeking social support, illness support, and information on treatment protocols. Nurses have been instrumental in initiating and developing opportunities through which AIDS patients can access unconventional modes of health care.

The University of Virginia, in collaboration with community agencies, established the Jefferson Area Rural Elder Health Consortium, a database system designed to manage a nursing outreach program for rural elderly individuals (Currie & Abraham, 1994). They had 514 unique variables that were used to track the activities and care for a complex group of patients who received not only full nursing assessment and case management but also community-based services, informal care, and volunteer efforts. The database was designed to allow nurses to monitor the patients' status and provide extensive data for research purposes. Thirteen different forms, surveys, and indices are included in this database.

Brennan and her colleagues established unique nursing interventions in their research on the use of computers in clients' homes, coupled with personal electronic communication, a computerized decision

support system, and online information resources for persons with AIDS and caregivers of Alzheimer's patients (Brennan and Ripich, 1994; Brennan and Smyth, 1994). She has been studying not only how individuals use computers placed in their home to access information and resources, but also what effect the medium has on decision-making skills.

CAREERS IN NURSING INFORMATICS

It is becoming more evident that the diversity of informatics projects and programs leads to tremendous professional career opportunities. Managers in the rapidly changing health-care environment are demanding more and more information, patients are receiving care in many settings, and organizations are reengineering how they define their services and provide care. All of these changes mean continued growth for nursing and general health information systems and the creation of new positions in nursing informatics.

Many of the future informatics jobs are yet to be defined. As the technology changes, so too will the work necessary to maintain and further the acquisition of information and knowledge. Currently, informatics nurses are working in health-care organizations, for software and hardware vendors, in educational settings, and for insurance companies, to name only a few. In any position, the informatics specialist works closely with professionals from all other health-care disciplines.

Positions in Health-Care Organizations

A variety of roles exist for the specialist in nursing informatics within hospitals, home health agencies, nursing homes, and other health-care institutions. As organizations implement information systems, informatics nurses serve an important function in assessing the institution's information needs, evaluating available products and vendors, and assisting with product installations. There are often ongoing needs for liaison between the nursing staff and the information systems people, a service well handled by a nursing informatics specialist.

Many health-care organizations, particularly hospitals, are undergoing restructuring. As work is redefined, units reconfigured, and services redefined, the nursing informatics expert has many opportunities to work with the data needed to handle staffing and scheduling changes and productivity measures, to establish databases for quality assurance and quality improvement, and to provide training on system changes for new users. The increasing use of computer-aided educational tools offers a whole array of possibilities for developing patient and staff education programs. The role of chief information officer is certainly one that could be held by a specialist in nursing informatics.

Positions with Systems and Software Vendors

Many of the producers of software and information systems seek to hire nursing informatics specialists. Nurses work in the development of new products, marketing of products and services, and installation of systems. Nursing informatics experts serve as liaisons between the vendor and the health-care organization, because they are able to articulate the issues for both parties.

Positions in Educational Settings

The integration of computers and computerized learning applications is now a reality in a cross-section of educational settings. Nursing informatics experts are developing new computer-aided instruction programs and teaching faculty about using and incorporating computer applications in course work and other programmatic offerings. A promising shift in the number of computer-literate nurses and nursing educators is well underway and appears to be shaping the next generation of nursing professionals. Nursing informatics itself is becoming more common as a subject in curricula on both the undergraduate and graduate levels. Only a few schools in the country currently offer master's and doctoral preparation in nursing informatics, but that number continues to grow. Research efforts regarding nursing language and taxonomy, the uses of databases, expert decision making, and artificial intelligence applications are being led by nursing informatics researchers.

Positions in Managed Care Organizations and Insurance Companies

As forms of managed care continue to develop, the demand for data and information will increase, as will the opportunities for informatics specialists. Informatics nurses are now working directly with care delivery institutions in developing data and information systems, and with the mechanisms involved in the internal reporting processes. New roles are emerging continuously, many of which have been designed and articulated by the informatics nurse as this burgeoning new specialty evolves.

Defining and describing the evolving and expanding nature of the nursing informatics specialty promises to be a constantly changing process. The process is linked to the rapid advances in technology and the needs of health-care patients and clients. The challenges confronting the field of informatics reflect the issues facing all of health care. Significant challenges awaiting the attention of informatics specialists include identifying and testing methods for tracking and managing patients across settings, exploring systems that allow information sharing with other institutions, dealing with advances in telemedicine, enabling long-distance education, fostering the delivery of care in nontraditional sites and nontraditional ways, and engaging in the continued introduction of more sophisticated computer systems.

FINDING MORE INFORMATION

Information on hardware, software, or the complexities of networking systems can be found in any introductory computer science textbook. In addition, many books and articles on computing resources are specifically written for nurses, and some references are included in the bibliography at the end of this chapter.

KEY POINTS

- Nursing informatics combines knowledge in computer science, information science, and nursing science.
- The role of the informatics specialist includes the analysis, design, development, modification, evaluation, and maintenance of information and the technology needed to acquire that information and transform it to knowledge to further the practice of nursing and the delivery of nursing care.
- Nursing informatics is one component of a health management information system.

- Nursing informatics specialists work in collaboration with all other health-care professionals in many settings.
- The Minimum Nursing Data Set (NMDS) is one important attempt to define those nursing and patient data elements that are critical for the creation of a nursing-focused information system.
- The computerized patient record (CPR) is in various stages of development across health-care facilities. Nursing informatics specialist can offer valuable input in the development and application of a CPR, particularly as it relates to nursing-specific data, information used in the delivery of nursing care, and ethical considerations in the implementation and evaluation of a CPR.
- A number of innovative nursing care applications have been instituted by nursing informatics specialists, such as the free-net. Nursing informatics specialists will be the creators of new techniques for identifying potential clients, communicating with patients, and establishing ongoing methods of providing nursing care.

CHAPTER EXERCISES

1. Interview someone in a hospital management information system department and ask: (a) What kinds of data are collected? (b) What types of reports are routinely generated? and (c) What are the future plans for information systems in the hospital? Now interview someone in nursing administration and ask the same types of questions. Compare and contrast your findings. What recommendations would you make for their information system based on what you have learned?

2. Obtain a medical record for a hospitalized patient and for a home health-care patient. Review all of the information contained in the records. Identify the major data elements in the records. How do the records differ? If you were to design a computerized version of the records, what would the major considerations be?

3. Interview a hospital risk manager, a risk manager in a physician's office, an attorney, a medical record (or clinical information) specialist, a staff nurse, an advanced practice nurse, a nursing professor, and a patient regarding the following:

   From their perspective, what are the most important issues related to the development and use of a CPR?

   What ethical issues do they consider important in developing and using a CPR?

   From the results of your interviews, write a brief argument for and against the further development and use of a computerized patient record.

REFERENCES

American Nurses Association. (1995). *Standards of practice for nursing informatics*. Washington, DC: ANA.

American Nurses Credentialing Center. (1995). *Informatics nurse certification catalog*. Washington, DC: ANCC.

Bakker, A. R. (1994). "Open system: Perspective or fata morgana?" Paper presented at the Fifth IMIA International Confer-ence on Nursing Use and Information Science: Nursing Informatics: An International Overview for Nursing in a Technological Era, San Antonio, TX.

Brennan, P. F., & Ripich, S. (1994). Use of a home-care computer network by persons with AIDS. *International Journal of Technology Assessment in Health Care, 10* (2), 258–272.

Brennan, P. F., & Smyth, K. (1994). Elders' attitudes and behavior regarding ComputerLink. *Proceedings/The Annual Symposium on Computer Applications in Medical Care,* 1011.

Currie, L. J., & Abraham, I. L. (1994). "Where high-tech and high-touch meet: A custom-designed database system for a nursing outreach program to rural elderly." Paper presented at the Fifth IMIA International Conference on Nursing Use and Information Science: Nursing Informatics: An International Overview for Nursing in a Technological Era, San Antonio, TX.

Dick, R. S., & Steen, E. B. (1991). *The computer-based patient record: An essential technology for health care.* Washington, DC: National Academy Press.

Dick, R. S., & Steen, E. B. (1992). Essential technologies for computer-based patient records: A summary. In M. J. Ball & M. F. Collen (Eds.), *Aspects of the computer-based patient record* (pp. 229–261). New York: Springer-Verlag.

Galvin, J. R. (1994, October 30–November 3). "The virtual hospital: The future of information distribution in medicine." Paper presented at the Symposium on Computer Applications in Medical Care: Patient-Centered Computing, Washington, DC.

Graves, J. R. & Corcoran, S. (1989). The study of nursing informatics. *Image: Journal of Nursing Scholarship, 21*(4), 227–231.

Grobe, S. J. (1994). Nursing informatics: State of the science. In J. H. van Bemmel & A. T. McCray (Eds.), *Yearbook 94 of medical informatics: Advanced communication in health care.* Stuttgart: Schattauer.

Hannah, K. J., Ball, M. J., & Edwards, M. J. A. (1994). *Introduction to nursing informatics.* New York: Springer-Verlag.

Hodson, K., Hanson, A., & Brigham, C. (1994, June 17–22). "Development of technological access to RN degree-completion students at distant learning sites." Paper presented at the Fifth IMIA International Conference on Nursing Use and Information Science: Nursing Informatics: An International Overview for Nursing in a Technological Era, San Antonio, TX.

Jones, A., Skiba, D. J., & Phillips, S. (1994, June 17–22). "Creating a twenty-first century learning lab environment for nursing." Paper presented at the Fifth IMIA International Conference on Nursing Use and Information Science: Nursing Informatics: An International Overview for Nursing in a Technological Era, San Antonio, TX.

McCormick, K. A., Lany, N., Zielstorff, R., Milholland, D. K., Saba, V., & Jacox, A. (1994). Toward standard classification schemes for nursing language: Recommendations of the American Nurses Association Steering Committee on Databases to Support Clinical Practice. *Journal of American Medical Informatics, 1*(6), 421–427.

McHugh, M. L. (1992). Nurses' needs for computer-based patient records. In M. J. Ball & M. F. Collen (Eds.), *Aspects of the computer-based patient record* (pp. 16–29). New York: Springer-Verlag.

Mills, M. E. (1995). Order communications/Nursing system requirements questionnaire. In M. J. Ball, K. J. Hannah, S. K. Newbold, & J. V. Douglas (Eds.), *Nursing informatics: Where caring and technology meet* (2nd ed.) (pp. 365–374). New York: Springer-Verlag.

National Center for Nursing Research. (1993). *Nursing informatics: Enhancing patient care* (NIH Publication No. 93-2419). Bethesda, MD: National Center for Nursing Research.

Newbold, S. K., & Jaffe, M. (1995). Electronic resources for nursing. In M. J. Ball, K. J. Hannah, S. K. Newbold, & J. V. Douglas (Eds.), *Nursing informatics: Where caring and technology meet* (2nd ed.) (pp. 54–68). New York: Springer-Verlag.

Ozbolt, J. G., Fruchtnight, J. N., & Hayden, J. R. (1994). Toward data standards for clinical nursing information. *Journal of the American Medical Informatics Association, 1*(2), 175–185.

Parietti, E. S., & Atav, A. S. (1994). AIDSNET: An innovative strategy of nursing outreach. In S. J. Grobe & E. S. P. Pluyter-Wenting (Eds.), *Nursing informatics: An international overview for nursing in a technological era* (p. 816). New York: Elsevier.

Skiba, D. J., & Mirque, D. T. (1994). "The electronic community: An alternative health care approach." Paper presented at the Fifth IMIA International Conference on Nursing Use and Information Science: Nursing Informatics: An International Overview for Nursing in a Technological Era, San Antonio, TX.

Tan, J. K. H. (1995). *Health management information systems: Theories, methods, and applications.* Gaithersburg, MD: Aspen Publishers.

Werley, H. H. (1988). Introduction of the nursing minimum data set and its development. In H. H. Werley & N. M. Lang (Eds.), *Identification of the nursing minimum data set* (pp. 1–21). New York: Springer.

Werley, H. H., & Lang, N. M. (1988). The consensually derived nursing minimum data set: Elements and definitions. In H. H. Werley & N. M. Lang (Eds.), *Identification of the nursing minimum data set* (pp. 402–411). New York: Springer.

BIBLIOGRAPHY

American Nurses Association. (1992). *Computers in nursing research: A theoretical perspective.* Washington, DC: American Nurses Association.

Arnold, J. M., & Pearson, G. A. (Eds.). (1992). *Computer application in nursing education and practice* (Pub. No. 14-2406). New York: National League for Nursing.

Ball, M. J., & Collen, M. F. (1992). *Aspects of the computer-based patient record.* New York: Springer-Verlag.

Hannah, K. J., Ball, M. J., & Edwards, M. J. A. (1994). *Introduction to nursing informatics.* New York; Springer-Verlag.

Saba, V. K., Rieder, K. A., & Pocklington, D. B. (Eds.). (1989). *Nursing and computers: An anthology.* New York: Springer-Verlag.

Section VI

NURSES WITH VISION

Chapter 24

PROFESSIONAL ETHICS

Joseph T. Catalano

CHAPTER OBJECTIVES

On completion of
this chapter, the reader
will be able to:

1. Analyze and define the key terms used in ethics.
2. Distinguish between the two primary systems used in ethical decision making.
3. Apply the steps of the ethical decision-making model in resolving ethical dilemmas.
4. Analyze and discuss the key ethical principles involved in (a) organ transplantation, (b) end of life decisions, (c) advanced directives, and (d) staffing and delegation.

KEY TERMS

Autonomy	Obligations	Normative Ethics
Justice	Legal Obligations	Utilitarianism
Distributive Justice	Moral Obligations	Deontology
Fidelity	Rights	Code of Ethics
Beneficence	Welfare Rights	Euthanasia
Nonmaleficence	Ethical Rights	Advanced Directives
Veracity	Option Rights	Restructuring
Standard of Best Interest		

A s a registered nurse who has been in professional practice for some years, you are aware of the many changes that are occurring in the current health-care system, such as rapid advances in technology, changes in health-care delivery systems, decreased personalization of health care, and increasing costs. You have also likely encountered some of the difficult ethical dilemmas associated with these changes. By definition, ethical dilemmas present problems that defy a simple solution (Catalano, 1991).

If you are the graduate of a typical associate degree or diploma nursing program, the curriculum of your school probably had little if any content on professional ethics and ethical decision making. For some reason, many nursing education programs presume that students are able to resolve ethical dilemmas from their past experiences and home moral training. As a result, many nurses faced with difficult ethical dilemmas attempt to deal with them in several less-than-satisfactory ways (French, 1991). They may decide to do nothing at all, with the hopes that the problem will resolve itself or someone else will solve it. If that fails, some nurses may use the "it just feels right" technique, choosing the solution that produces the lowest degree of internal discomfort (Catalano, 1995).

In truth, ethical decision making is a skill that can be learned just like any skill, such as inserting a catheter, starting an IV, or writing a nursing diagnosis (Thompson & Thompson, 1985; Jameton, 1984). And as with any learned skill, the more you practice it, the more proficient you become.

ETHICAL PRINCIPLES

Although no two ethical dilemmas are exactly alike, when you begin to analyze them, you will find a few key ethical principles that seem to reoccur and often serve as the underpinnings for very different situations. At the heart of the dilemma is often a conflict between one or more of these basic principles (Davis & Aroskar, 1978). Understanding what the principle is and how it relates to the client's situation is the beginning of resolving the dilemma.

Autonomy is the right of self-determination, independence, and freedom. Autonomy refers to the clients' right to make health-care decisions for themselves, even if you do not agree with those decisions (Mappes & Zembaty, 1991).

Autonomy, as with most rights, is not absolute, and under certain conditions, limitations can be imposed on it. Generally, these limitations occur when one individual's autonomy interferes with others' rights, health, or well-being. For example, a client can generally use his or her right to autonomy by refusing any or all treatments. However, in the case of contagious diseases that affect society, such as tuberculosis (TB), the individual can be forced by the health-care and legal systems to take medications to cure the disease (Aiken & Catalano, 1994). The individual can also be forced into isolation, to prevent the spread of the disease.

Justice is the obligation to be fair to all people. The concept is often expanded to what is called **distributive justice,** or social justice, which refers to the individual's right to be treated equally regardless of race, sex, marital status, medical diagnosis, social standing, economic level, or religious belief (Thompson & Thompson, 1989). The principle of justice underlies the first statement in the ANA Code for Nurses: "The nurse provides services with respect for human dignity and the uniqueness of the client unrestricted by considerations of social or economic status, personal attributes, or the nature of health problems" (ANA, 1985). Distributive justice sometimes includes ideas such as equal access to health care for all citizens. As with other rights, limits can be placed on justice when it interferes with the rights of others.

Fidelity is the obligation to be faithful to commitments made to yourself and others. In health care, fidelity includes your faithfulness or loyalty to agreements and responsibilities accepted as part of the practice of the profession. Fidelity is the main support for the concept of accountability, although conflicts in fidelity might arise from obligations to different individuals or groups (Dohney, Cook, & Stopper, 1987). For example, a nurse who is just finishing a very busy and tiring 12-hour shift may experience a conflict of fidelity when she is asked by a supervisor to work an additional shift because the unit is understaffed. The nurse would have to weigh her fidelity to herself against fidelity to the employing institution and fidelity to the profession and clients to do the best job possible, particularly if she felt that her fatigue would interfere with the performance of those obligations.

Beneficence is a very old requirement for health-care providers that views the primary goal of health care as doing good for clients under their care (Catalano, 1991). In general, the term "good" means more that just technically competent care for clients. Good care requires a holistic approach to the client, including his or her beliefs, feelings, and wishes as well as those of the family and significant others. The main problem you will encounter in implementing the principle of beneficence is determining exactly what is good for another and who can best make the decision about this good.

Nonmaleficence requires that health-care providers do no harm to their clients, either intentionally or unintentionally. In a sense, it is the opposite side of the coin of beneficence, and it is difficult to speak of one concept without the other. In current health-care practice, the principle of nonmaleficence is often violated in the short run to produce a greater good in the long-term treatment of the client (Quinn & Smith, 1987). For example, a client may undergo a very painful and debilitating surgery to remove a cancerous growth that will prolong her or his life in the long term.

By extension, the principle of nonmaleficence also requires you to protect those from harm who cannot protect themselves. This protection from harm is particularly important in such groups as children, the mentally incompetent, the unconscious, and those who are too weak or debilitated to protect themselves, such as the frail elderly. For example, very strict regulations have developed to deal with medication experimentation with groups such as the mentally handicapped, children, and prisoners (Fiesta, 1988).

Veracity is the principle of "truthfulness." It requires you to tell the truth, and not intentionally deceive or mislead clients. As with other rights and obligations, there are limitations to this principle. The primary limitation is when telling the client the truth would seriously harm (principle of nonmaleficence) his or her ability to recover or produce greater illness. You may often feel uncomfortable giving clients "bad news," and may avoid answering their questions truthfully. Feeling uncomfortable is not a good enough reason to avoid telling clients the truth about their diagnosis, treatments, or prognosis. Clients have a right to know this information.

Standard of best interest involves decisions made about clients' health care when they are unable to make informed decisions about their own care. The standard of best interest is based on what the health-care provides and the family decide is best for that individual (Aiken & Catalano, 1994). It is very important that you consider the individual's expressed wishes, either formally in a written declaration (such as a living will) or informally in what may have been said to family members.

The standard of best interest should be based on the principle of beneficence. Unfortunately, in situations in which clients are unable to make decisions for themselves, the dilemma may be resolved by a unilateral decision made by the health-care providers.

Unilateral decisions that disregard the clients' wishes, implying that the health-care providers alone know what is best, are examples of paternalism.

Obligations are demands made on individuals, professions, society, or government to fulfill and honor the rights of others. Obligations are often divided into two categories:

Legal obligations are those that have become formal statements of law and are enforceable under the law. For example, you have a legal obligation to provide safe and adequate care for clients to whom you are assigned.

Moral obligations are based on moral or ethical principles, but are NOT enforceable under the law. For example, if you are on vacation and encounter an automobile accident, you have no legal obligation, but as a nurse you have a strong moral obligation to stop and help the victims.

Rights are generally defined as something due to an individual according to just claims, legal guarantees, or moral and ethical principles. Although the term "right" is frequently used in both the legal and ethical systems, its meaning is often blurred in everyday usage. Individuals tend to claim things as rights that are really privileges, concessions, or freedoms. Several classification systems for rights delineate different types of rights. The following three types of rights are included in most of these systems:

Welfare rights (also called *legal rights*) are based on a legal entitlement to some good or benefit. These rights are guaranteed by laws (such as the Bill of Rights) and, if violated, can come under the power of the legal system. For example, citizens of the United States have a right to equal access to employment regardless of race, sex, or religion.

Ethical rights (also called *moral rights*) are based on a moral or ethical principle. Ethical rights usually do not have the power of law to be enforced. Ethical rights are, in reality, often privileges allotted to certain individuals or groups of individuals. Over time, popular acceptance of ethical rights can give them the force of a legal right. For example, in America and South Africa, the right to health care is really a long-standing privilege whereas in many other industrialized countries it is a legal right.

Option rights are based on a fundamental belief in the dignity and freedom of human beings. Option rights are particularly evident in free and democratic countries such as the United States, and much less evident in totalitarian and restrictive societies such as Iraq. Option rights give individuals freedom of choice and the right to live their lives as they choose, but within a set of prescribed boundaries. For example, in America, you may wear whatever clothes you choose, as long as you do wear some type of clothing.

TWO ETHICAL SYSTEMS

Every time you interact with a client in a health-care setting, an ethical situation exists. You may not realize it, but you are continually making ethical decisions in your daily practice. This is known as **normative ethics.** Normative ethical decisions deal with questions and dilemmas requiring a choice of actions in which the rights or obligations of the nurse and the client, the nurse and the client's family, or the nurse and the physician conflict. In resolving these ethical questions, you are probably using one of two, or perhaps a combination of two or more, ethical systems.

The two fundamental systems most used in health care–related ethical decision making are utilitarianism and deontology (Catalano, 1992). Both systems apply to "bioethics"—the ethics of life (or death, in some cases). "Bioethics" and "bioethical issues" are terms that are in common use, which have become synonymous with health-care ethics, including not only questions of life and death, but also questions of quality of life, life-sustaining and -altering technologies, and bioscience in general (Catalano, 1994). It is in this context of bioethics that the following discussion of these two ethical systems is undertaken.

Utilitarianism

ETHICAL PRECEPTS

Utilitarianism (also called teleology, consequentialism, or situation ethics) is defined as the ethical system of utility. As a system of normative ethics, utilitarianism defines "good" as happiness or pleasure. It is based on two underlying principles. The first is principle of "The greatest good for the greatest number." The second principle is "The end justifies the means." Based on these two principles, utilitarianism is sometimes subdivided into rule utilitarianism and act utilitarianism. According to *rule utilitarianism,* you draw on your past experiences to formulate internal rules that are useful in determining the greatest good. With *act utilitarianism,* the particular situation that you find yourself in determines the rightness or wrongness of a particular act. In practice, the true follower

of utilitarianism does not believe in the validity of any system of rules, because the rules change depending on the circumstances surrounding the decision to be made (O'Rourke & Brodeur, 1989).

Situation ethics is probably the most publicized form of act utilitarianism. Joseph Fletcher, one of the best known proponents of act utilitarianism, outlines a method of ethical thinking in which the situation determines whether the act is morally right or wrong. Fletcher views acts as good to the extent that they promote happiness and wrong to the degree that they promote unhappiness. Happiness is defined as the happiness of the greatest number of people, yet the happiness of each person has equal weight (Fletcher, 1966). For example, abortion is considered ethical in this system in a situation where an unwed welfare mother with four other children becomes pregnant with her fifth child. The greatest good and the greatest amount of happiness may be produced by aborting this unwanted child, for whom this mother can not provide adequate food or care.

Based on the concept that moral rules should not be arbitrary but serve a purpose, ethical decisions derived from a utilitarian framework weigh the effect of alternative actions that influence the overall welfare of present and future populations. As such, this system is oriented toward the good of the population in general, and the individual as he or she participates in that population.

Advantages

The major advantage of the utilitarian system of ethical decision making is that many individuals find it easy to use in most situations. Utilitarianism is built around an individual's own happiness needs in which he or she has an immediate and vested knowledge. Another advantage is that utilitarianism fits well into a society that shuns rules and regulations. The follower of utilitarianism can justify many decisions based on the "happiness" principle. Its utility orientation also fits well into Western society's belief in the work ethic and the behavioristic approach to education, philosophy, and life.

For example, the follower of utilitarianism holds to a general prohibition against lying and deceiving because ultimately, truth telling will lead to more happiness than lying. Yet truth telling is not an absolute requirement to the follower of utilitarianism. If telling the truth would produce widespread unhappiness for a great number of people and future generations, then it would be ethically better to tell a lie that would yield more happiness than to tell the truth that would lead to unhappiness. Although such behavior might appear to be unethical at first glance, the follower of strict act utilitarianism would have little difficulty in arriving at this decision as logical.

DISADVANTAGES

Utilitarianism has some serious limitations as a system of health-care ethics or bioethics. An immediate question is whether "happiness" refers to the average happiness of all or the total happiness of a few? Because individual happiness is also important, you must consider how to make decisions when the individual's happiness conflicts with the larger group's happiness. More fundamental is the question of what constitutes "happiness." Similarly, what constitutes the "greatest good for the greatest number?" Who determines what is "good" in the first place? Is it society in general? the government? governmental policy? the individual? In health-care delivery and the formulation of health-care policy, the general guiding principle often seems to be the greatest good for the greatest number. Yet where do minority groups, such as African-Americans or Native Americans, fit into this system?

The "ends justify the means" principle has also been historically rejected as a method of justifying actions. It is generally unacceptable to allow any type of action as long as the final goal or purpose is good. The Nazis used this aphorism to justify a variety of actions that may be viewed by others as less than "good."

The other difficulty in determining what is good lies in the attempt to quantify such concepts as "good," "harm," "benefits," and "greatest." This problem becomes especially acute when dealing with health-care issues that involve individuals' lives. For example, an elderly family member has been sick for a long period of time, and that illness has placed great financial hardship on her family. It would be ethical under utilitarianism to allow this client to die, or even euthanize her, to relieve the financial stress created by her illness.

The use of utilitarianism as an ethician system in health-care decision making requires additional principle of distributive justice as an ultimate guiding point. Unfortunately, whenever you combine an unchanging principle with this system, you negate the basic concept of pure utilitarianism. Pure utilitarianism, though easy to use as a general decision-making system, does not always work well as an ethical decision-making system in health care because of its arbitrary, self-centered nature. In the everyday delivery of health care, utilitarianism is often combined with other types of ethical decision making to resolve ethical dilemmas.

Deontology

ETHICAL PRECEPTS

Deontology is a system of ethical decision making based on moral rules and unchanging principles. This system is also called the formalistic system, the principle system of ethics, or duty-based ethics. A follower of a pure deontological system of ethical decision making believes in the ethical absoluteness of principles, regardless of the consequences of the decision. This strict adherence to an ethical theory in which the moral rightness or wrongness of human actions is considered separately from the consequences is based on a fundamental principle called the categorical imperative. It is not the results of the act that make it right or wrong, but the principles on which the act is based. These fundamental principles are ultimately unchanging and absolute and are derived from the universal values that underlie all major religions. The concern for right and wrong in the moral sense is the basic premise of the system. Deontology's goal is the survival of the species and social cooperation. The deontological system is also divided into rule deontology and act deontology.

Rule deontology is based on the belief that there are standards for the ethical choices and judgments made by individuals. These standards are fixed and do not change when the situation changes. Although the number of standards or rules is potentially unlimited, in reality, and particularly in dealing with bioethical issues, many of these principles can be grouped together into a few general or cover principles. These principles can also be arranged into a type of hierarchy of rules including such maxims as "Persons should always be treated as ends and never as means"; "Human life has value"; "One is always to tell the truth"; "Above all in health care, do no harm"; "The human person has a right to self-determination"; "All persons are of equal value" and so on. These principles echo such fundamental documents as the Bill of Rights and the Hospital Patient's Bill of Rights.

Act deontology places the highest value on the moral values of the individual. It requires that you make the same decision in any similar situation, regardless of time, place, individuals involved, or external circumstances. Act deontology does not depend on unchanging external rules as rule deontology does. Rather, you obtain all the data you can about the dilemma, then make the decision. The decision (act) makes it correct simply because it was made. For example, a community health nurse working in a prenatal clinic believes that birth control methods are moral, and therefore gives birth control information and pills to a sexually active teenager. The nurse would also give the same types of information to the next sexually active teenager who came into the clinic for care, without regard to the teenager's beliefs or background.

ADVANTAGES

Rule deontology is useful in making ethical decisions in health care because it holds that an ethical judgment you make is based on principles that will be the same in a variety of similar situations, regardless of time, location, or particular individuals involved. In addition, deontological terminology and concepts are similar to the terms and concepts used by the legal system. The legal system stresses rights and duties, principles, and rules. But there are significant differences between the two. Legal rights and duties are enforceable under the law, whereas ethical rights and duties usually are not. In general, ethical systems are much wider and more inclusive than the system of laws they underlie. It is difficult to have an ethical perspective on law without it leading to an interest in making laws that govern health care and nursing practice. When you evaluate and work to change laws from an ethical perspective, you should no longer be placed in situations in which your practice is unsupported by the legal system (Thompson & Thompson, 1985).

DISADVANTAGES

The deontological system of ethical decision making is not perfect. Some of the more troubling questions are "What do you do when the basic guiding principles conflict with each other?" "What is the source of the principles?" and "Is there ever a situation in which an exception to the rule applies?"

Although various approaches have been proposed to circumvent these limitations, it may be difficult for nurses to resolve situations in which duties and obligations conflict, particularly when the consequences of following a rule end in harm to a client. In reality, there are probably few followers of pure deontology, because most people do consider the consequences of their actions in the decision-making process.

Act deontology negates the underlying philosophy of the deontological system, and is difficult to use in resolving ethical dilemmas because of its lack of rules. It requires you to judge each situation individually and arrive at the same decision in similar cases. You may not have the time or energy to thoroughly analyze each situation you encounter in providing care to clients.

APPLYING ETHICAL THEORIES

Ethical theories do not provide you with cookbook solutions for resolving ethical dilemmas. Instead, they give you a framework for decision making, which you can apply to individual ethical situations.

At times, you may find ethical theories too abstract or general to be of much use in specific ethical situations. Without them, however, ethical decision making often becomes an exercise in personal emotions. Many nurses attempting to make ethical decisions use elements from both of the two theories presented here.

THE DECISION-MAKING MODEL IN ETHICS

Nurses, by definition, are problem solvers, and one of the important tools regularly used in problem solving is the nursing process. The nursing process is, if nothing else, a systematic, step by step, approach to resolving problems that deal with a client's health and well-being.

Although you routinely deal with problems related to the physical or psychological needs of clients, you may feel inadequate when dealing with their ethical problems. No matter what the health-care setting, however, you can develop the decision-making skills necessary to make sound ethical decisions if they learn and practice using an ethical decision-making model.

An ethical decision-making model provides a method for answering key questions about ethical dilemmas and organizing your thinking more logically and sequentially. Although several ethical decision-making models exist, the problem-solving method presented here is based on the nursing process. It should be a relatively easy transition for you to move from the nursing process used in resolving clients' physical problems to the ethical decision-making model to resolve ethical problems.

The chief goal of the ethical decision-making model is to determine right from wrong in situations with no clear or readily apparent demarcations. This process presupposes that a system of ethics exists, that you know what the basic ethical principles are, and that the system applies to similar ethical decision-making problems, despite multiple variables. At some point, you need to undertake the task of clarifying your own values, if you have not done it already (Figure 24–1). You also need an understanding of the possible ethical systems that may be used in making decisions about ethical dilemmas (Catalano, 1991).

The following five-step ethical decision-making model is presented as a tool for resolving ethical dilemmas (Table 24–1).

Step 1. Collect, Analyze, and Interpret the Data. Obtain as much information as possible concerning the particular ethical dilemma you are facing. Unfortunately, information is sometimes very limited. Among the issues important for you to know are the client's wishes, the family's wishes, the extent of the physical

or emotional problems causing the dilemma, the physician's beliefs about health care, and your own orientation to life-and-death issues.

For example, many nurses must deal with the question of whether or not to initiate resuscitation efforts when a terminally ill client is admitted to the hospital. Physicians often leave verbal instructions indicating that you really should not resuscitate the client, but merely go through the motions to make the family feel better. Your dilemma becomes whether to seriously attempt to revive the client or let him or her die quietly.

Important information that would help you make the best decision include the mental competency of the client to make a no resuscitation decision, the client's desires, the family's feelings, and whether the physician sought input from the client and family before leaving his orders. Many institutions have policies concerning no resuscitation orders, and you should consider these in the data collection stage.

PART I — Rank the following from 1 to 5, with 1 being the item with the highest priority and 5 being the item with lowest priority.

A. A hospital must cut back its budget or go bankrupt. Which of the following clients should be given priority for care?
_____ A newborn with multiple birth defects who is likely to be retarded for life.
_____ A 47-year-old male scientist with an acute MI who has just discovered a new medication that might cure HIV.
_____ An 88-year-old retired female grade-school teacher who was recently diagnosed with liver cancer.
_____ A 17-year-old runaway who is addicted to cocaine and is pregnant.
_____ A 58-year-old construction worker who has severe emphysema due to his 2½ pack a day smoking habit.

B. The nurse assigned to a client who has a bleeding ulcer secondary to stress. Which aspects of his care would receive highest priority?
_____ Give him pain medications to make him comfortable.
_____ Explain the relationship between stress and ulcers.
_____ Involve him as much as possible in his self-care.
_____ Encourage him to talk about his job, family, etc.
_____ Teach him about diet and medication to control ulcers.

PART II — Rate the following statements on a scale of 1 to 5.
(1 = strongly support; 2 = support; 3 = no opinion; 4 = reject; 5 = strongly reject).
_____ 1. Abortion is always wrong, no matter what the circumstances.
_____ 2. People who receive the death penalty deserve it.
_____ 3. Life support should be terminated for clients when they are not likely to live.
_____ 4. Street drugs should be made legal.
_____ 5. Prisoners, genetically defective, and mentally retarded persons should be sterilized.
_____ 6. Premature, drug addicted newborns should be allowed to die.
_____ 7. Condoms should be given out in high schools to prevent pregnancy and HIV.
_____ 8. All hospitalized clients should be routinely screened for HIV and AIDS.
_____ 9. Scientists should be allowed to use aborted fetuses for fetal tissue research.
_____ 10. All newborn infants should be genetically screened for inherited diseases.

FIGURE 24-1. Values clarification tool.

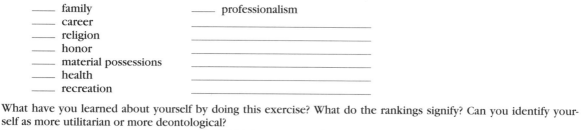

PART III — Complete the following sentences.

1. The one thing I have always wanted to do is _____
2. If I just inherited 5 million dollars, I would _____
3. As president of the United States, I would _____
4. If I died today, I would like my obituary to say _____
5. If I could control the world and its destiny, I would _____

PART IV — Below is a partial list of things people value. Complete the list, then rank each item from 1 (highest value) to ? being the lowest value.

____ family	____ professionalism
____ career	_____
____ religion	_____
____ honor	_____
____ material possessions	_____
____ health	_____
____ recreation	_____

What have you learned about yourself by doing this exercise? What do the rankings signify? Can you identify yourself as more utilitarian or more deontological?
How do they feel about your ethical standards? high, average, or low? Why? What areas could be improved?

FIGURE 24-1. *Continued.*

After collecting as much information as possible, you need to bring the pieces of information together into a form that will give the dilemma the clearest and sharpest focus.

Step 2. State the Dilemma. After you have collected and analyzed as much of the information as is available, you need to state the dilemma as clearly and succinctly as possible. Recognizing the key aspects of the dilemma helps focus your attention on the important ethical principles. Most of the time, the dilemma can be reduced to a statement or two revolving around key ethical principles. These ethical principles often involve a question of conflicting rights, obligations, or basic ethical principles.

In the question of slow resuscitation or no resuscitation, the dilemma might be stated as "The client's right to self-determination and death with

TABLE 24-1. Steps of Ethical Decision Making

1. Collect, analyze, and interpret the data
2. State the dilemma
3. Consider the choices of action
4. Analyze the advantages and disadvantages of each course of action
5. Make the decision

dignity versus the nurse's obligation to preserve life and do no harm." In general, the principle that the competent client's wishes must be followed is unequivocal. If the client has become unresponsive before expressing his or her wishes, then the family members' input must be given serious consideration. Additional questions can arise if the family's wishes conflict with those of the client.

Step 3. Consider the Choices of Action. After you have stated the dilemma as clearly as possible, you should attempt to list, without consideration of their consequences, all the possible courses of action that you can take to resolve the dilemma. This brainstorming activity, in which you consider all possible courses of action, may require input from outside sources such as colleagues, supervisors, or even experts in the ethical field. The consequences of the different actions are considered later.

Some of the possible courses of action to consider include resuscitating the client to your fullest capabilities, despite what the physician has requested; not resuscitating the client at all; just going through the motions without any real attempt to revive the client; seeking another assignment to avoid dealing with the situation; reporting the problem to a supervisor; attempting to clarify the question with the client; attempting to clarify the question with the family; and confronting the physician about the question.

Step 4. Analyze the Advantages and Disadvantages of Each Course of Action. Some of the courses of actions you developed in the previous step are more realistic than others. The unrealistic actions become readily evident during this step in the decision-making process, when you consider the advantages and the disadvantages of each action in detail. Along with each option you must consider the consequences of taking each course of action. You should evaluate the advantages and disadvantages of the consequences thoroughly.

For example, you should consider whether initiating discussion about the order would anger the physician or cause him to distrust you in the future. Either of these responses might make practicing at that institution difficult. The same result might occur if you successfully resuscitate the client despite orders to the contrary. Not resuscitating the client has the potential to involve you in a lawsuit if no clear order for no resuscitation exists. Presenting the situation to a supervisor may, if the supervisor supported the physician, cause you to be labeled a troublemaker and have a negative effect on your future evaluations. The same process can be applied to the other possible courses of action.

By thoroughly considering the advantages and disadvantages of each possible action, you should be able to reduce your realistic choices of action. An important factor to include in your deliberations is the American Nurses Association Code for Nurses (1985).

Step 5. Make the Decision. The most difficult part of the process is actually making the decision and living with the consequences. By their nature, ethical dilemmas produce differences of opinion, and not everyone will be pleased with your decision.

In the attempt to solve any ethical dilemma, there is always a question of the correct course of action. The client's wishes almost always supersede independent decisions on your part. Collaborative decision making among the client, physician, nurses, and family about resuscitation is the ideal solution and tends to produce fewer complications in the long-term resolution of such questions.

NURSING CODE OF ETHICS

A **code of ethics** is generally defined as the ethical principles that govern a particular profession. Codes of ethics are presented in general statements, and do not give specific answers to every possible ethical dilemma that might arise. These codes do, however, offer you guidance in your ethical decisions (Figure 24–2).

Ideally, codes of ethics should undergo periodic revision to reflect changes in the profession and society as a whole. Although codes of ethics are not legally enforceable as laws, consistently violating the code of ethics is taken as an indication of an unwillingness to act in a professional manner, and often results in disciplinary actions ranging from reprimands and fines to suspension and revocation of licensure (Sawyer, 1989).

The ANA Code for Nurses has been acknowledged by other health-care professions as one of the

1. The nurse provides services with respect for human dignity and the uniqueness of the client unrestricted by considerations of social or economic status, personal attributes, or the nature of the health problems.
2. The nurse safeguards the client's right to privacy by judiciously protecting information of a confidential nature.
3. The nurse acts to safeguard the client and the public when health care and safety are affected by the incompetent, unethical, or illegal practice of any person.
4. The nurse assumes responsibility and accountability for individual nursing judgments and actions.
5. The nurse maintains competence in nursing.
6. The nurse exercises informed judgment and uses individual competence and qualifications as criteria in seeking consultation, accepting responsibilities, and delegating nursing activities to others.
7. The nurse participates in activities that contribute to the ongoing development of the profession's body of knowledge.
8. The nurse participates in the profession's efforts to implement and improve standards of nursing.
9. The nurse participates in the profession's efforts to establish and maintain conditions of employment conducive to high-quality nursing care.
10. The nurse participates in the profession's efforts to protect the public from misinformation and misrepresentation and to maintain the integrity of nursing.
11. The nurse collaborates with members of the health care professions and other citizens in promoting community and national efforts to meet the health needs of the public.

FIGURE 24–2. ANA Code for Nurses.

most complete. It is sometimes used as the benchmark against which other codes of ethics are measured. Yet a careful reading of this code of ethics reveals only a set of clearly stated principles that you must apply to actual clinical situations. For example, if you are involved in the resuscitation situation described earlier, you will find no specific mention of "no resuscitation" orders. Rather, you must apply general statements, such as "The nurse provides services with respect for human dignity . . ." and "The nurse assumes responsibility and accountability for individual nursing judgments and actions" to the particular situation.

COMMON ETHICAL DILEMMAS IN NURSING

Although the potential ethical dilemmas you might face in your career are almost unlimited, a number of issues are much more likely to be encountered in your practice. A complete analysis of each of these issues is beyond the scope of this book, but the important ethical features are presented so that you will be better able to analyze the dilemma and make an informed decision. Resolving ethical dilemmas is never an easy task, and it is likely that you will displease someone by your decision, no matter how carefully and thoughtfully you made it.

Access to Care

Although access to health care has been a concern in the United States for many years, it is only with recent proposed changes in the health-care system that it has been pushed into the headlines as an important ethical and social issue. In today's health-care system, some individuals obtain the best care that medicine and technology can provide, while others can neither afford to see a physician nor purchase the medications that are prescribed. The underlying ethical principle involved in access to care is that of justice, particularly distributive justice. The basic question is whether health care is a universal right to be allotted to all citizens, or a privilege limited to those who can pay for it?

On the surface, the current health-care system seems to be based on the belief that health care is a privilege. Yet the government recognizes the needs of some of those who cannot afford health care, such as the elderly, poor, and disabled, and subsidizes their health care through a variety of programs, such as Medicaid. The end result is that the United States spends more on health care than any

country in the world, with most of that money coming from the pockets of taxpayers.

However, those who support universal access and health care as a basic right of every citizen are faced with the specter of health-care rationing. The reality of the situation is that if universal access becomes the law of the land, some form of restricted access to services will be likely to control the flow of money. De facto, a system of universal access to health care in the United States means that some health-care goods must be rationed.

Ideally, under the ethical principle of distributive justice, everybody should have open access to every type of health care. Because that type of access is unrealistic, a decision needs to be made on what health-care services will be restricted to which groups of individuals. Current proposals for universal coverage all include limiting those health-care services that generally fall into the tertiary category, including highly specialized diagnostic and treatment regimens, organ and tissue transplants, and procedures that merely prolong life temporarily.

The group that is most often targeted for rationing is the elderly because they are a rapidly growing, easily identified group, that has high health-care costs. Over the past few years, the cost of health care for the elderly in the last year of their life has amounted to 1 percent of the total gross national product (GNP) each year since 1984 (Callahan, 1990). Also, the traditional role of the elderly in society is to care for the young and future generations, not to absorb a large portion of their heritage in the form of expensive resources.

However, there is a strong prohibition in this country against using age alone as a criterion for restriction of services. Allocation of health-care services based on need seems to be a more equitable way to arrive at the decision. It would make more sense to restrict the use of expensive technologies by all age groups rather than all sources for the elderly only. The elderly have also contributed a great deal to this country over the years, compared to the younger members of society, and it seems only fair that they receive the care they have earned. Many nurses find it difficult to reconcile their personal and professional codes of ethics with limiting resources for just one group, such as the elderly. It is unlikely that professional groups, such as nurses, would abide by a policy that restricted care to the elderly.

What is the solution to this dilemma? As with most ethical dilemmas, there is no perfect solution, yet nurses can contribute a great deal to resolving this question. Underlying any resolution to the access to care problem is the requirement for a fundamental shift in attitude and philosophy about health care. No longer can curing disease and extending life be the primary focuses of health care. Rather, the health-care system needs to adopt *caring* as a central goal of health care. Nurses understand caring as a mode of treatment. Physicians and other health-care providers can learn it. Caring will refocus the goals of health-care toward a more equitable and rational use of health-care resources.

Organ Transplantation

Despite the widespread public and medical acceptance of organ transplantation as a highly beneficial procedure, ethical questions still remain. Whenever a human organ is transplanted, a large number of people are involved, including the donor, the donor's family, and medical and nursing personnel, as well as the recipient and the recipient's family. Society in general could also be added to this mix, because of the high cost of organ transplantation, which is usually borne directly by tax monies or indirectly in the form of increased insurance premiums. Each one of these persons or groups have rights that may conflict with the rights of others.

Most institutions that perform transplants, or organizations that are involved in obtaining organs, have developed elaborate, detailed, and involved procedures to help deal with the ethical and legal issues involved in transplantation (Stoeckle, 1993). Despite these efforts, some ethical issues still arise whenever organ transplantation is considered.

One particularly sensitive issue arises when a child is involved. Although parents are legally permitted to give consent for medical procedures for their children, the child needs to have some input in the decision also, particularly if it poses a risk to her or his life such as with a kidney transplantation. By legal definition, a child under the age of 18 cannot give informed consent to such a procedure. Yet it seems unethical to coerce the child into donating a kidney if she or he really did not want to do it. The proposed and experimental use of fetal tissue for transplantation also raises ethical questions about permission, informed consent, and viability (Verklin, 1993).

Despite the best efforts of the medical and legal community to establish criteria for death, ethical questions about when a person is really dead remain (Evans, 1993). Does brain death, the most widely accepted criterion for death, really indicate that a person no longer exists as a human being? Or is there some other criterion that should be examined? Such organs as hearts, lungs, and livers need

to come from a beating heart donor. Might there be the tendency to declare brain death before it actually occurs?

One of the most difficult ethical issues involved in organ transplantation is selecting recipients. The number of people who need organs far exceeds the number of available organs. Many potential ethical dilemmas arise from this fact (Thomas, 1993). Should someone get an organ because he or she is rich or famous or knows the right people? The national organ recipient list attempts to list and rank all persons who need organs in a nondiscriminatory manner. Some of the important criteria are need, length of time on the list, potential for survival, prior organ transplantation, value to the community, and tissue compatibility.

Nurses can be, and often are, involved in some aspects of the organ donation process. Many states have passed laws requiring that health-care workers ask the family members of potential organ donors if they have ever thought about organ donation for their dead or dying loved one. Many nurses, particularly nurses in critical care units, provide care for clients who are potential organ donors. Nurses in operating rooms may help in the actual surgical procedures that remove organs from a cadaver and transplant them into a recipient's body. Many floor nurses provide the postoperative care for clients who have received a transplanted organ. Home health care nurses give the follow-up care of these clients at home.

Nurses working with organ transplantation need to be sensitive to the potential for manipulation. Most people who are seeking organ transplantation are desperately ill, or near death. They and their families can be very easily manipulated, or be very manipulating. On the other side, the families of potential organ donors are usually emotionally distraught due to the sudden and traumatic loss of a loved one. They, too, are vulnerable to manipulation. As a general rule, neither the donor nor his family should play any part in selecting a recipient. Nurses need to avoid making statements or giving nonverbal indications of their approval or disapproval of potential recipients. For example, a statement such as "I hope the teenager gets the kidney rather than the old lady" may prejudice the whole process.

End-of-Life Decisions

The term **"euthanasia"** generally means a painless or peaceful death. A distinction is often made between passive and active euthanasia. *Passive eu-*

thanasia usually refers to the practice of allowing an individual to die without any extraordinary intervention. Under this umbrella definition, such practices as DNR orders, living wills, and withdrawal of ventilators or other life support are usually included. *Active euthanasia,* on the other hand, describes the practice of speeding an individual's death through some act or procedure. This practice is also sometimes referred to as mercy killing, and takes many forms, ranging from using large amounts of pain medication for terminal cancer clients to using poisons, carbon monoxide, guns, or knives to end a person's life.

Assisted suicide, recently brought to public attention by Dr. Kevorkian, a Michigan physician, is really a type of active euthanasia or mercy killing. The central issue that has been pushed to the forefront by Dr. Kevorkian's public practice of assisted suicide is whether it is ever ethically permissible for health-care personnel to assist in taking a life. In most states the practice is illegal. The definition of *homicide,* bringing about a person's death or assisting him or her to do so, seems to fit the act of assisted suicide. Yet there is a great deal of hesitation on the part of the legal system to prosecute persons who are involved in assisted suicide for terminally ill clients.

The fundamental ethical issue is the *right to self-determination* (Evans, 1993). In almost every other health-care situation, a client, as long as he or she is competent, can make decisions about what care is acceptable and what care he or she will refuse. Yet, when it comes to the termination of life, this right no longer seems to apply. Supporters of the practice of assisted suicide hold to the belief that the right to self-determination remains intact, even to the decision to end life. It is the last act of a very sick individual to control his or her own fate. Medical personnel, many feel, should be allowed to assist these clients in this procedure, just as they are allowed to assist clients in other medical and nursing procedures.

Those who oppose assisted suicide find these arguments lacking in ethical principle. Legally, ethically, and morally, suicide in American society has never been accepted. Health-care staff go to great lengths to prevent clients from injuring themselves when they are identified as suicidal. In addition, it would seem that individuals in the terminal states of a disease who are overwhelmed by pain, and depressed by the thought of prolonged suffering, might not be able to think clearly enough to give informed consent for assisted suicide. Also, the termination of life is final. It does not allow for spontaneous cures, or the development of new treatments or medications.

Although nurses are unlikely to be employed in assisted suicide clinics, the reality of active euthanasia has and will continue to exist in modern-day health care. Nurses need to remember the principle of nonmaleficence. There is a very strong obligation to do no harm to clients. Assisting in or causing the death of a client would seem to be an obvious violation of this principle.

HIV and AIDS

Few diseases have the power to raise strong opinions as do HIV and AIDS. Nurses, who for years held strongly to the ethical principle that all clients, regardless of race, sex, religion, age, or disease process, should be cared for equally, are now questioning their obligation to take care of clients who have AIDS.

Several ethical issues underlie the AIDS controversy. One of the most important is the right to privacy. Some feel that this issue has been carried to extremes. Many diseases such as tuberculosis, gonorrhea, syphilis, and hepatitis, which are highly contagious and sometimes fatal, must be reported to public health officials. Although there is a general requirement to report infection with HIV or AIDS to the Centers for Disease Control (CDC), many states have strict laws regarding the confidentiality of the diagnosis. Revealing the diagnosis of HIV or AIDS even to other health-care personnel brings the possibility of a lawsuit against the health-care provider or institution. It is important to remember that the right to privacy is not an absolute right. If the right to privacy can be violated when the public welfare is threatened by such diseases as TB, syphilis, or gonorrhea, isn't logical to include AIDS in this group? Is it unjust to ask health-care providers to care for clients with this disease without knowing that the client has it? A parallel question involves the client's right to know when a health-care provider is infected with HIV or AIDS?

Another important ethical issue is the right to care. Can a nurse refuse to care for a client with a highly contagious, and potentially lethal disease, such as HIV, hepatitis B, or medication-resistant TB? Obviously, a fundamental right of being a client is receiving care, just as a fundamental obligation of a nurse is to provide care. The first statement of the ANA Code for Nurses states that a nurse must provide care unrestricted by any considerations. There may be some exceptions, for example, if the nurse were pregnant, or receiving chemotherapy, or had other immunity problems, they might be able to refuse an assignment because of safety considerations. But in most situations, the nurse would be obligated to provide the best nursing care possible for all clients, including ones with dangerous diseases (Trought & Moore, 1989).

What about the tremendous cost involved in treating individuals who have AIDS? Recent studies estimate that the medical cost of treating an AIDS client from the time of diagnosis to the time of death will be in the neighborhood of $750,000 per client (Catalano, 1996). In the face of this crisis, governmental agencies, who bear the brunt of the cost of AIDS treatment will have to make some hard decisions concerning this issue. With in excess of one million people already infected with this disease, the cost to society is astronomical. Nurses are obligated to care for all clients, including those with AIDS, but are physicians, hospitals, or governmental agencies also held to this same precept? Is the right to health care really a privilege?

Advanced Directives

A relatively new development in health care during the past decade is **advanced directives.** Originally developed as a means for clients to express their wishes about the type and amount of health care they desired if they became unable to make decisions at a future date (right to self-determination), advanced directives are now a required part of the health care of all clients. Under the Omnibus Budget Reconciliation Act of 1990, all hospitals, nursing care facilities, home care agencies, and care providers are required by law to ask clients about advanced directives, and provide information about them if so desired (Catalano, 1994).

Advanced directives can take the form of living wills and medical durable power of attorney (MDPOA). Living wills are defined as a directive from a competent individual to medical personnel and family members regarding the treatment he or she wishes to receive when he or she is no longer able to make decisions (Guido, 1988). This directive is ideally in the form of a written document, but it may also take the form of verbal directions to a health-care provider that are documented in the client's health-care record. Unfortunately, no one form is accepted by all states. Some living wills are very specific as to the treatments you can and cannot use, but other forms provide only general directions, such as "no extraordinary measures."

As a nurse, you can play an important part in identifying potential problems in a client's living will. If a client has a living will already written, you need to make sure it is signed and witnessed properly or notarized. Generally, health-care providers, and the client's family members are excluded from witnessing a living will. In addition, if the living will is very old (more than 2 years), you should encourage the client to review it, and update it if needed. Also see how clear and detailed the statements are about which treatments are to be used or excluded. Often clients do not understand such modes of treatment as intubation, ventilation, defibrillation, medication administration, and resuscitation. Also explain to them any new modes of treatment that may have been developed since they first composed their living will. Finally, encourage the client to give copies of the document to the next of kin, primary physician, and attorney. Some states even allow the client to register a living will with certain agencies in the state, such as the secretary of state (Catalano, 1996).

Although the use of the living will seems to be a relatively simple way to resolve a complicated situation in health care, you need to be aware of a number of ethical pitfalls. One of the most common ethical questions revolves around the client's level of knowledge of potential and future health-care problems he or she may encounter. Living wills are often composed while the client is in a relatively positive state of health, and may be directed toward only a few "common" problems with which he or she is familiar. For example, the client may anticipate a myocardial infarction (MI), and give specific directions for treatments to be excluded in this condition, such as "no CPR," or "no defibrillation." Then the client is in an automobile accident, has a crushed chest and needs to be on a ventilator for proper healing of the ribs. If he is unconscious, and cannot give directions to the health-care team, should they not intubate him and put him on the ventilator because of his living will? Did he really intend to exclude this situation? In general, if there is any indication that the client did not fully understand the implications or use of possible therapies, then the validity of the whole living will is in question and can probably be disregarded (O'Rourke & Brodeur, 1989).

Nurses working with clients who have a living will sometimes encounter ethical questions revolving around the principles of beneficence and nonmaleficence. As defined earlier, the principle of beneficence states that your primary duty as a nurse is to do good for the client, and the principle of nonmaleficence requires you to protect the client from any harm. From the perspectives of beneficence and nonmaleficence, you may feel that following a client's living will violates these principles. Some nurses feel ethically uncomfortable in situations where implementing a client's living will involves the termination of life-sustaining treatments already in use. When you "pull the plug" on a ventilator or tube feeding, you seem to be doing definite harm to that client, namely, causing his or her death.

A third difficulty that you may encounter with a living will is actually enforcing it. The legal and ethical systems overlap a great deal in this dilemma. Strictly speaking, unless a state has enacted into law a special type of living will called a "natural death act," the living will is *not* legally enforceable (Guido, 1988). Although 44 states have this type of act, they vary widely in wording and requirements. Some of these laws recognize the living will only if it is in accord with the physician's plan of treatment. Other states have laws that are so specific in defining "terminal illness" they require the client to die within a few hours of implementing the living will. Very few of these laws have any provisions to protect nurses and other health-care providers from criminal or civil actions if they do carry out the living will. You need to know not only if your state has a "natural death act," but also what it says specifically about living wills.

The other form of advanced directive, used less frequently than the living will, is the medical durable power of attorney or health-care proxy. This type of advanced directive allows the client to designate another person to make health-care choices should he or she become unconscious or otherwise unable to make decisions (Catalano, 1996). Like the living will, the MDPOA has difficulties. State laws vary widely as to who can be given this power, for how long it is good, and the legal process involved in verifying the person with the power of attorney. The ethical issues surrounding MDPOA are very similar to those found with living wills. In addition, some clients may designate two or more persons as MDPOAs. Making health-care decisions when these individuals disagree about the care they think the client wanted is extremely complicated.

Staffing and Delegation

You have probably already encountered "health-care restructuring" at your workplace. No matter how it may have been presented, or how it was phrased, all **restructuring** has as its primary goal cost containment. Almost all health-care facilities are attempting to find ways to cut their costs, while maintaining at least minimal standards of care. You may have been exposed to such terms as "managed care," "resource allocation," and "change in provider mix." Be cautious when these terms are used because they usually mean that the ratio between professional staff and unlicensed staff is changing, and this has the potential to produce ethical conflicts that challenge your role as a professional nurse.

The current trend to use more unlicensed assistive personnel (UAP) poses ethical and legal concerns for you in attempting to carry out your ethical and professional responsibilities. As a nurse, your main goal is to provide respectful, competent, and compassionate care for your clients using your expertise, knowledge, and professional skill. Professional nurses in most settings have always relied on some UAP type of help, but as the mix of professional to nonprofessional care provider changes, your ethical and legal obligations also change.

The professional nurse's primary commitment has always been, and should always be, to the health, well-being, and safety of the client. Nurses act as advocates for clients, and should always be aware of, and take appropriate action regarding, situations in which incompetent, unethical, or illegal practice is performed by any one providing care. Although it is possible for UAPs to provide safe care within their scope of practice, they tend to carry out skills that are not appropriate for their level of training. It is your ethical and legal responsibility to identify situations where client care is adversely affected, and take action to change or eliminate the potential for harm.

Legally and ethically, professional nurses are responsible for the actions taken and judgments made by those they supervise in the provision of care. Neither physician's orders nor the employing agency's policies release nurses from the responsibility for actions taken or judgments made by subordinates (Aroskar, 1995). Nurses can protect themselves from unethical or illegal situations by constantly evaluating how staffing changes affect the safety and quality of the care being provided. By becoming involved in the formulation of institutional policies through active participation on various in-house committees, nurses can have a major influence on the staffing practices at that institution. It is also ethically permissible, and even desirable, that nurses protest and take appropriate action when they judge UAPs that are being used inappropriately or unsafely in client care situations.

Similarly, nurses are ethically and legally accountable for the appropriate delegation of nursing care activities to other health-care workers. It is important that nurses know the level of training of each UAP assigned to them and evaluate their competency when assigning client care tasks. It is ethically irresponsible to assign a nursing care function to a UAP for which he or she is not prepared or qualified. Again, employer policy statements do NOT release the nurse from accountability for inappropriately assigning an unprepared UAP to a task that ultimately results in harm to the client. The educator role of the professional nurse has new importance in helping to prepare and instruct UAPs in the work setting. Professional nurses will also be spending more and more of their time evaluating the competency of other health-care workers as they provide care to protect clients from harm.

In our rapidly changing health-care system, the use of UAP-type workers will only increase. Correspondingly, you will need to understand your growing professional and legal obligations regarding these workers. As with most ethical questions, there is no single right answer to the dilemma posed by UAPs, yet you, as a professional nurse, must always keep in mind the ultimate goal of safe and high-quality care for all clients.

Ethical issues and ethics are a part of your day-to-day practice as a nurse. In today's world, with rapidly advancing technology and unusual health-care situations, ethical dilemmas are increasing. You can be prepared to deal with most of these dilemmas if you keep current with the issues and are able to use a systematic process for making decisions about them. Hiding from ethical issues is not a solution. At some point, you are going to have to make difficult decisions. One of the most difficult parts of ethical decision making is that someone is likely to be unhappy about your decision. But if you made the decision after analyzing the situation, and your decision is based on sound ethical principles, you should be able to defend it to anyone.

KEY POINTS

- Ethical decision making is a skill that can be learned and developed through practice.
- The steps in the ethical decision-making process are to collect and analyze the data; state the dilemma; consider the choices of action; analyze the choices and consider the consequences; and make the decision.
- Utilitarianism is a system of ethical decision making based on the principle of the greatest good for the greatest number of people. It is situation oriented, and has no established or unchanging rules. Deontology is a system of ethical decision making based on unchanging rules and principles, without consideration of the consequences.
- The ANA Code for Nurses serves as the ethical guidelines for the profession of nursing. It provides the nurse with general statements about nursing ethics, which the nurse needs to interpret and apply to individual ethical situations.
- The key ethical issues involved in organ transplantation revolve around the ethical principles of distributive justice, informed consent, and determination of death.
- Ethical questions concerning end-of-life decisions often involve a conflict between the client's right to self-determination and the nurse's obligations of beneficence and nonmaleficence.
- A number of ethical principles are involved in ethical dilemmas created by the HIV and AIDS issue. These include the right to privacy, self-determination, the right to care, and distributive justice in the form of health-care worker's and society's right to protection from dangerous diseases.
- Although advanced directives are now a legal part of the health-care system, a number of ethical issues still plague their use. The primary ethical concern is that of informed consent. Many clients have only a limited knowledge about the types of treatments possible for various conditions.
- A relatively new ethical concern for nurses involves current trends in health care for the increased use of UAPs.
- Professional nurses are ethically and legally accountable for the care provided by these individuals.

CHAPTER EXERCISES

1. Discuss the ethical, financial, treatment, and additional issues that surround the following *Case of the Elderly Lady*. Relate the case to the principles of distributive justice.

Clara, 108 years old, is admitted through the hospital emergency room for nonspecific complaints of chest pain and dizziness. This was the third time she came into the hospital with this complaint in the last month, and although previous examinations and tests showed no acute disease process, the ER physician felt that, due to her age and long history of coronary artery disease, she should be monitored and evaluated more closely. She has no private insurance, but is covered under Medicare, parts A and B, with a supplemental from a small insurance company in her state.

Despite her age, Clara is mentally alert and competent, lives by herself in a small apartment, and manages basic daily care, including shopping and cleaning, with only minimal assistance from friends. She has no living family members except for a few aging cousins in a distant state. She is taking several medications at home, including diltiazem (Cardizem) for her heart problems, ranitidine (Zantac) for a hiatal hernia, and papaverine (Pavabid) to increase her general circulation.

After a complete physical examination, including several tests and an ECG, she is scheduled for a cardiac catheterization. A significant block is seen in one of the major coronary arteries, and it is decided to perform angioplasty on the artery. She is admitted to the ICU after the procedure, where she also receives two units of blood for an anemia problem. She recovers without incident and is discharged 5 days after her admission.

Total cost for her hospitalization, including tests and angioplasty is in excess of $15,000.

2. Consider the ethical dilemmas inherent in the following case study:

Bill Z, a 6'3", 135-lb, 76-year-old retired college professor was admitted to a medical unit in a large metropolitan hospital. He had been diagnosed 6 months previously as having metastatic cancer that had spread from his lungs to the liver, gastrointestinal system, and bones. He had received some chemotherapy, but with little effect. He was admitted to the hospital because he had become too weak to walk or care for himself at home, and the large doses of oral narcotic medications were having little effect on his generalized pain.

His physician had decided that further chemotherapy would be useless, and ordered Mr. Z was to be kept comfortable with medications. A continuous morphine sulfate IV drip was started to help control the pain. Although talkative and friendly by nature, as Mr. Z's cancer spread, he would cry out and beg the nurses not to move him. Because he was very tall and underweight, his bony prominences quickly became reddened and showed signs of breakdown. The hospital standards of care for bedridden patients required that they be turned from side to side every 2 hours. Mr. Z yelled so loudly when he was turned that the nursing staff wondered if they were helping him or hurting him.

To decide what should be done, a client care conference was called by the nurses most often involved in providing care for Mr. Z. The head nurse of the unit stated very clearly that the hospital standards of care required that he be turned at least every 2 hours to prevent skin breakdown, infections, and perhaps sepsis. In his already weakened condition, an infection or sepsis would most likely be fatal. Melanie F, who had been an RN for some 15 years, disagreed with the head nurse. Her feeling was that causing this obviously terminal client as much pain as he was having by turning him was cruel and violated his dignity as a human being. She stated that she could not stand to hear him yell any more and refused to take care of him until some other decision was made about his nursing care. Susan B, a new graduate nurse, felt that the client should have some say in his own care and that perhaps some type of compromise could be reached about turning him, even if less frequently. Ellen R, who had worked on the unit for 2 years, felt that the physician should make the decision on turning this patient and then the nurses would only have to follow the order. This last suggestion was met with strong negative comments by the other nurses present. Client comfort and turning are nursing measures (Aiken & Catalano, 1995, pp. 74–75).

What should they decide? Violation of a standard of care can leave a nurse open to a lawsuit. What about the client's right to decide when a standard of care should be violated? Are there ever any situations when a nurse might legally and ethically violate a standard of care? What are the consequences?

3. Evaluate the following case study on staffing and standards of care:

Maggie C, RN and head nurse of a busy neurological intensive care unit, was reviewing the weekend staffing for the unit on a Friday afternoon. As usual, the unit's nine beds were full with clients in various levels of recovery from brain surgery or head injuries. The staffing on the weekend was "short," with only enough staff to safely care for eight clients. After a great deal of time reworking the schedule, calling nurses on the phone, and trading days off, Maggie finally managed to arrange sufficient coverage for the unit.

As Maggie was closing her office for the weekend, Dr. West, a neurosurgeon, approached her and related the following situation. Mrs. P, a 63-year-old client with a brain tumor, had been scheduled for surgery 3 days earlier. She had a very rare blood type that was difficult to match, so the surgery was delayed. Although a few day's wait would not likely worsen her condition drastically, she had become very anxious when informed about the delay in surgery. The blood bank had just obtained the necessary units for the surgery and had informed Dr. West that he could now operate on Mrs. P. Dr. West was wondering if the neuro unit would be able to safely care for Mrs. P over the weekend. This was the only unit in the hospital equipped to monitor brain surgery and provide appropriate nursing care for this type of client. The neuro step-down unit was also full, so it would be difficult getting a bed to transfer one of the neuro unit's clients to "make" a bed for Mrs. P. Mrs. P would most likely require one-to-one care for 18 to 24 hours after surgery (Aiken & Catalano, 1995, pp. 187–188).

Should Maggie tell Dr. West that he can go ahead with the surgery, and she will make the adjustments to provide care for this client? What ethical obligations does Maggie have to the client? How about her obligations to Dr. West and the hospital?

REFERENCES

Aiken, T. D., and Catalano, J. T. (1994). *Legal, ethical, and political issues in nursing*. Philadelphia: Davis.

American Nurses Association. (1985). *Code for nurses with interpretive statement*. Washington, DC: American Nurses Association.

Aroskar, M. A. (1995). Nurses and unlicensed assistive personnel: Ethical perspectives. *ANA Center for Ethics and Human Rights, 4,* 2–4.

Callahan, D. (1990). *What kind of life? The limits of medical progress*. New York: Simon & Schuster.

Catalano, J. T. (1996). *Contemporary professional nursing*. Philadelphia: Davis.

Catalano, J. T. (1991). Critical care nurses and ethical dilemmas. *Critical Care Nurse, 11,* 16–21.

Catalano, J. T. (1994). Ethics of cadaver experimentation. *Critical Care Nursing, 14,* 81–85.

Catalano, J. T. (1995). *Ethical and legal aspects of nursing* (2nd ed.). Springhouse, PA: Springhouse.

Catalano, J. T. (1992). Systems of ethics. *Critical Care Nurse 12,* 91–96.

Catalano, J. T. (1994). Treatments not specifically listed in the living will: The ethical dilemmas. *Dimensions of Critical Care Nursing, 13,* 142–150.

Curtin, L. H. (1994). How much is enough? *Nursing Management 25,* 30–31.

Davis, A. J., & Aroskar, M. S. (1978). *Ethical dilemmas and nursing practice*. New York: Appleton-Century-Crofts.

Doheny, M., Cook, C., & Stopper, C. (1987). *The discipline of nursing*. Norwalk, CT: Appleton & Lange.

Evans, M. (1993). Moral costs: Brain stem death ethics. *Nursing Times, 15,* 34–35.

Fiesta, J. (1988). *The law and liability: A guide for nurses* (2nd ed.). Albany, NY: Delmar.

Fletcher, J. (1966). *Situation ethics*. Philadelphia: Westminster.

French, P. A. (1991). *The spectrum of responsibility*. New York: St. Martin's Press.

Guido, G. W. (1988). *Legal issues in nursing*. Norwalk, CT: Appleton & Lange.

Jameton, A. (1984). *Nursing practice: The ethical issues*. Englewood Cliffs, NJ: Prentice-Hall.

Mappes, T. A., & Zembaty, J. S. (1991). *Biomedical ethics* (3rd ed.). New York: McGraw-Hill.

O'Rourke, K., & Brodeur, D. (1989). *Medical ethics*. St. Louis: Catholic Health Association of the United States.

Quinn, C. A., & Smith, M. D. (1987). *The professional commitment: Issues and ethics in nursing*. Philadelphia: Saunders.

Sawyer, L. M. (1989). Nursing code of ethics: An international comparison. *International Nurse Review 3,* 145–148.

Stoeckle, M. L. (1993). Issues of transplantation: The ethics of potential legislative change. *Dimensions of Critical Care Nursing, 12,* 158–166.

Thomas, D. J. (1993). Organ transplantation in people with unhealthy lifestyles. *AACN Clinical Issues, 4,* 665–668.

Thompson, J. E., & Thompson, H. O. (1985). *Bioethical decision making for nurses*. Norwalk, CT: Appleton & Lange.

Thompson, J. E., & Thompson, H. O. (1989). Teaching ethics to nursing students. *Nursing Outlook, 37,* 84–88.

Trought, E. A., & Moore, F. (1989). *Guidelines for the registered nurse in giving, accepting, or rejecting a work assignment*. Orlando: Florida Nurses Association.

Verklin, M. T. (1993). The ethical use of fetal tissue for transplantation and research. *Journal of Advanced Nursing, 18,* 1172–1177.

Chapter 25

EXPANDING THE VISION

Rose Kearney Nunnery

We have seen nursing and health-care change radically in the past few years. With restructuring of health care, nursing professionals have responded with refinements, advancements, and innovations in practice, education, research, and administration. Nursing has moved from the functional service mode of the mid-1900s to a cost, community, quality, and consumer-focused orientation in the late 1990s. Presently, to address the health of people, all health professions are now faced with the challenges of transformation, innovation, and collaboration. Although no clear images have emerged for the vision of health care and nursing in the twenty-first century, we have some direction. We are in the process of a major paradigm shift.

HEALTH-CARE PROFESSIONALS OF THE TWENTY-FIRST CENTURY

The Pew Charitable Trust Foundation established the Pew Health Professions Commission in 1989 to address issues of health-care reform and health policy across the professions. At this time, the health-care industry was in the midst of redesigning services and containing costs. Health professionals were dealing with redefined roles and declining resources. Everyone was attempting to envision the future. In the fall of 1995, reports from the commission produced strong reactions and responses through the professional communities. The work of this commission was becoming a driving force for change.

The mission or charge of the Pew Commission (1995) is to "assist workforce policy makers and educational institutions to produce health care workers who meet the changing needs of the American health care system" (p. ii). Predictions on the closure of hospitals, the surplus of physicians, nurses, and pharmacists, and the redesign needed in education, health care, and research received much attention. The Pew Health Professions Commission (1995) proposed four challenges, with the identified need for a rapid transformation in the health professions workforce:

Redesign the ways in which health professional work is organized in hospitals, clinics, private offices, community practices, and public health activity.

Re-regulate the ways in which health professionals are permitted to practice, allowing more flexibility and experimentation, but ensuring that the public's health is genuinely protected.

Right-size the health professional workforce and the institutions that produce health professionals; for the most part this will mean reducing the size of the professions and programs.

Restructure education to make efficient use of the resources that are allocated to it (p. vi).

The view of the future health-care system presented by the commission is market-driven and integrated with more managed and primary care. In addition, this new health-care system and its professionals would be more accountable to the public and responsive to consumers; more efficient, effective, and innovative; and focus primarily on education, prevention, and care management rather than treatment (Pew Health Professions Commission, 1995). The goals in our revised health-care system are thus cost reduction, enhanced consumer satisfaction, and improved health-care outcomes. To meet such goals, health professionals must demonstrate accountability, responsibility, competence, and collaboration while celebrating diversity and consumer individuality.

Earlier, in 1991, the Pew Commission identified specific competencies for health professionals in 2005 (Table 25–1). **Competencies** are those qualities that illustrate effectiveness and appropriateness in our respective professional roles. The characteristics of a profession described in Chapter 1 direct us in our professional competencies. The individual competencies for all health professionals identified by the Pew

TABLE 25–1. Pew Commission on Health Professions Competencies Needed by Health-Care Providers in 2005

Care for the community's health	Improve the health-care system
Expand access to effective care	Manage information
Provide clinically competent care	Understand the role of the physical environment
Emphasize primary care	Provide counseling on ethical issues
Participate in coordinated care	
Ensure cost effective and appropriate care	Accommodate expanded accountability
Practice prevention	Participate in a racially and culturally diverse society
Involve patients and families in decision-making process	
Promote healthy lifestyles	Continue to learn
Access and use technology appropriately	

Source: Pew Health Professions Commission. (1995). *Critical challenges: Revitalizing the health professions for the twenty-first century.* San Francisco: UCSF Center for the Health Professions. Reprinted with permission.

Commission focus on the abilities to provide effective, sensitive, and appropriate care and health promotion. The ultimate goal is a healthier society.

The work of the Pew Commission continued, concentrating on the assets and needs of each of the health professions to address the nation's health. In December 1993, education in the health professions was targeted, with strategies recommended for schools and practitioners. The following six major trends in nursing that would have major influences on the profession and professional education were identified:

- The aging population
- Health promotion and disease prevention
- Cost-effective care
- Management of care
- Community organization
- Differentiation of practice and education (O'Neil, 1993, pp. 85–86).

Five strategies were proposed to prepare nurses with the professional competencies that would be essential in the year 2005 (Table 25–2). These strategies involve change in curricula, faculty, teaching methods, and training sites, along with intensive planning and evaluation.

In a report presented in September 1995 and published in December, the Pew Commission made ten recommendations aimed at states for protecting and promoting the public's health. These recommendations concerned standardization of terms and regulations, entry-to-practice requirements, scopes of practice, assessment of continuing competence and disciplinary processes, professional boards, providing information and public accountability, data collection, evaluation processes, and development of state, federal, and private partnerships to streamline regulation.

In November 1995, the commission presented six overall recommendations related to education, clinical training, future skills, cultural diversity, development of partnerships, and collaboration with regulatory systems needed across all professions. In this report, specific recommendations were aimed at allied health, dentistry, medicine, nursing, pharmacy, and public health. Table 25–3 lists the Pew Health Professions Commission's seven recommendations for nursing. Following are the evident threads running through these recommendations:

- Our accountability to the public, both consumers of nursing and society in general
- Recognition of our assets
- The need for clarity in our roles and functions
- Meeting the demands of the marketplace

COLLABORATION AND COLLEGIALITY

One of the commission's recommendations was recognition of our assets in the nursing profession. One way to do this is by valuing our colleagues who provide clinical nursing care, specialty care, advanced clinical practice, education, or administration. This involves both collaboration and collegiality.

The health-care team is an ideal example for collaboration. **Collaboration** involves actively working together to meet some identified goal, such as the client's treatment goals. Nurses from each area of nursing contribute to that goal, whether as the admission nurse or discharge planner, student in a clinical rotation, operative or postanesthesia nurses, acute care nurse practitioners, or other professional nurses providing care to raise the client's level of well-being. In times of limited staffing and growing responsibilities, seeing the broader picture with collaboration may appear to be time-consuming. Special efforts may be needed initially, to ensure effective collaboration, but the cooperative spirit will bring more efficient achievement of goals and greater personal reward for both colleagues and clients. Questions of authority and responsibility arise with this cooperative or collaborative spirit.

TABLE 25–2. Pew Health Profession Commission (1993) Strategies for Education in Nursing

- Develop programs at the various levels of nursing education that reflect the contributions needed in the changing patient care system. Change licensing and care delivery regulations to ensure that nurses are employed in roles for which they have received appropriate training and are rewarded for their contributions. Model new nursing arrangements in the care delivery system using these differentiated nursing roles, and evaluate their impact on patient and health-care system outcomes.

- Restructure faculty positions in nursing schools and programs to involve them more directly with the patient care system and nursing practice.

- . Develop interdisciplinary teaching, practice, and research programs for maintenance care of chronic patient populations.

- . Redirect a significant part of all nursing programs and schools to the health-care needs of community-based patients.

- . Continue the development of graduate-level clinical training programs for nurses in areas where health-care services can reduce costs and improve access and quality.

- . Conduct comprehensive and ongoing programs of strategic planning within each nursing school and program.

Source: O'Neil, E. H. (1993). *Health professions education for the future: Schools in service to the nation.* San Francisco: Pew Health Professions Commission. Reprinted with permission.

TABLE 25–3. Pew Health Profession Commission (1995) Recommendations for Nursing

Topic	Recommendation
Educational diversity	Value the multiple entry points to professional practice: ADN, BSN, MSN.
Professional titles	Consolidate professional nomenclature, e.g., single title for each level of nursing preparation and service.
Career ladders	Differentiate the responsibilities between these different levels of nursing, and strengthen existing career ladder programs to facilitate movement through the levels: ADN: entry level, hospital, and nursing home care BSN: hospital care management and community practice MSN: specialty practice in hospitals and independent practice
Education programs	Reduce the size and number of basic nursing programs by 10 to 20%, especially ADN and diploma programs, with further consideration of areas with existing shortages or surpluses of nurses.
Training programs	Expand MSN nurse practitioner programs with increased federal support for students.
Integration	Develop new models of integration between education and managed care systems for education, research, and practice that encourage continual improvement, innovation, and redesign.
Management role	Recover the clinical management role of nursing

Source: Pew Health Professions Commission. (1995). *Critical challenges: Revitalizing the health professions for the twenty-first century.* San Francisco: UCSF Center for the Health Professions.

Collegiality is the sharing of responsibility and authority to achieve a goal or prescribed outcome. Power and responsibility for outcomes related to clients' health and well-being are invested in more than one person. Respect and collaboration are important components of a collegial relationship. Tappen (1995) describes the function of collegial relationships, with all members being regarded as having equal worth as individuals and recognized for their contributions to the team rather than their status (p. 296). All colleagues contribute to the intended goals and are accountable for the outcomes.

Taking this idea a step further, through valuing our colleagues within the profession, we also are responsible for collaboration and collegiality among the professions. As described in Chapter 15, health-care delivery systems are becoming more integrated and interdisciplinary as we address needs and resources and monitor cost-effectiveness, outcomes, and consumer satisfaction. The ANA (1995) has defined collaboration as follows:

> the process whereby physicians and nurses plan and practice together as colleagues, working independently within the boundaries of their scopes of practice with shared values and acknowledgement and respect for each other's contributions to care for individuals, their families, and their communities. (p. 28)

Although this definition addresses only nurses and physicians, in our present multidisciplinary health-care system, collaboration must be effective among all members of the various health professions, with collegiality based on abilities and functions in the different roles for the client's care.

INVOLVEMENT

When we think of **involvement,** we think of our function as advocates and health-care providers for our clients. This is one form of involvement. The focus in not on a clock. Rather, our professional involvement focuses on the individual attributes and needs of our clients, the consumers of nursing and health care. This is involvement as individual professionals with the clients and families who are the consumers of nursing care.

But our involvement is also as members of the health-care team. Collaboration and collegiality have been described in relation to nursing and interdisciplinary practice. In Chapter 13, the importance of group dynamics and group skills was described. Additional skills such as the art of negotiation are involved in leading and managing, as was described in Chapter 9. All of these functions relate to active involvement with a defined group to attain specified goals for the consumers of health care.

A third form of professional involvement is as a member of the professional group. This form of involvement requires time and commitment for advancement of the profession. **Professional contributions** result from participation in professional organizations, research, publications, theory evaluation, and promotion of the further development of the profession. Recall from Chapter 1 the nine areas of professionalism identified by Miller, Adams, and Bell (1993):

- Educational background
- Adherence to the code of ethics
- Participation in the professional organization
- Continuing education and competency

- Communication and publication
- Autonomy and self-regulation
- Community service
- Theory use, development, and evaluation
- Research involvement (p. 291)

Personal contributions in clinical practice occur through your education, competency, ethical behaviors, use of theory, and communication. Further contributions to the profession result from participation in professional organizations, research, publications, theory evaluation, and promotion of the development of the profession.

REVISITING YOUR PHILOSOPHY OF NURSING

Now is the time to reflect on your personal contributions and philosophy of nursing. Nurses are talented, creative, and visionary when they allow themselves to be. They are frequently viewed as leaders and risk takers as they advocate for the perceived good of their clients. But what skills required of professionals do we need to refine? Step back and think of the vital and basic skills needed to demonstrate our professional competencies. These skills are what we continually strive to refine:

- Our knowledge base
- Critical thinking skills
- Technical skills
- Interpersonal skills
- Articulation skills

Clinical practice requires the skills of assessment, diagnosis, outcome identification and planning, implementation, and evaluation. These skills are enhanced through the professional attributes of dedication, collaboration, collegiality, and involvement in the health of society. Concern for the health of people, whether individual clients, families, communities, or groups in their environment, is the core of professional nursing. Individuals like you are dedicated and exemplify those characteristics of a professional described here. Your philosophy of nursing will evolve and develop, just as you do as a professional.

CREATING NEW TRADITIONS AND PARADIGMS

The Pew Commission recommendations have had the beneficial effect of opening up the discussion for needed changes in the health-care system and the professions. At national, state, and local meetings, discussions have started with reactionary comments, but the discussions continued. In profes-sional newsletters, journals, and the Internet, debate and discussion are ongoing. Communication and critical thinking are taking place. The restraining and driving forces of change are present. We are at the point of a paradigm shift. Practice and education can no longer serve the needs of their consumers without change. All professionals are shareholders in the process of improving the health of society at large.

The topics that you have embraced through this book have presented you with some of the issues involved in this change, and the new traditions being created. Facing the responsibilities inherent in professional practice is a way of revisiting our present roles and considering how they meet the needs of our clients and the intent of our profession. Addressing opportunities as a student is always a challenge, but the student role provides the setting for analyzing information related to current practices. Theories that guide practice continue to be tested and refined, as appropriate to their utility in practice, education, and research. Communication and critical thinking are vital components of this activity as we function as leaders, managers, and care providers in organizations and communities. We function as change agents, teachers, and group leaders in practice settings. As change agents, knowledge of research and the political process provides direction for addressing the changes needed for a healthier society. Consider the following characteristics of the emerging health-care system identified by the Pew Health Professions Commission (1995):

- Orientation toward health
- Population perspective
- Intensive use of information
- Focus on the consumer
- Knowledge of treatment outcomes
- Constrained resources
- Coordination of services
- Reconsideration of human values
- Expectations of accountability
- Growing independence (p. x)

Current health-care agendas and initiatives must be evaluated for applicability, acceptability, and appropriateness for meeting the needs of the population, with due consideration given to economic and quality indicators. All of these issues are addressed within the ethical parameters of professional nursing practice.

The information presented here has been designed to address the challenge of the book's title, *Advancing Your Practice: Concepts of Professional Practice*. We are all challenged to advance our professional practice.

KEY POINTS

- The Pew Health Professions Commission, established through a charitable trust in 1989, was designed to "assist workforce policy makers and educational institutions to produce health care workers who meet the changing needs of the American health care system" (p. ii). Predictions included the closure of hospitals, the surplus of physicians, nurses, and pharmacists, and the redesign of education, health care, and research.

- The Pew Health Professions Commission (1995) described the emerging health-care system with the following characteristics:

Orientation toward health	Constrained resources
Population perspective	Coordination of services
Intensive use of information	Reconsideration of human values
Focus on the consumer	Expectations of accountability
Knowledge of treatment outcomes	Growing independence (p. x)

- The following six trends in nursing were identified as major influences: the aging population, health promotion and disease prevention, cost-effective care, management of care, community organization, and differentiation of practice and education (O'Neil, 1993, pp. 85–86). Seven recommendations specifically for nursing proposed by the Pew Health Professions Commission are focused on our accountability to the public, the recognition of our assets, the need for clarity in our roles and functions, and the need to meet the demands of the marketplace.

- The Pew Health Professions Commission recommended 17 competencies for all health professionals by 2005. **Competencies** are those qualities that illustrate effectiveness and appropriateness in our respective professional roles.

- **Collaboration** involves actively working together to meet some identified goal, such as the client's treatment goals.

- **Collegiality** is the sharing of responsibility and authority toward a goal or prescribed outcome. Power and responsibility are invested in more than one person to achieve the outcome related to the client's health and well-being. Respect and collaboration are important components of a collegial relationship.

- **Involvement** as a professional takes three forms:
  (a) As an individual professional with clients, families, and communities who are the consumers of nursing care,
  (b) As a group member or leader of an interdisciplinary health-care team, and
  (c) As an active member of the professional group.

- **Personal contributions** as a professional occur in clinical practice, demonstrated through educational preparation, competency, ethical behaviors, use of theory, and communication.

- **Professional contributions** result from participation in professional organizations, research, publications, theory evaluation, and promotion of the further development of the profession.

- Vital and basic skills needed and continually refined by professionals include expanding one's knowledge base, critical thinking, and technical, interpersonal, and articulation skills.

CHAPTER EXERCISES

1. Reevaluate your personal philosophy, developed following Chapter 1. What changes do you suggest? Rewrite your philosophy statement, and describe any additions or deletions from the original statement.

2. Develop a personal plan for how you will demonstrate in 2005 the following list of 17 competencies for health professionals identified by the Pew Health Professions (1995):

Care for the community's health

Expand access to effective care

Provide clinically competent care

Emphasize primary care

Participate in coordinated care

Ensure cost-effective and appropriate care

Practice prevention

Involve patients and families in the decision-making process

Promote healthy lifestyles

Access and use technology appropriately

Improve the health-care system

Manage information

Understand the role of the physical environment

Provide counseling on ethical issues

Accommodate expanded accountability

Participate in a racially and culturally diverse society

Continue to learn (p. xii).

3. Give examples of the ways your practice setting demonstrates the following characteristics of the emerging health-care system (Pew, 1995):

Orientation toward health

Population perspective

Intensive use of information

Focus on the consumer

Knowledge of treatment outcomes

Constrained resources

Coordination of services

Reconsideration of human values

Expectations of accountability

Growing independence (p. x)

4. Develop three personal goals to be met in your professional nursing practice during the next 5 years.

5. Describe your plans for two specific personal contributions to professional nursing practice that you will attempt during the next 10 years.

REFERENCES

American Nurses Association. (1995). *Scope and standards of gerontological nursing practice* (Publication Number GE-14 7.5 M 6/95). Washington, DC: American Nurses Publishing.

Miller, B. K., Adams, D., & Beck, L. (1993). A behavioral inventory for professionalism in nursing. *Journal of Professional Nursing, 9,* 290–295.

O'Neil, E. H. (1993). *Health professions education for the future: Schools in service to the nation.* San Francisco: Pew Health Professions Commission.

Pew Health Professions Commission. (1995). *Critical challenges: Revitalizing the health professions for the twenty-first century.* San Francisco: UCSF Center for the Health Professions.

Tappen, R. M. (1995). *Nursing leadership and management: Concepts and practice* (3rd ed.). Philadelphia: Davis.

BIBLIOGRAPHY

Duncan, K. A. (1994). *Health information and health reform: Understanding the need for a national health information system.* San Francisco: Jossey-Bass.

Finocchio, L. J., Dower, C. M., McMahon, T., Gragnola, C. M., & the Taskforce on Health Care Workforce Regulation. (1995). *Reforming health care workforce regulation: Policy considerations for the 21st century.* San Francisco: Pew Health Professions Commission.

Shugars, D. A., O'Neil, E. H., & Bader, J. D. (Eds.) (1991). *Healthy America: Practitioners for 2005, an agenda for action for U.S. health professional schools.* Durham, NC: Pew Health Professions Commission.

Appendix A

PROFESSIONAL NURSING ORGANIZATIONS

Academy of Medical Surgical Nurses (AMSN)
N. Woodbury Road, Box 56
Pitman, NJ 08071
(609) 589-6677   (609) 589-7463 (FAX)

American Academy of Ambulatory Care Nursing
 (AAACN)
N. Woodbury Road, Box 56
Pitman, NJ 08071
(609) 582-9617   (609) 589-7463 (FAX)
http://www.inurse.com/member.htm

American Academy of Nurse Practitioners
Capital Station, LBJ Bldg.
P.O. Box 12846
Austin, TX 78711

American Assembly for Men in Nursing (AAMN)
P.O. Box 31753
Independence, OH 44131
dosprouse@aol.com

American Association of Colleges of Nursing
 (AACN)
1 Dupont Circle, NW, Suite 530
Washington, DC 20036
(202) 463-6930   (202) 785-8320 (FAX)
http://www.aacn.nche.edu

American Association for the History of Nursing
 (AAHN)
P.O. Box 90803
Washington, DC 20090-0803
(202) 543-2127   (202) 543-0724 (FAX)
http://users.aol.com/nsghistory/AAHN.html

American Association of Critical-Care Nurses
 (AACN)
101 Columbia
Aliso Viejo, CA 92656-1491
(714) 362-2000   (714) 362-2020 (FAX)
http://www.aacn.org

American Association of Legal Consultants
P.O. Box 3616
Phoenix, AZ 85030-3616

American Association of Neuroscience Nurses
 (AANN)
224 N. Des Plaines, Suite 601
Chicago, IL 60661
(312) 993-0043   (312) 993-0362 (FAX)
AssnNeuro@aol.com

American Association of Nurse Anesthetists
 (AANA)
222 South Prospect Ave.
Park Ridge, IL 60068-4001
(708) 692-7050   (708) 692-6968 (Fax)
http://www.aana.com

American Association of Nurse Attorneys
720 Light St.
Baltimore, MD 21230

American Association of Occupational Health
 Nurses (AAOHN)
50 Lenox Pointe
Atlanta, GA 30324
(404) 262-1162   (404) 262-1165 (FAX)

American Association of Office Nurses
1089 Kinderkamack Rd.
Montvale, NJ 07645
(201) 391-2600

American Association of Spinal Cord Injury Nurses
(AASCIN)
75-20 Astoria Blvd.
Jackson Heights, NY 11370-1177
(718) 803-3782   (718) 803-0414 (FAX)

American College of Nurse-Midwives (ACNM)
1522 K St., NW, Suite 1120
Washington, DC 20005
(202) 289-0171   (202) 289-4395 (FAX)

American College of Nurse Practitioners
2401 Pennsylvania Ave., NW, Suite 350
Washington, DC 20037-1718
(202) 466-4825   (202) 466-3826 (FAX)
ANCP@aol.com

American Holistic Nurses Association
4101 Lake Boone Trail, Suite 201
Raleigh, NC 27607
(919) 787-5181

American Medical Informatics Association (AMIA)
4915 St. Elmo Ave., Suite 401
Bethesda, MD 20814
(301) 657-1291   (301) 657-1296 (FAX)
http://www.amia.org/

American Nephrology Nurses' Association (ANNA)
ANNA National Office
East Holly Ave., Box 56
Pitman, NJ 08071-0056
(609) 256-2320   (609) 589-7463 (FAX)
http://www.inurse.com/~anna/about.htm

American Nurses Association (ANA)
600 Maryland Ave., SW, Suite 100 West
Washington, DC 20024-2571
(202) 651-7000 or (800) 637-0323
    (202) 651-7001 (FAX)
http://www.nursingworld.org/

American Organization of Nurse Executives
AHA Bldg., 840 N. Lake Shore Dr.
Chicago, IL 60611
(312) 280-4190

American Psychiatric Nurses Association (APNA)
1200 19th St., NW
Washington, DC 20036-2422
(202) 857-1133   (202) 223-4579 (FAX)

American Radiologic Nurses Association
502 Forrest Ct.
Greenville, NC 27834

American Society of Ophthalmic Registered Nurses,
    Inc. (ASORN)
P.O. Box 193030
San Francisco, CA 94119
(415) 561-8513   (415) 561-8575 (FAX)

American Society of PeriAnesthesia Nurses (ASPAN)
6900 Grove Rd.
Thorofare, NJ 08086
(609) 845-5557   (609) 848-1881 (FAX)
http://www.aspan.org/aspan.htm

American Society of Plastic and Reconstructive
    Surgical Nurses, Inc. (ASPRSN)
N. Woodbury Rd., Box 56
Pitman, NJ 08071
(609) 589-6247   (609) 589-7964 (FAX)

American Society of Post Anesthesia Nurses
    (ASPAN)
11512 Allecingie Pkwy.
Richmond, VA 23235
(804) 379-5516   (804) 379-1386 (FAX)

American Thoracic Society
Section on Nursing
1740 Broadway
New York, NY 10019-4374

American Urological Association Allied, Inc.
11512 Allecingie Pkwy.
Richmond, VA 23235
(804) 379-1306   (804) 379-1386 (FAX)

Association for Practitioners in Infection Control
    (APIC)
505 E. Hawley St.
Mundelein, IL 60060
(708) 949-6052   (708) 566-7282 (FAX)

Association of Operating Room Nurses, Inc.
    (AORN)
2170 S. Parker Rd., Suite 300
Denver, CO 80231-5711
(303) 755-6300   (303) 750-2927 (FAX)
http://www.aorn.org

Association of Nurses in AIDS Care
704 Stonyhill Rd., Suite 106
Yardley, PA 10967

Association of Pediatric Oncology Nurses (APON)
11512 Allecingie Pkwy.
Richmond, VA 23235
(804) 379-9150   (804) 379-1386 (FAX)

Association of Rehabilitation Nurses (ARN)
5700 Old Orchard Rd., First Floor
Skokie, IL 60077-1057
(708) 966-3433   (708) 966-9418 (FAX)

Association of Women's Health, Obstetric, & Neonatal Nurses (AWHONN—formerly NAACOG)
700 14th St., NW, Suite 600
Washington, DC 20005-2019
(202) 662-1600   (202) 737-0575 (FAX)

Canadian Intravenous Nurses Association
4433 Sheppard Ave. E., Suite 200
Agincourt, Ontario, Canada M1S IV3
(416) 292-0687   (416) 292-1038 (FAX)
http://web.idirect.com/~csotcina

Canadian Nurses Association
50 the Driveway
Ottawa, Ontario, Canada K2P 1E2
(613) 237-2133

Dermatology Nurses' Association (DNA)
N. Woodbury Rd., Box 56
Pitman, NJ 08071
(609) 589-6247   (609) 589-7964 (FAX)
http://www.inurse.com/member.htm

Drug and Alcohol Nurses Association, Inc.
720 Lime St.
Baltimore, MD 21230

Emergency Nurses' Association (ENA)
216 Higgins Rd.
Park Ridge, IL 60068-5736
(708) 698-9400   (708) 698-9406 (FAX)
http://www.ena.org

International Society of Nurses in Genetics, Inc.
(ISONG)
3020 Javier Rd.
Fairfax, VA 22031

Intravenous Nurses Society, Inc. (INS)
2 Brighton St.
Belmont, MA 02178
(617) 489-5205   (617) 484-6992 (FAX)

National Association of Directors of Nursing
Administration in Long Term Care
(NADONA/LTC)
10999 Reed Hartman Hwy., Suite 234
Cincinnati, OH 45242

National Association of Hispanic Nurses
6905 Alamo Downs Pkwy.
San Antonio, TX 78238

National Association of Neonatal Nurses
1304 Southpoint Blvd., Suite 280
Petaluma, CA 94954-6861
(800) 451-3795   (707) 762-0401 (FAX)
http://ajn.org/ajnnet/nursorgs/naan/
naan84@aol.com

National Association of Nurse Massage Therapists
(NANMT)
4172 Shiloh Ridge Trail
Kennesaw, GA 30144

National Association of Nurse Practitioners in
Reproductive Health (NANPRH)
2401 Pennsylvania Ave., NW, Suite 350
Washington, DC 20003
(202) 466-4825   (202) 466-3826 (FAX)

National Association of Orthopaedic Nurses
(NAON)
NAON National Office
East Holly Ave., Box 56
Pitman, NJ 08071-0056
(609) 256-2310   (609) 589-7463 (FAX)
http://www.inurse.com/~naon/about.htm

National Association of Pediatric Nurse Associates
& Practitioners (NAPNAP)
1101 Kings Hwy., N, Suite 206
Cherry Hill, NJ 08034
(609) 667-1773   (609) 667-7187 (FAX)

National Association of School Nurses (NASN)
P.O. Box 1300
Scarborough, ME 04070-1300
(203) 883-2177   (203) 883-2683 (FAX)
NASN@mail. VRmedia.com

National Black Nurses Association
1012 10th St., NW
Washington, DC 20003

National Flight Nurses Association (NFNA)
6900 Grove Rd.
Thorofare, NJ 08086-9447
(609) 384-6725   (609) 848-5274 (FAX)

National Gerontological Nursing Association
3100 Homewood Pkwy.
Kensington, MD 20895

National League for Nursing (NLN)
350 Hudson Street
New York, NY 10014
(800) 669-1656 or (212) 989-9393
(212) 989-3710 (FAX)
http://www.nln.org/

National Nurses Society on Addictions (NNSA)
5700 Old Orchard Rd., First Floor
Skokie, IL 60077-1057
(708) 966-5010   (708) 966-9418 (FAX)

National Nursing Staff Development Organization
437 Twin Bay Dr.
Pensacola, FL 32534-1350

National Organization of Philippine Nurses in the
  US
4459 Joan St.
S. Plainfield, NJ 07080
(201) 548-6000

North American Nursing Diagnosis Association
3535 Caroline St.
St. Louis, MO 63104

Nurse Consultants Association, Inc.
414 Plaza Dr., Suite 209
Westmont, IL 60559

Nurses Association of Veterans Affairs (NOVA)
Gregg Gordon email
  Gordon.David@dayton.va.gov

Nurses Organization of Veterans Affairs
1311 A Dolly Madison Blvd., Suite 3A
McLean, VA 22101
(703) 556-9222

Oncology Nursing Society (ONS)
501 Holiday Dr.
Pittsburgh, PA 15220-2749
(412) 921-7373   (412) 921-6565 (FAX)
http://nauticom.net//www/onsmain

Respiratory Nursing Society
5700 Old Orchard Rd., First Floor
Skokie, IL 60077-1057

Sigma Theta Tau International
Center for Nursing Scholarship
550 West North St.
Indianapolis, IN 46202-3191
(317) 634-8171
http://stti-bl.iupui.edu

Society of Gastroenterology Nurses & Associates,
  Inc. (SGNA)
1070 Sibley Tower
Rochester, NY 14604
(716) 546-7241   (716) 546-5141 (FAX)

Society of Otorhinolaryngology & Head-Neck
  Nurses, Inc. (SOHN)
116 Canal St., Suite A
New Smyrna Beach, FL 32168-7004
(904) 428-1695   (904) 423-7566 (FAX)

Society of Pediatric Nurses
P.O. Box 626
Danville, CA 94526-0626

Society of Peripheral Vascular Nursing
309 Winter St.
Norwood, MA 02062
(617) 762-3630

Society of Urologic Nurses & Associates, Inc.
  (SUNA)
East Holly Ave., Box 56
Pitman, NJ 08071-0056
(609) 589-7463 (FAX)
http://www.inurse.com/~suna/about.htm

Transcultural Nursing Society
College of Nursing & Health
Madonna University
36600 School Croft Rd.
Livonia, MI 48150
Barbara Sullivan email   sullibmh@seattleu.edu

Appendix B

NURSING INTERVENTIONS CLASSIFICATION (NIC)

NIC Taxonomy

	Domain 1	**Domain 2**	**Domain 3**
Level 1 Domains	1. **Physiological: Basic** Care that supports physical functioning	2. **Physiological: Complex** Care that supports homeostatic regulation	3. **Behavioral** Care that supports psychosocial functioning and facilitates lifestyle changes
Level Classes	A *Activity and Exercise Management:* Interventions to organize or assist with physical activity and energy conservation and expenditure	G *Electrolyte and Acid-Base Management:* Interventions to regulate electrolyte/acid base balance and prevent complications	O *Behavior Therapy* **2** Interventions to reinforce or promote desirable behaviors or alter undesirable behaviors.
	B *Elimination Management:* Interventions to establish and maintain regular bowel and urinary elimination patterns and manage complications due to altered patterns	H *Drug Management:* Interventions to facilitate desired effects of pharmacologic agents	P *Cognitive Therapy:* Interventions to reinforce or promote desirable cognitive functioning or alter undesirable cognitive functioning
	C *Immobility Management:* Interventions to manage restricted body movement and the sequelae	I *Neurologic Management:* Interventions to optimize neurologic functions	Q *Communication Enhancement:* Interventions to facilitate delivering and receiving verbal and nonverbal messages
	D *Nutrition Support:* Interventions to modify or maintain nutritional status	J *Perioperative Care:* Interventions to provide care before, during, and immediately after surgery	R *Coping Assistance:* Interventions to assist another to build on own strengths, to adapt to a change in function, or to achieve a higher level of function
	E *Physical Comfort Promotion:* Interventions to promote comfort using physical techniques	K *Respiratory Management:* Interventions to promote airway patency and gas exchange	S *Patient Education:* Interventions to facilitate learning
	F *Self-Care Facilitation:* Interventions to provide or assist with routine activities of daily living	L *Skin/Wound Management:* Interventions to maintain or restore tissue integrity	T *Psychological Comfort Promotion:* Interventions to promote comfort using psychological techniques
		M *Thermoregulation:* Interventions to maintain body temperature within a normal range	
		N *Tissue Perfusion Management:* Interventions to optimize circulation of blood and fluids to the tissue	

Domain 4	Domain 5	Domain 6
4. Safety Care that supports protection against harm	**5. Family** Care that supports the family unit	**6. Health System** Care that supports effective use of the health-care delivery system
U *Crisis Management:* Interventions to provide immediate short-term help in both psychological and physiologic crises V *Risk Management:* Interventions to initiate risk-reduction activities and continue monitoring risks over time	W *Childbearing Care:* Interventions to assist in understanding and coping with the psychological and physiologic changes during the childbearing period X *Lifespan Care:* Interventions to facilitate family unit functioning and promote the health and welfare of family members throughout the lifespan	Y *Health System Mediation:* Interventions to facilitate the interface between patient/family and the health-care system a *Health System Management:* Interventions to provide and enhance support services for the delivery of care b *Information Management:* Interventions to facilitate communication among health-care providers

Level 1 Domains	*1. Physiological: Basic* **Care that Supports Physical Functioning**		
Level 2 Classes	A **Activity and Exercise Management** Interventions to organize or assist with physical activity and energy conservation and expenditure	B **Elimination Management** Interventions to establish and maintain regular bowel and urinary elimination patterns and manage complications due to altered patterns	C **Immobility Management** Interventions to manage restricted body movement and the sequelae
Level 3 Interventions	0140 Body Mechanics Promotion 0180 Energy Management 0200 Exercise Promotion 0202 Exercise Promotion: Stretching 0221 Exercise Therapy: Ambulation 0222 Exercise Therapy: Balance 0224 Exercise Therapy: Joint Mobility 0226 Exercise Therapy: Muscle Control 5612 Teaching: Prescribed Activity/Exercise **S***	0410 Bowel Incontinence Care 0412 Bowel Incontinence Care: Encopresis **X** 0420 Bowel Irrigation 0430 Bowel Management 0440 Bowel Training 0450 Constipation/Impaction Management 0460 Diarrhea Management 0470 Flatulence Reduction 0480 Ostomy Care **L** 0490 Rectal Prolapse Management 0550 Bladder Irrigation 0560 Pelvic Floor Exercise 1876 Tube Care: Urinary 0570 Urinary Bladder Training 0580 Urinary Catheterization 0582 Urinary Catheterization: Intermittent 0590 Urinary Elimination Management 0600 Urinary Habit Training 0610 Urinary Incontinence Care 0612 Urinary Incontinence Care: Enuresis **X** 0620 Urinary Retention Care 1804 Self-Care Assistance: Toileting **F**	0740 Bed Rest Care 0762 Cast Care: Maintenance 0764 Cast Care: Wet 6580 Physical Restraint **V** 0840 Positioning 0846 Positioning: Wheelchair 0910 Splinting 0940 Traction/Immobilization Care 0960 Transport
	0100 to 0399	0400 to 0699	0700 to 0999

*Letter indicates another class where the intervention is also included.

D Nutrition Support Interventions to modify or maintain nutritional status	**E Physical Comfort Promotion** Interventions to promote comfort using physical techniques	**F Self-Care Facilitation** Interventions to provide or assist with routine activities of daily living
1020 Diet Staging 1030 Eating Disorders Management 1050 Feeding **F** 1056 Enteral Tube Feeding 1080 Gastrointestinal Intubation 1100 Nutrition Management 1120 Nutrition Therapy 5246 Nutritional Counseling 1160 Nutritional Monitoring 1803 Self-Care Assistance: Feeding **F** 1860 Swallowing Therapy **F** 5614 Teaching: Prescribed Diet **S** 1200 Total Parenteral Nutrition (TPN) Administration **G** 1874 Tube Care: Gastrointestinal 1240 Weight Gain Assistance 1260 Weight Management 1280 Weight Reduction Assistance	1320 Acupressure 1340 Cutaneous Stimulation 6482 Environmental Management: Comfort 1380 Heat/Cold Application 1400 Pain Management 1460 Progressive Muscle Relaxation 1480 Simple Massage 5465 Therapeutic Touch 1540 Transcutaneous Electrical Nerve Stimulation (TENS)	1610 Bathing 1620 Contact Lens Care 1630 Dressing 1640 Ear Care 1650 Eye Care 1050 Feeding **D** 1660 Foot Care 1670 Hair Care 1680 Nail Care 1710 Oral Health Maintenance 1720 Oral Health Promotion 1730 Oral Health Restoration 1750 Perineal Care 1770 Postmortem Care 1780 Prosthesis Care 1800 Self-Care Assistance 1801 Self-Care Assistance: Bathing/Hygiene 1802 Self-Care Assistance: Dressing/Grooming 1803 Self-Care Assistance: Feeding **D** 1804 Self-Care Assistance: Toileting **B** 1850 Sleep Enhancement 1860 Swallowing Therapy **D** 1870 Tube Care
1000 to 1299	**1300 to 1599**	**1600 to 1899**

Level 1 Domains	*2. Physiological: Complex* **Care that Supports Homeostatic Regulation**	
Level 2 Classes	G **Electrolyte and Acid-Base Management** Interventions to regulate electrolyte/acid base balance and prevent complications	H **Drug Management** Interventions to facilitate desired effects of pharmacologic agents
Level 3 Interventions	1910 Acid-Base Management 1911 Acid-Base Management: Metabolic Acidosis 1912 Acid-Base Management: Metabolic Alkalosis 1913 Acid-Base Management: Respiratory Acidosis **K*** 1914 Acid-Base Management: Respiratory Alkalosis **K** 1920 Acid-Base Monitoring 2000 Electrolyte Management 2001 Electrolyte Management: Hypercalcemia 2002 Electrolyte Management: Hyperkalemia 2003 Electrolyte Management: Hypermagnesemia 2004 Electrolyte Management: Hypernatremia 2005 Electrolyte Management: Hyperphosphatemia 2006 Electrolyte Management: Hypocalcemia 2007 Electrolyte Management: Hypokalemia 2008 Electrolyte Management: Hypomagnesemia 2009 Electrolyte Management: Hyponatremia 2010 Electrolyte Management: Hypophosphatemia 2020 Electrolyte Monitoring 2080 Fluid/Electrolyte Management **N** 2100 Hemodialysis Therapy 2120 Hyperglycemia Management 2130 Hypoglycemia Management 2150 Peritoneal Dialysis Therapy 4232 Phlebotomy: Arterial Blood Sample **N** 1200 Total Parenteral Nutrition (TPN) Administration **D**	2210 Analgesic Administration 2214 Analgesic Administration: Intraspinal 2840 Anesthesia Administration **J** 2240 Chemotherapy Management **S** 2260 Conscious Sedation 2300 Medication Administration 2301 Medication Administration: Enteral 2302 Medication Administration: Interpleural 2303 Medication Administration: Intraosseous 2304 Medication Administration: Oral 2305 Medication Administration: Parenteral 2306 Medication Administration: Topical 2307 Medication Administration: Ventricular Reservoir 2380 Medication Management 2390 Medication Prescribing 2400 Patient-Controlled Analgesia (PCA) Assistance 5616 Teaching Prescribed Medication **S** 2440 Venous Access Devices (VAD) Maintenance **N**
	1900 to 2199	2200 to 2499

*Letter indicates another class where the intervention is also included.

I	**Neurologic Management** Interventions to optimize neurologic function	**J**	**Perioperative Care** Interventions to provide care before, during, and immediately after surgery

I   Neurologic Management
Interventions to optimize neurologic function

2540 Cerebral Edema Management
2550 Cerebral Perfusion Promotion
2560 Dysreflexia Management
2590 Intracranial Pressure (ICP) Monitoring
2620 Neurologic Monitoring
2660 Peripheral Sensation Management
0844 Positioning: Neurologic
2680 Seizure Management **V**
2690 Seizure Precautions
2720 Subarachnoid Hemorrhage Precautions
1878 Tube Care: Ventriculostomy/Lumbar Drain
2760 Unilateral Neglect Management

J   Perioperative Care
Interventions to provide care before, during, and immediately after surgery

2840 Anesthesia Administration **H**
2860 Autotransfusion **N**
6545 Infection Control: Intraoperative
0842 Positioning: Intraoperative
2870 Postanesthesia Care
2880 Preoperative Coordination **Y**
2900 Surgical Assistance
2920 Surgical Precautions **V**
2930 Surgical Preparation
5610 Teaching: Preoperative **S**
3902 Temperature Regulation: Intraoperative **M**

2500 to 2799

2800 to 3099

Level 1 Domains	*2. Physiological: Complex* **Care that Supports Homeostatic Regulation—Cont'd**	
Level 2 Classes	K **Respiratory Management** Interventions to promote airway patency and gas exchange	L **Skin/Wound Management** Interventions to maintain or restore tissue integrity
Level 3 Interventions	1913 Acid-Base Management: Respiratory Acidosis **G** 1914 Acid-Base Management: Respiratory Alkalosis **G** 3120 Airway Insertion and Stabilization 3140 Airway Management 3160 Airway Suctioning 3180 Artificial Airway Management 3200 Aspiration Precautions **V** 3230 Chest Physiotherapy 3250 Cough Enhancement 4106 Embolus Care: Pulmonary **N** 3270 Endotracheal Extubation 3300 Mechanical Ventilation 3310 Mechanical Ventilatory Weaning 3320 Oxygen Therapy 3350 Respiratory Monitoring 1872 Tube Care: Chest 3390 Ventilation Assistance	3420 Amputation Care 3440 Incision Site Care 3460 Leech Therapy 0480 Ostomy Care **B** 3500 Pressure Management 3520 Pressure Ulcer Care 3540 Pressure Ulcer Prevention **V** 3584 Skin Care: Topical Treatments 3590 Skin Surveillance 3620 Suturing 3660 Wound Care 3662 Wound Care: Closed Drainage 3680 Wound Irrigation
	3100 to 3399	3400 to 3699

*Letter indicates another class where the intervention is also included.

M	Thermoregulation	N	Tissue Perfusion Management
	Interventions to maintain body temperature within a normal range		Interventions to optimize circulation of blood and fluids to the tissue

3740 Fever Treatment	2860 Autotransfusion **J**
3780 Heat Exposure Treatment	4010 Bleeding Precautions
3800 Hypothermia Treatment	4020 Bleeding Reduction
3840 Malignant Hyperthermia Precautions **U**	4021 Bleeding Reduction: Antepartum Uterus **W**
3900 Temperature Regulation	4022 Bleeding Reduction: Gastrointestinal
3902 Temperature Regulation: Intraoperative **J**	4024 Bleeding Reduction: Nasal
	4026 Bleeding Reduction: Postpartum Uterus **W**
	4028 Bleeding Reduction: Wound
	4030 Blood Products Administration
	4040 Cardiac Care
	4044 Cardiac Care: Acute
	4046 Cardiac Care: Rehabilitative
	4050 Cardiac Precautions
	4060 Circulatory Care
	4064 Circulatory Care: Mechanical Assist Device
	4070 Circulatory Precautions
	4090 Dysrhythmia Management
	4104 Embolus Care: Peripheral
	4106 Embolus Care: Pulmonary **K**
	4110 Embolus Precautions
	2080 Fluid/Electrolyte Management **G**
	4120 Fluid Management
	4130 Fluid Monitoring
	4140 Fluid Resuscitation
	4150 Hemodynamic Regulation
	4160 Hemorrhage Control
	4170 Hypervolemia Management
	4180 Hypovolemia Management
	4190 Intravenous (IV) Insertion
	4200 Intravenous (IV) Therapy
	4210 Invasive Hemodynamic Monitoring
	4220 Peripherally Inserted Central (PIC) Catheter Care
	4232 Phlebotomy: Arterial Blood Sample **G**
	4234 Phlebotomy: Blood Unit Acquisition
	4238 Phlebotomy: Venous Blood Sample
	4250 Shock Management
	4254 Shock Management: Cardiac
	4256 Shock Management: Vasogenic
	4258 Shock Management: Volume
	4260 Shock Prevention
	2440 Venous Access Devices (VAD) Maintenance **H**

3700 to 3999	4000 to 4299

Level 1 Domains	*3. Behavioral* **Care that Supports Psychosocial Functioning and Facilitates Lifestyle Changes**		
Level 2 Classes	**O Behavior Therapy** Interventions to reinforce or promote desirable behaviors or alter undesirable behaviors	**P Cognitive Therapy** Interventions to reinforce or promote desirable cognitive functioning or alter undesirable cognitive functioning	**Q Communication Enhancement** Interventions to facilitate delivering and receiving verbal and nonverbal messages
Level 3 Interventions	4310 Activity Therapy 4320 Animal-Assisted Therapy **Q*** 4330 Art Therapy **Q** 4340 Assertiveness Training 4350 Behavior Management 4352 Behavior Management: Overactivity/Inattention 4354 Behavior Management: Self-Harm 4356 Behavior Management: Sexual 4360 Behavior Modification 4362 Behavior Modification: Social Skills 4370 Impulse Control Training 4380 Limit Setting 4390 Milieu Therapy 4400 Music Therapy **Q** 4410 Mutual Goal Setting 4420 Patient Contracting 4430 Play Therapy **Q** 4470 Self-Modification Assistance 4480 Self-Responsibility Facilitation 4490 Smoking Cessation Assistance 4500 Substance Use Prevention 4510 Substance Use Treatment 4512 Substance Use Treatment: Alcohol Withdrawal 4514 Substance Use Treatment: Drug Withdrawal 4516 Substance Use Treatment: Overdose	4640 Anger Control Assistance 4680 Bibliotherapy 4700 Cognitive Restructuring 4720 Cognitive Stimulation 5520 Learning Facilitation **S** 5540 Learning Readiness Enhancement **S** 4760 Memory Training 4820 Reality Orientation 4860 Reminiscence Therapy	4920 Active Listening 4320 Animal-Assisted Therapy **O** 4330 Art Therapy **O** 4974 Communication Enhancement: Hearing Deficit 4976 Communication Enhancement: Speech Deficit 4978 Communication Enhancement: Visual Deficit 5000 Complex Relationship Building 4400 Music Therapy **O** 4430 Play Therapy **O** 5100 Socialization Enhancement
	4300 to 4599	**4600 to 4899**	**4900 to 5199**

*Letter indicates another class where the intervention is also included.

R Coping Assistance	S Patient Education	T Psychological Comfort Promotion
Interventions to assist another to build on own strengths, adapt to a change in function, or to achieve a higher level of function	Interventions to facilitate learning	Interventions to promote comfort using psychological techniques
5210 Anticipatory Guidance **W**	2240 Chemotherapy Management **H**	5820 Anxiety Reduction
5220 Body Image Enhancement	6784 Family Planning: Contraception **W**	5840 Autogenic Training
5230 Coping Enhancement	5510 Health Education	5860 Biofeedback
5240 Counseling	5520 Learning Facilitation **P**	5880 Calming Technique
5242 Genetic Counseling **W**	5540 Learning Readiness Enhancement **P**	5900 Distraction
5248 Sexual Counseling	5562 Parent Education: Adolescent **X**	5920 Hypnosis
6160 Crisis Intervention **U**	5564 Parent Education: Childbearing	5960 Meditation
5250 Decision-Making Support **Y**	Family **W**	6000 Simple Guided Imagery
5260 Dying Care	5566 Parent Education: Childrearing	6040 Simple Relaxation Therapy
5270 Emotional Support	Family **X**	
5290 Grief Work Facilitation	5580 Preparatory Sensory Information	
5294 Grief Work Facilitation: Perinatal	5602 Teaching: Disease Process	
Death **W**	5604 Teaching: Group	
5300 Guilt Work Facilitation	5606 Teaching: Individual	
5310 Hope Instillation	5608 Teaching: Infant Care **W**	
5320 Humor	5610 Teaching: Preoperative **J**	
5330 Mood Management	5612 Teaching: Prescribed	
5340 Presence	Activity/Exercise **A**	
5360 Recreation Therapy	5614 Teaching: Prescribed Diet **D**	
5370 Role Enhancement **X**	5616 Teaching: Prescribed Medication **H**	
5380 Security Enhancement	5618 Teaching: Procedure/Treatment	
5390 Self-Awareness Enhancement	5620 Teaching: Psychomotor Skill	
5400 Self-Esteem Enhancement	5622 Teaching: Safe Sex	
5420 Spiritual Support	5624 Teaching: Sexuality	
5430 Support Group		
5440 Support System Enhancement		
5450 Therapy Group		
5460 Touch		
5470 Truth Telling		
5480 Values Clarification		
5200 to 5499	**5500 to 5799**	**5800 to 6099**

Level 1 Domains	4. *Safety* **Care that Supports Protection against Harm**	
Level 2 Classes	U **Crisis Management** Interventions to provide immediate short-term help in both psychological and physiologic crises	V **Risk Management** Interventions to initiate risk-reduction activities and continue monitoring risks over time
Level 3 Interventions	6140 Code Management 6160 Crisis Intervention **R*** 6200 Emergency Care 6240 First Aid 3840 Malignant Hyperthermia Precautions **M** 6260 Organ Procurement 6300 Rape-Trauma Treatment 6320 Resuscitation 6340 Suicide Prevention **V** 6360 Triage	6400 Abuse Protection 6402 Abuse Protection: Child 6404 Abuse Protection: Elder 6410 Allergy Management 6420 Area Restriction 3200 Aspiration Precautions **K** 6440 Delirium Management 6450 Delusion Management 6460 Dementia Management 6470 Elopement Precautions 6480 Environmental Management 6484 Environmental Management: Community 6486 Environmental Management: Safety 6487 Environmental Management: Violence Prevention 6489 Environmental Management: Worker Safety 6490 Fall Prevention 6500 Fire-Setting Precautions 6510 Hallucination Management 6520 Health Screening 6530 Immunization/Vaccination Administration 6540 Infection Control 6550 Infection Protection 6560 Laser Precautions 6570 Latex Precautions 6580 Physical Restraint **C** 6590 Pneumatic Tourniquet Precautions 3540 Pressure Ulcer Prevention **L** 6600 Radiation Therapy Management 6610 Risk Identification 6630 Seclusion 2680 Seizure Management **I** 6340 Suicide Prevention **U** 2920 Surgical Precautions **J** 6650 Surveillance 6654 Surveillance: Safety 6680 Vital Signs Monitoring
	6100 to 6399	6400 to 6699

*Letter indicates another class where the intervention is also included.

Level 1 Domains	5. *Family* **Care that Supports the Family Unit**		
Level 2 Classes	W **Childbearing Care** Interventions to assist in understanding and coping with the psychological and physiologic changes during the childbearing period		X **Lifespan Care** Interventions to facilitate family unit functioning and promote the health and welfare of family members throughout the lifespan
Level 3 Interventions	6700 Amnioinfusion 5210 Anticipatory Guidance **R*** 6710 Attachment Promotion 6720 Birthing 4021 Bleeding Reduction: Antepartum Uterus **N** 4026 Bleeding Reduction: Postpartum Uterus **N** 1052 Bottle Feeding 1054 Breastfeeding Assistance 6750 Cesarean Section Care 6760 Childbirth Preparation 6771 Electronic Fetal Monitoring: Antepartum 6772 Electronic Fetal Monitoring: Intrapartum 6481 Environmental Management: Attachment Process 7104 Family Integrity Promotion: Childbearing Family 6784 Family Planning: Contraception **S** 6786 Family Planning: Infertility 6788 Family Planning: Unplanned Pregnancy 5242 Genetic Counseling **R** 5294 Grief Work Facilitation: Perinatal Death **R** 6800 High-Risk Pregnancy Care	6820 Infant Care 6830 Intrapartal Care 6834 Intrapartal Care: High-Risk Delivery 6840 Kangaroo Care 6850 Labor Induction 6860 Labor Suppression 5244 Lactation Counseling 6870 Lactation Suppression 6880 Newborn Care 6890 Newborn Monitoring 6900 Nonnutritive Sucking 5564 Parent Education: Childbearing Family **S** 6924 Phototherapy: Neonate 6930 Postpartal Care 5247 Preconception Counseling 6950 Pregnancy Termination Care 6960 Prenatal Care 7886 Reproductive Technology Management 6972 Resuscitation: Fetus 6974 Resuscitation: Neonate 6612 Risk Identification: Childbearing Family 6656 Surveillance: Late Pregnancy 5608 Teaching: Infant Care **S** 1875 Tube Care: Umbilical Line 6982 Ultrasonography: Limited Obstetric	0412 Bowel Incontinence Care: Encopresis **B** 7040 Caregiver Support 7050 Developmental Enhancement 7100 Family Integrity Promotion 7110 Family Involvement 7120 Family Mobilization 7130 Family Process Maintenance 7140 Family Support 7150 Family Therapy 7160 Fertility Preservation 7180 Home Maintenance Assistance 7200 Normalization Promotion 5562 Parent Education: Adolescent **S** 5566 Parent Education: Childrearing Family **S** 7260 Respite Care 5370 Role Enhancement **R** 7280 Sibling Support 0612 Urinary Incontinence Care: Enuresis **B**
	6700 to 6999		7000 to 7299

*Letter indicates another class where the intervention is also included.

Level 1 Domains	6. *Health System* **Care that Supports Effective Use of the Health-Care Delivery System**		
Level 2 Classes	**Y Health System Mediation** Interventions to facilitate the interface between patient/family and the health-care system	**a Health System Management** Interventions to provide and enhance support services for the delivery of care	**b Information Management** Interventions to facilitate communication among health-care providers
Level 3 Interventions	7310 Admission Care 7330 Culture Brokerage 5250 Decision-Making Support **R*** 7370 Discharge Planning 7400 Health System Guidance 7410 Insurance Authorization 7440 Pass Facilitation 7460 Patient Rights Protection 2880 Preoperative Coordination **J** 7500 Sustenance Support 7560 Visitation Facilitation	7610 Bedside Laboratory Testing 7620 Controlled Substance Checking 7640 Critical Path Development 7650 Delegation 7660 Emergency Cart Checking 7680 Examination Assistance 7690 Laboratory Data Interpretation 7700 Peer Review 7710 Physician Support 7722 Preceptor: Employee 7726 Preceptor: Student 7760 Product Evaluation 7800 Quality Monitoring 7820 Specimen Management 7830 Staff Supervision 7840 Supply Management 7880 Technology Management	7920 Documentation 7960 Health-Care Information Exchange 7970 Health Policy Monitoring 7980 Incident Reporting 8020 Multidisciplinary Care Conference 8060 Order Transcription 8100 Referral 8120 Research Data Collection 8140 Shift Report 8180 Telephone Consultation
	7300 to 7599	7600 to 7899	7900 to 8199

Source: McCloskey & Bulecheck (1996). Nursing interventions classification (NIC). St. Louis: Mosby-Yearbook, with permission.
*Letter indicates another class where the intervention is also included.

INDEX

Note: Page numbers followed by f refer to figures; page numbers followed by t refer to tables.